lonely planet

Denmark

Andrew Bender, Michael Grosberg, Sally O'Brien, Rick Starey, Andrew Stone

Contents

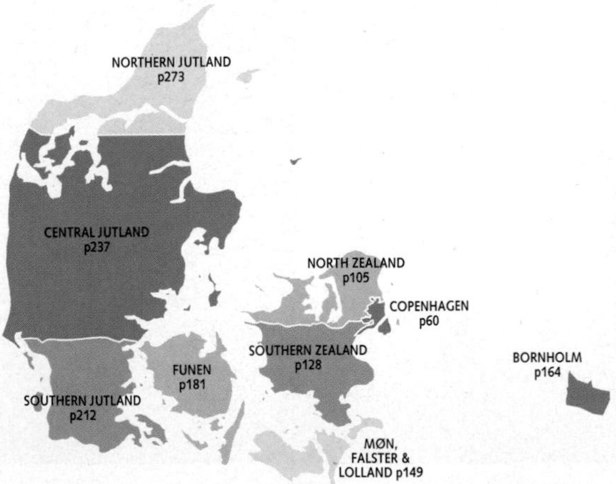

NORTHERN JUTLAND p273
CENTRAL JUTLAND p237
NORTH ZEALAND p105
COPENHAGEN p60
SOUTHERN ZEALAND p128
FUNEN p181
SOUTHERN JUTLAND p212
BORNHOLM p164
MØN, FALSTER & LOLLAND p149

Lonely Planet books provide independent advice. Lonely Planet does not accept advertising in guidebooks, nor do we accept payment in exchange for listing or endorsing any place or business. Lonely Planet writers do not accept discounts or payments in exchange for positive coverage of any sort.

Lonely Planets bøger giver uafhængige råd. Lonely Planet accepterer ikke reklame i rejseguiderne, og vi tager ikke imod betaling for at medtage eller anbefale steder eller forretninger. Lonely Planet skribenter tager ikke imod rabatter eller betaling til gengæld for positiv dækning af nogen som helst form.

Destination Denmark

The world first took notice of Denmark over a millennium ago when Danish Vikings took to the seas and ravaged vast tracts of Europe. My, how things have changed! These days Denmark is the epitome of civilised society, noted for progressivism, tolerance and a liberal social-welfare system.

The smallest and southernmost of the Scandinavian countries, Denmark offers a mix of lively cities and rural countryside, medieval churches, Renaissance castles and tidy 18th-century villages. Quaint country towns are lined with half-timbered houses that feel like the sets of Hans Christian Andersen fairytales. Copenhagen, Denmark's vibrant capital, is Scandinavia's largest, most cosmopolitan city. The Little Mermaid basks on Copenhagen's waterfront while the grand old Tivoli amusement park enlivens the heart of the city which boasts renowned museums, a wealth of cultural activities and a spirited music scene.

Denmark is still a maritime nation, bordered by the North Sea to the west and the Baltic to the east – there's 7314km of coastline. No place in Denmark is more than an hour's drive from its lovely seashore, much of it lined with splendid white-sand beaches.

Visitors are likely to find festivals pretty much whenever they visit – from jazz in Copenhagen to contemporary music in Roskilde and *Hamlet* performances in a castle in Helsingør. History seekers can marvel at preserved 2000-year-old 'bog people', Neolithic dolmens and impressive Viking ruins.

Whether you're relaxing over a glass of beer at an outdoor café, cycling the countryside or club-hopping the night away, this tiny country is a great escape for just about any taste.

ANDERS BLOMQVIST

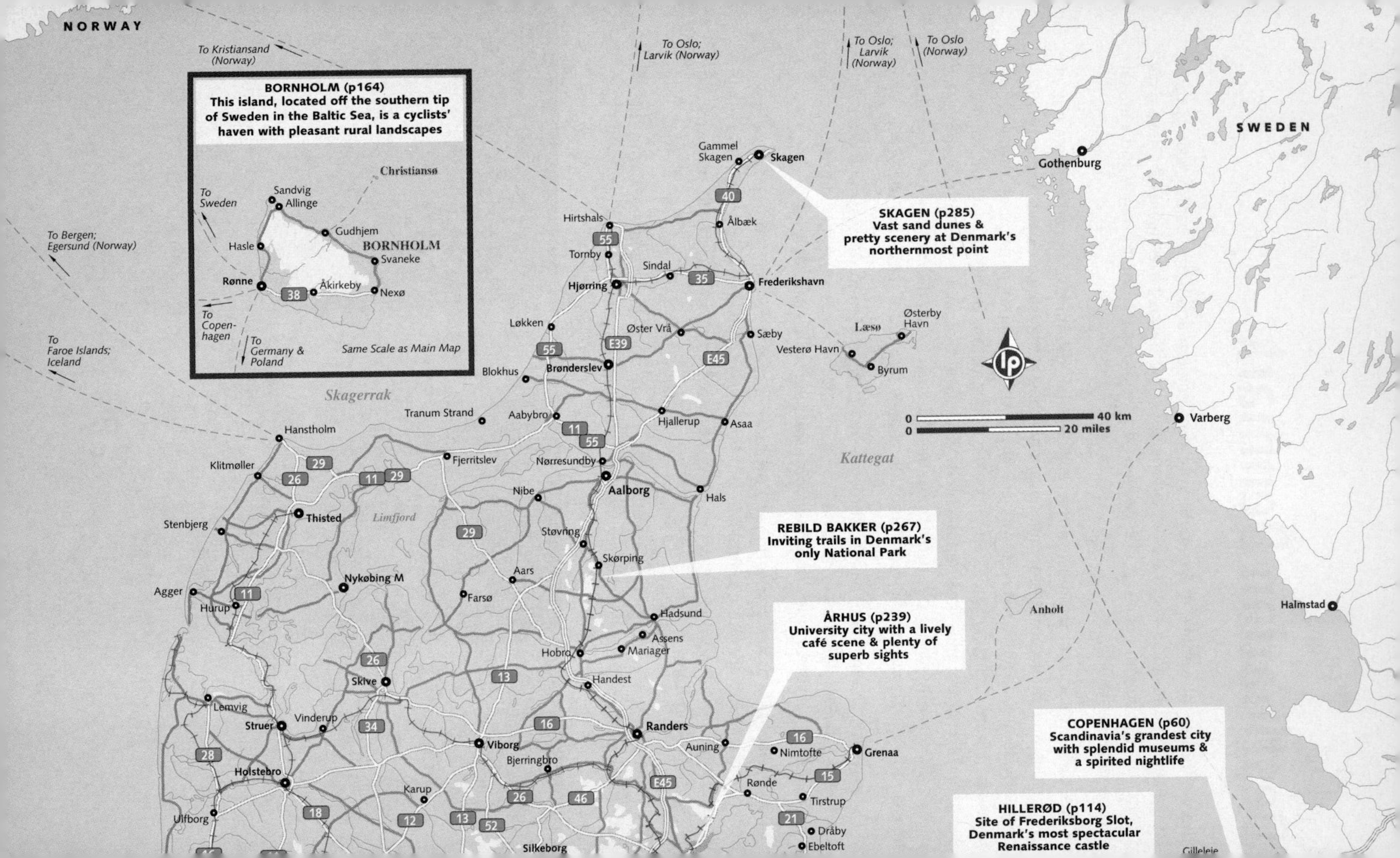

NORWAY
SWEDEN
To Kristiansand (Norway)
To Oslo; Larvik (Norway)
To Oslo; Larvik (Norway)
To Oslo (Norway)
To Bergen; Egersund (Norway)
To Faroe Islands; Iceland
BORNHOLM (p164)
This island, located off the southern tip of Sweden in the Baltic Sea, is a cyclists' haven with pleasant rural landscapes
Christiansø
To Sweden
Sandvig
Allinge
Gudhjem
BORNHOLM
Hasle
Svaneke
Rønne
38
Åkirkeby
Nexø
To Copenhagen
To Germany & Poland
Same Scale as Main Map
SKAGEN (p285)
Vast sand dunes & pretty scenery at Denmark's northernmost point
REBILD BAKKER (p267)
Inviting trails in Denmark's only National Park
ÅRHUS (p239)
University city with a lively café scene & plenty of superb sights
COPENHAGEN (p60)
Scandinavia's grandest city with splendid museums & a spirited nightlife
HILLERØD (p114)
Site of Frederiksborg Slot, Denmark's most spectacular Renaissance castle
Gammel Skagen
Skagen
Gothenburg
Hirtshals
Ålbæk
Tornby
Sindal
Hjørring
Frederikshavn
Løkken
Øster Vrå
Sæby
Læsø
Østerby Havn
Vesterø Havn
Byrum
Blokhus
Brønderslev
Skagerrak
Tranum Strand
Aabybro
Hjallerup
Asaa
Hanstholm
Klitmøller
Fjerritslev
Nørresundby
Aalborg
Nibe
Hals
Kattegat
0 40 km
0 20 miles
Varberg
Thisted
Limfjord
Stenbjerg
Støvring
Skørping
Nykøbing M
Aars
Agger
Hurup
Farsø
Hadsund
Anholt
Halmstad
Assens
Mariager
Hobro
Skive
Handest
Lemvig
Vinderup
Struer
Randers
Viborg
Auning
Nimtofte
Grenaa
Bjerringbro
Holstebro
Rønde
Tirstrup
Karup
Ulfborg
Dråby
Ebeltoft
Silkeborg
Gilleleje
40
55
35
E39
E45
11
29
26
13
16
34
28
18
12
52
46
15
21

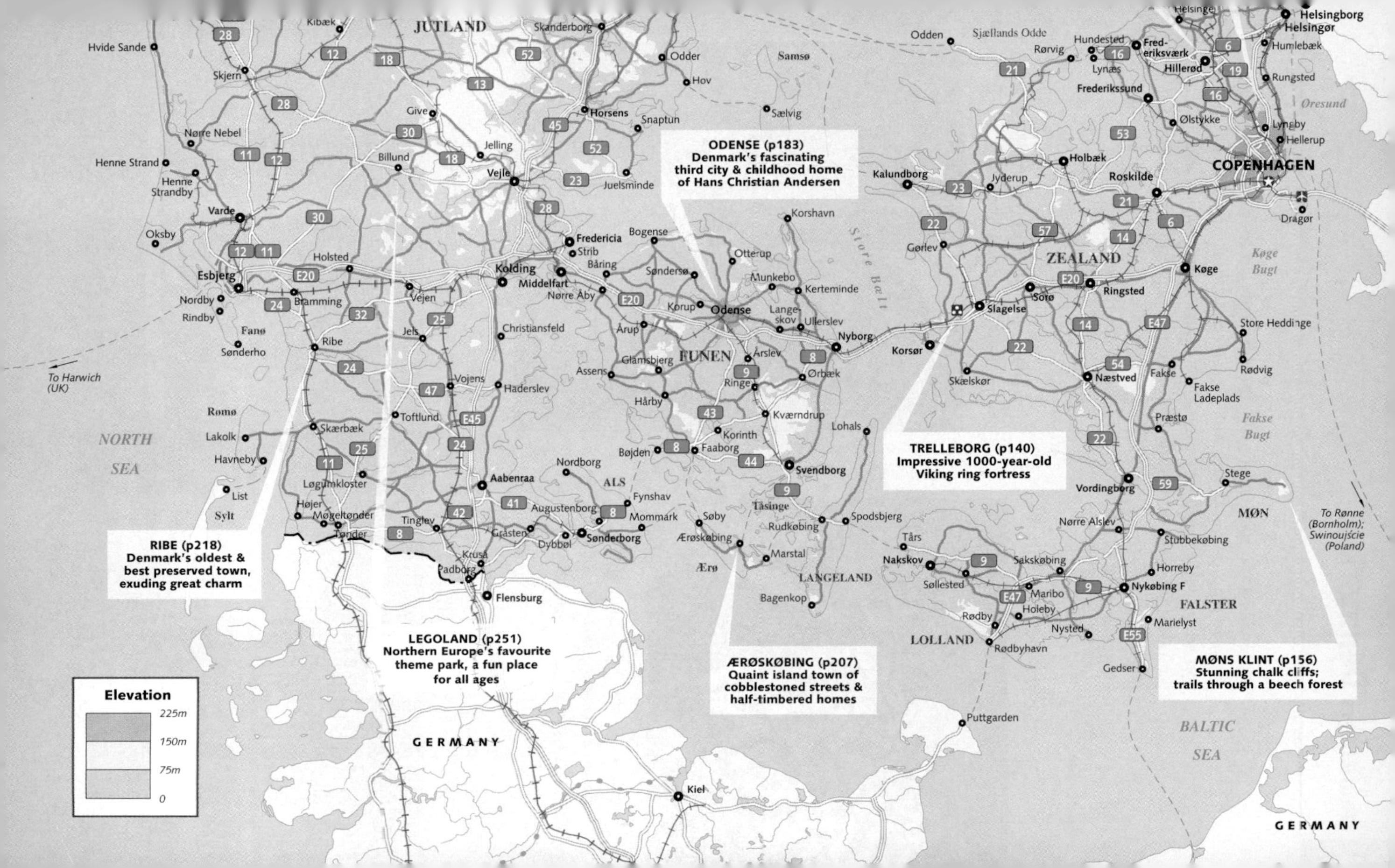

ODENSE (p183)
Denmark's fascinating third city & childhood home of Hans Christian Andersen
TRELLEBORG (p140)
Impressive 1000-year-old Viking ring fortress
RIBE (p218)
Denmark's oldest & best preserved town, exuding great charm
LEGOLAND (p251)
Northern Europe's favourite theme park, a fun place for all ages
ÆRØSKØBING (p207)
Quaint island town of cobblestoned streets & half-timbered homes
MØNS KLINT (p156)
Stunning chalk cliffs; trails through a beech forest
Elevation
225m
150m
75m
0
JUTLAND
FUNEN
ZEALAND
COPENHAGEN
LANGELAND
LOLLAND
FALSTER
MØN
ALS
Ærø
Samsø
Rømø
Fanø
Sylt
NORTH SEA
BALTIC SEA
GERMANY
Store Bælt
Øresund
Køge Bugt
Fakse Bugt
To Harwich (UK)
To Rønne (Bornholm); Swinoujście (Poland)
Hvide Sande
Skjern
Nørre Nebel
Henne Strand
Henne Strandby
Varde
Oksby
Esbjerg
Nordby
Rindby
Sønderho
Ribe
Bramming
Holsted
Vejen
Jels
Vojens
Haderslev
Christiansfeld
Kolding
Middelfart
Fredericia
Strib
Vejle
Jelling
Give
Billund
Horsens
Skanderborg
Odder
Hov
Snaptun
Juelsminde
Kibæk
Toftlund
Skærbæk
Lakolk
Havneby
List
Løgumkloster
Højer
Møgeltønder
Tønder
Tinglev
Aabenraa
Kruså
Padborg
Flensburg
Gråsten
Dybbøl
Sønderborg
Augustenborg
Nordborg
Fynshav
Mommark
Kiel
Bogense
Båring
Nørre Åby
Årup
Assens
Glamsbjerg
Hårby
Bøjden
Faaborg
Korinth
Ringe
Årslev
Odense
Korup
Søndersø
Otterup
Munkebo
Kerteminde
Langeskov
Ullerslev
Nyborg
Ørbæk
Kværndrup
Svendborg
Tåsinge
Rudkøbing
Spodsbjerg
Lohals
Søby
Ærøskøbing
Marstal
Bagenkop
Korshavn
Sælvig
Odden
Sjællands Odde
Kalundborg
Jyderup
Gørlev
Korsør
Slagelse
Skælskør
Sorø
Ringsted
Holbæk
Rørvig
Hundested
Lynæs
Frederiksværk
Frederikssund
Hillerød
Helsinge
Helsingør
Helsingborg
Humlebæk
Rungsted
Ølstykke
Lyngby
Hellerup
Roskilde
Dragør
Køge
Store Heddinge
Rødvig
Fakse
Fakse Ladeplads
Næstved
Præstø
Vordingborg
Stege
Nørre Alslev
Stubbekøbing
Horreby
Nykøbing F
Marielyst
Gedser
Nysted
Sakskøbing
Maribo
Holeby
Rødby
Rødbyhavn
Puttgarden
Tårs
Nakskov
Søllested

The smallest and southernmost of the Scandinavian countries, Denmark is an appealing mix of lively cities, well-preserved villages and pristine countryside and coastlines. From the stylish capital, Copenhagen, visitors fan out across the country's 400 odd islands and onto the peninsula of Jutland – its only mainland territory – to explore Viking fortresses and grand castles or to simply enjoy the great outdoors – on foot, by bike or by boat

ICASSO
ANDINSKY
HARFF
AGALL
ERINI

MARTIN LLADÓ

Explore the Statens Museum for Kunst – a fabulous collection of Scandinavian and European art (p78)

Step back in time in Ribe, Denmark's oldest and best-preserved town (p218)

TIN LLADÓ

Enjoy the easy-going waterside atmosphere of vibrantly painted Nyhavn (p74)

CRAIG PERSHC

15kr

ANDERS BLOMQVIST

Explore sleepy Bornholm the old-fashioned way – from its wooded interior to its fabulous coastline (p164)

CHARLOTTE HINDLE

Borrow a bike for free through Copenhagen's Bycykler city bike deal (p99)

Visit magnificent Frederiksborg Slot, superbly set across three islets on the edge of a lake (p114)

JON DAVISON

NED FRIARY

Hike along the gleaming white chalk cliffs of Møns Klint and stroll the beach below (p156)

See Denmark in miniature at Legoland, the country's most-visited family destination (p251)

JOHN BORTHWICK

Discover the Rundkirke (fortified Round Churches), which are unique to the island of Bornholm (p177)

NED FRIARY

Explore the Viking past at the fascinating Trelleborg ring fortress site (p140)

NED

Getting Started

Denmark is an easygoing, easy to manage country with lots of options for many tastes. The big problem is that it's expensive compared to most other countries, though some careful planning – especially of accommodation – can help keep costs down.

WHEN TO GO

July and August are peak season, with open-air concerts, street activity and basking on the beach. Other bonuses: longer hours at museums and other attractions, and potential savings on accommodation (some hotels drop their rates). Downsides: lots of other travellers celebrating midsummer with gusto. Mitigating factor: in late August, Danish kids are back in school – there's still summer weather but fewer crowds.

See Climate Charts (p297) for more information.

May and June can also be delightful for a visit. The land is a rich green, accented with fields of yellow rapeseed flowers, the weather is generally warm and comfortable, and you'll beat the rush of tourists. Although autumn can also be pleasant, it's not nearly as scenic as the rural landscape has by then largely turned brown. Winter, with its cold weather and long nights, is pretty inhospitable to tourism (see Climate p297). Many destinations close up in October and don't open again until late April.

Some attractions and businesses such as those in the accommodattion and hospitality services, use the terms 'high season' and 'low season'. The usage depends on the type of business, but generally the high season (longer opening hours and higher prices) coincides with

DON'T LEAVE HOME WITHOUT...

- Adapter plug – if you're coming from a country with different electrical outlets (p293).
- Bottle opener – there are no twist top beers, so unless you are born Danish and can pop a bottle with a lighter...
- Bike lock – a small one can be useful when locking up hire bikes or stabilising your luggage.
- Cameras, mini disks etc – very expensive in Denmark.
- Change purse – you may accumulate a lot of coins (p301).
- Eye mask – to help you sleep during the long days of summer.
- Mobile phone sim-cards and sending international text messages are very cheap (see p303)
- Motion-sickness pills – if you're sensitive and plan to ride ferries.
- Prescriptions – for any medicine you bring in. Customs officials are very strict on prescription drugs.
- Reading material – books in English can be expensive.
- Warm sleeping clothes – it can get cold at night even on mild days, especially if you're camping.
- Swiss army knife – though note that Denmark's anti-gang laws make it illegal to carry a knife with a blade more than 7cm long.
- Umbrella – it may be your constant companion.
- Water bottle – can save a bundle on bottled drinks.
- Your punctuality – trains run on time, and tours aren't a minute late. Danes operate similarly in social situations and don't wait for the unorganised.

the school summer holiday, from about mid-June to mid-August. 'Low season' generally means any time outside that period.

COSTS & MONEY

Unless you're Scandinavian, British or Japanese, you'll probably find Denmark an expensive country. Partly this is due to the 25% value-added tax (VAT), called *moms* in Danish, which is included in every price from hotel rooms and restaurant meals to car rentals and shop purchases.

Still, your actual costs will depend on how you travel and it is possible to see Denmark without spending a fortune. Staying in modest hotels and eating at inexpensive restaurants, you can expect to spend about 500kr per day assuming double occupancy, or 700kr if you're travelling alone (less in the countryside). Interestingly, top-end hotels, which commonly have good weekend and holiday rates, often cost only 30% more than regular rates at budget hotels.

If you're on a budget, consider Denmark's extensive network of camping grounds and hostels. Hostels are widely used by all age groups and are usually set up more like small hotels than cavernous drop-in centres. Travelling this way and preparing your own meals, you might get by on 250kr per day.

Expect to pay 650kr per day to hire the cheapest economy car; the daily rate drops to around 500kr on longer rentals. One advantage of travelling by car is that you can often find economical accommodation options outside the city centre, so you may save a bit on hotel bills. Car ferries are reasonable, but the charges can add up.

Long-distance public transport is reasonably priced, and it helps that Denmark is small – the most expensive train ticket between two points in Denmark costs about 300kr.

You can save money by purchasing a municipal discount card such as the Copenhagen Card, with free or discounted admissions to sights and activities, plus use of public transportation. See local listings.

HOW MUCH?

Row-your-own Viking ship in Roskilde: 50kr

Cycle hire: 60-75kr for 24hr (or free in Copenhagen, if you're lucky)

Locker in train station: 20kr for 24hr

Copenhagen Card: 199/399kr for 24/72hr

Windsurfing lesson: 400kr for 3hr, incl equipment rental

LONELY PLANET INDEX

Litre of gas/petrol: 8.2kr

Litre of bottled water: 11kr

Bottle of Carlsberg: 6-25kr

Souvenir T-shirt: 80kr

Hot sausage from a street vendor: 22kr

TRAVEL LITERATURE

General

Danmark by John Roth Andersen is an attractive hardback coffee-table book. A multilingual commentary complements the colour photography.

Discover Denmark – on Denmark and the Danes; Past, Present and Future by the Danish Cultural Institute provides a comprehensive overview of Danish society, covering topics such as history, politics, arts, culture and social issues.

Copenhagen Architecture Guide by Olaf Lind and Annemarie Lund is a substantial soft-cover book covering more than 300 noteworthy buildings in Copenhagen with interesting descriptions and colour photos.

A Kierkegaard Anthology by Robert Bretall (1973) is considered the definitive work on Denmark's famed philosopher, comprising a broad cross section of Kierkegaard's major works and somehow making it not too heavy. To read in more depth, look into Kierkegaard's *Sickness unto Death*, *Fear and Trembling* or *Either/Or*. In *Concluding Unscientific Postscript to the Philosophical Fragments* (1846), Kierkegaard passionately laid the groundwork for existentialism.

There's an avalanche of books by and about Hans Christian Andersen. The definitive biography is *Hans Christian Andersen* by Elias Bredsdorff. *Just as Well I'm Leaving – Around Europe with Hans Christian Andersen* by Michael Booth is about the newest, a funny, entertaining travelogue following in the footsteps of the amazing, peculiar, troubled writer.

TOP TENS

FILMS & PLAYS

- *Pelle the Conqueror* (1988) Director: Bille August
- *Babette's Feast* (1987) Director: Gabriel Axel
- *Italian for Beginners* (2000) Director: Lone Scherfig
- *The One and Only* (1978) Director: Susanne Bier
- *The Green Butchers* (2004) Director: Anders Thomas Jensen
- *The Idiots* (1998) Director: Lars von Trier
- *De Fem benspænd* aka *The Five Obstructions* (2003) Director: Jørgen Leth
- *Miss Smilla's Feeling for Snow* aka *Smilla's Sense of Snow* (1997) Director: Bille August
- *Copenhagen* (1998) Playwright: Michael Frayn
- *Hamlet* (er…1603 & 1604) Playwright: William Shakespeare

DANISH ICONS

- Carlsberg beer (p80)
- the Dannebrog (Danish flag, p24)
- Queen Margrethe II (p83)
- Little Mermaid (p76)
- Lars von Trier, film director (p11)
- Tivoli (p66)
- Arne Jacobsen's chairs (p38)
- Smørrebrød (p44)
- Anything Viking
- Viggo Mortensen (p37)

FESTIVALS

- Roskilde Festival (p299)
- Århus Festival (p300)
- Frederikssund Viking Festival (p299)
- Copenhagen Fashion & Design Festival (p83)
- Aalborg Carnival (p299)
- Hamlet Summer Plays (p299)
- Tønder Festival (p299)
- Silkeborg Riverboat Jazz Festival (p299)
- Copenhagen Jazz Festival (p84)
- Copenhagen Pride (p300)

The Golden Age of Danish Art by Hans Edvard Norregard-Nielsen takes a look at the art of the early 19th century; it's full of colour illustrations.

Children love *The Magic Hat and other Danish Fairy Tales* (edited by Clara Stroebe) and anything by Hans Christian Andersen.

For novels about Denmark and by Danish authors see p34.

History

There are numerous books about Viking-era culture and history. *The Viking World* by James Graham-Campbell is a book with handsome photos that outlines the history of the Vikings by detailing excavated sites and artefacts. *The Viking* by Bertil Almgren is an authoritative book tracing Viking history in both the Old and New Worlds.

In Denmark It Could Not Happen: The Flight of the Jews to Sweden in 1943 is a personal narrative of Jewish author Herbert Pundik's escape to Sweden during WWII and the assistance he received from fellow Danes.

The hardback *Denmark: A Modern History* by W Glyn Jones is one of the more comprehensive and insightful accounts of contemporary Danish society.

Women in Denmark, Yesterday and Today by Inga Dahlsgård traces Danish history from a woman's perspective.

INTERNET RESOURCES

Crown Prince Frederik (www.hkhkronprinsen.dk/english.php) Learn about the crown prince and his lovely new Australian-born crown princess.

Danish Tourist Board (www.visitdenmark.com) Comprehensive site, with lots of handy preplanning tips and links to all the regional tourist offices.

Danish Ministry of Foreign Affairs (www.denmark.dk) Official site, with information about doing business, studying, living and playing in Denmark, and useful links all around.

Lego (www.lego.com) All you ever wanted to know about the little plastic bricks – plus virtual games, on-line shopping, and up-to-date information on the Legoland parks including, of course, at Billund (p251).

Lonely Planet (www.lonelyplanet.com) Succinct summaries on travel to Denmark and almost anyplace on earth. Don't forget to visit the Thorn Tree for updates from fellow Lonely Planet readers and fans.

Wonderful Copenhagen (www.visitcopenhagen.com) The city tourist board's site is useful even if you're just transiting through the capital and surrounds.

Itineraries

CLASSIC ROUTES

JUTLAND'S CRÈME DE LA CRÈME

Two Weeks

Experience exquisite food, medieval architecture and Viking times down south at **Ribe** (p218), Denmark's oldest town. You need at least two days to walk through this living, well-preserved medieval town. Explore the narrow cobblestone alleys, enjoy Danish cuisine at some excellent restaurants, and just soak up the medieval spirit that is Ribe.

The seductive city of **Kolding** (p230), will dazzle with its edgy museums and gallant old castle. Allow at least a day and a night to explore before swinging into the middle of Jutland to **Legoland** (p251), home of the world's most popular children's toy. The **Lake District** (p253) follows before you hit the student capital in **Århus** (p239). You'll need at three days. Wild nights lie ahead at **Aalborg** (p275) on Jomfru Ane Gade. Dig a little deeper and discover some fine architecture. Give yourself two days to unravel this city on the Limfjord. **Skagen** (p285) tops off a route that takes you from Jutland's south to Denmark's northernmost tip. At least two days are needed to appreciate the magnificent artwork, indulge in fine seafood, and soak in its incredible northern light. Your senses will truly be awakened.

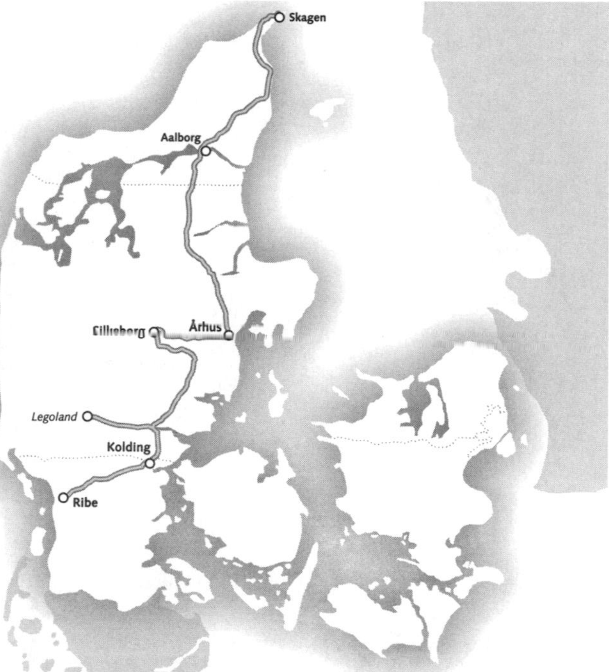
Skagen
Aalborg
Århus
Legoland
Kolding
Ribe

This classic route exposes Jutland's rich cultural history, gives you a magical night out along the hottest street in Denmark and culminates in an unforgettable moment seeing the majestic northern light with your own eyes.

NORTHERN SMORGASBORD

10 Days

Deservedly popular, this compact loop from Copenhagen around North Zealand is best approached in a leisurely fashion. Our trip starts west of the capital but it's just as easy to start the circle heading north.

After leaving fast-paced Copenhagen, you'll be in **Roskilde** (p122, at the edge of a fjord and paddling a Viking ship in no time. For the less galley-slave inclined, the hands-on museum dedicated to Viking ship building is fascinating, as is the church housing the tombs of Denmark's royalty.

North from here is magnificent **Frederiksborg Slot** (p114), dominating the unassuming town of Hillerød. It's hard to decide which is more impressive, the baroque interiors or the regal grounds, perfect for a stroll.

To truly appreciate the northern lights and sunbathing Scandinavian-style, head to the northern beaches: **Tisvildeleje** (p120) is pristine; **Gilleleje** (p119), a modern harbour, has its fair share of sand and surf; and **Hornbæk** (p117) is the place where the young and good-looking go to appreciate the natural beauty and their own.

When the pleasures of the sun and sea become just too much to bear, continue east, then south along the coast to Hamlet's **Kronborg Slot** (p109) in Helsingør. The actual history of this massive fortress/toll booth may provoke existential questions like 'to jump on the ferry to Sweden or not?'

Be sure to skip the highway and take the spectacular coastal road south to Humlebæk and the **Louisiana Museum** (p109), whose splendid architecture rivals it's collection of contemporary art from around the world. It's a short but picturesque drive along the 'Danish Riviera' back to Copenhagen and big city life.

This 175km northern loop has it all, from Viking ships to royal castles, from sun worshipping hedonism to cutting-edge video installations. This route deserves more than a day-tripping mentality, so allow yourself more than a week to do each place justice.

Gilleleje
Hornbæk
Tisvildeleje
Helsingør
Humlebæk
Copenhagen
Roskilde

ROADS LESS TRAVELLED

A CASTLE, A LAKESIDE TOWN, WINDSURFING & A REMOTE ISLAND

One Week

This unique adventure follows a horse-shoe route around the northern half of Jutland. It ignores the clichéd Denmark while presenting a plethora of contrasting sights which will change your perception of the country. A slice of Jutland untouched by the footprints of high-scale tourism, combining romantic bliss with adventure and a bunch of charismatic towns.

Sitting on the edge of two idyllic lakes is **Viborg** (p268), a city that is both romantically green and historically religious. **Støttrup Slot** (p270) comes next, an impressive castle that delights inside and out. It's a double-moated castle high on character and great to explore. Flowers, butterflies and good times await a little further north on the island of Mors where you will find **Flowers Jesperhus** (p270). The colourful park will delight the romantic at heart as 1000 different butterflies fly freely in Scandinavia's largest enclosed habitat. Wild times can be had up on the brazen, windy west coast in the surfing hamlet of **Klitmøller** (p291). Windsurfing is the main player in these parts, so it's an ideal place to learn the basics on the inland lake and chow down some fresh seafood. Contrasting beautifully just off the east coast is **Læsø** (p282), an island embedded in tradition and festive atmosphere. Læsø is rarely visited by international tourists but is well worth the effort as it boasts some fine landscapes and remarkable characters.

Læsø
Klitmøller
Flowers Jesperhus
Støttrup Slot
Viborg

See a different side to Denmark with this leisurely tour. It's not one of the usual tourist get aways but it has loads of charm, adventure and romance.

SOUTHERN HIDEAWAYS

One Week

Most travellers head north or west from Copenhagen but this trip takes you to islands south of Zealand where it's possible to feel like you're far from civilisation, quite a feat in this otherwise densely developed part of the country.

On E55 it's almost a straight shot south to Møn and the charming town of **Stege** (p152). There's a bird-watching tower on the untouched small island of **Nyord** (p154) only a few minutes away. Driving east from Stege you pass the **Keldby Kirke** (p155), worth a stop for its remarkable frescoes. It's best to base yourself here or further east to truly feel like you've left the rest of the world behind. The eastern side of the island is dominated by forests great for hiking and the white chalk Møns Klint. Climb down to the waters' edge to appreciate the spectacular view. A short drive north of here is peaceful **Liselund Park** (p156), designed to spark reveries in the most jaded. South of both is the town of **Klintholm Havn** (p157), where you'll find a narrow sandy beach and a welcoming vibe from the locals.

Rather than returning the same way, take the 287 west from Stege to the island of Bogø and cross over to the island of Falster from where it's only a short drive south to the beach resort of **Marielyst** (p160).

You can return to Copenhagen the same way you came or take a slight detour to the forests and lakes between **Sorø** (p136) and **Næstved** (p143) – an ideal place to park the car and test your pedal power.

Leave your troubles and your taste for nightlife behind and experience small towns, island life and a touch of the back country – well, as close to it as you can get in this part of Denmark. After all, it's only a short drive back to Copenhagen.

Ulvshale
Nyord
Udby
Elmelunde
Keldby
Borre
Kalvehave
Stege
Koster
Busemarke
Tjørnemarke
Neble
Klintholm Havn
Kraneled
Damsholte
Bogø By
Tostenæs
Askeby
Nyby

TAILORED TRIPS

HISTORICAL JUTLAND WITH A SPLASH OF ROYALTY One Week

This journey starts in **Sønderborg** (p234) for your initial introduction to Denmark's war-torn past with Germany. A couple of brilliantly presented museums stand on the fields that bore the brunt of Germany's successful invasion during the Battle of Dybbøl in 1864.

From there it's time to reflect in the classically English-style gorgeous gardens of Gråsten's **royal summer palace** (p233). Then head west to the intimate and visually enchanting village of **Møgeltønder** (p229) and yet another royal castle. A tour of the garden, a prayer in the church and a coffee on one of the prettiest streets in Denmark are all elementary before kicking on to historic **Ribe** (p218).

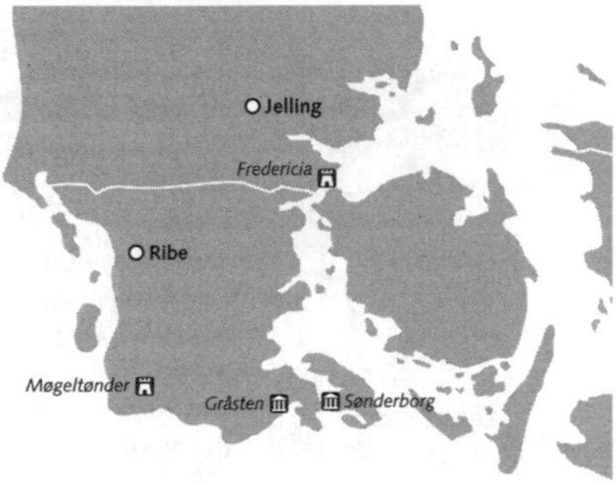
Jelling
Fredericia
Ribe
Møgeltønder
Gråsten
Sønderborg

Fredericia (p249) is next and is where Denmark's war-torn past comes to the forefront. The Danes successfully defended the town, and the border, against a formidable German assault. Its ramparts are still intact and portray the harsh simplicity of 19th-century warfare.

To finish, you end in **Jelling** (p250) where, in a sense, it all began. It was in this picturesque village that historians were able to piece together the beginnings of the Danish monarchy and draw an effective connection between Gorm the Old and today's royals. It's little wonder that its rune stones are called Denmark's birth certificate.

KID FRIENDLY, ADULT APPROVED One Week

Sometimes it's best to cater to their needs, indulge their fantasies, just outright spoil the little buggers, especially when it's fun for adults too. The destinations for this trip take you beyond the obvious attractions of **Legoland** (p251). They are scattered around Zealand and Lolland, an island to the south, and may best be thought of as vacations from your vacation and not necessarily a route to follow step by step.

The beaches on the northern coast from **Tisvildeleje** (p120) to **Rågeleje** (p107) are family oriented; the water is gentle and the kids will find plenty of playmates.

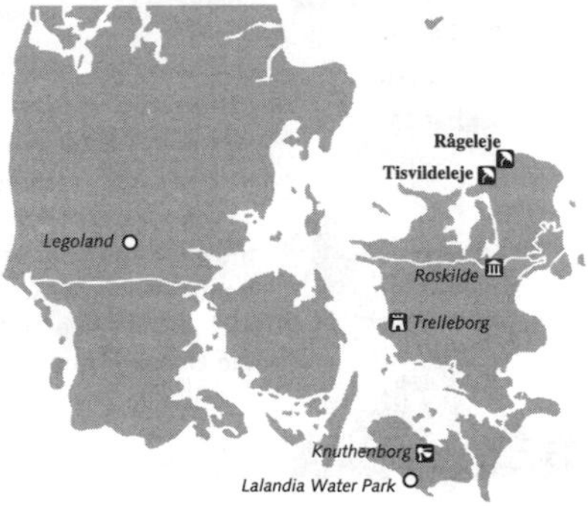
Rågeleje
Tisvildeleje
Legoland
Roskilde
Trelleborg
Knuthenborg
Lalandia Water Park

History always goes down easier when you can touch things. With that in mind, kid-friendly Museum Island at the **Viking Ship Museum** (p123) in Roskilde and the **Viking fortress** (p140) at Trelleborg, both in central Zealand, will make them want to be scholars.

For a taste of African wildlife take the toddlers to **Knuthenborg Safari Park** (p163) in north central Lolland, and you might as well pop down to enormous **Lalandia Water Park** (p163) near Rodby in southern Lolland. Even if it's not hot, the combination of water and slides brings out the juvenile in all of us.

The Authors

ANDREW BENDER

Coordinating Author

Yet another LP author with an MBA, Andy left the business world and now does what every MBA secretly dreams of: travelling and writing about it. Since then, his writing has appeared in *Travel + Leisure, Fortune, Men's Journal* and various Lonely Planet titles. Andy's been drawn to Denmark since childhood, when his parents brought him a tiny wooden Viking from their Danish holiday (he still has it). When at home in Los Angeles, he bikes at the beach, obsesses over Japanese and Korean food and schemes over ways to spoil his nieces and nephews.

MICHAEL GROSBERG

Michael was raised in the Washington DC area, studied philosophy in Michigan and Israel and then worked in business on a small island in the Northern Marianas. After a long trip through Asia and across the US, he left for journalism and NGO work in South Africa. Michael then pursued graduate work in comparative literature in New York City, where he discovered the philosophy of Kierkegaard and wanted to know what kind of country could produce such a well-adjusted person. Post academia, he has since taken many random jobs and currently teaches at university in between trips abroad. Michael updated the North Zealand, Southern Zealand and Møn, Falster & Lolland chapters.

SALLY O'BRIEN

Sally grew up surrounded by Danish furniture, Danish jewellery and Danish pastries, thus making her a logical choice to spend some time in Copenhagen on the trail of more bits and pieces to add to her various collections (the pastries keep getting eaten…). Ruddy enough to pass for a Dane before she opens her mouth and starts mangling the language, Sally adored almost every part of this job, especially the great English-language skills of the locals and their love of herring, bacon and pâté. Jaywalking dilemmas and bicycle-lane fiascos still haunt her though. Sally updated the Copenhagen chapter.

RICK STAREY

Rick became infatuated with Denmark when Bjarne Riis stormed home to win the Tour de France in 1996. Since then he's cycled the islands, explored the towns and commenced this project the day Australian/Danish ties were bound forever as Crown Princess Mary sealed the deal with Danish royalty. All in all, it's been a fairytale. Rick updated the Jutland chapters along with the Outdoor Activities section.

ANDREW STONE

Andrew first visited Denmark in the 1990s to see friends who had married on Funen. He has been back regularly since then to visit them, to enjoy the country's fantastic café culture and its charming natives, to feed his interest in Denmark's history and to feed his face on pastries. Andrew updated the Bornholm and Funen chapters.

Snapshot

To misquote *Hamlet,* if Shakespeare were alive today, we think he'd be hard pressed to find much rotten in the state of Denmark.

Denmark has the highest per-capita gross domestic product in the European Union, and its citizens enjoy a high standard of living. Literacy is 100%, unemployment is low, and its social welfare programmes are the envy of much of the rest of the world. The country's main exports are natural gas and crude oil. Education is free, and about half of all Danish students who graduate from secondary school continue on to higher education.

Not that everything's *all* pastries and cream.

The last few years have been turbulent ones – by Danish standards anyway – in the social and political realms. Not unlike other European nations, there's been a gradual shift to the right in this famously liberal nation. It's been reflected in a growing concern over immigration – particularly from Muslim countries – and an erosion of traditional values.

Perhaps there's no clearer illustration of this change than the rise of the Danish People's Party (DPP). Although it was founded only in 1995, it's already the third-largest party in the Danish parliament with 12% of the seats which make it an important swing vote. The DPP's platform supports, among other things, the monarchy, the national church, strong defence, law and order, and the preservation of Danish cultural heritage. Also significantly, the party's website states 'Denmark is not an immigrant country and has never been so. We will not accept a transformation to a multiethnic society.'

In practical terms, the DPP's participation has made the difference in Denmark's joining the US, UK and other allies in the 2003 Iraq War. Domestically, too, Denmark took what would have been a distinctly un-Danish move a decade ago: restrictions on immigration and on foreigners marrying Danes.

The next national election is due in 2005; it's one we'll be watching with keen interest.

FAST FACTS

Unified as a state: 10th century AD

Population: 5.4 million (July 2004)

Type of government: constitutional monarchy

Parliament: Folketing (179 seats)

Comprises 14 counties, 2 boroughs, 273 municipalities

Important crops: wheat, barley, sugar beet, rapeseed (for canola oil)

Coastline: 7314km

Unemployment (May 2004): 5.9% (versus 9% for Euro-Zone)

History

Today's Denmark may seem like the paragon of all that is civilised and worthy. But this tiny nation sits at the crossroads of northern Europe, anything but placid over the years. Scratch the surface, and you'll find Vikings plundering, wars being fought, and empires and alliances built and fallen.

THE STONE AGE

Indications are that present-day Denmark was inhabited intermittently by humans during the interglacial period. The first permanent settlements, though, were probably founded in about 12,000 BC. Glacial ice had by then receded and the lichen and mosses of the low-lying tundra attracted herds of reindeer, followed by nomadic hunters.

Stone Age culture relied primarily on hunting, but as the climate gradually warmed and the tundra gave way to forest, the reindeer migrated further north. Eventually hunters resettled near the sea and subsisted by fishing and catching sea birds and seals.

A History of Denmark by Palle Lauring is a well-written excursion through the lives and times of the Danish people.

By 4000 BC, people began to grow more food crops, and agriculture and the keeping of animals became common. Woods were cleared by slash-and-burn and grain was sown in the resulting ash.

Villages developed around the fields and the villagers began to bury their dead in dolmens, a type of grave monument comprising upright stones and topped by a large capstone; you can still find a number of these ancient dolmens in Denmark's meadows.

THE BRONZE AGE (1800–500 BC)

Bronze was introduced to Denmark in about 1800 BC, giving rise to skilled artisans who fashioned weapons, tools, jewellery and finely crafted works of art. New trade routes to the south brought a supply of bronze – and influences from as far away as Crete and Mycenae.

Valuable objects were often buried in bogs as sacrificial offerings. One superb artefact is the Sun Chariot, crafted 3500 years ago by followers of a sun cult and found by a farmer in a Zealand field in 1902. It's now on display at Nationalmuseet (p68) in Copenhagen, along with Bronze Age lurs that are among the world's oldest surviving musical instruments.

THE IRON AGE (500 BC–AD 800)

With the arrival of locally-available iron, long-distance trade trickled off. New iron ploughs to till fields enabled the development of large-scale agricultural communities.

Present-day Denmark's linguistic and cultural roots date to the late Iron Age and the arrival of the Danes, a tribe thought to have migrated south from Sweden about AD 500.

THREAT OF THE FRANKS

At the dawn of the 9th century, the territory of present-day Denmark was on the perimeter of Europe, but Charlemagne (768–814) extended the power of the Franks northward to present-day northern Germany.

TIMELINE

c 1500 BC
Sun Chariot is crafted

AD 793
Vikings invade Lindisfarne monastery, Northumbria (present-day England)

Hoping to ward off a Frankish invasion, Godfred, king of Jutland, reinforced an impressive earthen rampart called the Danevirke, that ran the length of his southern border from the North Sea coast to the town of Hedeby (present-day Schleswig, now part of Germany). However, the Franks breached the rampart, later combining their military adventures in Denmark with establishment of Christian missions.

Denmark's reaction: Viking expeditions (at least the southward ones).

EARLY VIKING ERA

Although unrecorded raids had probably been occurring for decades, the start of the Viking Age is generally dated from AD 793, when Nordic Vikings brutally raided Lindisfarne Monastery, off the coast of Northumbria in northeastern England. Survivors of the Lindisfarne attack described the Vikings' sleek square-rigged vessels as 'dragons flying in the air' and the raiders as 'terrifying heathens'.

The Vikings were, by and large, adventurous opportunists who took advantage of the turmoil and unstable political conditions that prevailed elsewhere in Europe. In time their campaigns evolved from the mere forays of pirates into organised expeditions that established far-flung colonies overseas.

Different Viking groups came from the territories that now make up Denmark, Norway and Sweden, and each group had its own dominant sphere. The Swedes colonised the Baltic countries, which became the bases for expeditions deep into present-day Russia. The Norwegian domain included Scotland, Ireland and the Shetland, Orkney and Hebrides island groups. It was a Norwegian explorer, Erik the Red, who colonised Iceland and Greenland; his son, Leif Eriksson, went on to explore the coast of North America.

DID YOU KNOW?

So fearsome were the Vikings that the English introduced a special prayer into church services: 'From the fury of the Northmen, good Lord, deliver us'.

Danish Vikings primarily visited the coast of Western Europe and northeastern England, with the first documented raid by Danish Vikings occurring in 835. England was particularly vulnerable because it comprised a number of warring kingdoms.

Early Viking raiders often targeted churches and monasteries, not for their religious significance but for their rich repositories of gold and jewels. Because the churches also served as centres of learning, many irreplaceable documents, books and other cultural artefacts went up in flames during the raids.

By 850, Danish Vikings had established a settlement in Kent, and soon sizeable groups of Danish colonists came to control northwestern England (a region that became known as the Danelaw). But the Anglo-Saxon king Alfred the Great (871–99) successfully repelled the Danes and forced them to accept a boundary that recognised his reign over the kingdom of Wessex.

UNIFICATION OF DENMARK

Denmark's lands, like the rest of Scandinavia, have a long history of being ruled by rival regional kings, although by the early 9th century Jutland (and parts of southern Norway) appears to have been more or less united under a single king. In the late 9th century a move towards Danish unification occurred when warriors led by the Norwegian chieftain Hardegon conquered

950–985
King Harald I (Bluetooth) unifies Denmark

1219
The Dannebrog (Danish flag) is raised for the first time

THE VIKINGS SLEPT HERE

A fascinating legacy of Denmark's rich Viking history are the four impressive ring fortresses discovered in the Danish countryside, which date from about AD 980.

Although the purpose of these Viking camps is not entirely understood, the current popular theory suggests that they were used by the monarchy to strengthen its domestic position, rather than as staging grounds for Viking forays overseas. Their locations are rather remote for easy use in naval expeditions, and in any case their design suggests a defensive function rather than an offensive one.

The fortresses are notable for their massive earthen walls, moats and gates at the four points of the compass, constructed with mathematical precision and symmetrical forms. Long, wooden stave buildings inside the walls were all of an equal measure. The lack of houses for nobles indicates that these were barracks for soldiers.

The fortress at Trelleborg (p140) and the Fyrkat fortress near Hobro (p264) are open to the public, with educational displays, reconstructed Viking-style buildings, and symmetrical walls still intact after more than 1000 years. Two other fortress sites on Funen and Jutland have not been developed for visitors.

the Jutland peninsula; Hardegon then began to extend his power base across the rest of Denmark's territory.

The Danish monarchy can be traced back to Gorm the Old, Hardegon's son, who established his reign in the early 10th century, ruling from Jelling in central Jutland.

Gorm's son, Harald Bluetooth, was throned in 950 and, during his 35-year rule, completed the conquest of Denmark. He spearheaded the conversion of Danes to Christianity, partly to appease his powerful Frankish neighbours to the south who, a century earlier, had sent the missionary Ansgar to build churches in the Danish towns of Ribe and Hedeby.

DID YOU KNOW?

Denmark is the oldest monarchy in Europe.

END OF THE VIKING ERA

Under the reigns of Harald Bluetooth's son Sweyn Forkbeard (985–1014) and grandsons Harald II (1014–18) and Canute the Great (1018–35), England was conquered and a short-lived Anglo-Danish kingdom formed.

Canute the Great was the first true Danish king to sit on the throne of England, reigning in much the same manner as an English king except that he employed Scandinavian soldiers to maintain his command. The period of Danish rule in England ended in 1042 with the death of Canute's son Hardecanute, after which the balance of power shifted to the English heirs of Alfred the Great. Many of the Danes who had settled in England elected to stay on to live under English rule.

There were a couple of later, unsuccessful attempts by the Danes to reclaim England, but the Viking era was clearly on the wane. The defeat of Norwegian Vikings by Harold II of England at the Battle of Stamford Bridge in 1066 marked the end of the Viking Era.

THE MIDDLE AGES

During the medieval period, Denmark was plagued by internal strife, plots, counter plots and assassinations involving rival nobles, wealthy landowners and corrupt church leaders.

1375

Five-year-old Oluf becomes King of Denmark

1397

Queen Margrethe I establishes the Kalmar Union of Denmark, Norway and Sweden

Probably the most notable incident involved the imposition of a personal tax by King Canute II and his dispatch of heavy-handed bailiffs to collect it. Resistance was so widespread that in 1086 Canute was chased from Jutland by a band of rebellious farmers, cornered in an Odense church and stabbed to death.

The monarchy was again thrown into turmoil in 1131 when Magnus the Strong, son of the ageing King Niels and heir to the throne, slew his cousin Knud Lavard out of fear that Knud Lavard's popularity would make him king.

This murder touched off a bitter civil war that resulted in the death of Magnus the Strong, Niels and five of his bishops. Knud's brother Erik Emune ascended the throne in 1134 but his tyrannical rule ended abruptly with his assassination just three years later. Civil strife continued unabated until Valdemar, son of Knud Lavard, took the throne in 1157.

King Valdemar I united the war-weary country and enacted Denmark's first written laws, known as the *Jyske Lov* (Jutland Code). His successors enacted other laws that were quite progressive for their times: no imprisonment without just cause, an annual assembly of the *hof* (national council), and the first supreme court.

THE KALMAR UNION

In 1363 Norway's King Haakon married Margrethe, daughter of the Danish king Valdemar IV. When Valdemar IV died in 1375, Oluf, the five-year-old son of Haakon and Margrethe, was chosen king of Denmark. After the death of King Haakon five years later, Oluf became king of Norway as well.

However, Oluf was still too young to take charge, so his mother Margrethe assumed de facto control of the Crown. And after Oluf died in 1387, Margrethe became the official head of state.

The next year Swedish nobles turned to Margrethe for assistance in a rebellion against their unpopular German-born king (there were already longstanding royal ties between Sweden and Norway). The Swedes hailed Margrethe as their regent, and in turn she sent Danish troops to Sweden, securing victory over the king's forces.

In 1397 Margrethe established an alliance between Denmark, Norway and Sweden known as the Kalmar Union, to counter the powerful German-based Hanseatic League that had come to dominate regional trade.

FLYING THE FLAG

The Danish flag, the Dannebrog, is the oldest national flag in the world. Legend has it that in 1219, during an invasion of Estonia by Valdemar II (the Victorious), an imminent Danish defeat was reversed when a red banner with a white cross fell from the sky. A voice from the mist announced that if the banner was raised, the Danes would win. The Danes raised the banner, won their battle, and proclaimed the banner their national flag. Its central design element, the cross on a solid background, was later adopted by the other Nordic countries.

Danes continue to take pride in their flag and display it whenever possible. The flag can be seen hanging pennant-style in shopping streets, as a graphic device in magazine ads, flying high on the flagpoles that stand beside virtually every home in the countryside, and flying low on tables at parties in private homes.

1523
Kalmar Union is dissolved

1665
King Frederik III establishes absolute monarchy and crowns himself king

In 1410 King Erik of Pomerania, Margrethe's grandson, staged an unsuccessful attack on the Hanseatic League, which exhausted the resources of the Kalmar Union. Erik's penchant for appointing Danes to public office in Sweden and Norway soured relations with aristocrats in those countries. In 1438 the Swedish council withdrew from the union, whereupon the Danish nobility deposed Erik.

Erik's successor, King Christopher III, made amends by pledging to keep the administrations of the three countries separate. However, the union continued to be a rocky one, and in 1523 the Swedes elected their own king, Gustav Vasa. The Kalmar Union was permanently dissolved, but Norway would remain under Danish rule for another three centuries.

DID YOU KNOW?

The Order of the Elephant was instituted by King Christian 1 in the 1470s to celebrate the battle elephants of the Christian Crusades.

THE LUTHERAN REFORMATION & CIVIL WAR

A pivotal power struggle involving the monarchy and the Catholic Church was played out during the Danish Reformation.

Over some 10 years beginning in 1523, King Frederik I went from promising to fight heresy against Catholicism to inviting Lutheran preachers to Denmark. When Frederik died 10 years later, the lack of a clear successor left the country in civil war.

In 1534, Hanseatic mercenaries from Lübeck (now Germany) invaded southern Jutland and Zealand. By and large the Lübeckers were welcomed as liberators by peasants and members of the middle class, who were in revolt against the noble classes.

Alarmed by the revolt, a coalition of aristocrats and Catholic bishops crowned the Lutheran Christian III as king. Still, the rebellion raged on.

In Jutland, manor houses were set ablaze and the peasants made advances against the armies of the aristocracy. Christian's general, Rantzau, took control and quickly cut Lübeck off from the sea. He then made a sweeping march northward through Jutland, brutally smashing peasant bands. Copenhagen, where merchants supported the uprising and welcomed the prospect of becoming a Hanseatic stronghold, was besieged by Rantzau's troops for more than a year. Cut off from the outside world, Copenhagen's citizens suffered starvation and epidemics before surrendering in 1536, marking the end of the civil war.

Christian III quickly consolidated his power. He took a surprisingly lenient approach to the merchants and Copenhagen burghers who had revolted, and in turn they pledged their allegiance to the Crown. Catholic bishops, on the other hand, were arrested and monasteries, churches and other ecclesiastical estates became the property of the Crown.

Thus the Danish Lutheran Church became the only state-sanctioned denomination and was placed under the direct control of the king. For all practical purposes, church officials became civil servants.

Buoyed by a treasury enriched by confiscated Church properties, the monarchy emerged from the civil war stronger than ever.

WARS WITH SWEDEN

The first part of Christian IV's long reign (1588–1648) was a period of prosperity and growth. Then in 1625 the king entered the ill-advised Thirty Years War, hoping to neutralise Swedish expansion. The war resulted in substantial losses for Denmark.

late 18th century
Feudal obligations abolished

1807
Battle of Copenhagen

In 1655 the Swedish king invaded Poland, and although the victory was swift, the Swedes found themselves bogged down trying to secure that vast country. Denmark had been seething for revenge against Sweden, and word of Swedish troubles ignited nationalistic fervour. Christian IV's successor, Frederik III, once again declared war on Sweden in 1657. For the Danish government, ill-prepared for battle, it was a tremendous miscalculation.

Sweden's King Gustave, looking for an honourable way out of Poland, gladly withdrew but led his troops through Germany and into Jutland, plundering his way north.

A romantic historical novel *Music and Silence* by Rose Tremain is set in the time of Christian IV and has some wonderfully evocative descriptions of courtly life in Copenhagen.

During the winter of 1657–58 – the most severe in Danish history – King Gustave marched his soldiers across the frozen seas of the Lille Bælt between Fredericia and the island of Funen. King Gustave's uncanny success unnerved the Danes and he proceeded without serious resistance across the Store Bælt to Lolland and then on to Falster.

The Swedish king had barely made it across the frozen waters of the Storstrømmen to Zealand when the thawing ice broke away behind him, precariously separating him and his advance detachment from the rest of his forces. However, the Danes failed to recognise their sudden advantage; instead of capturing the Swedish king, they sued for peace and agreed to yet another disastrous treaty.

In February 1658 the Treaty of Roskilde, the most lamented treaty in Denmark's history, was signed – Denmark lost a third of its territory, including the island of Bornholm and all territories on the Swedish mainland. Only Bornholm, which eventually staged a bloody revolt against the Swedes, would again fly the Danish flag.

ABSOLUTE MONARCHY

In 1660, King Frederik III cunningly convened a gathering of nobles, placed them under siege, and forced them to nullify their powers of council. Then Frederik conferred upon himself the right of absolute rule. In 1665, he enshrined the new system in an absolutist constitution called the *Kongeloven* (Royal Act), which became the law of the land for almost two centuries.

DID YOU KNOW?

A polar bear was included in the Danish coat of arms in the 1660s to symbolise the country's claim of sovereignty over Greenland.

In the spirit of the day, the exact content of the constitution was not made public at the time, and for nearly 50 years no copies were allowed to be printed. But in essence the document said this: the king was the highest head on earth, above all human laws and inferior to God alone, and the king had supreme legislative, judicial and military authority. You might say it was a fairly liberal document. So concentrated were royal powers that Frederik's successor had to place the crown upon his own head during the church service – nobody else was deemed worthy!

The monarchy managed to rebuild the military and put up a reasonable fight in three more wars with Sweden (1675–79, 1699–1700 and 1709–20), but the lost territories remained lost. Still, throughout the rest of the 18th century, Danes and Swedes managed to coexist without serious hostilities.

THE AGE OF REFORMS

The peace of the 18th century gave Denmark a much needed economic boost and set the stage for political and social change. In 1784, crown prince Frederik VI, then just 16, assumed control. More benevolent

1849

Danish constitution enacted

1864

Prussian prime minister Otto von Bismarck declares war on Denmark than his predecessors, Frederik VI brought progressive landowners into government and introduced a sweeping series of reforms.

With the French Revolution brewing, the government saw the value in improving the lot of the Danish peasantry. Under Frederik VI's leadership, all feudal obligations were abolished, including those that had required peasants to reside within prescribed boundaries and provide labour. Large tracts of land were broken up and redistributed to the landless, and education was made compulsory for all children under the age of 14.

DID YOU KNOW?

The 1759 Gråsten Castle is now home for Crown Prince Frederik and Crown Princess Mary, a wedding gift from Queen Margrethe and Prince Henrik.

THE NAPOLEONIC WARS (1796–1815)

By the turn of the 19th century, Denmark's foreign trade was growing and Britain, which controlled the seas, was concerned. In 1800 Denmark signed a pact of armed neutrality with Sweden, Prussia and Russia. Britain regarded the act as hostile and in 1801 sent a naval expedition to attack Copenhagen, inflicting heavy damage on the Danish fleet and forcing Denmark to withdraw from the pact.

Denmark managed to avoid further conflicts and actually profited from the war trade until 1807, when a new treaty between France and Russia once again drew the Danes closer to the conflict. However, the British, wary of Napoleon's growing influence in the Baltic, feared that Denmark might support France. So the British fleet unleashed a sudden, brutal bombardment on neutral Copenhagen, setting much of the city ablaze, destroying its naval yard and confiscating the entire Danish fleet: nearly 170 vessels. The only ship left standing in Copenhagen harbour was a private yacht that the king of England had given his nephew, Denmark's then-crown prince Frederik.

DID YOU KNOW?

The village of Trankebar (Tranquebar) in India was the sixth-largest Danish settlement in the world, including Denmark, in the 1700s.

Although the unprovoked attack was unpopular enough back home to have been roundly criticised by the British parliament, Britain nonetheless kept the Danish fleet. The British then offered the Danes an alliance – something that might have been accepted by Denmark a few months earlier but had since become unthinkable.

Later that year the Danes joined the continental alliance against Britain, and Britain blockaded both Danish and Norwegian waters, causing poverty in Denmark and famine in Norway.

When Napoleon fell in 1814, the Swedes, then allied with Britain, successfully demanded that Denmark cede Norway to them.

THE GOLDEN AGE

Although the 19th century started out dismal and lean, by the 1830s Denmark had a cultural awakening as a flourishing centre of arts, literature and

ICELAND, GREENLAND & THE FAROE ISLANDS

When Norway broke its political ties with Denmark, the former Norwegian colonies of Iceland, Greenland and the Faroe Islands stayed under Danish administration.

Iceland became an independent state within the Danish realm in 1918 and became completely independent in 1944, while Greenland and the Faroe Islands (p40) remain part of the Kingdom of Denmark to this day. The Faroe Islands have had home rule since 1948, Greenland since 1979, and each has two parliamentary representatives in the Danish Folketing (p72).

1940 Germany invades Denmark

1943 Resistance smuggles 7200 Jews into Sweden

philosophy. Philosopher Søren Kierkegaard, theologian Nikolaj Frederik Severin Grundtvig and writer Hans Christian Andersen emerged as prominent figures. Sculptor Bertel Thorvaldsen bestowed his grand neoclassical statues on Copenhagen, and Christoffer Wilhelm Eckersberg introduced the Danish school of art, which paid homage to everyday life.

DID YOU KNOW?

A monkey killed in a 1755 Lisbon earthquake is buried in Liselund Slot, Møn; its agitation before the disaster apparently saved its owners' lives.

Spurred by these new ideas and the rising expectations of a growing middle class, the Crown began to see the need for democratic principles. Provincial assemblies were formed, providing a vehicle for debate and giving rise to political parties. Two growing factions – farmers and liberals – joined forces to form a united liberal party in 1846.

The powers of the monarchy were already on the wane when revolution swept across Europe in the spring of 1848. The new Danish king, Frederik VII, under pressure from the liberal party, convened a national assembly to abolish the absolute monarchy and draw up a democratic constitution.

The constitution, enacted 5 June 1849, established a parliament with two chambers, Folketing and Landsting, whose members were elected by popular vote. Although the king retained a limited voice, parliament took control of legislative powers. The constitution also established an independent judiciary and guaranteed the rights of free speech, religion and assembly. Denmark changed overnight from a virtual dictatorship to one of the most democratic countries in Europe.

SCHLESWIG & HOLSTEIN

The duchies of Schleswig and Holstein in southern Jutland, long under Danish rule, became restless during the nationalist fervour of the 1840s. Holstein, which was linguistically and culturally German, had already affiliated itself with the German Federation, while Schleswig was inhabited by people of both Danish and German heritage. When Denmark's new constitution threatened to incorporate Schleswig as an integral part of Denmark, the German population in the duchy allied with Holstein, sparking a war against the Danes. The three-year revolt ended in 1851, only when Denmark agreed not to further tighten bonds with Schleswig.

In 1864 the Prussian prime minister, Otto von Bismarck, declared war on a militarily weak Denmark and captured Schleswig within months. This further erosion of Denmark's domain raised doubts about Denmark's survival as a nation.

In the wake of that defeat, a conservative government took power in Denmark – and retained power until the end of the century. The conservatives oversaw a number of economic advances: the railway was extended throughout the country; Danish farmers found a ready grain market in Britain; and Denmark's major industries – shipbuilding, brewing and sugar refining – developed to maturity.

Tove Ditlevsen's childhood in Vesterbro during the Depression is recounted in his memoir *Early Spring*.

EARLY 20TH CENTURY

In 1901, the Venstrereformparti (Left Reform Party) came into power and carried through a number of broad-minded reforms, including revising the constitution to extend the right to vote to women.

Denmark remained neutral during WWI. Northern Schleswig was returned to Denmark following a 1920 plebiscite. In the period between the two world wars a social-democratic government emerged, passing

1953
Danish constitution is amended to allow a female monarch

1971
Protesters proclaim the Free State of Christiania

some landmark legislation that softened the effects of the Great Depression and laid the foundations for a welfare state.

WWII

Denmark again declared neutrality at the outbreak of WWII, but Germany, which felt threatened by the growing Allied presence in Norway, coveted coastal bases in northern Jutland.

In the early hours of 9 April 1940, German forces simultaneously crossed into southern Jutland and landed troops at a half-dozen strategic points throughout Denmark. They captured a military airfield in Copenhagen, sent commandos into the city and issued an ultimatum: that Copenhagen would be bombed if the Danes resisted.

With only a nominal military at their disposal and German warplanes flying overhead, King Christian X and parliamentary heads hastily met at Amalienborg and, under protest, decided to yield to the Germans. The Danish government did manage to obtain assurances from the Nazis that Denmark would be allowed to retain some degree of internal autonomy. Before nightfall Denmark was an occupied country.

The Danes managed to tread a thin line, running domestic affairs under close Nazi supervision, until August 1943 when the Germans took outright control.

A Danish resistance movement quickly mushroomed. In October 1943, as the Nazis were preparing to round up Jewish Danes, the Resistance, using night-running fishing boats, quickly smuggled some 7200 Jews – about 90% of those remaining in Denmark – into neutral Sweden.

Although the island of Bornholm was heavily bombarded by Soviet forces, the rest of Denmark emerged from WWII relatively unscathed.

DID YOU KNOW?

In recognition of its actions in saving its Jewish population, Denmark is remembered as one of the Righteous Among the Nations at the Yad Vashem Holocaust Memorial in Jerusalem.

POSTWAR & PROTESTS

The Social Democrats led a comprehensive social-welfare state in postwar Denmark and the cradle-to-grave securities that guarantee medical care, education and public assistance were expanded. As the economy grew and the labour market increased, women entered the workforce in unprecedented numbers, and household incomes reached new heights.

King Frederik IX (1899–1972) had no sons, so a 1953 referendum amended the Danish constitution to allow women to succeed to the throne. Margrethe II was proclaimed queen in 1972, Denmark's first female monarch since the 14th century. That same year, the Landesting was eliminated and the Folketing made the nation's unicameral parliament.

In the 1960s, a rebellion by young people, disillusioned with growing materialism, the nuclear arms race and an authoritarian educational system, took hold in the larger cities. Student protests broke out on university campuses, and squatters occupied vacant buildings.

The movement came to a head in Copenhagen in 1971, when protesters tore down the fence of an abandoned military base at the east side of Christianshavn and turned the site into a commune, the 'free state of Christiania' (p76). Thousands of people flocked here, and the government let Christiania stand as a 'social experiment'. More than three decades later, Christiania is still a bastion for alternative lifestyles, with a population around 800.

DID YOU KNOW?

The Danish tanker S/S *Sejero* sank in January 1942 after colliding in the Baltic en route from Rotterdam to Copenhagen, filled with Coca Cola.

1973
Denmark joins the European Community (now the EU)

1993
Maastricht Treaty accepted in second referendum

MODERN-DAY ISSUES

One of the most controversial issues of recent decades has been Denmark's role in the European Union (EU). Denmark joined the European Community, the predecessor of the EU, in 1973, but Danes have been hesitant to support expansion of the EU's powers. Denmark rejected the 1992 Maastricht Treaty (which set the terms for economic and political cooperation) and, in 2000, also rejected adoption of the euro – the latter decision saw a remarkable 87% voter turnout.

Opponents of the euro convinced the Danish people they had more to lose than gain, that local control would be ceded to a European bureaucracy dominated by stronger nations, including Denmark's generous welfare-state programs.

Meanwhile, Denmark maintained its leadership stance for socially liberal policies, including same-sex marriage (instituted in 1989) and aggressive implementation of alternative power sources (p42).

These days, though, Denmark is not universally liberal; as the conservative Danish People's Party (currently a minority in the Folketing) has gained in power, in 2002 Denmark imposed some of the toughest immigration laws in Europe, including restrictions on marriage between Danes and foreigners. The next national general election is scheduled for 2005.

2000
Denmark votes against adopting the euro

2004
Crown Prince Frederik weds Australian-born Mary Elizabeth Donaldson

The Culture

THE NATIONAL PSYCHE

Perhaps nothing captures the Danish perspective more than the concept of *hygge* which, roughly translated, means cosy and snug. It implies shutting out the turmoil and troubles of the outside world and striving instead for a warm, intimate mood. *Hygge* affects how Danes approach many aspects of their personal lives, from the design of their homes to their fondness for small cafés and pubs. There's no greater compliment that a Dane can give their host than to thank them for a cosy evening.

Given all that, it may surprise some visitors that the Danes pride themselves on being thoroughly modern. The wearing of folk costumes, the celebration of traditional festivals and the tendency to cling to old-fashioned customs is less prevalent in Denmark than in other European countries, and many big-city dwellers especially have an independent, don't-tell-me-what-to-do streak.

There is a wealth of interesting information on the comprehensive state-sponsored website www.denmark.dk.

LIFESTYLE

Danish family life has changed dramatically in the past few decades. These days, about 20% of all couples who live together aren't married and the average age for those who do tie the knot has risen to 35 years. The average number of children per family has dropped to 1.8.

Denmark was an early adopter of gay rights with the Danish National Association for Gays & Lesbians established back in 1948. In 1989, Denmark became the first European country to legalise same-sex marriages and to offer gay partners most of the same rights as heterosexual couples. In 1999 a further step in recognising a broader definition of the family was taken when the decade-old Registered Partnership Act was amended to allow married gays to legally adopt the children of their partners.

If you're interested in learning more about the struggles leading up to the 1989 law, go online to users.cybercity.dk/~dko12530/, a website produced by Axel and Eigil Axgil, the first of more than 5000 same-sex couples to be married in Denmark.

Women are often well established in their careers by the time they have their first child, and generous leave schemes make it easy to take a temporary pause from the workplace. The traditional role of homemaker, in which a woman stays home to care for children, has all but disappeared in Denmark. Fewer than 5% of Danish women remain at home full-time after the end of their maternity leave. Maternity leave is four weeks pre-birth and 14 weeks after. Men are entitled to two weeks' paternity leave. Parents have an additional 32 weeks which they may share between them with full benefits.

Today more than 80% of all Danish women are in the workplace. The Danish law prevents sex discrimination, yet women hold fewer than 10% of the top management positions in the private sector.

DID YOU KNOW?

Prince Joachim and his Princess Alexandra are the first Danish royals to divorce since 1846.

DID YOU KNOW?

Denmark was the first European nation to end its participation in the slave trade on moral grounds.

THEY LOVE THE NIGHTLIFE...

Denmark's cities have some of the most active nightlife in Europe, with live music wafting through numerous side-street cafés, especially in the university cities of Copenhagen, Århus and Odense. You'll find a wide range of music, including alternative, rock, folk, jazz and blues. Not much begins before 10pm or ends before 3am.

DOS & DON'TS

- If you have a meeting or appointment scheduled, it's best to arrive on time and not before or after. If you show up late or not at all, you'd better have a good reason.
- Danes generally queue by a number system. When you go to the post office, a bakery, the tourist office – just about any place there can be a queue – there's invariably a machine dispensing numbered tickets. Grab one as you enter and wait until your number is called.
- Danes love to joke, and although irony and gentle teasing are common ways of showing respect, some visitors may find it jarring at first. Similarly, Danes are often quite frank, but that's not meant to be insulting. There's a high degree of respect for the queen, and any flippant remark about the royal family is apt to offend.
- Casual dress is usually perfectly fine. You rarely have to dress up to do anything in Denmark, other than for the fanciest of fine dining. Nonetheless, Danes themselves are often very stylish dressers. If you want to blend in and hit the club scene, black clothing is the key.

From infancy, Danish children spend a significant amount of time away from home – day-care centres and nursery schools are a normal part of daily life for the vast majority of preschoolers.

Perhaps because of spending so much time away the family from an early age, Danes are notably tolerant and have a high degree of social responsibility. Visitors will find Danes relaxed, casual and not given to extremes. Danes think of themselves as a classless society and there are seldom any hints of chauvinism, sexism or any other -ism. They tend to be more involved in club activities and organisations than most other societies.

DID YOU KNOW?

Because no photo ID is required, a number of prisoners have hired temps to serve their sentences – 30 days for drunk driving, 60 days for violent crime and 18 months for drug dealing.

POPULATION

Denmark's population is about 5.4 million, making it the most densely populated nation in northern Europe. Some 70% of people live in urban areas with Copenhagen (1,700,000), Århus (300,000), Odense (185,000) and Aalborg (169,000) the four largest cities. Life expectancy is about 75 years for men, and almost 80 for women.

Denmark is almost entirely inhabited by ethnic Danes, people of the Teutonic ancestry common to all of Scandinavia. Foreign nationals account for approximately 5% of the population, an increase from just 2% in 1984 but still one of the lowest in Europe. Approximately 12% of all foreign nationals come from Nordic countries, 43% from other parts of Europe, 25% from Asia, 12% from Africa and 5% from the Americas.

Follow the ultimate Danish fairy tale at www.denmark.dk, the official royal website.

A relaxation of immigration policies during the economic expansion of the 1960s attracted 'guest workers', many of whom established a permanent niche. There are now sizable Turkish and Pakistani populations. New humanitarian policies – in response to famine and war crises – have resulted in small Somalian and Ethiopian immigrant communities and there is a growing number of refugees from the former Yugoslavia.

Although Denmark has long been viewed as one of Europe's most tolerant nations – and one with the most generous social benefits – in recent years there has been a movement away from that stance, promoted in part by the Danish People's Party (DPP). While the DPP don't control the Parliament, they are known for being able to swing votes… and for voicing concern over the degradation of traditional Danish character due to immigration and asylum-seekers from abroad, particularly Muslim countries. In 2002, Denmark implemented some of Europe's most restrictive – and controversial – immigration laws, particularly governing marriage between Danes and foreigners.

DID YOU KNOW?

The tax ceiling for individuals in Denmark is 59%.

WHAT'S IN A NAME?

Of the five million-plus Danes on the planet today, two-thirds have a surname ending in 'sen'. The three most common – Jensen, Nielsen and Hansen – account for 23% of all Danish surnames. Next, in order of frequency, are Pedersen, Andersen, Christensen, Larsen and Sørensen.

This is because up until the mid-19th century most peasants and other rural folk did not have a permanent family name but simply added 'sen' ('son') onto their father's first name. Thus if your father was Peder Hansen and your name was Eric, you would be known as Eric Pedersen.

On the other hand, it was announced in mid-2004 that Copenhagen schools would begin offering Arabic language classes.

Some 92% of Danes officially belong to Folkekirken (Danish People's Church), an Evangelical Lutheran denomination that is the state-supported national church; however, fewer than 5% of Denmark's citizens are regular churchgoers. The second largest religion is Islam (3%), followed by Roman Catholicism.

Danes enjoy freedom of religion and in most of the larger cities there are places of worship for Muslims (though not in official mosques as of this writing), Catholics, Anglicans and Jews in addition to the Folkekirken.

DID YOU KNOW?

Arctic explorer Knud Rasmussen's first language was Inuit. He didn't learn Danish until he went to school.

SPORT

Despite the country's small size, over the years Denmark has won Olympic gold medals in cycling and in water sports such as sailing, rowing, kayaking, swimming and platform diving. In 2004, Denmark won two gold medals, one each for women's handball (they also won gold in 2000) and the men's lightweight four rowing.

Denmark is the adopted home of runner Wilson Kipketer, a native of Kenya who took up Danish citizenship in 1990 after completing his studies here. He's been winning medals for Denmark since 1997. Notable races include a few first place finishes in the 800m world championships, a silver medal in the 2000 Olympics, and making three world records.

Football and handball are the two leading spectator sports in the country. Although the premier football league does not have the bottomless bank account of Europe's elite, it is fiercely competitive and attracts a number of international players. The two leading teams are FC København and Brøndy, both of which hail from Zealand. The matches are renowned for their festive, relaxed atmosphere and families attend in droves. You can watch a match at København Parken (the national stadium) or at the København Brøndby Stadion for around 100kr (season

DID YOU KNOW?

The nation with a mere five million people beat the heavyweights of England, France and Italy to win football's Euro 2002.

HOME GROUNDS & CONTACT DETAILS FOR MAIN SUPERLIGA CLUBS

- **AB (Akademisk Boldklub) Gladsaxe Idrætspark** (☎ 44 98 98 42; Skovdiget 1, 2880 Bagsværd)
- **Aalborg Boldspiklub Aalborg Stadion** (☎ 98 15 72 22; Hornevej 2, 9220 Aalborg Øst)
- **AGF Århus Stadion** (☎ 86 11 27 33; Terp Skovvej 16-18, 8260 Viby J)
- **Brøndby IF Brøndby Stadion** (☎ 43 63 08 10; Brøndbyvester Blvd 8, 2605 Brøndby)
- **FC København Parken** (☎ 35 43 31 31; Øster Allé 50, 2110 København)
- **Lyngby FC Lyngby Stadion** (☎ 45 88 40 60; Lundtoftevej 61, 2800 Lyngby)
- **Silkeborg IF Silkeborg Stadion** (☎ 86 80 44 77)

August–May). The Danish national team reflects the population in many ways, always accountable, respectable and every now and then claiming the golden prize (European Champions 1992). The national football team is usually rated in the top 20 worldwide.

Women's handball is a very popular spectator sport, and the ongoing success of the national team has ensured its crowd pulling ability. The National Womens Handball Team has won Olympic Gold as well as all other major championships. One of the most respected teams in the national league, Viborg HK, is from Jutland. They have won a lot of silverware and feed many players into the national side. See p269 for details about catching a game (season September–April).

DID YOU KNOW?

The Danish women's handball team collected their third straight Olympic gold medal in Athens 2004.

Cycling, rowing and sailing are popular in all parts of the country; there are many regional competitions throughout Denmark.

ARTS

Fine Arts

Prior to the 19th century, Danish art tended to revolve around formal portraits of the bourgeoisie, the aristocracy and the royal family. One of the most highly regarded portrait painters was Jens Juel (1745–1802).

Denmark's 'Golden Age' of the arts, from 1800 to 1850, produced luminaries such as Christoffer Wilhelm Eckersberg (1783–1853), who depicted more universal scenes of everyday Danish life, and Eckersberg's student Christen Købke (1810–48), who was little known in his time but is now regarded as one of the most important painters of the era. The leading Danish sculptor in this period was Bertel Thorvaldsen (1770–1844) who re-created classical sculptures during a long sojourn in Rome. Thorvaldsen later returned to Copenhagen in order to establish his own museum.

DID YOU KNOW?

Danish painter Einar Wegener became the first man to undergo a sex-change operation in 1931.

The Skagen school was active in the late 18th and early 19th centuries and specialised in romantic seaside subjects with an emphasis on the effects of natural light. Leading Skagen (p274) painters included PS Krøyer, Michael Ancher and Anna Ancher.

The CoBrA movement was formed in 1948 by artists from three European capitals (Copenhagen-Brussels-Amsterdam) with the aim of exploiting the free artistic expression of the unconscious, and it left a significant impact on 20th-century Danish art. One of its founders, Danish artist Asger Jorn (1914–73), achieved an international following for his abstract paintings, many of which evoke vivid imagery from Nordic mythology.

Literature

The first half of the 19th century has been characterised as the 'Golden Age' of Danish literature. The foremost writers in that prolific period included Adam Oehlenschläger (1779–1850), a romantic lyric poet who also wrote short stories and plays; Steen Steensen Blicher (1782–1848), a writer of tragic short stories; Hans Christian Andersen (see boxed text opposite), whose fairy tales have been translated into more languages than any other book except the Bible; and the noted philosopher Søren Kierkegaard (1813–55, p120), considered the father of existentialism.

A Copenhagen man pieces together his wife's disappearance and his own inner life in Jens Christian Grøndahl's book *Silence in October*.

A trend towards realism emerged in about 1870, focusing on contemporary issues of the day. A writer of this genre, novelist Henrik Pontoppidan (1857–1943), won the Nobel Prize for Literature in 1917 shortly after publishing the epic *The Realm of the Dead*, which attacked materialism. Another Danish author who won the Nobel Prize for Literature (in 1944) was Johannes Vilhelm Jensen (1873–1950), who penned the six-volume novel *The Long Journey* and *The Fall of the King*, a story about Danes during Renaissance times. Better known outside Denmark is Martin Andersen

ONCE UPON A TIME...

Some people seem to be born with greatness; others take their time and find it within. Guess which describes Hans Christian Andersen.

Denmark's most celebrated author (1805–75) entered the world humbly, the son of a cobbler and a washerwoman in Odense. But, like so many of his characters, he wanted more. He was only 11 when his father died, and three years later he ran away to Copenhagen 'to become famous'. You might say he showed promise even at this young age: studying at the Royal Danish Theatre, attending university, travelling abroad and self-publishing a chronicle of his journeys.

Yet like the late-bloomers of whom he so famously wrote, he did not hit his stride until much later, when he was in his 30s – and what a stride it was. His first volume of fairytales, *Tales, Told for Children* (1835), contained such classics as 'The Tinderbox' and 'The Princess and the Pea', and in subsequent years this series was published at Christmastime, with new stories each year. Try to imagine the world today without 'The Little Mermaid', 'The Ugly Duckling', 'Thumbelina' or 'The Emperor's New Clothes'.

Andersen infused his animals, plants and inanimate objects with a magical humanity that somehow still remained true to their origins. His antagonists are not witches or trolls, but human foibles such as indifference and vanity, and it's often his child characters who see the world most clearly. The result is a gentleness that crosses borders and generations. His work is said to have influenced Charles Dickens, Oscar Wilde and innumerable modern-day authors.

Yet, despite his success, he led a troubled, largely unhappy life: unlucky at love, sexually ambivalent, high-strung and hypochondriacal.

Andersen's collected works (156 in all) include poems, novels, travel books, dramatic pieces and two autobiographies. He died of liver cancer at a villa outside Copenhagen and is buried in the capital's Assistens Kirkegård (p79). Celebrations in early 2005 marked the 200th anniversary of Hans Christian Andersen's birth.

Nexø (1869–1954), whose novels about the proletariat – the four-volume *Pelle the Conqueror* and *Ditte, Child of Man* – helped draw attention to the conditions of the poor and spurred widespread reform in Denmark.

The most famous Danish writer of the 20th century, Karen Blixen (1885–1962, p108), started her career with *Seven Gothic Tales* published in New York under the pen name Isak Dinesen. She is best known for *Out of Africa*, the memoirs of her farm life in Kenya which she wrote in 1937. It was made into an Oscar-winning movie (1985) starring Meryl Streep and Robert Redford. Blixen's other works include *Winter's Tales* (1942), *The Angelic Avengers* (1944), *Last Tales* (1957), *Anecdotes of Destiny* (1958) and *Shadows on the Grass* (1960).

Denmark's foremost contemporary novelist is Peter Høeg, whose works focus on nonconformist characters on the margins of society. In 1992 he published the bestseller *Miss Smilla's Feeling For Snow* (published as *Smilla's Sense of Snow* in the USA and made into a movie in 1997), a suspense mystery about a Greenlandic woman living in Copenhagen. Other Høeg novels published in English include *The History of Danish Dreams*, a narrative that sweeps through many generations of a Danish family; *Borderliners*, which deals with social issues surrounding private schooling in Denmark; and *The Woman and the Ape*, the main character of which saves a rare primate from the clutches of scientists. An earlier collection of his short stories has also been translated under the title *Tales of the Night*.

Danish colonialism and the struggle for Greenlandic cultural identity are touched on in *Miss Smilla's Feeling for Snow* by Peter Høeg. The excellent screen adaptation *Smilla's Sense of Snow* (1997), directed by Bille August, has some beautiful skyline shots.

Theatre, Dance & Orchestral Music

Det Kongelige Teater (Royal Theatre) in Copenhagen first opened in 1748 as a court theatre, staging the plays of Denmark's most famous playwright, Ludvig Holberg (1684–1754). Today its repertoire encompasses

THE CLOWN PRINCE OF DENMARK

Victor Borge (1909–2000) was the face of Denmark to the world for much of the 20th century. Born Børge Rosenbaum, this son of musicians showed an early ear for music and began to study piano at the Royal Danish Music Conservatory at age nine, making his professional debut at 13. By his twenties he was called Scandinavia's leading entertainer, blending classical musical perfection with screwball comedy.

Borge's rise coincided with that of one Adolf Hitler, a frequent – and popular – target of Borge's humour. But Borge, as a Jew, was a target of a much more sinister form of persecution, and in 1940, when Germany invaded Denmark, he abandoned his worldly possessions and went to America.

It was in New York that he honed his craft, first playing for Rudy Vallee and Bing Crosby, and later refining such trademark bits as playing 'Happy Birthday' in the style of famous composers and reciting stories with audible punctuation marks (some of which sound like bodily functions). His patter was peppered with groaners (eg 'Brahms spelled backwards is Smharb'; calling a character a 'Portugoose' because 'you can't have one geese') all delivered in English with a pleasant Danish lilt. His solo performance *Comedy in Music* became one of the longest-running shows in Broadway history. Eventually Borge became an American citizen and in 1999 he received a Kennedy Centre award for lifetime achievement in the arts. Even after his death, his videotaped performances remain a favourite on Public TV in the US.

international works, including Shakespearean plays, as well as classical and contemporary Danish plays.

In the mid-19th century, Den Kongelige Ballet (Royal Danish Ballet) took its present form under the leadership of the French choreographer and ballet master August Bournonville (1805–79). Today it's one of the leading dance companies in northern Europe, with nearly 100 dancers. It still performs a number of Bournonville's romantic ballets, such as *La Sylphide* and *Napoli*, along with more contemporary works.

A firm favourite the world over, *The Complete Fairy Tales* by Hans Christian Andersen has many Copenhagen locales at centre stage.

Den Kongelige Opera (Royal Danish Opera) has an ensemble of 32 singers and a renowned 60-member opera chorus.

Traditionally these groups have performed at Det Kongelige Teater, but a new venue, the Opera House (p77), set on its own special island near Copenhagen's Christianshavn district is to open in 2005. Productions other than opera and ballet will still be staged at Det Kongelige Teater.

Det Kongelige Kapel (Royal Danish Orchestra) was founded in 1448, giving it claim to be the oldest orchestra in the world; it accompanies the ballet and opera performances.

Larger Danish cities have concert halls with their own symphony orchestras; these halls also double as venues for big-name Danish and international musicians of all genres.

Lars Von Trier's immensely influential film production company has its own website – www.zentropa.sk.

Contemporary Music

The Danish band Kashmir has a cult following at home and cleans up at awards ceremonies with tremendous regularity. They sing all their songs in English and sound very much like Radiohead.

Another band that has withstood the test of time is TV2, a product of the late '70s – and still immensely popular around the country – singing light rock/pop Danish-lyric songs. Their charismatic front man Steffan Brandt still captures female hearts even with his grey hair.

A good primer for the thriving Danish jazz scene can be found at www.dansk.jazz.dk.

Cinema

Denmark's best-known director of the early 20th century was Carl Theodor Dreyer (1889–1968), whose films included the 1928 French masterpiece *La*

Passion de Jeanne d'Arc, acclaimed for its rich visual textures and innovative use of close-ups. In the midst of WWII, Dreyer boldly filmed *Vredens Dag* (Day of Wrath), which made so many allusions to the tyranny of Nazi occupation that he was forced to flee to Sweden.

It wasn't until the 1980s that Danish directors attracted a broader international audience. In 1988 *Babette's Feast*, directed by Gabriel Axel, won the Academy Award for Best Foreign Film. *Babette's Feast* was an adaptation of a story written by Karen Blixen.

In 1989, director Bille August won the Academy Award for Best Foreign Film as well as the Cannes Film Festival's Palme d'Or for *Pelle the Conqueror*, a film adapted from Martin Andersen Nexø's book about the harsh life of an immigrant in 19th-century Denmark. August also directed *The House of the Spirits* (1993), with Meryl Streep, Glenn Close and Jeremy Irons, which was based on the novel by Isabel Allende; *Smilla's Sense of Snow* (1997), based on the bestseller by Peter Høeg, starring Julia Ormond and Gabriel Byrne; and *Les Miserables* (1998), adapted from Victor Hugo's classic tale, with Liam Neeson and Geoffrey Rush.

Film buff's choice www.dfi.dk is the website of Det Danske Filminstitut (Danish Film Institute), based in Copenhagen.

The leading Danish director of the new millennium is Lars von Trier, whose better-known films include the melodrama *Breaking the Waves* (1996) featuring Emily Watson, which took the Cannes Film Festival's Grand Prix, *Dancer in the Dark* (2000) starring Icelandic pop singer Björk and Catherine Deneuve, and *Dogville* (2003) starring Nicole Kidman. *Dancer in the Dark* won the Cannes Palme d'Or in 2000. Von Trier is closely associated with Dogma '95, a minimalist style of film-making using only hand-held cameras, shooting on location with natural light and refraining from the use of special effects and pre-recorded music. Von Trier also worked with Jørgen Leth, one of Denmark's leading directors since 1963, to create *The Five Obstructions (De Fem benspænd)* (2004), in which von Trier challenged Leth to tell the same story five ways in the same film.

The Danish Directors: Dialogues on a Contemporary National Cinema, edited by Mette Hjort and Ib Bondebjerg, features interviews with 20 Danish film makers exploring general contemporary film issues

Another Dogma '95 director is Lone Scherfig, whose romantic comedy *Italian for Beginners* (2000) dealt with diverse but damaged Danes learning the language of love and became an international hit. She also directed the 2002 dark comedy *Wilbur Wants to Kill Himself*, shot in Scotland, in English.

One of Hollywood's current heart-throbs is Viggo Mortensen, who catapulted to fame as Aragorn in the *Lord of the Rings* trilogy. Although he was born in New York and has lived outside Denmark for most of his life, he retains Danish citizenship. Mortensen is also a painter, a photographer and a poet. Two female Danish actors on the international film scene are Iben Hjejle, who made her Hollywood debut with a leading role in the quirky romantic comedy *High Fidelity* (2000) opposite John Cusack, and Connie Nielsen, who co-starred in the Oscar-winning epic *Gladiator* (2000) with Russell Crowe and the thriller *One Hour Photo* (2001) with Robin Williams.

I Kina spiser de hunde (1999), directed by Lasse Spang Olsen, is a love-it-or-hate-it heist flick set in Copenhagen and filmed in English.

Most Danish towns have cinemas showing first-run English-language films. Foreign films are not dubbed – movies are shown in their original language with Danish subtitles.

DANISH MODERN DESIGN

Denmark is a leader in the field of applied design, characterised by cool clean lines, graceful shapes and streamlined functionality. These concepts have been applied to everything from concert halls to coffeepots to Lego blocks (p253).

Architecture

In the second half of the 20th century, a number of Danish architects introduced new designs both at home and abroad. Perhaps the most influential is Jørn Utzon (1918–), winner of the 2003 Pritzker Prize. He is chiefly known for the world-famous Sydney (Australia) Opera House constructed in the 1960s, but he's also known for incorporating elements as wide-reaching as Mayan, Japanese and Islamic into traditional Danish design. In the 1950s, he took the basic elements of a Californian ranch-house design and modified them into a popular style of suburban Danish house that can be found throughout Denmark today; an open floor plan and an abundance of windows and glass doors are designed to merge indoor spaces with the outdoors and utilise precious sunlight during long winters. Utzon was also behind a number of eminent public buildings in Denmark, such as the performing arts centre Musikhuset Esbjerg in southern Jutland.

Other notable contemporary Danish architects include Johan von Spreckelsen (1929–87), who in 1984 designed the huge cube-like La Grande Arche in Paris, and Arne Jacobsen (1902–71), an innovator in international modernism, producing Danish interpretations of the Bauhaus style. Some of Jacobsen's best-known works are additions at St Catherine's College in Oxford, England, and the Herrenhaus concert hall in Hanover, Germany, the latter created in collaboration with his partner Otto Weitling (1930–). Weitling himself has designed some significant European buildings, including the much-acclaimed Museum of Art in Düsseldorf in 1986.

Furniture

Danish architects place such great emphasis on 'form following function' that they typically design a room only after considering the styles of furniture that are most likely to be used there. So it's not surprising that several Danish architects have crossed over to the field of furniture design, where their work has had an even broader impact.

'Modern Danish furniture focuses on a practical style ... tailored to the comfort of the user'

Modern Danish furniture focuses on a practical style and the principle that its design should be tailored to the comfort of the user. The smooth, unadorned style of contemporary Danish furniture design traces its roots back to Kaare Klint (1888–1954), who both worked as an architect and founded the furniture design department at the Royal Academy of Fine Arts in Copenhagen. He spent much of his career studying the human form and modified a number of chair designs to add functionality.

In 1949 one of Klint's contemporaries, Hans Wegner (1914–), created the Round Chair, the fluid, curving lines of which made it an instant classic and a model for many furniture designers to follow. So popular was the chair at the time that it appeared on the cover of a number of international interior-design magazines, helping to establish the first successful overseas export market for Danish furniture.

A decade later architect Arne Jacobsen (1902–71) created the Ant, a form chair designed to be mass produced, which became the model for the stacking chairs found in schools and cafeterias worldwide. Jacobsen also designed the Egg and the Swan; both are rounded, uncomplicated upholstered chairs with revolving seats perched on pedestal stands.

Danish design prevails in stylish lamps as well. The country's best-known lamp designer was Poul Henningsen (1894–1967), who emphasised the need for lighting to be soft, for the shade to cast a pleasant shadow and for the light bulb to be blocked from direct view. His PH-5 lamp created in 1958 remains one of the most popular hanging lamps sold in Denmark today.

The trademark clean lines and gentle curves of Danish design are also evident in avant-garde sound systems and televisions produced by Bang & Olufsen.

Silverware & Porcelain

The clean lines of industrial design are also evident in Danish silver, which combines aesthetics with function. Danish silverwork is highly regarded both at home and abroad, the chief design criteria being that the item is attractive yet simple, as well as easy to use. The father of modern Danish silverwork was the sculptor and silversmith Georg Jensen, who artistically incorporated curvilinear designs; his namesake company is still a leader in the field, with a flagship Copenhagen store (p98). Two of Jensen's students, Kay Bojesen and Henning Koppel, are also leading names in Danish silverwork.

One of the world's most famous sets of porcelain is the Flora Danica dinner service created by Royal Porcelain Manufactory (now Royal Copenhagen). No two pieces of this 1800-piece set are alike; each is hand-painted with a different native wildflower or other plant, then rimmed with gold. Some of the pieces have *trompe l'oeil* features, such as cup handles that look like flower stems. Commissioned in 1790, the original set took 13 years to complete and is still part of the Danish royal collection; pieces of that original set are on display at Copenhagen's Rosenborg Slot (p78). You can also see examples – or, if money is no obstacle, purchase your own reproduction set – at the Royal Copenhagen porcelain shop in Copenhagen (p98).

The other leader in Danish porcelain is Bing & Grøndahl, founded in 1853 to compete with Royal Copenhagen. It too produces a variety of tableware, much of it decorated with finely painted floral designs. Bing & Grøndahl is perhaps best known for its annual Christmas plates, which have been issued for more than 100 years. These plates, which are cobalt blue and white with a traditional winter design, are collected worldwide.

ART FIT FOR A QUEEN

Queen Margrethe is an accomplished artist. She has illustrated a number of books, including Tolkien's *Lord of the Rings*, and designed stamps for the Danish postal service.

Environment

THE LAND

Denmark is a small country, with a land area of 43,094 sq km, slightly larger than Switzerland or about half the size of the US state of Maine.

The Jutland (Jylland) peninsula encompasses more than half the land area of the country, stretching 360km from north to south. It's also where you'll find Denmark's only land connection to the European mainland, the 69km-long border with Germany. In addition, Denmark has 406 islands, about 90 of which are inhabited. The capital city, Copenhagen, is on the largest island, Zealand (Sjælland). The next largest islands are Funen (Fyn), the twin islands of Falster and Lolland, and Bornholm to the east.

DID YOU KNOW?

In 1917, during WWI, Denmark sold its Caribbean colonies to the USA for US$25 million.

Denmark is bordered on the west by the North Sea and on the east by the Baltic Sea. To the north, separating Denmark from Norway and Sweden, are the Skagerrak and Kattegat straits. Sweden is just 5km away at its closest point, across a narrow strait called the Øresund, although a bridge over the Øresund now makes for easy connections between Copenhagen and the Swedish city of Malmö.

Most of Denmark is a lowland of fertile farms, rolling hills, beech woods and heather-covered moors. The country hasn't a single mountain; the highest elevation, at Yding Skovhøj in Jutland's Lake District (called Søhøjlandet), is a mere 173m.

There are numerous small rivers, lakes and streams. The largest lake is Arresø on the island of Zealand and the longest river is the 158km Gudenå in Jutland.

The 7314km coastline includes many inlets and bays. No place in Denmark is more than 52km from the sea.

Denmark also retains administrative control over Greenland and the Faroe Islands. Greenland is the world's largest island (if Australia is regarded as a continent), with a total area of 2,166,086 sq km (of which 81% is under permafrost) and a population of about 56,400. Greenland has no arable land, but is rich in fisheries and mining resources. The Faroe Islands have a land area of 1399 sq km and a population of about 46,600. The Faroes are largely supported by fishing and have a standard of living similar to that of Denmark.

DID YOU KNOW?

The North Sea island Rømø was formed by wind, water and sand. There's not a single rock on its beaches.

WILDLIFE

Elk, bears and wolves – these don't exist in Denmarat least not in the wild. However, you're apt to come across gentle woodland creatures in a woodland and coastal setting, and a good assortment of birds for birdwatching.

Animals

The loss of so much natural wilderness habitat to cultivated farmland has spelt the end for numerous animal species in Denmark. Almost 30% of all mammal species and breeding birds are listed as either threatened, vulnerable or rare. Elk, bear, wolf, wild boar and beaver have all disappeared.

Today the most endangered mammal in the country is the freshwater otter, which was plentiful as late as the 1950s and shot by hunters until 1967. By the time protections for the otter were put in place its population had dropped to around 100, although it's now making a comeback with the latest estimate around 400.

The largest wild species is the red deer, which can weigh more than 200kg. Denmark is also home to the roe and fallow deer, wild hare, fox, squirrel, hedgehog and badger.

Approximately 400 bird species have been observed in Denmark; of these about 160 breed in the country. Some of the more commonly seen birds include the magpie, crow, sparrow, pigeon, coot, goose and duck.

The western coast of Jutland attracts migrating water birds and breeding waders such as the avocet, dunlin, ruff, redshank, lapwing and black-winged godwit. The gull-billed tern, which is a threatened species in Europe, breeds on the uninhabited fjord island of Fjandø, as do some of the country's largest colonies of the sandwich tern, arctic tern and black-headed gull.

Bornholm, the easternmost island, is home to nightingales and rooks and is a resting spot for migratory ducks and waders. The nearby Ertholmene Islands provide a bird refuge that hosts breeding eider ducks, razorbills, guillemots and other sea birds.

Birds threatened by extinction – mostly because of the destruction of their habitat – include the wood sandpiper, golden plover and black grouse. One of the country's faunal emblems is the swan, commonly found in urban parks and suburban ponds.

There are 68 indigenous species of butterfly, though many are rare and nine species have vanished since 1950. A small tortoiseshell butterfly is Denmark's other faunal emblem, a pretty brownish-orange in colour with a blue fringe. It's common in all areas of the country from early July and is unusual in that it hibernates as a fully grown insect.

Eleven species of frogs and toads can be found in Denmark, including the common toad, green tree frog and fire-bellied toad; however, because of the loss of wetlands, amphibians have disappeared from half of their breeding sites in the past 50 years. Efforts are being made to turn the situation around, most notably on Bornholm where 400 water holes have been restored to create a habitat for the green tree frog.

Plants

About 12% of Denmark is treed, but primary forest is rare. Instead, most woods are planted, the bulk of them having been reforested either for conservation and recreation purposes or for timber production. Most of the commercial forests are now planted with fast-growing conifers such as spruce and fir.

The natural woodlands are largely deciduous with a prevalence of beech and oak trees. Other species in mixed woodlands include hazel, maple, pine, birch, aspen, lime (linden) and horse chestnut. Elm trees are common, but the 1993 outbreak of Dutch elm disease devastated these stately trees in a number of areas. In Copenhagen virtually all of the city's 10,000 or so elm trees contracted the disease – most have been felled.

Heath, bogs and dunes cover about 7% of land area and are particularly common in western Jutland. To stem coastal erosion, large tracts of the dunes have been planted with the deep-rooted lyme and marram grasses. Wild pink and white beach roses *(Rosa rugosa)* are common on sand dunes as well.

In spring, cultivated fields of massed brilliant yellow rapeseed flowers, a member of the mustard family, are a particularly lovely addition to the farm-belt areas.

In summer, gardens throughout Denmark are planted with a colourful mix of temperate-climate flowers. The country's floral emblem is the marguerite, a white daisy with a yellow centre that is prolific in sunny open spaces, such as along roadways.

NATIONAL PARKS

Given that Denmark does not have large expanses of wilderness, it's no surprise that it does not have a system of national parks. Its largest contiguous area of woodlands is Rold Skov, a 77-sq-km public forest in central Jutland that contains Denmark's only national park, Rebild Bakker (p267).

Numerous state-administered nature conservation areas around the country, collectively encompass about 4% of the nation's land area. These include beaches, coastal forests, heath lands and inland woods and lakes. Many are quite scenic and have been selected for a particular natural quality or historical significance. Most are crossed with hiking and biking trails and, although the majority can be walked in an hour or two, some areas are long and narrow and thus suitable for longer outings.

As we went to press, seven areas were under consideration as part of a pilot phase of an expanded national park program, with evaluations to be made in late 2005. You can find out the latest at www.sns.dk.

ENVIRONMENTAL ISSUES

Centuries of deforestation and overgrazing meant that by the early 19th century less than 4% of Denmark's land remained forested – encroaching heathlands and meadows covered nearly 50% of the total land area. In the late 19th century much of that heathland was turned into agricultural land, with heavy use of fertilisers and modification of natural waterways.

Today about 20% of Danish farmland is at or near sea level, much of it on environmentally sensitive wetlands made arable by draining the water with pumps. The landscape has been so intensely altered that only about 2% of Denmark's naturally winding streams remain intact, the rest having been artificially straightened.

However, a concerted effort is being made to restore the environment. International trade agreements and EU quotas have brought an end to many agricultural subsidies for Danish farmers; consequently some farmland is no longer economically viable. This, along with a growing environmental awareness, has created a favourable backdrop for restoration.

Under a nature management act passed in 1990, the government has instituted an ambitious program to restore wetlands, re-establish the salt marshes and realign streams to their original courses. The act also called for the doubling of forest cover over the next 100 years.

On another front, popular sentiment is strongly against nuclear power and Denmark has one of the world's most extensive networks of alternative energy sources. Most notable is wind power (see boxed text below),

DID YOU KNOW?

Denmark hopes to claim the North Pole for oil exploration by scientifically proving that the seabed beneath the North Pole was a natural extension of Greenland.

DID YOU KNOW?

Wind energy provides over 20% of Denmark's electricity, more than any other country in the world.

HOLD ON TO YOUR HAT!

Given that there have been windmills in northern Europe for about eight centuries, perhaps it's little surprise that wind power has, pardon the expression, taken off here. But you may not know that Denmark leads the way. Its wind industry is the world's largest, employing 20,000 people and exporting some 90 per cent of the equipment produced. Wind power already accounts for a world-leading 20% of Danish power needs, en route to 25% by 2008.

A single two megawatt turbine can provide enough energy for 2000 households for a year. Rows of sleek wind turbines are an increasingly common sight on the Danish landscape, particularly in breezy coastal areas. In 2001 the world's largest offshore windmill park was built outside Copenhagen harbour, and its 20 giant windmills now generate 3% of the capital's electricity.

If you're looking for more information on wind farms – more than you ever thought there was to know – go to the Danish Wind Industry Association website, www.windpower.org.

and Denmark has also been harnessing solar energy – the island of Ærø (p207) boasts one of Europe's largest solar power stations, despite Denmark's often cloudy weather!

Denmark also has active recycling programs. More than 80% of all paper produced comes from used paper and roughly half of all waste is recycled. Over recent decades many air-pollution levels – including sulphur dioxide – have dropped by nearly 50%. Since 1993 Danish businesses have been required to pay a tax based on their carbon dioxide emissions.

In 1971 Denmark created a cabinet-level ministry to deal specifically with environmental issues, the first industrialised country to do so. The EU has based its European Environment Agency in Copenhagen, and the Danes have taken an active role in international efforts to reduce pollution.

Food & Drink

Like the cuisines of its neighbouring countries, the cuisine of Denmark is homely and hearty and relies heavily on fish, meat and butter. But you'll also find options for vegetarians as well as a variety of cuisines from other world regions.

STAPLES & SPECIALITIES

Madjournal by Paul Cunningham is a food journal from the man behind Michelin-starred The Paul, in Tivoli.

Although Denmark does not have the culinary diversity of other world cultures, it's possible to find choices from around the world, from East Asia to India, the Middle East, France and Italy. A distinctively Danish presentation is the *koldt bord* (cold table), a buffet-style spread of cold foods – such as cold sliced meats, smoked fish, cheeses, vegetables, salads, condiments, breads and crackers – plus usually a few hot dishes such as meatballs and fried fish. The cornerstone of the *koldt bord* is herring, which comes in pickled, marinated and salted versions. Generally a serving of herring with raw onions is treated as a starter, because it's thought to prime the stomach for the meal. Pickled herring is almost invariably washed down with cold *akvavit* (aquavit or schnapps, p45), a type of spirit.

TRAVEL YOUR TASTE BUDS

Nothing epitomises Danish food more than smørrebrød, an open sandwich that ranges from very basic to elaborate and sculptural. Your basic smørrebrød is a slice of sourdough rye bread topped, for example, with roast beef, tiny shrimps, roast pork, or fish fillet, and finished off with a variety of garnishes, but they can get as creative as the imagination allows, with ingredients from fruit preserves to aspic to pâté. Smørrebrød is served in most restaurants at lunchtime, although it's cheapest in bakeries or specialised smørrebrød takeaway shops found near train stations and office buildings.

'Ritt Bjerregaard'

½ slice of rye bread with butter
2 slices of smoked leg of lamb
2 tbsp. of scrambled eggs
1 tbsp. of chopped herbs (parsley, lovage & chive)

Put the two slices of leg of lamb on the bread. Place the scrambled eggs diagonally on the bread. Sprinkle the chopped herbs over the scrambled eggs.

Smørrebrød with 'Modern' Roast Beef

½ slice of rye bread with butter
3 slices of very thin roast beef
3 slices of tomato
1 hard-boiled egg
A handful of fried crisp onion

Put the three slices of roast beef on the bread, the three slices of tomato down the middle. Peel and slice the hard-boiled egg lengthwise into six wedges, and arrange three wedges on either side of the tomato slices. To finish it off, put the fried onion on the tomato slices.

Recipes courtesy of Ida Davidsen Restaurant, Copenhagen

In Denmark the sweet pastry known elsewhere in the world as 'Danish' is called *wienerbrød* ('Viennese bread', ironically), and nearly every second street corner has a bakery with mouthwatering varieties. As legend has it, the naming of the pastry can be traced to a Danish baker who moved to Austria in the 18th century, where he perfected the treats of flaky, butter-laden pastry.

DRINKS

Non-Alcoholic Drinks

All cafés serve *kaffe* (coffee) and *te* (tea), though caffeine-rich coffee is clearly the more popular. In addition to the common brew, expect to find a good variety of cappuccino, espresso and other coffee drinks.

Mineralvand (mineral water) and the standard *sodavand* (soft drinks) such as Coca-Cola are widely available. The tap water anywhere in Denmark is safe to drink.

WE DARE YOU

Saltakrids (salty liquorice) is a favourite among Danes. One popular type is *Piratos*, which comes in a flat coin shape.

Alcoholic Drinks

The most popular spirit in Denmark is the Aalborg-produced *akvavit*. There are several dozen types, the most common of which is spiced with caraway seeds. In Denmark *akvavit* is not sipped but is swallowed straight down as a shot, usually followed by a chaser of beer. A popular Danish liqueur made from cherries is Peter Heering, which is good sipped straight or served over vanilla ice cream.

Danes are prodigious producers and consummate consumers of *øl* (beer). Carlsberg Breweries, based in Copenhagen, markets the Carlsberg and Tuborg labels and is the largest exporter of beer in Europe. Not all of the brew leaves home, however: Danes themselves down some seven million hectolitres (roughly two billion bottles) of brew a year, ranking them sixth among the world's greatest beer drinkers.

DID YOU KNOW?

Carlsberg's logo was designed by sculptor, house painter and Skagen resident, Thoruand Bindesboll; he charged 100kr for his artwork – imagine if he'd got royalties!

The best-selling beers in Denmark are pilsners, a lager with an alcohol content of 4.6%, but there are scores of other beers to choose from. These range from light beers with an alcohol content of 1.7% to hearty stouts that kick in at 8%. You'll find the percentage of alcohol listed on the bottle label. Danish beers are classified with ascending numbers according to the amount of alcohol they contain, with *klasse 1* referring to the common pilsners and *klasse 4* to the strongest stouts.

Here's a short list of beer terms:

- *øl* – beer
- *fadøl* – draught
- *lagerøl* – dark lager
- *lyst øl* – light beer
- *pilsner* – lager
- *porter* – stout

Also note that you get a cash refund when returning empty beer bottles to any supermarket (eg Netto). That 1.5kr per bottle can add up if you're having a session or just broke and looking for secondary income!

Common *vin* (wine) terms used in Denmark include *hvidvin* (white wine), *rødvin* (red wine), *mousserende* (sparkling wine) and *husets vin* (house wine). *Gløgg* is a mulled wine that's a favourite speciality during the Christmas season.

HIDDEN COSTS

If you're used to a bottomless cup of coffee, get unused to it – each cup costs. And while tap water is generally free, we've heard of rare instances of restaurants charging for it – 15kr in one case! Be sure to ask if it's not obvious.

HOW TO HAVE YOUR OWN ROYAL WEDDING

If you're a fan of the Danish Crown Prince Frederik and Crown Princess Mary, you might try some of these specialities from their wedding banquet:

- timbale of shellfish from the Nordic seas, sea urchin sauce
- roast venison from the royal Danish forests, with rissole potatoes from Samsø and peas à la Parisienne, sauté morel and mushroom sauce
- vol-a-vent Perfect Union, with white Danish asparagus and Bornholm chicken and a sprinkling of apple cider
- champagne Mercier, Cuvée Frederik & Mary
- book the Fredenborg Palace, add music courtesy of the Royal Lifeguards, and you're all set

Beer, wine and spirits are served in most restaurants and cafés. They can also be purchased at grocery shops during normal shopping hours. Prices are quite reasonable compared with those in other Scandinavian countries. The minimum legal age for consuming alcoholic beverages is 18 years.

CELEBRATIONS

Weddings

A traditional Danish wedding cake is a ring-shaped almond cake made with marzipan (almond paste), filled with goodies like candies and fresh fruit, and decorated with sugar. According to custom, good luck will come if the bride and groom cut the cake together and all guests eat a piece of the cake.

DID YOU KNOW?

Never fail to make eye contact during a toast – it's a breach of etiquette, and custom says it'll mean seven years of bad sex.

Christmas

The year's big festival is often preceded by Christmas 'lunches', particularly in workplaces, though in practice they often take place in the evening. The menu for a Christmas lunch might include herring, a curry salad with eggs, and ham or sausages.

The centrepiece of the traditional Christmas Eve dinner with family is roast duck or goose stuffed with apples and prunes – though turkey and roasts are not uncommon – served with red cabbage.

Another Christmas Eve tradition is rice pudding, sometimes eaten warm before the meal. Hidden inside the rice pudding is a single whole almond – the person who finds the almond in his or her bowl gets a prize (eg a sweet made of marzipan). Tradition holds that the winner does not announce it until everyone has finished their rice pudding. And of course, Denmark is famous for Christmas sweets including *brune kager* (ginger cookies), *klejner* (deep fried knotted dough), *pebernødder* (spiced cookies).

On 25 December, the leftovers make for an excellent *koldt bord* lunch. Special Christmastime drinks include *gløgg*, beers brewed for the season, and *aqvavit*.

DID YOU KNOW?

If a Danish bride or groom has deceased parents, the bride's bouquet is traditionally placed on the grave, so it's not uncommon for part of the wedding day to be spent at a cemetery.

Other Celebrations

At children's birthday parties, you can expect a multilayered birthday cake and hot chocolate (or soft drinks). Guests always bring a gift.

At private ceremonies such as birthday or anniversary dinners, as well as public ceremonies in Denmark, people often fly the national flag or place small flags on the table – or in Christmas trees.

WHERE TO EAT & DRINK

Generally the most prominent top-end restaurants feature what's dubbed 'Danish-French' cuisine, a creative fusion combining the flavoursome sauces characteristic of French fare with the addition of fresh Danish vegetables and seafood that are not typical in traditional French recipes.

The *dagens ret* (daily special) is usually the best deal on the menu, whereas the *børnemenu* is for children. Typical opening hours for restaurants and cafés are 11am and 11pm.

Frøken Jensens Kogebog, by Kristine Marie Jensen, was first published in 1901 and is a classic of Danish cooking.

Cheap Eats

Mediterranean buffets and Italian restaurants that serve the standard pizza-and-pasta fare are good for cheap eats. Simple Greek, Egyptian, Lebanese and Moroccan eateries selling inexpensive *shawarma* (a filling pitta-bread sandwich of shaved meat) are a favourite alternative to the ubiquitous fast-food chains. You can also find a cheap, if not particularly healthy, munch at one of the *pølsemænd* (the wheeled carts that sell a variety of hot dogs and sausages – pork, for those for whom it matters).

Sodas can be expensive at restaurants, so if you're on a budget you can get takeaway and save a bundle buying drinks at supermarkets.

As for tipping, a 15% service charge is included in your restaurant bill. However, rounding up the bill is not uncommon when the service has been particularly good.

Dejligt by Camilla Plum, concentrates on sweet treats; Plum is as close to a Danish Martha Stewart as you can get.

VEGETARIANS & VEGANS

Although strictly vegetarian restaurants are generally limited to larger cities, vegetarians should be able to get by reasonably comfortably throughout Denmark. Danish cafés commonly serve a variety of salads, and vegetarians can often find something suitable at the smørrebrød counter as well.

In addition, there are a growing number of Middle Eastern restaurants with buffets that have separate meat and vegetarian dishes, the latter including sautéed vegetables, salads, rice and couscous. Most Italian restaurants will have vegetarian pasta options, and for those who eat cheese, there are scores of pizzerias all around Denmark. Of course all Indian and Pakistani restaurants will have some vegetarian-only dishes.

Enjoy *Lyst* by Claus Meyer, another local chef with an eye for fresh ingredients and inventive variations of Danish staples.

WHINING & DINING

Taking your kids out to eat in Denmark is rarely a problem. Many cafés and restaurants have high chairs and *børnemenu* (children's menus). If you're out for a quick bite, kids will love the pastry shops, or you can stop at one of the *pølsemandens* (hot dog stands).

HABITS & CUSTOMS

Dinner is the main meal of the day. If you're at a dinner where toasts are expected, it's best to let the first toast come from someone senior to you.

DENMARK'S TOP FIVE RESTAURANTS

- **Rogeriet i Svaneke** excellent smoked fare (p174)
- **Restaurant Klitgaard** locally grown and clever cooking (p189)
- **Restaurant Koch** flamboyant fresh seafood (p246)
- **Pakhuset** for discerning seafood lovers (p287)
- **Skipperhuset** idyllic alfresco dining (p117)

COPENHAGEN'S TOP FIVE RESTAURANTS

- **Ida Davidsen** lip-smacking smørrebrø (p94)
- **Kommandanten** it's out of this world (p93)
- **Langelinie Pavillonen** fabulously upmarket (p94)
- **The Paul** a meal to remember (p92)
- **Peder Oxe** wonderful country grub (p93)

Although Danes can be quite gregarious, don't feel that you have to fill up time with conversation during a meal. Many Danes are comfortable with silence, and if you're constantly talking it may seem that you're overly chatty or, worse, pushy.

If you're invited to someone's home, be prompt since dinner is often served right away. If there's a cocktail hour, it may come after the meal rather than before. Dinners at a Danish home are prone to last long – as much as four hours – and it is considered rude to leave right when dinner ends. It's a nice idea to take along flowers and chocolates as gifts.

The quickest way to set the teeth of fellow diners on edge is to pick things up with your fingers and then noisily lick your fingers. It's the one big Danish dining *faux pas*. The Danes even sometimes eat burgers with knives and forks. If in doubt, follow their lead.

An excellent search engine for Copenhagen's eating, drinking, sleeping and entertainment options is www.aok.dk.

Before you leave the table, *always* thank your host or hostess for any food or drink, even if it's just a cup of coffee.

EAT YOUR WORDS

Useful Phrases

I'd like today's special, please. — *Jeg vil gerne have dagens ret, tak.*
yai vi *ger*·ne ha *daa*·ens ret tag

A table for two, please. — *Et bord til to, tak.*
it bor ti to tag

I'd like to reserve a table. — *Jeg vil gerne reservere et bord.*
yai vi *ger*·ne re·suh·*vi*·re it bor

Do you have a menu in English? — *Har De en menu på engelsk?*
har dee in *eng*·elsg mi·*new*

I'd like a local speciality. — *Jeg vil gerne have en lokal specialitet.*
yai vi *ger*·ne ha in lo·*kal* spi·sya·lee·*tit*

I'd like to order the ... — *Jeg vil gerne bestille ...*
yai vi *ger*·ne bi·*sdi*·le ...

Could you recommend something? — *Kan De anbefale noget?*
kan dee an·bi·*fa*·le *no*·eth

Renowned Copenhagen chef Nikolaj Kirk turns his hand to interesting twists on daily dining – and shows you how to do it too in his book *Hverdagsmad*.

I'm a vegetarian. — *Jeg er vegetar.*
yai er ve·ge·*tar*

I don't eat ... — *Jeg spiser ikke ...*
yai *spee*·suh ig ...

meat — *kød*
kerth

fish — *fisk*
fisg

seafood — *skaldyr*
sgal·dewr

The bill, please. — *Regningen, tak.*
rai·ning·en tag

Menu Decoder

Following is a list of Danish dishes you'll probably come across; see the following Food Glossary for more staples.

Flæskeæggekage – scrambled egg dish with bacon
Flæskesteg – roast pork, usually with crackling, served with potatoes and cabbage
Frikadeller – fried minced-pork meatballs, commonly served with boiled potatoes and red cabbage
Fyldt hvidkålshoved – minced beef wrapped in cabbage leaves
Gravad laks – cured or salted salmon marinated in dill and served with a sweet mustard sauce
Hakkebøf – a minced-beef burger, usually covered with fried onions and served with boiled potatoes, brown sauce and beets
Hvid labskovs – Danish stew made from cubes of beef boiled with potatoes, bay leaves and pepper
Kogt torsk – poached cod, usually with mustard sauce and served with boiled potatoes
Mørbradbøf – small pork fillets, commonly in a mushroom sauce
Stegt flæsk – crisp-fried pork slices, generally served with potatoes and a parsley sauce
Stegt rødspætte – fried, breaded plaice, usually served with parsley potatoes

Food Glossary

BASICS

børnemenu	children's menu
dagens middag	set menu
dagens ret	daily special
diabetes mad	dishes for diabetics
forretter	starters, appetisers
frokost	lunch
hovedretter	main dishes
middag	dinner
morgenmad	breakfast
retter	dishes, courses
spisekort	menu
tag selv buffet	self-serve buffet
udvalg af	assorted

COOKING TERMS

bagt	bagd	baked
benfri	*ben*·free	boneless
dampet	*dam*·peth	steamed
fiskeretter	*fis*·ge·rad	fish dishes
frisk	frisg	fresh
friturestegt	free·*tew*·uh·stegd	deep fried
fromage	fror·*ma*·she	pudding
fyld	fewl	stuffing
fyldt	fewld	stuffed
gennemstegt	*ge*·nem·stegd	well-done
glasur	gla·*soor*	glaze, frosting
grilleret, grillstegt	greel·*ye*·reth, *greel*·stegd	grilled
gryderet	*grew*·the·rad	casserole or stew
hakket	*ha*·geth	chopped, minced
hjemmebagt	*yem*·e·bagd	home-baked
hjemmelavet	*yem*·e·la·veth	home-made
hvide	*vee*·the	white (as in white potatoes, rice etc)
iskold	*ees*·korl	ice cold
karry	*ka*·ree	curry
kød	kerth	meat
kødbolle	*kerth*·bol·e	meatball

kogt	kogd	boiled
kold	korl	cold
kotelet	ko·de·*led*	cutlet
marineret	ma·ree·*ni*·reth	marinated
mellemstegt	*me*·lem·stegd	medium cooked
ovnstegt	*own*·stegd	roasted
pocheret	por·*she*·reth	poached
rå	ror	raw
ristet	*res*·deth	toasted
røget	*roy*·yeth	smoked
salat	sa·*lad*	salad, lettuce
saltet	*sal*·deth	salted, cured
skive	*skee*·ve	slice
stegeretter	stai·*e*·ra·da	meat dishes
stegt	stegd	fried
suppe	*sor*·be	soup
tilberedt	til·bi·*red*	cooked
varm	varm	warm, hot
vegetar, vegetarianer	ve·ge·*ta*, ve·ge·ta·ree·*a*·na	vegetarian

DRINKS

alkoholfri	*al*·ko·hol·free	non-alcoholic
citronvand	cee·*trorn*·van	lemonade
fadøl	*fath*·erl	draught (draft) beer
kærnemælk	*ker*·ne·melg	buttermilk
kaffe	*ka*·fe	coffee
koffeinfri	kor·fe·*een*·free	caffeine-free
letmælk	*led*·melg	low-fat milk
mælk	melg	milk
mineralvand	mee·ne·*ral*·van	mineral water
øl	erl	beer
skummetmælk	*skor*·meth·melg	skimmed (nonfat) milk
sodavand	*so*·da·van	soft drink, carbonated water
sødmælk	*serth*·melg	whole milk
te	ti	tea
vand	van	water

FISH

ål	orl	eel
ansjoser	an·*shor*·sa	anchovies
blæksprutte	*blerg*·sproo·duh	octopus
fisk	fisg	fish
fiskefilet	*fis*·ge·fee·le	fish fillet
fiskefrikadelle	*fis*·ge·fri·ka·de·le	fried fishball
flynder	*flern*·nuh	flounder
forel	for·*rel*	trout
helleflynde	*hel*·e·fler·ne	halibut
hummer	*hor*·ma	lobster
klipfisk	*kleeb*·fisg	dried salt cod
krabbe	*kra*·be	crab
kryddersild	*rer*·tha·seel	herring pickled in various marinades
kuller	*kool*·a	haddock
laks	lags	salmon
makrel	ma·krel	mackerel
marineret sild	ma·ree·*ni*·reth seel	marinated herring

musling	*moos*·ling	mussel
ørred	*er*·eth	trout
østers	*ers*·das	oyster
rejer	*rai*·ya	shrimp
rødspætte	*rerth*·sper·de	plaice
røget laks	*roy*·yeth lags	smoked salmon
røget sild	*roy*·eth seel	smoked herring
sild	seel	herring
skaldyr	*sgal*·dewr	shellfish
søtunge	*ser*·tor·ng·e	sole
torsk	torsg	cod
torskerogn	*tors*·ge·rorwn	cod roe
tun, tunfisk	toon, *toon*·fisg	tuna

FRUIT & VEGETABLES

abrikos	a·bree·*kors*	apricot
æble	*e*·ble	apple
ærter	*er*·da	peas
agurk	a·*goorg*	cucumber
agurkesalat	a·*goor*·ge·sa·lad	sliced cucumber with vinegar dressing
ananas	*a*·na·nas	pineapple
appelsin	a·pel·*seen*	orange
asparges	a·*spars*	asparagus
bagt kartoffel	bagd ka·*tof*·el	baked potato
banan	ba·*nan*	banana
blåbær	*blor*·ber	blueberry
blomkål	*blom*·korl	cauliflower
blomme	*blo*·me	plum
bønner	*ber*·na	beans
brombær	*brom*·ber	blackberry
champignon	*sham*·peen·yong	mushroom
citron	see·*tron*	lemon
dild	deel	dill
fersken	*fer*·sgen	peach
frugt	frorgd	fruit
grapefrugt	*grap*·frorgd	grapefruit
grøn bønne	grern *ber*·ne	green bean
gulerødder	*goo*·le·rer·tha	carrots
hasselnød	*ha*·sel·nerth	hazelnut
hindbær	*heen*·ber	raspberry
jordbær	*jor*·ber	strawberry
jordnød	*jor*·nerth	peanut
kål	korl	cabbage
kartoffel	ka·*tof*·el	potato
kartoffelmos	kar·*to*·fel·mors	mashed potatoes
kartoffelsalat	kar·*to*·fel·sa·lad	potato salad
kirsebær	*keer*·se·ber	cherry
løg	loy	onion
majs	mais	corn
pære	*pe*·a	pear
porre	por·e	leek
rødbeder	rerth·*be*·tha	beets, commonly served pickled
rødkål	*rerth*·korl	red cabbage
selleri	*si*·luh·ree	celery
snittebønner	*snee*·de·ber·na	string beans

spinat	spee·*nad*	spinach
surt	soord	pickled cucumbers or zuchini
vandmelon	*van*·me·lon	watermelon

MEAT

and, andesteg	an, *an*·e·sdai	duck, roast duck
dyresteg	*dew*·re·sdai	roast venison
engelsk bøf	*eng*·elsg berf	steak, commonly served with onions
fårekød	*for*·uh·kerth	mutton
gås	gors	goose
hakkebøf	*ha*·ge·berf	ground-beef burger
haresteg	*ha*·re·sdai	roast hare
høns, hønsekød	herns, *hern*·se·kerth	hen, chicken meat
hønsebryst	*hern*·se·brersd	chicken breast
kalkun	kal·*koon*	turkey
kalvekød	*kal*·ve·kerth	veal
kylling	*kew*·ling	chicken
lam, lammekød	lam, *la*·me·kerth	lamb
lammesteg	*la*·me·sdai	roast lamb
lever	*li*·wa	liver
oksehaleragout	*og*·se·ha·le·ra·goo	oxtail stew
oksekød	*og*·se·kerth	beef
oksemørbrad, oksefilet	*og*·se·mer·brath, *og*·se·fee·*le*	fillet of beef, tenderloin
oksesteg	*og*·se·sdai	roast beef
pølse	*perl*·se	sausage, hot dog
skinke	*sging*·ge	ham
svinekød	*svee*·ne·kerth	pork
tunge	*tor*·nge	tongue
vildt	veeld	game

STAPLES

æg	eg	egg
æggeblomme	*e*·ge·blor·me	egg yolk
blødkogt æg	*blerth*·kogd eg	soft-boiled egg
bolle	*bol*·e	soft bread roll; also a meatball or fishball
brød	brerth	bread
chokolade	sho·go·*la*·the	chocolate, also hot chocolate
creme fraiche	krem·fresh	sour cream
eddik	*eth*·ge	vinegar
fløde	*fler*·the	cream
flødeøst	*fler*·the orsd	cream cheese
flødeskum	*fler*·the·sgorm	whipped cream
flute	flewt	type of French bread
forårsrulle	*for*·or	spring roll, egg roll
grøn salat	grern sa·*lad*	green salad
grøntsager	*grern*·sa·uh	vegetables
gule ærter	*goo*·le *er*·da	split pea soup served with pork
hårdkogt æg	*hor*·kogd eg	hard-boiled egg
honning	*hor*·ning	honey
hønsekødsuppe	*hern*·se·kerth·sor·be	chicken soup
hvidløg	*veeth*·loy	garlic
hytteost	*hew*·duh·orsd	cottage cheese
ingefær	ing·e·fer	ginger
jordnødsmør	*yor*·nerth·smer	peanut butter
klar suppe	klar *sor*·be	clear soup

krydder	*krerth*·uh	crispy bread roll
krydderi	krer·tha·*ree*	spice
leverpostej	*li*·wa·por·sdai	liver paté
mandel, mandler	*ma*·nel, *man*·la	almonds
nødder	*ner*·tha	nuts
nudler	*nooth*·la	noodles
olie	*orl*·ye	oil
oliven	o·*lee*·wen	olive
ost	orsd	cheese
parisertoast	pa·*ree*·suh·torwsd	toasted ham and cheese sandwich
peber	*pi*·wa	pepper
pebermynte	pi·wa·*mern*·de	peppermint
peberrod	*pi*·wa·rorth	horseradish
persille	per·*see*·le	parsley
pommes frites	porm freed	French fries, chips
purløg	*poor*·loy	chives
remoulade	re·moo·*la*·the	mayonnaise-based tartar sauce
ris	rees	rice
røræg	*rer*·eg	scrambled eggs
rugbrød	*roo*·brerth	rye bread
rundstykke	*rorn*·ster·ge	crispy poppyseed roll
sennep	*se*·nob	mustard
sky	sgew	beef jelly
skysovs	*sgew*·sows	gravy
smør	smer	butter
smørrebrød	*smer*·re·brerth	open sandwich
sovs	sows	sauce
spejlæg	*spail*·eg	fried egg, sunny-side up
sukker	*sor*·ga	sugar
syltetøj	*sewl*·de·toy	jam
tykmælk	*tewg*·melg	pourable yoghurt
valnød	*val*·nerth	walnut

SWEET THINGS

ingefærbrød	*eeng*·e·fer·brerth	gingerbread
is	ees	ice cream, ice
kage	*ka*·e	cake
kringle	*kreng*·le	type of Danish pastry
lagkage	*low*·ka·e	layer cake
pandekage	*pa*·ne·ka·e	pancake or crepe
ris à l'amande	rees a la·mang	rice pudding with almonds (equal stress)
sød	serd	sweet
tærte	*ter*·de	tart
vaffel	*va*·fel	waffle
vanilleis	va·*neel*·ye·ees	vanilla ice cream

Outdoor Activities

Danes, by nature, are active souls who enjoy nothing more than getting out and revelling in the great outdoors. Be it cycling, hiking, horse riding or canoeing, you'll notice many Danes out and among it. Their backyard, although small, has some great diversity for such activities, from island-hopping bike adventures, to canoeing through the Lake District along Denmark's longest river, or horse riding into a magical sunset on the west coast of Jutland. Denmark may be modest in size but, don't be deceived, it has quality to burn.

CYCLING

Denmark is a superb country for the cyclist, as the roads are relatively quiet and the country features an attractively undulating landscape. Biking holidays are becoming increasingly popular, reflecting the Danes' own love of the great outdoors.

Cycling is a very common means of transport in Denmark as it keeps people fit, is environmentally friendly and an easy option for city folk.

Due to cycling's standing and popularity, cyclists enjoy a variety of well-established and well-maintained routes around towns and in the country. These cycling routes are very well suited for recreational cyclists, including families with children.

DID YOU KNOW?

It is estimated that, on average, each Dane rides 3km per day.

Danish cyclists enjoy rights that, in most other countries, are reserved for motorists. There are bicycle lanes along major city roads and through central areas, road signs are posted for bicycle traffic, and bicycle racks can be found at grocery shops, museums and many other public places. Drivers are so accommodating to cyclists in this country that cycling is an almost surreal experience.

When touring the country by bike, accommodation is easy to find, be it at a small country inn or at a basic camping ground. One advantage of the small scale of the country is that you're never far from a bed and a hot shower, which can be greatly needed after a tough day on the road.

Ever since Bjarne Riis stormed home to win the Tour de France in 1996 Danes have embraced the competitive aspect of cycling. So much so that nowadays 150 races are held around the country, with the most heavily contested being the annual Århus–Copenhagen Race (www.aarhus-koebenhavn.dk) every June.

For quality rental bikes, Copenhagen (p99) and Århus (p249) are your best bets. For more information on bicycle transport see p311.

Maps & Resources

The best map for planning a trip is *Cykelferiekort* (49kr), a 1:500,000-scale map published by Dansk Cyklist Forbund. Each county produces its own detailed map, and these are readily available at tourist offices.

The Danish cycling federation, **Dansk Cyklist Forbund** (☎ 33 32 31 21; www.dcf.dk; Rømersgade 7, Copenhagen K), has its headquarters in Copenhagen. Quality cycling maps can be ordered direct; jump on the Internet or call.

There are two excellent free regional cycling publications available in English, *Cycling Holidays in West Jutland* and *Funen and the Isles – a bike's eye view*, that suggest routes, things to see and do, and accommodation options along the way. They're available from all major tourist offices in Denmark.

Cycling Routes & Tours

There are 10 major bike routes that run throughout the country, all of which are in immaculate condition. In addition to the 'top 10' each county has an extensive network of bike routes which literally enables you to explore every inch of the country.

Routes 1, 3 and 5 run the length of Jutland, with route 1 covering the windswept west coast, route 3 cutting through the middle and route 5 hugging the east coast. Routes 2 and 4 take you out of the capital and over to Jutland's ferocious west coast while route 6 comes out of Copenhagen, across Funen and through to the fishing stronghold of Esbjerg. Routes 7 and 9 comprehensively cover Zealand and Lolland while route 8 sweeps across the southern leg of the country. Route 10 runs around the coast of Bornholm.

The best way to tour Denmark is by grabbing a map and planning it yourself. The routes are easy to follow and make for a great adventure. Tours, not surprisingly, are also available and are exceptionally well run although they tend to be rather pricey affairs. Denmark's cycling maps make it easy to self-plan your tour as they detail places to stay as well as all sorts of sightseeing spots, such as castles, museums and historic sights.

'The best way to tour Denmark is by grabbing a map and planning it yourself.'

However, if you're interested in joining a packaged cycling tour, Dansk Cyklist Forbund (opposite) arranges tours, as do the following companies.

BikeDenmark (☎ 48 48 58 00; www.bikedenmark.com; Oluf Poulsens Allé 1, 3480 Fredensborg) Operating since 1991 and well established in the industry, BikeDenmark offers a wide array of tours ranging from '10 islands in 10 days' (7500kr) to a '5 night tour north of Copenhagen' (5000kr). A big player in this growing Danish industry and renowned for consistent quality.

City Safari (☎ 33 23 94 90; Strandgade 27B, Copenhagen C; tours from 200kr) For innovative tours of the capital this company has it covered, from the relaxed informative historical viewpoint through to the Copenhagen-by-night experience. They do it well and their tours pedal to the beat of their groups.

Euro Bike and Walking (www.eurobike.com; tours from 8000kr) The tours are family friendly and although a little pricey they do deliver top-notch accommodation on their eight-day tour of the Danish Isles.

Scantours (www.scantours.com; 10-day tour 8200kr) A US-based company that offers seven different tours around the islands.

Classic Rides

There is incredible biking diversity on offer in Denmark. Here are three classic rides that use both national and local bike routes to give you an unforgettable biking adventure.

THE ZEALAND ISLANDS LOOP

Duration: 10–21 days

This ride is great if you have landed in the capital and want to explore the islands of the south at your own leisurely pace. The ride takes in six islands and there is plenty to see and do. You will be using three main bike routes (9, 8 and 6). Depending on how much you want to pedal, and how much you want to absorb, this ride can take anywhere between 10 days and three weeks.

It begins by taking route 9 south out of the capital and along the east coast of Zealand passing through the historic port town of Køge (p130), the yacht-infested Præstø (p146) and the medieval stronghold of Vordingborg (p147). The terrain is relatively mild and the bike tracks are tailor-made for easy riding.

SKAGERRAK
Skagen
Skiveren
Hirtshals
Frederikshavn
Løkken
Øster Vrå
Sæby
Blokhus
Hjallerup
Dronninglund
Aalborg
Hanstholm
Nørre Vorupør
Thisted
Stenbjerg
Hals
Egense
Støvring
KATTEGAT
Agger
Nykøbing M
Thyborøn
Harboøre
Hadsund
Hobro
Skive
Udbyhøj
Viborg
Randers
Grenaa
JUTLAND
Ebeltoft
Århus
Søndervig
Ringkøbing
Ry
Skanderborg
Hvide Sande
Skjern
Sønder Felding
Nørre Snede
Sjællands Odde
Hov
Nykøbing S
Horsens
Snaptun
Jelling
Juelsminde
Vejle
Kalundborg
Jyderup
Roskilde
COPENHAGEN
Bække
Fredericia
Kolding
Esbjerg
Vejen
Middelfart
Odense
ZEALAND
Lejre
Køge
Sorø
Slagelse
Ringsted
Korsør
Nyborg
Vojens
FUNEN
Næstved
Fakse
Haderslev
Bøjden
Faaborg
Præstø
Aabenraa
Ballebro
Svendborg
MØN
Stege
Fynshav
Tønder
Sønderborg
Vordingborg
Rudkøbing
Spodsbjerg
Rudbøl
Tårs
Saks-købing
Stubbekøbing
Nakskov
FALSTER
Padborg
LANGELAND
Maribo
Holeby
LOLLAND
Nykøbing F
Rødby
GERMANY
Gedser
BALTIC SEA
Helsingør
Humlebæk
Rungsted
SWEDEN
Allinge
Gudhjem
Hasle
Svaneke
Rønne
Nexø
BORNHOLM
Same Scale as Main Map

When you reach the southern tip, cross the bridge to Falster (p158) and you can ride around the northwest of the island through the tiny hamlets of Nr Vedby, Vålse and Alstrup before you jump on another bridge and over to the pastorally rich island of Lolland.

Once on Lolland you can take in the towns of Skaskøbing and Maribo before switching onto route 8 and heading west through the town of Nakskov and on to the ferry terminal at Tårs.

Hop on the ferry over to the seaside town of Spodsbjerg and then, depending on your time frame, you could cut a quick lap of the island or make a beeline for Tåsinge and the island of Funen.

On arrival at Funen head north, hugging the east coast, to the town of Nyborg. Note that this route is marked as 50 and is not one of the main trails; it is, however, in good shape and cycle friendly. It's a relaxing 40km. You will pass through a number of pretty villages and some gently rolling hills. At Nyborg you should part company with Funen and rejoin Zealand at Korsor. From there it's a couple of days riding on route 6 back to the capital.

SOUTHERN JUTLAND

Duration: 7–12 days

This ride takes in two glorious castles, a typically relaxed Danish island, and two wonderfully contrasting towns in Ribe (p218) and Kolding (p230). The cycling is relatively easy unless the west coast wind flexes its muscle.

The tour starts at Sønderborg where you can head off for a day of exploring the cycle friendly island of Als. There's a castle, lighthouse and quaint villages to see and it's well worth a day trip.

You then head west to the royal castle of Gråsten (p233), which is an ideal spot for a picnic lunch in the gardens, before cycling down to Padborg (p233) on the German border.

From Padborg you will pass through plenty of mellow fields on your way to Tønder (p227), a town rich in history. It's also 4km from Møgeltønder (p229), where you can take in what is arguably the most beautiful street in Denmark, and also see Prince Joachim's castle. Just north, the intriguing tale of the Golden Horns (p228) is waiting to beguile you.

Continue west through the town of Højer (p229) and past its impressive windmill and swing up the coast 30km to the island of Rømø (p225). On your trip you will notice many windmill farms, a money-spinner in these parts. Rømø is normally pretty quiet but well worth a day of relaxed touring and sightseeing.

When you leave the island make a beeline for Ribe, the oldest and quite possibly prettiest town in the land. While this ride is often windy, its flat surface makes it a highly pleasurable, stress-free ride.

For the final leg, you will cross a large chunk of Southern Jutland to the ever improving Kolding (p230).

BORNHOLM ODYSSEY

Duration: 4–7 days

Unique is the word to use when biking on Bornholm (p164). There is a total of 105km of cycling paths around the island. They run along former railway lines and through forest trails and offer an enchanting experience. Bornholm is also home to Denmark's third-largest forest, and an impressive

RULES OF THE ROAD

Just as cyclists' rights are taken seriously in Denmark, so too are their responsibilities. Here are some of the traffic regulations that are directly relevant to cyclists.

- All traffic in Denmark, both bicycle and motor vehicle, drives on the right-hand side of the road.
- Cyclists are obliged to obey traffic lights, pedestrian right-of-ways and most other road rules that apply to motor vehicles.
- Lights are required for night riding.
- When making a left turn at crossings, a large left turn is mandatory; that is, you must cycle straight across the intersecting road, staying on the right, before turning left into the right-hand lane of the new road. Do not cross diagonally.
- Use hand signals to indicate turns: your left arm should be outstretched prior to a left turn, and your right arm outstretched before a right turn.
- When entering a roundabout yield to vehicles already in the roundabout.
- If you're transporting children, the bicycle must have two independent brakes. A maximum of two children under the age of six can be carried on the bicycle or in an attached trailer.

waterfall awaits in Dondalen. In the south the ground is covered by a 550 million-year-old layer of sandstone. You will find granite rocks on this island which are also unique to Bornholm. There's a multitude of picturesque coastal villages and medieval round churches on offer just to highlight the striking contrast that is Bornholm. You can experience it all at your own leisurely pace and can spend anywhere from five to ten days exploring the island. Pick up a copy of the English-language *Bicycle Routes on Bornholm* from the tourist office.

WINDSURFING

The wild winds of the west coast have gained a lot of attention from windsurfers as the consistently good southwest–northwest conditions attract many Europeans to Klitmøller (p291) and Hvide Sande (p270).

Not only do these towns hold numerous contests each year, but they boast great terrain for all levels. Experts can carve up the wild North Sea breakers, while beginners can master the basics on the inland fjords. Klitmøller has a lovely bay that appears tailor-made for this activity, while Hvide Sande's most popular point is just off the end of the man-made lock.

Kite surfing, the latest fad, can be carried out at both these destinations. It is a whole new concept, and is doing what snowboarding did to skiing, revolutionising the boundaries of the sport.

Windsurfers with their own equipment can pick and choose where to set sail, but for beginners the best areas are the inland lakes. You can hire equipment from Hvide Sande and Klitmøller (300kr per day hire; 500kr per 4 hour lesson with gear).

SAILING

Yachting around Denmark is an ever popular activity, but basically limited to people with their own boats. During the summer months, all major towns along the southern coast of Funen (p181) offer sailing cruises either at sunset or during the day. On some of them you can actively take part in the running of the ship, while on others you're invited to sit back and enjoy a glass of bubbly.

Eager yachtsmen can get hold of a boat or organise a private cruise through the Maritimt Center www.maritimt-center.dk

HORSE RIDING

Horse riding is excellent in Denmark, with fantastic trails and scenic rides spread throughout the country. Jutland is full of opportunities, be it up north meandering along some forest paths, or down south on the island of Rømø (p225) galloping into the glorious sunset. Icelandic horses, whose forebears were once used by the Vikings as a key mode of transport, can now be found all over the country. Rides can be organised through riding companies (see Rømø p225) at very moderate prices (85kr per hour).

DID YOU KNOW?

Strong, steady and rather intelligent, Icelandic horses are said to reflect the character of Vikings.

GOLF

Although Denmark has produced only one world-class golfer, namely Tomas Bjorn, it boasts a number of top-quality courses. Here's a selection of some of the best that are open year round for a round:

Copenhagen Golf Club (☎ 39 63 04 83; Dyrehaven 2; 18 holes Mon-Fri 280kr, Sat & Sun 350kr; club hire 200kr) Scandinavia's oldest golf club is beautifully located just outside the capital in the deer park. Golfers can stroll (or buggy) through woodlands and meadows while either hunting for lost balls or waiting for others to match their hole in one.

Odense Golf Club (☎ 65 95 90 00; Hestehrven 200; 18 holes Mon-Fri 250kr, Sat & Sun 300kr) A spaciously laid out undulating course that is immaculately kept and offers some of the best holes on Fyn. A great course if you are not the straightest off the tee.

Royal Oak Golf Club (☎ 74 55 32 94; Golfvej 2, Jels; 18 holes Mon-Fri 350kr, Sat & Sun 380kr) An impeccable golfing experience awaits you here. This course has been specifically designed in accordance with American USGA standards. In effect this means that among other obstacles there are 78 bunkers to contend with.

Harre Vig Golf Club (☎ 97 57 11 66; Harrebjergvej 13; 18 holes Mon-Fri 225kr, Sat & Sun275kr) Laid out next to the idyllic Harre Vig, this course would have to go close to being the most beautiful in Denmark. It's a favourite of many of the locals and a lazy 18 holes here should win most over in a hurry.

Bornholm Golf Club (☎ 56 95 68 54; Plantagevej 3B; 18 holes 250kr) A big advantage of this course is the lack of wind due to its sheltered location. It's a wonderfully laid out course with plenty of wildlife to keep you entertained.

CANOEING

The best canoeing in Denmark can be experienced along its longest river, Gudenå. For more information about paddling a boat, check out the Lake District section (p253).

WALKING

Walking in Denmark is not as widespread a phenomenon as cycling, but is popular nonetheless. For hikers, there are some picturesque trails through Denmark's only national park, Rebild Bakker (p267). Along with some good, if not very taxing, hikes within the Lake District (p253) there are also some decent tracks in southern Zealand. Aside from that, beaches are great for a stroll and none are better than those up at Denmark's most northern tip, Grenen (p286). Walkers in Denmark are allowed to explore any stretch of coast, irrespective of who owns it. Forests are fair game too, but you must stick to the paths.

SWIMMING

Although the water temperature would worry even brass monkeys most of the year, enjoyable seaside swimming can be had in the warmer months (July and August). Outside of that nearly all regional towns have an aqua centre with heated pools. The quality of the beaches is outstanding as the majority have clean water, silky sand, and plenty of room. If you are swimming on the west coast of Jutland caution needs to be taken with currents and undertows from the ever-dangerous North Sea.

'The quality of beaches is outstanding, the majority have clean water, silky sand and plenty of room.'

FISHING

Denmark abounds with streams and lakes, all well stocked with pike, perch and trout. In addition, with so much shoreline the saltwater fishing possibilities are endless, with the most common saltwater fish being cod, mackerel, plaice and sea trout. Fly fishing enthusiasts will find the best spots are the rivers in Jutland.

Anglers between the age of 18 and 67 are required to carry a fishing licence (25kr per day, 75kr per week) and these are sold at most tourist offices. There are also a number of privately run 'put and take' fishing holes enabling you to fish in well-stocked rivers and lakes for a fee.

Copenhagen

CONTENTS

Copenhagen (København), one of the world's most liveable cities, is an immensely appealing blend of everything you want to find in a place to visit – beautifully preserved historic architecture, copper-covered church steeples punctuating the generally low-rise skyline, cobblestone streets with understated charm, and excellent sightseeing choices that cater to all tastes.

The city packs a delicate punch – it's easy to get around and is a pleasant place for walking, as many areas in the city centre are reserved for pedestrians. For those who prefer to move at a slightly faster pace, there are bicycle lanes, as well as an excellent metropolitan bus and train system and a metro system that could have come straight from a sci-fi flick.

Populated by easy-going, tolerant (albeit taciturn and introverted) people who practice consideration towards virtually everyone, Copenhagen's inclusive quality can also be seen in the country's royal family – who are known for their relaxed approach to duties. This city-wide appreciation of variety means that Copenhagen offers cosmopolitan dining and cultural options that alleviate any sense of homogeneity that may strike you while strolling (it's true: the gene pool, although good-looking, does seem to be a tad uniform in some quarters).

One very pleasant surprise is that Copenhagen is not as hideously expensive as some would have you believe. It survives comparisons to London, Paris, New York and Tokyo with ease. In fact, Copenhagen is the sort of city that'll have you itching to tell everyone you know that they should get over there – fast.

HIGHLIGHTS

- Lose yourself in **Statens Museum for Kunst** (p78) – a fabulous collection of European and Scandinavian art.
- Catch sight of the copper-bedecked roofs sandwiched between the city's canals and clear skies, particularly on charming **Christianshavn** (p76).
- Copenhagen's flat topography and abundance of cycle lanes make **biking** (p99) a breeze.
- Push yourself to squeeze in one last piece of the famous open-faced sandwiches at **Ida Davidsen** (p94).
- Whether it's jazz, dance, opera, electronica or theatre, Copenhagen places a high value on its arts scene. Don't miss the **Copenhagen Jazz Festival** (p85) if you're in town in July.

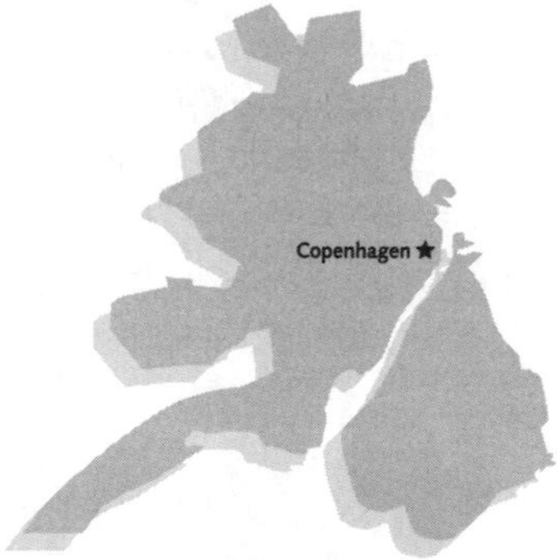
Copenhagen

- POPULATION: 1.7 MILLION

COPENHAGEN

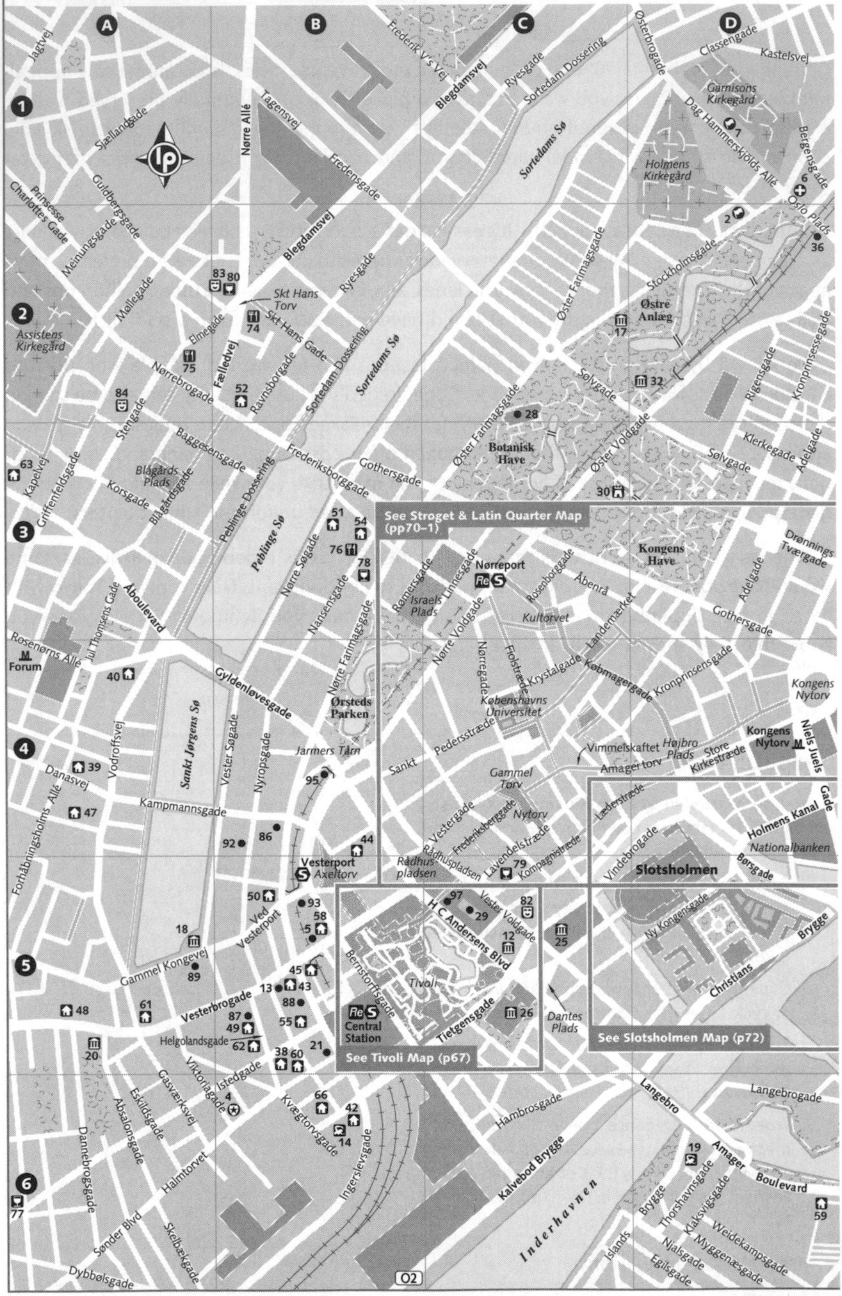
A
B
C
D
1
2
3
4
5
6
Jagtvej
Frederik V's Vej
Blegdamsvej
Ryesgade
Sortedam Dossering
Østerbrogade
Classensgade
Kastelsvej
Garnisons Kirkegård
Dag Hammerskjölds Allé
Bergensgade
Holmens Kirkegård
Oslo Plads
Tagensvej
Nørre Allé
Sjællandsgade
Sortedams Sø
Fredensgade
Prinsesse Charlottes Gade
Guldbergsgade
Meinungsgade
Blegdamsvej
Ryesgade
Skt Hans Torv
Skt Hans Gade
Øster Farimagsgade
Stockholmsgade
Østre Anlæg
Møllegade
Elmegade
Fælledvej
Sortedam Dossering
Sortedams Sø
Assistens Kirkegård
Nørrebrogade
Ravnsborggade
Sølvgade
Kronprinsessegade
Rigensgade
Stengade
Baggesensgade
Frederiksborggade
Gothersgade
Øster Farimagsgade
Botanisk Have
Øster Voldgade
Klerkegade
Sølvgade
Adelgade
Kapelvej
Griffenfeldsgade
Blågårds Plads
Blågårdsgade
Korsgade
Peblinge Dossering
Peblinge Sø
See Stroget & Latin Quarter Map (pp70–1)
Kongens Have
Dronnings Tværgade
Nørre Søgade
Nørreport
Rømersgade
Linnésgade
Israels Plads
Rosenborggade
Åbenrå
Landemærket
Kultorvet
Adelgade
Gothersgade
Åboulevard
Jul Thomsens Gade
Nansensgade
Nørre Farimagsgade
Nørre Voldgade
Rosenørns Allé
Forum
Gyldenløvesgade
Nørregade
Fiolstræde
Krystalgade
Købmagergade
Kronprinsensgade
Kongens Nytorv
Københavns Universitet
Ørsteds Parken
Vodroffsvej
Sankt Jørgens Sø
Vester Søgade
Nyropsgade
Jarmers Tårn
Sankt Pedersstræde
Vimmelskaftet
Højbro Plads
Amagertorv
Store Kirkestræde
Kongens Nytorv
Niels Juels Gade
Danasvej
Gammel Torv
Lædersstræde
Holmens Kanal
Nationalbanken
Kampmannsgade
Forhåbningsholms Allé
Vestergade
Frederiksberggade
Nytorv
Lavendelstræde
Kompagnistræde
Vindebrogade
Slotsholmen
Børsgade
Vesterport
Axeltorv
Rådhuspladsen
Rådhus-pladsen
Ved Vesterport
H C Andersens Blvd
Vester Voldgade
Ny Kongensgade
Brygge
Christians
Gammel Kongevej
Bernstorffsgade
Tivoli
Vesterbrogade
Helgolandsgade
Central Station
Tietgensgade
Dantes Plads
See Tivoli Map (p67)
See Slotsholmen Map (p72)
Istedgade
Gasværksvej
Viktoriagade
Eskildsgade
Absalonsgade
Kvægtorvsgade
Hambrosgade
Langebro
Langebrogade
Dannebrogsgade
Halmtorvet
Ingerslevsgade
Kalvebod Brygge
Amager Boulevard
Sønder Blvd
Skelbækgade
Inderhavnen
Islands Brygge
Thorshavnsgade
Klaksvigsgade
Weidekampsgade
Njalsgade
Myggenæsgade
Egilsgade
Dybbølsgade
O2

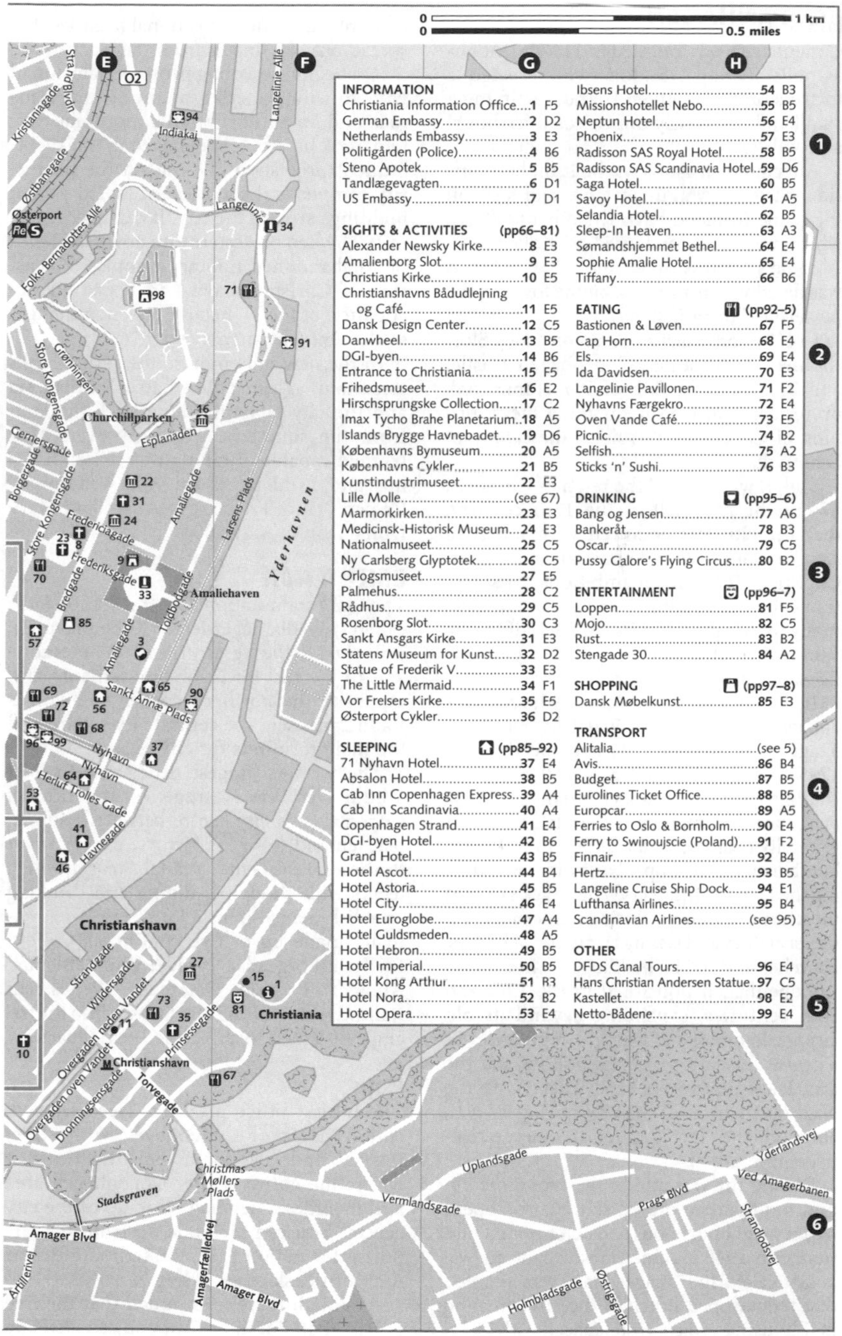

0 1 km
0 0.5 miles
E
F
G
H
1
2
3
4
5
6
O2
Strandblvd
Kristianiagade
Østbanegade
Østerport
Folke Bernadottes Allé
Indiakaj
Langelinie Allé
Langelinie
Store Kongensgade
Grønningen
Churchillparken
Esplanaden
Gernersgade
Borgergade
Fredericiagade
Frederiksgade
Bredgade
Amaliegade
Toldbodgade
Amaliehaven
Larsens Plads
Yderhavnen
Sankt Annæ Plads
Nyhavn
Herluf Trolles Gade
Havnegade
Christianshavn
Strandgade
Wildersgade
Overgaden neden Vandet
Overgaden oven Vandet
Prinsessegade
Christiania
Dronningensgade
Torvegade
Christmas Møllers Plads
Stadsgraven
Amager Blvd
Artillerivej
Amagerfælledvej
Uplandsgade
Vermlandsgade
Prags Blvd
Yderlandsvej
Ved Amagerbanen
Strandlodsvej
Holmbladsgade
Østrigsgade

INFORMATION
- Christiania Information Office....**1** F5
- German Embassy....**2** D2
- Netherlands Embassy....**3** E3
- Politigården (Police)....**4** B6
- Steno Apotek....**5** B5
- Tandlægevagten....**6** D1
- US Embassy....**7** D1

SIGHTS & ACTIVITIES (pp66–81)
- Alexander Newsky Kirke....**8** E3
- Amalienborg Slot....**9** E3
- Christians Kirke....**10** E5
- Christianshavns Bådudlejning og Café....**11** E5
- Dansk Design Center....**12** C5
- Danwheel....**13** B5
- DGI-byen....**14** B6
- Entrance to Christiania....**15** F5
- Frihedsmuseet....**16** E2
- Hirschsprungske Collection....**17** C2
- Imax Tycho Brahe Planetarium..**18** A5
- Islands Brygge Havnebadet....**19** D6
- Københavns Bymuseum....**20** A5
- Københavns Cykler....**21** B5
- Kunstindustrimuseet....**22** E3
- Lille Molle....(see 67)
- Marmorkirken....**23** E3
- Medicinsk-Historisk Museum....**24** E3
- Nationalmuseet....**25** C5
- Ny Carlsberg Glyptotek....**26** C5
- Orlogsmuseet....**27** E5
- Palmehus....**28** C2
- Rådhus....**29** C5
- Rosenborg Slot....**30** C3
- Sankt Ansgars Kirke....**31** E3
- Statens Museum for Kunst....**32** D2
- Statue of Frederik V....**33** E3
- The Little Mermaid....**34** F1
- Vor Frelsers Kirke....**35** E5
- Østerport Cykler....**36** D2

SLEEPING (pp85–92)
- 71 Nyhavn Hotel....**37** E4
- Absalon Hotel....**38** B5
- Cab Inn Copenhagen Express..**39** A4
- Cab Inn Scandinavia....**40** A4
- Copenhagen Strand....**41** E4
- DGI-byen Hotel....**42** B6
- Grand Hotel....**43** B5
- Hotel Ascot....**44** B4
- Hotel Astoria....**45** B5
- Hotel City....**46** E4
- Hotel Euroglobe....**47** A4
- Hotel Guldsmeden....**48** A5
- Hotel Hebron....**49** B5
- Hotel Imperial....**50** B5
- Hotel Kong Arthur....**51** B3
- Hotel Nora....**52** B2
- Hotel Opera....**53** E4
- Ibsens Hotel....**54** B3
- Missionshotellet Nebo....**55** B5
- Neptun Hotel....**56** E4
- Phoenix....**57** E3
- Radisson SAS Royal Hotel....**58** B5
- Radisson SAS Scandinavia Hotel..**59** D6
- Saga Hotel....**60** B5
- Savoy Hotel....**61** A5
- Selandia Hotel....**62** B5
- Sleep-In Heaven....**63** A3
- Sømandshjemmet Bethel....**64** E4
- Sophie Amalie Hotel....**65** E4
- Tiffany....**66** B6

EATING (pp92–5)
- Bastionen & Løven....**67** F5
- Cap Horn....**68** E4
- Els....**69** E4
- Ida Davidsen....**70** E3
- Langelinie Pavillonen....**71** F2
- Nyhavns Færgekro....**72** E4
- Oven Vande Café....**73** E5
- Picnic....**74** B2
- Selfish....**75** A2
- Sticks 'n' Sushi....**76** B3

DRINKING (pp95–6)
- Bang og Jensen....**77** A6
- Bankerât....**78** B3
- Oscar....**79** C5
- Pussy Galore's Flying Circus....**80** B2

ENTERTAINMENT (pp96–7)
- Loppen....**81** F5
- Mojo....**82** C5
- Rust....**83** B2
- Stengade 30....**84** A2

SHOPPING (pp97–8)
- Dansk Møbelkunst....**85** E3

TRANSPORT
- Alitalia....(see 5)
- Avis....**86** B4
- Budget....**87** B5
- Eurolines Ticket Office....**88** B5
- Europcar....**89** A5
- Ferries to Oslo & Bornholm....**90** E4
- Ferry to Swinoujscie (Poland)....**91** F2
- Finnair....**92** B4
- Hertz....**93** B5
- Langeline Cruise Ship Dock....**94** E1
- Lufthansa Airlines....**95** B4
- Scandinavian Airlines....(see 95)

OTHER
- DFDS Canal Tours....**96** E4
- Hans Christian Andersen Statue..**97** C5
- Kastellet....**98** E2
- Netto-Bådene....**99** E4

HISTORY

Copenhagen was founded in 1167 by tough-as-nails Bishop Absalon, who erected a fortress on Slotsholmen Island, fortifying a small and previously unprotected harbour-side village.

After the fortification was built, the harbour-side village grew in importance and took on the name Kømandshavn (Merchant's Port), which was later condensed to København. Absalon's fortress stood until 1369, when it was destroyed in an attack on the town by the powerful Hanseatic states.

In 1376 construction began on a new Slotsholmen fortification, Copenhagen Castle, and in 1416 King Erik of Pomerania took up residence at the site, marking the beginning of Copenhagen's role as the capital of Denmark.

Still, it wasn't until the reign of Christian IV, in the first half of the 17th century, that the city was endowed with much of its splendour. A lofty Renaissance designer, Christian IV began an ambitious construction scheme, building two new castles and many other grand edifices, including the Rundetårn observatory and the glorious Børsen, Europe's first stock exchange.

In 1711 the bubonic plague reduced Copenhagen's population of 60,000 by one-third. Tragic fires, one in 1728 and the other in 1795, wiped out large tracts of the city, including most of its timber buildings. However, the worst scourge in the city's history is generally regarded as the unprovoked British bombardment of Copenhagen in 1807, during the Napoleonic Wars. The attack targeted the heart of the city, inflicting numerous civilian casualties and setting hundreds of homes, churches and public buildings on fire.

Copenhagen flourished in the 19th and 20th centuries, expanding beyond its old city walls and establishing a reputation as a centre for culture, liberal politics and the arts. Dark times were experienced with the Nazi occupation of the city during WWII, although the city managed to emerge relatively unscathed.

During the war and in the economic depression that had preceded it, many Copenhagen neighbourhoods had deteriorated into slums. In 1948 an ambitious urban renewal policy called the 'Finger Plan' was adopted that redeveloped much of the city, creating new housing projects interspaced with green areas of parks and recreational facilities that spread out like fingers from the city centre.

A rebellion by young people disillusioned with growing materialism, the nuclear arms race and an authoritarian educational system, took hold in Copenhagen in the 1960s. Student protests broke out on the university campus and squatters occupied vacant buildings around the city. It came to a head in 1971 when protesters tore down the fence of an abandoned military camp at the east side of Christianshavn and began an occupation of the 41-hectare site, naming this settlement Christiania (see p76).

In the new millennium, the future looks uncertain, as riot police patrol Christiania and the city talks of taking back the land from the squatters. The only event that seemed capable of taking this topic off the lips and front pages was the wedding of Crown Prince Frederik to Australian Mary Donaldson in May 2004.

ORIENTATION

The main train station, Central Station (also called Hovedbanegården or København H), is flanked to the west by the main hotel zone and to the east by Tivoli amusement park. Opposite the northern corner of Tivoli is Rådhuspladsen, the central city square and the main terminus for city buses.

The world's longest pedestrian mall at a little over 1km – Strøget – runs through Copenhagen's city centre between Rådhuspladsen and Kongens Nytorv, the square at the head of the Nyhavn canal. Strøget, which teems with shopping, dining and drinking establishments – plus a lot of locals – is actually made up of five continuous streets: Frederiksborggade, Nygade, Vimmelskaftet, Amagertorv and Østergade. Pedestrian walkways run north from Strøget into the triangle of streets forming the Latin Quarter.

Maps

The tourist office produces free, detailed, colour maps of Copenhagen with street indexes and keys for major attractions. It covers the entire greater Copenhagen area and includes a detailed blow-up of the city centre. You can pick one up from the airport information desk, the tourist office or the front desk of most hotels.

Although there's not much that the free tourist map doesn't show, you can also buy commercial maps and street directories at bookshops. These maps are larger and have expanded indexes; one of the best is the street directory *Kraks Kort over København og Omagn*, which costs 229kr.

INFORMATION

Bookshops

Arnold Busck (Map pp70-1; ☎ 33 73 35 00; Købmagergade 49) General and specialist titles in the Latin Quarter.

GAD (Map pp70-1; ☎ 77 66 60 00; Vimmelskaftet 32; 🕓 10am-7pm Mon-Fri, 10am-5pm Sat) An excellent range of Danish- and English-language titles, plus plenty of guidebooks in a central location.

Nordisk Korthandel (Map pp70-1; ☎ 33 38 26 38; Studiestræde 26; 🕓 10.30am-5.30pm Mon-Fri, 9.30am-3pm Sat) Sells guidebooks as well as an extensive range of cycling and hiking trail maps of Denmark and elsewhere in Europe.

Politiken Boghallen (Map pp70-1; ☎ 33 47 25 60; Rådhuspladsen 37; 🕓 10am-7pm Mon-Fri, 10am-4pm Sat) Great shop with a large range of travel guides, coffee-table books and novels.

Emergency

Dial ☎ 112 to contact police, ambulance or fire services; the call can be made without coins from public phones.

Politigården (Map pp62-3; ☎ 33 14 14 48; Polititorvet; 🕓 24hr) Police headquarters.

Internet Access

Boomtown (Map p67; ☎ 33 32 10 32; Axeltorv 1; per 30 min 20kr; 🕓 24hr) Large, modern and the most convenient by a long shot.

Hovedbiblioteket (Map pp70-1; ☎ 33 73 60 60; Krystalgade 15; 🕓 10am-7pm Mon-Fri, 10am-4pm Sat) The main public library – computers can be used free for up to 30 minutes, but queuing can take an hour.

Kongelige Bibliotek (Map p72; ☎ 33 47 47 47; www.kb.dk; Christians Brygge; 🕓 10am-5pm Mon-Fri, 10am-2pm Sat) Library on the southern side of Slotsholmen, where visitors can make a quick online run as long as no-one else is waiting.

Use It (Map pp70-1; ☎ 33 73 06 20; Rådhusstræde 13; 🕓 11am-4pm Mon-Wed, 11am-6pm Thu, 11am-2pm Fri 16 Sep-14 Jun; 9am-7pm Mon-Fri 15 Jun-15 Sep) Budget travel information centre offering free Internet access on four computers for 20 minutes at a time. Bookings advised.

Internet Resources

Five websites that will link you to a wealth of information in English are

www3.aok.dk/Copenhagen/Visiting_Copenhagen In association with the *Copenhagen Post* newspaper.

www.cphpost.dk The online edition of the *Copenhagen Post*, with plenty of news and listings.

www.hur.dk The website of the Greater Copenhagen Authority.

www.useit.dk Run by Use It, the budget travel centre, with tips on all things Copenhagen and cheap.

www.woco.dk Run by Wonderful Copenhagen, the tourism office.

Left Luggage

Central Station Left-luggage office (☎ 33 69 21 15; per 24hr, max 10 days suitcase, bag, parcel 30kr per piece, rucksack, pram, bike 40kr per piece ; Luggage lockers (per 24hr, max 72hr small/large 25/35kr); 🕓 5.30am-1am Mon-Sat, 6am-1am Sun)

Copenhagen Airport Luggage Lockers (from 20kr per piece per 24hr); Left-luggage Room (☎ 32 47 47 32; 30kr per piece per day; 🕓 6am-10pm) Near the airport's post office.

Use It (Map pp70-1; ☎ 33 73 06 20; www.useit.dk; Rådhusstræde 13; no charge; 🕓 11am-4pm Mon-Wed, 11am-6pm Thu, 11am-2pm Fri 16 Sep-14 Jun; 9am-7pm Mon-Fri 15 Jun-15 Sep)

Medical Services

The following hospitals have 24-hour emergency wards:

Amager Hospital (Map p103; ☎ 32 34 32 34; Italiensvej 1)

Bispebjerg Hospital (Map p103; ☎ 35 31 35 31; Bispebjerg Bakke 23)

Frederiksberg Hospital (Map p103; ☎ 38 16 38 16; Nordre Fasanvej 57)

Private doctor visits vary but usually cost from around 500kr. Dentists' fees must be paid in cash.

City General Practice & Travel Medicine (Map pp70-1; ☎ 70 27 57 57; Ny Østergade) Behind the Hotel d'Angleterre, English spoken.

Tandlægevagten (Map pp62-3; ☎ 35 38 02 51; Oslo Plads 14) Emergency dental service.

There are numerous pharmacies around the city; look for the sign *apotek*.

Steno Apotek (Map pp62-3; ☎ 33 14 82 66; Vesterbrogade 6; 🕓 24hr) Opposite Central Station.

Money

Banks are plentiful and can be found on nearly every second corner in central Copenhagen. Most are open 10am to 4pm weekdays (to 6pm on Thursday). Most banks in Copenhagen have ATMs accessible 24 hours per day.

Danske Bank at Airport (Arrival & Transit Halls; 6am-10pm)
Forex (Map p67; Central Station ☎ 33 11 21 13; Central Station; 7am-9pm; Map pp70-1; Nørreport ☎ 33 32 81 00; Nørre Voldgade 90; 9am-7pm Mon-Fri, 9am-4pm Sat; Map pp70-1; opposite Tivoli ☎ 33 93 77 70; Vesterbrogade 2B; 9am-7pm Mon-Fri, 9am-4pm Sat)

Post

Post office (Map pp70-1; ☎ 33 89 90 00; Købmagergade 33; 10am-5.30pm Mon-Fri, 10am-2pm Sat) A handy post office just near Strøget and in the Latin Quarter.
Post office in Central Station (☎ 33 41 56 00; 8am-9pm Mon-Fri, 9am-4pm Sat, 10am-4pm Sun)

Tourist Information

Copenhagen Right Now (Map p67; ☎ 70 22 24 42; www.woco.dk; Vesterbrogade 4A; 9am-4pm Mon-Fri, 9am-2pm Sat Jan-Apr; 9am-6pm Mon-Sat May & Jun; 9am-8pm Mon-Sat, 10am-6pm Sun Jul & Aug; 9am-4pm Mon-Fri, 9am-2pm Sat Sep-Dec) Brand-new information office with a café, free Internet access, gift shop and multilingual staff. Opened mid-2004, it's the best source of information in town – free maps, booking services and hotel reservation available for a fee.
Use It (Map pp70-1; ☎ 33 73 06 20; www.useit.dk; Rådhusstræde 13; 11am-4pm Mon-Wed, 11am-6pm Thu, 11am-2pm Fri 16 Sep-14 Jun; 9am-7pm Mon-Fri 15 Jun-15 Sep) A terrific alternative information centre catering to young budget travellers but open to all. Books accommodation, stores luggage, holds mail and provides information on everything, all free of charge.

SIGHTS

Copenhagen has been the Danish capital since the early 15th century. Most of the city's foremost historical and cultural sites remain concentrated within a relatively small area of the city's centre. A variety of parks, gardens, water fountains, squares and green areas lace the city centre. Along the waterfront you'll discover the scenic row houses that line Nyhavn, the famed statue of the Little Mermaid and the canal-cut district of Christianshavn.

Rådhuspladsen & Tivoli

The large central square of **Rådhuspladsen** is flanked on one side by the city hall and on another by Copenhagen's municipal bus terminus, and marks the heart of Copenhagen. The bustling shopping street Strøget begins at the northeast side of Rådhuspladsen and while the entertainment centre Tivoli glitters to the southwest.

Rådhuspladsen is laid out in an open format without barriers such as fences, which tends to give it a rather barren appearance. The unobstructed openness of the square, however, makes it a great place to stop and observe the buildings that surround it.

RÅDHUS

Copenhagen's grand red-brick **Rådhus** (City Hall; Map pp62-3; admission free; 7.45am-5pm Mon-Fri) was completed in 1905. Designed by the Danish architect Martin Nyrop, it reflects many of the trends of its period, displaying elements of 19th-century national Romanticism, medieval Danish design and northern Italian architecture, the last-mentioned most not-able in the central courtyard.

Adorning the façade above the main entrance is a golden statue of Bishop Absalon, who founded the city in 1167. The entrance leads to the main hall, a grand room that serves as a polling station during municipal elections.

You can poke around the main hall on your own but it's more interesting to make the climb up the 105m clock tower for **Jens Olsens Clock** (adult/child 10/5kr; 8.30am-4.30pm Mon-Fri, 10am-1pm Sat), which tops city hall, but expect a decent workout as there are some 300 steps along the way. The clock, designed by Danish astromechanic Jens Olsen (1872–1945) and built at a cost of one million krone, is of special note to chronometer buffs, displaying not only the local time, but also solar time, sidereal time, sunrises and sunsets, firmament and celestial pole migration, planet revolutions, the Gregorian calendar and even changing holidays, such as Easter.

TIVOLI

Situated in the heart of the city, **Tivoli** (Map p67; ☎ 33 15 10 01; www.tivoligardens.com; Vesterbrogade 3; adult/child 65/40kr; 11am-11pm Sun-Wed, 11am-midnight Thu & Sat, 11am-1am Fri 16 Apr-17 Jun & 16 Aug-19 Sep; 11am-midnight Sun-Thu, 11am-1am Fri & Sat 18 Jun-15 Aug) is a tantalising combination of amusement rides, flower gardens, food pavilions, carnival games and open-air stage shows. This genteel, ever-popular entertainment park, which dates from 1843, is delightfully varied and one of Denmark's most popular attractions. Visitors can ride the new roller coaster (named 'The Demon' – and Denmark's biggest), take in the famous fireworks display at night or simply watch the happy crowds

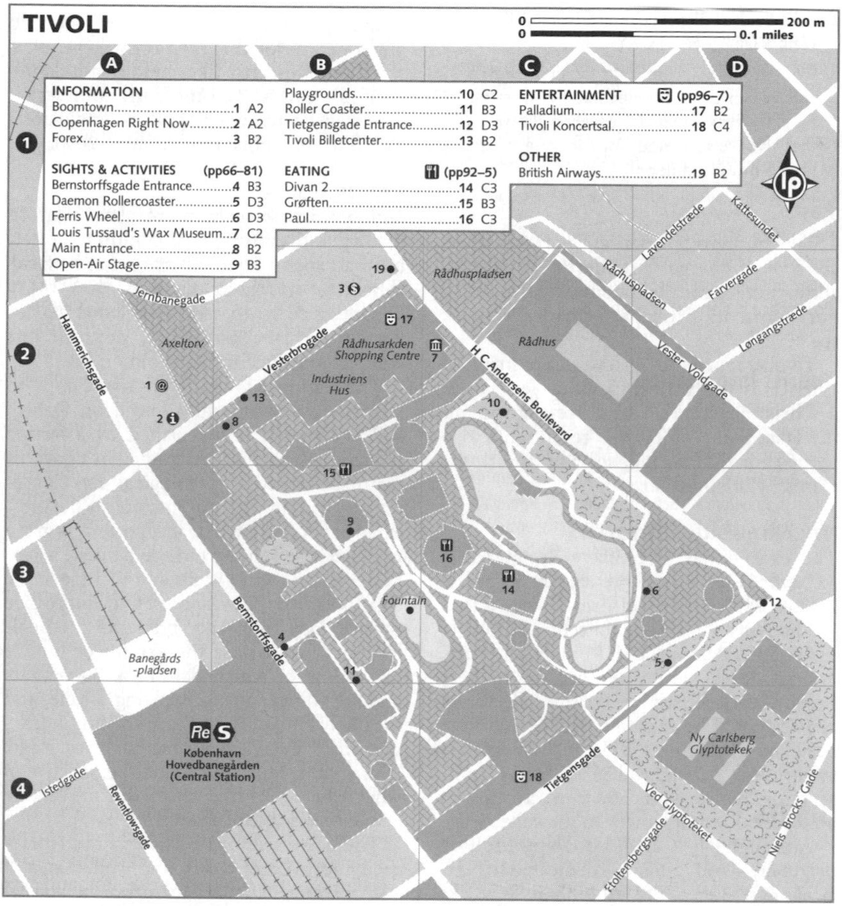
TIVOLI
0 200 m
0 0.1 miles
A
B
C
D
1
2
3
4
INFORMATION
Boomtown....1 A2
Copenhagen Right Now....2 A2
Forex....3 B2
SIGHTS & ACTIVITIES (pp66–81)
Bernstorffsgade Entrance....4 B3
Daemon Rollercoaster....5 D3
Ferris Wheel....6 D3
Louis Tussaud's Wax Museum...7 C2
Main Entrance....8 B2
Open-Air Stage....9 B3
Playgrounds....10 C2
Roller Coaster....11 B3
Tietgensgade Entrance....12 D3
Tivoli Billetcenter....13 B2
EATING (pp92–5)
Divan 2....14 C3
Grøften....15 B3
Paul....16 C3
ENTERTAINMENT (pp96–7)
Palladium....17 B2
Tivoli Koncertsal....18 C4
OTHER
British Airways....19 B2
Jernbanegade
Hammerichsgade
Axeltorv
Vesterbrogade
Rådhusarkden Shopping Centre
Industriens Hus
Rådhuspladsen
H C Andersens Boulevard
Rådhus
Vester Voldgade
Lavendelstræde
Kattesundet
Farvergade
Løngangstræde
Fountain
Bernstorffsgade
Banegårds -pladsen
København Hovedbanegården (Central Station)
Istedgade
Reventlowsgade
Tietgensgade
Ny Carlsberg Glyptotekek
Ved Glyptoteket
Stoltenbergsgade
Niels Brocks Gade

cavort in this most beloved of Copenhagen's tourist attractions, which is bathed in a near-permanent glow of nostalgia.

During the day children and the young-at-heart flock to Tivoli's Ferris wheel and other rides. In the evening Tivoli takes on a more romantic aura as the thousands of fairy lights are switched on and the cultural activities unfold, with one stage hosting traditional folk dancing as another prepares a theatrical performance.

Each of Tivoli's numerous entertainment venues has a different character. Perhaps best known is the open-air pantomime theatre, which features mime and ballet, and was built in 1874 by Vilhelm Dahlerup, the Copenhagen architect who also designed the royal theatre. Tivoli also has an indoor cabaret theatre and a large concert hall that features performances by international symphony orchestras and ballet troupes.

Between all the nightlights and glorious flowerbeds, Tivoli is a sweet place to stroll around, and if you feel like eating there are some decent (and even some very good) restaurants that make for a memorable dining experience.

Saturday is the best night to visit as it includes a fireworks display at 11.45pm. There's a nightly sound and light display on Tivoli Lake, 30 minutes before closing. Amusement ride tickets cost 15kr (some rides require up to four tickets), but there are multi-ticket schemes and passes as well.

FIREWORKS FACTORY

Tivoli has its own fireworks factory – with a crack team of 10 pyrotechnicians working hard to ensure that the dazzling fireworks that Tivoli is so famous for continue to uphold a proud tradition.

The numerous open-air performances are free of charge, but there's usually an admission fee for the indoor performances. For information on performance venues, see p97.

Tivoli reopens for a few weeks prior to Christmas for various holiday festivities, a Christmas market and ice-skating on the lake. Some of Tivoli's restaurants also reopen for that period, serving traditional Danish Christmas fare.

NY CARLSBERG GLYPTOTEK

The exceptional **Ny Carlsberg Glyptotek** (Map pp62-3; ☎ 33 41 81 41; www.glyptoteket.dk; Tietgensgade 25; adult/child 20kr/free, free Wed & Sun; 🕙 10am-4pm Tue-Sun) houses an excellent collection of Greek, Egyptian, Etruscan and Roman sculpture and art. It was built a century ago by beer baron Carl Jacobsen, an ardent collector of classical art. The museum's main building, designed by architect Vilhelm Dahlerup, is set around a delightful glass-domed conservatory replete with palm trees, creating an atmospheric complement to the collection.

Although Ny Carlsberg Glyptotek was originally – and remains – dedicated to classical art, a later gift of more than 20 works by Paul Gauguin (whose wife was Danish) led to the formation of an impressive 19th-century French and Danish art collection. The Danish collection includes paintings by JC Dahl, CW Eckersberg, Christian Købke and Jens Juel.

The French collection is centred on the Gauguin paintings, which now number 45. These are displayed along with works by Cézanne, Van Gogh, Pissarro, Monet and Renoir in the stunning new wing of the museum that opened in 1996. This 'French Wing' also boasts one of only three complete series of Degas bronzes.

A treat for off-season visitors are the chamber concerts given on Sundays from October to March in the museum's concert hall, which is lined by life-size statues of Roman patricians. And you won't have to pay a penny for this high-brow experience since the concerts, like Sunday admission itself, are gratis. The museum is undergoing extensive remodelling, with certain areas closed to the public until 28 June 2006.

NATIONALMUSEET

If you want to learn more about Danish history and culture, you couldn't do better than spending an afternoon at **Nationalmuseet** (National Museum; Map pp62-3; ☎ 33 13 44 11; www.natmus.dk; Ny Vestergade 10; adult/child 50kr/free, free Wed; 🕙 10am-5pm Tue-Sun), opposite the western entrance to Slotsholmen.

The National Museum has first claims on virtually every antiquity found on Danish soil, whether it be unearthed by a farmer ploughing his field or excavated in a government-sponsored archaeological dig. Consequently this quality museum boasts the most extensive collection of Danish artefacts in the world. These range from the Upper Palaeolithic period to the 1840s and include Stone Age tools, Viking weaponry and impressive Bronze Age, Iron Age and rune-stone collections. Don't miss the exhibit of bronze lurs, some of which date back 3000 years and are still capable of blowing a tune, and the finely crafted 3500-year-old Sun Chariot, unearthed in a Zealand field a century ago. If you want to get an outdoor perspective of what a lur looks like, check out the Viking statue on Rådhuspladsen.

There are sections related to the Norsemen and Inuit of Greenland, collections of 18th-century Danish furniture, a special children's wing and a 'Please Touch' exhibition for sight-impaired visitors.

The museum also hosts a fine collection of Greek, Roman and medieval coins, and a Classical Antiquities section complete with Egyptian mummies. There's a café as well as a gift shop on the premises.

DANSK DESIGN CENTER

You may as well face up to it, the **Dansk Design Center** (Map pp62-3; ☎ 33 69 33 69; www.ddc.dk; HC Andersens Blvd 27; adult/child 40/20kr; 🕙 10am-5pm Mon, Tue, Thu & Fri, 10am-9pm Wed, 11am-4pm Sat & Sun) is only going to highlight how unbearably cluttered, poorly designed and daggy your own living space is. The centre showcases Danish industrial design alongside international design trends.

The five-storey building was designed by senior Danish architect Henning Larsen and incorporates a double-glass wall of windows. The ground floor holds an exhibit of classic Danish chairs (chairs are one of the Danes great obsessions), while upstairs are changing exhibits on a variety of design-related topics. There's a handy café on site and a natty little gift shop.

Strøget & the Latin Quarter

Billed as 'the world's longest pedestrian mall', **Strøget** (Map pp70-1) runs through the city centre between Rådhuspladsen and Kongens Nytorv, the square at the head of the Nyhavn canal.

Copenhagen's most popular shopping strip, Strøget consists of five continuous streets and hums with activity.

Strøget is a lively place to stroll, its broad squares bustling with buskers, tourists, students, protesters and urbanites, who play off each other's energies. It's a particularly vibrant scene on sunny days, when people seem to pour out of the woodwork and the air is buzzing.

With its cafés and second-hand book and clothes shops, the **Latin Quarter** (north of Strøget, around the old campus of Københavns Universitet or Copenhagen University) is a good place for some leisurely ambling. The university, which was founded in 1479, has largely outgrown its original quarters and moved to a new campus on Amager, but parts of the old campus, including the law department, remain here.

In the north of the Latin Quarter is **Kultorvet**, a lively pedestrian plaza and summer gathering place with beer gardens, flower stalls and produce stands. On sunny days you'll usually find impromptu entertainment here, which can range from the ever-present sounds of the Andean flute to street theatre. Consider yourself warned…

UNIVERSITY LIBRARY

Climb the stairs of the **university library** (Map pp70-1; ☎ 33 47 47 47; Fiolstræde 1; admission free; 🕑 10am-7pm Mon-Fri) to see one quirky remnant of the 1807 British bombardment of Copenhagen: a glass case containing a cannonball in five fragments and the target it hit, ironically a book entitled *Defensor Pacis* (Defender of Peace).

VOR FRUE KIRKE

Opposite the university is **Vor Frue Kirke** (Map pp70-1; ☎ 33 37 65 40; www.koebenhavnsdomkirke.dk; Nørregade 8; admission free; 🕑 8am-5pm Mon-Sat, noon-5pm Sun), Copenhagen's cathedral, which was founded in 1191 and rebuilt three times after devastating fires. The current structure dates from 1829 and was designed in neoclassical style by CF Hansen. With its high-vaulted ceilings and columns, Vor Frue Kirke seems as much museum as church – quite apropos because it's also the showcase for sculptor Bertel Thorvaldsen's statues of Christ and the 12 apostles, his most acclaimed works, which were completed in 1839. Thorvaldsen's depiction of Christ, with comforting open arms, became the most popular worldwide model for statues of Christ and remains so today. In May 2004, Vor Frue Kirke was the site of Denmark's biggest wedding – that of Crown Prince Frederik to Mary Donaldson. Access to the cathedral for people with disabilities can be arranged quite easily.

SANKT PETRI KIRKE

Another handsome place of worship in the Latin Quarter is **Sankt Petri Kirke** (Map pp70-1; ☎ 33 13 38 33; www.sankt-petri.dk; Sankt Pedersstræde 2; admission free; 🕑 10am-1pm Tue-Thu), a German church that dates from the 15th century – making it the oldest church building in the city.

RUNDETÅRN

The **Rundetårn** (Round Tower; Map pp70-1; ☎ 33 73 03 73; www.rundetaarn.dk; Købmagergade 52A; adult/child 120/5kr; 🕑 10am-5pm Mon-Sat, noon-5pm Sun) is a splendid vantage point (perhaps the city's best) from which to admire the old city's red-tiled rooftops and abundant church spires. This vaulted brick tower, 35m high, was built by Christian IV in 1642 and used as an astronomical observatory in conjunction with the nearby university. Although the university erected a newer structure in 1861, amateur astronomers have continued to use the Rundetårn each winter, which gives credence to its claim to be the oldest functioning observatory in Europe.

A 209m spiral walkway winds up the tower around a hollow core; about halfway up is a small exhibition hall housing changing displays of art and culture that is worth a visit if open.

STRØGET & LATIN QUARTER

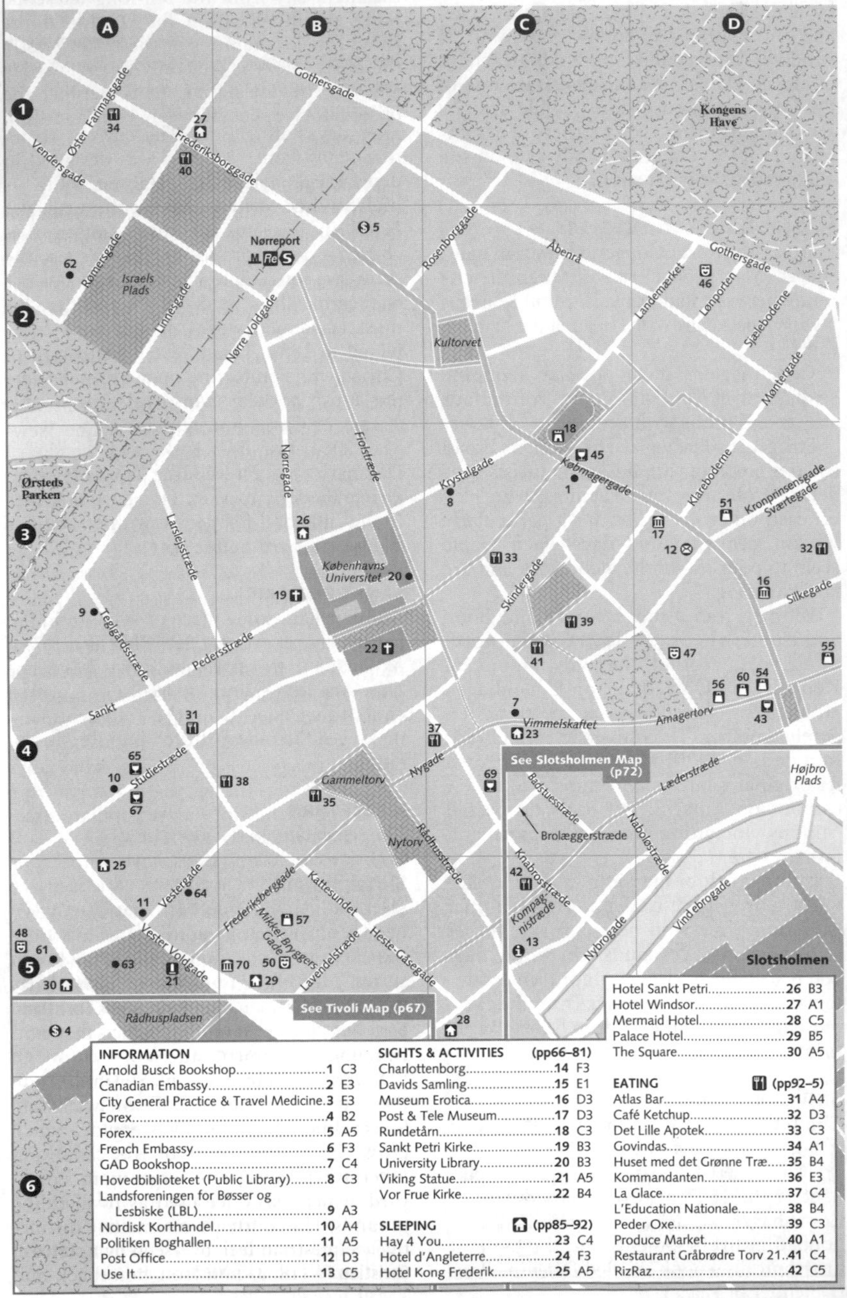
A
B
C
D
1
2
3
4
5
6
Gothersgade
Kongens Have
Øster Farimagsgade
Vendersgade
Frederiksborggade
Nørreport
Rosenborggade
Åbenrå
Romersgade
Israels Plads
Linnesgade
Nørre Voldgade
Kultorvet
Landemærket
Lønporten
Sjæleboderne
Møntergade
Ørsteds Parken
Nørregade
Fiolstræde
Krystalgade
Købmagergade
Klareboderne
Kronprinsensgade
Sværtegade
Larslejsstræde
Københavns Universitet
Skindergade
Silkegade
Teglgårdsstræde
Pedersstræde
Sankt
Studiestræde
Vimmelskaftet
Amagertorv
Højbro Plads
Nygade
Gammeltorv
Nytorv
Rådhusstræde
See Slotsholmen Map (p72)
Badstuestræde
Brolæggerstræde
Læderstræde
Nabolostræde
Knabrostræde
Kompagnistræde
Nybrogade
Vindebrogade
Slotsholmen
Vestergade
Frederiksberggade
Kattesundet
Mikkel Bryggers Gade
Lavendelstræde
Heste-Gåsegade
Vester Voldgade
Rådhuspladsen
See Tivoli Map (p67)

INFORMATION

Arnold Busck Bookshop....................1 C3
Canadian Embassy....................2 E3
City General Practice & Travel Medicine.3 E3
Forex....................4 B2
Forex....................5 A5
French Embassy....................6 F3
GAD Bookshop....................7 C4
Hovedbiblioteket (Public Library)..........8 C3
Landsforeningen for Bøsser og Lesbiske (LBL)....................9 A3
Nordisk Korthandel....................10 A4
Politiken Boghallen....................11 A5
Post Office....................12 D3
Use It....................13 C5

SIGHTS & ACTIVITIES (pp66–81)

Charlottenborg....................14 F3
Davids Samling....................15 E1
Museum Erotica....................16 D3
Post & Tele Museum....................17 D3
Rundetårn....................18 C3
Sankt Petri Kirke....................19 B3
University Library....................20 B3
Viking Statue....................21 A5
Vor Frue Kirke....................22 B4

SLEEPING (pp85–92)

Hay 4 You....................23 C4
Hotel d'Angleterre....................24 F3
Hotel Kong Frederik....................25 A5
Hotel Sankt Petri....................26 B3
Hotel Windsor....................27 A1
Mermaid Hotel....................28 C5
Palace Hotel....................29 B5
The Square....................30 A5

EATING (pp92–5)

Atlas Bar....................31 A4
Café Ketchup....................32 D3
Det Lille Apotek....................33 C3
Govindas....................34 A1
Huset med det Grønne Træ.....35 B4
Kommandanten....................36 E3
La Glace....................37 C4
L'Education Nationale....................38 B4
Peder Oxe....................39 C3
Produce Market....................40 A1
Restaurant Gråbrødre Torv 21..41 C4
RizRaz....................42 C5

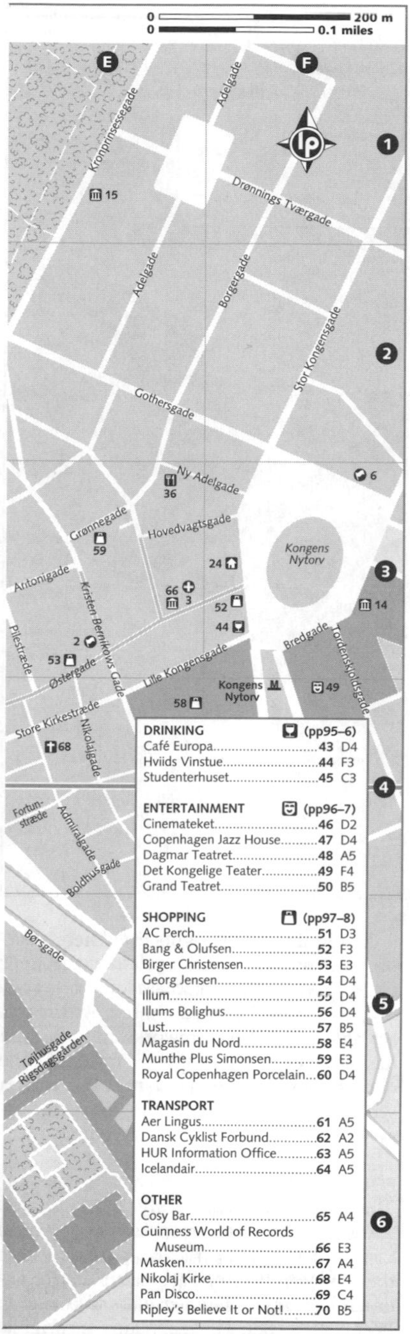
0 200 m
0 0.1 miles
E
F
1
2
3
4
5
6
Kronprinsessegade
Adelgade
Drønnings Tværgade
Borgergade
Stor Kongensgade
Gothersgade
Ny Adelgade
Hovedvagtsgade
Grønnegade
Antonigade
Kristen Bernikows Gade
Pilestræde
Østergade
Lille Kongensgade
Bredgade
Tordenskjoldsgade
Kongens Nytorv
Store Kirkestræde
Nikolajgade
Fortunstræde
Admiralgade
Boldhusgade
Børsgade
Tøjhusgade
Rigsdagsgården
15
36
6
59
24
66
3
52
14
44
2
53
58
49
68
DRINKING (pp95–6)
Café Europa 43 D4
Hviids Vinstue 44 F3
Studenterhuset 45 C3
ENTERTAINMENT (pp96–7)
Cinemateket 46 D2
Copenhagen Jazz House 47 D4
Dagmar Teatret 48 A5
Det Kongelige Teater 49 F4
Grand Teatret 50 B5
SHOPPING (pp97–8)
AC Perch 51 D3
Bang & Olufsen 52 F3
Birger Christensen 53 E3
Georg Jensen 54 D4
Illum 55 D4
Illums Bolighus 56 D4
Lust 57 B5
Magasin du Nord 58 E4
Munthe Plus Simonsen 59 E3
Royal Copenhagen Porcelain 60 D4
TRANSPORT
Aer Lingus 61 A5
Dansk Cyklist Forbund 62 A2
HUR Information Office 63 A5
Icelandair 64 A5
OTHER
Cosy Bar 65 A4
Guinness World of Records Museum 66 E3
Masken 67 A4
Nikolaj Kirke 68 E4
Pan Disco 69 C4
Ripley's Believe It or Not! 70 B5

Winter visitors who would like to view the night sky from the 3m-long telescope that's mounted within the rooftop dome should make inquiries at the ticket booth; the observatory is generally open Tuesday and Wednesday nights. In September the observatory opens between 1pm and 4pm on Sunday.

POST & TELE MUSEUM

Get out your cardigan for the **Post & Tele Museum** (Map pp70-1; ☎ 33 41 09 00; www.ptt-museum.dk; Købmagergade 37; adult/child 30kr/free, free Wed; 10am-5pm Tue & Thu-Sun, 10am-8pm Wed, noon-4pm Sun), 300m north of Strøget, which depicts the history of the Danish postal and telecommunications system with displays of historic postal vehicles, uniforms, letter boxes and the like. Not surprisingly, it also boasts a fine stamp collection. Fine views can be had from its rooftop café.

MUSEUM EROTICA

A cross between a museum and a peep-show, **Museum Erotica** (Map pp70-1; ☎ 33 12 03 11; www.museumerotica.dk; Købmagergade 24; admission 1/2 adults 99/178kr; 10am-11pm May-Sep, 11am-8pm Oct-Apr), is full of supposedly erotic paintings, posters, photographs, statues and sex toys. These items range from hand-coloured daguerreotype photographs from the 1850s to a multiscreen video room playing modern porn movies that are not for the easily shocked. In our opinion, this place is overpriced, exploitative and a little sad – but that doesn't stop it from being one of the city's most popular attractions. It's two blocks north of Strøget.

Slotsholmen

Slotsholmen is the seat of national government and a veritable repository of historical sites. Located on a small island and separated from the city centre by a moat-like canal, Slotsholmen's centrepiece is **Christiansborg Slot**, a large rambling palace that now contains government offices.

Several short bridges link Slotsholmen to the rest of Copenhagen. If you walk into Slotsholmen from Ny Vestergade, you'll cross the western part of the canal and enter Christiansborg's large main courtyard, which was once used as royal riding grounds. The courtyard maintains a distinctively equestrian feel, overseen by a **statue of Christian IX** (1863–1906) on horseback and

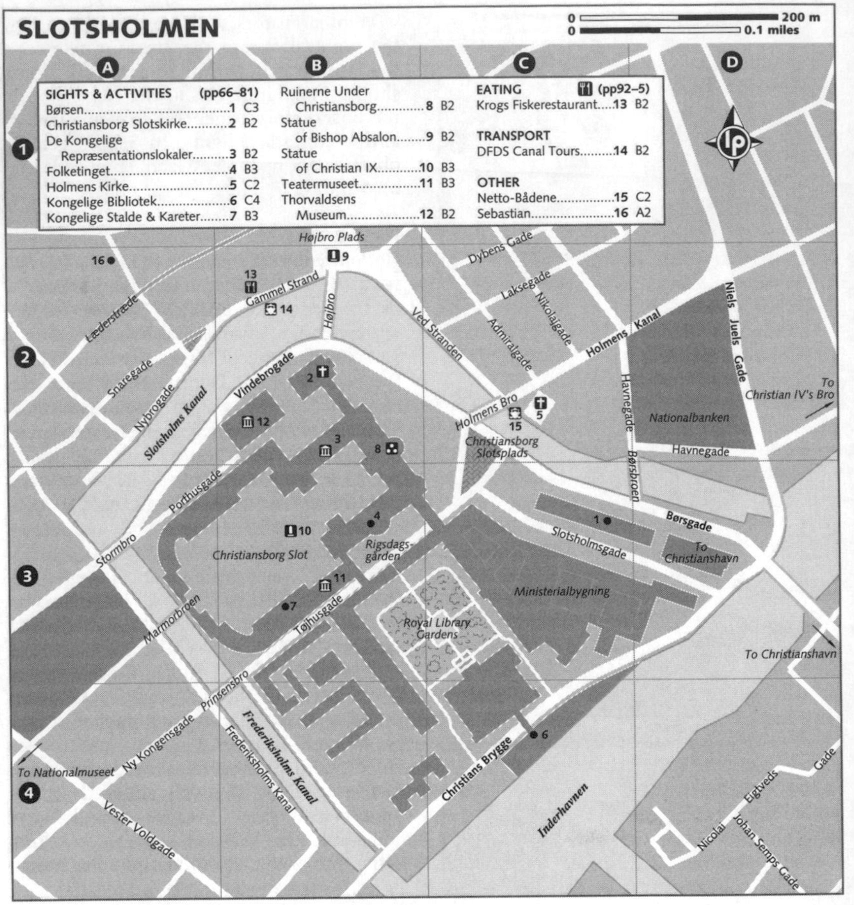
SLOTSHOLMEN
0 200 m
0 0.1 miles
A
B
C
D
1
2
3
4
SIGHTS & ACTIVITIES (pp66–81)
Børsen.....1 C3
Christiansborg Slotskirke.....2 B2
De Kongelige Repræsentationslokaler.....3 B2
Folketinget.....4 B3
Holmens Kirke.....5 C2
Kongelige Bibliotek.....6 C4
Kongelige Stalde & Kareter.....7 B3
Ruinerne Under Christiansborg.....8 B2
Statue of Bishop Absalon.....9 B2
Statue of Christian IX.....10 B3
Teatermuseet.....11 B3
Thorvaldsens Museum.....12 B2
EATING (pp92–5)
Krogs Fiskerestaurant.....13 B2
TRANSPORT
DFDS Canal Tours.....14 B2
OTHER
Netto-Bådene.....15 C2
Sebastian.....16 A2
Højbro Plads
Dybens Gade
Laksegade
Nikolajgade
Admiralgade
Ved Stranden
Gammel Strand
Højbro
Læderstræde
Snaregade
Nybrogade
Slotsholms Kanal
Vindebrogade
Holmens Kanal
Niels Juels Gade
To Christian IV's Bro
Havnegade
Nationalbanken
Holmens Bro
Christiansborg Slotsplads
Børsbroen
Porthusgade
Stormbro
Christiansborg Slot
Rigsdagsgården
Børsgade
Slotsholmsgade
To Christianshavn
Ministerialbygning
Marmorbroen
Tøjhusgade
Royal Library Gardens
To Christianshavn
Prinsensbro
Ny Kongensgade
Frederiksholms Kanal
To Nationalmuseet
Vester Voldgade
Christians Brygge
Inderhavnen
Eigtveds Gade
Nicolai
Johan Semps Gade

flanked to the north by stables and to the south by carriage buildings.

The stables and buildings surrounding the main courtyard date back to the 1730s when the original Christiansborg palace, was built by Christian VI to replace the more modest Copenhagen Castle that previously stood there. The grander west wing of Christian VI's palace went up in flames in 1794, was rebuilt in the early 19th century and was once again destroyed by fire in 1884. In 1907 the cornerstone for the third (and current) Christiansborg palace was laid by Frederik VIII and, upon completion, the national parliament and the Supreme Court moved into new chambers there.

In addition to the sights listed here, visitors can enter **Christiansborg Slotskirke** (Map p72; admission free; noon-4pm Sun Aug-Jun, noon-4pm daily July), the castle's domed church, which was set ablaze by stray fireworks in 1996 and has since been painstakingly restored. The church reopened in January 1997 with a service to commemorate the 25th anniversary of Queen Margrethe II's reign.

FOLKETINGET

The **Folketinget** (Map p72; ☎ 33 37 55 00; www.folketinget.dk; Rigsdagsgården; admission free; guided tours 2pm daily Jul & Aug, 2pm Sun Sep-Jun), is where the 179 Members of Parlimaent debate national legislation. Guided tours also take in Wanderer's Hall, which contains the original copy of the Constitution of the Kingdom of Denmark, enacted in 1849.

DE KONGELIGE REPRÆSENTATIONSLOKALER

The grandest part of Christiansborg are the **De Kongelige Repræsentationslokaler** (Royal Reception Chambers; Map p72; ☎ 33 92 64 92; www.ses.dk; adult/child 50/20kr; 🕒 English guided tours 11am, 1pm & 3pm Tue-Sun May-Sep; 3pm Tue, Thu, Sat & Sun Oct-Apr), an ornate Renaissance hall where the queen holds royal banquets and entertains heads of state.

Of particular note are the very colourful (almost cartoonish) wall tapestries depicting the history of Denmark from Viking times to the present day. Created by tapestry designer Bjørn Nørgaard, the tapestries took a full 10 years (until 2000) to complete. Tapestries to pay particular attention to include the representation of the queen and her husband Adam-and-Eve-style (albeit clothed) in a Danish Garden of Eden. The queen's admirable qualities of creativity, intelligence and compassion are embodied by the symbolic enlargement of her hands, forehead and arms respectively.

KONGELIGE STALDE & KARETER

At the **Kongelige Stalde & Kareter** (Royal Stables & Coaches; Map p72; ☎ 33 40 10 10; www.kongehuset.dk; adult/child 20/10kr; 🕒 2-4pm Fri-Sun May-Sep, 2-4pm Sat & Sun Oct-Apr) visitors can view a collection of antique coaches, uniforms and riding paraphernalia, some of which are still used for royal receptions. You can also see the royal family's carriage and saddle horses. And who knows? You may spy Crown Princess Mary, a keen and accomplished horsewoman.

RUINERNE UNDER CHRISTIANSBORG

A walk through the crypt-like bowels of Slotsholmen, known as **Ruinerne under Christiansborg** (Ruins under Christiansborg; Map p72; ☎ 33 92 64 92; www.ses.dk; adult/child 25/10kr; 🕒 10am-4pm Tue-Sun Oct-Apr, 10am-4pm May-Sep), offers a unique perspective on Copenhagen's lengthy history. In the basement of the current palace, beneath the tower, are the remains of two earlier castles. The most notable are the ruins of Absalon's fortress, Slotsholmen's original castle, built by Bishop Absalon in 1167. The excavated foundations, which consist largely of low limestone sections of wall, date back to the founding of the city.

Absalon's fortress was demolished by Hanseatic invaders in 1369. Its foundations, as well as those of Copenhagen Castle that replaced it and stood for more than three centuries, were excavated when the current tower was built in the early 20th century.

TEATERMUSEET

The **Teatermuseet** (Theatre Museum; Map p72; ☎ 33 11 51 76; www.teatermuseet.dk; Christiansborg Ridebane 18; adult/child 30kr/free; 🕒 11am-3pm Tue-Thu, 1-4pm Sat & Sun) occupies the Hofteater (Old Court Theatre), which dates from 1767 and drips with historic character. Performances have ranged from Italian opera and pantomime to shows by local ballet troupes, one of which included fledgling ballet student Hans Christian Andersen. The theatre, which took on its current appearance in 1842, drew its final curtain in 1881 but was reopened as a museum in 1922. The stage, boxes and dressing rooms can be viewed, along with displays of set models, drawings, costumes and period posters tracing the history of Danish theatre. Royal-watchers will enjoy peeking into the royal boxes – Christian VIII's entertainment area is even equipped with its own commode!

THORVALDSENS MUSEUM

Greek and Roman mythology prevail at **Thorvaldsens Museum** (Map p72; ☎ 33 32 15 32; www.thorvaldsensmuseum.dk; Bertel Thorvaldsens Plads 2; adult/child 30kr/free, free Wed; 🕒 10am-5pm Tue-Sun) which exhibits the works of famed Danish sculptor Bertel Thorvaldsen (1770–1844). Heavily influenced by mythology, after four decades in Rome, Thorvaldsen returned to Copenhagen and donated his private collection to the Danish public. In return the royal family provided this site for the construction of a museum to house Thorvaldsen's drawings, plaster moulds and beautiful statues. The museum also contains antique art from the Mediterranean region that Thorvaldsen collected during his lifetime. You'll find the entrance to the museum on Vindebrogade.

KONGELIGE BIBLIOTEK

The largest library in Scandinavia, **Kongelige Bibliotek** (Royal Library; Map p72; ☎ 33 47 47 47; www.kb.dk; Søren Kierkegaards Plads; admission free, exhibition adult/child 31/10kr; 🕒 10am-7pm Mon-Sat) is a fascinating blend of the original classical style

AN AUTHOR APPLIES HIMSELF...

In 1834, Hans Christian Andersen applied for work at the Royal Library in Copenhagen 'to be freed from the heavy burden of having to write in order to live'. Apparently the library administrators weren't too impressed with his résumé, as he was turned down. Ironically, Andersen's unsuccessful application is now preserved as part of the library's valued archives, along with many of his original manuscripts. They can be viewed with advance notice.

building near parliament and a new ultramodern extension on the waterfront.

The seven-story extension, dubbed the 'Black Diamond', sports a shiny black granite facade, smoked black windows and a leaning parallelogram design. This sleek canal-side addition gives the once solidly historic waterfront a curious futuristic juxtaposition. An enclosed overhead walkway straddles the motorway, connects the Black Diamond with the library's historic wing.

The Royal Library not only serves as a research centre for scholars, but doubles as a repository for manuscripts and rare books. As Denmark's national library it contains a complete collection of all Danish printed works produced since 1482 and houses some 21 million items in all.

Not an ordinary library, it is well worth a visit. You'll find a spacious lobby with canal views, a 210-sq-metre ceiling mural by the celebrated Danish artist Per Kirkeby and various exhibition areas. The lobby contains a bookshop, café and restaurant.

BØRSEN

Another striking Renaissance building is **Børsen** (Map p72; Børsgade; ⌚ closed to public), the stock exchange, at the eastern corner of Slotsholmen. Constructed under Christian IV's in the 1620s, it's of note for its ornate spire, formed from the entwined tails of four dragons, and for its richly embellished gables. This still-functioning chamber of commerce, which first opened during the bustling reign of Christian IV, is the oldest in Europe. One of its doors is adorned with the following words from Christian himself: 'The House that you see here has not been built for Mercury's secret arts, but first and foremost for the glory of God and secondly for the profitable use of Buyer and Seller.'

HOLMENS KIRKE

Just across the canal to the northeast of Slotsholmen is **Holmens Kirke** (Church of the Royal Danish Navy; Map p72; ☎ 33 13 61 78; www.holmenskirke.dk, in Danish; Holmens Kanal 9; admission free; ⌚ 9am-2pm Mon-Fri). This historic brick structure, with a nave that was originally built in 1562 to be used as an anchor forge, was converted into a church for the Royal Navy in 1619. Most of the present structure, which is predominantly in Dutch Renaissance style, dates from 1641. The church's burial chapel contains the remains of some important naval figures, including Admiral Niels Juel, who beat back the Swedes in the crucial 1677 Battle of Køge Bay.

It was at Holmens Kirke that Queen Margrethe II took her marriage vows in 1967 (a gesture of respect for her thalassocrat father). The interior of the church has an intricately carved 17th-century oak altarpiece and pulpit.

Nyhavn to the Little Mermaid

Long a haunt for sailors and writers (including Hans Christian Andersen, who lived in the house at No 67 for nearly 20 years), Nyhavn is a half-salty and half-gentrified tourist magnet of bright colours, herring buffets and foaming beers. The canal is lined with restored gabled townhouses and trendy pavement cafés that pack in a crowd whenever the weather is warm and sunny. The Amalienborg area has upmarket residences, including that of the royal family, a grand marble church and other historic sites. The northern Kastellet area includes a 17th-century citadel and the city's best-known statue, the Little Mermaid, making this is a popular spot on the tour-bus circuit.

CHARLOTTENBORG

Fronting Kongens Nytorv and competing for your attention with this central square's other grand buildings is **Charlottenborg** (Map pp70-1; ☎ 33 13 40 22; www.charlottenborg-art.dk, in Danish; Nyhavn 2; adult/child 30kr/free; ⌚ 10am-7pm Wed, 10am-5pm Thu-Tue), built in 1683 as a palace for the royal family. Since 1754 Charlottenborg has housed Det Kongelige Kunstakademi. The academy's exhibition hall, on the eastern side of the central courtyard, features changing exhibitions of modern art by Danish and international artists.

AMALIENBORG SLOT

Visitors can enter one wing of the **Amalienborg Slot** (Map pp62-3; ☎ 33 12 21 86; www.rosenborg-slot.dk; Amalienborg Plads; adult/child 45/10kr; 🕑 11am-4pm Tue-Sun 2 Jan-30 Apr & 1 Nov-30 Dec, 10am-4pm daily 1 May-31 Oct), which features exhibits of the royal apartments used by three generations of the monarchy from 1863 to 1947.

The reconstructed rooms have heavy oak furnishings, gilt-leather tapestries, family photographs and old knick-knacks. They include the study and drawing room of Christian IX (1863–1906) and Queen Louise, whose six children wedded into nearly as many royal families – one ascending the throne in Greece and another marrying Russian tsar Alexander III. Also on show is the study of Frederik VIII (1906–12), who decorated it in a lavish neo-Renaissance style, and the study of Christian X (1912–47), the grandfather of the present queen Margrethe II. Don't miss this – it may well be the only chance you get to nose around royal quarters.

MARMORKIRKEN

The **Marmorkirken** (Marble Church; Map pp62-3; ☎ 33 15 01 44; www.marmorkirken.dk; Frederiksgade 4; admission to church free, to dome adult/child 20/10kr; 🕑 noon-5pm Fri-Sun, 10am-5pm Mon-Thu, to dome 1pm & 3pm Sat & Sun), also called Frederikskirken, is a stately neo-Baroque church on Frederiksgade, a block west of Amalienborg Slot. The church's massive dome, which was inspired by St Peter's in Rome and measures more than 30m in diameter, is one of Copenhagen's most dominant skyline features.

The plans for the church were ordered by Frederik V and drawn up by Nicolai Eigtved as part of a grand design that included the Amalienborg mansions. Although church construction began in 1749, it encountered problems as costs overran, due in part to the prohibitively high price of Norwegian marble, and the project was soon shelved.

It wasn't until Denmark's wealthiest 19th-century financier, CF Tietgen, bankrolled the project's revival that it was finally taken to completion. It was consecrated as a church in 1894.

The church's exterior is ringed by statues of Danish theologians and saints. In addition to viewing the interior, with its huge circular nave, you can tour the dome and catch a broad view of the city from its rim.

ALONG BREDGADE

There is a cluster of sights along the posh street known as Bredgade. Heading north, first is **Alexander Newsky Kirke** (Map pp62-3; ☎ 33 13 60 46; Bredgade 53; admission free; 🕑 only for services), which was built in Russian Byzantine style in 1883 by Tsar Alexander III.

Next sight to the north is the **Medicinsk-Historisk Museum** (Map pp62-3; ☎ 35 32 38 00; www.mhm.ku.dk; Bredgade 62; adult/concession 30/20kr; 🕑 guided tours 11am & 1pm Wed-Fri, 1pm Sun Nov-Jan; 7pm Wed & Thu Feb-Apr & Aug-Oct; 11am Wed & Thu, 2pm Sun 16 Jun-17 Aug), housed in a former surgical academy dating from c 1786 and deals with the history of medicine, pharmacy and dentistry over the past three centuries. Guided tours are conducted in English.

Sankt Ansgars Kirke (Map pp62-3; ☎ 33 13 37 62; Bredgade 64; admission free; 🕑 10am-4pm Tue-Fri) is Copenhagen's Roman Catholic cathedral. It was built in 1841 in the neo-Romanesque style and has a colourfully painted apse. There's also a small museum on the history of Danish Catholicism.

Kunstindustrimuseet (Museum of Decorative Art; Map pp62-3; ☎ 33 18 56 56; Bredgade 68; adult/child 40kr/free; 🕑 10am-4pm Tue-Fri, noon-4pm Sat & Sun) is based in the former Frederiks Hospital (c 1752). This large, rambling place feels like an oversized antiques shop, with an eclectic collection of nearly 300,000 items from Asia and Europe, dating from the Middle Ages.

The displays include a fairly extensive collection of Danish silver and porcelain and lots of coverage of innovations in contemporary Danish design, making its location on Bredsgade (one of the shopping strips for Danish design collectibles) particularly apt. One exhibit, for example, shows Denmark's contribution to chair design, displaying chairs by influential 20th-century designers Kaare Klint, Hans Wegner and Arne Jacobsen. There's a café on site and is reasonably accessible to people in wheelchairs.

FRIHEDSMUSEET

The **Frihedsmuseet** (Museum of Danish Resistance; Map pp62-3; ☎ 33 13 77 14; www.natmus.dk; Churchillparken; adult/child 25kr/free, free Wed; 🕑 10am-4pm Tue-Sat, 10am-5pm Sun 1 May-15 Sep; 11am-3pm Tue-Sat, 11am-4pm Sun 16 Sep-30 Apr) features exhibits on the Danish resistance movement from the time of the German occupation in 1940 to liberation in 1945. There are displays on the Danish underground press, the clandestine radio operations that maintained links with England and the smuggling operations that saved 7200 Danish Jews from capture by the occupying Nazis.

THE LITTLE MERMAID

Further north, you'll find Copenhagen's most famous landmark, the **Little Mermaid** (Den Lille Havfrue; Map pp62-3). In 1909 the Danish beer baron Carl Jacobsen was so moved after attending a ballet performance of *The Little Mermaid* that he commissioned sculptor Edvard Eriksen to create a statue of the fairytale character to grace Copenhagen's harbour front.

The face of the famous statue was modelled after the ballerina Ellen Price, while Eline Eriksen, the sculptor's wife, modelled for the body.

The Little Mermaid survived the Great Depression and the WWII occupation unscathed, but modern times haven't been so kind to Denmark's leading lady. She's frequently defaced and vandalised. Pundits have made the supposition that frustration with the sheer 'so effing what?' reaction that the statue inspires (it's top of our list for overrated tourist sights) could be the reason for such savagery.

Christianshavn

The island of **Christianshavn** is on the eastern flank of Copenhagen. It was established by Christian IV in the early 17th century as a commercial centre and also a military buffer for the expanding city. It's cut with a network of canals, modelled after those in Holland, which often leads Christianshavn to be dubbed 'Little Amsterdam', and it's not hard to see why.

Still surrounded by its old ramparts, Christianshavn today is an appealing mix of standard-issue public housing complexes, cooler-than-thou period warehouses that have found second lives as upmarket housing and restored government offices. The neighbourhood attracts an interesting mix of boho-chic artists, biz-kid yuppies, anarchist dropouts and a sizable Greenlandic community. It was the setting for many parts of the deservedly popular novel and movie *Miss Smilla's Feeling for Snow*. To get to Christianshavn, you can walk over the copper-toned, funky-looking Knippelsbro from the northeastern part of Slotsholmen or catch bus No 2A, 19, 48 or 350S, or take the metro to the stop of the same name.

CHRISTIANIA

In 1971 an abandoned 41-hectare military camp on the eastern side of Christianshavn was taken over by squatters who proclaimed it the 'free state' of **Christiania** (Map pp62-3; ☎ 32 95 65 07; www.christiania.org; Prinsessegade), subject to their own laws. The police tried to clear the area but it was the height of the hippie revolution and an increasing number of alternative folk from throughout Denmark continued to pour in, attracted by the concept of communal living and the prospect of reclaiming military land for peaceful purposes.

Bowing to public pressure, the government allowed the community to continue as a social experiment. About 1000 people settled into Christiania, turning the old barracks into schools and housing, and starting their own collective businesses, workshops and recycling programs.

As well as hosting progressive happenings, Christiania also became a magnet for runaways and junkies. Christiania residents, self-governing, ecology-oriented and generally tolerant, did, in time, find it necessary to modify their free-law/anything goes approach. A new policy was established that outlawed hard drugs in Christiania, and the heroin and cocaine pushers were expelled, although for many years a blind eye was turned to the sale of marijuana and hash on 'Pusher St'.

Some Danes resent the community's rent-free, tax-free situation and more than a few Christianshavn neighbours would like to see sections of Christiania turned into public parks and school grounds. The sheer size and incredible location of the land means that chances are Christiania won't last much longer – the government has put the wheels in motion to take back what it's been 'lending' to the Christiania locals for the last 30-odd years.

At the time of writing the police, decked out in riot gear, were patrolling Christiania and staging numerous organised raids on the community, leading to some ugly confrontations and arrests.

Visitors are welcome to stroll or cycle in car-free Christiania. A crackdown on the sale of drugs has meant that a stroll through the area will be under the watchful eyes of police. Christiania has a small market, a couple of craft shops and a few places where you can get coffee and something to eat. The main entrance into Christiania is on Prinsessegade, 200m northeast of its intersection with Bådsmandsstræde. You can take a **guided tour** (☎ 32 57 96 70; 30kr per person; 3pm 20 Jun-31 Aug, 3pm Sat & Sun 1 May-31 Oct) of Christiania. Meet just inside the main entrance. There's a Pusher St **information office of sorts** (☎ 32 95 65 07; nytforum@christiania.org; noon-6pm Mon-Thu, noon-4pm Fri) – it's just next to the Oasen café.

VOR FRELSERS KIRKE

A few minutes southwest of Christiania is the 17th-century **Vor Frelsers Kirke** (Our Saviour's Church; Map pp62-3; ☎ 32 57 27 98; Sankt Annæ Gade 29; admission to church free, to tower adult/child 20/10kr; 11am-4.30pm Mon-Sat, noon-4.30pm Sun). The church, which once benefited from close ties with the Danish monarchy, has a grand interior that includes an elaborately carved pipe organ dating from 1698 and an ornate Baroque altar with marble cherubs and angels.

For a soul-stirring panoramic city view (many of the attractions listed in this chapter will be visible from these dizzy heights), make the head-spinning 400-step ascent up the church's 95m-high spiral tower – the last 150 steps run along the outside rim of the tower, narrowing to the point where they literally disappear at the top. If heights or confined spaces make you panic, then you should probably avoid this particular hike. The colourful spire was added to the church in 1752 by Lauritz de Thurah, who took his inspiration from Boromini's tower of St Ivo in Rome. It was climbed in 1752 by King Frederik V on inauguration day.

If you'd like to hear the organ, it's used in church services, including an English-language one that's held at noon on Sunday. Piped music is often played in the church anyway, making it a rather nice spot to collect your thoughts before resuming a tour of the area.

ORLOGSMUSEET

The Orlogsmuseet (**Royal Danish Naval Museum**; Map pp62-3; ☎ 32 54 63 63; www.orlogsmuseet.dk; Overgaden oven Vandet 58; adult/child 40/25kr; noon-4pm Tue-Sun) occupies a former naval hospital on Christianshavn Kanal. This museum has more than 300 model ships, many dating from the 16th to the 19th century – meaning that if you are, or someone you know is, the type to get high from tooling around with hobby glue, then you have stumbled upon the mother lode. Some were built by naval engineers to serve as design prototypes for the construction of new ships; consequently the models take many forms, from cross-sectional ones detailing frame proportions to full-dressed models with working sails.

The museum also displays figureheads, navigational instruments, ship lanterns and the propeller from the German U-boat that sank the *Lusitania*.

CHRISTIANS KIRKE

Designed by the Danish architect Nicolai Eigtved **Christians Kirke** (Map pp62-3; ☎ 32 54 15 76; Strandgade 1; admission free; 8am-6pm Sun-Thu, 8am-5pm Fri & Sat) was completed in 1759. It once served the local German congregation and has a large, theatre-like rococo interior.

LILLE MOLLE

The 17th-century **Lille Molle** (Map pp62-3; ☎ 33 47 38 38; www.natmus.dk; Christianshavn Voldgade 54; adult/child 50kr/free; guided tours 1pm, 2pm & 3pm Tue-Sun May-Sep) is a windmill that was turned over to the National Museum in the 1970s and has been preserved as its last owners left it – and they left it in a very interesting state. It's situated on the ramparts that are southeast of Christiana, and if you time your visit just right, it's perfect for a guided tour preceded or followed by an excellent meal at Bastionen & Løven, the attached restaurant/café (p94).

OPERA HOUSE

The finishing touches were being added to the stupendous new **Opera House** (www.kgl-teater.dk) when we visited. Construction commenced in November 2001, lasting until January 2005, and the state-of-the-art structure features no fewer than six stages (with 1400 seats in the main auditorium) and a 'floating' roof with a 32m-long cantilever. The Opera House, which takes up its own specially constructed 'island' north of Christianshavn can be seen from many waterside vantage points in the city.

Nørreport to Nørrebro

This area takes in some of the city's most interesting royal sites and an increasingly gentrified working-class neighbourhood – a nicely democratic mix in this most egalitarian of cities.

ROSENBORG SLOT

The beautiful early-17th-century **Rosenborg Slot** (Map pp62-3; ☎ 33 15 32 86; www.rosenborg-slot.dk; Øster Voldgade 4A; adult/child 60/10kr; 🕒 11am-2pm Tue-Sun 2 Jan-30 Apr, 10am-4pm daily May & Sep, 10am-5pm daily Jun-Aug, 11am-3pm daily Oct, 11am-2pm Tue-Sun Nov & Dec) with its fairytale moat-and-garden setting, was built between 1606 and 1633 by King Christian IV in Dutch Renaissance style to serve as his summer home. A century later King Frederik IV, who felt cramped at Rosenborg, built a roomier palace north of the city in the town of Fredensborg. In the years that followed, Rosenborg was used mainly for official functions and as a place in which to safeguard the monarchy's heirlooms.

In the 1830s the royal family decided to open the castle to visitors as a museum, while still using it as a treasury for royal regalia and jewels. It continues to serve both functions today.

The 24 rooms in the castle's upper levels are chronologically arranged, housing the furnishings and portraits of each monarch from Christian IV to Frederik VII; however, it's the lower level, where the treasury remains, that's the main attraction, with its dazzling collection of crown jewels. There's Christian IV's ornately designed crown, the jewel-studded sword of Christian III and Queen Margrethe II's emeralds and pearls; the latter are displayed here when the queen is not wearing them to official functions. You'll want to wear your sunglasses for some displays – the glittering, winking diamonds and precious stones are quite dazzling.

Kongens Have (King's Gardens; Map pp70-1), the expansive green space behind Rosenborg Slot, is the city's oldest public park. It has manicured box hedges, lovely rose beds and plenty of shaded areas. Kongens Have is a very popular picnic spot on sunny days and the site of a free marionette theatre that performs on summer afternoons.

DAVIDS SAMLING

If you time your outing well, you can include a visit to **Davids Samling** (Map pp70-1; ☎ 33 73 49 49; www.davidmus.dk; Kronprinsessegade 30; admission free; 🕒 1-4pm Tue & Thu-Sun, 10am-4pm Wed), east of Kongens Have, a delightful little museum housing Scandinavia's largest collection of Islamic art.

BOTANISK HAVE

In the 10-hectare **Botanisk Have** (Botanical Garden; Map pp62-3; ☎ 35 32 22 40; www.botanic-garden.ku.dk; Gothersgade 128; admission free; 🕒 8.30am-6pm May-Sep, 8.30am-4pm Tue-Sun Oct-Apr) you can wander along fragrant paths amid arbours, terraces, rock gardens and ponds. Within the Botanisk Have is the **Palmehus** (Palm House; 🕒 10am-3pm Tue-Sun Oct-Apr), a large walk-through glasshouse containing a lush collection of tropical plants. There's also a **cactus house** (🕒 1-2pm Wed, Sat & Sun) and an **orchid greenhouse** (🕒 2-3pm Wed, Sat & Sun). One entrance to the Botanisk Have is at the intersection of Gothersgade and Øster Voldgade, while the other is off Øster Farimagsgade.

You can get to the gardens and Rosenborg Slot by taking the S-train or metro to Nørreport station and walking north for two blocks, or via numerous buses.

STATENS MUSEUM FOR KUNST

Denmark's national gallery, **Statens Museum for Kunst** (Royal Museum of Fine Arts; Map pp62-3; ☎ 33 74 84 94; www.smk.dk; Sølvgade 48; adult/child 50kr/free, free Wed; 🕒 10am-8pm Wed, 10am-5pm Tue & Thu-Sun), was founded in 1824 to house art collections belonging to the royal family. Originally sited at Christiansborg Slot, the museum opened in its current location in 1896. Statens Museum now lays claim to being the largest art museum in Denmark, thanks to an enormous, light-filled modern extension constructed in recent times.

Its collection covers seven centuries of European art, ranging from medieval works with stylised religious themes to free-form modern art. There's an interesting collection of old masters by Dutch and Flemish artists, including Rubens and Frans Hals, as well as more contemporary European paintings by Matisse, Picasso and Munch. The museum also has an extensive collection of drawings, engravings and lithographs representing the works of such prominent artists as Degas and Toulouse-Lautrec.

As might be expected, the museum has a wonderful collection of Danish fine art, including works by CW Eckersberg, Jens

Juel, Christen Købke, PS Krøyer and Per Kirkeby. There's plenty to keep children amused too, with special programs year-round. Accessibility to people in wheelchairs is generally very good.

DEN HIRSCHSPRUNGSKE SAMLING

Dedicated to Danish art of the 19th and early 20th centuries **Den Hirschprungske Samling** (Hirschsprung Collection; Map pp62-3; ☎ 35 42 03 36; www.hirschsprung.dk; Stockholmsgade 20; adult/child 35kr/free, free Wed; 11am-4pm Thu-Mon, 11am-9pm Wed) is an excellent little museum. Originally the private holdings of tobacco magnate Heinrich Hirschsprung, it contains works by 'Golden Age' painters such as Christen Købke and CW Eckersberg, a notable selection by Skagen painters PS Krøyer and Anna and Michael Ancher, and also works by the Danish symbolists and the Funen painters.

The Nørrebro quarter of the city in the mid-19th century was a working-class neighbourhood. In more recent times it's attracted a large immigrant community and has become a haunt for students, musicians and artists and a few yuppies looking to be classified as edgy.

ASSISTENS KIERKEGÅRD

The serene **Assistens Kierkegård** (Map pp62-3; ☎ 35 37 19 17; www.assistens.dk, in Danish; Kapelvej 4; admission free; 8am-5pm 1 Jan-28 Feb, 8am-6pm 1 Mar-30 Apr & 1 Sep-31 Oct, 8am-8pm 1 May-31 Aug, 8am-4pm 1 Nov-31 Dec) in the heart of Nørrebro is the final resting place of some of Denmark's most celebrated citizens, including philosopher Søren Kierkegaard, physicist Niels Bohr, author Hans Christian Andersen and artists Jens Juel, Christen Købke and CW Eckersberg. It's an interesting place to wander around – as much a park and garden as it is a graveyard.

The cemetery is divided into sectors, which helps in locating specific sites. A good place to start is at the main entrance on Kapelvej, which has an office where you can pick up a brochure mapping famous grave sites.

ZOOLOGISK MUSEUM

The modern **zoologisk museum** (Map p103; ☎ 35 32 10 01; www.zoologiskmuseum.dk, in Danish; Universitetsparken 15; adult/child 40/10kr; 11am-5pm Tue-Sun; bus No 18, 42, 43, 185, 150S or 173E), 1km north of Assistens Kierkegård, is the sort of place where once magnificent wild creatures, from North Zealand deer to Greenlandic polar bears, get well and truly stuffed. There are also interesting dioramas, recorded animal sounds, a whale skeleton and insect displays.

Vesterbro to Frederiksberg

The Vesterbro district has a varied character that's readily observed by walking along its best-known street, Istedgade, which runs west from Central Station. The first few blocks are lined with rows of hotels that mingle with the city's main red-light area. When Denmark became the first country to legalise pornography in the late 1960s, Vesterbro's porn shops and seedy nightclubs became a magnet for tourists and voyeurs.

About halfway down Istedgade the red-light district recedes and the neighbourhood becomes increasingly multiethnic, with a mix of Pakistani and Turkish businesses plus the new wave of funky boutiques and cafés filled with earnestly fashionable young artists, designers and students. You'll find good places to eat, drink and loiter around here.

KOBENHAVNS BYMUSEUM

True to its name the **Københavns Bymuseum** (Copenhagen City Museum; Map pp62-3; ☎ 33 21 07 72; www.bymuseum.dk; Vesterbrogade 59; adult/child 20kr/free, free Fri; 10am-4pm Wed-Mon May-Sep, 1-4pm Wed-Mon Oct-Apr) in the Vesterbro district has displays about the history and development of Copenhagen – mainly paintings and scale models of the old city. Of particular interest is the small room dedicated to philosopher Søren Kierkegaard, who was born in Copenhagen in 1813 and died in the city in 1855.

IMAX TYCHO BRAHE PLANETARIUM

Copenhagen's **Planetarium** (Map pp62-3; ☎ 33 12 12 24; www.tycho.dk; Gammel Kongevej 10; adult/child 85/65kr; 10.30am-8.30pm Fri-Tue, 9.45am-8.30pm Wed & Thu), 750m northwest of Central Station, has a domed space theatre that offers shows of the night sky using state-of-the-art equipment capable of projecting more than 7500 stars, planets and galaxies. The planetarium's 1000-sq-metre screen also shows Omnimax natural science films on subjects ranging from astronauts to Australia.

The planetarium was named after the famed Danish astronomer Tycho Brahe (1546–1601), whose creation of precision astronomical instruments allowed him to make exact observations of planets and stars, and paved the way for the discoveries made by later astronomers.

ZOOLOGISK HAVE

Copenhagen's **Zoologisk Have** (Zoo; Map p103; ☎ 70 20 02 80; www.zoo.dk; Roskildevej 32; adult/child 95/55kr; ⌚ 9am-6pm Jun-Aug, 9am-5pm Apr-May & Sep-Oct, 9am-4pm Nov-Mar; bus No 28 or 39), located in the Frederiksberg area, has a large (over 2500 critters) collection of nature's lovelies, including lions, elephants, zebras, hippos, gorillas and polar bears. Special sections include various thematic displays, making it both an enjoyable and educational experience, especially for children.

CARLSBERG VISITORS CENTER

Adjacent to the famed Carlsberg brewery, the **Carlsberg Visitors Center** (Map p103; ☎ 33 27 13 14; www.carlsberg.com; Gamle Carlsberg Vej 11; admission free; ⌚ 10am-4pm Tue-Sun), has an exhibition area on the history of Danish beer from 1370 BC (yes, they carbon-dated a bog girl who was found in a peat bog caressing a jug of well-aged brew). Dioramas give the low-down on the brewing process and en route to your final destination you'll pass antique copper vats and the stables with a dozen Jutland dray horses. The self-guided tour ends at a little pub where you get two free beers.

ACTIVITIES

Despite high levels of drinking and smoking, and a diet rich in fats, salts and other goodies, the Danes are big on physical activity. Cycling is the most obvious choice – it's both a mode of transport and a fitness regimen. You might be surprised to stumble upon good swimming options, both indoors and out.

Swimming

BEACHES

If brisk water doesn't deter you, the greater Copenhagen area has several bathing areas. The water is tested regularly and if sewage spills or other serious pollution occurs the beaches affected are closed and signposted.

Amager Strandpark Popular beach south of Copenhgen. Playground facilities and shallow water make it ideal for children, while deeper water can be reached by walking out along the jetties. Take the Metro to Lergravsparken.

Bellevue An attractive, popular beach at Klampenborg – this coast is known as the Danish Riviera. The northern end of the beach is popular with gays and lesbians. To get there take S-train C to Klampenborg.

Charlottenlund An accessible beach north of central Copenhagen. Take S-train C to Charlottenlund.

POOLS

Copenhagen has a handful of swimming pools that visitors can use; the following are the most central ones.

DGI-byen (Map pp62-3; ☎ 33 29 80 00; www.dgibyen.dk; Tietgensgade 65; adult/child 49kr/free; ⌚ 6.30am-9pm Mon-Thu, 6.30am-7pm Fri, 9am-5pm Sat & Sun) An extravagant swim centre with several pools, including a grand ellipse-shape affair with 100m lanes, a deep 'mountain pool' with a climbing wall, a hot water pool and a children's pool. If you've forgotten your togs or towels, they can be hired for 25kr each.

Islands Brygge Havnebadet (Map pp62-3; ☎ 23 71 31 89; Islands Brygge; admission free; ⌚ 7am-7pm 1 Jun-31 Aug) You'll not have a more authentically local swimming experience than at this natty outdoor pool, which is actually in one the city's famous canals. Red-and-white striped barriers, interesting architectural shapes and a great mix of locals makes for a refreshing and captivating dip. Green flags mean good quality water, so don't worry about pollution.

Vesterbro Svømmehal (Map p103; ☎ 33 22 05 00; Angelgade 4; adult/child 26/12kr; ⌚ 10am-7pm Mon, 7am-7pm Tue-Thu, 7am-2.30pm Fri, 9am-2pm Sat & Sun) This is a handy 25m-long indoor swimming pool (there's also a sports centre on the premises).

Boating

Christianshavns Bådudlejning og Café (Map pp62-3; ☎ 32 96 53 53; Overgaden neden Vandet 29; boats per hr 80kr; ⌚ 10am-sunset May–mid-Sep) If you want to explore Christianshavn's historic canals this place rents out rowing boats on the canal. An added bonus is the sweet little café on the premises.

Cycling

If you didn't bring a bike with you, you can readily hire one in Copenhagen. In addition to the rental rates, expect to pay a refundable deposit of around 500kr for a regular bike, 1000kr for a mountain bike or tandem.

Danwheel (Map pp62-3; ☎ 33 21 22 27; Colbjørnsensgade 3; bicycle hire per day/week 40/175kr; ⌚ 9am-5.30pm Mon-Fri, 9am-2pm Sat & Sun) A couple of blocks northwest of Central Station, Danwheel hires out bargain-basement older bikes.

Københavns Cykler (Map pp62-3; ☎ 33 33 86 13; www.rentabike.dk; Reventlowsgade 11; bicycle hire per day/week from 75/340kr; ⌚ 8am-6pm Mon-Fri, 9am-1pm Sat year round, 10am-1pm Sun May-Sep) One of the most convenient rental options is at the Reventlowsgade side of Central Station. The bicycles are in good working order and children's seat are available for hire.

Østerport Cykler (Map pp62-3; ☎ 33 33 85 13; www.oesterport-cykler.dk; Oslo Plads 9; bicycle hire per day/week from 75/340kr; ⏲ 8am-6pm Mon-Fri, 9am-1pm Sat), at Østerport S-train station near track 13, is a sister business to the above listing and has the same good standards.

WALKING TOUR

> **WALKING TOUR**
>
> **Distance** 3.4km
>
> **Duration** 3hr

From **Rådhuspladsen** the large central square fronting city hall, walk down the famous **Strøget (1)** which, after a couple of blocks, cuts between two spirited pedestrian squares, **Gammel Torv (2)** and **Nytorv (3)**. A popular summertime gathering spot in Gammel Torv is the gilded **Caritas Fountain (4)**, erected in 1608 by Christian IV and marking what was once the old city's central market. As in days past, pedlars sell jewellery, flowers and fruit on the square. At the southwestern corner of Nytorv is **Domhuset (5)**, an imposing neoclassical building that once served as the city hall and now houses the city's law courts.

Eventually you'll reach **Højbro Plads (6)**. At the southern end of this elongated square is a **statue of Bishop Absalon (7)**, the city's founder, on horseback; behind it, the fitting backdrop is **Slotsholmen (8)**, where the bishop erected Copenhagen's first fortress.

At the end of Strøget you'll reach **Kongens Nytorv (9)**, a square with an equestrian statue of its designer, Christian V, and circled by gracious old buildings. Notable structures are **Charlottenborg (10)**, a 17th-century Dutch Baroque palace that houses the Royal Academy of Fine Arts, and **Det Kongelige Teater (11**; the Royal Theatre), fronted by statues of the playwrights Adam Oehlenschläger and Ludvig Holberg. The theatre, which is the home of Den Kongelige Ballet (the Royal Danish Ballet) and Den Kongelige Opera (the Royal Danish Opera), has two stages, on either side of Tordenskjoldsgade. An **archway (12)** with a mosaic depicting Danish poets and artists spans the road connecting the two stages.

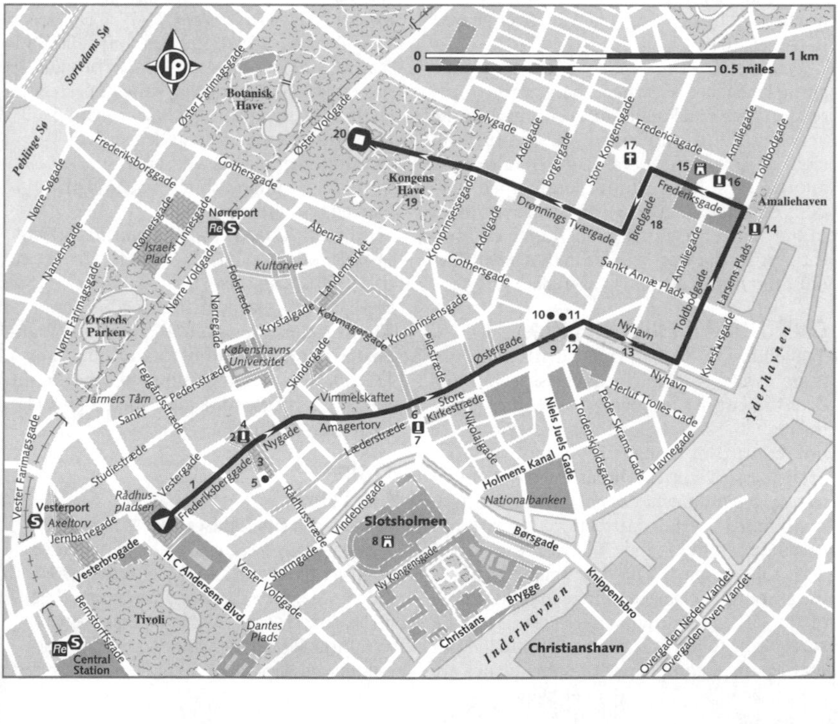
0
0
1 km
0.5 miles
Sortedams Sø
Peblinge Sø
Botanisk Have
Øster Farimagsgade
Øster Voldgade
Sølvgade
Adelgade
Borgergade
Store Kongensgade
Fredericiagade
Amaliegade
Toldbodgade
Frederiksborggade
Gothersgade
Kongens Have
Nørreport
Nørre Søgade
Rømersgade
Israels Plads
Linnésgade
Åbenrå
Kronprinsessegade
Dronnings Tværgade
Bredgade
Frederiksgade
Amaliehaven
Nansensgade
Kultorvet
Landemærket
Sankt Annæ Plads
Larsens Plads
Nørre Farimagsgade
Nørre Voldgade
Fiolstræde
Nørregade
Krystalgade
Købmagergade
Kronprinsensgade
Ørsteds Parken
Københavns Universitet
Pilestræde
Østergade
Nyhavn
Kvæsthusgade
Yderhavnen
Teglgårdsstræde
Pedersstræde
Skindergade
Jarmers Tårn
Sankt
Vimmelskaftet
Store Kirkestræde
Nikolajgade
Niels Juels Gade
Tordenskjoldsgade
Peder Skrams Gade
Herluf Trolles Gade
Havnegade
Vester Farimagsgade
Studiestræde
Vestergade
Nygade
Amagertorv
Læderstræde
Holmens Kanal
Nationalbanken
Rådhus-pladsen
Frederiksberggade
Rådhusstræde
Vesterport
Axeltorv
Jernbanegade
Vindebrogade
Slotsholmen
Vesterbrogade
H C Andersens Blvd
Vester Voldgade
Stormgade
Ny Kongensgade
Børsgade
Knippelsbro
Bernstorffsgade
Tivoli
Dantes Plads
Christians Brygge
Inderhavnen
Christianshavn
Overgaden Neden Vandet
Overgaden Oven Vandet
Central Station

To the east of Kongens Nytorv is the picturesque **Nyhavn (13)** canal, which was dug 300 years ago to allow traders to bring their wares into the heart of the city. Long a haunt for sailors and writers (including Hans Christian Andersen, who lived in the house at No 67 for nearly two decades), Nyhavn today is half salty and half gentrified, with a line of pavement cafés and restored gabled townhouses. It makes an invitingly atmospheric place to break for lunch or an afternoon beer.

From the northern side of Nyhavn, head north along Toldbodgade. When you reach the fountain that graces **Amaliehaven (14**; Amalie Gardens), turn inland to get to **Amalienborg Slot (15)**, home of the royal family since 1794. The palace's four nearly identical rococo mansions, designed by architect Nicolai Eigtved, surround a central cobblestone square and an immense **statue of Frederik V (16)**, 1746–66, on horseback sculpted by JFJ Saly. Looking west from the square you'll get a head-on view of the imposing **Marmorkirken (17**; Marble Church), which was designed in conjunction with the Amalienborg complex as part of an ambitious plan by Frederik to extend the city northward by creating a new district geared to the affluent.

From this point make a short detour along **Bredgade (18)**, where there are a couple of churches and small museums, plus some very good furniture stores, before turning right at Drønnings Tværgade. You're now approaching the beautiful landscaped gardens of **Kongens Have (19)**, an ideal spot to sit in the sunshine with a picnic lunch or for a catnap. To the west you'll find **Rosenborg Slot (20)**, the home of the royal treasury.

COPENHAGEN FOR CHILDREN

Travelling in Copenhagen with children is no sweat – many businesses accommodate the enormous prams that Danes wield through the streets, children's portions are not unheard-of in many restaurants and babysitting services can be arranged at many hotels. Neighbourhood play areas are well maintained, certain attractions are geared specifically for kids and children are regarded with fond respect. The only major hassle is the amount of cigarette smoke that fills many of the city's restaurants and cafés. Don't be surprised either by the sight of a pram left out on the street, complete with baby! Danes are relaxed about such things – and assume no-one will kidnap their child while they duck indoors for a coffee.

The extensive hands-on technology and natural **Experimentarium** (Map p103; ☎ 39 27 33 33; www.experimentarium.dk; Tuborg Havnevej 7, Hellerup; adult/child 105/70kr; 🕒 9.30am-5pm Mon, Wed-Fri, 9.30am-9pm Tue, 11am-5pm Sat & Sun) is housed in a former bottling hall of Tuborg Breweries in Hellerup, north of the city. Containing some 300 exhibits, it's a fun place for kids, featuring such time-honoured standards as the hall of mirrors, as well as computer-enhanced activities that make it possible to compose water music, stand on the moon or ride an inverted bicycle. To get here take the S-train to Hellerup from Central Station.

The touristy **Guinness World of Records Museum** (Map pp70-1; ☎ 33 32 31 31; www.guinness.dk; Østergade 16; adult/child 80/40kr; 🕒 10am-6pm Sun-Thu, 10am-2pm Fri & Sat 1 Jan-9 May & 13 Sep-31 Dec; 10am-8pm daily 10 May-31 May & 1 Sep-12 Sep; 9.30am-10.30pm daily 1 Jun-31 Aug) on Strøget uses displays, film and photos to depict the world's superlatives – the tallest, fastest, oddest and so on.

Whacky **Ripley's Believe It or Not! museum** (Map pp70-1; ☎ 33 91 89 91; Rådhuspladsen 57; adult/child 80/40kr; 🕒 10am-8pm 10 May-31 May, 9.30am-10pm 1 Jun-31 Aug, 10am-8pm 1 Sep-12 Sep, 10am-6pm Sun-Thu & 10am-8pm Fri & Sat 2 Jan-9 May, 10am-6pm Sun-Thu & 10am-8pm Fri & Sat 13 Sep-31 Dec) displays the expected collection of unexpected oddities from around the world (such as a six-legged calf) replicated in wax figures and tableaux. Revelling in its own outlandish clichés, this place gets packed with young folk.

At **Louis Tussaud's Wax Museum** (Map p67; ☎ 33 11 89 00; www.tussaud.dk; HC Andersens Blvd 22; adult/child 79/34kr; 🕒 10am-11pm daily mid-Apr–mid-Sep, until 6pm rest of year), on the northern edge of Tivoli, celebrities such as Elvis and Frankenstein can be found in the company of Danish notables, including the royal family, Søren Kierkegaard, Karen Blixen and Hans Christian Andersen.

TOURS

Bus Tours

Copenhagen City Sightseeing (☎ 32 66 00 00; www.citysightseeing.dk; departs from Rådhuspladsen; tickets adult/child from 120/60kr; 🕒 departures 9.45am-4.15pm) Many major cities have a hop-on/hop-off red double-decker bus tour operator, and Copenhagen is no different. Themed tour options include Christiania, Carlsberg and Mermaid, and manage to include the most popular sights in the city. If you buy a 140kr 'all line' ticket, you can take part in every tour on offer over two days, which is handy for those short on time. Multilingual tape recordings make sure everyone gets the picture.

Copenhagen Vintage Experience (☎ 38 10 20 48; www.vico.dk; departs from Rådhuspladsen; 1hr tour for max 15 people 2800kr, private tour for max 4 people per hr 680kr) A pricey way to explore the city even if you're part of a group, but lovers of vintage vehicles will get a kick out of cruising Copenhagen in style. Sights include the Little Mermaid, Nyhavn, Amalienborg Palace and Christiansborg Palace. English is spoken and departures occur at 9.30am, 11.30am and 1.30pm daily between May and September.

Canal Tours

For a somewhat relaxingly different angle on the city, hop on to one of the boat tours that wind through Copenhagen's canals. All the tours follow a similar loop route, passing by Slotsholmen, Christianshavn and the Little Mermaid.

DFDS Canal Tours (Map p72; ☎ 33 42 33 20; www.canaltours.com; 50min tours adult/child from 50/20kr; 🕑 10am-5pm late Mar–mid-Dec) DFDS, the biggest company of its kind, operates boats that leave around twice an hour from two locations – one at the head of Nyhavn and the other on Gammel Strand, north of Slotsholmen. Tours are enjoyable and informative.

DFDS Waterbus (Map pp62-3; ☎ 33 42 33 20; www.canaltours.com; s ticket adult/child 30/20kr; 🕑 10.15am-4.45pm 7 May-5 Sep, to 5.45pm 18 Jun-22 Aug) DFDS Canal Tours operates a summertime 'waterbus' that runs along a route similar to its guided tours but has no commentary. These boats leave Nyhavn every 30 minutes and make 10 stops, including Slotsholmen, Christianshavn and the Little Mermaid. A day pass, which costs adult/child 45/20kr allows you to get on and off as often as you like.

Netto-Bådene (Map pp62-3; ☎ 32 54 41 02; www.havnerundfart.dk; Holmens Kirke jetty; 1hr tour adult/child 25/10kr; 🕑 10am-5pm mid-Apr–mid-Oct) A better deal than many organised tours of this kind is this local operator, whose cruises, which last an hour, leave from Holmens Kirke, east of Slotsholmen (see the Slotsholmen map), as well as from Nyhavn, between two and five times per hour, with the greatest frequency in the summer high season, ie July and August.

Walking Tours

Copenhagen Walking Tours (☎ 40 81 12 17; www.copenhagen-walkingtours.dk; Vesterbrogade 4A; per person 100kr; 🕑 11am Sat & Sun) This tour follows in the footsteps of Hans Christian Andersen, allowing tourists to learn more about his life and times, and also gain a real feel for Copenhagen life, past and present. There's no need to book – simply show up at the tourist office and look for a red-suited guide.

The Old Night Watchman (☎ 39 61 48 94; www.viseknud.dk; Gråbrødretorv; per person 40kr; 🕑 9pm, Thu-Sat 29 May-30 Aug) Dressed in period clothing (from the early 19th century – the time of Frederik VI's reign) the old night watchman takes tourists (no booking needed) through the historic streets of the city, with commentary and song in both Danish and English. Tours last about 1½ hours. Meet at 9pm at Gråbrødre Torv, the small square fronting Peder Oxe restaurant.

FESTIVALS & EVENTS

Following is a list of some of the larger Copenhagen-area annual events. Since the dates and venues can change a bit from year to year, check with the tourist office for current schedule information.

JANUARY

New Year concerts Performed at various venues in the greater Copenhagen area.

MARCH-APRIL

NatFilm Festival A Night Film Festival held at various Copenhagen cinemas. Features more than 100 films by Danish and international directors, shown in original languages, over a 10-day period from late March. See www.natfilm.dk.

Copenhagen Fashion & Design Festival Held at the end of March or early April, it focuses on Danish design and the latest in fashions. There are special displays in many shops and exhibits at Nikolaj Kirke (Map pp70-1) on Strøget.

Queen Margrethe II's birthday 16 April. Celebrated at Amalienborg Slot with the royal guards in full ceremonial dress and the queen waving from the palace balcony at noon. Buses are adorned with Danish flags too.

Tivoli Copenhagen's venerable amusement park Tivoli reopens after a long slumber in mid-April.

MAY

Labour Day Celebrated on 1 May, this is not officially a public holiday. Try telling that to thousands of people who take the day off, many ending up in Fælledparken, where there's often a big bash (read: big booze-up).

Copenhagen Marathon This 42km race through the streets of Copenhagen is held on a Sunday in mid-May and is open to both amateur and professional runners. See www.copenhagenmarathon.dk.

Copenhagen Carnival This three-day event in the heart of the capital takes place on Whitsunday weekend (usually late May or early June) and sees the Danes try to go Brazilian. Highlights include a parade and dancing in the streets. There are special events for children too. See www.karneval.dk.

JUNE

Midsummer Eve Held on 23 June and also called Sankt Hans eve, this is a time for evening bonfires at beaches all around Denmark. Copenhagen's Fælledparken is the site of a big bonfire, and there are special activities at Tivoli and Bakken.

Danish Derby Denmark's most important horse race is held in late June at Klampenborg.

JULY

Copenhagen Jazz Festival Held for 10 days in early July this is one of the world's major jazz festivals, with indoor and outdoor concerts all around the city, featuring local and big-name artists. See www.jazzfestival.dk and opposite.

Klokkespilskoncerter i Vor Frelsers Kirke Features free carillon recitals each Saturday during July at the atmospheric Vor Frelsers Kirke in Christianshavn.

AUGUST

Copenhagen International Ballet Festival Held from the first week to the third week in August. Features top solo dancers from the Royal Danish Ballet as well as visiting performers from international ballet companies, with an emphasis on modern choreography. See www.copenhageninternationalballet.com.

Cultural Harbour First week in August. A range of free cultural events on and around Copenhagen's harbour. See www.kulturhavn.dk.

Sommerkoncerter i Vor Frue Kirke Features free classical music performances throughout the month at Vor Frue Kirke, the city's theatre-like cathedral.

Mermaid Pride Parade Held on the first or second Saturday in August, this festive gay pride parade marches with Carnival-like extravagance through the city to Slotsholmen. See www.mermaidpride.dk.

GAY & LESBIAN COPENHAGEN

Denmark (and therefore Copenhagen) is a relatively easy place to be gay. The Danish Law of Registered Partnership took effect in October 1989, allowing people of the same sex to tie the knot. Since that time more than 5000 couples have taken advantage of the law and registered their partnership with city hall. Adoption laws are liberal compared with other Western countries, and public displays of affection between people of the same sex are unlikely to provoke ire. The Danish national organisation for gays and lesbians, **Landsforeningen for Bøsser og Lesbiske** (LBL; Map pp70-1; ☎ 33 13 19 48; www.lbl.dk; Teglgårds-stræde 13) is based in the Latin Quarter. The facility includes a library, bookshop, informal café, various gay and lesbian support groups and counselling services.

See our review for the Hotel Windsor (p88) for gay-friendly sleeping options.

A network of gay and gay-friendly businesses in the city is Copenhagen Gay Life (www.copenhagen-gay-life.dk). The website includes useful tourist information and listings in English, as well as links to LBL and other gay organisations.

Copenhagen has one of the liveliest gay and lesbian scenes in Europe. Copenhagen has dozens of gay bars, clubs and cafés, nearly half of them concentrated along Studiestræde in the two blocks between Vester Voldgade and Nørregade. For a complete list pick up a copy of *PAN-bladet,* which is available at gay businesses, including the clubs mentioned here. This monthly newspaper has information on gay organisations, saunas and other places of interest. Another read worth keeping an eye out for is newish *Out & About* (free), which lists gay venues and events. Its website is at www.out-and-about.dk. Good gay venues include the following:

Cosy Bar (Map pp70-1; ☎ 33 12 74 27; www.cosybar.dk; Studiestræde 24; 🕑 10pm-6am Sun-Thu, 10pm-8am Fri & Sat) A very popular late-night place for men, with DJs playing Tuesday to Saturday and a serious attitude to picking up, and quickly.

Masken (Map pp70-1; ☎ 33 91 09 37; Studiestræde 33; 🕑 4pm-2am Mon-Thu, 4pm-5am Fri & Sat, 3pm-2am Sun) Here you'll find a pretty mellow, easy-going atmosphere, with cheap beer and good snacks. It's mainly a hang-out for gay men, but Thursday is Ladies Night. Entertainment options include drag acts, live music and football telecasts.

Pan Disco (Map pp70-1; ☎ 33 11 37 84; www.pan-cph.dk; Knabrostræde 3; 🕑 disco 10pm-5am Fri, 10pm-6am Sat) On the southern side of Strøget, this is the city's main mixed gay and lesbian danceteria, with multiple bars and two (frequently packed) dance floors. Typically one disco spins current house tunes and the other focuses on camp/romantic pop classics that bring out the inner Karaoke queen in all of us.

Sebastian (Map p72; ☎ 33 32 22 79; Hyskenstræde 10; 🕑 noon-midnight Mon-Wed, noon-2am Thu-Sat) Pleasant bar/café attracts a mixed gay and lesbian crowd. It's a good spot to visit in the late afternoon, when 'happy hour' attracts a relaxed crowd.

COPENHAGEN JAZZ FESTIVAL

The Copenhagen Jazz Festival is the biggest entertainment event of Copenhagen's year, with 10 days of music beginning on the first Friday in July. It's a cornucopia of hundreds of indoor and outdoor concerts, with music wafting out of practically every public square, park, club and café throughout the city. All types of jazz are to be found, from Dixieland that makes you tap your toes to free jazz improvisations that will have your head spinning.

Jazz first arrived in Copenhagen in the 1920s and Danes quickly took to it, producing some fine local jazz musicians and band leaders of their own. Jazz reached its height of popularity in Copenhagen during the Nazi occupation of WWII, when it dominated the music scene in virtually every club and café in the city. Musical tastes began to change after the war. Jazz slipped in popularity and many of the old jazz musicians found it tough to eke out a living.

With jazz securely footed in the Copenhagen music scene, in 1978 the city kicked off the first Copenhagen Jazz Festival, a citywide event that featured Denmark's top jazz musicians and many international names.

Since that time the Copenhagen Jazz Festival has mushroomed into one of Europe's leading jazz events. Over the years, performers have included such renowned names as Dizzy Gillespie, Miles Davis, Sonny Rollins, Oscar Peterson, Ray Charles and Wynton Marsalis.

During festival time, the whole city turns into a massive venue dedicated to nothing but jazz, with musical performances occurring in Copenhagen's numerous clubs and small cafés, in the city's public squares and alongside the canals. And there are also plenty of street parades and special events such as midnight concerts at Nationalmuseet and daily children's jazz programs at Kongens Have.

Most of the open-air events are free. Those held in the cafés are either free or have small cover charges and it's only the largest big-name events that have significant ticket prices.

Note that events and venues can change a bit from year to year. For the latest in schedules, contact **Copenhagen Jazz Festival** (☎ 33 93 20 13; www.festival.jazz.dk; Nytorv 3, 1450 Copenhagen K).

Golden Days in Copenhagen Held over two weeks in late August and early September, it features art exhibits, poetry readings, theatre, ballet and concerts that focus on Denmark's 'Golden Age' (1800–50).

Copenhagen Film Festival Highlighting Danish and international film, it is held during the second half of September. See www.copenhagenfilmfestival.com.

OCTOBER

Cultural Night in Copenhagen Held on the first night of the autumn school holidays (typically the second Friday in October), when museums, theatres, galleries and even the Rosenborg Slot throw open their doors to one and all. Free buses transport visitors between the various sites. Then it's time to hibernate till next year… See www.kulturnatten.dk.

Copenhagen Gay & Lesbian Film Festival Spread over a week from mid-October, it shows contemporary films from around the world and is Copenhagen's longest-running film festival. See www.cglff.dk.

NOVEMBER

Copenhagen Irish Festival Traditional Irish folk music at various venues in the city for three days in early November.

Copenhagen Autumn Jazz , Features top jazz musicians performing at clubs around the city for four days in early November. Produced by the Copenhagen Jazz Festival folks.

Great Christmas Parade Held on the last Saturday in November. 'Father Christmas' parades through the city followed by jazz musicians, costumed fairytale characters and scores of children, lighting Christmas trees in public squares and ending in Rådhuspladsen to light up the city's largest tree.

DECEMBER

Tivoli Reopens its gates from mid-November to a few days before Christmas with a holiday market and fair. There's ice skating on the pond and some Tivoli restaurants offer menus with hot mulled wine and traditional holiday meals.

Christmas fairs Held throughout December and featuring food booths, arts and crafts stalls, and often parades. Check the tourist office for the latest venues.

SLEEPING

Copenhagen is an extremely popular convention city and if you happen to arrive when one is taking place, finding a room could be a challenge. The main hotel quarter (and slowly-getting-gentrified red-light district) is conveniently located along the western side of Central Station in Vesterbro, where rows of six-storey, early-20th-century buildings house one hotel after the other.

TOP FIVE COPENHAGEN SLEEPS

- **Best Waterside** 71 Nyhavn (p89)
- **Coolest Boutique Hotel** Hotel Guldsmeden (p90)
- **Best Fitness Facilities** DGI-Byen (p90)
- **Nicest Newcomer** The Square (p88)
- **Hippest Hotspot** Hotel Sankt Petri (p91)

Although this Central Station area is jammed with mid-range hotels, Copenhagen has very few hotels that are priced to really warrant the term 'budget'. However, you'll find a good range of spotless budget options in the tony Frederiksberg neighbourhood, which lies west of Vesterbro. Mid-range and top-end hotels are of the highest standard – with comfort and stylish design featuring heavily. After all, this is the city where people get in earnest discussions about their favourite chairs…

The hotel rates quoted in this section include service charge, the 25% value-added tax (VAT). It's a good idea to book in advance – rooms in many of the most popular mid-range hotels fill quickly, particularly during the summer season of June to September. Our listings reflect prices as follows: Budget (doubles with bathroom under 975kr per night), Mid-Range (doubles with bathroom between 1000kr and 1700kr) and Top End (doubles over 1700kr).

The city tourist office, **Copenhagen Right Now** (Map p67; ☎ 70 22 24 42; www.woco.dk; Vesterbrogade 4A; 🕑 9am-4pm Mon-Fri, 9am-2pm Sat Jan-Apr; 9am-6pm Mon-Sat May & Jun; 9am-8pm Mon-Sat, 10am-6pm Sun Jul & Aug; 9am-4pm Mon-Fri, 9am-2pm Sat Sep-Dec) can help you find accommodation (for free if you book via the phone or Internet). Rooms in private homes around the city cost from around 300kr for singles and 400kr for doubles. This office also books unfilled hotel rooms, typically at discounted rates that vary from around 100kr off for budget hotels to as much as 50% off for top-end hotels. These discounts, however, are based on supply and demand, and are not always available during busy periods. There's a 75kr to 100kr fee per booking.

Just outside customs, **Tourist Information Copenhagen Airport** (🕑 6am-midnight) also books unfilled Copenhagen hotel rooms at similarly discounted rates for a 60kr booking fee. If you're flying in and looking for a hotel, this is definitely the way to go.

Use It (Map pp70-1; ☎ 33 73 06 20; www.useit.dk; Rådhusstræde 13; 🕑 11am-4pm Mon-Wed, 11am-6pm Thu, 11am-2pm Fri 16 Sep-14 Jun; 9am-7pm Mon-Fri 15 Jun-15 Sep) books rooms in private homes, which cost from around 200kr for singles and 250kr for doubles. There's no booking fee for the service. Use It also keeps tabs on which hostel beds are available and is a good source of information on subletting student housing and other long-term accommodation.

If you're staying for more than a week, it's worth looking into services such as **Hay 4 You** (Map pp70-1; ☎ 33 33 08 05; www.hay4you.dk; Vimmelskaftet 49; apt per day/week/month from 450/2200/7500kr), which provides excellent central apartments (whose owners are on holiday elsewhere) at very good prices.

Budget

HOSTELS

The two closest hostels under the auspices of Hostelling International (Danhostel) are listed below. These hostels often fill early in summer so it's best to make reservations in advance. When the HI hostels are full you can almost always find a bed at one of the city-sponsored hostels. Although they tend to be more of a crash-pad scene than the HI hostels, they're also more central and don't require hostel membership.

Sleep-In (Map p103; ☎ 35 26 50 59; www.sleep-in.dk; Blegdamsvej 132A, Østerbro; dm 99kr; 🕑 Jul & Aug; 💻) Seasonal budget place, a few kilometres north of the city centre in the Østerbro district, is Copenhagen's largest summer hostel with some 280-plus beds occupying a sports hall that's curtained off into 'rooms' with four to six beds; there are no doors, but curtains offer a little privacy. There are free lockers, a guest kitchen and a café. You can use your own sleeping bag or rent bed linen (30kr). From the city centre take bus No 1 or 15, get off at Trianglen and walk 300m southwest on Blegdamsvej. Bakeries, shops and restaurants are within easy walking distance.

Sleep-In Heaven (Map pp62-3; ☎ 35 35 46 48; www.sleepinheaven.com; Struenseegade 7, Nørrebro; dm with shared bathroom 125kr, breakfast 30kr, sheets 30kr; 🕑 year-round; 💻) Privately run hostel, in the Nørrebro area, has 76 beds in a basement dorm. There's no group kitchen but there are a number of cheap eating places within walking distance. There are even 'bridal suites' for couples – and they cost 445kr.

Danhostel Copenhagen Bellahøj (Map p103; ☎ 38 28 97 15; bellahoej@danhostel.dk; Herbergvejen 8, Brønshøj; dm/d/tr 95/300/390kr; 1 Feb-2 Jan;) The most easily accessible HI-hostel, this place is in the quiet suburban neighbourhood known as Bellahøj, 4km northwest of the city centre. Although it has 250 beds, it's quite cosy for its size. Facilities include a laundry room, cafeteria, TV room and table tennis, plus reception is open 24 hours. To get here, take bus No 2A.

Danhostel Copenhagen Amager (Map p103; ☎ 32 52 29 08; copenhagen@danhostel.dk; Vejlands Allé 200, Amager; dm/d 95/300kr; 2 Jan-15 Dec) In an isolated part of Amager just off the E20, about 5km from the city centre, this place ranks as one of Europe's largest hostels, with 528 beds in a series of low-rise wings containing cells of two-bed and five-bed rooms. There's a laundry room, Internet access and a cafeteria. It's accessible to people in wheelchairs. To get there, take the metro to Bella Center.

Belægningen Avedørelejren (Map p103; ☎ 36 77 90 84; www.belaegningen.dk; Avedøre Tværvej 10, Hvidovre; dm bed 110kr, s/d with bathroom 360/460kr; P) About 7km southwest of the city centre, this hostel in the well-renovated barracks of a former military camp has friendly staff, high standards and quite cosy rooms with only four beds in the dorm rooms. Breakfast is available for 55kr, and the hostel also offers cheap bicycle rentals and a good group kitchen. As an added perk you might spot some of Denmark's hottest screen stars, as the camp's rear buildings have been turned into a Danish 'Hollywood' housing the country's main movie companies, including Lars von Trier's Zentropa production company. Take bus No 650S from Central Station.

HOTELS

Missionshotellet Nebo (Map pp62-3; ☎ 33 21 12 17; www.nebo.dk; Istedgade 6, Vesterbro; s/d/tr/q 760/860/1100/1250kr;) Good old Nebo is very convenient, a mere stone's throw from Central Station, and has been tarted up to within an inch of its budget life. A real bargain in this category and friendly to boot – mind you, you're in the thick of the sex shops here if you're looking for salubrious surrounds. There's free Internet access in the hotel's lobby, and all rooms have bathroom, TV and a desk.

Saga Hotel (Map pp62-3; ☎ 33 24 49 44; booking@sagahotel.dk; Colbjørnsensgade 18, Vesterbro; s/d from 550/650kr) With 76 rooms, most of which look shipshape thanks to a navy-and-white paint job, this is a handy little spot close to the main train station (and some of the red-light district sex shops). There's no lift and it's multistorey, so you may have to climb some stairs, but the minimalist approach to luxuries helps keep the rates relatively low (rooms without bathroom are much cheaper still). The rooms have phone and TV (singles are quite small though), and the service is friendly and personal.

Hotel Sankt Thomas (Map p103; ☎ 33 21 64 64; www.sctthomas.com; Frederiksberg Allé 7, Frederiksberg; s/d 595/795kr; P) Groovy little Sankt Thomas lies tucked away off busy Vesterbrogade in a 19th-century building that just scored a well-earned facelift. It's close to the area's new bars, restaurants and theatres, and it's charmingly run. There are some cheaper rooms (without toilet) for s/d 495/595kr (even less in the low season).

Selandia Hotel (Map pp62-3; ☎ 33 31 46 10; www.hotel-selandia.dk; Helgolandsgade 12, Vesterbro; s/d from 795/975kr) Recently renovated Selandia has 84 spiffy rooms, each with a desk, trouser press and TV. Cheapest are the two-dozen-or-so rooms with shared bathroom (s/d 525/650kr). Service is quintessentially helpful, and it's worth perusing the website for special deals that make Selandia quite the bargain. When the lobby gets a facelift, there'll be no stopping this place.

Sømandshjemmet Bethel (Map pp62-3; ☎ 33 13 03 70; fax 33 15 85 70; Nyhavn 22, Nyhavn; s/d 795/895kr) Once a seamen's hotel, the well-managed Bethel is now open to all. This simple but effective little place has a nice location, a lift to all floors, and two dozen good-sized rooms with serviceable, tidy furnishings. All rooms have TV and a phone. Many also have unbeatable views of Nyhavn – for the best, ask for a corner room. For a good night's sleep in summer, ask for a room at the back (about 100kr to 200kr less).

Cab Inn Scandinavia (Map pp62-3; ☎ 35 36 11 11; scandinavia@cabinn.dk; Vodroffsvej 57, Frederiksberg; s/d/tr/q 510/630/750/870kr; P) Modern, well managed and accessible to people in wheelchairs, the Scandinavia has 201 sleekly compact rooms that resemble cabins in a cruise ship, complete with upper and lower bunks, but no seasickness. Although small, the rooms are very comfortable and have cable TV, phone, complimentary tea and bathroom. Reception is open 24 hours and the neighbourhood is quiet and safe, making this place ideal for budget-conscious families. There are about 25 rooms equipped for people with disabilities.

Hotel Nora (Map pp62-3; ☎ 3537 2021; www.hotelnora.dk; Nørrebrogade 18B, Nørrebro; s/d 850/975kr; 💻 🅿) An excellent low-cost addition to Copenhagen's hotel scene is the Nora, which is squeaky clean and situated in Nørrebrogade. While it's not as flash and focused on design as many of the local places to stay, it's very comfortable and service is considerate and reliable. Breakfast is included in the price.

Cab Inn Copenhagen Express (Map pp62-3 ☎ 33 21 04 00; express@cabinn.dk; Danasvej 32, Frederiksberg; s/d/tr/q 510/630/750/870kr; 💻 🅿) A few blocks to the southwest of the Cab Inn Scandinavia, this sister operation has the same type of rooms and rates, although it has less than 100 rooms, making it a little more intimate than the Scandinavia. Reception is open 24 hours and standards are solid. Two rooms here are accessible to people in wheelchairs.

Hotel Hebron (Map pp62-3; ☎ 33 31 69 06; www.hebron.dk; Helgolandsgade 4, Vesterbro; s/d & tw from 750/975kr, ste from 1125kr; ❄ ⊠) A quiet hotel in an attractive early-20th-century building, the Hebron has about 100 quite cosy, renovated rooms, each with desk, TV and phone. Despite its proximity to both the main train station and the red-light district, you should sleep soundly, thanks to the miracle of double-glazing. Staff are good with sightseeing tips and transport information. The hotel shuts down for Christmas between 22 December and 3 January.

Hotel Euroglobe (Map pp62-3; ☎ 33 79 79 54; www.hoteleuroglobe.dk; Niels Ebbesens Vej 20, Frederiksberg; s/d/tr/q with shared bathroom 450/550/650/800kr) The Euroglobe has 28 budget rooms, is in an old building that's been splashed with a fresh coat of paint and is in reasonable (if minimalist) condition. Rooms are pretty basic but sparsely stylish, with beds, an end table, chairs and washbasin. Hotel Euroglobe is about a 20-minute walk from Central Station, or take bus No 3 or 29, which stop a few blocks away.

Hotel Windsor (Map pp70-1; ☎ 33 11 08 30; www.hotelwindsor.dk; Frederiksborggade 30, Nørreport; s/d/tr 600/650/700kr) An exclusively gay hotel in an older building opposite Israels Plads, the Windsor's two dozen rooms are straightforward and a bit worn but all have TV and some have VCRs and refrigerators. Communal areas are a tad shabby, but this actually adds to the appeal, providing a welcome antidote to the Scandi obsession with neat and stylish. Also a good place to get information about the gay scene in Copenhagen.

CAMPING

Absalon Camping (Map p103; ☎ 36 41 06 00; Korsdalsvej 132, 2610 Rødovre; camping per adult 62kr; 🕑 year-round) Well-maintained three-star facility near Brøndbyøster station on S-train line B is 9km west of the city centre in the Rødovre suburb. Facilities on site include a coin laundry, food kiosk, playground and group kitchen, plus it's only 8km from the beach.

Charlottenlund Fort (Map p103; ☎ 39 62 36 88; www.campingcopenhagen.dk; Strandvejen 144B; camping per adult 70kr; 🕑 1 May-15 Sep) Eight kilometres north of central Copenhagen, this friendly camping ground, on Charlottenlund beach, is set in the tree-lined grounds of an old moat-encircled coastal fortification. Space is limited so advance bookings are recommended. There's a snack kiosk, showers and a coin laundry on site; a bakery and a supermarket are just a few hundred metres away. To get here, take bus No 6A.

Mid-Range

RÅDHUSPLADSEN & TIVOLI

The **Square** (Map pp70-1; ☎ 33 38 12 00; www.thesquare.dk; Rådhuspladsen 14; s/d from 1260/1560kr; ❄ 💻) Ultra-modern and so hip it almost hurts (Jacobsen chairs, cowhide fabric, red leather), The Square is an excellent three-star hotel with design touches and amenities generally associated with greater expense and more stiffness. Rooms are beautifully equipped, and some have sterling views of the main square – plus all the city's main sights are in walking distance.

Hotel Kong Frederik (Map pp70-1; ☎ 33 12 59 02; www.remmen.dk; Vester Voldgade 25; s/d from 1040/1240kr; ❄ 💻 🅿) Classic English-style hotel with four stars on its door and a solidly historic character including dark woods, antique furnishings and paintings of Danish royalty. Its 110 rooms are poshly comfortable and each has a TV, phone, minibar and hairdryer, plus there's free access to the spa/fitness centre at the Hotel d'Angleterre, p91.

Mermaid Hotel (Map pp70-1; ☎ 33 12 65 70; www.mermaid-hotel.dk; Løngangstræde 27; s/d from 1199/1399kr; Ⓟ) You'll find this little three-star Mermaid tucked behind the Rådhuspladsen area and you certainly won't be disappointed. Nicely renovated rooms are functional and stylish, while there's a very attractive rooftop area where you can unwind when the sun's shining. It is the sister hotel to the nearby four-star Palace, but we think this is a better option for those wanting to stay in this neck of the woods.

Hotel Astoria (Map pp62-3; ☎ 33 42 99 00; www.astoriahotelcopenhagen.dk; Banegårdspladsen 4; s/d from 990/1290kr) It's housed in a Funkis-style building that's loaded with character but showing its age a tad. The Astoria is a handy three-star choice for those into architecture and design that hasn't been tampered with too radically. Rooms have good amenities and are comfortable, although the hotel's location is very close to the main train station.

Hotel Ascot (Map pp62-3; ☎ 33 12 60 00; www.ascothotel.dk; Studiestræde 61; s/d from 900/1200kr; 💻 Ⓟ) The friendly Ascot occupies a former bathhouse erected 100 years ago by the same architect (Martin Nyrop) who designed Copenhagen's city hall. The lobby boasts some interesting bas-reliefs depicting scenes from the bathhouse days. Most of the 155 rooms are large and decorated in a hotchpotch of styles, although each has a deep soaking tub in the bathroom, and some have a kitchen and Internet access. Not easily accessible to people in wheelchairs though.

NYHAVN

71 Nyhavn Hotel (Map pp62-3; ☎ 33 43 62 00; www.71nyhavnhotelcopenhagen.dk; Nyhavn 71; s/d from 1390/1650kr; 💻) Well, you certainly won't forget your address if you stay here, and you won't forget the experience either. Slicker than grease and housed in a fabulous 200-year-old canal-side renovated warehouse, this wonderful hotel has incorporated some of the building's period features and great views of both the harbour and Nyhavn canal. Everything runs like clockwork, and the location is unbeatable. Popular with business travellers, and therefore a real bargain on weekends (s/d 990/1290kr).

Copenhagen Strand (Map pp62-3; ☎ 33 48 99 00; www.copenhagenstrand.dk; Havnegade 37; s/d from 1260/1560kr; 💻 ⊠) The Strand is an excellent mid-range hotel overlooking Copenhagen Harbour. Its 174 rooms, with a suitably maritime décor, are equipped with cable TV, minibar and phone. There's an onsite business centre and a lobby bar, making this a good choice for business travellers. Parking shouldn't be a hassle in the street, although it is metered.

Hotel Opera (Map pp62-3; ☎ 33 47 83 00; www.operahotelcopenhagen.dk; Tordenskjoldsgade 15; s/d from 1160/1490kr; ⊠) Just south of Det Kongelige Teater (hence the name), this hotel has an inviting English-style character that is reminiscent of a gentleman's club and befits its theatre-district location. Although it's not strictly as fancy as other top-end period hotels, the 91 three-star rooms are very pleasant, each with phone and TV. Weekend rates drop substantially.

Sophie Amalie Hotel (Map pp62-3; ☎ 33 13 34 00; booking.has@remmen.dk; Sankt Annæ Plads 21; s/d from 875/1075kr; ✱ 💻 Ⓟ) Popular with business travellers and the sort of person who has decided that the two-star joint they're staying at near the red-light district just ain't worth it. The 134 rooms are modern and each has the standard amenities plus sauna and solarium. What really sets this place apart is the service, which is charming and incredibly helpful. Go for a 6th-floor split-level suite with harbour views; each has a living room with a sofa bed on the lower level and a loft bedroom above (2075kr).

Hotel City (Map pp62-3; ☎ 33 13 06 66; www.hotelcity.dk; Peder Skramsgade 24; s/d from 995/1250kr; ⊠) This relatively small hotel has 81 pleasant (and green-keyed) rooms, each with cable TV, phone and trouser press. Most contain two single beds, placed side by side. The lobby has Jacobsen chairs and a water feature that would have him turning in his grave, but we give the place thumbs up for friendliness and patience with children.

NØRREPORT

Ibsens Hotel (Map pp62-3; ☎ 33 13 19 13; www.ibsenshotel.dk; Vendersgade 23; s/d from 925/1025kr) Ibsens has 118 rooms spread across four floors of a renovated period building. The place has the character of a 'boutique hotel' with creative décor and no two rooms looking exactly the same. Décor styles vary between modern (with contemporary Scandinavian design features), romantic and traditional (loads of antiques and plush fabric details). All boast a comfortable bed, telephone and TV. There are also suites with kitchenettes for 2100kr. Situated near happening Nansensgade, this is a great location for those who are in Copenhagen to experience more than the tourist sights.

Hotel Kong Arthur (Map pp62-3; ☎ 33 11 12 12; www.kongarthur.dk; Nørre Søgade 11; s/d from 1145/1400kr; P) The Kong Arthur is a 107-room establishment in an attractive 19th-century building that fronts the lake Peblinge Sø. Throughout the building you'll find such period details as suits of armour and stylish Persian rugs. Room amenities include TV, minibar, trouser press and attractive bathroom. The hotel also has a stylish inner courtyard, but there's also a lovely glassed-in atrium for breakfast in inclement weather. Ask about possible discounts for Internet bookings or slow periods.

VESTERBRO

Hotel Guldsmeden (Map pp62-3; ☎ 33 22 15 00; www.hotelguldsmeden.dk; Vesterbrogade 66; s/d 995/1295kr) Wonderful 64-room, three-star hotel deserves more stars and repeat stays. It's got an arty, Montmartre feel about it, and oozes intimacy and style. Many of the rooms have a four-poster bed, some feature claw-footed bathtubs and all have original (and pretty damn good) art on the walls. Charming touches such as Persian rugs, clubby leather chairs and sisal matting only add to its rare appeal. A bargain.

Savoy Hotel (Map pp62-3; ☎ 33 26 75 00; www.savoyhotel.dk; Vesterbrogade 34; s/d & tw 975/1275kr, f 1795kr) The lovely Savoy is a century-old hotel that was renovated a few years ago but still retains some of its period character and Art Nouveau décor. Although the hotel fronts a busy road, all of its 66 rooms face a winningly quiet courtyard, and each room has cable TV, a minibar and coffee maker. Plus, the service is some of the sweetest and most efficient we came across – no mean feat in a town used to hosting conventions.

Tiffany (Map pp62-3; ☎ 33 21 80 50; www.hoteltiffany.dk; Colbjørnsensgade 28; s/d/tr/q 895/1095/1295/1495kr;) The Tiffany, which proudly bills itself as a 'Sweet Hotel' is a pleasant little place filled with character and warmth. The 29 rooms each have a TV, a phone, a trouser press, a private bathroom and a kitchenette with refrigerator and microwave oven. A buffet breakfast (at Tiffany's – groan) is not included, but coffee, tea and fresh pastries are available each morning and you can help yourself to fruit in the lobby. Service is kind and considerate, making this little jewel excellent value for money in this price range.

DGI-byen Hotel (Map pp62-3; ☎ 33 29 80 50; www.dgi-byen.dk; Tietgensgade 65; s/d from 1295/1495kr; P) Part of a late-millennium sports complex development 200m south of Central Station, in the old cattle market district (the smell has long gone), this hotel consists of 104 rooms on three storeys of the complex. The rooms have modern Scandinavian décor with blond hardwood floors and sleek, modest furnishings. Rates drop by a very decent amount on weekends, making this a very good choice for a mini-break (from s/d 825/925kr). For 100kr more you can opt for a superior room, which is slightly larger and has a bathtub rather than a shower.

Grand Hotel (Map pp62-3; ☎ 33 27 69 00; www.grandhotelcopenhagen.dk; Vesterbrogade 9; s/d from 1290/1590kr;) A pleasant 100-year-old hotel with about 160 rooms, conveniently located just north of Central Station. Nonsmoking rooms are available and various discount schemes mean you can sometimes get a steeply reduced last-minute price through the tourist office's room-booking counter, the website or on a weekend. Not much soul in the décor, but plenty of polish.

Absalon Hotel (Map pp62-3; ☎ 33 24 22 11; www.absalon-hotel.dk; Helgolandsgade 15; s/d/tr 1005/1235/1435kr;) At the three-star 165-room Absalon you'll find chintz-laden rooms with good amenities, including cable TV and office facilities available to guests. Cheaper rooms without shared bathroom facilities are good value if you're pinching pennies (s/d/tr 550/725/925kr), but not nearly as attractive as the other rooms in the main wing. If you want a little more luxury, there are rooms on the top floor for a few hundred krone more. Parking is available nearby.

Top End

RÅDHUSPLADSEN & TIVOLI

Hotel Imperial (Map pp62-3; ☎ 33 12 80 00; www.imperialhotel.dk; Vester Farimagsgade 9; s/d from 1495/2450kr; P) Despite its rather nondescript (grotty, rather ugly) façade, opposite an S-train station, the Imperial has one of the best reputations for service among the city's top-end establishments. Each of the

164 rooms has good-looking modern décor (with some very nice Danish furnishings) and a deep Japanese-style bathtub. Definitely worth booking for a weekend of escapism and quality bath time.

Palace Hotel (Map pp70-1; ☎ 33 14 40 50; www.palace-hotel.dk; Rådhuspladsen 57; s/d 1825/2025kr;) In a picturesque period building overlooking Rådhuspladsen, the 162 rooms at the Palace are spacious and well equipped. The decor is old-fashioned, with upholstered chairs, heavy curtains and brass lamps in what's considered the 'English style'. It's incredibly handy to the centre of town, without the somewhat grubby surrounds of Vesterbro's hotel district just across the square. Service is whip-smart and incredibly helpful.

Radisson SAS Royal Hotel (Map pp62-3; ☎ 33 42 60 00; www.radissonsas.com; Hammerichsgade 1; s/d from 1595/1895; P) Centrally located, famous as all get out (Arne Jacobsen designed it and Room 606 – a tidy 3940kr per night – has been left intact), this 265-room, multistorey hotel is popular with well-to-do business travellers and visiting dignitaries, and, dare we say it, has been resting on its laurels for some time. While rooms are in good order and some of the views breathtaking, service seems a little slack and many communal areas are just plain bland. That said, the hotel has computer work stations with Internet access, well-regarded restaurants and a fitness centre, and we couldn't fault the 23,000kr per night Royal Panorama Suite.

STRØGET & THE LATIN QUARTER

Hotel Sankt Petri (Map pp70-1; ☎ 33 45 91 00; www.hotelsktpetri.com; Krystalgade 22; s/d from 2095/2395kr; P) Swanky is as swanky does, and this place is so hot right now that you'll get burnt walking past it. Fabulous rooms (many with charming views over the Latin Quarter's rooftops) in classic Scandinavian 21st-century style and amenities you didn't know you needed (anti-allergy quilts and the like). Plus there's a fantastic bar on the premises (Bar Rouge – see p95).

NYHAVN

Phoenix (Map pp62-3; ☎ 33 95 95 00; www.phoenixcopenhagen.dk; Bredgade 37; s/d from 1490/2190kr;) A block north of Nyhavn, the Phoenix is one of the city's more fastidious deluxe hotels and fairly hums with efficient (yet discreet) service. The 200-plus plush rooms have heavy carpets, upholstered chairs, chandeliers and the like, all in keeping with a Louis XVI feel. Business facilities are excellent, as is its proximity to Copenhagen's financial district. Weekend prices plummet by at least 30%.

Neptun Hotel (Map pp62-3; ☎ 33 96 20 00; info.neptun@clarion.choicehotels.dk; Sankt Annæ Plads 18; s/d from 1375/1775kr; P) The Neptun is a well-regarded and secure four-star hotel a block north of Nyhavn (without the noise). Each of the 122 rooms and 12 suites has TV, phone, an electronic room safe, a minibar and a trouser press, and almost half are non-smoking. The Neptun is an affiliate of Choice Hotels, meaning that you can find good deals for Internet bookings and weekend stays.

Hotel d'Angleterre (Map pp70-1; ☎ 33 12 00 95; www.dangleterre.dk; Kongens Nytorv 34; s/d from 2170/2470kr; P) Visiting high-profile celebrities often opt for the exclusive, reassuringly five-star d'Angleterre, which has enough chandeliers, marble floors and history (dating back to the 18th century) to give you a gilt complex. It also has some of Copenhagen's highest rates, with 14,870kr for the royal suite. Breakfast is an extra 135kr per person. Despite its lengthy history, the hotel no longer enjoys the solidly pre-eminent reputation it once had among Copenhagen's top hotels, and service, while perfectly pleasant, is not quite up to the bow-and-scrape standards we've come to expect when we pop our scruffy heads into these sorts of places. That said, the gym and spa are top class, and business facilities are excellent.

ELSEWHERE IN COPENHAGEN

Radisson SAS Scandinavia Hotel (Map pp62-3; ☎ 33 96 50 00; www.radissonsas.com; Amager Blvd 70, Amager; s/d from 1695/1895kr; P) In an unmissable high-rise building in the northern part of Amager, the Scandinavia offers all the luxury hotel amenities and goodies that any business traveller could want and Copenhagen's only casino. Its 542 rooms offer generous weekend reductions and plenty of comfort, but we got the distinct feeling that service was a 'by numbers' deal and cosiness (that most Danish of qualities) was distinctly lacking.

Hilton Copenhagen Airport (Map p103; ☎ 32 50 15 01; www.hilton.dk; Ellehammersvej 20, Kastrup; s/d from 1400/1900kr; P) Newish hotel, right at the airport, has around 375 very large rooms with full amenities including top-end touches such as Bang & Olufsen TVs. There's a fitness centre, a swimming pool and conference facilities. As airport hotels go – it's an excellent one, and service is impeccable. Children are also welcome, with babysitting services available.

EATING

Copenhagen's dining options cover every taste and budgetary base – from street-stall hot dogs (about 24kr) of dubious parentage to Michelin-starred gastrodomes purveying such imaginative fare as a bouillon of stinging nettle with baked sea bass (about 200kr). While Copenhagen does not have the culinary diversity of cities such as London or New York, it does manage to marry Danish dining traditions (herring, *frikadeller* and smørrebrød) with international influences to great effect.

Areas known for eating include Nyhavn (popular for its outdoor tables and Danish staples, plus seafood), Nørrebro (Asian and Middle Eastern and fare), Christianshavn (charming canal-side dining without the tourists of Nyhavn), the Latin Quarter (student eats and cosy cafés) and the area around Kongens Nytorv (fine dining, often with a strong French influence).

The Danes are not Mediterraneans, meaning that if you like to eat late, you'll have trouble finding a place to accommodate you after about 10pm at night, when many restaurants close their kitchens. Restaurants that open during the day will commence business at 11am or noon, and keep the kitchen serving lunch until about 3pm, before opening again at about 6 pm.

Tivoli

TOP END

Tivoli boasts nearly 30 places to eat, from simple stalls offering typical amusement-park fare such as hot dogs, to some of the most respected eating establishments in the city. You need to pay Tivoli admission (or have a Copenhagen Card) to eat at these places – and they only open during the Tivoli season.

The Paul (Map p67; ☎ 33 75 07 75; www.thepaul.dk; 5-course menu 600kr, 5-wine menu 600kr; dinner) White-hot inside and out, the Michelin-starred restaurant with the terrible name is a must for anyone who wants a memorable meal in relaxed yet beautiful surrounds. English-born Chef Paul Cunningham is highly acclaimed, and a look at the menu shows why. The pavilion itself is reminiscent of a wealthy friend's beach-house. Dishes such as warm quail salad with truffle butter vinaigrette are downright sublime. Reservations essential.

Divan 2 (Map p67; ☎ 33 12 51 51; mains 195-365kr; lunch & dinner) Long considered to be one of Tivoli's finest restaurants for both food and service, Divan 2 has been in operation since Tivoli opened in 1843 and serves gourmet French food (a wonderful fillet of sole is on the menu) with a vintage wine collection. A very decent tasting menu will set you back 465kr for three courses. The tacky practice of adding a 5% surcharge for credit-card payment is alive and well here, so you may want to bring some cash. Vegetarians should get their fill of greens elsewhere.

Grøften (Map p67; ☎ 33 75 06 75; mains 150-225kr; lunch & dinner) The speciality here (since 1974) is a type of smørrebrød with lip-smacking tiny fjord shrimps spiced with lime and fresh pepper; other smørrebrød are priced from 40kr apiece. When we popped in, this place was doing a roaring trade, but we got the feeling that we'd stumbled into the 'early bird special'.

TOP FIVE EATS IN COPENHAGEN

- **A Meal to Remember:** The Paul (p92)
- **Best choice of smørrebrød:** Ida Davidsen (p94)
- **Best sushi shoebox:** Selfish (p95)
- **Nicest escape:** Bastionen & Løven (p94)
- **Coolest décor:** Langeline Pavilonen (p94)

Strøget & the Latin Quarter

The area around this pedestrianised mall is filled with dining choices just waiting to be made. From cheap Middle Eastern hole-in-the-wall takeaways to vegetarian stalwarts at the budget end, and wonderful traditional Danish restaurants and modern international cafés at the pricier end.

BUDGET

Huset med det Grønne Træ (Map pp70-1; ☎ 33 12 87 86; Gammel Torv 20; smørrebrød from 40kr; lunch noon-4pm Mon-Fri year-round, noon-3pm Sat Sep-Mar)

Excellent lunch café at the northwestern corner of Gammel Torv and beside the linden tree from which it takes its name. Housed in a period building dating from 1796, it offers quintessential Danish fare, with smørrebrød sandwiches, draught beer and a dozen brands of schnapps.

La Glace (Map pp70-1; ☎ 33 14 46 46; www.laglace.com, in Danish; Skoubogade 3; pastries from 40kr; 🕒 8.30am-5.30pm Mon-Thu, 8.30am-6pm Fri, 9am-5pm Sat) It's *the* classic *konditori* (bakery-café) in town, and it has been serving tea and fancy cakes to socialites for more than a century. A rite of passage if you have a sweet tooth, or are looking to develop one.

MID-RANGE

Peder Oxe (Map pp70-1; ☎ 33 11 00 77; www.pederoxe.dk; Gråbrødre Torv 11; mains 79-199kr; 🕒 lunch & dinner) Fronting Gråbrødre Torv, this stalwart of rustic dining offers wonderful Danish country grub. The smørrebrød (three for 128kr) is a popular option for those at lunch. We fell in love with the solid wood floors, Portuguese tiles and groovy little system whereby you let the wait-staff know you're ready to order by flicking on a light above your table. Copenhagen's oldest monastery was built on this site in 1238 and the restaurant's wine cellar retains part of the old stone foundations.

Restaurant Gråbrødre Torv 21 (Map pp70-1; ☎ 33 11 47 07; www.graabroedre21.aok.dk; Gråbrødre Torv 21; mains 130-225kr; 🕒 lunch & dinner Mon-Sat, dinner Sun) Traditional Danish restaurant has excellent service and a welcoming ambience – with bare wooden floors, clean white walls and rustic furniture. Heart-warming dishes feature, such as roasted chicken with rhubarb, pickled cucumber and parsley.

Café Ketchup (Map pp70-1; ☎ 33 32 30 30; www.cafeketchup.dk; Pilestræde 19; mains 99-155kr; 🕒 lunch & dinner 11am-midnight Mon-Wed, 11am-1am Thu, 11am-3am Fri & Sat) Taking a leaf straight out of the Parisian bistro book, this bustling spot offers excellent hunger-assuaging sandwiches and scrummy lunch/dinner options. We plumped for the grilled salmon with lime and sesame marinade on a bed of celery-parsnip puree, topped with a Noilly Prat sauce – and we sat in utter contentment nursing our wine and watching the well-dressed locals come and go. On Friday and Saturday nights there's a DJ.

Atlas Bar (Map pp70-1; ☎ 33 15 03 52; Larsbjørnstre-stræde 18; mains 95-175kr; 🕒 lunch & dinner Mon-Sat) Casual basement café, festooned with maps from around the world, in the heart of the gay district, has a changing blackboard menu that includes salads, vegetarian fare and a good range of organic meat dishes, mostly with some sort of international influence. Service is brisk and friendly, and the place can get very popular in the evening, so you may want to reserve a table.

RizRaz (Map pp70-1; ☎ 33 15 05 75; Kompagnistræde 20; mains 99-169kr; 🕒 lunch & dinner) Just south of Strøget, this airy basement café will have you feasting on a Mediterranean-style vegetarian buffet that groans under the weight of felafel, pasta, hummus and salads, served daily to 5pm (to 4pm at weekends). You can also order from the menu, which includes lamb kebabs, grilled fish or fried calamari for the meat lovers among us. A frequent winner of 'best and cheapest' awards.

L'Education Nationale (Map pp70-1; ☎ 33 91 53 60; Larsbjørnstæde 12; mains 129-159kr; 🕒 lunch & dinner noon-4pm & 6pm-midnight Mon-Sat) Oozing a certain *je ne sais quoi*, this French-right-down-to-its-tennis-shoes (actually, they belonged to Arthur Ashe…) joint offers good bistro fare, such as warm goat cheese salad and other French staples. Service is just like in France (ie disinterested).

Det Lille Apotek (Map pp70-1; ☎ 33 12 56 06; Store Kannikestræde 15; mains 98-188kr; 🕒 lunch & dinner) The Little Pharmacy is a well-known standby for traditional Danish food at moderate prices in an old-fashioned environment. Multi-item meals that include pickled herring, fish fillet, smørrebrød and other solid batten-the-hatches fare are available for lunch and dinner. By some claims, Det Lille Apotek, which traces its history to 1720 (it was a pharmacy, or apotek, before that), is the oldest restaurant in Copenhagen.

TOP END

Kommandanten (Map pp70-1; ☎ 33 12 09 90; www.kommandanten.dk; Ny Adelgade 7; mains 320-340kr; 🕒 dinner Mon-Sat) Just west of Kongens Nytorv, Kommandenten has received numerous accolades, including the Michelin Guides' highest rating among Copenhagen's restaurants – two big fat shining stars – and that means that if you're in Copenhagen for a few days, haven't made a reservation and fancy eating here then you're in fantasy land. The food is beautifully prepared and presented according to the seasons and what's available locally is superb, and easily matched by a wonderful wine list (mostly French). Chef Kaspar Rune Sørensen has every reason to be proud.

Krogs Fiskerestaurant (Map p72; ☎ 33 15 89 15; www.krogs.com; Gammel Strand 38; mains 340-490kr; 🕑 dinner Mon-Sat) North of Slotsholmen Kanal, the famous Krogs specialises in fresh seafood plus organic produce in smart, subdued surroundings where relaxed good taste rules the roost. Choose from a selection of menus, with matching wines for about 730kr. Imaginative fishy fare includes cod braised in Burgundy with pork jaw and scallops.

Nyhavn to the Little Mermaid

BUDGET

Nyhavns Færgekro (Map pp62-3; ☎ 33 15 15 88; Nyhavn 5; herring buffet 89kr; 🕑 lunch & dinner) An atmospheric café right on the canal, this popular spot has an all-you-can-eat buffet with 10 different kinds of herring, including baked, marinated and rollmops, with condiments to sprinkle on top and boiled potatoes to round out the meal. If you're not a herring lover, then there's something very wrong with you. But there's also a variety of smørrebrød for around 50kr. Dinner, served from 5pm to 11.30pm, betrays French influences, like many Danish restaurants in this area.

MID-RANGE

Cap Horn (Map pp62-3; ☎ 33 12 85 04; www.caphorn.dk, in Danish; Nyhavn 21; mains 160kr; 🕑 breakfast, lunch & dinner) A deservedly popular spot, this canal favourite specialises in Danish fare and uses mainly organic ingredients. Grab a lunch plate of three open-faced sandwiches, a two-course meal of herring, steak and potatoes, wash it all down with a river of beer and revel in your 'localness'. Open until the crowds die down, which is usually late.

Ida Davidsen (Map pp62-3; ☎ 33 91 36 55; Store Kongensgade 70; smørrebrød 50-150kr; 🕑 lunch 10am-5pm Mon-Fri) Ida's is widely considered the top smørrebrød purveyor in not just Copenhagen, but all Denmark. It has a nearly limitless variety of open-faced sandwiches – the only limit is Ida's imagination and the actual dimensions of the piece of (home-made) rye bread that you're dealing with. A rite of passage – skip a museum to get here if time is tight.

TOP END

Langelinie Pavillonen (Map pp62-3; ☎ 33 12 12 14; www.langelinie.dk; Langelinie; set menu from 198kr; 🕑 lunch & dinner) Generally we'd walk a mile to avoid this is the sort of place – the only place to eat within spitting distance of a wildly overrated tourist attraction with an industrial backdrop masquerading as a 'water view'? No thanks – but to tell you the truth, this place (designed by architects Eva and Niels Koppel) is a fabulously upmarket-looking 2nd-floor restaurant with some great design flourishes and Philippe Privat at the stove. Lunch choices include a club sandwich or a two-course meal. At dinner there's a changing menu of French-Danish fare.

Els (Map pp62-3; ☎ 33 14 13 41; Store Strandstræde 3; mains 198-258kr; 🕑 lunch & dinner Mon-Sat, dinner Sun) If you're into formal dining, Els has been dishing out formal food (mind your manners) in a classic upmarket Danish-meets-French setting. Although the décor is solidly (and in some ways, stolidly) 19th century, the menu blends contemporary Danish and French influences to good effect where it counts – the food. Oh, and there's a good wine list, although the 4.75% surcharge on foreign credit cards is a bit rich.

Christianshavn

MID-RANGE

Oven Vande Café (Map pp62-3; ☎ 32 95 96 02; Overgade Oven Vandet 44; mains 159-189kr; 🕑 lunch & dinner) We loved this place so much we felt like wrapping it up, taking it home and making it the little restaurant on *our* corner. An upmarket, well-run café with a solidly French kitchen, plus the sort of low-key, local feel that sees all types popping in for a coffee or beer in an outdoor setting. We scoffed a baked salmon fillet stuffed with scallops and accompanied by spuds (159kr) and washed it down with an excellent glass of wine (available by the glass) and felt utterly satisfied.

Bastionen & Løven (Map pp62-3; ☎ 32 95 09 40; www.bastionen-loven.dk; Lille Molle, Christianshavns Voldgade 50; mains 105-170kr; 🕑 lunch & dinner) The elegant Scandinavian interior of this charming establishment is reason enough to come, but on a sunny day you'll find yourself yearning to sit outside in this tranquil windmill-by-the-water setting. And possibly, the fact that the interior seems to be riddled with smoke (cigars are popular) might push you out. The whole place feels like a wonderful secret – although the weekend brunch sessions can get mighty packed with local regulars.

Nørreport to Nørrebro

BUDGET

Picnic (Map pp62-3; ☎ 35 39 09 53; Fælledvej 22; mezze from 28kr; lunch & dinner) Delightful little place is a casual, cosy operation with deli-style dishes, including a variety of vegetable and Mediterranean/Middle Eastern salads. Most everything they serve is organic and it's a charming spot for a Turkish coffee or tea. The décor, a blend of Scandi-meets-souq is another bonus.

Govindas (Map pp70-1; ☎ 33 33 74 44; Nørre Farimagsgade 82; thali 69kr; dinner 4.30-9.30pm Mon-Sat) Govinda's serves savoury Indian-style vegetarian food in a pleasant setting with mellow music. Hare Krishna devotees cook up a nine-dish thali meal of basmati rice, soup, salad and a few hot dishes such as eggplant casserole for bargain prices, meaning that the place is very popular with students and travellers. Govindas is run as a business rather than a venue for converting new members, so there's no religious hard-sell, just good, wholesome food.

MID-RANGE

Selfish (Map pp62-3; ☎ 35 35 96 26; www.selfish.dk; Elmegade 4; sushi menu 70-230kr; lunch & dinner noon-9pm Tue-Sat, 5-9pm Sun) Great name this, although space is at a premium and there's no alcohol licence. If you don't fancy fighting for one of the five seats on the premises, you can easily order sushi (and Japanese beers) to take away – and it's very good sushi too. Hand rolls cost 60kr, but if you're sharing, go for the 'xx large platter' (230kr) and try and find room inside yourself, let alone here.

TOP END

Sticks 'n' Sushi (Map pp62-3; ☎ 33 11 14 07; www.sushi.dk; Nansensgade 59; menus 265-485kr; dinner) Handy Japanese restaurant has added some local twists to its menu to make things more appealing to Danes. Many of the items, such as sushi rolls, are served on sticks popsicle-style, similar to the way grilled items such as yakitori are served in Japan. The range of menus is extensive – our favourite (which is happily shared between two people) was the Pay Day Menu (485kr) – we're still salivating at the thought of its melt-in-the-mouth beef tenderloin foie gras.

> **TO MARKET, TO MARKET...**
>
> Copenhagen's main produce market is at Israels Plads, a few minutes' walk west of Nørreport station. Stalls are set up until 5pm Monday to Friday and until 2pm on Saturday, when it doubles as a flea market.

DRINKING

When locals want to go out for a drink (and they pretty much always do), they generally head for cosy places (read: candlelit and full of cigarette smoke), and consequently cafés play a leading role in the city's social scene. They not only serve alcohol, but also brunch, meals and snacks. Some cafés add music to the mix, particularly at weekends. Areas famed for their café/bar scenes include Vesterbro and Nørrebro for hip hangouts that cater to the experimental/fashion-forward set, the area around Kronprinsensgade for the glossy beautiful people and the streets around Strøget or Nyhavn for *hygge*-hugging quintessentially Danish boltholes.

Bankeråt (Map pp62-3; ☎ 33 93 69 88; Ahlefeldtsgade 27; 10am-midnight Mon-Fri, 11am-midnight Sat & Sun) Our fave bar in all Copenhagen features taxidermied critters in outlandish get-ups in the windows and pickled customers in outlandish get-ups at the tables. Nurse a drink, a hangover, artistic pretensions or your secret crush in lugubrious style.

Bang og Jensen (Map pp62-3; ☎ 33 25 53 18; Istedgade 130; 8am-2am Mon-Fri, 10am-2am Sat, 10am-midnight Sun) Reborn chemist's serves fabulous brunches and treats all day and Danish eye candy all night, when DJs play and so do the patrons of this very cool spot.

Bar Rouge (☎ 33 45 98 23; www.barrougenights.com; Krsytalgade 22; 3pm-2am Fri & Sat) Aimed squarely at the cocktail set who like getting gussied up to hear smooth lounge sounds, this bar is a haven from the sometimes exuberant but immature drinking dens of the Latin Quarter. It might be a good idea to reserve a table.

Hviids Vinstue (Map pp70-1; ☎ 33 15 10 64; Kongens Nytorv 19; 1pm-1am Sun-Fri, 1pm –2am Sat) The city's oldest wine bar (from 1723) is a cosy, sometimes cramped, affair, with plenty of old-world ambience.

Oscar (Map pp62-3; ☎ 33 12 09 99; www.oscarbar café.dk; Rådhuspladsen 77; ⏰ noon-2am) Oscar is a stylish, easy-going spot where you'll find gay men and their female friends having a bite to eat or a drink. It's an airy space, with room to breathe and good meals of the day (generally pasta and soup dishes) in substantial quantities. Oscar can seem so low-key in daylight hours that you may not realise it's a 'gay' place till you spy the wall of fame, with portraits of Oscar Wilde (of course), and other friends of the Wizzard of Oz's Dorothy.

Pussy Galore's Flying Circus (Map pp62-3; ☎ 35 24 53 00; Sankt Hans Torv 30; ⏰ 8am-2am Mon-Fri, 9am-2am Sat & Sun) Jacobsen chairs, outdoor seating, an excellent cocktail list and some serious queues mean this place has still got some sort of 'it' factor for many locals.

Café Europa (Map pp70-1; ☎ 33 12 04 28; Amagertorv 1; ⏰ 9am-midnight Mon-Thu, 9am-1am Fri & Sat, 10am-midnight Sun) With an unbeatable location, this modern continental-style café sets up tables right on Højbro Plads on sunny days, making it a great place for people-watching.

Studenterhuset (Map pp70-1; ☎ 35 32 38 60; www.studenterhuset.ku.dk, in Danish; Købmagergade 52; ⏰ noon-6pm Mon, noon-midnight Tue, noon-2am Wed-Fri) Low-key student hang-out near the Rundetårn features some good light meals to soak up all the cheap beer that's on offer. Not a bad spot to catch some live music either, or the eye of feverish types with Che posters on their bedroom walls.

ENTERTAINMENT

Copenhagen is Scandinavia's party HQ. There are scores of backstreet cafés and clubs with live music and great DJs, cinemas are popular with film-literate locals, the 'high-brow' arts are often generously subsidised by the state and those into the more avant garde side of things won't have to look far to be stimulated. As a general rule, entry to bars and clubs is free from Monday to Thursday, while there's usually a cover charge at weekends or any time someone special is playing. Danes tend to be late-nighters and many places don't really start to get going until 11pm or midnight.

The free publications *Musik Kalenderen, Film Kalenderen* and *Teater Kalenderen* list entertainment and concert schedules in detail; they're available at the tourist office and various clubs, cafés and bars.

Most events can be booked through **BilletNet** (☎ 38 48 11 22; www.billetnet.dk), a service that's also available at all post offices.

Live Music

Copenhagen Jazz House (Map pp70-1; ☎ 33 15 03 66; www.jazzhouse.dk; Niels Hemmingsensgade 10; ⏰ 6pm-midnight Sun-Thu, 6pm-5am Fri & Sat) The city's leading jazz spot, featuring top Danish musicians and occasional international performers. The music runs the gamut from bebop to fusion jazz, and there's a large dance floor.

Loppen (Map pp62-3; ☎ 32 57 84 22; www.loppen.dk, in Danish; Bådsmandsstræde 43; admission 40-120kr; ⏰ Wed-Sat) Housed in an old warehouse in Christiania, this is a popular spot with some of the city's top bands, ranging from funk and soul to punk rock. At weekends, the live concerts are followed at 2am to 5am by a disco.

Mojo (Map pp62-3; ☎ 33 11 64 53; www.mojo.dk, in Danish; Løngangstræde 21; admission 30-60kr; ⏰ 8pm-5am) East of Tivoli, this is a great spot for blues, with live entertainment nightly and draught beer aplenty.

Night Clubs

Rust (Map pp62-3; ☎ 35 24 52 00; www.rust.dk; Guldbergsgade 8; admission 50-120kr; ⏰ 9pm-5am Wed-Sat) A thriving, smashing place that attracts one of the largest and coolest club crowds in Copenhagen. There's a choice of spaces here from nightclub to concert hall, and a wide variety of edgy modern music. Weekends see some earnest queuing. You'll need to be over 21 to enter the nightclub.

Stengade 30 (Map pp62-3; ☎ 35 36 09 38; www.stengade30.dk; Stengade 18; admission 30-90kr) In the Nørrebro area, Stengade 30 has a frequently lively alternative scene with everything from electronica and hip hop to Berlin-style techno and edgy international DJs like Miss Kittin and Ned Flanders. Big nights last until about 5am or thereabouts.

Vega (Map p103; ☎ 33 25 70 11; www.vega.dk; Enghavevej 40; admission 50-120kr; ⏰ nightclub: 11pm-5am Fri & Sat) In the Vesterbro area, this is one of Copenhagen's hippest spots with big-name rock, pop and jazz bands performing on its main stage (Store Vega) and underground acts on a smaller stage (Lille Vega). It's also home to a cool club that gets packed with seriously good-looking Vesterbro locals. Or you could try the heavenly Ideal Bar (⏰ 7pm-4am Thu, 7pm-5am Fri & Sat).

Ballet, Opera, Theatre & Classical Music

There are also a few smaller theatres in Copenhagen that stage performances of popular plays and musicals; programs are published in the daily newspapers, *Copenhagen This Week* and *Teater Kalenderen*.

Det Kongelige Teater (Map pp70-1; ☎ 33 69 69 69; www.kgl-teater.dk; Kongens Nytorv; tickets 60-1000kr) Den Kongelige Ballet (the Royal Ballet) and Den Kongelige Opera (the Royal Opera) perform at this theatre. The season runs from mid-August to late May, skipping the main summer months.

Tivoli Koncertsal (Concert Hall; Map p67; ☎ 33 15 10 12; www.tivoli.dk; Tietgensgade 30) is the venue for symphony orchestra, string quartet and other classical music performances by Danish and international musicians. There's a ballet festival each season with top international troupes, as well as cabaret performances. They also have modern dance performances by such big names as the Alvin Ailey dance troupe. Tickets are sold at the Tivoli Billetcenter (below).

BOOKING OFFICES

The **Tivoli Billetcenter** (Map p67; ☎ 33 15 10 12; Vesterbrogade 3; 🕑 10am-8pm Mon-Fri, 11am-5pm Sat & Sun) At the main Tivoli entrance and good for tickets of any kind. Not only does it sell Tivoli performance tickets, but it's also the box office for ARTE, which handles tickets for plays in Copenhagen; and an agent for BilletNet, which sells tickets for concerts and music festivals nationwide.

Cinemas

First-release movies are shown on about 20 screens in the group of cinemas along Vesterbrogade between Rådhuspladsen and Central Station. Tickets for movies range from around 50kr for weekday matinees to 75kr for weekend evenings. As in the rest of Denmark, movies are generally shown in their original language with Danish subtitles.

Cinemateket (Map pp70-1; ☎ 33 74 34 12; www.dfi.dk; Gothersgade 55; admission 50kr; 🕑 10am-10pm Tue-Fri, noon-10pm Sat & Sun) The Danish Film Institute's wonderful cinema plays classic Danish and foreign films. There's also an excellent shop and restaurant on the swanky premises.

Dagmar Teatret (Map pp70-1; ☎ 33 14 32 22; www.sandrewmetronome.dk, in Danish; Jernbanegade 2; admission 50-70kr; 🕑 11.30am-9.45pm) A good central theatre that plays mostly art house films, although a few mainstream gems sneak into the mix.

Grand Teatret (Map pp70-1; ☎ 33 15 16 11; www.grandteatret.dk, in Danish; Mikkel Bryggersgade 8; admission 50-70kr; 🕑 noon-9.40pm) Just off Strøget, this comfortable theatre shows films from the mainstream end of cinema.

Palladium (Map p67; ☎ 70 13 12 11; www.biobooking.dk; Vesterbrogade 1; admission 50-75kr; 🕑 11.30am-10pm) Shows current-release films in their original language. The cinema is in the Rådhusarkden Shopping Centre.

SHOPPING

Along Copenhagen's touristy main shopping street, Strøget, you can find numerous shops selling everything from chain-store clothing to exquisite Danish porcelain, silverware and electronics. Other prime shopping strips include Kronprinsensgade for designer labels and cutting-edge fashion, streets such as Elmgade, Blågårdsgade and Ravnsborggade in Nørrebro for streetwear, edgy fashion and retro Danish home wares, Istedgade for crazy kitsch gifts, Frederiksborggade for outdoorsy accessories, Vændemsvej for gourmet providores, Pisserenden (Piss Streets) – the chunk of town in the Latin Quarter that is hemmed in by Strøget, Norre Voldgade and Nørregade – which is good for books, music and fashion.

Danish Delights

AC Perch (Map pp70-1; ☎ 33 15 35 62; www.perchs-the.dk; Kronprinsensgade 5; 🕑 9am-5.30pm Mon-Thu, 9am-7pm Fri, 9.30am-2.30pm Sat; bus No 350S) North of Strøget, this fabulously beautiful family-run tea shop (since 1835) is much loved for its blends and quality leaves (the Darjeeling First Flush is justifiably famous). And it's been given the royal seal of approval to boot. Coffee fiends need not apply.

Birger Christensen (Map pp70-1; ☎ 33 11 55 55; Østergade 38; 🕑 10am-6pm Mon-Thu, 10am-7pm Fri, 10am-4pm Sat; metro Kongens Nytorv) Long-running temple of style stocks international heavy-hitters such as Prada, Chanel, YSL and other assorted labels that leave you reeling with fashionitis. Animal lovers take note: they still sell fur here. And lots of it come winter.

Lust (Map pp70-1; ☎ 33 33 01 10; www.lust.dk; Mikkel Bryggersgade 3A; 🕑 11am-7pm Mon-Thu, 11am-9pm Fri, 11am-6pm Sat; train Central Station, bus Nos 2A, 5A, 6A, 250S, among others) If Istedgade's sex shops are a little too red-light for your tastes, then this soothing pink-hued 'boudoir' will calm your nerves. Run by two women and catering to tastes that are more into, well, lust, than hard-core porn, this is the spot where you can find the writings of the Marquis de Sade, blindfolds and leopard-print vibrators.

Munthe Plus Simonsen (Map pp70-1; ☎ 33 32 03 12; Grønnegade 10; ⏰ 10am-6pm Mon-Thu, 10am-7pm Fri, 10am-4pm Sat; bus No 350S) Local gals flock to this stunning flagship store of local label Munthe Plus Simonsen. The look is part boho-chic, part ethno-dress ups, part luxe detailing, part Stevie Nicks at her most coke-addled.

Danish Design & Homewares

Bang & Olufsen (Map pp70-1; ☎ 33 15 04 22; www.bang-olufsen.com; Østergade 3; ⏰ 10am-5.30pm Mon-Thu, 10am-6pm Fri, 10am-2pm Sat) For sleek, top-priced audio and televisual equipment, it's hard to go past this uber-stylish brand. The shop itself is a high-tech marvel that has design nuts drooling.

Dansk Møbelkunst (Map pp62-3; ☎ 33 32 38 37; Bredgade 32; 10am-6pm Mon-Fri, 10am-3pm Sat) Filled with the very best of 20th-century Scandinavian furniture and design, this excellent shop had us wondering: 'Would they mind if we moved in?'

Georg Jensen (Map pp70-1; ☎ 33 11 40 80; www.georgejensen.dk; Amagertorv 4; ⏰ 10am-6pm Mon-Thu, 10am-7pm Fri, 10am-5pm Sat) Beautifully modern store features wonderful Danish silverwork, including cutlery, watches and jewellery.

Royal Copenhagen Porcelain (Map pp70-1; ☎ 33 13 71 81; Amagertorv 6; ⏰ 10am-6pm Mon-Thu, 10am-7pm Fri, 10am-5pm Sat) Famous for its Flora Danica pattern, Royal Copenhagen Porcelain is in an imposing Renaissance house (c 1616) near Højbro Plads. Lovingly crafted porcelain items inspire much self-conscious care when handled by everyone.

Department Stores

Illums Bolighus (Map pp70-1; ☎ 33 13 71 81; Amagertorv 10; ⏰ 10am-6pm Mon-Thu, 10am-7pm Fri, 10am-5pm Sat) Fabulous-looking store, by appointment to Queen Margrethe II, stocks wonderful Danish-designed furniture, down comforters, ceramics, silverware and glass, and is also a good place to look for simple yet stylish gifts such as a quality toy or kitchen utensil. There's a small but natty selection of clothes and shoes.

Illum (Map pp70-1; ☎ 33 14 40 02; www.illim.dk; Østergade 52; ⏰ 10am-7pm Mon-Thu, 10am-8pm Fri, 9am-5pm Sat) Large department store has a fabulous range of essential wares arranged around its central glass dome. It has a slightly more upmarket feel than Magasin du Nord.

Magasin du Nord (Map pp70-1; ☎ 33 11 44 33; www.magasin.dk; Kongens Nytorv 13; ⏰ 10am-7pm Mon-Thu, 10am-8pm Fri, 10am-5pm Sat) The city's largest (and oldest) department store, it covers an entire block on the southwestern side of Kongens Nytorv, and stocks everything from clothing and luggage to books and groceries.

GETTING THERE & AWAY

Air

Copenhagen's wonderful airport is Scandinavia's busiest hub, with flights from over 100 cities across the world. There are direct flights to Copenhagen from Europe, Asia and North America, as well as a handful of Danish cities. For more details about flying to and from Copenhagen see p305.

COPENHAGEN AIRPORT

The modern international airport is in Kastrup, 9km southeast of Copenhagen city centre, and sees about 1.7million passengers each year. It has good eating, retail and information facilities.

If you're waiting for a flight, note that this is a 'silent' airport and there are no boarding calls, although there are numerous monitor screens throughout the terminal.

Boat

A daily sailing between Oslo and Copenhagen and Bornholm and Copenhagen, leaves from Kvæsthusbroen, north of Nyhavn. See www.dfdsseaways.com or www.bornholmferries.dk for more details, or p310. **Polferries** (www.polferries.com.pl) operates boats to Świnoujście in Poland, leaving from Nordre Toldbod, east of Kastellet five times a week. Cruise ships use Langelinie harbour.

Bus

International buses to several European cities are operated by **Eurolines** (Map pp62-3; ☎ 33 88 70 00; www.eurolines.dk; Reventlowsgade 8), which has a ticket office behind Central Station. Long-distance buses leave from Central Station, though some buses, including those to Oslo, also stop at Copenhagen airport. For more information see p312.

Car & Motorcycle
The main highways into Copenhagen are the E20 from Jutland and Funen (and continuing towards Malmö in Sweden) and the E47 from Helsingør and Sweden. If you're coming from the north on the E47, exit onto Lyngbyvej (Rte 19) and continue south to reach the heart of the city.

Train
All long-distance trains arrive at and depart from Central Station, a huge complex with numerous services including currency exchange, a post office and a supermarket. There are showers at the underground toilets opposite the police office.

GETTING AROUND
To/From the Airport
If you judge a city by how easy it is to get to/from the airport, Copenhagen takes top marks. The rail system speedily (and cheaply) links the airport arrival terminal directly with Copenhagen's Central Station. The trains run every 20 minutes until midnight from 4.55am on weekdays, 5.35am on Saturday and 6.35am on Sunday. The trip takes just 12 minutes and costs 25.50kr.

By taxi, it's about 15 minutes between the airport and the city centre, as long as traffic isn't too heavy. The cost is about 170kr.

Bicycle
Despite the motor traffic Copenhagen, with all its cycle paths, is a great city for getting around by bicycle.

Except during weekday rush hours, it's possible to carry bikes on S-trains (10kr per ticket). You can load your bicycle in any carriage that has a cycle symbol and you must stay with the bike at all times.

Cycle lanes are found along many city streets and virtually all of Copenhagen can be toured by bicycle, except for pedestrian-only streets such as Strøget. Bicycles are allowed to cross Strøget at Gammel Torv and Kongens Nytorv.

When touring the city, cyclists should be cautious of bus passengers who commonly step off the bus into the cycle lanes, and of pedestrians (particularly tourists) who sometimes absent-mindedly step off the kerb and into the path of oncoming cyclists.

Cycling maps, including a 1:50,000-scale map of the greater Copenhagen area called *Københavns Amt*, are produced by the Danish cycling federation, **Dansk Cyklist Forbund** (Map pp70-1; www.dcf.dk), and can be purchased at bookshops. For information on bicycle hire, see p80.

FREE CITY BIKES
The city of Copenhagen has a generous scheme, called **Bycykler** (City Bikes; ☎ 35 43 01 10; www.bycyklen.dk), in which anyone can borrow a bicycle for free. In all there are over 1000 bikes available from 1 May to 15 December.

Although these bicycles are not streamlined and are certainly not practical for long-distance cycling, that's part of the plan – use of the cycles is limited to the city centre. To deter theft and minimise maintenance, the bicycles have a distinctive design that includes solid spokeless wheels with puncture-resistant tyres. The bikes can be found at 125 widely scattered street stands in public places, including S-train stations.

The way it works is that if you're able to find a free bicycle, you deposit a 20kr coin in the stand to release the bike. When you're done using the bicycle, you can return it to any stand and get your 20kr coin back.

Car & Motorcycle
Except for the weekday-morning rush hour, when traffic can bottleneck coming into the city (and vice versa around 5pm), traffic in Copenhagen is generally manageable. Getting around by car is not problematic, except the usual challenge of finding an empty parking space in the most popular places.

To explore sights in the centre of the city, you're best off on foot or using public transport, but a car is convenient for getting to the suburban sights.

RENTAL
The following car hire companies have booths at the airport in the international terminal. Each also has an office in central Copenhagen:

Avis (Map pp62-3; ☎ 33 73 40 99; www.avis.dk; Kampmannsgade 1)

Budget (Map p62-3; ☎ 33 55 05 00; www.budget.dk; Helgolandsgade 2)

Europcar (Map p62-3; ☎ 33 55 99 00; www.europcar.dk; Gammel Kongevej 13)

Hertz (Map pp62-3; ☎ 33 17 90 21; www.hertzdk.dk; Ved Vesterport 3)

PARKING

For street parking, you buy a ticket from a kerbside *billetautomat* (automated ticket machine) and place it inside the windscreen. Copenhagen parking is zoned so that the spaces most in demand, such as those in the central commercial area, are the most costly. Your best bet is to search out a blue zone, where parking costs just 7kr per hour. If you can't find an empty blue space then opt for a green zone, where the fee is 12kr per hour. Avoid red zones, where the parking fee is 20kr per hour. Parking fees must be paid on weekdays from 8am to 6pm (to 8pm in red zones) and also on Saturday to 2pm in green zones and 8pm in red zones.

If you can't find street parking, there are car parks at the main department stores, at the Radisson SAS Royal Hotel and on Jernbanegade, east of Axeltorv. *Parkeringforbudt* means 'no parking' and is generally accompanied by a round sign with a red diagonal slash. You can stop for up to three minutes to unload bags and passengers. A round sign with a red 'X', or a sign saying *Stopforbud*, means that no stopping at all is allowed. Parking ticket fines will set you back 510kr.

Public Transport

Copenhagen has an extensive public transit system consisting of a metro, rail and bus

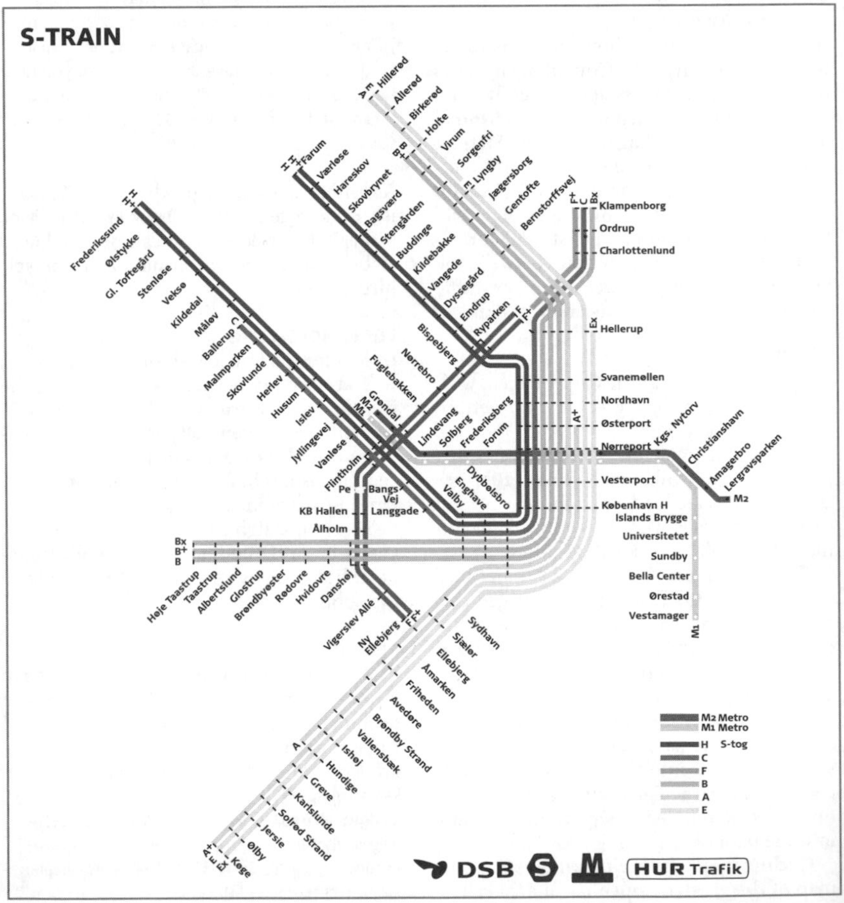
S-TRAIN
Hillerød
Allerød
Birkerød
Holte
Virum
Sorgenfri
Lyngby
Jægersborg
Gentofte
Bernstorffsvej
Klampenborg
Ordrup
Charlottenlund
Hellerup
Svanemøllen
Nordhavn
Østerport
Nørreport
Kgs. Nytorv
Christianshavn
Amagerbro
Lergravsparken
M2
Vesterport
København H
Islands Brygge
Universitetet
Sundby
Bella Center
Ørestad
Vestamager
M1
Farum
Værløse
Hareskov
Skovbrynet
Bagsværd
Stengården
Buddinge
Kildebakke
Vangede
Dyssegård
Emdrup
Ryparken
Bispebjerg
Nørrebro
Fuglebakken
Grøndal
Lindevang
Solbjerg
Frederiksberg
Forum
Frederikssund
Ølstykke
Gl. Toftegård
Stenløse
Veksø
Kildedal
Måløv
Ballerup
Malmparken
Skovlunde
Herlev
Husum
Islev
Jyllingevej
Vanløse
Flintholm
Pe
Bangs Vej
KB Hallen
Langgade
Ålholm
Valby
Enghave
Dybbølsbro
Høje Taastrup
Taastrup
Albertslund
Glostrup
Brøndbyøster
Rødovre
Hvidovre
Danshøj
Vigerslev Allé
Ny Ellebjerg
Sydhavn
Sjælør
Ellebjerg
Amarken
Friheden
Avedøre
Brøndby Strand
Vallensbæk
Ishøj
Hundige
Greve
Karlslunde
Solrød Strand
Jersie
Ølby
Køge
M2 Metro
M1 Metro
H S-tog
C
F
B
A
E
DSB
HUR Trafik

network. The brand-new metro system – which is driverless – connects the east and west of Copenhagen via the city centre. Parts of the system are still under construction until 2007, when it will finally connect with the airport. The S-train network has 11 lines passing through Central Station (København H), and a vast bus system called HUR (Hovedstadsens Udviklingsråd), the main terminus of which is at Rådhuspladsen, a couple of blocks to the northeast.

BUSES & TRAINS

Buses and trains use a common fare system based on the number of zones you pass through. The basic fare of 17kr for up to two zones covers most city runs and allows transfers between buses and trains on a single ticket as long as they're made within an hour. Third and subsequent zones cost 8.50kr more, with a maximum fare of 59.50kr for travel throughout North Zealand. DSB, the national railway, also includes its lines in the common fare system as far north as Helsingør, west to Roskilde and south to Køge.

On buses, you board at the front and pay the fare to the driver (or stamp your clip card in the machine next to the driver). On S-trains, tickets are purchased at the station and then punched in the yellow time clock on the platform before boarding the train.

Instead of buying a single destination ticket, you can buy a *klippekort* (clip card) that is valid for 10 rides in two zones (105kr) or three zones (145kr), or you can get a 24-hour ticket valid for unlimited travel in all zones (100kr). Passengers who are stopped and found to be without a stamped ticket are liable to a fine of 500kr.

Up to two children aged under 10 travel free when accompanied by an adult. Otherwise those aged under 16 travel half-price.

COPENHAGEN CARD

The Copenhagen Card is a tourist pass that allows unlimited travel on buses and trains in Copenhagen and throughout North Zealand, as well as free admission to about 60 of the region's museums and attractions.

An adult card costs 199/399kr for 24/72 hours; a child's card costs 129/229kr for the same period. Cards can be purchased at Central Station, at tourist offices and in some hotels. Days are calculated on a 24-hour basis; for example, if you begin a one-day card on Saturday at 6pm, it's valid until Sunday at 5:59pm.

If you want to run through a lot of sightseeing in a few days, the Copenhagen Card can be a real bargain. For a more leisurely exploration of select places it may work out cheaper to pay individual admission charges and use one of the transport passes.

Trains and buses generally run from about 5am (6am on Sunday) to around 12.30am, though buses continue to run through the night (charging double the usual fare) on a few main routes.

The free Copenhagen city maps that are distributed by the tourist office show bus routes (with numbers) and are very useful for finding your way around the city. If you plan to use buses extensively, you might want to buy HUR's hefty timetable book *Busser og tog* (40kr), which comes with a colour-coded bus route map (covering the entire HUR route throughout North Zealand), or get just the map for 5kr. Both are sold at HUR's information office on Rådhuspladsen.

Throughout this chapter the bus numbers of some of the more frequent buses to individual destinations are listed, but since there can be as many as a dozen buses passing any particular place, our listing is often only a partial one.

For schedules or more details try: **HUR** (☎ 36 13 14 15; www.hur.dk, in Danish; 🕑 7am-9.30pm), **DSB S-tog** (☎ 33 14 17 01; www.dsb.dk/s-tog, in Danish; 🕑 6.30am-10pm), **DSB trains** (☎ 70 13 14 15; www.dsb.dk, in Danish; 🕑 7am-10pm) or **Metro** (☎ 70 15 16 15; www.m.dk; 🕑 9am-4pm Mon-Fri).

Taxi

Taxis with signs saying *fri* can be flagged down or you can call **Københavns Taxa** (☎ 35 35 35 35) or **Taxa Motor** (☎ 38 10 10 10). The cost is 23kr at flag fall, plus about 10kr per kilometre (13kr at night and at weekends). Most taxis accept credit cards. A service charge is included in the fare, so tips are not expected.

AROUND COPENHAGEN

Many places in the greater Copenhagen area make for quick and easy excursions from the city. If you're hankering for woodlands, lakes, beaches and historic areas, the mix of destinations that follows should satisfy. For other day-trip possibilities a bit further afield, see the North Zealand chapter (p105).

ARKEN MUSEUM OF MODERN ART

Sometimes controversial, the **Ark** (Map p103; ☎ 43 54 02 22; www.arken.dk; Skovvej 100; adult/child 70/30kr; 🕑 10am-5pm Tue & Thu-Sun, 10am-9pm Wed) is a substantial contemporary art museum on the coast at Ishøj, 17km south of central Copenhagen. Opened in 1996, the stark modernist building rises above the beach and is as much a work of art as the exhibits inside. The Arken collection features the works of leading Danish artists since 1945 (such as Per Bak Jensen, Per Kirkeby and Asger Jorn), with an emphasis on photo-based art, sculpture and installations. Changing exhibits showcase works such as those by the artists from the regional Cobra (Copenhagen-Brussels-Amsterdam) movement and paintings by the Norwegian artist Edvard Munch. There's plenty to keep children intrigued too. To get here, take S-train to Ishøj station, then bus No 128 from there.

DRAGØR

If Copenhagen begins to feel crowded, consider an afternoon excursion to Dragør, a maritime town on the island of Amager, a few kilometres south of the airport. In the early 1550s Christian II allowed Dutch farmers to settle in Amager to provide his court with flowers and produce, and the town of Dragør still retains a bit of Dutch flavour.

Along the waterfront you'll find smokehouses, fishing boats and the **Dragør Museum** (Map 103; ☎ 32 53 41 06; www.dragoermuseum.dk, in Danish; Havnepladsen 2; adult/child 20/10kr; 🕑 noon-4pm Tue-Sun 1 May-30 Sep), a half-timbered house featuring model ships and period furnishings.

A fun way to spend time is to simply wander the narrow, winding cobblestone streets leading up from the harbour, which are lined with the thatch-roofed, mustard-coloured houses comprising the **old town**. One interesting little ramble is to take Strandgade, a pedestrian alley that begins opposite the museum, and continue up to Badstuevælen, an old square lined with some attractive houses dating from the 1790s (especially house Nos 8 and 12).

If you're in Dragør for lunch, you'll find several places near the waterfront serving sandwiches, fish and chips and other fare.

You can get to Dragør via bus No 30, 36 or 350S from central Copenhagen.

CHARLOTTENLUND

Charlottenlund is a well-to-do coastal suburb just beyond the northern outskirts of Copenhagen. Despite being so close to the city, it has a decent **sandy beach**, although the smokestacks of Hellerup to the south are part of the backdrop.

Danmarks Akvarium (Map 103; ☎ 39 62 32 83; www.akvar ium.dk; Kavalergården 1; adult/child 70/35kr; 🕑 10am-6pm mid-Feb–mid-Oct, 10am-4pm mid-Oct–mid-Feb) is 500m north of the beach on the inland side of the road. By Scandinavian standards it's a fairly large aquarium. The collection is well-presented and includes both cold-water and tropical fish, colourful live corals, nurse sharks, sea turtles, crocodiles and piranhas.

To get here, take S-train Line C to Charlottenlund.

KLAMPENBORG

Klampenborg, being only 20 minutes from Central Station on S-train line C, is one of the favourite spots for Copenhageners on family outings.

A few hundred metres east of Klampenborg station is **Bellevue beach** (see p80), a sandy stretch that gets packed with sunbathers in summer.

An 800m walk west from Klampenborg station is the 400-year-old **Bakken** (Map p103; ☎ 39 63 55 44; www.bakken.dk, in Danish; Dyrehavevej 62; admission free; 🕑 Vary but generally open by 2 pm, until 10 pm & often midnight daily. Closed Sep-Apr), the world's oldest amusement park (it opened in the 16th century). A blue-collar version of Tivoli, it's a honky-tonk carnival of bumper cars, roller coasters, slot machines and beer halls. Children's rides cost around 25kr, adult rides about double that and there are discounted multi-use passes.

Bakken is at the southern edge of **Dyrehaven** (more formally called Jægersborg Dyrehave), an expansive 1000-hectare area of beech trees and meadows crisscrossed by an alluring network of walking and cycling trails. Dyrehaven was established as a royal hunting ground in 1669 and has evolved into the capital's most popular picnicking area.

At the centre of Dyrehaven is the old manor house **Eremitagen**, a good vantage point to spot herds of grazing deer, which

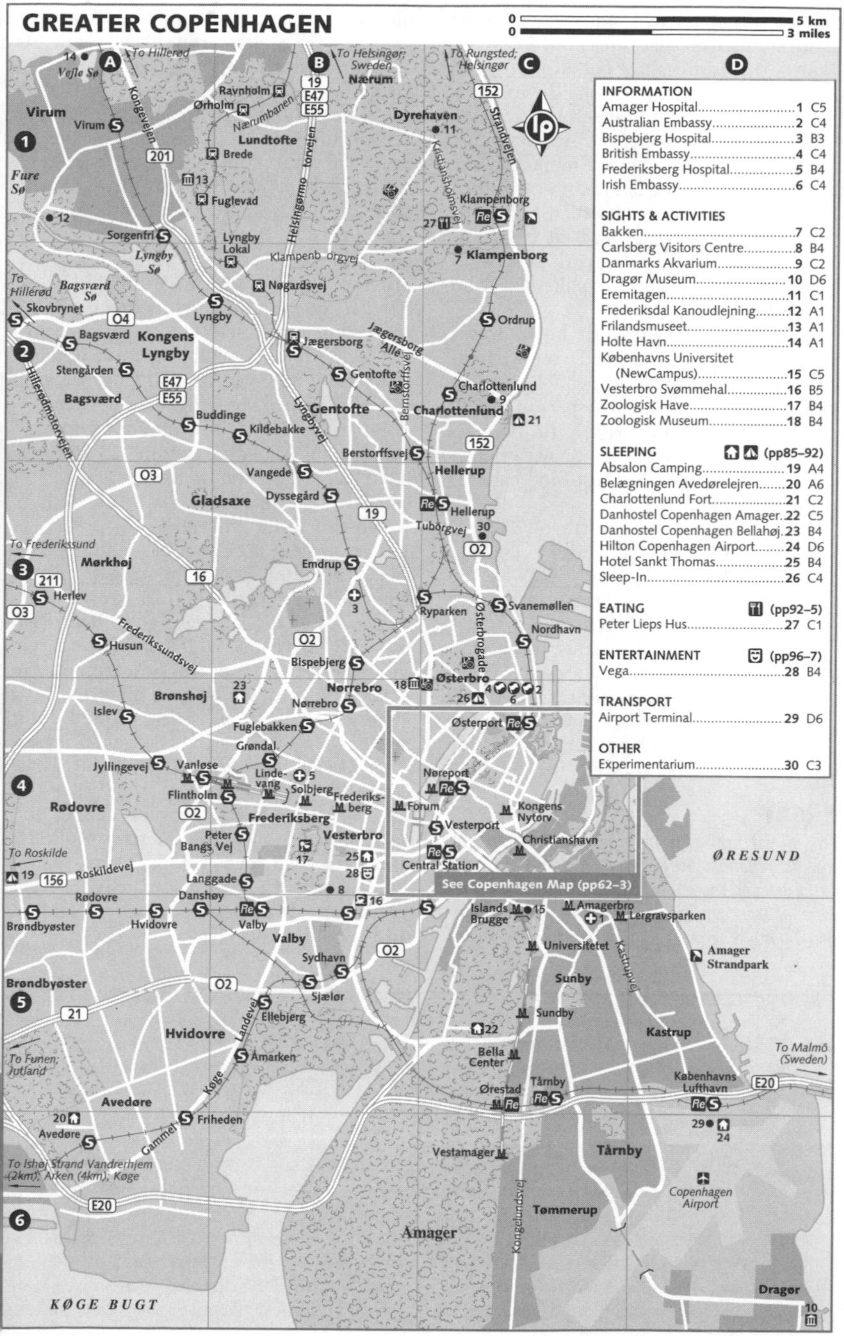
GREATER COPENHAGEN
0 5 km
0 3 miles
INFORMATION
Amager Hospital 1 C5
Australian Embassy 2 C4
Bispebjerg Hospital 3 B3
British Embassy 4 C4
Frederiksberg Hospital 5 B4
Irish Embassy 6 C4
SIGHTS & ACTIVITIES
Bakken 7 C2
Carlsberg Visitors Centre 8 B4
Danmarks Akvarium 9 C2
Dragør Museum 10 D6
Eremitagen 11 C1
Frederiksdal Kanoudlejning 12 A1
Frilandsmuseet 13 A1
Holte Havn 14 A1
Københavns Universitet (NewCampus) 15 C5
Vesterbro Svømmehal 16 B5
Zoologisk Have 17 B4
Zoologisk Museum 18 B4
SLEEPING (pp85–92)
Absalon Camping 19 A4
Belægningen Avedørelejren 20 A6
Charlottenlund Fort 21 C2
Danhostel Copenhagen Amager 22 C5
Danhostel Copenhagen Bellahøj 23 B4
Hilton Copenhagen Airport 24 D6
Hotel Sankt Thomas 25 B4
Sleep-In 26 C4
EATING (pp92–5)
Peter Lieps Hus 27 C1
ENTERTAINMENT (pp96–7)
Vega 28 B4
TRANSPORT
Airport Terminal 29 D6
OTHER
Experimentarium 30 C3
See Copenhagen Map (pp62–3)
ØRESUND
KØGE BUGT
To Hillerød
To Helsingør; Sweden
To Rungsted; Helsingør
To Frederikssund
To Roskilde
To Funen; Jutland
To Ishøj Strand Vandrerhjem (2km); Arken (4km); Køge
To Malmö (Sweden)
Virum
Lundtofte
Dyrehaven
Klampenborg
Kongens Lyngby
Bagsværd
Gentofte
Charlottenlund
Hellerup
Gladsaxe
Mørkhøj
Brønshøj
Nørrebro
Østerbro
Rødovre
Frederiksberg
Vesterbro
Valby
Brøndbyøster
Hvidovre
Avedøre
Sunby
Kastrup
Tårnby
Tømmerup
Amager
Dragør
Copenhagen Airport
Amager Strandpark

are especially abundant in the meadows west of the house. In all, there are about 2000 deer in the park, mostly fallow but also some red and Japanese sika deer. Among the red deer are a few rare white specimens, descendants of deer imported in 1737 from Germany, where they are now extinct. Eremitagen can be reached by walking 2km north of Bakken along the main route, Kristiansholmsvej, although it can also be reached from numerous other points in the park as most of the largest trails radiate like spokes out from Eremitagen.

Hackney carriages provide horse-drawn rides into the park from the Dyrehaven entrance just north of Klampenborg S-train station. Rides cost 60kr per person for 30 minutes; the coaches carry up to five passengers, but it's most romantic with two…

Bakken has numerous fast-food eateries selling carnival fare.

A few minutes' walk north of Bakken, **Peter Lieps Hus** (Map p103; ☎ 39 64 07 86; Dyrehaven 8; mains 96-188kr; ⌚ 11am-9pm Tue-Sun), is the quintessential Danish country restaurant occupies an historic thatch-roofed house and is good for a nice relaxing meal, with smørrebrød, venison specialities and other Danish food (including children's portions of *frikadeller* – meatballs – and chips). On sunny days it's a popular place to sit outside and watch the horse and buggies go by.

LYNGBY

The main sight of interest in the Lyngby area is **Frilandsmuseet** (Map p103; ☎ 33 13 44 11; www.natmus.dk; Kongevejen 100; adult/child 25kr/free, free Wed; ⌚ 10am-5pm Tue-Sun 3 Apr-30 Sep, 10am-4pm Tue-Sun 1-24 Oct), a sprawling open-air museum of old countryside dwellings that have been gathered from sites around Denmark. Its 100-plus historic buildings are arranged in groupings that provide a sense of Danish rural life as it was in various regions and across different social strata. The houses range from rather grand affairs to meagre, sod-roofed cottages. Many of the buildings are furnished from the period: the smithy is equipped with irons and a hearth, and the post mill still has functioning sails. Grazing farm animals, selected from old Danish breeds, and costumed field workers add an element of authenticity (mostly in odour) to the scene. There's a light schedule of demonstrations such as folk dancing, weaving and pottery making, mostly on weekends.

Frilandsmuseet is a 10-minute signposted walk from Sorgenfri station, 25 minutes from Central Station on S-train line B. You can also take bus No 184 or 194, both of which stop at the entrance.

The Lyngby area also has a number of lakes, including **Furesø**, the deepest lake in Denmark. It's possible to hire rowing boats or canoes at the lakeside kiosk, **Holte Havn** (Map p103; ☎ 45 42 04 49; 22 Vejlesøvej; per hr 80kr; ⌚ 10am-9pm), and row around Furesø or the smaller Vejlesø, which are connected by a channel. Holte Havn is near Holte S-train station, two stops north of Sorgenfri. **Frederiksdal Kanoudlejning** (Map p103; ☎ 45 85 67 70; www.frdal.dk; Nybrovej 520; boat hire from 100kr; ⌚ 10am-8pm Tue-Sun), by the locks, hires out canoes and rowing boats for use on the river Mølleåen and the lakes Lyngby Sø, Bagsværd Sø and Furesø, which are interconnected. To get there, get off at Sorgenfri S-train station and take bus No 191.

North Zealand

CONTENTS

Compact, congested with historical sights and beaches, Sweden just across the sound, pastoral idylls interrupted only by picture postcard vistas – North Zealand deserves to be the most travelled region in the country. Almost all its destinations are easily accessible from Copenhagen by public transport and, if you blink while driving, you'll miss your turn-off.

The geography is fortuitous, lending itself to an easy loop north to Kronborg Slot, Hamlet's castle in Helsingør, to Hornbæk where the rich and beautiful sunbathe and then west along the coast to more subdued but equally beautiful Tisvildeleje. From there it's a short way south to impressive Frederiksborg Slot in Hillerød and then to the fjord town of Roskilde, where you can learn about the country's Viking past. There are other worthy stops along the way, including Louisiana, the modern-art museum in Humlebæk, Fredensborg Slot where Danish royalty still resides and several other relaxing north-shore beaches.

Keep in mind that the Copenhagen Card allows free access to trains, buses and most sightseeing attractions throughout North Zealand.

If you're driving between Helsingør and Copenhagen, ignore the motorway and take the coastal road, Strandvej (Route 152), which is far more scenic.

Information on Charlottenlund, Lyngby and Klampenborg, just north of Copenhagen, is in the Around Copenhagen section at the end of the Copenhagen chapter.

HIGHLIGHTS

- Soak up the rays on the broad sandy beaches at Hornbæk and **Tisvildeleje** (p120)
- Marvel at the magnificent lakeside **Frederiksborg Slot** and its glorious gardens (p114)
- Stroll through history at massive Kronborg Slot, the setting for Shakespeare's **Hamlet** (p111)
- Browse Denmark's most renowned modern-art collection at **Louisiana**, where the museum itself is an architectural delight (p109)
- Paddle your own Viking ship and party at northern Europe's largest **rock music event** (p125)

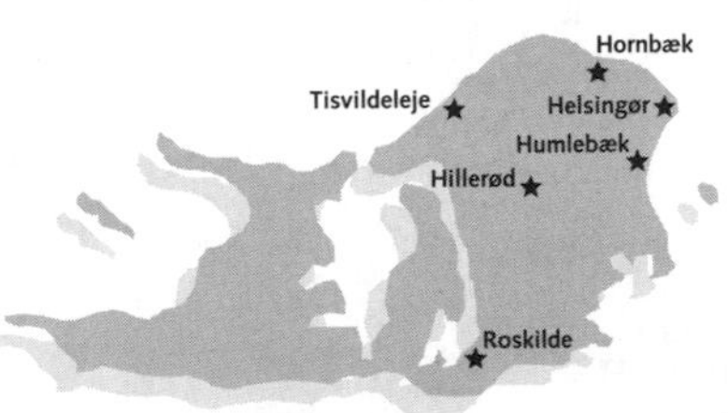
Hornbæk
Tisvildeleje
Helsingør
Humlebæk
Hillerød
Roskilde

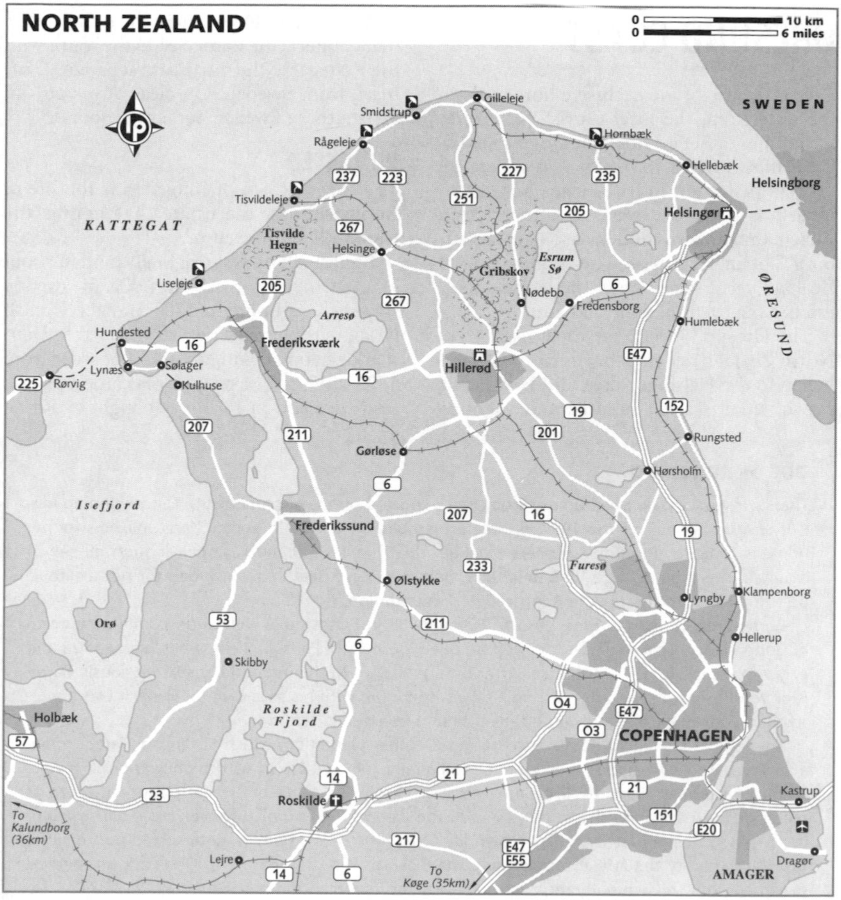
NORTH ZEALAND
0 10 km
0 6 miles
SWEDEN
Helsingborg
KATTEGAT
ØRESUND
Gilleleje
Smidstrup
Rågeleje
Hornbæk
Hellebæk
Helsingør
Tisvildeleje
Tisvilde Hegn
Helsinge
Esrum Sø
Gribskov
Nødebo
Fredensborg
Liseleje
Arresø
Humlebæk
Hundested
Frederiksværk
Hillerød
Lynæs
Sølager
Rørvig
Kulhuse
Gørløse
Rungsted
Hørsholm
Isefjord
Frederikssund
Furesø
Ølstykke
Lyngby
Klampenborg
Orø
Hellerup
Skibby
Roskilde Fjord
Holbæk
COPENHAGEN
Roskilde
Kastrup
To Kalundborg (36km)
Lejre
To Køge (35km)
Dragør
AMAGER
237
223
227
235
251
205
267
6
16
225
E47
207
211
152
19
201
53
233
O4
O3
57
14
21
23
151
E20
217
E55
lp

Getting There & Away

Almost all parts of North Zealand can be reached from Copenhagen in less than an hour – and usually quicker if you have your own transportation. The Copenhagen Card (see p101) can be used for many trips via bus or train in the area.

A few trains leave every hour travelling north from Copenhagen – however, you'll miss the beautiful view of the water. Take bus No 388 from Klampenborg (the last stop on C or F line of the S-train system) north to Helsingør for the full experience although it's slightly slower than the train.

Helsingør train station handles both thr DSB trains and the privately operated HHGB, which runs a regional service in North Zealand. Frequent trains operate throughout the day connecting the city with Copenhagen in 55 minutes.

Getting Around

A joint zone fare system embraces all HT/Copenhagen Transport buses and DSB/State Railway and S-trains in Metropolitan Copenhagen and North Zealand as well as some privately operated railway routes in the area (within an approximately 40km radius of Copenhagen). It's possible to change between train and bus routes on the same ticket.

To reach most of the north coast you must switch trains in either Hillerød or Helsingør.

ØRESUND COAST

Partly because of the exclusive homes along the waterfront, the local tourist authorities sometimes rather grandly refer to this area as the Danish Riviera. In reality its main appeal to visitors lies not in its beaches but in two museums – one dedicated to author Karen Blixen, the other to modern art – and Kronborg Slot in Helsingør. The annual Round Zealand yacht race, one of the world's largest, is a big event here in mid-June.

The Øresund Coast, the eastern shore of North Zealand, extends north from Copenhagen to the Helsingør area and is largely a run of small seaside suburbs and yachting harbours. The Øresund itself is the sound that connects the Baltic Sea to the south with the Kattegat to the north and separates Denmark from Sweden. On clear days you can see southern Sweden across the sound.

RUNGSTED

The coastal town of Rungsted is the site of Rungstedlund, the estate that houses the Karen Blixen museum.

Rungstedlund was originally built in about 1500 as an inn. King Karl XII of Sweden stayed there in about 1700 and the Danish lyric poet Johannes Ewald, who wrote Denmark's national anthem, was a boarder from 1773 to 1776. The property became a private residence and in 1879 was bought by Karen

OUT OF RUNGSTED

Thanks in part to the posthumous book sales spurred by the success of the Oscar-winning film *Out of Africa,* based on the 1937 landmark memoirs of her life in Kenya, Karen Blixen's former home is today a museum. For years after her death in 1962 there was only enough money to maintain the grounds as a bird sanctuary. Before Blixen's death she arranged for her estate to be turned over to the private Rungstedlund Foundation.

Born Karen Christenze Dinesen on 17 April 1885 in Rungsted, a well-to-do community north of Copenhagen, she studied art in Copenhagen, Rome and Paris. In 1914, when she was 28 and eager to escape from the confines of her bourgeois family, she married her second cousin Baron Bror von Blixen-Finecke, after having a failed love affair with his twin brother Hans. It was a marriage of convenience – she wanted his title and he needed her money.

The couple moved to Kenya and started a coffee plantation, which Karen was left to manage. The baron, who had several extramarital affairs, infected Blixen with syphilis though several medical historians claim her ill health was more likely the result of arsenic poisoning taken as medicine for the syphilis she feared she had. The diagnosis was probably even more damaging to her psyche since her father took his own life after contracting syphilis, determined not to suffer from the insanity thought to accompany the disease. She came home to Denmark for medical treatment, but subsequently returned to Africa and divorced the baron in 1925.

In 1932, after Blixen's coffee plantation had failed, the great love of her life, Englishman Denys Finch-Hatton, with whom she lived for six years, died in a tragic plane crash. The couple were played by Meryl Streep and Robert Redford in the film adaptation of *Out of Africa*. Soon after this Blixen left Africa, returned to the family estate in Rungsted and began to write. Danes were slow to take to Blixen's writings, in part because she consistently wrote about the aristocracy in approving terms and used an old-fashioned idiomatic style that some thought arrogant. Her insistence on being called 'Baroness' also took its toll on her popularity in a Denmark bent on minimising class disparity.

Following rejection by publishers in Denmark and England, Blixen's first book, *Seven Gothic Tales,* a compilation of short stories set in the 19th century, was published in New York in 1934 (under the pseudonym Isak Dinesen) and was so well received that it was chosen as a Book-of-the-Month selection. It was only after her success in the USA that Danish publishers took a serious interest in her works.

After the commercial success of *Out of Africa,* published in both Danish and English, other books followed: *Winter's Tales* in 1942, *The Angelic Avengers* in 1944, *Last Tales* in 1957, *Anecdotes of Destiny* in 1958 and *Shadows on the Grass* in 1960. Another Oscar-winning film, *Babette's Feast,* was based on her story about culinary artistry in small-town Denmark (see p37).

Blixen's father, Wilhelm Dinesen. Blixen was born at Rungstedlund in 1885 and lived there off and on until her death in 1962.

Sights

KAREN BLIXEN MUSEET

Karen Blixen's former home in Rungsted is now the **Karen Blixen museum** (☎ 45 57 10 57; www.karen-blixen.dk; Rungsted Strandvej 111; adult/child 40kr/free; 10am-5pm Tue-Sun May-Sep; 1-4pm Wed-Fri, 11am-4pm Sat & Sun Oct-Apr). It remains much the way she left it with photographs, Masai spears, paintings, shields and other mementoes of her time in Africa, such as the gramophone given to Blixen by her lover Denys Finch-Hatton. On her desk is the old Corona typewriter she used to write her novels.

One wing of the museum, a converted carriage house and stables, houses a library of Blixen's books, a café and bookshop; there's also an audiovisual presentation on her life. The grounds contain gardens and a wood, part of which has been set aside as a bird sanctuary. Blixen is buried near a sprawling beech tree, the grave marked by a simple stone slab inscribed with her name.

The museum is opposite the yacht harbour and 1.25km from the train station. To get there, walk north from the train station up Stationsvej, turn right at the lights onto Rungstedvej and then, at its intersection with Rungsted Strandvej, walk south about 300m and you'll come to the museum.

If you'd like to walk through the museum's bird sanctuary on the way back to the train station, ask at the museum desk for the free *Garden and Bird Sanctuary* brochure, which maps out the route.

Getting There & Away

Trains to Rungsted run every 20 minutes from Copenhagen (45.50kr, 30 minutes) and Helsingør (27.50kr, 25 minutes).

HUMLEBÆK

pop 8600

The coastal town of Humlebæk has a couple of harbours and bathing beaches and some wooded areas, but the main focus for visitors to the area is the modern-art museum called Louisiana.

Louisiana

Denmark's renowned modern-art museum, **Louisiana** (☎ 49 19 07 19; www.louisiana.dk; Gammel Strandvej 13; adult/student/child 74/67/20kr; 10am-5pm Thu-Tue, 10am-10pm Wed), is on a seaside knoll in a strikingly modernistic complex with sculpture-laden grounds. The sculptures on the lawns, which include works by Henry Moore, Alexander Calder and Max Ernst, create an engaging interplay between art, architecture and landscape. Louisiana is a fascinating place to visit even for those not passionate about modern art.

Selections from the museum's permanent collection, mainly paintings and graphic art from the postwar era, are creatively displayed and grouped. There are sections on constructivism, Cobra movement artists, minimalist art, abstract expressionism, pop art and staged photography. Works on display include those by such international luminaries as Pablo Picasso, Francis Bacon and Alberto Giacometti. Some of the more prominent Danish artists represented are Asger Jorn, Carl-Henning Pedersen, Robert Jacobsen, and Richard Mortensen. The museum also has top-notch temporary exhibitions.

If you're travelling with kids this is one museum that can be real fun. It has an entire children's wing where kids can explore their artistic talents using interactive computers and various hands-on mediums; ask about the free Friday afternoon workshops that attract lots of international youngsters.

The museum has a café with a picturesque setting and a shop selling art books, prints and motif mugs.

Louisiana is 1km from Humlebæk train station, a 10-minute signposted walk along Gammel Strandvej.

Getting There & Away

DSB trains leave Copenhagen frequently for Humlebæk, a ride that takes 40 minutes and costs 45.50kr. The train from Helsingør takes 12 minutes and costs 19.50kr.

HELSINGØR

pop 34,700

Helsingør (Elsinore), at the narrowest point of the Øresund, is a busy port but the top sight, perched across the harbour, is the imposing Kronborg Slot. It was made famous as Elsinore Castle in Shakespeare's *Hamlet,* which is performed in the castle courtyard almost every night in August. Kronborg Slot, on the northern side of town, was designated a Unesco World Heritage Site in 2000.

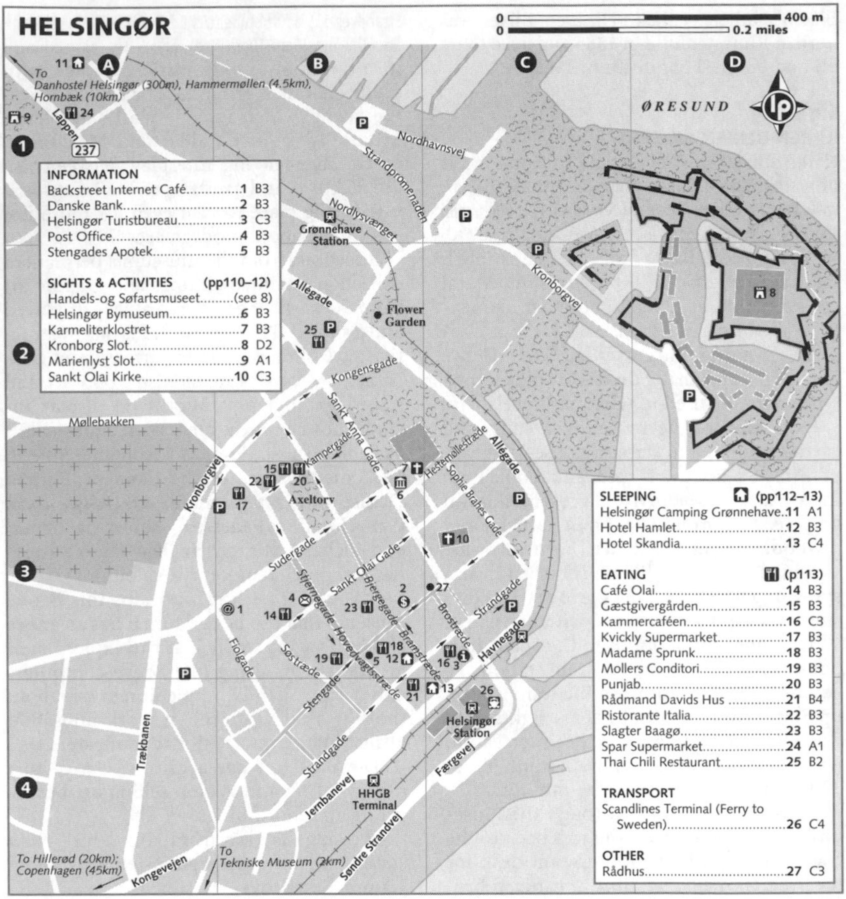
HELSINGØR
0 400 m
0 0.2 miles
ØRESUND
To Danhostel Helsingør (300m), Hammermøllen (4.5km), Hornbæk (10km)
INFORMATION
Backstreet Internet Café 1 B3
Danske Bank 2 B3
Helsingør Turistbureau 3 C3
Post Office 4 B3
Stengades Apotek 5 B3
SIGHTS & ACTIVITIES (pp110–12)
Handels-og Søfartsmuseet (see 8)
Helsingør Bymuseum 6 B3
Karmeliterklostret 7 B3
Kronborg Slot 8 D2
Marienlyst Slot 9 A1
Sankt Olai Kirke 10 C3
SLEEPING (pp112–13)
Helsingør Camping Grønnehave 11 A1
Hotel Hamlet 12 B3
Hotel Skandia 13 C4
EATING (p113)
Café Olai 14 B3
Gæstgivergården 15 B3
Kammercaféen 16 C3
Kvickly Supermarket 17 B3
Madame Sprunk 18 B3
Mollers Conditori 19 B3
Punjab 20 B3
Rådmand Davids Hus 21 B4
Ristorante Italia 22 B3
Slagter Baagø 23 B3
Spar Supermarket 24 A1
Thai Chili Restaurant 25 B2
TRANSPORT
Scandlines Terminal (Ferry to Sweden) 26 C4
OTHER
Rådhus 27 C3
Lappen
Nordhavnsvej
Strandpromenaden
Nordlysvænget
Grønnehave Station
Allégade
Flower Garden
Kronborgvej
Kongensgade
Møllebakken
Sankt Anna Gade
Kampergade
Axeltorv
Hestemøllestræde
Sophie Brahes Gade
Sudergade
Sankt Olai Gade
Stjernegade
Bjergegade
Brostræde
Strandgade
Havnegade
Fiolgade
Søstræde
Hovedvagtsstræde
Bramstræde
Stengade
Helsingør Station
Færgevej
Trækbanen
Jernbanevej
HHGB Terminal
Søndre Strandvej
To Hillerød (20km); Copenhagen (45km)
Kongevejen
To Tekniske Museum (2km)

Ferries shuttle to and from Sweden during the day, the passengers mostly Swedish shoppers on day trips to Helsingør looking to snap up large quantities of relatively inexpensive alcohol – which accounts for the plethora of liquor shops to be found near the harbour.

Helsingør has maintained some of its historic quarters, including a block of old homes and warehouses known as Sundtoldkarreen (Sound Dues Square) towards the northeastern end of Strandgade.

Information

DSB terminus at Helsingør train station and the **Scandlines ferry terminal** have lockers where you can store your bags while you tour the town.

Danske Bank (☎ 49 25 52 00; Stengade 55; 9.30am-4pm Mon-Fri, to 6pm Thu) has ATMs.

Helsingør Turistbureau (☎ 49 21 13 33; www.visithelsingor.dk; Havnepladsen 3; 9am-5pm Mon-Fri & 10am-3pm Sat Jun-Aug , 9am-4pm Mon-Fri & 10am-3pm Sat Sep-May) is opposite the train station.

Post office (☎ 80 20 70 30; Stjernegade 15; 9.30am-5pm, 10am-1pm Sat)

Stengades Apotek (☎ 49 21 86 00; Stengade 46) For pharmaceuticals.

Sights

Massive Kronborg Slot, which is only a short walk on the northern side of town from the narrow, cobblestone streets of the town centre, anchors Helsingør's sights. There are several museums within walking distance and a narrow beach that runs along the shoreline to the north.

KRONBORG SLOT

Despite the attention **Kronborg Slot** (☎ 49 21 30 78; www.kronborgcastle.com; Kronborgvej; adult/child 50/15kr, incl Maritime Museum 75/25kr; ⏰ 10.30am-5pm May-Sep, 11am-4pm Tue-Sun Apr & Oct, 11am-3pm Tue-Sun Nov-Mar) has received as the setting of *Hamlet*, its primary function was not as a royal residence but rather as a grandiose tollhouse, wresting taxes from foreign-flagged ships passing through the narrow Øresund. The castle's history dates from the 1420s, when the Danish king Erik of Pomerania introduced the 'sound dues' – the first tax of its kind anywhere – and built a small fortress, called Krogen, on a promontory at the narrowest part of the sound.

Financed by the generous revenue from shipping tolls – a progressive tax based on the size of the cargo – the original medieval fortress was rebuilt and enlarged by Frederik II in 1585 to form the present Kronborg Slot. Kronborg was ravaged by fire in 1629 – in fact almost all that remained were the outer walls – but Christian IV rebuilt it, preserving the castle's earlier Renaissance style. In 1658, during the war with Sweden, the Swedes occupied Kronborg and removed practically everything of value, leaving the interior in a shambles. After that, Danish royalty rarely visited the castle, although the sound dues continued to be collected for another 200 years. Slavery was introduced in Kronberg in 1739 and in 1785, the same year as a minor slave revolt, it was converted into barracks; that remained its chief function until 1922 (slavery was abolished in 1851) when the restoration process began and it was transformed into a museum. Since then the Danish and Swedish governments have cooperated to return all of the looted items. It's still sometimes used by Danish royalty and in theory at least can be rented for private functions – guides are understandably reluctant to quote a price.

Some of Kronborg's more interesting quarters include the king's and queen's chambers, which have marble fireplaces and detailed ceiling paintings; the small chamber, which boasts royal tapestries, including an especially interesting one (the eyes of the king seem to follow you across the room); and the great hall, one of the longest Renaissance halls in Scandinavia. Banquets held here consisted of no fewer than 65 courses and each guest was given their own bucket for vomiting. The chapel is one of the best-preserved parts of the castle and has some choice woodcarvings, while the gloomy dungeons make for more unusual touring.

In the dungeon you'll pass the resting statue of the legendary Viking chief Holger Danske (Ogier the Dane) who is said to watch over Denmark, ever-ready to come to her aid should the hour of need arrive. The low-ceilinged dungeon includes areas that once served as soldiers' quarters and storerooms for salted fish, and which these days attract nesting bats. Before entering the dungeon take some time to read the fascinating explanations on the life of soldiers at the fort – how they lived, died and even revolted.

Tracing the history of Danish shipping and trade and the little known overseas Danish colonies, **Handels-og Søfartsmuseet** (Danish Maritime Museum; ☎ 49 21 06 85; www.maritime-museum.dk

TO BE OR NOT TO BE

Shakespeare never visited Kronborg Slot in Helsingør but he did use it as the setting for his tragedy *Hamlet*. Word of the imposing castle completed in 1585 had already spread far and wide by the time the play was penned in 1602. It apparently struck Shakespeare as a fitting setting, and he renamed it Elsinore Castle. Although the play was fiction, Shakespeare did include in his plot two actual Danish nobles – Frederik Rosenkrantz and Knud Gyldenstierne (Guildenstern), both of whom had visited the English court in the 1590s.

English merchants used to visit the castle out of curiosity and respect for the tragic Hamlet, Prince of Denmark, convinced the play was a retelling of actual historical events and personages. Due to the fame bestowed on it by Shakespeare, Kronborg is the most widely known castle in all of Scandinavia.

The courtyard of Kronborg is still used to stage performances of *Hamlet*, which have in the past featured such prominent actors as Sir Laurence Olivier, Richard Burton and Michael Redgrave.

in Danish; adult/child 40/15kr, or part of combined ticket to castle; 10.30am-5pm May-Sep, 11am-4pm Tue-Sun Apr & Oct, 11am-3pm Tue-Sun Nov-Mar), also housed in the castle, is well worth a visit. Mostly comprising a collection of model ships, paintings, nautical instruments and sea charts, the exhibit helps one to appreciate the impact of the sea on Danish culture and history. Oh, and it has the oldest preserved ship biscuit, c 1352, probably no longer edible. The remains of the original Krogen fortress can be seen in the masonry of the museum's showroom Nos 21 and 22.

Although you have to pay to enter the castle's interior, you can cross the moat and walk around the courtyard free of charge, which can be a fun experience in itself.

MARIENLYST SLOT

About 1.5km northwest of the town centre is **Marienlyst Slot** (49 28 18 30; www.helsingor.dk/museum in Danish; Marienlyst Allé 32; adult/student/child 30/20kr/free; noon-4pm), a stately-looking three-storey manor house, set back from the road in a manicured garden. Built in 1763 in the Louis Seize neoclassical style by French architect NH Jardin, it encompasses parts of an early summer house constructed by Frederik II. Highlights include contemporary artworks and several interesting pieces from the original furnishings, such as two huge mirrors shipped from France and a painting on the 2nd floor that is half Venice and half Copenhagen. Look out the 2nd-floor window for the naturally designed view of the sea. 'Hamlet's grave' can be found in the garden out the back, added because every good romantic garden needs ruins or other signs of mortality to provoke melancholic thoughts and also as a tourist attraction for visiting English merchants convinced Hamlet was an actual historical figure. The Hornbæk-bound train stops at Marienlyst station, 100m north of the manor house.

DANMARKS TEKNISKE MUSEUM

If you'd like to examine innovative technological inventions from the late 19th and early 20th centuries, the **Danmarks Tekniske Museum** (49 22 26 11; www.tekniskmuseum.dk/; Fabriksvej 25; adult/child 65/35kr; 10am-5pm Tue-Sun) displays early gramophones, radios, motor vehicles and a 1906 Danish-built aeroplane that, it's claimed, was the first plane flown in Europe (it stayed airborne for 11 seconds!).

HELSINGØR BYMUSEUM

One block further north of the cathedral is **Helsingør Bymuseum** (49 28 18 00; www.helsingor.dk/museum in Danish; Sankt Anna Gade 36; adult/child 10kr/free; noon-4pm), built by the monks of the adjacent monastery in 1516 to serve as a sailors' hospital. It was a poorhouse before becoming a history museum in 1973. The hotchpotch of exhibits includes about 200 dolls and a model of Helsingør in 1801.

SANKT OLAI KIRKE

The 15th-century Gothic cathedral **Sankt Olai Kirke** (admission free) occupies the block between Stengade and Sankt Olai Gade. The cathedral has an ornate altar and baptistry and is open to the public.

HAMMERMØLLEN

Five kilometres west in the village of Hellebæk is **Hammermøllen** (49 70 88 67; www.hammermollen.dk in Danish; Bøssemagergade 21; adult/child 10/5kr; 10am-4pm Tue-Sun), an old smithy that was founded by Christian IV. Dating from 1765, it has also been a water wheel-operated copper mill and textile mill. It's 500m south of Hellebæk train station.

KARMELITERKLOSTRET

One of Scandinavia's best-preserved medieval monasteries, **Karmeliterklostret** (Carmelite monastery; 49 21 17 74; www.sctmariae.dk; Sankt Anna Gade 38; admission 10kr; noon-3pm), is housed in the red-brick buildings north of the Bymuseum. Christian II's mistress, Dyveke, is thought to have been buried at the monastery when she died in 1517.

Sleeping

Tourist office staff can book **rooms** in many private homes for 250/400kr for singles/doubles, plus a 50kr booking fee.

Helsingør Camping Grønnehave (49 28 12 12; www.helsingorcamping.dk; Strandalleen 2; camp site per person 55kr; year-round; bus No 340) Easy to reach two-star camping ground on the beach about 1.5km northwest of the town centre.

Danhostel Helsingør (49 21 16 40; www.helsingorhostel.dk; Nordre Strandvej 24; dm/r without bathroom 110/350kr; Feb-Nov; bus No. 340) A stately looking renovated coastal manor house right on a small beach looking directly across to Sweden houses this 180-bed hostel. It's 2km northwest of the town centre. Dorm rooms have up to ten beds and are in one of the smaller attached buildings. Ping pong and pool are available.

Hotel Skandia (☎ 49 21 09 02; www.hotel-skandia.dk; Bramstræde 1; s/d without bathroom 395/495kr) The most affordable choice in the centre of town.

Hotel Hamlet (☎ 49 21 05 91; Bramstræde 5; s/d 695/915kr) Best choice for a central hotel is the Hamlet, which has 36 rather nondescript rooms, all with private bathroom and TV.

Eating

You'll find the main cluster of eateries around Axeltorv, four blocks northwest of the train station, as well as beer gardens selling Helsingør's own Wiibroe pilsner.

Slagter Baagø (☎ 49 21 11 84; Bjergegade 3; shrimp salad 45kr; lunch & dinner) Pick and choose from the selection of fresh vegetable and meat dishes to make your own picnic.

Kammercaféen (☎ 49 28 20 52; Havnepladsen 1; snacks & meals 30-90kr; lunch & dinner) In the old customs house behind the tourist office, this café specialises in organic fare, including sandwiches, salads and a few hot dishes.

Café Olai (☎ 49 20 16 07; Sankt Olai Gade 19; sandwiches 50kr; lunch & dinner) Reasonably priced quality salads and sandwiches.

Rådmand Davids Hus (☎ 49 26 10 43; Strandgade 70; mains 60kr; lunch & dinner) A 300-year-old half-timbered building houses this popular café. The special is the 'shopping lunch' (68kr), a generous plate of traditional Danish foods, typically salmon pâté, salad and slices of lamb, cheese and bread.

Gæstgivergården (☎ 49 21 19 78; Kampergade 9; daily specials 69kr; lunch & dinner) A pub-like atmosphere with everything from burgers and salads to traditional Danish fare, including some good-value specials.

Thai-Chili Restaurant (☎ 49 21 31 75; Sct. Anna Gade 48; mains 85kr; lunch & dinner) Does all the standbys but you can't beat the take-away box (39kr) for value.

Madame Sprunck (☎ 49 26 48 49; Stengade 48F; pasta 82kr; lunch & dinner) An old cottage with cosy dining room and charming courtyard seating, Madame Sprunck does Danish, French and Italian fare.

Ristorante Italia (☎ 49 21 60 22; Kampergade 7; mains 70-100kr; lunch & dinner) Pleasant Italian restaurant with all of the usual pasta choices as well as seafood dishes.

Punjab (☎ 49 21 17 86; Bjergegade 27A; veg meals for two 199kr; lunch & dinner) Chic Indian venue right on the northeast corner of Axeltorv.

Møllers Conditori (Stengade 39) sells tasty muffins and bread. There's a bakery opposite the train station and one in the **Kvickly** supermarket (Stjernegade 25), west of Axeltorv, and a **Spar** supermarket (Lappen) near the hostel.

Getting There & Away

Helsingør train station has two adjacent terminals: the DSB terminal for national

NORTH ZEALAND

THE WORLD ACCORDING TO TYCHO

It was on the island of Hven, in the sound between Denmark and Sweden, that the 16th-century Danish astronomer Tycho Brahe collected evidence that the sun and moon revolved around the earth. Despite the fact that he was wrong – and proven so by Johannes Kepler, his former assistant, no less – Brahe's observations and calculations were still significant achievements. He was the first to measure planetary movement and designed instrumentation light years more sophisticated than his predecessors.

While Brahe's mind may have been on the stars, his ambitions were decidedly worldly. Part of his nose was sliced off in a duel, reputedly over claims that his opponent was a better mathematician. In order to keep Brahe from continuing to teach abroad, King Frederik of Denmark gave Hven to the astronomer as a gift and helped finance the building of Uraniborg, a dual-purpose observatory and castle. Brahe reportedly treated both his assistants and the people of the island in a lordly manner, not helped by his belief that he was Ptolemy's rightful successor and perhaps more important than the king. After falling out with Frederik's son Christian, Brahe closed down the observatory in 1597, left the island and later left Denmark for good.

Unfortunately he wasn't granted much time to enjoy his next appointment as the Imperial Mathematician to the Holy Roman Emperor, a title bound to turn anyone's head. He died in Prague in 1601, the result of complications from holding in his urine for too long out of respect for his royal host. He thought it bad etiquette to leave the table first. No doubt a valuable lesson for everyone: etiquette be damned when you gotta go.

trains and the smaller Helsingør–Hornbæk–Gilleleje Banen (HHGB) terminal for the private railway that runs along the north coast. The DSB trains to and from Copenhagen (59.50kr, 55 minutes) run about three times hourly from early morning to around midnight while DSB trains to and from Hillerød (51kr, 30 minutes) run at least once hourly until around midnight. The HHGB train from Helsingør to Gilleleje (51kr, 40 minutes) via Hornbæk (25.50kr, 20 minutes) runs an average of twice hourly, with the last train pulling out of Helsingør at 10.54pm.

Helsingør is 64km north of Copenhagen and 24km northeast of Hillerød. There's free parking throughout the city, including at car parks northeast of the tourist office, to the west of the Kvickly supermarket and outside Kronborg Slot.

For information on the frequent ferries to Helsingborg in Sweden (34kr return, 20 minutes), see p311. Visitors arriving by train can make a beeline to the Scandlines ferry office by walking through the back exit of the DSB railway terminal.

INLAND TOWNS

Hillerød and Fredensborg are the heartland of the heartland, the two towns of special interest to visitors in this part of North Zealand.

HILLERØD

pop 27,800

Hillerød, 30km north of Copenhagen, isn't especially quaint in itself but the grand lakeside castle of Frederiksborg Slot and the surrounding gardens are splendid. You can enjoy picturesque views of the castle by following the path that skirts the lake. If you feel like taking a longer stroll, paths run through Slotshaven, an expansive Baroque-style private garden immediately north of the castle and lake. The Slotshaven paths connect with trails in the woodlands of Lille Dyrehave and Indelukket which, taken together, could easily make a pleasant hour's outing.

Hillerød is also a transport hub for North Zealand, where you make connections to trains heading to the beaches on the north coast.

If you arrive at Hillerød by train, follow the signs to the central square, Torvet. The main street through town, Slotsgade, leads directly from Torvet to the gate of Frederiksborg Slot, 500m to the northwest.

The helpful **Hillerød Turistbureau** (☎ 48 24 02 00; www.hillerodturist.dk; Møllestræde 9; 🕒 10am-5pm Mon-Fri &10am-1pm Sat, mid-Jun–Aug 10am-6pm Mon-Fri & 10am-3pm Sat) is a short walk from the castle entrance.

Sights

Combining history, beauty and strength, the impressive Dutch Renaissance-styled **Frederiksborg Slot** (☎ 48 26 04 39; www.frederiksborgmuseet.dk in Danish; Slotsgade 1; family/adult/student/child 120kr/60/50/15; 🕒 10am-5pm Apr-Oct, 11am-3pm Nov-Mar) is one of the most interesting destinations in the region. Spread across three islets on the eastern side of the castle lake, Slotsø, the imposing exterior and ornate rooms inside hide the marvellous Baroque gardens out the back. Graceful patterns and designs are carved out of the vegetation and a narrow stream runs through several fountains, finally emptying into the lake.

The oldest part of Frederiksborg Slot dates from the reign of Frederik II, after whom it is named, but most of the present structure was built in the early 17th century by Frederik II's more extravagant son, Christian IV.

As you enter the main gate you'll pass old stable buildings dating from the 1560s and then cross over a moat to the second islet, where you'll enter an expansive central courtyard with a grandly ornate Neptune fountain. The relatively modest wings that flank the fountain once served as residences for court officers and government officials. A second bridge crosses to the northernmost islet, the site of the main body of the castle, which served as the home of Danish royalty for more than a century.

Frederiksborg Slot was ravaged by a fire in 1859. The royal family, unable to undertake the costly repairs, decided to give up the property. Carlsberg beer baron JC Jacobsen then stepped onto the scene and spearheaded a drive to restore the castle as a national museum, a function it still serves today.

The sprawling castle has a magnificent interior boasting gilded ceilings, wall-sized tapestries and fine paintings, with exhibits occupying 70 of its rooms. The richly embellished **Riddershalen** (Knights Hall) and the **Slotskirken** (Coronation Chapel), where the Danish monarchs were crowned from 1671

BRILLIANT BUILDER, FAULTY FIGHTER

No Danish monarch has made such a lasting impact on the Danish landscape as Christian IV (1588–1648). Many of Denmark's most lavish structures were erected during his reign and you'll find his fancy handiwork when touring Frederiksborg Slot and Kronborg Slot.

Christian inherited the throne in 1596 when he was just 10 years old and ruled for the next 52 years. Denmark had a robust economy and a seemingly boundless treasury when Christian took power. The ambitious king established trading companies and a stock exchange, and built splendid new Renaissance cities, castles and fortresses throughout his kingdom. Unfortunately, the king's foreign policies weren't nearly as brilliant as his domestic undertakings. In 1625 Christian IV dragged Denmark into the ill-fated Thirty Years' War with Sweden. By the end of the war Denmark was bankrupt and so much territory had been lost to Sweden that there were doubts Denmark would even survive as a nation. The king himself lost an eye to shrapnel when his flagship was attacked in battle. A vivid oil painting of that scene, with the king's eye covered by a bloody handkerchief and his sword raised in defiance, can be seen above Christian IV's crypt in the Roskilde cathedral.

to 1840, are alone worth the admission fee. The chapel, incidentally, was spared serious fire damage and retains the original interior commissioned by Christian IV, including a priceless **Compenius organ** built in 1610. The organ is played between 1.30pm and 2pm each Thursday and there are free concerts every Sunday at 5pm in July and August.

The 3rd floor of the castle houses the **Moderne Samling** (Modern Collection), a chronologically arranged exhibition of history paintings, portraits and photography of Denmark in the 20th century.

Outside opening hours, visitors are free to stroll around the gardens and enter the castle courtyard. If you arrive by car, there's free parking off Frederikværksgade, west of the castle.

During the Middle Ages, the sick came to **Æbelholt Klostermuseum** (☎ 48 24 34 48; Æbelholt 4; adult/child 15kr/free; 🕑 11am-4pm, closed Mon May-Oct) hoping to be healed at the grave site of the first abbot. The Augustinian monastery 15km north of Hillerød was founded in 1175. It's mainly only ruins that now remain as most of the building was demolished after the Protestant reformation, but the museum explains medieval living conditions, discovered in part by scientists studying the skeletons of the former monks.

Sleeping

Hillerød Camping (☎ 48 26 48 54; www.hillerodcamping.dk; Blytækkervej 18; camp site per person 60kr; 🕑 Apr–mid-Sep) A two-star camping ground about a 20-minute walk directly south of the castle along Slangerupgade.

Hotel Hillerød (☎ 48 24 08 00; www.hotelhillerod.dk; Milnersvej 41; s/d incl breakfast 965/1080kr Mon-Fri, 800/900kr Sat & Sun). With an atrium filled with flowering plants and 62 modern rooms with bath and kitchenette, this hotel is about 2km south of the castle. Bikes can be borrowed.

Eating

Several restaurants are clustered just outside the castle entrance while others are only a few minutes' walk away on Slotsgade.

Brassiere Kong Christian (☎ 48 24 53 50; Slotsgade 59; sandwiches 50kr; 🕑 lunch & dinner) On the corner directly across from the castle, Kong Christian does reasonably priced sandwiches.

El Castillo's Cantina (☎ 48 26 19 11; Slotsgade 6; tacos 81kr; 🕑 dinner) Although the design scheme is a little heavy on the sombreros and cactuses, the food is authentic Mexican.

Ristorante La Perla (☎ 48 24 35 33; Torvet 1; pastas 80kr; 🕑 lunch & dinner) Sitting outside in the cobblestone courtyard makes the homestyle Italian food taste even better.

Getting There & Away

The S-train (A & E lines) runs every 10 minutes between Copenhagen and Hillerød (45.50kr), a 40-minute ride.

Trains from Hillerød run eastward to Fredensborg (17kr, 12 minutes) and Helsingør (51kr, 30 minutes), north to Gilleleje (42kr, 31 minutes) and west to Tisvildeleje (42kr, 31 minutes); all services operate at least hourly.

Buses also link Hillerød with North Zealand towns but they are much slower than the train and cost just as much.

Getting Around

Bus Nos 701 and 702 depart frequently from the train station and can drop you near the castle gate (15kr).

The little ferry *Frederiksborg* sails across the castle lake about every 30 minutes daily from June to August, landing at three small piers: one just north of Torvet, another near the castle entrance and the third north of the castle on the road to Slotshaven. The fare is 20/5kr for adults/children.

Bikes can be hired at **Skansen Cykler** (☎ 48 26 17 27; Skanseevej 31; per day 50kr).

FREDENSBORG

pop 8000

The real draws of small and quiet Fredensborg are the gardens and grounds of the royal palace and the shaded lake-shore path that make it a pleasant stay for a day or two.

Bordering the southeastern shore of Esrum Sø, Denmark's second-largest lake, Fredensborg offers swimming, boating and fishing. Along the shore you can sometimes spot ospreys and cormorants, and the surrounding woods are the habitat of roe deer.

Fredensborg Turistbureau (☎ 48 48 21 00; www.visitfredensborg.dk; Slotsgade 2; 11am-4pm Jun-Aug, closed rest of year) is just outside the palace.

Sights

FREDENSBORG SLOT

The royal family's residence during most of the Danish summer, **Fredensborg Palace** (☎ 33 40 31 87; Slotsgade 1), was built in 1720 by Frederik IV. It was named Fredensborg – meaning Peace Palace – to commemorate the peace that Denmark had recently achieved with its Scandinavian neighbours. The palace certainly reflects the more tranquil mood of that era and is largely in the style of a country manor house, an abrupt contrast with the moat-encircled fortresses of Kronborg and Frederiksborg that preceded it.

Partly because of its spread-out design, the palace is not as impressive as some other Danish royal palaces in North Zealand. Fredensborg's interior can only be visited during July, when the royal family holidays elsewhere. Guided palace tours (40kr) run every 30 minutes between 1pm and 4.30pm daily. The grounds are open sunrise to sunset year-round.

The main mansion was designed by the leading Danish architect of the day, JC Krieger, and is in Italian Baroque style with marble floors and a large central cupola. It's fronted by an expansive octagonal courtyard framed by two-storey buildings.

The palace is backed by 120 hectares of **wooded parkland**, crisscrossed by trails and open free to the public year-round. Take a stroll through **Normandsdalen**, west of the palace, to a circular amphitheatre with 70 life-sized sandstone statues of Norwegian folk characters – fisherfolk, farmers and so on – in traditional dress. If you continue walking a few minutes west from there you'll reach **Esrum Sø**, a lake skirted by another trail.

To get to Fredensborg Slot from the train station, turn left onto Stationsvej and then right onto Jernbanegade, which merges with Slotsgade near the palace gate; the 1km walk takes only 10 minutes.

OTHER SIGHTS

It's a 10-minute walk west from the palace gate along Skipperallé to **Skipperhuset** (opposite), a lakeside restaurant where there's a summer ferry service and rowing boats for hire. The main beach is nearby. The ferry can take you to **Gribskov**, a forested area with trails and picnic grounds that borders the western side of Esrum Sø.

Founded in 1151, making it one of the oldest monasteries in Denmark, **Esrum Kloster** (☎ 48 36 04 00; www.esrum.dk; Klostergade, Esrum; adult/child 40/20kr; 10am-4pm Tue-Sun) has been immaculately restored. Exhibitions are on the history of the abbey and other medieval subjects.

Sleeping

Tourist office staff can book **rooms** in private homes, with doubles costing on average 350kr including breakfast, plus a 25kr booking fee.

Danhostel Fredensborg (☎ 48 48 03 15; www.fredensborghostel.dk; Østrupvej 3; dm/s/d without bathroom 110/185/260kr; Jan–mid-Dec; P) The hostel has 88 beds that are mostly in double rooms. It occupies a prime location just 300m south of Fredensborg Slot and 50m west of Hotel Store Kro.

Pension Bondehuset (☎ 48 48 01 12; www.bondehuset.dk in Danish; Sørup-vej 14; s/d 790/1350kr; P) An upmarket rural getaway, this 18th-century manor house offers comfortable rooms and free rowing boats for guests' use. It's right on the lake on the western side of town.

Hotel Store Kro (☎ 48 40 01 11; www.fredensborg.storekro.dk; Slotsgade 6; per person per night with dinner & breakfast 995kr; P) Classic inn, just outside the palace gate, was originally built by Frederik IV in 1723 to accommodate palace guests. Not surprisingly, no two rooms are alike, but all have traditional décor and full amenities.

Eating

Ristorante La Princesa (☎ 48 48 01 25; Slotsgade 3A; pasta 70kr; lunch & dinner) La Princesa's delicious tiramisu is a good way to end the meal. Mains are hearty portions.

Skipperhuset (☎ 48 48 17 17; Skipperallé 6; dinner mains 160kr; lunch & dinner, closed Mon) It's hard to imagine a more idyllic setting for alfresco dining than this restaurant on Lake Esrum. Fish is delicately prepared and topped with fresh seasonal vegetables.

Hotel Store Kro (☎ 48 40 01 11; Slotsgade 6; 3-course dinner 385kr; breakfast, lunch & dinner) Old-world charm at this top-end option which offers a three-course Danish dinner with a menu that changes nightly.

You'll pass a **kiosk** for ice cream and sandwiches right before the palace gate. **Drachmann's Pavilion** is another kiosk serving ice cream and drinks down by the lake, a short walk from Skipperhuset.

Getting There & Away

Fredensborg is midway on the train line between Hillerød (17kr, 12 minutes) and Helsingør (42kr, 20 minutes). Trains run about twice hourly from early morning.

NORTH COAST

Strung out along the north coast of Zealand, also known as the Kattegat coast, are several small towns connected by vacation homes perched over white sand beaches, wide in parts, the water shallow and gentle and good for swimming. Just inland from the shore there's a mix of heathlands and woodlands and a generally laid-back holiday air. Although the towns have only a few thousand residents in winter, the population swells with throngs of beach-goers in summer.

HORNBÆK

pop 3300

The young, beautiful and wealthy are attracted to Hornbæk's beach, probably the best on the north coast – a vast expanse of soft, white sand that runs the entire length of the town. It's backed by sand dunes with beach grass and thickets of *Rosa rugosa*, a wild pink seaside rose that blooms all summer. Even though it borders the town, the beach is pleasantly undeveloped, with all the commercial facilities on the inland side of the dunes.

Poet Holger Drachmann, who passed away in Hornbæk in 1908, is memorialised by a harbourside monument. These days the salty fisherfolk, about whom Drachmann often wrote, share their harbour with scores of sailing boats and yachts.

Orientation

From the train station it's a five-minute walk – about 200m – directly north along Havnevej to the harbour. Climb the dunes to the left and you're on the beach.

Information

Danske Bank (☎ 49 76 01 20; Nordre Strandvej 350) is in the town centre.

Hornbæk Turistbureau is inside the library (☎ 49 70 47 47; www.hornbaek.dk; Vester Stejlebakke 2A; 2-7pm Mon, Tue & Thu, 10am-5pm Wed & Fri, 10am-2pm Sat). To reach it take the walkway at the side of Danske Bank. Three computers provide free Internet access.

Post office (☎ 70 00 12 25) is opposite the train station.

Public toilets and shower facilities are at the harbour.

Sights & Activities

The **beach** is without a doubt Hornbæk's main attraction and offers some good swimming conditions and plenty of space for sunbathing. If you're interested in **windsurfing**, contact **Hornbæk Surfudlejning** (☎ 49 70 33 75;

AN INSPIRING RESCUE

In 1774, Hornbæk fishermen came to the rescue of British captain Thomas Brauwn, whose ship was being battered by a raging storm. These unhesitating Danes, braving treacherous seas, so inspired their country folk that a popular play, *Fiskerne*, was written about them by the lyricist poet Johannes Ewald. A song taken from the play became Denmark's national anthem. The rescue was also immortalised by the painter CW Eckersberg, who used it as a theme in a number of his paintings.

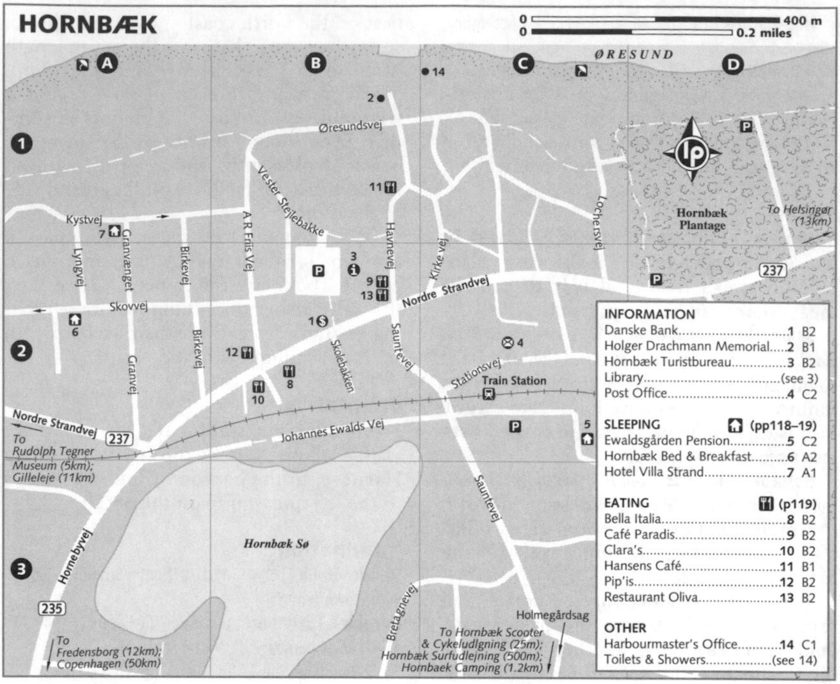

HORNBÆK
0 400 m
0 0.2 miles
ØRESUND
Øresundsvej
Vester Stejlebakke
Kystvej
Lyngvej
Granvænget
Birkevej
A R Friis Vej
Havnevej
Kirke vej
Lochersvej
Hornbæk Plantage
To Helsingør (13km)
237
Skovvej
Nordre Strandvej
Skolebakken
Sauntevej
Granvej
Stationsvej
Train Station
Johannes Ewalds Vej
To Rudolph Tegner Museum (5km); Gilleleje (11km)
Hornbæk Sø
Homebyvej
235
To Fredensborg (12km); Copenhagen (50km)
Bretagnevej
Holmegårdsag
To Hornbæk Scooter & Cykeludlgning (25m); Hornbæk Surfudlejning (500m); Hornbaek Camping (1.2km)
INFORMATION
Danske Bank....1 B2
Holger Drachmann Memorial....2 B1
Hornbæk Turistbureau....3 B2
Library....(see 3)
Post Office....4 C2
SLEEPING (pp118–19)
Ewaldsgården Pension....5 C2
Hornbæk Bed & Breakfast....6 A2
Hotel Villa Strand....7 A1
EATING (p119)
Bella Italia....8 B2
Café Paradis....9 B2
Clara's....10 B2
Hansens Café....11 B1
Pip'is....12 B2
Restaurant Oliva....13 B2
OTHER
Harbourmaster's Office....14 C1
Toilets & Showers....(see 14)

Drejervej 19), which rents gear for 250kr per day. To charter a boat to go **fishing**, contact the tourist office or the harbourmaster's office on the southern side of the harbour; prices average 600kr (per boat per day) for up to three passengers. You can rent **bicycles** for 50kr per day at **Hornbaek Scooter & Cykeludlejning** (☎ 20 78 03 43; Holmegaardsag 52).

If you're up to an enjoyable nature stroll, **Hornbæk Plantage**, a public woodland that extends 3.5km along the coast east from Hornbæk, has numerous interconnecting trails branching out either side of Rte 237. One trail hugs the coast from Lochersvej in Hornbæk to the eastern end of the plantage. There are several areas along Nordre Strandvej (Rte 237) where you can park a car and start your wanderings. A free forestry map *Vandreture i Statsskovene, Hornbæk Plantage* shows all the trails and is available from the tourist office.

The **Rudolph Tegners Museum** (☎ 49 71 91 77; www.rudolphtegner.dk in Danish; Museumsvej 19, Villingerød; adult/child 40kr/free; noon-5pm Tue-Sun) exhibits more than 200 pieces by the eponymous sculptor, some installed in the surrounding nature park. Most are bronze and done in his distinctive monumental style. The artist Rudolph Tegners died in 1950 and is buried in the centre of the museum in a vaulted octagonal chamber.

Sleeping

The tourist office can book single/double **rooms** from 250/450kr in nearby bed and breakfasts.

Hornbæk Camping DCU (☎ 49 70 02 23; www.camping-hornbaek.dk; Planetvej 4; camp site per person 62kr; year-round). This three-star camping ground is on the outskirts of town off Sauntevej, about 1.5km southeast of the centre

Ewaldsgården Pension (☎ 49 70 00 82; www.ewaldsgaarden.dk in Danish; Johannes Ewaldsvej 5; s/d incl breakfast 450/675kr) A light and airy interior with a cosy mix of antiques and cottage-style furnishings. This friendly pension, southeast of the train station and about a 10-minute walk from the harbour, is an early-18th-century country house. All 12 rooms have a washbasin; showers and toilets are off the hall. There's also a simple guest kitchen.

Hornbæk Bed & Breakfast (☎ 49 76 19 10; www.hornbaekbandb.dk; Skovvej 15C; r incl breakfast 595kr; P) Renovated country villa a short walk from the beach has well-maintained, spacious rooms. Electric bikes available for hire.

Hotel Villa Strand (☎ 49 70 00 88; www.villastrand.dk in Danish; Kystvej 12; s/d incl breakfast 500/750kr; P) A variety of rooms can be found at this small hotel on the western side of town. The cheaper ones are small and the pricier ones quite large, but all have private bathroom. It's opposite the beach and there's a lovely private garden.

Eating

Bella Italia (☎ 49 70 31 60; Nordre Strandvej 335; pizzas 40kr; lunch & dinner) The Italian usual standbys of pizzas, pastas plus kebab pitta bread sandwiches.

Hansens Café (☎ 49 70 04 79; Havnevej 19; mains 70-90kr; lunch & dinner) Hansens is in the town's oldest house, an earthen-roofed half-timbered building with a pleasant pub-like atmosphere. The menu changes daily but you can expect to find good Danish food at moderate prices.

Clara's (☎ 49 76 10 20; Nordre Strandvej 357; sandwiches 42kr; lunch & dinner) Burgers and sandwiches best taken away – to the beach.

Café Paradis (☎ 49 70 04 25; Havnevej 3; burgers 39kr; lunch & dinner) Wraps and bagel sandwiches, live music and that Danish speciality, stand-up comedy, performed on weekends make Paradis popular.

Restaurant Oliva (☎ 49 76 11 77; www.oliva.dk in Danish; Havnevej 1; buffet 290kr; lunch & dinner) Upmarket restaurant that serves meticulously prepared Danish dishes best washed down with a glass of wine from the extensive selection. Garden seating out back.

There's a charcuteri (butcher) on Nordre Strandvej and eating opportunities down at the harbour include a little shop, a fish market and **Havnegrillen**, a fast-food stand selling hot dogs and ice cream – although **Pip'is** (AR Friisvej 1) is the best place for frozen desserts. Within 100m of each other on Nordre Strandvej you'll find three supermarkets, Favør, Super Brugsen and Netto, as well as the bakery Wiener Bageriet.

Getting There & Away

Trains connect Hornbæk with Helsingør (25.50kr, 25 minutes) and Gilleleje (25.50kr, 15 minutes) about twice hourly.

BEST BEACHES

- Hornbæk – Best-looking beach-goers (p117)
- Tisvildileje – Families, picnics and plenty of sand (p120)
- Liseleje – Less crowded, backed by dunes (p127)
- Gilleleje – Not as beautiful as others, close to the harbour (p119)
- Hundested – Isolated, end of the line (p127)

GILLELEJE

pop 5300

Zealand's northernmost town, Gilleleje, has the island's largest fishing harbour and, despite its modern facilities, still possesses a certain timeless character, filled as it is with colourful wooden-hulled fishing boats. During WWII many Jews escaped to neutral Sweden from Gilleleje with the help of local fishermen. Today, there's a little dock-side fish auction that can be viewed by early-risers while the smokehouses and restaurants along the harbour bustle during the day. A small monument on a nearby hill is dedicated to Kierkegaard, who was a frequent visitor.

It's a five-minute walk north from the train station to the harbour. Although they are not as pristine or as long as those at Hornbæk or Tisvildeleje, there are public beaches on both sides of town.

The Gilleleje **tourist office** (☎ 48 30 01 74; www.gilleleje-turistbureau.dk; Hovedgade 6F; 10am-6pm Mon-Sat Jun-Aug, 10am-4pm Sep-May & 10am-noon Sat) is in the town centre, 200m east of the train station.

Sights & Activities

The **Gilleleje Museum** (☎ 48 30 16 31; www.holbo.dk in Danish; Vesterbrogade 46; adult/child incl entry to eastern lighthouse 25kr/free; 1-4pm mid-Jun–mid-Sep, closed Thu, Sep-Jun closed Mon & Thu) is on the western side of the town centre. The museum is dedicated to Gilleleje's history from the Middle Ages to the advent of summer tourism. It includes a 19th-century fisherman's house.

Of the two **coastal trails**, the one to the west, which starts near the intersection of Nordre Strandvej and Vesterbrogade, leads 1.75km to a stone **memorial** (see boxed text

EUREKA! LIFE IS DREADFUL

There can't be too many memorials around the world marking intellectual epiphanies. So the stone in the harbour town of Gilleleje marking the centenary of the Danish philosopher Søren Kierkegaard's very own is at least of some interest.

Inscribed on the stone is the question/response, 'What is truth but to live for an idea', words taken from his own notebooks. Kierkegaard retreated to Gilleleje, a peaceful harbour town on Zealand's north coast, in the summers of 1834 and 1835 when he was 21, tormented by personal doubt and anxiety with age-old questions: what to do with one's life and what kind of life is worth living?

And for Kierkegaard, as for others since the dawn of time, a vacation at a coastal resort helped him to focus on what really mattered. While in Gilleleje he wrote, 'It is a matter of understanding my destiny, of seeing what the Divinity actually wants me to do; what counts is to find a truth, which is true for me, to find that idea for which I will live and die.'

Like most epiphanies, his did not lead to immediate action, but up to that point his pursuits had been relatively dissolute and unfocused. It took his father's death to finally inspire him to action, albeit studious action, and he returned to university to earn a theology degree in 1840.

p120) dedicated to the Danish philosopher Søren Kierkegaard, who used to make visits to this coast.

The trail to the east begins just off Hovedgade and leads 2.5km to the site where two lighthouses with coal-burning beacons were erected in 1772. The western lighthouse was modernised in 1899 with rotating lenses and the eastern one, no longer needed, was abandoned. The eastern lighthouse, **Nakkehoved Østre Fyr** (☎ 48 30 16 31; Fryvejen 20; adult/child incl entry to the Gilleleje Museum 25kr/free; ⌚ 1-4pm Wed-Mon mid-Jun–mid-Sep), has been restored as a museum. You can get to this lighthouse on the coastal footpath or by turning north off Rte 237 onto Fyrvejen.

Sleeping

Tourist office staff can book **rooms** in private homes at around 350/800kr for singles/doubles, plus a 25kr booking fee.

Hotel Strand (☎ 48 30 05 12; fax 48 30 18 59; Vesterbrogade 4; s/d incl breakfast without bathroom 410/610kr, with bathroom 470/720kr). This 25-room hotel is in the centre of town, a short walk west from the harbour. The cheaper rooms are a tad small but have showers (toilets are off the hall); the higher-priced rooms are larger and more modern with full amenities.

Gilleleje Badehotel (☎ 48 30 13 47; www.gillelejebadehotel.dk; Hulsøvej 15; r 490-1190kr) Originally built as a beach hotel in 1895, this luxurious waterfront property is truly special. All the rooms are bright and sunlit and most have balconies with views of Sweden. Sauna and Jacuzzi available for guests.

Eating

Adamsen's Fisk (☎ 48 30 09 27; Gilleleje Havn; sandwiches 35kr; ⌚ lunch & dinner) Deservedly popular, with tasty fish cakes, shrimp sandwiches and salads. Tables right on the harbour.

Rogeriet Bornholm (☎ 48 30 01 10; Gilleleje Havn; fish 30kr; ⌚ lunch) Simple smokehouse that sells inexpensive smoked fish by the piece.

Hos Karen & Marie (☎ 48 30 21 30; Nordre Havnevej 3; mains from 70kr; ⌚ lunch & dinner) Excellent little seafood restaurant in a period building overlooking the harbour. At lunchtime there's a generous sampler plate (139kr) that includes pickled herring, butter-fried plaice, salmon, pork tenderloin and brie.

Gilleleje Havn (☎ 48 30 30 39; Havnevej 14; mains 90kr; ⌚ lunch & dinner) Another excellent option a stone's throw from Hos Karen & Marie but with a more modern look. Gilleleje Havn's innovative menu includes burgers among the fish dishes.

Getting There & Away

Trains run between Hillerød and Gilleleje (50kr, 31 minutes) about twice hourly on weekdays, hourly at weekends, and between Helsingør and Gilleleje (50kr, 40 minutes) about twice hourly every day.

TISVILDELEJE

The drive down the hill through the pleasant seaside village of Tisvildeleje with its cafés, restaurants, slow pace and air of prosperity leads to a wide, glorious sweep of sand backed by low dunes. That beach has a large car park, a changing room, toilets, and an ice-cream kiosk. Other beaches are accessible on short walks away from town and there are several nature trails in the area.

Inland from the beach is Tisvilde Hegn, a windswept forest of twisted trees and heather-covered hills that extends southwest from Tisvildeleje for more than 8km. Much of this enchanting forest was planted in the 18th century to stabilise the sand drifts that were threatening to turn the area into desert.

The seasonal tourist office (☎ 48 70 74 51; www.helsinge.com; Banevej 8; noon-5pm Mon-Fri, 10am-3pm Sat, Jun 15-Aug 31) operates from the Tisvildeleje train station.

Activities

From the beach parking area at the end of Hovedgaden you can walk, either along the beach or on a dirt path through the woods, about 3km south to **Troldeskoven** (Witch Wood), an area of ancient trees that have been sculpted by the wind into haunting shapes.

Tisvilde Hegn has numerous trails, including one to **Asserbo Slotsruin**, the moat-encircled ruins of a former manor house and a 12th-century monastery, which are near the southern boundary of the forest. The southwestern part of Tisvilde Hegn merges with **Asserbo Plantage**, a wooded area that borders Lake Arresø. Trail maps are available free from the tourist office.

Sleeping

Danhostel Tisvildeleje (☎ 48 70 98 50; www.helene.dk; Bygmarken 30; camping per person 30kr, dm/s/d 118/425/455kr; year-round; P) Within walking distance of a sandy beach, this modern 272-bed hostel is part of the Sankt Helene complex, 1km east of the town centre. Reservations are essential from June through to August. Its 12-hectare grounds have walking trails, sports fields and playgrounds and the complex is accessible to people in wheelchairs. Campers can pitch a tent in an adjacent field. If you are arriving by train, get off at Godhavns station, one stop before Tisvildeleje station; the hostel is a short walk north of the tracks. There's a nice **restaurant and café** on the grounds as well.

Bed & Breakfast Hårlandsgård (☎ 48 70 83 96; www.haarlandsgaard.dk; Harlands Allé; r 420kr; P) A country house originally built in 1788 with a sunny garden and comfy rooms. Former stables house an art gallery.

Borshøjgaard (☎ 48 70 26 24; www.borshojgaard.dk in Danish; Sankt Helenevej 10; r 500kr; P) Rooms in this bed and breakfast, a family-owned farm within walking distance of town, have TV and bathroom.

Tisvildeleje Strand Hotel (☎ 48 70 71 19; www.strand-hotel.dk in Danish; Hovedgaden 75; s/d incl breakfast without bathroom 425/640kr, with bathroom 525/750kr; P) Although within walking distance of the beach, this 29-room hotel is in the centre of town.

Eating

There's a small cluster of eateries in the town centre on Hovedgaden and a number of more affordable options 8km away in the town of Helsinge.

Chimos Pizzabar (☎ 48 70 21 27; Hovedgaden 78; pizzas 50kr; lunch & dinner) Opposite the Tisvildeleje Strand Hotel, this eatery caters to the summer crowds, selling ice cream, burgers and large individual pizzas.

Tisvilde Bio & Bistro (☎ 48 70 41 91; www.tisvildebio.dk; Hovedgaden 38; mains 70kr; lunch & dinner) A combination movie theatre and restaurant with live music at the weekend.

Tisvildeleje Cafeen (☎ 48 70 88 86; Hovedgaden 55; buffet dinner 195kr; lunch & dinner) Gorge yourself on the dinner buffet, a real treat of fresh fish, steaks, vegetables and piping hot bread.

Restaurant Højbohus (☎ 48 70 71 19; Hovedgaden 75; 3-course dinners 275kr; lunch & dinner) The Strand Hotel's restaurant is expensive but the vibe still casual – it's a beach resort, after all, and the patio is a pleasant place to watch the sunset.

There's also a good bakery, **Tisvildeleje Bageri** (☎ 48 70 71 22; Hovedgaden 60), and a little grocery shop on the opposite side of the street. Lines can be long for burgers, hot dogs and ice cream at the kiosk in the public car park at the beach.

Getting There & Around

Bus No 363 operates between Tisvildeleje and Gilleleje (25kr, one hour) every two hours. Trains run between Tisvildeleje and Hillerød (25kr, 31 minutes) once an hour; there are a few extra trains in the early morning and the late afternoon.

Bicycles can be hired at the Hydro Texaco petrol station (☎ 48 70 80 13; Hovedgaden 54), which is 200m west of the train station, for 65kr per day.

FJORD TOWNS

North Zealand has two interlinking fjords, the Isefjord and the Roskilde Fjord – to the naked eye both indistinguishable from lakes – that connect with the Kattegat at the town of Hundested. The largest towns in the region, Frederiksværk and Frederikssund, border the Roskilde Fjord and are along the main Tisvildeleje–Roskilde road route.

ROSKILDE

pop 52,000

Justly famous for its Viking Ship Museum and striking cathedral, Roskilde is Zealand's second-largest town and is the burial site of Danish royalty. It is a popular day trip from Copenhagen only 30km away. Students attending two large universities inject youthfulness and life into the town centre, a pleasant architectural mix of old and new and a good place to sit at a café and watch everyone else go about their business.

Roskilde, Denmark's first capital, was a thriving trade centre throughout the Middle Ages. It was also the site of Zealand's first Christian church, built by the Viking king Harald Bluetooth in 980. In 1026 Canute I, in a rage over a chess match, had his brother-in-law Ulf Jarl assassinated in that church. Ulf's widow, Canute's sister Estrid, insisted that the wooden stave church in which her husband was ambushed be torn down, and then donated property for the construction of a new stone church. The foundations of that early stone church are beneath the floor of the present-day Roskilde Domkirke (cathedral). Estrid and her son Svend Estridsen are among the multitude of Danish royals who are now buried there.

As the centre of Danish Catholicism, the medieval town of Roskilde was the site of not only a cathedral but also nearly 20 churches and monasteries. After the Reformation swept Denmark in 1536 the monasteries and most of the churches were demolished. Consequently the town, which had been in decline since the capital moved to Copenhagen in the early 15th century, saw its population shrink radically.

Information

Backstreet Internet Café (Netcenter (☎ 46 35 30 38; Grønnegade 2)

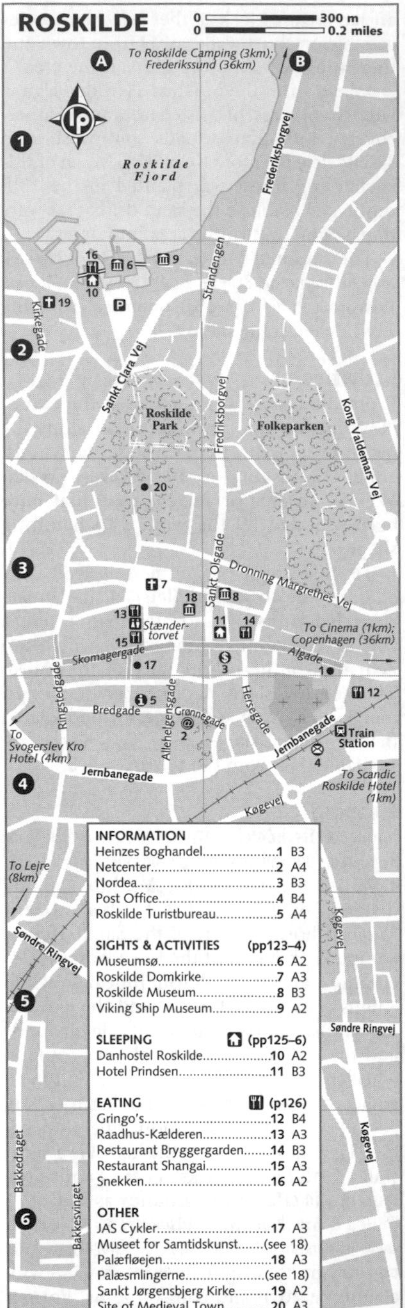
ROSKILDE
0 300 m
0 0.2 miles
To Roskilde Camping (3km); Frederikssund (36km)
Roskilde Fjord
Frederiksborgvej
Strandengen
Kirkegade
Sankt Clara Vej
Roskilde Park
Fredriksborgvej
Folkeparken
Kong Valdemars Vej
Sankt Olsgade
Dronning Margrethes Vej
Stændertorvet
Skomagergade
Algade
To Cinema (1km); Copenhagen (36km)
Ringstedgade
Bredgade
Allehelgensgade
Grønnegade
Hersegade
Jernbanegade
Train Station
To Svogerslev Kro Hotel (4km)
To Scandic Roskilde Hotel (1km)
Køgevej
To Lejre (8km)
Søndre Ringvej
Bakkedraget
Bakkesvinget
INFORMATION
Heinzes Boghandel 1 B3
Netcenter 2 A4
Nordea 3 B3
Post Office 4 B4
Roskilde Turistbureau 5 A4
SIGHTS & ACTIVITIES (pp123–4)
Museumsø 6 A2
Roskilde Domkirke 7 A3
Roskilde Museum 8 B3
Viking Ship Museum 9 A2
SLEEPING (pp125–6)
Danhostel Roskilde 10 A2
Hotel Prindsen 11 B3
EATING (p126)
Gringo's 12 B4
Raadhus-Kælderen 13 A3
Restaurant Bryggergarden 14 B3
Restaurant Shangai 15 A3
Snekken 16 A2
OTHER
JAS Cykler 17 A3
Museet for Samtidskunst (see 18)
Palæfløejen 18 A3
Palæsmlingerne (see 18)
Sankt Jørgensbjerg Kirke 19 A2
Site of Medieval Town 20 A3

Heinzes Boghandel (☎ 46 35 43 43; Algade 54), sells books and travel guides.
Nordea (☎ 46 32 32 33; Algade 4) is one of several banks in the centre.
Post office (☎ 70 12 40 00; Jernbanegade 3) is just southwest of the train station.
Roskilde Turistbureau (☎ 46 35 27 00; www.visitroskilde.com; Gullandsstræde 15; 9am-6pm Mon-Fri & 10am-2pm Sat Jul & Aug, 9am-5pm Mon-Fri, 10am-1pm Sat Sep-Jun).

Sights

VIKING SHIP MUSEUM

This intriguing museum (☎ 46 30 02 00; www.vikingeskibsmuseet.dk/; Vindeboder 12; adult/student/child/family 75/55/25/190kr; 8am-5pm May-Sep, 10am-5pm Oct-Apr) displays five reconstructed Viking ships (c 1000) excavated from the bottom of Roskilde Fjord in 1962. All are presumed to have been scuttled in order to block attacking ships. The wooden ship fragments have been reassembled on new skeleton frames to recreate the original shapes. As some of the wood was lost over the centuries, none of the ships is complete but all have been reconstructed sufficiently to provide a sense of their original features. The vessels include an 18m warship of the type used to raid England and a 16.5m trader that is thought to have carried cargo between Greenland and Denmark. Several rooms have fascinating exhibits explaining Viking history in Denmark, Scandinavia and, interestingly enough, Dublin in particular. Appropriately, the museum is on the eastern side of the harbour overlooking Roskilde Fjord, which provides a scenic backdrop for the displays.

Museumsø (Museum Island), a harbourfront facility adjacent to the main museum, is equally worthy of your time. On this pier-like island, craftspeople painstakingly use Viking-era techniques and tools to build replicas of Viking ships. Three substantial replicas, *Helge Ask*, *Kraka Fyr* and *Roar Ege*, are moored in the harbour, and numerous other reconstructions are in the works. *Skuledev 2*, a 30m-long warship launched in September 2004, took over 11 people 27,000 man hours. A 20-minute film documenting this process is screened in the museum basement. Museumsø also holds an **archaeological workshop** (10am-3pm Mon-Fri) where recent excavations are being preserved and analysed by researchers from the National Museum.

Summer is a fun time to visit the Viking Ship Museum as there are seasonal workshops where children can try their hand at sail-making and other maritime and Viking-related crafts. If you think you'd have been a good Viking – well, Viking *rower* – then you can take one of the five daily hour-long sailing trips on the fjord. You must buy a museum ticket in addition to the separate trip ticket (adult/child 50/30kr). Both can be purchased at the Museumsø ticket office.

ROSKILDE DOMKIRKE

The imposing **Roskilde Domkirke** (☎ 46 35 27 00; Domkirkepladsen; adult/child 25/15kr; 9am-4.45pm Mon-Fri, 9am-noon Sat, 12.30-4.45pm Sun Apr-Sep; 10am-3.45pm Tue-Fri, 11.30am-3.45pm Sat, 12.30-3.45pm Sun Oct-Mar) dominates the city centre. Begun in 1170 by Bishop Absalon, the cathedral has been rebuilt and added to so many times that it represents a millennium of Danish architectural styles.

Roskilde Domkirke boasts tall spires, a splendid interior and the crypts of 37 Danish kings and queens. Some of the crypts are spectacularly embellished and guarded by marble statues of knights and women in mourning, while others are simple unadorned stone coffins. There's something quite awesome about being able to stand next to the bones of so many of Scandinavia's most powerful historical figures. And of course the present living royals intend to be buried here as well.

Of particular interest is the chapel of King Christian IV, off the northern side of the cathedral. It contains the coffin of Christian flanked by his young son, Prince Christian, and his wife, Anne Cathrine, as well as the brass coffins of his successor, Frederik III, and his wife, Queen Sofie Amalie. The bronze statue of Christian IV beside the entrance is the work of Bertel Thorvaldsen, while the huge wall-sized paintings, encased in trompe l'oeil frames, were created by Wilhelm Marstrand and include a classic scene depicting Christian IV rallying the troops aboard the warship *Trinity* during the 1644 battle of Kolbergerheide.

Some of the cathedral's finest pieces were installed by Christian IV, including the intricately detailed pulpit made of marble, alabaster and sandstone in 1610 by Copenhagen sculptor Hans Brokman.

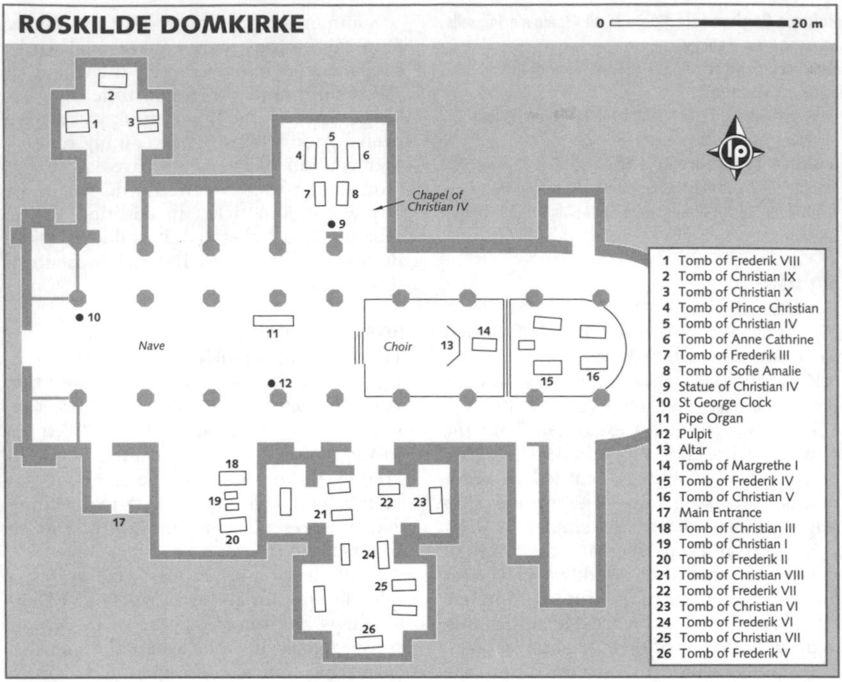
ROSKILDE DOMKIRKE
0
20 m
Chapel of Christian IV
Nave
Choir
1 Tomb of Frederik VIII
2 Tomb of Christian IX
3 Tomb of Christian X
4 Tomb of Prince Christian
5 Tomb of Christian IV
6 Tomb of Anne Cathrine
7 Tomb of Frederik III
8 Tomb of Sofie Amalie
9 Statue of Christian IV
10 St George Clock
11 Pipe Organ
12 Pulpit
13 Altar
14 Tomb of Margrethe I
15 Tomb of Frederik IV
16 Tomb of Christian V
17 Main Entrance
18 Tomb of Christian III
19 Tomb of Christian I
20 Tomb of Frederik II
21 Tomb of Christian VIII
22 Tomb of Frederik VII
23 Tomb of Christian VI
24 Tomb of Frederik VI
25 Tomb of Christian VII
26 Tomb of Frederik V

The enormous gilt 'cupboard-style' altarpiece, made in 1560 in Antwerp, is adorned with 21 plates depicting the life of Christ. The story of how it came to Roskilde is as interesting as the piece. Apparently when the altarpiece was being sent to its original destination Gdansk, its shipper tried to cheat on the sound dues in Helsingør by grossly undervaluing it; the shrewd customs officer, asserting his right to acquire items at the valuation price, snapped up the altarpiece.

It's not unusual for the cathedral to be closed on Saturday for weddings (particularly in spring) and occasionally on other days for funerals but you can always call in advance to check if it's open.

In summer, tours (30kr) are conducted by multilingual guides at 11.30am and 1.30pm Monday to Friday, 11am Saturday and 1.30pm Sunday. Free concerts using the splendid 16th-century Baroque pipe organ are held at 8pm on Thursday in June, July and August.

Unesco designated Roskilde Domkirke as a World Heritage Site.

MUSEET FOR SAMTIDSKUNST

Palæet (the Palace), an 18th-century building that fronts the central square, is a former bishops' residence that now houses **Museet for Samtidskunst** (Museum of Contemporary Art; ☎ 46 31 65 70; www.samtidskunst.dk in Danish; Stændertorvet 3D; adult/student & child 30kr/free; ⌚ 11am-5pm Tue-Fri, noon-4pm Sat & Sun), a small art museum with changing exhibits, and **Palæsamlingerne** (Palace Collections; ☎ 46 35 78 80; Stændertorvet 3E; adult/student & child 25/15kr; ⌚ 11am-4pm mid-May–mid-Sep, 11am-4pm Sat mid-Sep–mid-May), containing 18th- and 19th-century paintings that once belonged to the wealthy Roskilde merchants. **Palæfløejen** (☎ 46 32 14 70; Stændertovet 3C; admission free; ⌚ noon-6pm Tue-Sun), in a wing of the palace, has temporary exhibitions of ceramics, paintings and other artworks.

The well-presented **Roskilde Museum** (☎ 46 36 60 44; www.roskildemuseum.dk; Sankt Olsgade 18; adult/child 25kr/free; ⌚ 11am-4pm) covers Roskilde's history from the Stone Age up to the contemporary 'rock age' of the Roskilde Festival.

Festivals & Events

More than just music – it's a huge spirited bash with lots of drinking and partying. The

Roskilde Festival (☎ 46 36 66 13; www.roskilde-festival.dk), held since 1971, is northern Europe's largest music festival rocks and rocks Roskilde for four consecutive days each summer on the last weekend in June.

Some 150 rock, techno and world music bands play on seven stages. Metallica headlined in 2003 and the line-up in 2004, the festival's 34th year, included the Wu-Tang Clan, Santana, Morissey and the Royal Danish Opera. Over the years the promoters have also been particularly astute at presenting new trends in rock and at booking lesser-known groups (such as UB40 and Talking Heads) who have later gone on to stardom, so you can expect to see some hot bands who haven't yet come into the spotlight.

The average age of the festival-goers is 24 and about half come from other countries, particularly Germany, Sweden, Finland, the Netherlands, Norway and Belgium. There are stalls selling everything from tattoos to fast food but you may want to bring some food supplies of your own as prices are high.

The profits from the Roskilde Festival are distributed to charitable causes both at home and abroad. Four-day festival tickets cost around 1050kr, including camping near the site, and can be purchased in Denmark through BilletNet (☎ 70 15 65 65; www.billetnet.dk) or at Danish post offices. Tickets can also be purchased online at the official concert website.

Advance sales typically start in December and the festival does sell out, so the sooner the better. Even if you're late, however, you needn't miss it all, as it's possible to buy a ticket at the gate (350kr) for just the last day of the festival.

Sleeping

Being so close to Copenhagen, Roskilde is usually visited on a day trip, but there are a few options if you want to spend a night. Tourist office staff book rooms in private homes at 150/300kr for singles/doubles, plus a 25kr booking fee; rooms can be booked in town, in the suburbs and on farms.

Danhostel Roskilde (☎ 46 35 21 84; www.rova.dk in Danish; Vindeboder 7; dm/r 115/400kr; year-round; P) Architecturally, it's difficult to distinguish this modernist hostel from the buildings on Museum Island next to it. There are 152 beds in 40 immaculate rooms, some

SUNKEN SHIPS SURFACE

Towards the end of the Viking era, the narrower necks of Roskilde Fjord were purposely blocked to prevent raids by Norwegian fleets. The five Viking ships that are now displayed at Roskilde's Viking Ship Museum are thought to have been deliberately sunk in one such channel and then piled with rocks to make a reinforced barrier similar to an underwater stone wall. Although people had long suspected that there was a ship beneath the ridge of stones, folklore had led them to believe it was a single ship sunk by Queen Margrethe in the 15th century.

It wasn't until researchers from the National Museum made a series of exploratory dives in the late 1950s that it was discovered that there were several ships at the site and that they dated from the Viking period. Excavations began in 1962 when a cofferdam was built around the ships in the middle of the fjord and pumps were used to drain sea water from the site. Within just four months archaeologists were able to unpile the mound of stones and excavate the ships, whose wooden hulks were now in thousands of pieces. The ship fragments were then reassembled within the purpose-built museum that opened on the harbour front in 1969.

In the mid-1990s, during the deepening of the harbour and the construction of a new artificial island west of the museum, workers were stunned to discover nine more ships, seven dating from the Middle Ages and two from the Viking period. The largest is a 36m-long Viking ship thought to have been built in 1030. In response to these new finds, the National Museum established an archaeological workshop on the site where the recovered ship fragments are cleaned, preserved and documented.

Skuledev 2, the largest Viking ship reconstruction ever, was completed and launched into the water in September 2004. Craftsmen only had 25% or 1800 fragments of the original warship – displayed in the Viking Ship Hall – to work from. In 2007, the reconstruction of *Skuldelev 2* will sail to Dublin, where the original ship was built in 1042, to test and document the seaworthiness and manoeuvrability of the ship on the open sea.

with water views and each with its own shower and toilet.

Svogerslev Kro Hotel (☎ 46 38 30 05; www.svogerslevkro.dk; Svogerslev Hovedgave 45; s/d 650/800kr; P) Despite the old-fashioned façade the rooms and facilities are modern. This hotel is in a romantic red half-timbered building 4km west of town.

Hotel Prindsen (☎ 46 35 80 10; www.prindsen.dk; Algade 13; s/d 1175/1275kr ; P) First opened in 1695, the centrally located Prindsen is Denmark's oldest continuously operating hotel. It has a guest list which reads like a who's who of great Danes, from King Frederik VII to Hans Christian Andersen. As befits an old hotel, the rooms are different sizes and have varied décor, but all have modern amenities and include breakfast. The hotel is a member of the Best Western chain.

Scandic Roskilde Hotel (☎ 46 32 46 32; www.scandic-hotels.com; Søndre Ringvej; s/d 715/815kr; P) Only 1km east of the town centre close to a park and lake, this large modern facility is part of the Hilton hotels network.

Roskilde Camping (☎ 46 75 79 96; www.roskildecamping.dk; Baunehøjvej 7, Veddelev); camp site per person 60kr; early Apr–mid-Sep; bus No 603). Three-star camping ground is near a sandy beach right on Roskilde Fjord, 3km north of the Viking Ship Museum.

Eating

Most of the eating options are clustered on Skomagergade, the pedestrian street that runs west from Stændertorvet.

Gringos (☎ 46 36 14 47; Hestetorvet 10; mains 85kr; tacos 49kr; lunch & dinner) The all-you-can-eat taco lunch at this Mexican restaurant is a good deal and the burritos thick and juicy.

Café Ce'Ci (☎ 46 38 48 78; Stændertorvet; sandwiches 48kr; lunch & dinner) Ce'Ci is a trendy, fashionable café; a good place to sit and people watch.

Restaurant Shanghai (☎ 46 35 01 82; Skomagergade 4; dinner buffet 99kr; lunch & dinner) Busy family-run restaurant is the place to go for reasonably priced Chinese fare.

Restaurant Bryggorgarden (☎ 46 35 01 03; Algade 15; mains 48-160kr; lunch & dinner) French and Danish cuisine served in an elegant pub atmosphere; however, the service can be slow.

Raadhus-Kælderen (☎ 46 36 01 00; Stændertorvet; lunch specials 68kr, dinner mains 200kr; lunch & dinner). For a treat, try this atmospheric restaurant in the cellar of the old town hall (c 1430). Lunchtime specials include such dishes as fish fillet with shrimp and asparagus. Dinner features a changing menu of creative, French-inspired meat and seafood dishes.

Restaurant Snekken (☎ 46 35 98 16; Vindeboder 16; mains 82kr; lunch & dinner) Situated between the hostel and the Viking Ship Museum, Snekken has a large dining room and outdoor waterfront seating.

On Wednesday and Saturday mornings there's a market on Stændertorvet selling fresh produce as well as local handicrafts and flowers.

Getting There & Around

Trains from Copenhagen to Roskilde are frequent (59kr, 25 minutes). Trains also run between Roskilde and Køge (34kr, 25 minutes) and Næstved (49kr, 42 minutes).

If you're coming from Copenhagen by car, Rte 21 leads to Roskilde. Upon approaching the city, exit onto Rte 156, which leads into the centre. There are car parks south of Strandberg Supermarket and down by the Viking Ship Museum.

Bicycles can be hired from **JAS Cykler** (☎ 46 35 04 20; Gullandsstræde 3) for 50kr per day.

LEJRE

The countryside on the outskirts of Lejre, a village 8km southwest of Roskilde, has two sightseeing attractions that could be combined for an afternoon outing.

Sights

LEDREBORG SLOT

Visitors to the grand manor house **Ledreborg Slot** (☎ 46 48 00 38; www.ledreborgslot.dk; Ledreborg Allé; adult/child 60/35kr; 11am-5pm mid-Jun–Aug, 11am-5pm Sun May–mid-Jun & Sep), considered one of the finest in Denmark, are required to put on booties to prevent damage to the marble and parquet floors. Ledreborg Slot was built and decorated by Count Johan Ludvig Holstein in 1739 and has been home to the Holstein-Ledreborg family ever since. The interior has barely changed in all that time and is chockfull of antique furniture, gilded mirrors, chandeliers, oil paintings and wall tapestries. One of the most superb rooms is the banquet room, designed by architect Nicolai Eigtved, the creator of Copenhagen's Amalienborg Slot. Also in the manor house is a chapel, constructed by JC Krieger in 1745, which served as the parish church until 1899.

Outside are 80 hectares of lawns and woods and the Jungle Path, a series of ropes and logs and ladders designed for children but equally fun for adults.

LEJRE FORSØGSCENTER

The reconstructed Iron Age village **Lejre Forsøgscenter** (☎ 46 48 08 78; www.lejre center.dk; Slangeallen 2; adult/child 75/45kr; 🕑 10am-5pm May–mid-Sep) is an archaeological experimental centre where Danish families can volunteer to spend their summer holidays as 'prehistoric families', using technology and dressed in clothing from that period. The reconstructed houses they live in and the tools they use are modelled on finds from archaeological excavations around Denmark.

The centre has craft demonstrations and the lives of 19th-century Danish farmers are re-enacted at the small cottage-farm area. In summer, when the place is most active, children can paddle dugout canoes and partake in other hands-on activities such as grinding flour.

Getting There & Away

From Roskilde it's just a short train ride to Lejre station, where bus No 233 continues to both Ledreborg Slot and Lejre Forsøgscenter (17kr).

By car, from Roskilde take Ringstedvej (Rte 14), turn right on Rte 155 and then almost immediately turn left onto Ledreborg Allé. Follow the signs to Ledreborg, 6km away, where a long drive lined by old elm trees leads to the entrance. Lejre Forsøgscenter is 2km further west along the same road.

HUNDESTED

pop 8400

The main attraction in Hundested, a small town at the mouth of Isefjord, is the home built by Knud Rasmussen (1879–1933), Denmark's most famous arctic explorer. Near the lighthouse, the home has been turned into a museum, **Knud Rasmussens Hus** (☎ 47 93 71 61; Knud Rasmussensvej 9; adult/child 15/10kr; 🕑 11am-4pm Tue-Sun mid-Apr–mid-Oct). It contains original furnishings, but thousands of archaeological artefacts that Rasmussen collected on his expeditions are kept in Nationalmuseet in Copenhagen.

The Lynæs area, a few kilometres south of Hundested, is a **windsurfing** mecca with good wind conditions as well as shallow-water areas suitable for beginners. **Nautic Surf og Ski** (☎ 47 98 01 00; Lynæs Havnevej 15) has windsurfing gear for hire and also offers lessons.

Byaasgaard Camping (☎ 47 92 31 02; www.byaasgaard.dk; Amtsvejen 340; camp site per person 65kr, small cabins 200kr; 💻) Equidistant between Hundested and Frederiksværk, this camping ground is one of the few in all of Europe to offer free wireless Internet access.

The train between Hundested and Hillerød (45kr, 45 minutes) runs twice an hour.

FREDERIKSVÆRK

pop 11,600

Frederiksværk, on the northern side of the Roskilde Fjord, is Denmark's oldest industrial town, founded in 1756 by order of King Frederik V, from whom the town takes its name. At that time a canal was dug between the Roskilde Fjord and Arresø Lake to provide water power for mills, a gunpowder factory and a cannon foundry.

The **tourist office** (☎ 47 72 30 01; www.frvturist.dk/; Gjethusgade 5; 🕑 10am-5pm Mon-Fri, 1am-1pm Sat) is in Gjethuset, a former cannon foundry on Torvet converted into a **cultural centre** with changing art exhibits. You can reserve rooms in the area for a 25kr booking fee.

The town sits on the western shore of Arresø which, at 41 sq km, is Denmark's largest lake. Leisurely **boat excursions** (☎ 47 72 30 01) cruise the lake on summer afternoons (adult/child 60/30kr). The small beach town of **Liseleje** is only 6km away.

Danhostel Frederiksværk & Frederiksværk Campingplads (☎ 47 77 07 25; www.strandbo.dk; Strandgade 30; dm/s/d 100/300/400kr, camp site per person 58kr) Hostel and camping ground right by the canal in the centre of town. Canoes can be hired per hour (100kr) or per day (350kr).

Liselangen Bed & Breakfast (☎ 47 74 73 06; www.liselangen.dk in Danish; Liselejevej 62; s/d incl breakfast, without bathroom 390/595kr) Charming place on main street and a short walk to the beach. Reduced prices last two weeks of August. Relaxing garden and café attached.

Frederiksværk is on the railway line between Hundested (25kr, 18 minutes) and Hillerød (50kr, 28 minutes).

Southern Zealand

CONTENTS

A region mostly undisturbed by tourism, primarily modern towns contained in single strips, stretched out along pedestrian avenues for the convenience of Danes going about their everyday lives. Most people pass through on their way to the beaches further south or Jutland to the west. However, in places like Køge and Sorø, the age and history of the region reveals itself in the form of perfectly restored medieval churches and rough, cobblestone streets lined by yellow half-timbered houses.

The triangular region between Næstved in the south and Sorø and Korsør to the north is spotted with forests, small lakes and streams, as close to undomesticated nature as you'll find in Zealand. And standing atop the remains of a 1000-year-old Viking ring fortress at Trelleborg, it's possible to imagine a time when the land was wild and forbidding, and surveying the horizon as far as the eye can see was a journey in and of itself.

In medieval times southern Zealand was a stamping ground for significant historical characters such as Bishop Absalon and the royal Valdemar family. In the 17th century the area was the stage for some of the most important battles of the lengthy wars between Denmark and Sweden. The most pivotal defeat in Danish history was played out here in 1658 when the Swedish king Gustave marched across southern Zealand en route to Copenhagen, where he forced a treaty that nearly cost Denmark its sovereignty.

If you're travelling across the region between Køge and Korsør using your own transport, the rural Rte 150 makes an excellent alternative to zipping along on the E20 motorway. Not only is it a slower, greener route, but it will take you right into the most interesting towns and villages.

HIGHLIGHTS

- Wander around **Sorø** (p136), a charming town with a rich cultural background
- Explore the countryside around **Næstved** (p143), as close as you'll come to virgin nature
- Explore the Viking past at the fascinating ring fortress at **Trelleborg** (p140)
- Stroll through the well-preserved historic quarter of the ancient town of **Køge** (p130)
- Poke around the rural hamlet of **Vallø** (p134), with its castle and woodland

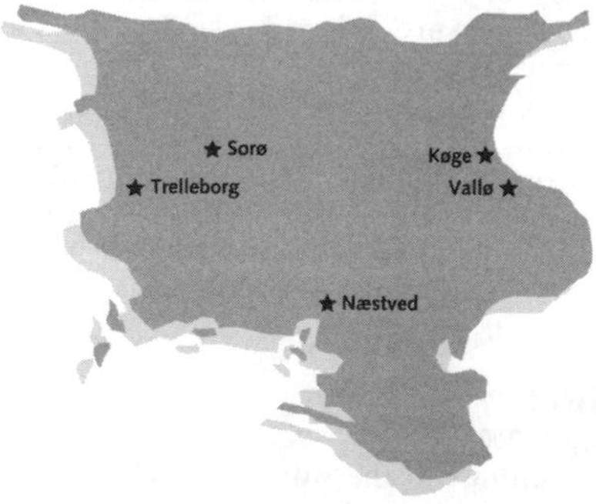
Sorø
Køge
Trelleborg
Vallø
Næstved

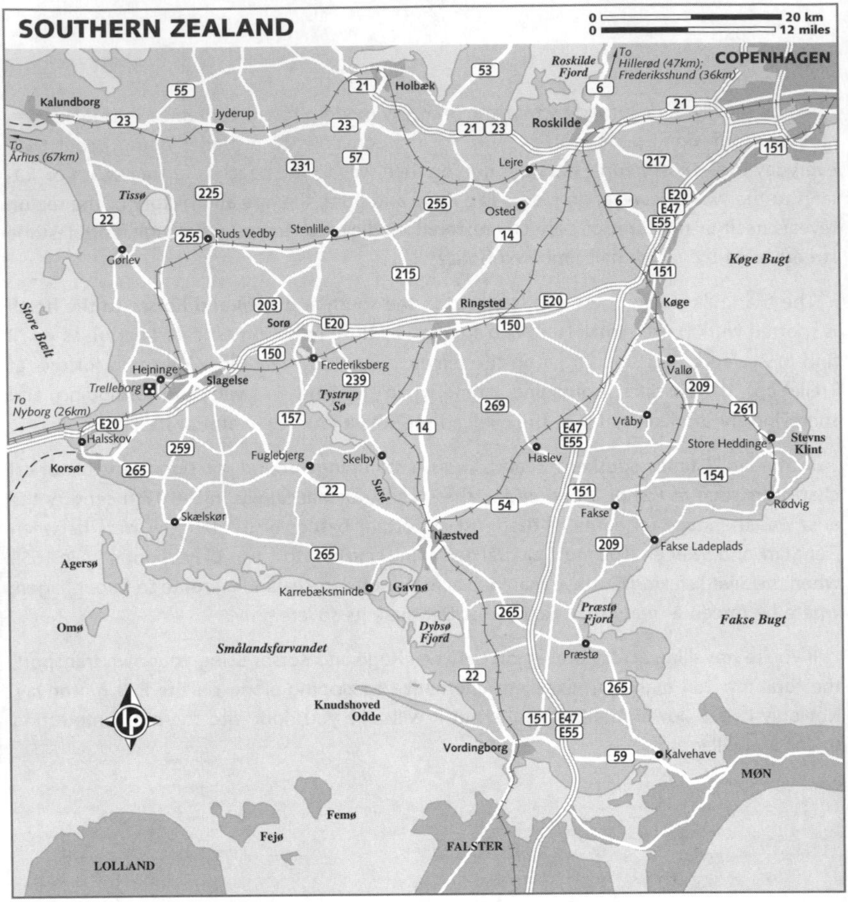
SOUTHERN ZEALAND
0 20 km
0 12 miles
COPENHAGEN
To Hillerød (47km); Frederiksshund (36km)
Roskilde Fjord
Roskilde
Holbæk
Kalundborg
To Århus (67km)
Jyderup
Tissø
Lejre
Osted
Gørlev
Ruds Vedby
Stenlille
Køge Bugt
Køge
Ringsted
Sorø
Store Bælt
Hejninge
Slagelse
Trelleborg
Frederiksberg
Tystrup Sø
To Nyborg (26km)
Halsskov
Korsør
Fuglebjerg
Skelby
Suså
Vallø
Vråby
Haslev
Store Heddinge
Stevns Klint
Rødvig
Fakse
Fakse Ladeplads
Skælskør
Næstved
Agersø
Karrebæksminde
Gavnø
Omø
Dybsø Fjord
Præstø Fjord
Præstø
Fakse Bugt
Smålandsfarvandet
Knudshoved Odde
Vordingborg
Kalvehave
MØN
Femø
Fejø
FALSTER
LOLLAND
55
53
21
23
6
231
57
225
255
22
14
217
E20
E47
E55
151
215
203
150
239
157
269
209
261
259
265
54
154
59

Getting There & Around

Like that of North Zealand, the transportation system in Southern Zealand is linked to Copenhagen and just about all of the region can be reached in an hour from the capital. Having your own transportation is more important, though, since the destinations are more scattered than in the north and a good amount of the region's appeal lies in the pastoral scenery witnessed as you travel through.

KØGE

pop 33,200

In contrast to the working, modern commercial harbour, Køge's small, but central historic quarter exudes much charm and a lost, slower pace of life. The narrow streets that radiate from Torvet, the town square, are lined with old buildings, some having survived a sweeping fire in 1633, and others built in the construction boom spawned by that blaze. Narrow beaches are along the bay both to the north and south of town.

Køge has a rich history stretching back to 1288, when it was granted its municipal charter by King Erik VI. With its large natural harbour, Køge quickly developed into a thriving fishing and trade centre. In 1677 one of the most important naval engagements of the Danish-Swedish wars was fought in the waters off Køge. Known as the Battle of Køge Bay, it made a legend of Danish admiral Niels Juel, who resoundingly defeated the attacking Swedish navy and thwarted the attempted invasion.

Information

Køge Turistbureau (☎ 56 65 58 00; www.visitkoege.com; Vestergade 1; ⌚ 9am-5pm Mon-Fri, Sat 9am-2pm Jun-Aug, 10am-1pm Sep-May) distributes a free 90-page booklet, with English translations, describing the town's sights.

Nordea (☎ 56 63 33 33; Torvet 14; ⌚ 9.30am-4pm Mon-Fri, to 6pm Thu) Bank has ATMs.

Post office (☎ 70 12 40 00; Jernstøbervænget 2; ⌚ 10am-5pm Mon-Fri, 10am-12.30pm Sat)

Sights

SANKT NICOLAI KIRKE

Named after the patron saint of mariners, the **Sankt Nicolai Kirke** (☎ 56 65 13 59; Kirkestræde 31; admission free; ⌚ 10am-4pm Mon-Fri, 10am-noon Sat mid-Jun–Aug; 10am-noon Mon-Sat Sep–mid-Jun) is two blocks north of Torvet. On the upper eastern end of the church tower there's a little brick projection called **Lygten**, which was used to hang a burning lantern as a guide for sailors returning to the harbour. It was from the top of the church tower that Christian IV kept watch on his naval fleet as it successfully defended the town from Swedish invaders during the Battle of Køge Bay.

The church dates from 1324 but was largely rebuilt in the 15th century. Most of the ornately carved works that adorn the interior were added later, including the altar and pulpit, which date from the 17th century. From June to August – the Danish summer – you can climb the tower between 10.30am and 1.30pm.

KØGE MUSEUM

Occupying a lovely building dating from 1619, the **Køge Museum** (☎ 56 63 42 42; www.dmol.dk; Nørregade 4; adult/student/child 30/15kr/free incl entry to Køge Skitsesamling; ⌚ 11am-5pm Jun-Aug, 1-5pm Sun-Fri, 11am-3pm Sat Sep-May) was once a wealthy merchant's home. Its rooms now feature exhibits illustrating the cultural history of the Køge area. As well as the expected furnishings and artefacts, there's an interesting hotchpotch of displays ranging from a Mesolithic-era grave to hundreds of recently discovered silver coins. The coins include those unearthed in the courtyard at **Brogade 17**,

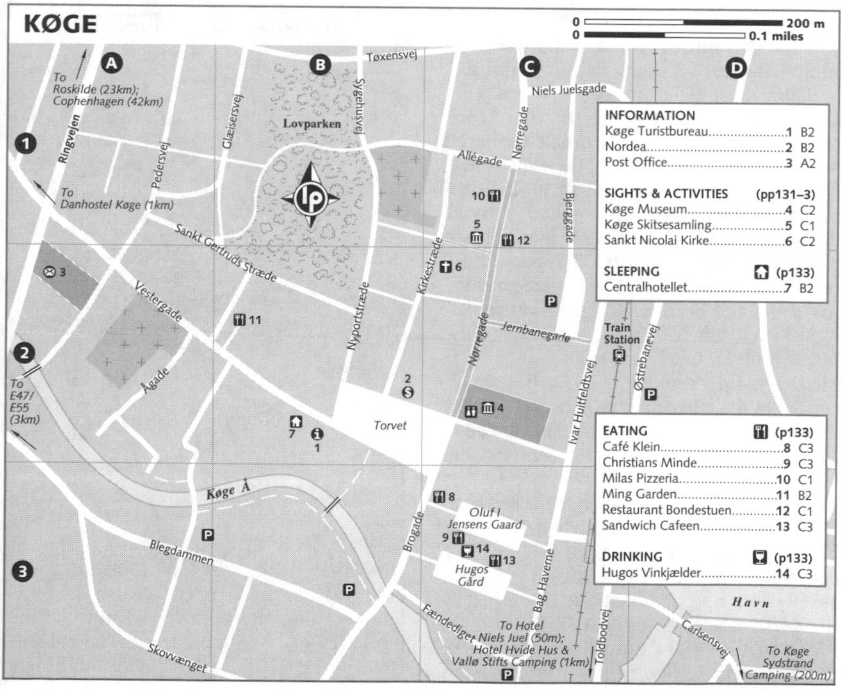
KØGE
0 200 m
0 0.1 miles
A
B
C
D
1
2
3
To Roskilde (23km); Cophenhagen (42km)
To Danhostel Køge (1km)
To E47/ E55 (3km)
Tøxensvej
Niels Juelsgade
Lovparken
Sygehusvej
Glæisersvej
Pedersvej
Ringvejen
Allégade
Nørregade
Bjerggade
Sankt Gertruds Stræde
Vestergade
Ågade
Nyportstræde
Kirkestræde
Jernbanegade
Train Station
Østrebanevej
Ivar Huitfeldtsvej
Torvet
Køge Å
Blegdammen
Brogade
Oluf I Jensens Gaard
Hugos Gård
Bag Haverne
Fændediget
Toldbodvej
Skovvænget
Havn
Carlsensvej
To Hotel Niels Juel (50m); Hotel Hvide Hus & Vallø Stifts Camping (1km)
To Køge Sydstrand Camping (200m)
INFORMATION
Køge Turistbureau 1 B2
Nordea 2 B2
Post Office 3 A2
SIGHTS & ACTIVITIES (pp131–3)
Køge Museum 4 C2
Køge Skitsesamling 5 C1
Sankt Nicolai Kirke 6 C2
SLEEPING (p133)
Centralhotellet 7 B2
EATING (p133)
Café Klein 8 C3
Christians Minde 9 C3
Milas Pizzeria 10 C1
Ming Garden 11 B2
Restaurant Bondestuen 12 C1
Sandwich Cafeen 13 C3
DRINKING (p133)
Hugos Vinkjælder 14 C3

part of a huge stash thought to have been hidden during the Swedish wars of the late 17th century.

The museum also has a desk used by Danish philosopher NFS Grundtvig, who lived on the outskirts of Køge, and a windowpane onto which Hans Christian Andersen, during an apparently stressed-out stay at a nearby inn, scratched the words 'Oh God, Oh God in Kjøge'.

KØGE SKITSESAMLING

The Køge Art and Sketch Collection – **Køge Skitsesamling** (☎ 56 67 60 20; www.skitsesamlingen.dk; Nørregade 29; adult/child incl entry to the Køge Museum 30/15kr; 🕓 11am-5pm Tue-Sun) is a unique art museum that specialises in outlining the creative process from an artist's earliest concept to the finished work. The displays include original drawings, clay models and mock-ups by 20th-century Danish artists.

Walking Tour

Most of Køge's finest historical sites are within easy walking distance of each other. A pleasant little stroll around these sites can be made in about an hour, although if you take your time, stopping at Sankt Nicolai Kirke and the two museums along the way, you could easily turn it into a half-day outing.

Begin the walk from Torvet by making a short detour west along the first block of **Vestergade**. There are two half-timbered houses on this street: **No 7 (1)**, which dates from the 16th century, and **No 16 (2)**, a remarkably well-preserved merchant's house dating from 1644, featuring old hand-blown glass in the doors and intricately carved detail on the timbers. From Vestergade, return to Torvet and head north on Kirkestræde.

At **Kirkestræde 3 (3)**, just near Torvet, is the house built by Oluf Sandersen and his wife Margareta Jørgensdatter in 1638, the date recorded in the lettering above the gate. Other timber-framed houses include **Kirkestræde 13 (4)**, which dates from the 16th century, and a 17th-century house at Kirkestræde 10 that has served as a kindergarten, **Køge Børneasyl (5)**, since 1856. The oldest half-timbered house in Denmark is a modest little place constructed in 1527 with a brick front and a steeply tiled roof at **Kirkestræde 20 (6)**. Just to the north is **Sankt Nicolai Kirke (7, p131)**.

If you turn right onto Katekismusgade, you'll immediately come to the art museum **Køge Skitsesamling (8)** art museum. In the grounds near the museum is a bronze sculpture by Svend Rathsack of a young boy with scurrying lizards.

Immediately north of the museum, at Nørregade 31, is an attractive red timbered house, built in 1612, that now holds a **goldsmith shop (9)**. Continuing south on Nørregade, you'll pass more houses built in the early 17th century: No 5, which now houses the **Arnold Busck bookshop (10)**, and No 4, home to the **Køge Museum (11)**.

Look for the marble plaque marked **Kiøge Huskors (12)** (Kiøge and Kjøge are old spellings of Køge) on the green corner building at Torvet 2, which honours the victims of a witch-hunt in the 17th century. Two residents of an earlier house on this site were among those burned at the stake.

Along the eastern side of Torvet is the yellow neoclassical **Køge Rådhus (13)**, said to be the oldest town hall in use in Denmark. At the rear of this complex is a building erected in 1600 to serve as an inn for King Christian IV on journeys between his royal palaces in Copenhagen and Nykøbing.

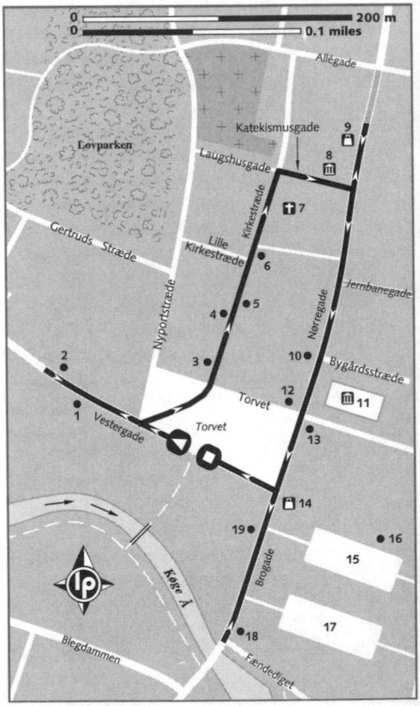
0
200 m
0
0.1 miles
Allégade
Katekismusgade
Løvparken
Laugshusgade
Kirkestræde
Gertruds Stræde
Lille Kirkestræde
Jernbanegade
Nyportstræde
Nørregade
Bygårdsstræde
Torvet
Vestergade
Torvet
Brogade
Køge Å
Blegdammen
Fændediget
1
2
3
4
5
6
7
8
9
10
11
12
13
14
15
16
17
18
19

At Brogade 1, by the southeastern corner of Torvet, is **Køge Apotek (14)**, a pharmacy that has occupied this site since 1660. Proceeding south, at Brogade 7 is **Oluf I Jensens Gård (15)**, a courtyard lined with a collection of typical 19th-century merchant buildings; one of these now houses **Køge Galleriet (16)**, a local art gallery.

At Brogade 19 there's an older courtyard, **Hugos Gård (17)**, with some 17th-century structures and a 14th century medieval brick building, the wine cellar of which now houses a wine bar, Hugos Vinkjælder. It's an enjoyable place to stop for a break. In the adjacent courtyard, at Brogade 17, workers unearthed a buried treasure in 1987 – an old wooden trunk filled with more than 30kg of 17th-century silver coins, the largest such find ever made in Denmark. Some of these coins are on display at the Køge Museum.

Cherubs carved by the famed 17th-century artist Abel Schrøder decorate the building at **Brogade 23** (**18**, c 1638). If you cross the street and return to Torvet along the western side of Brogade, you'll pass Køge's longest timber-framed house at **Brogade 16 (19)**, a yellow-brick structure erected in 1636 by the town's mayor.

Sleeping

The tourist office can book rooms in private homes for 375kr to 450kr per double, plus a 25kr booking fee.

Køge Sydstrand Camping (☎ 56 65 07 69; koege.sydstrand.camping@fritid.tele.dk; Søndre Badevej; camp site per person 50kr; Apr–mid-Sep) Two-star facility, south of the harbour, on a beach with an industrial backdrop, about a 20-minute (500m) walk from the train station.

Vallø Stifts Camping (☎ 56 65 28 51; www.valloecamping.dk; Strandvejen 102; camp site per person 62kr) Technically part of Vallø, this lovely camping ground is across the street from the Hotel Hvide Hus and the water.

Danhostel Køge (☎ 56 65 14 74; www.danhostel.dk/koege; Vamdrupvej 1; dm/r 100/440kr, r in low season 250kr; Apr–mid-Dec; P) A quiet area 2km northwest of the town centre (take bus No 210) is where you'll find this 80-bed hostel.

Centralhotellet (☎ 56 65 06 96; fax 56 66 02 07; Vestergade 3; s/d incl breakfast without bathroom 290/530kr, d with bath 630kr; P) Aptly named hotel adjacent to the tourist office has a dozen straightforward rooms above a small bar and in a separate wing at the back.

Hotel Niels Juel (☎ 56 63 18 00; www.hotelnielsjuel.dk; Toldbodvej 20; s/d incl breakfast 965/1195kr; P) Part of the Best Western chain, this 50-room modern hotel nevertheless looks distinctive and old-fashioned in a charming way. Niels Juel overlooks the harbour a couple of blocks south of the train station.

Hotel Hvide Hus (☎ 56 65 36 90; www.hotelhvidehus.dk; Strandvejen 111; s/d incl breakfast 775/975kr; P) A sprawling Best Western hotel near the beach at the less-developed end of town. Rooms and facilities are modern but both have seen better days. Caters to large groups.

Eating

Sandwich Cafeen (☎ 56 65 04 28; Brogade 19; sandwiches 36kr; lunch & dinner) Situated in Hugo's Gård, wide variety of sandwiches good for takeaway. A few small tables in the courtyard.

Milas Pizzeria (☎ 56 65 61 60; Nørregade 35; mains 50kr; lunch & dinner) Usual mix of pizzas, burgers and pitta sandwiches.

Café Klein (☎ 56 63 60 61; Brogade 7; mains 58kr; lunch & dinner) Modern and stylish café serving up healthy pasta salads and burgers too. Great garden out the back.

Ming Garden (☎ 56 65 12 23; Vestergade 20; meals or barbecues 120kr; lunch & dinner) Chinese restaurant offering a variety of three-item meals daily and an indulgent all-you-can-eat, Mongolian-style barbecue on Friday and Saturday.

Christians Minde (☎ 56 63 68 56; Brodgade 7; light lunches 60kr, full dinners 200kr; lunch & dinner) Menu features interesting mix of Danish, Chinese and big American-style steaks and full-course fish and beef dinners that include everything from soup to coffee. Dining room is elegant and slightly formal while outdoor seating is casual. Live music every Saturday.

On the eastern side of Torvet you'll find a fruit hut and a butcher shop with takeaway smørrebrød (open sandwiches). There's a produce, cheese and flower market at Torvet on Wednesday and Saturday mornings.

Drinking

Hugos Vinkjælder (☎ 56 65 58 50; Brogade 19; lunch & dinner) Dark and cosy little wine bar, in Hugos Gård in the cellar of a 14th-century building, sells half a bottle of wine for just 60kr and also serves beer from around the world. In summer, live jazz bands play in the courtyard at noon on Saturday.

Getting There & Away

Køge is at the end of the E and A+ lines, the southernmost station on greater Copenhagen's S-train network. Trains from Copenhagen (42kr, 32 minutes) run three to six times an hour. Køge is also on the rail line between Roskilde (37kr, 25 minutes) and Næstved (45kr, 34 minutes).

Køge is 42km southwest of Copenhagen and 25km southeast of Roskilde. If you're coming by road take the E47/E55 from Copenhagen or Rte 6 from Roskilde and then pick up Rte 151 south into the centre of Køge. There's free parking on Torvet with a one-hour limit during business hours as well as less-restricted parking off Havnen, north of the harbour.

VALLØ

Vallø is a charming little hamlet with cobblestone streets, a dozen mustard-yellow houses and an attractive moat-encircled Renaissance castle, Vallø Slot. Situated in the countryside about 7km south of Køge, Vallø makes an enjoyable little excursion for those looking to get off the beaten path. If old-world character and mildly eccentric surroundings appeal, it could also be a fun place to spend the evening.

Sights

The red-brick **Vallø Slot** dates from 1586 and retains most of its original style, even though much of it was rebuilt following a fire in 1893.

The castle has a rather unusual history. On her birthday in 1737 Queen Sophie Magdalene, who owned the estate, established a foundation that turned Vallø Slot into a home for 'spinsters of noble birth'. Until a few decades ago unmarried daughters of Danish royalty who hadn't the means to live in their own castles or manor houses were allowed to take up residence at Vallø, supported by the foundation and government social programs.

In the 1970s, bowing to the changing sentiments that had previously spared this anachronistic niche of the Zealand countryside, the foundation amended its charter to gradually make the estate more accessible to the general public. For now, the castle remains home solely to a handful of ageing blue-blooded women who had taken up residence prior to 1976.

Vallø Slot is surrounded by 2800 hectares of woods and ponds and 1300 hectares of fields and arable land reaching down to the coast. Although the main castle buildings are not open to the public, visitors are free to walk in the gardens and the adjacent woods.

Hestestalden (☎ 56 63 42 42; admission 15kr, free with a same-day Køge Museum ticket; ⌚ 11am-4pm, closed Mon mid-May–Aug), the stables at Vallø Slot, feature an exhibition on the history of the castle.

Sleeping & Eating

Vallø Slotskro (☎ 56 26 70 20; www.hotelvalloeslotskro.dk; Slotsgade 1; s/d incl breakfast without bathroom 475/750kr, with bathroom 745/925kr) Just outside the castle gate, this 200-year-old inn has 11 quite pleasantly decorated rooms that combine antique furnishings with modern conveniences such as minibars and TV. The inn's dining room serves Danish country fare featuring three-course meals from 100kr.

Getting There & Away

Take the train to Vallø station, two stops south of Køge, and from there it's an easy 1.25km stroll east down a tree-lined country road to the castle.

If you're travelling by road take Rte 209 south from Køge, turn right onto Billesborgvej and then left (south) onto Valløvej, which leads to Slotsgade.

There's a signposted cycle route from Køge that leads into Valløvej.

RINGSTED

pop 18,100

Situated at a crossroads in central Zealand, Ringsted was an important market town during the Middle Ages and also served as the site of the *landsting,* a regional governing assembly. The town grew up around Sankt Bendts Kirke, which was built during the reign of Valdemar I (1157–82). This historic church, which still marks the town centre, is Ringsted's most interesting sight.

Immediately east of the church is Torvet, the central square, which features a statue of Valdemar I, sculpted by Johannes Bjerg in the 1930s, as well as three sitting stones that were used centuries ago by the *landsting* members.

Ringsted's town centre is a short walk north from the train station and the **Ringsted Turistbureau** (☎ 57 62 66 00; www.met-2000.dk; Sankt

Bendtsgade 6; 9am-5pm Mon-Fri & 10am-2pm Sat mid-Jun–Sep, 10am-5pm Mon-Fri & 10am-1pm Sat Oct–mid-Jun) is just north of Sankt Bendts Kirke.

Sights

Erected in 1170 by Valdemar I, the imposing **Sankt Bendts Kirke** (57 61 14 01; Sankt Bendtsgade 1; admission free; 10am-noon & 1-5pm May–mid-Sep, 1-3pm mid-Sep–Apr) was to serve as a burial sanctuary for his father, Knud Lavard, who had been canonised by the Pope. It was also a calculated move to shore up the rule of the Valdemar dynasty and intertwine the influences of the Crown and the Catholic Church.

Although Sankt Bendts Kirke was substantially restored during the 1900s, it has retained much of its original medieval style and character. The building still incorporates travertine blocks from an 11th-century abbey church that had earlier occupied the same site.

The nave is adorned with magnificent frescoes, including a series depicting Erik IV (known as Erik Ploughpenny, for the despised tax he levied on ploughs), which were painted in about 1300 in a failed campaign to get the assassinated king canonised. These frescoes show Queen Agnes seated on a throne; on her left is a scene of Ploughpenny's murderers stabbing the king with a spear, while the right-hand scene depicts the king's corpse being retrieved from the sea by fishermen.

Sankt Bendts Kirke was a burial place for the royal family for 150 years. In the aisle floor beneath the nave are flat stones marking the tombs of many of Denmark's famous kings and queens (in order from the font) Valdemar III and his queen, Eleonora; Valdemar II, flanked by his queens Dagmar and Bengærd; Knud VI; Valdemar I, flanked by his queen, Sofia, and his son Christopher; and Knud Lavard. Also buried in the church are Erik VI (Menved) and Queen Ingeborg, whose remains lie in an ornate tomb in the chancel, although King Birger of Sweden and his queen Margarete, were buried in the former tomb of Erik Ploughpenny.

Some of the tombs, including the empty one that once held Queen Dagmar, have been disturbed over the centuries to make room for later burials. A few of the grave relics removed from these tombs can be found in the church's museum chapel, along with a copy of the Dagmar Cross.

The church has interesting carved works, including pews from 1591 (note the dragons on the seats near the altar), an elaborate altar-piece from 1699 and a pulpit from 1609. The church's oldest item is the 12th-century baptismal font which, despite its historical significance, once served a stint as a flower bowl in a local garden.

Note that the church is closed whenever there are weddings, a particularly common occurrence on Saturdays in April and May, the spring months.

A restored 1814 Dutch windmill is part of the **Ringsted Museum** (57 62 69 00; Køgevej 41; adult/child 25/10kr; 11am-4pm Tue-Sun). This small museum of local cultural history is on the eastern side of town, within walking distance of Torvet and the train station.

THE DAGMAR CROSS

Queen Dagmar, the first wife of Valdemar II, was born a princess in Bohemia. Although she lived in Denmark for only a few years before her premature death in 1212, she was much loved by the Danes and is revered in several ballads as a kind, good-hearted woman.

In 1683, as Queen Dagmar's tomb was being removed from Sankt Bendts Kirke in Ringsted, a small gold cross with finely detailed enamel work was found at the site. Now known as the Dagmar Cross, it is thought to date from AD 1000. One side shows Christ with arms outstretched on the cross and the other side depicts him with the Virgin Mary, John the Baptist, St John and St Basil.

This perfectly preserved cross of Byzantine design is now in Nationalmuseet in Copenhagen. It has been widely replicated as a pendant by Ringsted jewellery shops and is popularly worn as a necklace by brides who marry in Sankt Bendts Kirke.

Sleeping

Tourist office staff can book rooms in private homes for 180kr to 250kr per person; there's a 25kr booking fee.

Skovly Camping (57 52 82 61; www.skovlycamp.dk; Nebs Møllevej 65, Ortved; camp site per person 62kr;) Surrounded by forests. Also has small cabins for rent.

SOUTHERN ZEALAND

Danhostel Ringsted (☎ 57 61 15 26; www.amtstuegaarden.dk; Sankt Bendtsgade 18; dm/s/d with bathroom 115/290/360kr; mid-Jan–mid-Dec; P) Modern 78-bed hostel has an ideal location opposite Sankt Bendts Kirke.

Scandic Hotel Ringsted (☎ 57 61 93 00; www.scandic-hotels.com; Nørretorv 57; s/d incl breakfast 590/690kr; P) On the northern side of the town centre, this not especially attractive hotel – a member of the Scandic chain – has 75 modern rooms with 1st-class amenities. Breakfast included.

Sørup Herregaard (☎ 57 64 30 02; www.sorup.dk; Sørupvej 26; s/d incl breakfast 998/1198kr; P) Sørup is located on a beautiful estate 7km south of town, surrounded by forests and farmland. Modern rooms are in converted 13th-century buildings. Reduced rates are often available.

Eating

Rådhuskroen (☎ 57 61 68 97; Sankt Bendtsgade 8; steaks 130kr; lunch & dinner) A pub-style restaurant specialises in steaks of all sorts and fried fish. It's next to the tourist office.

Café Aspendos (☎ 57 67 05 09; Møllegade 11; sandwiches 45kr; breakfast, lunch & dinner) Airy café with a good brunch deal near the town centre.

Italy & Italy (☎ 57 61 53 53; Torvet 1C; multicourse lunch/dinner 89/198kr; lunch & dinner) Facing the southeastern side of the church, this place serves good Italian food ranging from pizzas and pasta to a mouthwatering cognac salmon.

Restaurant Kina (☎ 57 61 23 18; Sankt Bendtsgade 10; mains 50-70kr; lunch & dinner) Eatery just 20m east of the tourist office offers a variety of Chinese selections served with rice, as well as cheap hot dogs and chicken dishes.

Getting There & Away

Ringsted is on Rte 150 and just off the E20 motorway, 27km west of Køge and 16km east of Sorø. Roskilde is 30km to the north via Rte 14.

There are numerous trains throughout the day to Ringsted from Roskilde (29kr, 18 minutes) and Næstved (29kr, 20 minutes).

SORØ

pop 6800

Bordered by lakes and woodlands, Sorø is a delightful little town steeped in culture and history. The streets of the town centre are thick with old timber-framed houses, and the academy grounds and surrounding lakeside park are idyllic for a late afternoon stroll.

Bishop Absalon established a Cistercian monastery here in 1161, six years before he founded Copenhagen. The bishop and four Danish monarchs lie buried in Sorø Kirke, the church that Absalon erected in the monastery grounds.

After the Reformation, when Catholicism was banned and Church properties were turned over to the Crown, Frederik II set aside the monastery grounds to be used as a school. His successor, Christian IV, developed it into the Sorø Academy of Knights, an elite school dedicated to the education of the sons of the nobility.

The great Danish playwright Ludvig Holberg (1684–1754), a summer resident of Sorø and a patron of the academy, helped to revive the school during faltering times by bequeathing it his substantial estate.

During Denmark's 'Golden Age' (1800–50) of national romanticism, Sorø became a haunt for some of the country's most prominent cultural figures, including Bertel Thorvaldsen, NFS Grundtvig and Adam Oehlenschläger.

The streets of the town centre are thick with old timber-framed houses, and the academy grounds and surrounding lakeside park are open to the public.

Information

Cyber Net Café (☎ 57 84 57 33; Ostergade 4; noon-10pm, closed Sun) charges 15kr per hour.

Library (☎ 57 87 01 01; Storgade 7) has free Internet access.

Nordea (☎ 57 83 05 00; Storgade 22) is one of several banks in town.

Post office (☎ 58 56 78 00; Rådhusvej 6) is just south of the rådhus.

Sorø Turistbureau (☎ 57 82 10 12; www.set-soroe.dk in Danish; Storgade 15; 9.30am-5pm Mon- Fri & 9.30am-3pm Sat, 9.30am-noon Sat Sep-May) is in the town centre. In addition to the usual services, staff here can arrange bicycle rentals.

Sights

Although it's no longer reserved for the sons of the nobility, the **Sorø Akademi** remains a prominent Danish school. The extensive grounds are owned by a private foundation, though the school itself is still funded by the state.

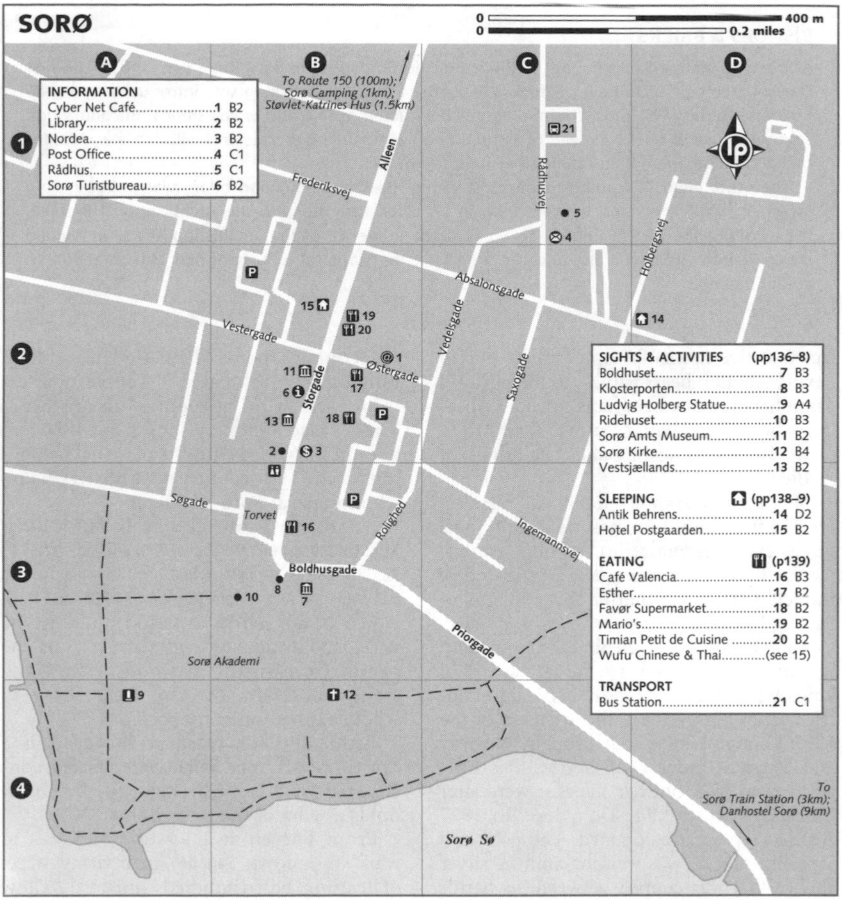
SORØ
0 400 m
0 0.2 miles
A
B
C
D
1
2
3
4
INFORMATION
Cyber Net Café.....1 B2
Library.....2 B2
Nordea.....3 B2
Post Office.....4 C1
Rådhus.....5 C1
Sorø Turistbureau.....6 B2
SIGHTS & ACTIVITIES (pp136–8)
Boldhuset.....7 B3
Klosterporten.....8 B3
Ludvig Holberg Statue.....9 A4
Ridehuset.....10 B3
Sorø Amts Museum.....11 B2
Sorø Kirke.....12 B4
Vestsjællands.....13 B2
SLEEPING (pp138–9)
Antik Behrens.....14 D2
Hotel Postgaarden.....15 B2
EATING (p139)
Café Valencia.....16 B3
Esther.....17 B2
Favør Supermarket.....18 B2
Mario's.....19 B2
Timian Petit de Cuisine.....20 B2
Wufu Chinese & Thai.....(see 15)
TRANSPORT
Bus Station.....21 C1
To Route 150 (100m); Sorø Camping (1km); Støvlet-Katrines Hus (1.5km)
Alleen
Frederiksvej
Rådhusvej
Holbergsvej
Absalonsgade
Vestergade
Østergade
Vedelsgade
Saxogade
Storgade
Søgade
Torvet
Rolighed
Ingemannsvej
Boldhusgade
Priorgade
Sorø Akademi
Sorø Sø
To Sorø Train Station (3km); Danhostel Sorø (9km)

The southern end of Sorø's main street, Storgade, leads directly to the academy via **Klosterporten**, the medieval gate that once served to cloister the monks from the outside world.

Although both Klosterporten and Sorø Kirke date back to the Middle Ages, other monastery buildings that once occupied the academy grounds were long ago demolished and replaced with Renaissance structures – thought to be more conducive to learning.

Ridehuset, immediately west of Klosterporten, was built by Christian IV to stable the horses and dogs used to train students in the art of hunting.

Boldhuset, just east of Klosterporten, also dates from the reign of Christian IV and now houses the library, which contains an outstanding collection of first editions of Ludvig Holberg's works.

A **statue** of Ludvig Holberg by the sculptor Vilhelm Bissen can be found in the garden area in the western part of the grounds. Walking **trails** lead west from the statue down to the lake, Sorø Sø.

The 12th-century **Sorø Kirke** (☎ 57 82 10 12; admission free; 🕒 10am-4pm Mon-Sat, noon-4pm Sun Apr–mid-Sep; reduced hr mid-Sep–Mar), in the centre of the academy grounds, is one of Denmark's oldest brick structures and the country's largest monastery church. It was built to serve as a sepulchral church for Bishop Absalon and his prestigious family, the Hvides, whose landholdings included the Sorø region. The

BISHOPS & BRICKS

Along with stately Sankt Bendts in Ringsted, the Romanesque Sorø Kirke was one of the first Danish churches to be built of brick. Before the art of brick-making was introduced by Italian builders around 1160, most churches were constructed from wood or calcareous tufa and rough stone. The use of bricks allowed construction on a much larger scale and within a few decades grand churches were being built all around Denmark.

The other element leading to the post-Viking era church-building boom was political. King Sweyn II (1047–74) found himself deep in a power struggle with the Archbishop of Bremen, the leader of the Danish Church. To weaken the influence of the archbishop, the king divided Denmark into eight separate dioceses, which set the stage for a flurry of new church and cathedral building.

fact that five monarchs opted to be buried next to Absalon bears witness to the bishop's prominence; many historians consider Absalon, who wielded both sceptre and sword, to be the most significant Danish statesman of medieval times.

The church stands largely as Absalon erected it, in the Romanesque style typical of Cistercian monasteries. Its huge central nave is flanked by two aisles. At the end of the left aisle is the marble sarcophagus of Ludvig Holberg.

Absalon lies directly behind the main altar; keeping him company are the sarcophagi of kings Valdemar IV, Christopher II and Oluf III. Queen Margrethe I, the architect of the 1397 Kalmar Union that brought Norway and Sweden under Danish rule, was buried here as well, but her remains were later transferred to Roskilde Domkirke. In 1827 Absalon's grave was opened. The gold and sapphire ring he was wearing and the silver chalice that was cupped between his hands were removed; they're now in a little display area to the right of the altar, along with some interpretive descriptions in English.

The church's grand interior includes medieval frescoes, a 6m-high crucifix by Odense sculptor Claus Berg and a beautifully detailed altar and pulpit, both carved in the 1650s in Baroque style.

The 16th-century organ, rebuilt by Christian IV's master organist Johan Lorenz, is the centrepiece of a classical concert series on Wednesday evening from late June to early September; advance tickets (90kr) are available from the tourist office.

The regional cultural **Sorø Amts Museum** (☎ 57 83 40 63; Storgade 17; adult/student/child 20/10kr/free; ⌚ 1-4pm Tue-Sun) is housed in a handsome half-timbered building dating from 1625.

It contains rooms with period furnishings, ranging from a peasant's simple quarters to the stylish living room of an aristocrat. There's also a grocery shop from 1880 and a room furnished with the personal belongings of the 19th-century poet BS Ingemann, who taught at Sorø Akademi.

Another worthwhile stop is **Vestsjællands Kunstmuseum** (Art Museum of West Zealand; ☎ 57 83 22 29; Storgade 9; admission free; ⌚ 10am-4pm Tue-Sun mid-May–mid-Aug, 1-4pm Tue-Sun mid-Aug–mid-May), which is housed in a period building. Its varied collection of regional art runs the gamut from medieval woodcarvings and stodgy portraits by CW Eckersberg to wildly expressionist modern art.

Inside the courtyard at **Storgade 7** is a fine timber-framed **Renaissance building**, constructed by King Christian IV, that now holds a wing of the town library.

From Torvet, an intersting option is to walk west down **Søgade**, an inviting street of leaning half-timbered, mustard-yellow houses with red tiled roofs. You can follow this street 400m down to the lake and its garden-like setting, where there are trails in both directions.

Sleeping

Tourist office staff can book rooms in private homes for 175/350kr for singles/doubles; there's a 25kr booking fee.

Sorø Camping (☎ 57 83 02 02; www.soroecamping.dk; Udbyhøj-vej 10; camp site per person 59kr; ⌚ Mar-Oct) Three-star camping ground borders the waters of Pedersborg Sø to the northwest of town, about 150m north of Slagelsevej. It's about a 20-minute walk from the town along a lakeside trail, or take bus No 234.

Danhostel Sorø (☎ 57 84 92 00; www.kongskildefriluftsgaard.dk in Danish; Skælskørvej 34; dm/r 110/495kr;

Apr-Oct; P) Set in a wonderful spot in the midst of a nature reserve, this lakeside place, also known as Kongskilde Friluftsgård, looks more like a country inn than a hostel. On Rte 157, 9km southwest of town (take bus No 83), it's a popular respite for both hikers and cyclists – two national cycle routes, Nos 6 and 7, cross right at the inn, and nature trails lead from the front door. Reasonably priced breakfast and dinner are available, but advance notice is needed for dinner.

Antik Behrens (☎/fax 57 83 53 52; Absalonsgade 19; s/d incl breakfast 250/400kr; P) A leisurely walk east of the town centre, this private home has four comfortable rooms. The owners are former antique dealers and the breakfast room is so laden with period paintings and furniture that it resembles a museum.

Hotel Postgaarden (☎ 57 83 22 22; www.hotelpostgaarden.dk; Storgade 25; s/d incl breakfast 600/700kr; P) Inn-style hotel with a 300-year history is in the town centre and has 23 rooms with private bathroom and TV.

Eating

There are several places to get cheap meals including a kiosk on Torvet, the town square, and a bakery on Storegade. You can buy groceries at the **Favør** supermarket (Storgade 28).

Marios (☎ 57 83 03 61: Storgade 44; pizzas 45kr; lunch & dinner) Better than the average pizza place found everywhere in Denmark. Menu includes burritos, calamari and nachos and there's comfortable seating.

Ristorante Valencia (☎ 57 83 16 13; Storgade 6; lunch mains 35-55kr, dinner mains 70-120kr; lunch & dinner) Upmarket Italian restaurant has a good variety of meat and fish dishes, including some French and Spanish options.

Wufu Chinese & Thai (☎ 57 83 53 88; Storgade 6; lunch mains 85kr; lunch & dinner). You can eat your meal in the courtyard at the restaurant at Hotel Postgaarden. It has a nightly buffet of Chinese and Thai dishes.

Timian Petit de Cuisine (Storgade 38; sandwiches 48-90kr, dinner mains 159kr; lunch & dinner) Upmarket but casual Italian restaurant, complete with white tablecloths, good wine and tasty dishes like grilled tuna.

Esther (☎ 57 83 41 14; Østergade 3; lunch mains from 65kr, dinner from 135kr; lunch & dinner Jun-Aug) The owners of this former cinema have created a superb dining experience. Chandeliers dangle from loft-like ceilings, light pours through windows and the décor is creative and personal. The menu is small but the attention given to each dish is high, emphasising seasonal ingredients. There's a garden in the back and the owners also provide advice and information for all your travel needs here and elsewhere in Denmark.

Støvlet-Katrines Hus (☎ 57 83 50 80; Slagelsevej 63; 3-course meals 285kr; lunch & dinner) Atmospheric restaurant on the western edge of town was originally built as a home for Christian VII's mistress. Today it serves splendid French-influenced Danish dishes such as smoked duck with apricot compote or poached turbot with ginger-lemongrass sauce. There's a daily selection of wines (35kr per glass) to match each course. It's an unbeatable spot for a night out.

Getting There & Away

Sorø is 15km east of Slagelse and 16km west of Ringsted via Rte 150 or the E20.

Trains run about hourly to Sorø from Slagelse (20kr, 10 minutes) and Ringsted (20kr, 8 minutes). Sorø train station is in Frederiksberg, 2km south of the town centre; bus Nos 806 and 807 run between the two at least hourly. There's also a frequent bus service (No 234) between Sorø and Slagelse (28kr, 24 minutes). The bus station is on Rådhusvej between Absalonsgade and Fægangen.

SLAGELSE

pop 31,400

Slagelse is best known to visitors as the starting point for outings to the nearby Viking fortress of Trelleborg (p140). There are a couple of local sights you could take in if time permits and it's an agreeable enough place to stay if you need to break for the night, although Slagelse itself doesn't have any particular allure.

The town centre is dominated by Sankt Mikkels Kirke, a Gothic church built of brick in the early 14th century. To the east of the church is Nytorv, the main commercial square. The **Slagelse Turistbureau** (☎ 58 52 22 06; www.vikingelandet.dk; Løvegade 7; 9am to 5pm Mon-Fri & 9am-3pm Sat mid-Jun–Aug, 10am-5pm Mon-Fri & 10am-1pm Sat Sep–mid-Jun) is a short walk south of the train station and 300m west of Nytorv.

Sights

The extensive local craft and industrial history-based **Slagelse Museum** (☎ 58 52 83 27;

www.slagelsemuseum.dk; Bredegade 11; adult/child 25/5kr; ⌚ noon-4pm, closed Fri) is a short walk southwest from Nytorv. It features the old tools and workshops of a grocer, barber, butcher, blacksmith and other tradespeople.

The brick **ruins of Antvorskov**, a monastery founded by Valdemar I in 1164, are about 2km south of the town centre. Antvorskov's most significant role in history is its connection with Hans Tausen, the renegade monk who took his monastic training here. Hans was vexed by the excessive privilege he found at Antvorskov, which was one of the wealthiest monasteries in Denmark and open only to those of noble birth. After touring Germany, where he heard Martin Luther preach, Hans returned to Antvorskov, and in 1525 delivered a fiery speech that helped spark the Danish Reformation.

After the Reformation, Antvorskov was confiscated by the Crown and became a favourite hunting manor of King Frederik II, who died here in 1588. Eventually it was sold off and the buildings, including the old monastery church, were demolished.

About half of the former monastery grounds are now buried under the E20 motorway, but remnants of the brick foundations can still be seen and interpretive plaques help explain the ruins. Although historically significant, the ruins are not overwhelmingly interesting and are pretty much out of the way if you don't have your own transport. You can get there by taking Slotsalléen from the town centre to its end, then turning right and proceeding about 200m to the car park opposite Munkebakken.

Sleeping

Tourist office staff can book rooms in private homes for around 200/400kr for singles/doubles, plus a 10kr booking fee.

Danhostel Slagelse (☎ 58 52 25 28; www.danhostel.dk/slagelse; Bjergbygade 78; dm/s/d 115/275/375kr; ⌚ mid-Jan–mid-Dec; P ♿) A rather unattractive hostel – it looks like a two-storey office building – is run by the same management as the adjacent Slagelse Campingplads. Bus No 303 goes there.

Slagelse Kommunes Campingplads (☎ 58 52 25 28; www.vikingelandet.dk; Bjergbygade 78; dm kr, camp site per person 58kr) Former villa converted into a hostel 2km south of the train station has basic rooms with four to six beds. Take bus No 303.

Bildsø Camping (☎ 58 54 76 17; Drøsseljergbvej 42A; camp site per person 60kr; ⌚ Jan-Oct) Close to the beach and surrounded by forests.

Hotel Frederik D II (☎ 58 53 03 22; www.frederik2.dk; Idagårdsvej 3; s/d incl breakfast 895/1218kr) Modern Best Western hotel, near the intersection of route 22 and the E20, at the south side of town, has comfortable rooms.

Eating

There are several choices on Nytorv, the central square, from bakeries and fast-food joints to sit-down restaurants.

Café Vivaldi (☎ 58 53 29 09; Rosengade 6; sandwiches 58kr; ⌚ lunch & dinner) A popular place, with cliché French café décor inside and plenty of outdoor seating where you can catch some sun. Salads, omelettes and sandwiches on the menu.

Café Radis (☎ 58 54 33 19; Fisketorvet 3; sandwiches 55kr, brunch 92kr; ⌚ lunch & dinner) Stylish and modern, Radis also serves up nachos, salads and omelettes.

Café Mikkel (☎ 58 58 13 66; Nytorv 5; salads 65kr; ⌚ lunch & dinner) Right on the pedestrian town square, this sunny café has a pleasant all-white interior and tables out front, a good place to people watch.

Siang Jiang (☎ 58 52 89 31; Fisketorv 3; dinner buffet 85kr, mains 75kr; ⌚ lunch & dinner) Restaurant on the square has tasty Chinese food and six good-value specials every day.

Getting There & Away

Slagelse is at the intersection of Rtes 150 and 22 and by the E20 motorway. It's 37km southeast of Kalundborg and 19km northeast of Korsør.

Slagelse is on the main east–west railway line between Copenhagen and Jutland and has frequent train services. From Slagelse, it's 33 minutes (58kr) to Roskilde, 12 minutes (36kr) to Korsør and 10 minutes (36kr) to Sorø.

Getting Around

Bicycle hire can be arranged at **HJ Cykler** (☎ 58 52 28 57; Løvegade 46; per day 50kr) near the tourist office.

TRELLEBORG

The best preserved of the four Viking ring fortresses in Denmark, **Trelleborg** (☎ 58 54 95 06; Trelleborg Allé 4; adult/child 45/30kr; ⌚ 10am-5pm Easter-Oct, 1-3pm Nov-Easter), is in the countryside

TRELLEBORG'S PRECISE DESIGN

It's difficult to imagine that people lived within the confines of Trelleborg's circular mound. From the top of the grassy rampart, the inside looks much the same as the farmland and pastures that stretch as far as the eye can see. And while Vikings aren't usually associated with scientific sophistication in the popular imagination, Trelleborg's military origins are visible in its precise mathematical layout and use of the Roman foot (29.33cm) as a unit of measure.

The Trelleborg compound consists of two wards that encompass about 7 hectares in all. The inner ward is embraced by a circular earthen rampart 6m high and 17m thick at its base. Four gates, one at each point of the compass, cut through the rampart. The ward is crossed by two streets, one east–west, the other north–south, which has the effect of dividing it into four symmetrical quadrants. In Viking times, each quadrant contained four long elliptical buildings surrounding a courtyard. Each of the 16 buildings was exactly 100 Roman feet long and contained a central hall and two smaller rooms.

Following the arc along the exterior of the inner rampart was an 18m-wide ditch; two bridges spanned the ditch, crossing over to the outer ward. This outer ward contained a cemetery holding about 150 graves and 15 houses, each of which was 90 Roman feet long and lined up radially with its gable pointing towards the inner rampart. A second earthen rampart separated the outer ward from the surrounding countryside.

7km west of Slagelse. Visitors may appreciate the small informative museum and bucolic countryside as much as the circular earthen mound which, despite the passing of a millennium since its construction, is amazingly intact. Naturally, the wooden structures that once stood within the fortress have long since decayed, but several Viking-era buildings have been reconstructed using materials and methods authentic to the period.

The most impressive is the longhouse, built in Viking stave style, using rough oak timbers erected above mud floors. The inside has benches of the type used by warriors for sleeping and a central hearth with a simple opening in the roof for venting smoke.

Other reconstructions are clustered together to give the sense of a Viking village, with costumed interpreters – mostly good-looking teenagers wearing peasant-like smocks – doing chores of the period such as sharpening axes, chopping wood and baking bread. They also answer the age-old question of whether a Viking re-enactor will continue to re-enact like a Viking when no one is watching. The reassuring answer seems to be yes. In the summer season – June through to August – the interpreters also conduct activities for children, such as archery demonstrations and pottery workshops.

In addition, the site has a small museum with exhibits of pottery, bronze jewellery, spearheads, human skeletons and other items excavated from the fortress grounds. It also shows a 20-minute video on Trelleborg's history.

Still, the highlight at Trelleborg is simply strolling the grounds. You can walk up onto the grassy circular rampart and readily grasp the geometric design of the fortress. From atop the rampart, Trelleborg appears strikingly symmetrical and precise; cement blocks have been placed to show the outlines of the elliptical house foundations. Grazing sheep wandering in from the surrounding farmland imbue the scene with a timeless aura.

Getting There & Away

Bus No 312 goes from Slagelse to Trelleborg (12kr, 12 minutes), but in summer it only runs to Trelleborg at 10am, noon and 2pm Monday to Friday, at 12.40pm on Saturday and not at all on Sunday. During the rest of the year, when it doubles as a school bus, the schedule is more frequent. Or just take a taxi to the site, which costs about 100kr.

To get to Trelleborg from Slagelse using your own transport, take Strandvejen to its end at the village of Hejninge and then follow the signs to Trelleborg, 1km further on.

A good alternative to relying on the bus is to cycle your way across the rural countryside between Slagelse and Trelleborg (see opposite for bike-hire details).

KORSØR

pop 14,800

Much of Korsør's character comes from its strategic location at the narrowest point of the Store Bælt (Great Belt), the channel that separates Zealand from Funen. The town boomed in the 1850s with the construction of the Zealand railway and until recently all vehicles – trains and cars alike – had to board ferries in Korsør to continue across the channel to Funen. In 1998 all that changed with the opening of the 18km-long Storebælts-forbindelsen (the Great Belt Fixed Link), which now connects Zealand and Funen, providing a 'land link' between the two islands.

With the new link and Korsør's new train station both 3km north of the town centre, Korsør itself is now largely bypassed by travellers. There are a couple of local sights in town that could be visited but, if time is tight, Nyborg, on the other side of the channel, holds far more allure. For more information go to the **Korsør Turistbureau** (☎ 58 35 02 11; www.korsoer.dk in Danish; Nygade 7; 🕒 10am-4pm Mon-Fri & 10am-2pm Sat).

SOUTHERN ZEALAND

Sights

The **Fæstning** (Fortress) tower, near the town centre on the southern side of the harbour, is one of Denmark's few remaining medieval towers. About 24m high and 9m wide, the tower was built using monkstone, a type of oversized brick. It's part of **Korsør By-og Overfartsmuseum** (Korsør Town & Ferry Service Museum; ☎ 58 37 47 55; Søbatteriet 3; adult/child 15/5kr; 🕒 11am-4pm Tue-Sun), which features ship models as well as displays on the history of the ferries and icebreakers that have crossed the Store Bælt over the past two centuries.

The works of Harald Isenstein, a Jewish sculptor who fled Nazi Germany in the 1930s, feature in **Kongegården** (☎ 58 37 78 90; Algade 25; admission free; 🕒 10am-4pm Thu-Tue, 10am-8pm Wed), a small art museum. It has one floor dedicated to Isenstein and there are also temporary exhibitions of regional work. Kongegården is in a neighbourhood of interesting 18th-century buildings in the town centre,

Sleeping

Danhostel Korsør (☎ 58 37 10 22; www.danhostel.dk/korsoer; Tovesvej 30F; dm/s/d without bathroom 115/250/350kr, s/d with bathroom 350/400kr; 🕒 Jan–mid-Dec; P 💻) Attractive 80-bed hostel on the eastern outskirts of town, midway between the train station and the city centre.

Jens Baggesen Hotel (☎ 58 35 10 00; www.hotel-jens-baggesen.dk; Batterivej 3; s/d incl breakfast 690/890kr; P) Converted period warehouse cum 40-room hotel, south of the fortress. Weekend discounts.

Halskov Camping (☎ 58 37 50 80; www.halskovcampingvip.cybercity.dk; Revvej 175; camp site per person 56kr; 🕒 year-round). Two-star camping ground on the beach just south of the E20.

Eating

In the town centre, near the intersection of Nygade and the pedestrian walkway Algade, you'll find several bakeries, cafés and restaurants.

Getting There & Away

As Korsør is on the main railway line between Zealand and Funen, there are fairly

LIFESTYLES OF THE RICH AND VIKING

Archaeologists continue to discover evidence of the Viking elite on the western shore of Lake Tissø, the fourth-largest lake in Denmark, between Slagelse and Kalundborg. A solid gold necklace weighing almost 2kg uncovered in 1977 is now displayed in the Danish National Museum in Copenhagen. Over 10,000 items have been found since digs began in earnest in 1995, but it's the high quality of items like the necklace, Arabian and Nordic coins, silver brooches, sword handles and stirrups dating from 500 to 1050 AD that lead scientists to believe that they are dealing with the lifestyles of the aristocratic and royal.

The foundation of the original 6th-century manor house complex, four times the size of any other so far discovered, is thought to have been a royal estate, vacation home, hunting lodge, banquet house or cult centre of the aristocracy, or possibly some combination of all of the above. Some experts think the site may have even been the ancient seat of Viking kings. Pieces from England, Ireland, Germany and Norway point to the fact that it was at least the temporary residence of those who planned military adventures and plundering – the very best of Viking society.

train services to Copenhagen (100kr, one hour) and Odense (110kr, 28 minutes). Local buses connect Korsør's town centre and train station.

On the northern outskirts of Korsør the E20 crosses the Store Bælt channel to Nyborg on Funen; the car toll for the 18km bridge is 250kr.

KALUNDBORG

pop 15,500

For those heading directly to Århus from Zealand, Kalundborg makes a convenient jumping-off point. The railway line ends at the central harbour, so you can walk off the train and right onto the boat.

If you have time to spare before catching a ferry, consider a stroll over to Vor Frue Kirke, an intriguing medieval church and Kalundborg's main site of interest.

Sights

With its five towers **Vor Frue Kirke** (Aldegade; admission free; ⌚ 9am-5pm Mon-Sat, noon-5pm Sun) was erected in the late 12th century and is unique among medieval churches in Denmark. Built as a castle church by Esbern Snare, Bishop Absalon's brother, it has a Byzantine-like design based upon the Greek cross. The cross shape takes the form of a square central tower connected by cross appendages to four equidistant octagonal towers. The church was originally part of an extensive fortress but in 1658 the townspeople tore down the fortress walls to minimise the risk of an attack by Swedish forces. The church is just west of Torvet and a short walk northwest from the harbour. The site of Snare's castle is in **Ruinparken**, a few minutes further west, but there's little left to decipher among the ruins.

If you make a loop around Vor Frue Kirke via Præstegade and Adelgade you'll pass through the oldest part of town, where there are cobbled streets and 16th-century homes, one of which houses the **Kalundborg-og Omegns Museum** (☎ 59 51 21 41; Adelgade 23; adult/child 20kr/free; ⌚ 11am-4pm Tue-Sun May-Aug, 11am-4pm Sat & Sun Sep-Apr), the local-history museum.

Sleeping & Eating

Danhostel Kalundborg (☎ 59 56 13 66; www.fridage.dk; Stadion Allé 5; dm/r up to 4 people 118/440kr; ⌚ year-round; P 🚭) Modern 118-bed hostel just northwest of Ruinparken, is within walking distance of the train station and the boats to Århus.

Restaurant Bispegården (☎ 59 51 25 35; Adelgade 6; lunch mains 78kr, 2-course dinners 240kr; ⌚ lunch & dinner Tue-Sat) Old-fashioned restaurant in a small yellow-painted building near Vor Frue Kirke serves up fresh fish dishes.

Getting There & Away

Rail services between Copenhagen and Kalundborg operate at least hourly, take 1¾ hours and cost 92kr.

For road travellers, Kalundborg is at the terminus of Rtes 22 and 23, some 51km north of Korsør and 69km west of Roskilde.

Mols-Linien (☎ 70 10 14 18; www.mols-linien.dk) runs ferries between Århus and Kalundborg six times daily Monday to Friday, three times daily at the weekend. The trip takes 2¾ hours. The fare is 250kr per car with up to five people, and 170kr per motorcycle and up to two people.

NÆSTVED

pop 45,000

Located at the mouth of the Suså River, Næstved has a bustling town centre, lively café culture and it's a convenient base from which to explore the lakes and forests to the south and west. Stroll through the streets and you chance come across medieval-era buildings, evidence of Næstved's long history as an important trading centre.

Industry grew following the introduction of the railway in the 19th century and with the later dredging of a new commercial harbour. Today Næstved is the largest town in southern Zealand. The town centre has some interesting historical buildings, including two medieval Gothic churches, all within easy walking distance of each other.

Orientation

The bus and train station are close together on Farimagsvej, opposite its intersection with Jernbanegade. To get to Axeltorv, the central square, take Jernbanegade west to Sankt Mortens Kirke and then continue west on Torvestræde; it's a walk of about five minutes in all. All of the town's sights are within a few minutes' walk of Axeltorv.

Information

Danske Bank (☎ 55 72 05 27; Axeltorv 2) is one of several in the town centre.

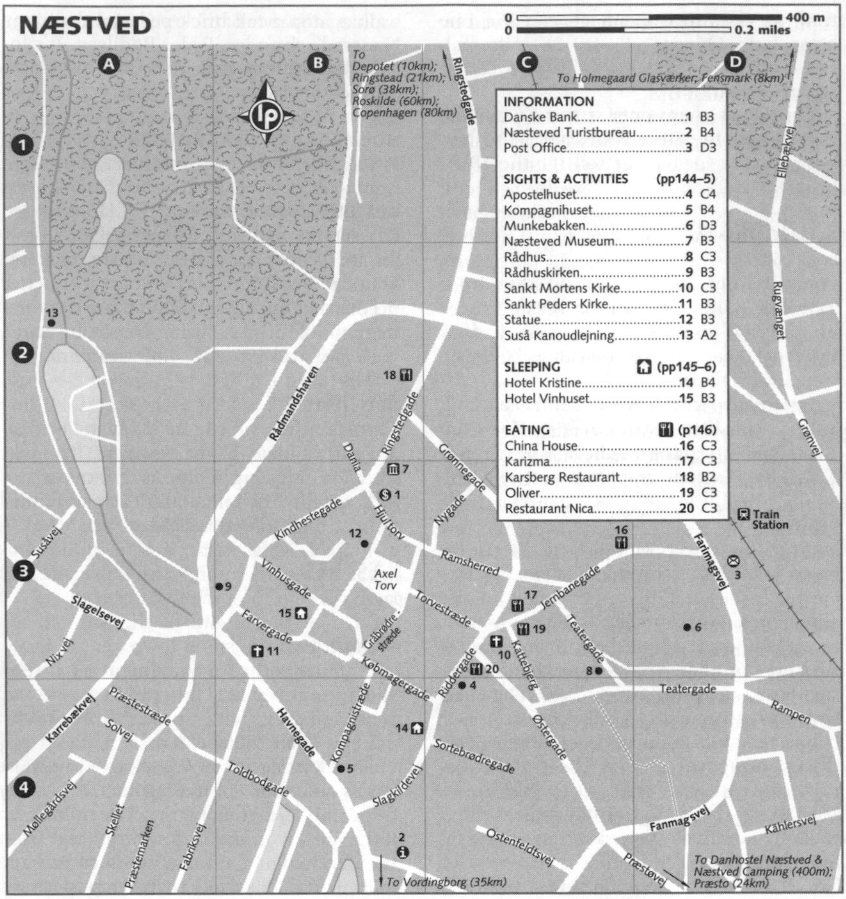
NÆSTVED
0 400 m
0 0.2 miles
A
B
C
D
1
2
3
4
To Depotet (10km); Ringstead (21km); Sorø (38km); Roskilde (60km); Copenhagen (80km)
To Holmegaard Glasværker; Fensmark (8km)
INFORMATION
Danske Bank 1 B3
Næsteved Turistbureau 2 B4
Post Office 3 D3
SIGHTS & ACTIVITIES (pp144–5)
Apostelhuset 4 C4
Kompagnihuset 5 B4
Munkebakken 6 D3
Næsteved Museum 7 B3
Rådhus 8 C3
Rådhuskirken 9 B3
Sankt Mortens Kirke 10 C3
Sankt Peders Kirke 11 B3
Statue 12 B3
Suså Kanoudlejning 13 A2
SLEEPING (pp145–6)
Hotel Kristine 14 B4
Hotel Vinhuset 15 B3
EATING (p146)
China House 16 C3
Karizma 17 C3
Karsberg Restaurant 18 B2
Oliver 19 C3
Restaurant Nica 20 C3
Ringstedgade
Ellebækvej
Rugvænget
Grønvej
Rådmandshaven
Dania
Grønnegade
Nygade
Kindhestegade
Hjultorv
Ramsherred
Axel Torv
Vinhusgade
Torvestræde
Jernbanegade
Farimagsvej
Train Station
Teatergade
Susåvej
Slagelsevej
Nixvej
Farvergade
Gråbrødre-stræde
Kattebjerg
Riddergade
Købmagergade
Karrebækvej
Præstestræde
Solvej
Kompagnistræde
Havnegade
Sortebrødregade
Østergade
Rampen
Toldbodgade
Slagkildevej
Fanmagsvej
Kählersvej
Møllegårdsvej
Skellet
Præstemarken
Fabriksvej
Ostenfeldtsvej
Præstøvej
To Vordingborg (35km)
To Danhostel Næstved & Næstved Camping (400m); Præsto (24km)

Næstved Turistbureau (☎ 55 72 11 22; www.visitnaestved.com; Det Gule Pakhus, Havnegade 1; 9am-5pm Mon-Fri & 9am-noon Sat mid-Jun–Aug, 9am-4pm Mon-Fri & 9am-noon Sat Sep–mid-Jun) is a few blocks south of Axeltorv.

Post office (☎ 55 78 75 00) is on the south side of the train station on Farimagsvej.

Sights

SANKT PEDERS KIRKE

The large Gothic **Sankt Peders Kirke** (☎ 55 72 31 90; Sct Peders Kirkeplads; admission free; 10am-noon & 2-4pm Tue-Fri May–mid-Sep, 10am-noon Tue-Fri mid-Sep–Apr), just south of Axeltorv, dominates Sankt Peders Kirkeplads, the church square. The church features notable 14th-century frescoes, including one depicting King Valdemar IV and Queen Helvig kneeling before God. The Latin inscription to the left of the king translates as 'In 1375, the day before the feast of St Crispin, King Valdemar died, do not forget it'.

SANKT MORTENS KIRKE

Also built with brick, the smaller **Sankt Mortens Kirke** (☎ 55 76 00 82; Kattebjerg 2; admission free; 9am-11am & 1-5pm Mon-Fri mid-Jun–mid-Sep, 9am-11am Mon-Fri mid-Sep–mid-Jun), midway between the train station and Axeltorv, has a strikingly similar design to Sankt Peders Kirke. The interior has period frescoes and a 6m-high altar created by the master Næstved carver Abel Schrøder in 1667. The pulpit, which dates from the early 17th century, is thought to have been carved by Schrøder's father.

NÆSTVED MUSEUM

The **Næstved Museum** (☎ 55 77 08 11; Sct Peders Kirkeplads; adult/child for both sections 20kr/free; ⏰ 10am-4pm Tue-Sun) has two sections. Fittingly, the local-history section is in Næstved's oldest building, the 14th-century **Helligåndshuset** (House of the Holy Ghost; Ringstedgade 4), just north of Axeltorv. It contains 13th- and 14th-century church carvings and exhibits of farm, trade and peasant life. The **Boderne section** (Sct Peders Kirkeplads) displays Næstved silverwork, Holmegaard glass and locally made pottery.

KOMPAGNIHUSET

Said to be the only medieval guildhall remaining in Denmark, **Kompagnihuset** (Kompagnistræde) is just southeast of Sankt Peders Kirke. This timber-framed building was constructed in 1493 and has been restored. Its architecture can be appreciated from the outside, but the interior is not open to the public.

APOSTELHUSET

A half-timbered medieval building just south of Sankt Mortens Kirke, **Apostelhuset** (Riddergade 5) takes its name from the 13 wooden exterior braces that separate the windows, each carved with the figure of Christ or one of the 12 apostles. Dating from about 1510, they are some of the oldest and best-preserved timber-frame carvings in Denmark.

RÅDHUSKIRKEN

Also with roots in the medieval period is the old town hall, **Rådhuskirken**, the brick and half-timbered building at the northern side of Sankt Peders Kirke.

Munkebakken is a hill with good views of the city and an interesting creation myth, see boxed text below.

The town's most novel curiosity is Denmark's smallest equestrian **statue**, a tiny bronze atop a tall brick pedestal depicting Næstved's founder, Peder Bodilsen. It's located at Hjultorv, a small square just north of Axeltorv.

> **FOR WHOM THE BELL TROLLS**
>
> According to legend, a troll who didn't like the sound of the church bells tried to bury Næstved with sand. However, his plans were foiled by a hole in the sandbag, and he subsequently dumped the leftovers on what is now Munkebakken (Monk's Hill).

HOLMEGAARD GLASVÆRKER

If you have your own transport you might want to drive to Fensmark, about 8km northeast of Næstved, to visit the Holmegaard Glassworks (☎ 55 54 50 00; Glasværksvej 1; admission free; ⏰ 10am-4pm Mon-Fri, 11am-4pm Sat & Sun). Founded in 1825, this is Denmark's principal producer of quality glass. Visitors can view the process of glass being blown by hand; there's also a shop and a little museum.

Activities

The Suså River, which runs through the western part of town, has calm waters that make for good canoeing. You can rent canoes for 80kr for the first hour, 50kr each additional hour, from **Suså Kanoudlejning** (☎ 57 64 61 44; www.kanoudlejning.dk; Næsbyholm Allé 6) at Slusehuset at the southern end of Rådmanshave, a large park north of the town centre.

Sleeping

The tourist office maintains a list of private rooms available for rent in the greater Næstved area, with singles from 150kr, doubles from 250kr.

Hotel Kirstine (☎ 55 77 47 00; www.hotelkirstine.dk; Købmagergade 20; s/d 675/850kr; Ⓟ) Truly charming and romantic architectural gem in the heart of Næstved. Everything, from the rooms to the lounges, is plush and comfy. Breakfast and coffee served in the sun-drenched arcade.

Danhostel Næstved & Næstved Camping (☎ 55 72 20 91; www.danhostelnaestved.dk; Frejasvej 8; dm/s/d 146/226/326kr, camp site per person 40kr; ⏰ hostel mid-Mar–mid-Nov, camping Jun-Aug; Ⓟ) Combined hostel and small one-star camping ground is 1km from the town centre. It's easy to reach – head south when you leave the train station and then continue east along Præstøvej.

Depotet (☎ 26 20 97 19; www.depotet-susaa.dk; Buen 18, Skelby; per person 125kr; Ⓟ) Almost halfway between Næstved and Sorø, this converted home has cosy rooms and a warm and inviting living room. Kitchen available for guests. Coming from Næstved, turn left down the only intersection in town. Hotel is a block away on the right.

Hotel Vinhuset (☎ 55 72 08 07; www.hotelvinhuset.dk; Sct Peders Kirkeplads 4; s/d incl breakfast 595/895kr; P) Large 18th-century hotel has pleasant rooms with modern amenities and a prime location on the square opposite Sankt Peders Kirke.

Eating

The central square, Axeltorv, has a few simple eateries where you can get a sandwich and beer. For something more upmarket, try one of the two romantic restaurants at Hotel Vinhuset (p146).

Oliver (☎ 55 77 88 81; Jernbanegade 15; pastas 50kr, chili con carne 88kr; breakfast, lunch & dinner) Trendy corner café occupies one of the best spots for hanging out. Creative menu including a fish fillet tortilla and extensive wine selection.

Restaurant Nica (☎ 55 77 78 73; Riddergade 1A; lunch mains 50kr, dinner mains 100kr; lunch & dinner) Danish cuisine served with class in brick-lined dining room.

Karsberg Restaurant (☎ 55 72 88 77; Ringstedgade 17; mains 140kr; lunch & dinner) Just north of the town centre, Karsberg has excellent full-course meals for about 189kr.

Karizma (☎ 55 77 07 70; Sct Mortensgade 3; pastas 55kr; lunch & dinner) Across the street from Oliver, Karizma is a casual restaurant with outdoor seating serving pastas, steaks and pizzas. Service can be slow.

China House (☎ 55 73 18 88; Jernbanegade 15; lunch specials 35kr, mains 80-100kr; lunch & dinner). A full range of Chinese dishes is served at China House, a few minutes' walk west of the train station.

Getting There & Away

Næstved is 25km south of Ringsted and 28km north of Vordingborg, at the crossroads of Rtes 14, 22, 54 and 265.

Trains run about hourly from Copenhagen (84kr, one hour), Roskilde (49kr, 42 minutes) and Ringsted (32kr, 20 minutes). There are also regular services to Vordingborg (39kr, 20 minutes) and to Køge (49kr, 34 minutes).

PRÆSTØ

pop 3500

This seaside village on the southern coast of the Præstø Fjord largely retains the look of a sleepy 19th-century provincial town. It has a small centre with older homes and handsome buildings that can make for a pleasant hour or so of wandering; however, the main activity is at the yacht harbour, which spreads across the northern side of the town centre. Although foreign tourists are few, Præstø attracts plenty of Danish visitors, particularly sailors with their own boats.

Præstø's bus station is in the village centre. The main commercial street, Algade, is on the southern side of the bus station, while the waterfront is to the north. **Præstø Turistinformation** (☎ 55 99 11 90; www.praestoe-turist.dk; Havnevej 19; 9am-4pm Mon-Fri & 9am-2pm Sat mid-Jun–Aug) is near the harbour.

Sights & Activities

On the eastern side of the town centre is **Præstø Kirke** (Klosternakken; admission free; varies), whose north nave dates from the 13th century. Before the Reformation it was an abbey church for monks of the order of St Anthony. Each of its two naves has an altar; most notable is the detailed altarpiece in the south nave, which was created by Abel Schrøder in 1657. The religious philosopher NFS Grundtvig was the parish rector here from 1821 to 1822.

A kilometre northwest of town is **Nysø**, a private manor house built in the 1670s. Baroness Christine Stampe, who owned Nysø in the mid-19th century, opened it as a retreat for Danish artists, including sculptor Bertel Thorvaldsen who set up a studio here. The manor isn't open to the public but a building in the grounds contains **Thorvaldsen-samlingen** (☎ 53 79 93 93; Nysøvej 1; adult/child 15kr/free; 11am-5pm Sat & Sun May, Jun & Aug, 11am-5pm Tue-Sun Jul), a collection of Thorvaldsen's works.

The waters around Præstø are mostly shallow – a challenge for sailors but quite suitable for waders. There's a public **beach** good for children on the northeastern side of town.

Sleeping

The tourist office can arrange accommodation in nearby bed and breakfasts. Singles/doubles from 250/300kr.

Strandhotel Frederiksminde (☎ 55 99 10 42; Klosternakken 8; s/d 550/675kr) Built in 1868, this hotel is set on a seaside knoll. Will open under new ownership in 2005 so prices could be subject to change. The two dozen rooms are all different, some quite spacious, some with ocean views, others with balconies.

Fjordkroen (☎ 55 96 58 10; www.fjordkroen.com; Bækkeskovstræde 23; r incl breakfast 700kr) A renovated inn 8km north of town, some rooms as well as the large outdoor terrace have a view of the fjord. Serves Danish and French cuisine with ingredients fresh from the market.

Præstø Camping (☎ 40 85 19 96; www.praestocamping.dk; Spangen 2; camp site per person 56kr; ⏰ Apr-Sep). Simple one-star facility 300m south of the town centre in a leafy setting.

Eating

There are half a dozen places to eat along Adelgade.

Restaurant Kaktus (☎ 55 99 12 46; Adelgade 45; pizzas or pasta 50kr, Mexican dishes 90kr; ⏰ lunch & dinner) Pleasant restaurant with a mix of Mexican and Italian fare.

Skipperkroen (☎ 55 99 22 00; Havnevej 1; mains 75kr; ⏰ lunch & dinner) Down at the harbour in the attractive old customs house, this is a sure winner for some really good fish dishes and an engaging atmosphere.

Getting There & Away

Route 265 passes Præstø on its way between Næstved (25km) and Møn (26km). Bus No 79 connects Præstø with Næstved (38kr, 40 minutes) hourly, and bus No 256 connects Præstø with Møn (38kr, 40 minutes) every two or three hours. There are no train services to Præstø.

VORDINGBORG

pop 8700

A pleasant stop on the way south to Falster and Møn, Vordingborg has a cosy pedestrian avenue lined with shops and cafés anchored by the train station at one end and the ruins of the old castle and fortress and greenery and water at the other. Only a short drive from the town centre, Knudshoved Odde peninsula juts out into the sound, and here you can find a few public parking spots with access to grassy lawns and very narrow rocky beaches, and can swim if the temperature's right. It's also the jumping-off point for trips to Møn if you are using public transport.

Strategically located on the strait between Zealand and Falster, Vordingborg played an important role in Denmark's medieval history. It was the royal residence of Valdemar I, whose ascension to the throne in 1157 marked the end of a contentious period of rebellion and served to reunite the Danish kingdom, and it continued to be a favoured residence of other kings of the Valdemar dynasty. With its large natural harbour, Vordingborg also served as the staging area for late-12th-century military campaigns led by Bishop Absalon against the Wends of eastern Germany.

During the 15th century Vordingborg slipped from prominence, in part because the Kalmar Union had so greatly expanded Danish rule elsewhere in Scandinavia that the royal family now took little interest in it.

Information

The **Vordingborg Turistkontor** (☎ 55 34 11 11; www.visitvordingborg.dk; Algade 96; ⏰ 9am-4pm Mon-Fri & 9am-2pm Sat Jun-Aug, 9.30am-5pm Mon-Fri & 9.30am-1pm Sat Sep-May) is just east of Gåsetåornet.

There are several banks on Algade, including a **Nordea** (☎ 55 34 33 33; Algade 78). The **post office** (☎ 80 20 70 30; Årsleffsgade 1) is just north of the train station.

Sights

The 14th-century **Gåsetårnet** (Goose Tower; ☎ 55 37 25 51; Slotsruinen 1; adult/child incl Sydsjællands Museum 40/10kr; ⏰ 10am-5pm Jun-Aug, 10am-4pm Tue-Sun Sep-May), once part of a huge royal castle and fortress, is Scandinavia's best-preserved medieval tower and the only intact structure remaining from the Valdemar era. The name stems from 1368, when Valdemar IV placed a golden goose on top of the tower to express his scorn for the German Hanseatic League's declaration of war (Valdemar referred to the league as 'cackling geese'). The rest of the fortress, including seven other towers, has been demolished over the centuries but the 36m-high Gåsetårnet was spared because of its function as a navigational landmark. The tower's 101 steps can be climbed for a good view of the surrounding area.

The fortress grounds, which have been turned into a pleasant park with walking paths, also contain various brick and stone **foundation ruins** and an attractive little **botanical garden** (admission free).

In addition, the grounds of Gåsetårnet hold the **Sydsjællands Museum** (☎ 55 37 25 54; adult/child 30/10kr; ⏰ 10am-5pm Jun-Aug, 10am-4pm Tue-Sun Sep-May). Southern Zealand's regional history museum, it has a Stone Age collection as well as sections on the Middle Ages and the Renaissance, including trade and craft exhibits, church decorations and textiles.

To get there from the train station, walk north to the nearby post office and then turn southeast onto Algade, which leads directly to the fortress grounds.

Along the way, on the western side of Algade, is **Vor Frue Kirke** (Kirketorvet; admission free; 10am-noon Mon-Sat), which has a nave dating from the mid-15th century, frescoes and a Baroque altarpiece carved by Abel Schrøder in 1642.

Activities

If you have your own transport and are up to a walk, **Knudshoved Odde**, the narrow 18km-long peninsula west of Vordingborg, offers some hiking opportunities in an area known for its 'Bronze Age landscape'. The peninsula also has a small herd of American buffalo brought in by the Rosenfeldt family who own Knudshoved Odde. There's a car park (10kr) about halfway down the peninsula, where the trail begins.

Sleeping

Ore Strand Camping (55 37 06 03; fax 55 37 23 20; Orevej 145; camp site per person 55kr) Modern facilities by the beach only 2km from town.

Danhostel Vordingborg (55 36 08 00; www.danhostel.dk/vordingborg; Præstedgårdsvej 18; dm/s/d without bathroom 100/250/300kr, r with bathroom 400kr; year-round; P) Located in the countryside, this 112-bed hostel is is about 2km north of town.

Hotel Kong Valdemar (55 34 30 95; www.hotelkongvaldemar.dk; Algade 101; s/d incl brunch buffet 499/629kr; P) Opposite Gåsetårnet in the town centre, this hotel has 60 slightly run-down rooms with bathroom and TV.

Eating

There are numerous cafés, bakeries and restaurants on Algade, the town's principal commercial street.

Café Einstein (55 37 61 61; Algade 66; sandwiches 56kr; breakfast, lunch & dinner) Duck into the shady courtyard to grab a meal or while the morning away. Dining room is light and airy and service is attentive.

Café Piaf (55 34 44 15; Algade 85; tapas 58kr; breakfast, lunch & dinner) Attractive and casual café decorated with work by local artists, with a few outdoor tables. Does a nice brunch for 69kr.

Restaurant Påfuglen (55 37 01 90; Algade 88; lunches 60kr, dinners 90kr; lunch & dinner) A good choice for traditional Danish food in a pleasant setting.

Babette (55 34 30 30; Kildemarksvej 4; 3-course meal 375kr; lunch & dinner) Named after the culinarily inspirational film *Babette's Feast*. If you're in the region it's worth the trip to come here for a full gastronomic and aesthetic experience. Blessed with a panoramic sea view and 1km north of the town centre, Babette is well known for its original pan-European cuisine.

Getting There & Away

Vordingborg is 28km south of Næstved via Rte 22, and 13km from Møn via Rte 59.

By train, Vordingborg is 80 minutes from Copenhagen (120kr) and 20 minutes from Næstved (56kr). If you're en route to Møn, you'll need to switch from the train to the bus at Vordingborg train station; see p152.

Møn, Falster & Lolland

CONTENTS

Most of Denmark is made up of islands and, like islanders everywhere, Danes talk about life in the big city – Copenhagen – as if it were a foreign capital and not only a few hours away. After all, it really wouldn't be too much of a hassle to commute to work there every day from Møn, Falster or Lolland, three islands all connected by bridges to southern Zealand.

Møn deserves the most attention since the others feel more like simply extensions of rural Zealand to the north than islands. On Møn it's possible to feel the impact of the sea even when driving through the interior of rolling wheat fields and farmhouses. Standing on the narrow rocky beach, pressed in by the sea, staring straight up at their tree-lined tops, the chalk sea cliffs at the easternmost extreme of the island seem like both the literal and figurative end of the road.

On Falster, the beach at Marielyst attracts Danish sun worshippers – that rare breed seen in captivity for only a few weeks each summer – while Lolland, the largest of the three islands, has a few scattered sights, including a safari and a water park that are only practical to explore if you have your own transport.

HIGHLIGHTS

- Hike along the gleaming white chalk cliffs at **Møns Klint** (p156) and to the beach below
- Dine outdoors at one of charming **Stege's fine cafés** (p154)
- Join the holiday-makers at Marielyst, Falster's premier summer **beach resort** (p160)
- Visit **Maribo** (p162) , a peaceful town with lakeside walking trails
- Drive through **Knuthenborg Safari Park** (p163) with its free-roaming animals

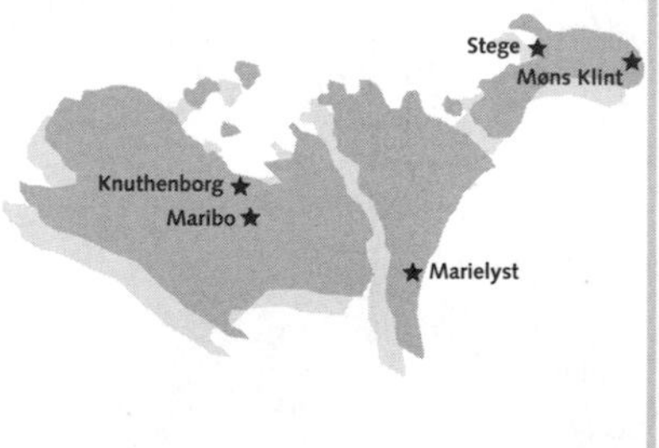
Stege
Møns Klint
Knuthenborg
Maribo
Marielyst

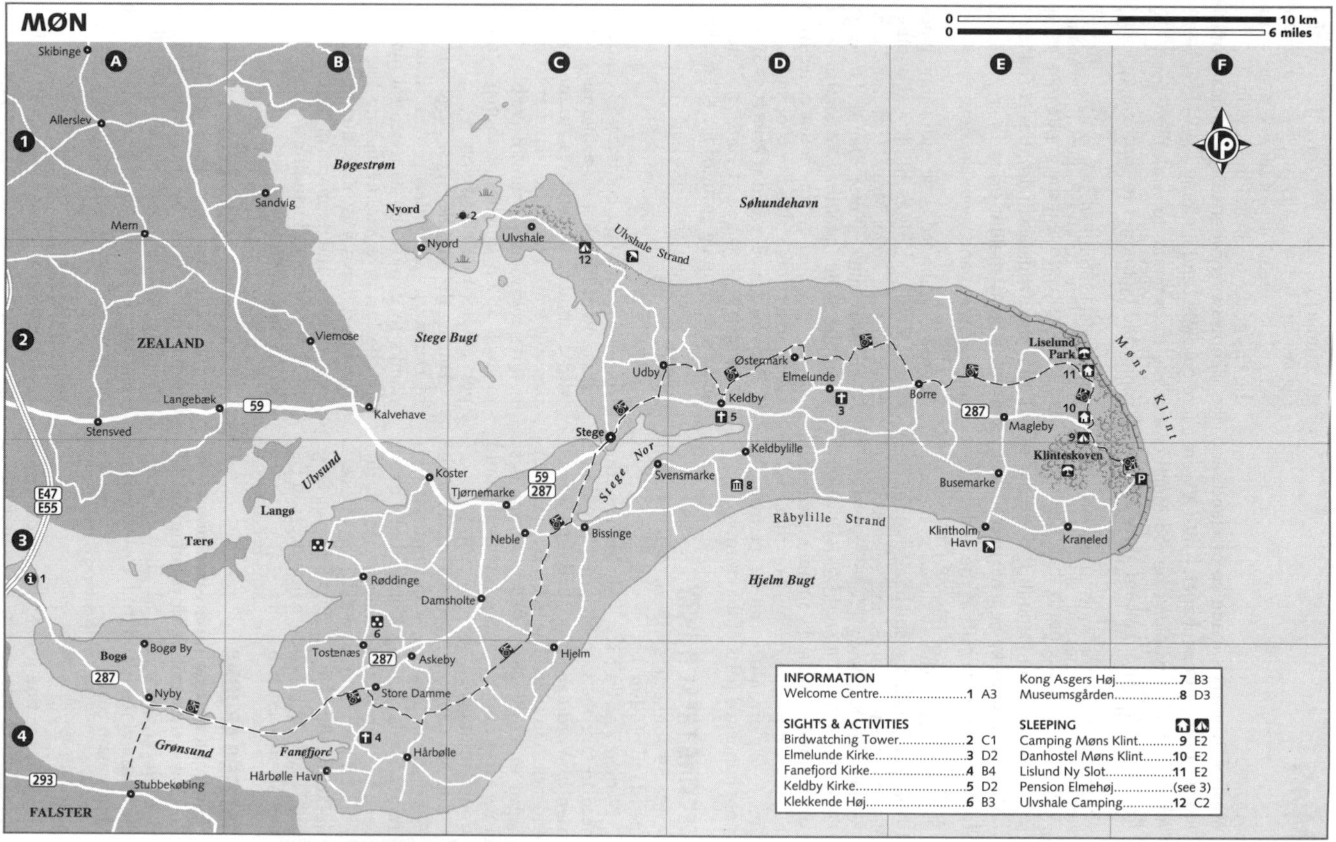
MØN
0 10 km
0 6 miles
A
B
C
D
E
F
1
2
3
4
Skibinge
Allerslev
Mern
Sandvig
Bøgestrøm
Nyord
Nyord
2
Ulvshale
12
Ulvshale Strand
Søhundehavn
ZEALAND
Viemose
Stege Bugt
Langebæk
59
Kalvehave
Stensved
Stege
Udby
Østermark
Elmelunde
Keldby
5
3
Borre
287
Magleby
Liselund Park
11
10
9
Klinteskoven
Møns Klint
Keldbylille
Svensmarke
8
Stege Nor
Ulvsund
Koster
Tjørnemarke
59
287
E47
E55
Langø
Tærø
7
1
Neble
Bissinge
Råbylille Strand
Busemarke
Klintholm Havn
Kraneled
Hjelm Bugt
Røddinge
Damsholte
6
Tostenæs
287
Askeby
Hjelm
Bogø
Bogø By
287
Nyby
Store Damme
4
Hårbølle
Grønsund
Fanefjord
Hårbølle Havn
293
Stubbekøbing
FALSTER
INFORMATION
Welcome Centre 1 A3
SIGHTS & ACTIVITIES
Birdwatching Tower 2 C1
Elmelunde Kirke 3 D2
Fanefjord Kirke 4 B4
Keldby Kirke 5 D2
Klekkende Høj 6 B3
Kong Asgers Høj 7 B3
Museumsgården 8 D3
SLEEPING
Camping Møns Klint 9 E2
Danhostel Møns Klint 10 E2
Lislund Ny Slot 11 E2
Pension Elmehøj .... (see 3)
Ulvshale Camping 12 C2

MØN

pop 12,000

Peregrine falcons have returned to the spectacular white cliffs of Møns Klint on the east coast after a 25-year absence, adding one more natural attraction to this thoroughly appealing island. Besides the beautiful scenery, which is both dramatic and bucolic, good beaches and slow pace there are also prehistoric passage graves and medieval churches with outstanding frescoes.

Møn's interior is largely given over to fields of rapeseed, grain and sugar beet, although agriculture has been in decline since the island's only sugar refinery closed in the early 1990s. Møn's rich clay soil has led to the rise of numerous workshops, and '*keramik*' signs are commonplace along its country roads.

Travellers using public transport should note that the island lacks a train system and the bus service is sketchy. For those with time to explore, Møn is an escape from the more populated parts of the country.

GETTING THERE & AWAY

Route 59 connects southern Zealand with the island of Møn.

As there's no train service to Møn, visitors need to take the Copenhagen–Nykøbing F train to Vordingborg in southern Zealand and switch to a bus. The trains from Copenhagen to Vordingborg (92kr, 80 minutes) leave about hourly from early morning until around midnight.

Bus No 62 from Vordingborg to Stege (32kr, 45 minutes), on Møn, connects with train arrivals, leaving Vordingborg about once an hour; there's a fuller service during weekday rush hours and a lighter service at weekends. Bus No 50 runs between Stege and Nykøbing F, (42kr, 55 minutes), on Falster, about every two hours.

GETTING AROUND

Numerous narrow rural roads branch off Rte 287 – they can be slow-going but fun to explore. Route 287, which cuts across the centre of the island from east to west, is Møn's main road.

Bus

Møn's bus station is in Stege, the departure point for all bus routes. Fares depend on the number of zones you travel in, with the highest fare between any two points on Møn being 22kr. Frequency of service varies with the day of the week and the season.

The most frequent service is bus No 52, which goes from Stege to Klintholm Havn (30kr) via Elmelunde and Magleby about hourly on weekdays and every couple of hours at weekends. The year-round bus service goes east only as far as Magleby, but from late June to mid-August the seasonal bus No 54 runs from Stege to Møns Klint (30kr) three times each day. Bus No 64 runs from Stege to Bogø (22kr).

Bicycle

There's a signposted cycle path running between Stege and Møns Klint, and another from Stege to Bogø. Møns Turistbureau at Stege distributes a free Danish-language pamphlet called *Cykelture på Møn* that maps out six suggested cycling tours collectively taking in all of the island's major sights.

Bicycles can be rented at **Points** (☎ 55 81 42 49; Storegade 91, Stege) and at Pension Elmehøj and most camping grounds for 45kr a day.

STEGE

pop 4000

Not only is Stege the commercial centre of the island of Møn but it's a charming town with a number of good restaurants and a pleasant sea breeze. The island is so small that it's always only a short drive back here to stock up on supplies or to make transport connections elsewhere.

During the Middle Ages, Stege was one of Denmark's wealthiest provincial towns, thanks to its position as a central market for the lucrative herring fishing business. The entire town was once surrounded by fortress walls, and remnants of the ramparts can still be found, including a section bordering Stege Camping.

In the mid-19th century a large sugar mill was erected on the western side of town but, with the demise of the sugar beet industry, the mill has been converted into a fledgling business zone where a handful of small enterprises, including an eel farm, are being encouraged.

Information

Library (☎ 55 81 43 54; Møllebrøndstræde 12; 🕑 11am-5pm Mon-Fri, 10am-1pm Sat) has online computers.

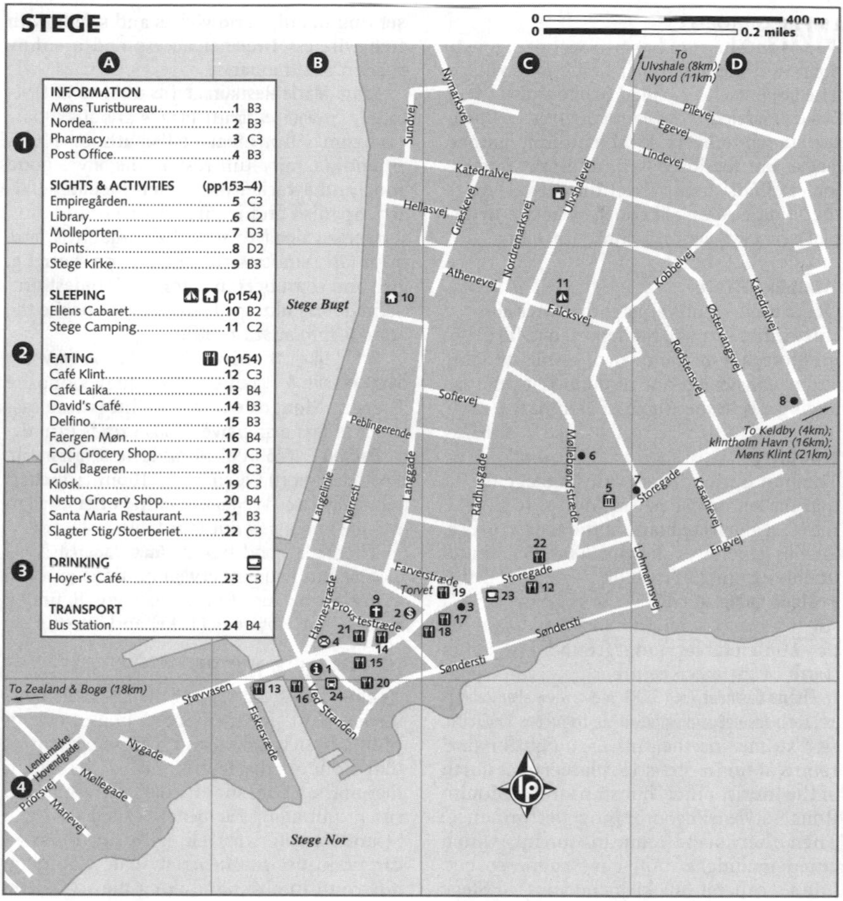
STEGE
0 400 m
0 0.2 miles
A
B
C
D
1
2
3
4
INFORMATION
Møns Turistbureau....1 B3
Nordea....2 B3
Pharmacy....3 C3
Post Office....4 B3
SIGHTS & ACTIVITIES (pp153–4)
Empiregården....5 C3
Library....6 C2
Molleporten....7 D3
Points....8 D2
Stege Kirke....9 B3
SLEEPING (p154)
Ellens Cabaret....10 B2
Stege Camping....11 C2
EATING (p154)
Café Klint....12 C3
Café Laika....13 B4
David's Café....14 B3
Delfino....15 B3
Faergen Møn....16 B4
FOG Grocery Shop....17 C3
Guld Bageren....18 C3
Kiosk....19 C3
Netto Grocery Shop....20 B4
Santa Maria Restaurant....21 B3
Slagter Stig/Stoerberiet....22 C3
DRINKING
Hoyer's Café....23 C3
TRANSPORT
Bus Station....24 B4
To Ulvshale (8km); Nyord (11km)
To Keldby (4km); klintholm Havn (16km); Møns Klint (21km)
To Zealand & Bogø (18km)
Stege Bugt
Stege Nor
Nymarksvej
Sundvej
Katedralvej
Hellasvej
Græskevej
Nordremarksvej
Ulvshalevej
Pilevej
Egevej
Lindevej
Athenevej
Falcksvej
Kobbelvej
Østervangsvej
Rødstensvej
Sofievej
Peblingerende
Langelinie
Nørresti
Langgade
Rådhusgade
Møllebrøndstræde
Storegade
Kasanievej
Engvej
Lohmannsvej
Farverstræde
Torvet
Provstestræde
Havnestræde
Sønderstí
Støvvasen
Fiskerstræde
Ved Stranden
Nygade
Lendemarke
Hovendgade
Møllegade
Priorsvej
Marievej

Møns Turistbureau (☎ 55 86 04 00; www.visitmoen.com; Storegade 2; ⌚ 9:30am-5pm Mon-Fri, 9am-6pm Sat), adjacent to the bus station, has information about the entire island.

Nordea (☎ 55 81 11 11; Storegade 23) is one of three banks in Stege centre that have an ATM. All are open 9.30am to 4pm Monday to Friday (to 6pm on Thursday).

Post office (☎ 55 81 40 31; Storegade 1; ⌚ 10am-5pm Mon-Fri, 10am-noon Sat).

Sights & Activities

STEGE KIRKE

The oldest part of the **Stege church** (☎ 55 81 43 35; Provstestræde; admission free; ⌚ 9am-5pm Tue-Sun) was built in Romanesque style in the early 13th century by Møn's ruler, Jakob Sunesen, a member of the powerful Hvide family that controlled much of southern Zealand. In the late 15th century this 60m-long church was expanded to its present dimensions.

The primitive-style ceiling frescoes are noteworthy, some with whimsical jester-like characters. The frescoes, which were covered with whitewash centuries ago, were exposed and restored in 1892. The church also has a splendidly carved pulpit dating from 1630, featuring reliefs of biblical scenes. Each relief is separated from the next by a narrow vertical panel depicting virtues such as hope and truth, and below each of those is a grotesque little caricature mask to serve as a reminder of the horrors that await the less virtuous.

EMPIREGÅRDEN

The Møn Museum has two sections, one in Stege and the other near Keldbylille village. The Stege section, called **Empiregården** (☎ 55 81 40 67; Storegade 75; adult/child 30kr/free; ⏰ 10am-4pm Tue-Sun), covers local cultural history. There are fossilised sea urchins, archaeological finds dating from the Stone Age to the Middle Ages, old coins, pottery and displays of 19th-century house interiors.

MØLLEPORTEN

Of the three medieval gates that once allowed entry into the town, Mølleporten (Mill Gate) on Storegade is the only one still standing and is considered one of the best-preserved town gates in the whole of Denmark.

Sleeping

The best option for staying in Stege or for that matter anywhere on Mon is to book a room in a private home at the tourist office. Singles generally run from 200 to 350kr and doubles from 250 to 400kr.

Stege Camping (☎ 55 81 84 04; Falcksvej 5; ⏰ 1 May-15 Sep; camp site per person 47kr) A pleasant little municipal camping ground just 500m north of the town centre.

Ellens Cabaret (☎ 55 81 54 54; www.ellenscabaret.dk; Langelinie 48; s/d with/without bathroom 500/700kr; Ⓟ) Come for the small, straightforward rooms at this motel-style place, 600m north of the tourist office, but stay for the Moulin Rouge-style show-stopping performance. Then there's the tempting menu, which could include a mint champagne sorbet. Life's a cabaret (400kr incl drinks) in Stege

.

Eating

Slagter Stig/Stoerberiet (☎ 55 81 42 67; Storegade 59; sandwiches 27kr, dinner mains from 65kr; ⏰ lunch & dinner) Open to 5pm Monday to Friday, to 1pm Saturday. A combination butcher shop and restaurant selling everything from smørrebrød (open sandwiches) and deli salads to salmon fillets and good bottles of wine. The dining area is quite charming, a beautiful glass-covered old home stocked with old sewing machines and other quaint furnishings. A beautiful small garden is out the back.

Café Klint (☎ 55 81 17 00; Storegade 68; mains 20-35kr; ⏰ breakfast, lunch & dinner) This café serves reasonably priced sandwiches and ice cream.

David's Café (☎ 33 13 80 57; Storegade 11; vegetable pies 52kr; ⏰ breakfast, lunch & dinner) A modern café serving mainly sandwiches and salads with free wireless Internet access and a sunny garden out the back.

Santa Maria Restaurant (☎ 55 81 18 55; Storegade 7; ⏰ lunch & dinner) Pizzas are 40kr, pastas from 50kr, meat & fish dishes 100kr. Friendly family-run restaurant offers good food and a varied menu that includes Italian, Spanish and Iranian dishes.

Faergen Møn (☎ 20 94 40 48; Stege Harbor; lunch mains 69kr; ⏰ lunch & dinner) Dine on herring, fish and roast beef in Denmark's oldest preserved ferry alongside the quay opposite the tourist information office.

Café Laika (☎ 55 81 46 07; Stege Harbor; sandwiches 50kr; ⏰ lunch & dinner) On the quay opposite Faergen Møn, this café is slightly more casual and less expensive. It also rents canoes.

Delfino (☎ 55 81 81 90; Storegade 10; pizzas 45kr; ⏰ lunch & dinner) Open until 10pm, which is relatively late for Stege, Delfino offers Italian cuisine and a few outdoor tables.

There's a good bakery **Guld Bageren** (Storegade 36) and two grocery shops **Netto** and **FOG** along Storegade. On Torvet you'll find a **kiosk** selling hot dogs (13kr) and burgers.

ULVSHALE & NYORD

The northeastern side of the Ulvshale peninsula, 6km north of Stege, boasts one of Møn's best beaches and a primeval forest that's one of the few virgin woods left in Denmark. The main road, Ulvshalevej, runs right along the beach, called Ulvshale Strand. If you're travelling by car, there's a car park just south of Ulvshale Camping, but you can also park along the road. The forest, which is crisscrossed by a network of walking trails, begins northwest of Ulvshale Camping and extends to the end of the peninsula, where there's a bridge to the island of Nyord.

Nyord has only been connected to the Møn mainland since the 1980s, and its former isolation served to safeguard the island from development. The sole village, also named Nyord, is a characteristic hamlet of 19th-century houses with well-tended gardens. Much of the island, particularly the eastern side, is given over to marshland and offers excellent bird-watching. There's a **bird-watching tower** on the northern side of the road about 1km west of the bridge. The bridge itself is also a good bird-watching site, as is the marsh on the Ulvshale side.

Birds spotted in the area include osprey, kestrel, rough-legged hawk, snow bunting, ruff, avocet, swan, black-tailed godwit, arctic tern, curlew and various ducks.

Sleeping & Eating

Ulvshale Camping (☎ 55 81 53 25; www.ulvscamp.dk; Ulvshalevej 236; ⏲ Apr-Oct; camp site per person 60kr) This two-star municipal camping ground is right by the beach and on the main road through Ulvshale. The complex includes a shop selling fresh bakery items and a small selection of groceries, and bicycles are available for hire.

Mizz Lizzi (☎ 55 81 85 03; Ulvshalevej 151; sandwiches 34-64kr; ⏲ breakfast, lunch & dinner) The only convenient place if spending the day at Ulvshale Strand, this kiosk offers reasonable burgers, ice cream and chicken and chips.

Lolles Gård (☎ 55 81 86 81; Hyldevej 1, Nyord; dishes 80-140kr; eels 135kr; ⏲ lunch & dinner) Walk down the only road in the village centre to find this pleasant lunch spot in a traditional home, specialising in fried eels. Omelettes and other light meals are on the menu.

KELDBY

The Keldby area, about 5km east of Stege, is noted mainly for its roadside church, but there's also a small farm museum 3km south of Rte 287.

Sights & Activities

KELDBY KIRKE

A splendid collection of fresco paintings splashed across its walls, arches and ceiling dominate Keldby's brick **church** (Rte 287; admission free; ⏲ 7am-5pm Apr-Sep, 8am-4pm Oct-Mar), the nave of which dates back to the early 13th century. The frescoes were painted over a period of two centuries, with the oldest (1275) decorating the chancel walls and depicting scenes from the book of Genesis. Scores of other expressionistic scenes, ranging from the vivid sacrifice of Cain and Abel to a large mural of doomsday, make this one of the most intriguing collections of church frescoes in Denmark.

MUSEUMSGÅRDEN

This low-key **museum** (☎ 55 81 30 80; Skullebjergvej 15; adult/child 25kr/free; ⏲ 10am-4pm Tue-Sun May-Oct), in a four-winged farmhouse south of Keldbylille, depicts life on a small Møn farm in the 19th century. The drive to it takes you, appropriately, through fields of sugar beet and wheat.

ELMELUNDE

Elmelunde is a small, rural hamlet with an appealing guesthouse and an ancient church, both on the main road between Stege and Møns Klint. Bus No 52 stops right in front of the church.

FRESCOES BY ANONYMOUS

When you visit Møn's churches you may notice a similar style in many of the frescoes. This is because most of those dating from the 15th century were painted by the same artist, whose exact identity is a mystery but who has come to be known over the centuries as Elmelundemesteren (the Elmelunde master) after the church of the same name.

The paintings are so splendid that the churches can be likened to medieval art galleries. The frescoes were a means of describing the Bible to illiterate peasants and run the gamut from light-hearted scenes from the Garden of Eden to depictions of grotesque demons and the fires of hell. This artist used distinctive warm earth tones: russet, mustard, sienna, brick red, chestnut brown and pale aqua.

Møn's church frescoes, created by painting with watercolours on newly plastered, still-wet walls or ceilings, are some of the best-preserved in Denmark. The frescoes in Stege Kirke were painted solely in black and ochre-red, whereas those in the other Møn churches employ a fuller range of colour.

Lutheran ministers who thought they represented Catholic themes of the pre-Reformation days whitewashed over the frescoes in the 17th century. Ironically, the whitewashing didn't destroy the paintings, but rather served to preserve this medieval art from soiling and fading, in part due to a protective layer of dust that separated the frescoes from the whitewash. The whitewash wasn't removed from most of the churches until the 20th century, at which time the frescoes were restored by artists under the auspices of Denmark's national museum.

Elmelunde Kirke

One of Denmark's oldest stone churches, the **Elmelunde Kirke** (Kirkebakken 41; admission free; 7am-5pm Apr-Sep, 8am-4pm Oct-Mar) has a section around the choir dating back to 1080. The church features wonderful frescoes whose subjects range from Adam and Eve's expulsion from the Garden of Eden to heavenly scenes. The three-pointed vaults were added in 1460 and painted by the 'Elmelunde master' (see boxed text p155).

Sleeping & Eating

Pension Elmehøj (55 81 35 35; www.elmehoj.dk; Kirkebakken 39, 4780 Stege; s/d incl breakfast 330/450kr; P) Situated right next door to Elmelunde Kirke, this pension makes a convenient base to explore the island. There are 23 pleasant rooms, all of which have shared toilets and showers. Guests have access to a shared kitchen and a TV lounge. Internet access is available for a nominal fee. In the high season, the pension operates a basement **restaurant and café** with cakes, sandwiches and meals if arranged in advance. There's also a children's playground in the large garden.

Kaj Kok (55 81 35 85; Klintevej 151; dishes 60-140kr; lunch & dinner) Located on the main road, this is the closest restaurant to the pension, which is 2km east. Kaj Kok serves steaks, schnitzels and chicken.

MØNS KLINT & AROUND

Gleaming white cliffs rising sharply 128m above an azure sea present one of the most striking landscapes in Denmark. Not only are Møns Klint's chalk cliffs a repository for fossilised Cretaceous-period shells – many of them from creatures long extinct – but legend has it this was the refuge for the Nordic god Odin, who was left homeless by Christianity. The chalk cliffs at **Møns Klint** were created some 5000 years ago when the calcareous deposits from aeons-worth of seashells were lifted from the ocean floor.

Møns Klint is a popular destination for Danish tourists. The main visitor area – Store Klint – has a cafeteria, a small hotel, souvenir shops, a car park (25kr) and picnic grounds. Still, none of this detracts from the natural beauty of the cliffs themselves.

You can walk down the cliffs to the beach – unsuitable for swimming because of strong tides and rocks – and directly back up again in about 30 minutes, although the return can be strenuous as it's almost straight up a wooden flight of stairs. Alternatively, you can head along the shoreline in either direction and then loop back up through a thick forest of wind-gnarled beech trees for a harder walk lasting about 1½ hours. Either way, start on the steps directly below the cafeteria – it's a quick route to the most scenic stretch of the cliffs.

You needn't limit your hiking to the coast. **Klinteskoven** (Klinte Forest), the woodland that extends 3km inland from the cliffs, is crisscrossed by an extensive network of footpaths and horse trails. Although most people start their hikes from the cliffs, there's a trail from Camping Møns Klint as well. One interesting track leads 1km west from Store Klint to Timmesø Bjerg, a hill top that is the site of castle ruins dating back to around AD 1100.

Liselund Park was built by Antoine de la Calmette in the late 1700s as a tribute to his wife. Inspired by the philosophical and aesthetic ideas of European romanticism, the grounds here combine the symmetry of human design and the sublime effects of uncorrupted nature. Walk the paths around the whitewashed and thatched mini chateau and along the sea cliffs. It's about 2km north of the hostel.

Sleeping & Eating

Danhostel Møns Klint (55 81 20 30; www.danhostel.dk/moen; Langebjergvei 1, 4791 Borre; dm/r without bathroom 105/300kr; May-15 Sep; P) With lots of shady trees and scurrying hares, Danhostel Møns Klint has a pleasant location, right on a lake. This hostel is in a former hotel 3km northwest of Møns Klint, opposite Camping Møns Klint. The 29 rooms contain 105 beds in all. From late June to mid-August you can take the Møns Klint bus No 54 from Stege, but during the rest of the year the nearest stop is in Magleby, 2.75km west of the hostel, where bus No 52 drops you off.

Liselund Ny Slot (55 81 20 81; www.liselundslot.dk; Langebjergvej 6, 4791 Borre; s/d incl breakfast with/without bathroom 800/1125kr; P) For those who would like to stay in a small manor-house hotel, Liselund Ny Slot occupies an upmarket 19th-century home in the midst of Liselund Park. The fine-dining **restaurant** (mains from 80kr) is worth a visit even if you don't stay the night. The dining area is ornate and sumptuous, the service first class and

MØNS KLINT'S UNUSUAL FLORA

Walking through Klinteskoven, the wood that backs the cliffs of Møn, you see wild orchids everywhere. In fact there are 20 species, the greatest variety anywhere in Denmark. Look but don't touch, as many of the orchids are rare and all are protected.

Two of the more beautiful flowers are the pyramidal orchid *(Anacamptis pyramidalis)*, which has a mounded, multi-blossomed pink head, and the dark red helleborine *(Epipactis atrorubens)*, which has an oval leaf and a tall stem with numerous crimson flowers.

The soil's high chalk content at Møns Klint provides ideal growing conditions for orchids. The unusual soil also means the beech trees along the coast keep their fresh spring-green hue throughout the summer. The calcareous soil inhibits their intake of iron and magnesium, the elements that cause leaves to darken.

The flowering season is from May to August and the grassy hills in the Mandemarke area in the southern part of the woods are particularly abundant with wild orchids.

the food – Danish lamb, Baltic fish, steaks and Asian dishes – delicious.

Camping Møns Klint (☎ 55 81 20 25; www.campingmoensklint.dk; camp site per person 65kr; ⏲ Apr-Oct; ♿) Bordering Klinteskoven, this three-star camping ground has a 25m swimming pool, a guest kitchen, a coin laundry, bicycles for hire and a shop selling bread, beer and other basics. It's 25kr for electricity and everyone pays a 5kr environment tax.

Møns Klint cafeteria (☎ 55 81 91 83; Store Klint; hamburgers 36kr; ⏲ lunch & dinner) Sandwiches 35kr, chicken & fish dishes 60kr. This place offers typical cafeteria fare such as chicken or fish with chips. There's a little kiosk below the cafeteria where you can buy ice cream.

KLINTHOLM HAVN

Half touristy, half local, Klintholm Havn has a harbour filled with fishing boats and another given over to yachts, many belonging to German tourists. It is a pleasant little harbourside village with a long sandy beach.

This one-road village has a grocery shop, a handful of eateries, a large harbourside resort and a little seaside inn.

Beyond that, it's mostly beach, which extends in two directions. The section that runs east is particularly appealing and pristine, with light grey sand backed by low dunes; it can be a fun place to stroll and also has the best surf. The safest swimming is found along the western section. There are public toilets and showers near the end of the road by the western part of the beach.

Sleeping

Klintholm Søbad (☎ 55 81 91 23; fax 55 81 91 01; Thyravej 19, 4791 Borre; s 400kr, cottages 495-795kr; Ⓟ) A small family can be accommodated in cottages with kitchens and TV. The small inn has a handful of double rooms with shared bathroom in the main building.

Danland Feriehotel Østersøen (☎ 55 81 90 55; www.dancenterferienparks.de; Klintholm Havn, 4791 Borre; apt from 939kr; Ⓟ ♿) Modern large apartment resort is spread across an artificial peninsula separating the two harbours. It has a pool, sauna, restaurant, coin laundrette and other conveniences. Each of the units has two bedrooms, bathroom, kitchen and TV.

Eating

Half a dozen restaurants line the waterfront road, ranging from a beachside hot-dog and burger joint to seafood restaurants. You can also stock up on supplies at the Spar Supermarket here.

Hyttefadet (☎ 55 81 92 36; Klintholm Havn; mains 75kr; ⏲ breakfast, lunch & dinner) This lively, if touristy, eatery is opposite the fishing harbour. Filling dishes, heavy on the fried foods. All-you-can-eat eel special for 132kr.

Klintholm Søbad (☎ 55 81 91 23; Thyravej 19; lunch specials 50kr, dinner fish meals 100kr; ⏲ lunch & dinner) For a typically Danish experience try this place which has a dining room with a sea view and fresh fish dishes.

Portofino (☎ 55 85 51 81; Thyravej 4A; pizzas 60kr; ⏲ lunch & dinner) Small but with a few classy touches. The all-you-can-eat dinner buffet (119kr) includes vegetables, meat, fish, pasta and salad.

Klintholm Røgeri (☎ 55 81 92 90; Margrethevej 14; fish buffet 100kr; ⏲ dinner) For Klintholm's best value, take the coastal road 250m east of the fishing harbour to the casual Klintholm Røgeri, where you can buy smoked and fried fish by the piece, enjoy a beer and sit down to feast at picnic tables.

WESTERN MØN

The western end of Møn is largely farmland crisscrossed by narrow country roads. This part of the island has a few worthwhile historic sights but you'll need your own transport to visit them, as the public bus system primarily serves Rte 287.

Passage Graves

Møn's two best-known Stone Age passage graves, Kong Asgers Høj and Klekkende Høj, are not far from each other on the western side of the island. Both are about 2km from the village of Røddinge and are signposted.

Kong Asgers Høj (Kong Asgers Vej) is in a farmer's field northwest of Røddinge; you can see the mound clearly from the road. This is Denmark's largest passage grave, with a burial chamber 10m long and more than 2m wide. Bring a torch (flashlight) and watch your head!

Klekkende Høj, southeast of Røddinge, is the only double passage grave mound on Møn. It has two entrances side by side, each leading to a 7m-long chamber.

Fanefjord Kirke

Overlooking the Fanefjord, the **Fanefjord Kirke** (Fanefjordvej; admission free; 8am-4pm Mon-Sat), was built in about 1250 in the early Gothic style but there have been several additions over the centuries. It is adorned with superb frescoes; the oldest, which date back to 1350, depict St Christopher carrying Christ across a ford. Most of the other frescoes date from around 1450 and were created by the Elmelunde master, whose mark (which resembles a stick man with rabbit ears) can be seen on an altar-facing rib in the northeastern vault.

BOGØ

The island of Bogø (west of Møn) is connected to Møn by a causeway, and to Zealand and Falster via the impressive Farø bridges.

Bogø chocolate, well known throughout Denmark, hails from the island. A car ferry shuttles between the southern side of the island and Stubbekøbing in Falster in summer. Bicycles are not allowed on the Farø bridges so cyclists will need to take the ferry (65kr), which operates once an hour.

Near the ramp to the Farø bridges is a welcome centre with a cafeteria, toilets, money exchange and the **Bogø chocolate production centre** (☎ 55 89 33 02; admission 35kr). There's also a tourist office where you can load up with brochures from 10am to 5pm daily.

FALSTER

pop 43,000

The island of Falster is almost completely given over to agriculture and its roads literally slice across farmers' fields. Although the scenery of the interior can become a bit repetitious, Falster's southeastern coast is a summer haven, with lovely white-sand

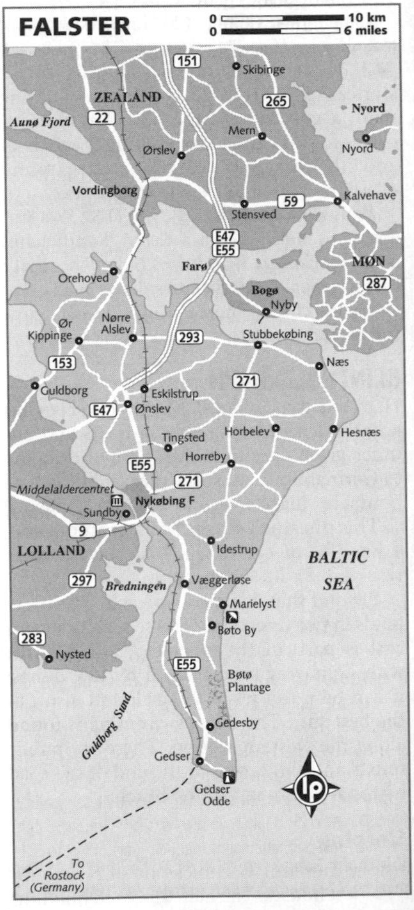
FALSTER
0 10 km
0 6 miles
151
Skibinge
ZEALAND
265
Nyord
Aunø Fjord
22
Mern
Nyord
Ørslev
Vordingborg
59
Kalvehave
Stensved
E47
E55
Farø
MØN
287
Orehoved
Bogø
Nyby
Ør
Kippinge
Nørre
Alslev
293
Stubbekøbing
153
Næs
271
Guldborg
Eskilstrup
E47
Ønslev
Tingsted
Horbelev
Hesnæs
Horreby
E55
271
Middelaldercentret
Nykøbing F
Sundby
9
LOLLAND
Idestrup
BALTIC
SEA
297
Bredningen
Væggerløse
Marielyst
Bøto By
283
Nysted
E55
Bøtø
Plantage
Guldborg Sund
Gedesby
Gedser
Gedser
Odde
To
Rostock
(Germany)

beaches that are a magnet for German and Danish holiday-makers.

If you're poking around Falster – and you'll need your own transportation to make this worthwhile – the rural hamlets and small towns contain a few sights, including a restored windmill in Gedesby and frescoes by the Elmelunde master at the church in Nørre Alslev.

NYKØBING F

pop 25,000

Surrounded by woods and large country houses, Nykøbing F is Falster's only large town. The F, incidentally, stands for Falster and is used to differentiate the town from Denmark's two other Nykøbings, one in Zealand and one in Jutland.

The grand medieval castle of Nykøbing F was torn down in the 18th century (you can see a model of it in the local-history museum) and with few exceptions the town has a predominantly modern façade. Still, if you need to stay overnight there is some reasonable accommodation and enough sights to occupy a day. Retail facilities include small speciality shops and large chain stores.

Torvet, the town centre, is a 10-minute walk west of the train station, and the **Nykøbing F Turistinformation** (☎ 54 85 13 03; www.tinf.dk; Østergågade 7; 🕑 10am-5pm Mon-Thu, 10am-6pm Fri & 10am-1pm Sat) is just south of Torvet.

Sights & Activities

The area's most popular attraction is **Middelaldercentret** (Medieval Centre; ☎ 54 86 19 34; www.middelaldercentret.dk; Ved Hamborgskoven 2, Sundby; adult/child 80/40kr; 🕑 10am-4pm May-Sep), which recreates a 14th-century medieval village with costumed interpreters demonstrating crafts, games, falconry and the like. There's a large wooden catapult, a distillery, a smithy and a number of buildings constructed as they would have been in the Middle Ages. A good time to visit is during one of the jousting tournaments, which occur at 2.30pm from mid-June to mid-August. It's on the outskirts of town, across the bridge on Lolland. Take bus No 2 from Nykøbing F train station.

Museet Falsters Minder (☎ 54 85 26 71; Langgade 2; admission 20kr; 🕑 11am-5pm Tue-Fri, 11am-3pm Sat, 2-4pm Sun May–mid-Sep; afternoons mid-Sep–Apr), the local-history museum, occupies one of Nykøbing F's oldest houses. The half-timbered building is referred to as Czarens Hus for the Russian tsar Peter the Great, who stayed here in 1716. It's on the western side of Torvet.

Sleeping

The tourist office keeps a list of rooms available in private homes; prices start at 150kr per person.

Danhostel Nykøbing F (☎ 54 85 66 99; www.danhostel.dk/vandrerhjem.asp; Østre Allé 110; dm 118kr, s & d 330kr; 🕑 mid-Jan–mid-Dec; Ⓟ) Modern 94-bed hostel is 1km east of the train station and opposite the zoo. Take bus No 42 (15kr) from the Nykøbing F station.

Hotel Falster (☎ 54 85 93 93; www.hotel-falster.dk; Skovalleen 2; s/d incl breakfast 670/815kr; Ⓟ) Family hotel has 69 comfortable, modern rooms and friendly management although its location just off a busy main road is hardly appealing. The hotel's restaurant serves such appetising dishes as whole roasted partridge, and smoked haunch of venison with cranberries.

Nykøbing F Camping (☎ 54 85 45 45; Østre Allé 112; camp site per person 56kr; 🕑 Apr-Sep) Two-star camping area is near the hostel.

Eating

Most of Nykøbing F's eating options are within a few blocks of Torvet, the central square.

Czarens Hus (☎ 54 85 28 29; Langgade 2; sandwiches 47kr, mains 150kr; 🕑 lunch & dinner) An upmarket option with a classic wood-panelled dining room and antique furnishings – from the days when it was a guest house and farm supply store 200 years ago. The steak specials are particularly filling.

Restaurant Italy (☎ 54 82 55 05; Langgade 23; pizzas 52kr; 🕑 lunch & dinner) Usual Italian fare, heaping portions of freshly made pasta and large personal pizzas, only a block from the action on Torvet.

Bjørnebageren (☎ 54 85 58 77; Torvet 2; pastries & desserts 15-40kr; 🕑 breakfast, lunch & dinner). Café is in a nice spot with outdoor seating where you can have a leisurely snack and coffee.

Teater Café (Østergågade 2; 🕑 lunch) An old school, where everything is wood and the Irish coffee (40kr) is strong. Across from the tourist office next to the theatre.

Getting There & Around

Nykøbing F is 128km southwest of Copenhagen and 24km north of Gedser. The north–south E55 highway goes directly through Nykøbing F, while Rte 9 connects Nykøbing F with Lolland via the Frederik IX bridge.

Trains leave Copenhagen hourly for Nykøbing F (108kr, two hours).

The bus stop is to the south of the train station. Bus Nos 40, 41 and 42 run to Marielyst (22kr, 25 minutes) frequently, particularly on weekdays.

MARIELYST

The most glorious stretch of beach in Falster is at Marielyst, which, with 6000 summer cottages, ranks as one of Denmark's prime holiday areas. Although summer crowds flock to the beach, it's long enough to find a relatively private patch of your own so that it doesn't feel too crowded. Follow the main street until it dead-ends for the most convenient parking and beach access. There are several other access roads down tree-lined streets but it's difficult to distinguish these from those preciously guarded by residents and summer holiday-makers. The town itself is really nothing more than a number of cafés, restaurants and hotels and a good number of ice cream kiosks perpendicular to the beach.

Information

Marielyst Møntvask (☎ 54 13 15 30; Marielyst Strandvej 23; 🕑 7am-10pm) is the town's coin laundrette.

Marielyst Turistbureau (☎ 54 13 62 98; www.marielyst.org; Marielyst Strandpark 3; 🕑 9am- 4pm Mon-Sat & 10am-2pm Sun mid-Jun–Aug, 9am to 4pm Mon-Fri Sep–mid-Jun) is next to the bowling alley on the northwestern outskirts of town. Internet access is available (15kr per half hour).

Nordea (☎ 54 13 60 85; Marielyst Strandvej 54; 🕑 10am-3pm Mon-Fri Jun-Sep, 10am-12.30pm Tue-Fri Oct-May) Is one of the many banks with ATM.

Sleeping

The tourist office maintains a list of rooms available in private homes for 250/410kr for singles/doubles. Staff there can also help you to book small apartments costing about 2000kr per week and summer houses starting at 4000kr per week. No booking fees.

Hotel Marielyst Strand (☎ 54 13 68 88; www.hotel-marielyst.dk; Marielyst Strandvej 61; s/d 745/898kr;

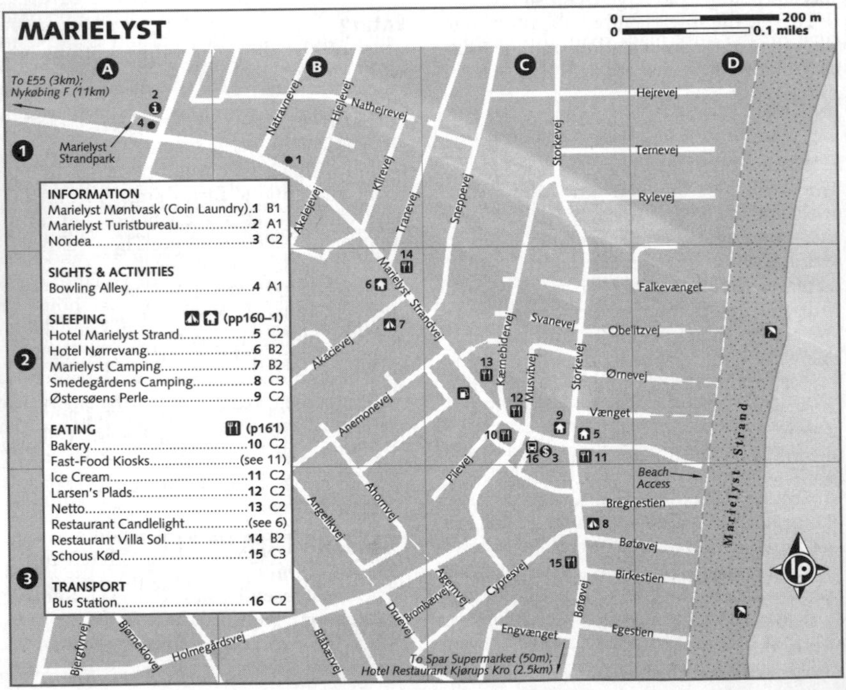
MARIELYST
0 200 m
0 0.1 miles
To E55 (3km); Nykøbing F (11km)
Marielyst Strandpark
INFORMATION
Marielyst Møntvask (Coin Laundry) 1 B1
Marielyst Turistbureau 2 A1
Nordea 3 C2
SIGHTS & ACTIVITIES
Bowling Alley 4 A1
SLEEPING (pp160–1)
Hotel Marielyst Strand 5 C2
Hotel Nørrevang 6 B2
Marielyst Camping 7 B2
Smedegårdens Camping 8 C3
Østersøens Perle 9 C2
EATING (p161)
Bakery 10 C2
Fast-Food Kiosks (see 11)
Ice Cream 11 C2
Larsen's Plads 12 C2
Netto 13 C2
Restaurant Candlelight (see 6)
Restaurant Villa Sol 14 B2
Schous Kød 15 C3
TRANSPORT
Bus Station 16 C2
Natravnevej
Hjejlevej
Nathejrevej
Akelejevej
Klirevej
Tranevej
Sneppevej
Storkevej
Hejrevej
Ternevej
Rylevej
Falkevænget
Marielyst Strandvej
Svanevej
Obelitzvej
Akacievej
Kærnebidervej
Musvitvej
Ørnevej
Vænget
Anemonevej
Pilevej
Beach Access
Ahornvej
Angelikvej
Bregnestien
Bøtøvej
Birkestien
Cypresvej
Agernvej
Brombærvej
Druevej
Engvænget
Egestien
Marielyst Strand
Bjergfyrvej
Bjørneklovej
Holmegårdsvej
Blåbærvej
To Spar Supermarket (50m); Hotel Restaurant Kjørups Kro (2.5km)

(P)) Close to the beach, this small hotel has a warm pastel-coloured design scheme. Rooms are tastefully done with attention to detail and several have their own patios.

Hotel Nørrevang (☎ 54 13 62 62; www.norrevang.dk; Marielyst Strandvej 32; r/bungalows 500/700kr; (P) (⊠)) Marielyst's most upmarket hotel looks like a low-slung Swiss chalet. Standard rooms have bathroom, phone and TV. There are 57 bungalows and apartments that also have kitchens and can accommodate from two to six people. The hotel also books and manages **Østersøens Perle** (Marielyst Strandvej 59), which has a handful of double rooms for 7000kr. It's closer to the beach.

Kjørupskro Hotel (☎ 54 13 62 43; www.kjorupskro.dk; Boto Møllevej 2; r incl breakfast 600kr; (P)) A few kilometres south of town, this hotel has spacious rooms and special deals if you stay longer than a week. A restaurant is attached.

Smedegårdens Camping (☎ 54 13 66 17; barklund@marieylst.dk; Bøtøvej 5; camp site per person 65kr; ⏰ Jun-Aug) A mere two-minute stroll from the beach, this simple one-star camping ground has cooking facilities.

Marielyst Camping (☎ 54 17 44 04; www.marielyst-camping.dk in Danish; Marielyst Strandvej 36; camp site per person 63kr; ⏰ Apr-Sep) Centrally located, just off the busy main road, this camping ground can feel cramped.

Eating

As is to be expected with a major holiday location, Marielyst has many cafés and fast-food joints, as well as pleasant restaurants.

Restaurant Candlelight (☎ 54 13 62 62; Hotel Nørrevang; dinner buffet 118kr; ⏰ lunch & dinner) An attractive restaurant attached to the Hotel Nørrevang has several vine-covered dining areas, some outside in a pleasant courtyard and garden. Candlelight's menu stresses seasonal ingredients.

Restaurant Villa Sol (☎ 54 13 05 04; Marielyst Strandvej 31; mains 80kr; ⏰ lunch & dinner) Sunny place on the commercial strip lives up to its name, dishing out filling fish and beef dishes. Service is especially friendly.

Larsen's Plads (☎ 54 13 21 70; Marielyst Strandvej 53; veg mains from 60kr, steaks from 147kr; ⏰ lunch & dinner) An idiosyncratic restaurant that abounds with character, and offers hearty beef and potato dishes as well as vegetarian offerings.

Schous Kød (☎ 54 13 64 69; Bøtøvej 12; fish & chips 30kr, chicken & chips 40kr; ⏰ lunch & dinner) A mere 200m south down Bøtøvej from the corner with Marielyst Strandvej, Schous Kød offers a good alternative to junk food. There's a little fruit and vegetable stand next door.

On the corner of Bøtøvej and Marielyst Strandvej you'll find an ice-cream shop and a handful of kiosks selling pizzas, burgers, hot dogs and beer. There's a good bakery just west of the bus station.

Getting There & Around

From Nykøbing F train station it's a 25-minute bus ride to Marielyst (26kr). Buses are frequent, particularly on weekdays; you can catch bus Nos 40, 41 or 42. Bus No 45 runs to Gedser (26kr, 20 minutes) during the summer period.

Bicycles can be hired from the Sydsol office next to the tourist information office or at the supermarket **Spar** (☎ 54 13 61 04; Lupinvej 1), 2km south of the centre, for 40kr per day.

LOLLAND

pop 72,000

Lolland has some of Denmark's best farming land, much of it planted with sugar beet. Think of it as a leisurely change of pace, although it's said that Lolland is the most popular vacation centre in the nation! Sights include a safari park, a water park with a tropical indoor swimming pool and a notable car museum.

Perhaps the most appealing of the island's towns is Maribo, in a little lake district in the central part of Lolland. Sakskøbing, about 9km northeast of Maribo, has a water tower painted with a cheery smiling face, and Nakskov, at the western end of Lolland, has a few half-timbered waterfront warehouses, a couple of local-history museums and a Russian U-359 submarine that can be toured.

The introduction of a direct ferry service to Puttgarden, Germany, saw the emergence of Rødbyhavn, a small harbourside town in the south, in the 1960s. That service now provides the link in the inter-Europe E47 highway between Germany and Denmark.

GETTING THERE & AROUND

There's a limited bus service on the island. The most useful route (No 47) connects Nykøbing F with Nakskov.

Of the two railway lines in Lolland the main east–west route cuts across the centre,

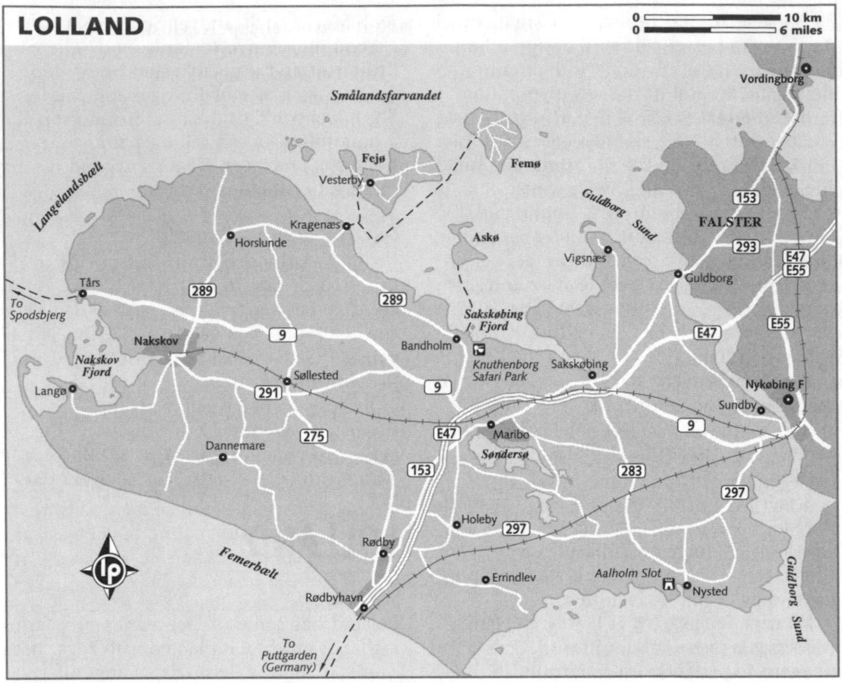
LOLLAND
0 10 km
0 6 miles
Smålandsfarvandet
Langelandsbælt
Fejø
Femø
Vesterby
Kragenæs
Horslunde
Askø
Guldborg Sund
FALSTER
Vordingborg
Vigsnæs
Guldborg
Tårs
To Spodsbjerg
289
289
153
293
E47
E55
E55
E47
Sakskøbing Fjord
Bandholm
Knuthenborg Safari Park
Sakskøbing
Nakskov
Nakskov Fjord
Langø
9
9
9
Søllested
291
Nykøbing F
Sundby
275
E47
Maribo
Søndersø
Dannemare
153
283
297
297
Holeby
Rødby
Femerbælt
Errindlev
Aalholm Slot
Nysted
Guldborg Sund
Rødbyhavn
To Puttgarden (Germany)

running between Nykøbing F and Nakskov (47kr, 48 minutes). Trains run about hourly during the week but less often at weekends.

The other railway line runs between Rødby and Nykøbing F (37kr, 23 minutes). Trains leave Rødbyhavn several times a day in conjunction with the ferry service from Puttgarden, Germany; most of the trains continue on from Nykøbing F to Copenhagen.

Route 9 cuts across central Lolland from Nykøbing F in the east to Tårs in the west (61km).

Scandlines (☎ 33 15 15 15; www.scandlines.dk) runs a car ferry between Tårs and Spodsbjerg (in Langeland; 230kr per car) about once every 30 minutes during the day and hourly in the early morning and late evening.

For information about the ferry between Rødbyhavn and Puttgarden, Germany, see p310.

Aalholm Slot & Automobil Museum

One of northern Europe's oldest inhabited castles, **Aalholm Slot**, dates back to the 12th century. The Danish king Christopher II was imprisoned in his own dungeon here in 1332 by his half-brother, Count Johan the Mild. The privately owned castle is not open to the public, but part of the estate houses the **Aalholm Automobil Museum** (☎ 54 87 19 11; www.aalholm.dk; Aalholm Parkvej 17, Nysted; adult/child 65/30kr; 10am-5pm Jun-Aug), which contains one of Europe's largest collections of antique cars.

Rare models include an 1899 Daimler, a 1900 Decauville, 1902 Renault, 1903 Ford Model A, 1905 Cadillac, 1911 Rolls Royce and a 1931 Bugatti.

The castle and museum are at the west side of the small town of Nysted, which is connected to Nykøbing F via Rte 297 and to Sakskøbing via Rte 283.

MARIBO

pop 5500

If you decide to stop for a night in Lolland, the town of Maribo, the island's centre is an agreeable place. It has a choice setting, nestled around the northern arm of a large inland lake, Søndersø. A historic cathedral sits on the eastern shore and Bangshave, a wood thick with beech trees, sits on the western shore.

The town centre, Torvet, is marked by Maribo's neoclassical 19th-century rådhus (town hall), fronted by a fountain and backed by a few 18th-century timber-framed houses. Beyond that the main attraction is the lake and woods; there are trails along both sides of the lake beginning only minutes from the town centre.

The train/bus station is north of Torvet, about a five-minute walk via Jernbanegade. **Maribo Turistbureau** (☎ 54 78 04 96; www.turistlolland.dk in Danish; Rådhuset, Torvet; ⏲ 9am-5pm Mon-Fri & 10am-1pm Sat) has info on all of the island.

Sights & Activities

MARIBO DOMKIRKE

Maribo's lakeside cathedral was erected in the 15th century and named after the Virgin Mary. Maribo Domkirke was part of a larger complex including the convent where Leonora Christine, the daughter of Christian IV, spent the rest of her life after her release from imprisonment in Copenhagen Castle in 1685. Her crypt is in the cathedral. Maribo Domkirke is 200m southwest of Torvet.

STORSTRØMS KUNSTMUSEUM & LOLLAND-FALSTER STIFTSMUSEUM

Maribo is home to a couple of small museums. The adjacent **Storstrøms Kunstmuseum** and **Lolland-Falster Stiftsmuseum** (☎ 54 78 11 01; Jernbanepladsen; admission incl both 20kr; ⏲ noon-4pm Tue-Sun), are beside the train station. The Kunstmuseum features regional art from the 18th to the 20th centuries, while the Stiftsmuseum exhibits church art.

MUSEUMSBANEN

An antique steam-engine train known as Museumsbanen (☎ 54 78 85 45; adult/child 40/20kr) makes a jaunt north to Bandholm on Tuesday, Thursday and Sunday from July to mid-August. It leaves Maribo station at 10.20am and the return trip takes 90 minutes.

Sleeping

Danhostel Maribo (☎ 54 78 33 14; www.danhostel.dk/maribo, Søndre Blvd 82B; dm/r 95/285kr; Ⓟ) About 2km southeast of Torvet, this modern hostel near Søndersø has 96 beds. There's a lakeside trail to the town centre.

Ebsens Hotel (☎ 54 78 10 44; www.ebsens-hotel.dk; Vestergade 32; s/d 350/550kr; Ⓟ) Although the rooms are straightforward, with shared bathrooms, this small local hotel is pleasant and relatively cheap. It is just a few minutes' walk southwest from the train station.

Park Inn Maribo Søpark (☎ 54 78 10 11; www.maribo-soepark.dk; Vestergade 27; s/d 845/895kr; Ⓟ ♿) This modern 63-room lakeside hotel, 500m west of Torvet, has rooms with full amenities and lake-view balconies.

Maribo Sø Camping (☎ 54 78 00 71; www.maribo-camping.dk; Bangshavevej 25; camp site per person 62kr; ⏲ Apr-Oct) Three-star camping ground right on Søndersø is 500m southwest of town It has a kitchen, laundry and TV lounge and is accessible to people in wheelchairs.

Eating

For a place to eat, it's worth trying the area in and around Vestergade, which runs west from Torvet.

Restaurant Bangs Have (☎ 54 78 19 11; Bangshavevej 23; mains around 100kr; ⏲ lunch & dinner) Popular for its lakeside setting, this restaurant is in an old manor house east of Maribo Sø Camping. There's a great view of Maribo Domkirke across the water.

Stegependen Steak House (☎ 54 78 10 10; Vesterbrogade 23; steaks from 125kr; ⏲ lunch & dinner) Another choice just a short walk from the camping ground. Stegependen is a small, elegant restaurant with all variety of steaks.

Café Maribo (☎ 54 78 39 76; Vestergade 6; burgers 35kr; ⏲ breakfast, lunch & dinner) This no-frills café has good food such as quiche with salad or Danish roast pork with potatoes and is one of the few places open on Sunday.

AROUND LOLLAND

The drive-through **Knuthenborg Safari Park** (☎ 54 78 80 88; www.knuthenborg.dk in Danish; Bandholm; adult/child 88/46kr; ⏲ 9am-5pm May-Sep), 7km north of Maribo via Rte 289, has free-roaming zebras, antelopes, llamas, giraffes, rhinoceroses, camels and other exotic creatures. The park occupies what was once Denmark's largest privately owned estate and has 500 species of trees and flowering bushes, an aviary, an enclosed tiger section and some simple amusement rides. Rødby to the south is the departure point for ferries to Puttgarden, Germany, but it also has beaches and **Lalandia** (☎ 54 61 05 00; www.lalandia.dk; adults/children 80/40kr; ⏲ 1-7:30pm), a huge water park that can keep the kids occupied even in inclement weather. The facilities at Lalandia include a tropical indoor swimming pool and Mediterranean restaurants.

Bornholm

CONTENTS

Life is pleasantly slow-paced on sleepy Bornholm, a leafy island stuck out in the middle of the Baltic 200km east of Copenhagen. It offers the best of rural Denmark in an enchanting and easily explored microcosm: wheat fields and forests, a coastline dotted with small fishing villages, picture-book thatched and half-timbered houses, sea cliffs and long stretches of powdery-white beaches.

The island is easy to explore, with both a good island-wide bus system and an impressive network of bicycle paths. Even if you're not a keen cyclist, it's well worth considering bicycle transport since Bornholm is reasonably flat and fairly small; a day's steady cycling will take you right across the island.

In addition to its unique fortified *rundkirke* (round churches) and medieval fortress, Bornholm is renowned for its smokehouses. Be sure to try Bornholm's smoked herring (*bornholmer)* and the spiced herring from the nearby island of Christiansø, considered the best in Denmark.

In fact there's an increasingly good selection of local produce, so however you decide to get around the island, you're sure to sample some locally prepared treats such as smoked fish of every kind, hand-made chocolate, micro-brewed beer and organic ice cream.

HIGHLIGHTS

- Wash down tender smoked fish with locally brewed ale at the island's best smokehouse in **Svaneke** (p174)
- Discover the utterly unique rundkirke, fortified round churches, at Nyker, Olsker, Østelars and **Nylars** (p168)
- Wiggle the finest white sand between your toes on the long, long beach at **Dueodde** (p172)
- Lose yourself in the bike and hiking trails in the **Almindingen** area (p172), part of Bornholm's forested heart
- Set sail for tiny Christiansø a well-preserved 17th-century island fortress and untouched **nature reserve** (p180)

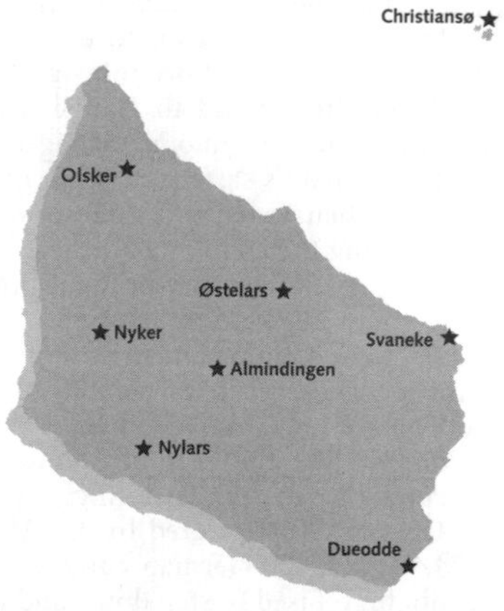
Christiansø
Olsker
Østelars
Nyker
Svaneke
Almindingen
Nylars
Dueodde

HISTORY

Given the fact that Bornholm is closer to Germany and Sweden than it is to Denmark and that it lies smack in the middle of the Baltic's key commercial and strategic shipping lanes, it's perhaps not surprising that the encircling nations have fought bitterly and repeatedly over ownership of the island for the past few centuries.

Bornholm's rich human history goes back much further than this though, by at least five millennia. Bronze and Iron-Age people left behind burial mounds, rock engravings, monoliths and items from around Europe such as numerous Roman coins, suggesting that by the Iron Age Bornholm was an important trading centre in the region. A rich bounty of finds from archaeological digs around the island are on display at the small but interesting Bornholms Museum in Rønne (p168).

In the Middle Ages Bornholm was administered by the archbishop of Lund (now part of southern Sweden, Lund was then Danish territory), who ruled from Hammershus, an expansive fortress on the island's northern coast, now a romantic, weather-beaten ruin (p179).

During the wars between Sweden and Denmark in the mid-17th century, Bornholm fell into Swedish hands, along with Danish territories at the southern end of the Swedish mainland. In 1658, when it looked likely that the island might become a permanent part of Sweden, the Swedish commandant on Bornholm was murdered in an uprising. The rebels, led by Bornholm native Jens Kofoed, went on to expel the Swedish garrison from Bornholm and in 1660 returned the island to Danish rule. As a consequence, Bornholm managed to prevail as Denmark's easternmost province in a period when Swedish conquests were steadily eroding the country's borders.

Peace in the 18th century brought prosperity to the island and to its merchants, who built timber-framed mansions along waterfront villages such as perfectly preserved Svaneke (p174) and Rønne.

Bornholm, like the rest of Denmark, was occupied by the Nazis during WWII. When Germany surrendered to the Allies on 4 May 1945, the German commander on Bornholm refused to step down and the Soviets bombed Rønne and Nexø, causing heavy damage. On 9 May the island was turned over to the Soviets, who occupied it until the spring of the following year.

GETTING THERE & AWAY

Bornholm can be reached by air, boat or a combination that couples the boat with a bus or train via Sweden.

Air

Cimber Air (☎ 70 10 74 74; www.cimber.dk) operates several flights a day between Copenhagen city and Rønne. The one-way fare for this route is 1010kr but return fares as low as 475kr are available if you book online at least seven days in advance.

The island's airport, Bornholms Lufthavn, is 5km southeast of Rønne, on the road to Dueodde. Bus No 7 stops on the main road in front of the airport.

Boat

Bornholmstrafikken (Copenhagen ☎ 33 13 18 66, Rønne ☎ 56 95 18 66) While not as fast as the boat/train option, the overnight sailing (departing daily at midnight and arriving in Rønne, at 6.30am) on the car ferry from Køge is worth considering. The bunk-style berths (76kr extra one way) and cabins (from extra 186kr one way) are reasonably inexpensive and it's a good use of time as you travel while you sleep. The downside is the arduous trip out to Køge, about 30 minutes by train south of Copenhagen. A peak return per person costs 325kr. A car with up to five people costs 1280kr. There are also a few (sporadic) daytime sailings each week.

For details on boats from Germany, Sweden and Poland, see p310.

Bus & Boat

Bornholmerbussen (☎ 44 68 44 00; www.bornholmerbussen.dk) runs a bus (No 866) between Copenhagen's Central Station and Ystad in Sweden, where it connects with a ferry. In summer, buses depart Copenhagen at 7am, 11am, 3pm and 7pm (adult/child 200/100kr, four hours).

Train & Boat

The national railway system **DSB** (☎ 70 13 14 15; www.dsb.dk) operates a combined train/boat service (adult/child 230/126kr, three hours, four times daily) to Rønne on Bornholm. You catch a train from Copenhagen's

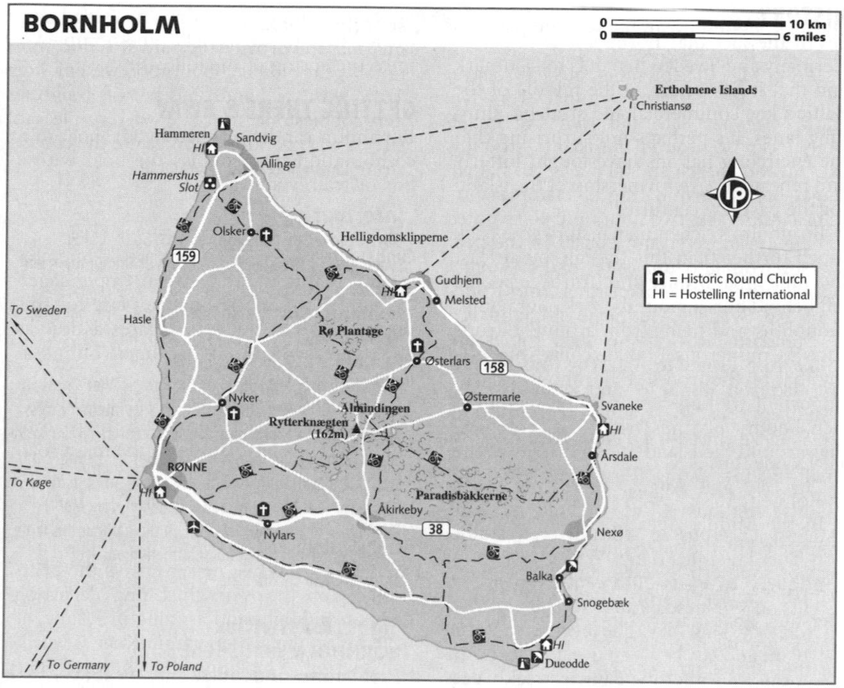
BORNHOLM
0 10 km
0 6 miles
Ertholmene Islands
Christiansø
Hammeren
Sandvig
HI
Allinge
Hammershus Slot
Olsker
Helligdomsklipperne
159
Gudhjem
HI
Melsted
= Historic Round Church
HI = Hostelling International
To Sweden
Hasle
Rø Plantage
Østerlars
158
Nyker
Østermarie
Svaneke
Almindingen
Rytterknægten (162m)
HI
Årsdale
RØNNE
To Køge
HI
Paradisbakkerne
Åkirkeby
38
Nexø
Nylars
Balka
Snogebæk
HI
To Germany
To Poland
Dueodde

Central Station to Ystad in Sweden, then connect with a ferry to Rønne.

GETTING AROUND

To/From the Airport

The island's airport, Bornholms Lufthavn, is 5km southeast of Rønne, on the road to Dueodde. Bus No 7 stops on the main road in front of the airport.

Bicycle

Cycling is a great way to get around Bornholm, which is crisscrossed by more than 200km of bike trails. Some of the trails go over former train routes, some slice through forests and others run alongside main roads. Together they connect Bornholm's largest towns, cross a wide variety of landscapes and lead to most of the island's sightseeing attractions.

You can start right in Rønne, where bike routes fan out to Allinge, Gudhjem, Nexø, Dueodde and the Almindingen forest.

If you don't feel like pedalling the entire way, you can take your bike on public buses for an additional 20kr.

The tourist office in Rønne sells the handy 60-page English-language *Bicycle Routes on Bornholm* (40kr), which maps out routes and describes sights along the way.

RENTAL

Bicycle hire ranges from about 60/240kr per day/week for three-speed bicycles; mountain bikes 70/350kr. Two of the larger Rønne rental shops are **Cykel-Centret** (☎ 56 95 06 04) at Søndergade 7, and **Bornholms Cykel-udlejning** (☎ 56 95 13 59), next to the tourist office at Nordre Kystvej 5. On the island most hostels and camping grounds hire out bicycles.

Bus

Bornholms Amts Trafikselskab (BAT; ☎ 56 95 21 21; www.bat.dk in Danish) runs a good, inexpensive round-island service. Fares are based on a zone system and cost 10kr per zone, with the maximum fare set at 10 zones. Ask the bus driver about the RaBATkort pass, which is good for 10 rides, can be used by more than one person and saves about 20%. There are also day/week passes for 130/440kr. Children travel for half-price.

Buses operate all year, but schedules are less frequent from October to April.

From May to September, bus No 7 leaves from the Rønne ferry terminal every two hours between 8am and 4pm and travels anticlockwise around the island, stopping at Dueodde beach and all major coastal villages before terminating at Hammershus. The circuit takes two hours and 40 minutes. There are more evening buses in the peak season from late June to the end of August. Other buses make direct runs from Rønne to Nexø, Svaneke, Gudhjem and Sandvig.

Standard fares on the main routes are: 30kr from Rønne to Åkirkeby (bus No 5 or 6); 40kr from Rønne to Sandvig (bus No 1) or Gudhjem (bus No 3); and 50kr from Rønne to Svaneke (bus No 4), Nexø (bus No 6) or Dueodde (bus No 7).

In July and August BAT runs special sightseeing buses for passholders: Kunsthåndværkerbussen stops at craft studios on Tuesday and Friday; Veteranbussen, an antique bus, visits 20th-century historical sights on Wednesday; and Havebussen visits gardens on Thursday. The tours leave Rønne at 10am and last between five and six hours. You can use either the daily or weekly pass; refreshments and admission fees (if applicable) are extra.

Car & Motorcycle

Europcar and Avis have offices within walking distance of the Rønne ferry terminal. **Avis** (☎ 56 95 22 08) is at Rønne Autoudlejning ApS, Snellemark 19. **Europcar** (☎ 56 95 43 00), Nordre Kystvej 1, is at the Q8 petrol station and rents motor scooters/open-topped mini four-wheel buggies/cars from 245/385/620kr per day. Both companies also serve the airport.

RØNNE

pop 15,000

A charming little town, Rønne has a number of engaging museums and an old quarter of cobbled streets flanked by very pretty, single-storeyed dwellings. It is the island's largest settlement and, although more of a place for a quick stopover than a compelling sightseeing destination, it is a pleasant enough town.

Spread around a large natural harbour, Rønne has been the island's commercial centre since the Middle Ages. Over the years the town has expanded and taken on a more suburban look, but a few well-preserved quarters still provide pleasant strolling, most notably the old neighbourhood west of Store Torv with its handsome period buildings and cobblestone streets. Two very pleasant streets with period buildings are the cobblestone **Laksegade** and **Storegade**.

Information

Bornholms Centralsygehus (☎ 56 95 11 65; Sygehusvej 9) The island's hospital is at the southern end of town.
Møntevask Laundrette (Norregade 11; 6am-10pm)
Nordeabank (☎ 56 95 14 20; Store Torv 18)
Post office (☎ 56 94 38 00; Lille Torv 18)
Public library (☎ 56 95 07 04; Pingels Allé; 10am-7pm Mon-Fri, 10am-2pm Sat) Offers free Internet access.
Tourist office (Bornholms Velkomstcenter; ☎ 56 95 95 00; www.bornholm.info; Nordre Kystvej 3; 9am-5pm Mon-Sat, 10am-3pm Sun late Jun-Aug; 9am-4pm Mon-Fri, 10am-1pm Sat Mar-May, Sep & Oct; 9am-4pm Mon-Fri Nov-Feb) A few minutes' walk from the harbour this large, friendly office has masses of information on all of Bornholm and Christiansø.

Sights & Activities

BORNHOLMS MUSEUM

Prehistoric finds including weapons, tools and jewellery are on show at **Bornholms Museum** (☎ 56 95 07 35, Sankt Mortensgade 29; adult/child 35/10kr; 10am-5pm Mon-Fri, 10am-2pm Sat May-Sep, shorter low-season hr) which has a surprisingly large and varied collection of local history exhibits. A good maritime section is decked out like the interior of a ship and a hotchpotch of nature displays, antique toys, Roman coins, pottery and paintings.

FORSVARSMUSEET

A 17th-century citadel called Kastellet houses the **Defence Museum** (☎ 56 95 65 83, Kastellet; adult/child 35/10kr; 11am-5pm Tue-Sat May-Oct), south of the town centre. The Forsvarsmuseet has extensive displays of guns, blades, bombs and military uniforms but the historical context they are given is usually scant, although some brief explanatory notes in English are available from the ticket desk. There are especially large displays on the Nazi occupation of the island and on the bombing of Rønne and Nexø by the Soviets at the end of WWII.

NYLARS RUNDKIRKE

The attractive **Nylars Rundkirke** (☎ 56 97 20 13, Kirkevej 17; 9am-5pm Mon-Sat), built in 1150, is

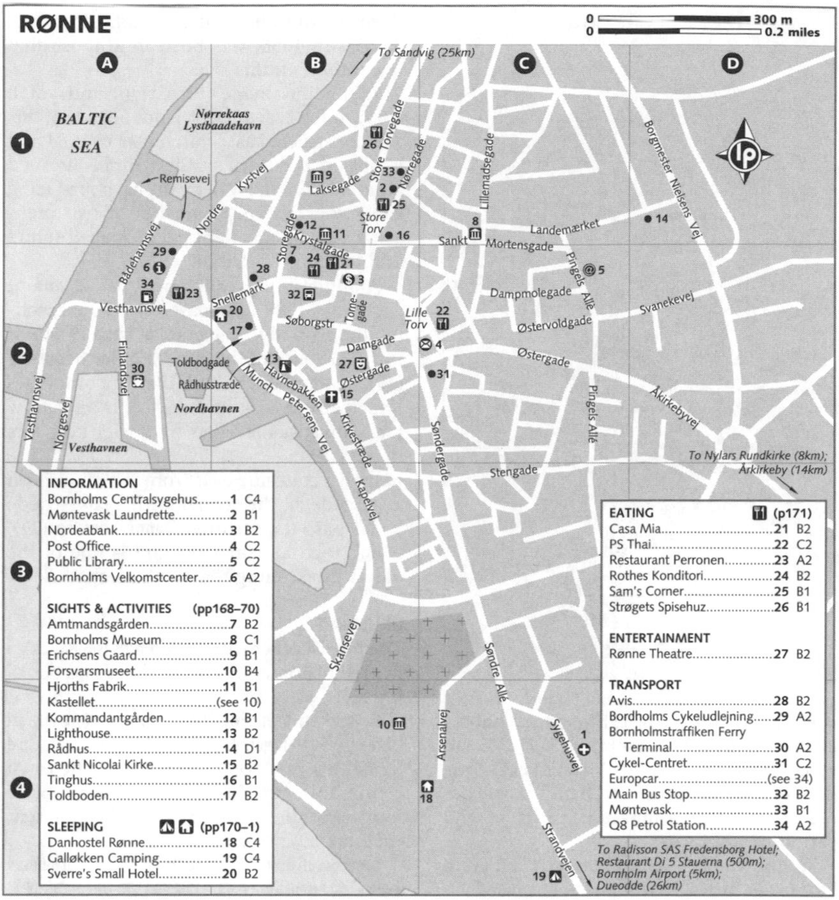
RØNNE
0 300 m
0 0.2 miles
To Sandvig (25km)
BALTIC SEA
Nørrekaas Lystbaadehavn
Nordhavnen
Vesthavnen
To Nylars Rundkirke (8km); Åkirkeby (14km)
To Radisson SAS Fredensborg Hotel; Restaurant Di 5 Stauerna (500m); Bornholm Airport (5km); Dueodde (26km)
INFORMATION
Bornholms Centralsygehus.........1 C4
Møntevask Laundrette...............2 B1
Nordeabank.................................3 B2
Post Office..................................4 C2
Public Library..............................5 C2
Bornholms Velkomstcenter.........6 A2
SIGHTS & ACTIVITIES (pp168–70)
Amtmandsgården......................7 B2
Bornholms Museum..................8 C1
Erichsens Gaard.........................9 B1
Forsvarsmuseet.........................10 B4
Hjorths Fabrik............................11 B1
Kastellet..................................(see 10)
Kommandantgården.................12 B1
Lighthouse.................................13 B2
Rådhus.......................................14 D1
Sankt Nicolai Kirke....................15 B2
Tinghus......................................16 B1
Toldboden..................................17 B2
SLEEPING (pp170–1)
Danhostel Rønne......................18 C4
Galløkken Camping...................19 C4
Sverre's Small Hotel..................20 B2
EATING (p171)
Casa Mia...................................21 B2
PS Thai.....................................22 C2
Restaurant Perronen.................23 A2
Rothes Konditori.......................24 B2
Sam's Corner.............................25 B1
Strøgets Spisehuz......................26 B1
ENTERTAINMENT
Rønne Theatre..........................27 B2
TRANSPORT
Avis...28 B2
Bordholms Cykeludlejning.........29 A2
Bornholmstraffiken Ferry Terminal.........30 A2
Cykel-Centret...........................31 C2
Europcar.................................(see 34)
Main Bus Stop..........................32 B2
Møntevask................................33 B1
Q8 Petrol Station......................34 A2

the most well preserved and easily accessible round church in the Rønne area. Its central pillar is painted with 13th-century frescoes, the oldest in Bornholm, depicting scenes from the Creation myth, including Adam and Eve's expulsion from the Garden of Eden. The cylindrical nave has three storeys, the top one a watchman's gallery that served as a defence lookout in medieval times.

Inside the church, the front door is flanked by two of Bornholm's 40 rune stones (carved memorial stones that date back to the Viking era).

It's about 8km from Rønne, on the road to Åkirkeby and a 15-minute ride from Rønne on bus No 6; alight at the bus stop near the Dagli Brugsen shop and turn north on Kirkevej for the 350m walk to the church. The cycle path between Rønne and Åkirkeby also passes the church.

Walking Tour

A good place to begin a walking tour of Rønne's older quarters is **Store Torv (1)**, formerly the military parade ground. Now the central commercial square, it's the site of a public market on Wednesday and Saturday mornings year-round. On the eastern side of the square, at Store Torv 1, is **Tinghus (2)**, a neoclassical building from 1834 that once housed Rønne's city hall, courthouse and jail.

Continue up Store Torvegade and turn left on Laksegade, a picturesque cobblestone

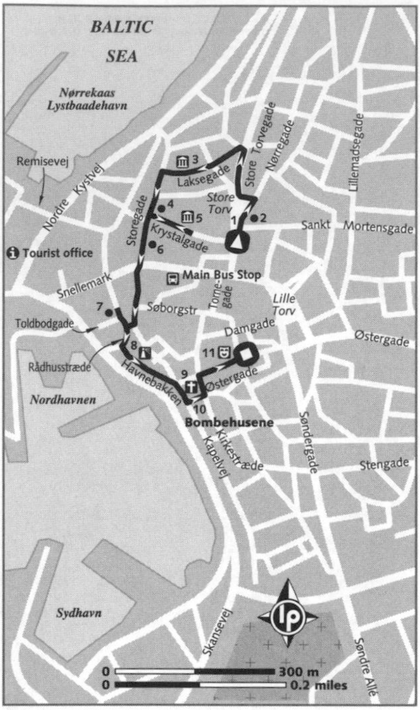
BALTIC
SEA
Nørrekaas
Lystbaadehavn
Remisevej
Nordre Kystvej
Tourist office
Laksegade
Store Torv
Store Torvegade
Nørregade
Lillemadsegade
Sankt Mortensgade
Krystalgade
Storegade
Snellemark
Main Bus Stop
Søborgstr
Tornegade
Lille Torv
Damgade
Østergade
Toldbodgade
Rådhusstræde
Havnebakken
Nordhavnen
Bombehusene
Kirkestræde
Kapelvej
Søndergade
Stengade
Sydhavn
Skansevej
Søndre Allé
300 m
0.2 miles

street lined with early 19th century houses including **Erichsens Gaard (3**; 56 95 87 35; Laksegade 7; adult/child 25/10kr; 10am-5pm Tue-Sat mid-May–mid-Oct). This 1806 merchant's house has been turned into a museum complete with period furnishings.

At the end of Laksegade turn left onto Storegade; at No 42 you'll find **Kommandantgården (4)**, an imposing building erected in 1846 as a residence for the Bornholm military commander.

Just around the corner on Krystalgade, **Hjorths Fabrik (5**; 56 95 01 60; Krystalgade 5; adult/child 30/10kr; 10am-5pm Mon-Fri, 10am-2pm Sat Apr-Oct) is a ceramics museum complete with working features. There are also some delicate, locally made wares for sale in the shop in front (which is free to enter) much of it exquisite, all of it fairly pricey. Some of it is made by the fourth generation of the Hjorth family of Bornholm ceramic artists who used to own the museum.

Return to Storegade and proceed south to **Amtmandsgården (6)**, a half-timbered 18th-century structure at Storegade 36 that is now the Bornholm prefect's residence. Jens Kofoed, who liberated Bornholm from the Swedes in 1658, was born in a house that once stood on this site.

At Rådhusstræde, turn right and you'll come to **Toldboden (7)**, at Toldbodgade 1; this was constructed as a storehouse in 1684 and is one of the town's oldest timber-framed buildings. On the wall by the harbour-facing gable you can spot figurines of two menacing Dalmatians flanking a cloaked figure said to represent Satan.

Along Havnebakken you'll pass a quaint octagonal 1880 **lighthouse (8)** before reaching the attractive **Sankt Nicolai Kirke (9)**, built in 1915. South of the church is **Bombehusene (10)**, a neighbourhood that encompasses Kapelvej and Kirkestræde; this is one of the areas that was levelled by Soviet bombers in May 1945.

If you continue east from the church on Østergade, at the corner with Teaterstræde you'll pass the restored **Rønne Theatre (11)**, which was built in 1823 and is one of the oldest functioning theatres in Denmark.

Sleeping

The tourist office can book **rooms** (s/d 200/290kr) in private homes in Rønne; there's no booking fee.

Galløkken Camping (56 95 23 20; www.gallokken.dk; Strandvejen 4; mid-May–Aug; adult/child 56/28kr; P) Just over 1km south of the town centre, this camping ground also has basic four-bed cabins (350kr) and bikes for rent (per day 60kr to 65kr).

Danhostel Rønne (56 95 13 40; www.danhostel-roenne.dk; Arsenalvej 12; dm 115kr, s/d 300/400kr; P) The immaculately kept 140-bed hostel near Galløkken Camping, is a secluded, whitewashed building with a neatly tended garden. It boasts typically small, tidy if rather soul-less dorms.

Sverre's Small Hotel (56 95 03 03; Snellemark 2; s/d incl breakfast 290/460kr) The only budget hotel in town but it's a good one run by a friendly jazz musician – and it's centrally located. The 24 rooms vary in size, but are all clean and adequate. Breakfast is included in the room rates.

Radisson SAS Fredensborg Hotel (56 95 44 44; www.bornholmhotels.dk, Strandvejen 116; s/d 995/1195kr;) Plush, comfortable and perched on a pleasant knoll overlooking wave-pounded rocks at the southern end of Rønne. The Fredensborg has 72 well-appointed and stylish rooms (all with sea views, some with rather pokey bathrooms and a few with wheelchair access). There's also a sauna, pool and tennis court.

Eating

There's a good variety of restaurants and cafées while for a quick breakfast, the ferry terminal has an upstairs caféteria serving pastries and coffee at reasonable prices.

Restaurant Perronen (☎ 56 95 84 40; mains 120-148kr; Munch Petersens Vej 3; ⌚ lunch & dinner daily Jun-Sep, closed Monday Oct-May) Southeast of the tourist office in an appealing period building this restaurant serves a patchy international menu but a rather better seasonal menu. The latter might include such treats as shrimp with asparagus, lemon and creamy tomato dressing or fresh plaice fillets with asparagus, lobster sauce and new potatoes.

Restaurant Di 5 Stauerna (☎ 56 95 44 44; www.bornholmhotels.dk; dinner mains 130-220kr; ⌚ lunch & dinner) One of the best (and priciest) places on the island for dinner, the influences here are Italian and French. There are plenty of dark meat choices (like sauté of Bornholm venison with mushrooms, onions, celery and bacon in cognac glacé) and a few fish choices (such as oak plate-baked halibut with mashed potatoes and pepper butter). There are light, yummy desserts (including apple sorbet with Calvados or an ice cream with local blueberries) and a very reasonable three-course, 75kr herring buffet lunch special.

TOP FIVE BORNHOLM TREATS

- Caramel sweetmeats from the tiny Gudhjem storybook candy factory **Karamel Kompagniet** (p178)
- Melt-in-the-mouth pastries and coffee on the rooftop terrace at **Gudhjem Bageri** (p178)
- Locally brewed ale from **Bryghuset** (p174) in Svaneke
- Great organic Bornholm ice cream by the beach from **Boisenøkologisk** (p172) in Snogebæk
- More sweet things from **Kjærstrup Chocolate By Hand** (p172) also in Snogebæk

Strøgets Spisehuz (☎ 56 95 81 69; Store Torvegade 39; mains lunch 70-120kr, dinner 122-160kr; ⌚ lunch & dinner) Subtlety is not the strong point of this quintessentially Danish restaurant, which serves hearty meat-and-potato dishes, including a good selection of steaks, in rather basic surroundings.

Casa Mia (☎ 56 95 95 73; Antoniestræde 3; pizza 66-72kr, pasta mains 66-110kr) Locals vote this the best place for pizza and pasta in town.

Rothes Konditori (☎ 56 95 04 39, Snellemark 41; snacks 8-25kr) Opposite the main bus stop, this small bakery serves good pastries, sandwiches and mini-pizzas to eat in or take away.

QUICK EATS & SELF-CATERING

Kvickly (☎ 56 95 17 77; Nordre Kystvej 28; sandwiches 40-50kr, meals 60-70kr) Supermarket has a good bakery that opens at 6.30am, and a handy bistro that offers sandwiches and hearty hot meals. It's opposite the tourist office.

You'll find a **Netto supermarket** (⌚ 9am-8pm Mon-Fri) and numerous fast-food places on Store Torv, the central square. **PS Thai** (☎ 56 96 25 01; takeaways from 35kr), next to the post office, has cheap Thai food takeaways, and **Sam's Corner** (☎ 56 95 15 23, Store Torv 2; pizza & café fare 40-70kr) is a generic but perfectly adequate pizza and burger place.

ÅKIRKEBY

pop 2400

Åkirkeby is an inland town with a mix of old half-timbered houses and newer homes with slightly less character.

The tourist office, car park and a couple of simple eateries are at the eastern side of the church on Jernbanegade. The town square, post office and bank are 150m east of the tourist office.

Sights

The town takes its name from its main sight, the 12th-century Romanesque stone church **Aa Kirke** (☎ 56 97 41 03; Nybyvej 2; admission 6kr; ⌚ 10am-4pm Mon-Sat spring & autumn, 9.30am-5pm summer) occupying a knoll overlooking the surrounding farmland. The largest church on Bornholm, its crossroads location made it a convenient place of assembly for islanders. The interior houses a number of historic treasures, including a 13th-century baptismal font of carved sandstone depicting scenes of Christ and featuring runic script.

The ornate pulpit and altar date from about 1600. For a 360-degree view of the town, climb the 22m-high bell tower, but watch your head on the low ceilings en route.

A centre dedicated to the geology and natural history of Bornholm might seem a worthy though slightly dull prospect, but **Natur Bornholm** (☎ 56 94 04 00; Grønningen 30; adult/child 40/20kr; 🕑 10am-5pm Apr-Oct) is a terrific geological and biological narrative of the island beginning from when it was just part of a bigger lump of cooling magma. It's packed with interesting facts and lively interactive displays. The dinosaur exhibits should interest children who can pretend to become fossilised Jurassic insects by 'sinking' into an eerily glowing bubble of 'amber'.

INTERIOR WOODLANDS

A fifth of Bornholm is wooded making it the most forested county in Denmark. Beech, fir, spruce, hemlock and oak are dominant. There are three main areas, each laid out with walking trails (you can pick up free maps at tourist offices). A single bicycle trail connects them all.

Almindingen, the largest forest (2412 hectares), is in the centre of the island and can be reached by heading north from Åkirkeby. It's the site of Bornholm's highest point, the 162m hill **Rytterknægten**, which has a lookout tower called Kongemindet from where you can view the surrounding countryside.

Paradisbakkerne (Paradise Hills), contains wild deer and a trail that passes an ancient monolithic gravestone. It's 2km northwest of Nexø. **Rø Plantage**, about 5km southwest of Gudhjem, has a terrain of heathered hills and woodlands.

DUEODDE

Dueodde, the southernmost point in Bornholm, is a vast stretch of beach backed by pine trees and expansive dunes. Its soft white sand is so fine-grained that it was once used in hourglasses and ink blotters.

There's no real village at Dueodde – the bus stops at the end of the road where there's a hotel, a restaurant, a couple of food kiosks and a footpath to the beach. The only 'sight' is a **lighthouse** on the western side of the dunes; you can climb the 197 stairs for a view of endless sand and sea.

The beach at Dueodde is a good place for children: the water is generally calm and is shallow for about 100m out, after which it becomes deep enough for adults to swim. It can be a crowded trek for a couple of hundred metres along boardwalks to reach the superb beach. Once there, though, head left or right to discover your own wide-open spaces.

Sleeping

Dueodde Vandrerhjem & Campground (☎ 56 48 81 19; info@dueodde.dk; 🕑 Apr-Oct; adult/child 54/30kr, tent 25kr; Ⓟ) A modern beachside place a 10-minute walk east of the bus stop, or it can be reached by car from the main road. It also has cabins for rent at 170/300kr for one/two persons, rising to 800kr for eight. There's an indoor swimming pool.

Dueodde Badehotel (☎ 56 48 86 49; www.dueodde-badehotel.dk, Sirenevej 2; s/d from 350/700kr, self-catering apt per wk 3500-6410kr; Ⓟ ♿) These smart, modern, Ikea-style apartments 150m from the beach have terraces or balconies overlooking the pleasant garden and are an especially good bet for families. The convenient one-bedroom units have a sofa bed in the living room and can sleep up to five people. There's a coin laundry, tennis court and sauna.

Eating

Restaurant Granpavillonen (☎ 56 48 81 75; Fyrvej 5; pizza 75kr, mains 130kr) As well as the ever popular pizza, basic Danish and German dishes are the staples here.

Dueodde Vandrerhjem & Camping (☎ 56 48 81 19, Skrokkegårdsvejen 17; fast-food mains 25-50kr) The cafeteria sells hamburgers and other simple fare while the minimarket sells ice cream, fresh bread and a few basic supplies.

There are a few kiosks selling ice cream, hot dogs and snacks at the end of the road opposite the bus stop.

SNOGEBÆK

pop 950

A quaint seaside village of older homes, Snogebæk makes a nice little detour if you are travelling by car or bike between Nexø and Dueodde. Down by the water, at the southern end of Havnevej and along Hovedgade, you'll find a good **smokehouse** where you can get smoked fish, deli items and cold beer. There's a cluster of shops nearby aimed at summer visitors, selling clothes and quality, reasonably priced hand-blown glass. Treat your sweet tooth to Bornholm-made organic ice cream at **Boisenøkologisk** (☎ 56 48 80 89; Hovegaden 4) or to scrumptious (and pricey) handmade chocolates at **Kjærstrup Chocolate By Hand** (☎ 56 48 80 89; Hovegaden 4). The end of the road beyond the glassworks is a good site for spotting migratory ducks and other water birds. If you want to explore more, there's a coastal footpath leading north along the beach.

NEXØ

pop 3800

Nexø (Neksø) is Bornholm's second-largest town. It has a large modern harbour where fishing vessels unload their catch. The town and harbour was reconstructed after being destroyed by Soviet bombing in WWII. Despite taking a back seat to more touristy towns such as Gudhjem and Svaneke, Nexø has its fair share of picturesque buildings. It's not an unpleasant town but lacks any compelling reason to linger.

Information

Nexø-Dueodde Turistbureau (☎ 56 49 32 00; www.bornholmonline.com; Åsen 4; 🕑 10am-5pm Mon-Fri year-round, 9am-2pm Sat May-Aug) In the centre of town, two blocks inland from the harbour, this office has information on Nexø, Snogebæk and Dueodde.

There are banks on Torvet, the central square, just south of the tourist office.

Sights & Activities

In a picturesque 1796 sandstone building opposite the waterfront the mildly diverting **Nexø Museum** (☎ 56 49 25 56; Havnen 2; adult/child 20/10kr; 🕑 10am-4pm Mon-Fri, 10am-2pm Sat mid-May–mid-Oct) features intriguing exhibits on Nexø's history with a maritime theme. There are also elaborate reconstructions of fishermen's dwellings. Check out the old-fashioned 150kg diving suit, model ships, old cannons and the lens and clock work from a nearby lighthouse.

Martin Andersen Nexø's House (☎ 56 49 45 52; cnr Andersen Nexøvej & Ferskeøstræde; adult/child 20/15kr; 🕑 10am-4pm Mon-Fri, 10am-2pm Sat mid-May–mid-Oct) is the childhood home of the author of *Pelle the Conqueror* (the book that inspired the 1988 Oscar-winning film). The house is in the southern part of town and displays photos of the author, along with some of his letters and other memorabilia.

Although Nexø's central waterfront is industrial, 2km south of town there's a popular seaside area called **Balka** with a gently curving, white-sand beach.

Sleeping

Because the beaches on the outskirts are much more appealing, few people stay in Nexø proper.

DELAYED LIBERATION

At the end of WWII, when Germany surrendered to the Allies, Bornholm was occupied by a German garrison of about 20,000 soldiers. At that time the German naval commander in charge of Bornholm, Captain von Kamptz, was fearful of Soviet reprisals against him and his men (justifiably so given the animosity and lack of mercy often shown by Germans and Russians to each other during the war) and insisted on surrendering his troops only to the British.

On 7 May 1945, when Soviet surveillance planes flew over the island, von Kamptz fired off a round from his anti-aircraft guns. Later that day the Soviets returned with a squadron of bombers, which released their loads onto the harbourfront towns of Nexø and Rønne. No warning was given to the islanders, who were still in the midst of celebrating the war's end, and 10 people died in the attack. There's little sign of the bomb damage these days, but in Rønne it's fairly evident where new housing has been built on bomb-damaged areas close to the harbour.

The Soviets gave the Germans until the next morning to surrender but von Kamptz held his ground, insisting once again on turning the island over to the British. He did, however, order a civilian evacuation of the two towns. The next morning the Soviets attacked Nexø and Rønne again, this time using incendiary bombs that levelled one-third of the houses. On 9 May the Germans finally capitulated and within a matter of days the Nazi soldiers had been repatriated from the island.

After the Germans left, the Soviets built up their forces and continued to occupy the island instead of turning Bornholm over to the Danish government. For a while it looked as if Stalin was going to wrap Bornholm within his Iron Curtain – but in March 1946 he abruptly announced plans to withdraw and within a month all the Soviet troops had left the island.

Hotel Balka Strand (☎ 56 49 49 49; www.hotelbalkastrand.dk, Boulevarden 9; r incl breakfast 410-1080kr, apt per wk 3136-7147kr; P ⊠ ▣) Only 200m from Balka's sandy beach, this hotel has double rooms and cheery apartments, all with modern décor. There's a sauna, pool, bar and restaurant.

Hotel Balka Søbad (☎ 56 49 22 25; www.hotel-balkasoebad.dk; Vester Strandvej 25; r incl breakfast per person 470-600kr; P ▣ ▣ ♿) Boasting its own bathing beach, this hotel has 106 commodious rooms in modern, two-storey buildings. Rooms have at least two twin beds, a sofa bed and a balcony; some have a second bedroom. There's also a tennis court, bar and restaurant.

Eating

Both of the beachside hotels have moderately expensive dinner restaurants.

Jørgens Cafe (☎ 56 49 49 45, Torvet 5; sandwiches 25-40kr, pizza 55-77kr) Cosy little café in the town centre specialises in smørrebrød (Danish open sandwiches).

Kvickly (☎ 56 49 21 37, Købmagerade 12) If you want to pack a lunch for the beach, head to this supermarket near the bus stop in the town centre, which has a good bakery and a deli section.

SVANEKE

pop 3740

Svaneke is an appealing town of red-tiled 19th-century buildings that has won international recognition for maintaining its historic character. The pretty harbourfront is lined with mustard-yellow half-timbered former merchants' houses, some of which have been turned into hotels and restaurants. Svaneke is also home to the island's best smokehouse and its only micro-brewery, both of them highly recommended.

Information

Nordeabank (☎ 56 49 64 20; Nansensgade 5)
Post office (☎ 56 94 38 00; Postgade 2)
Svaneke Turistbureau (☎ 56 49 63 50; fax 56 49 70 10; ⏲ noon-4.30pm Mon-Fri) Dispenses information from the rådhus, Storegade.

Sights & Activities

You'll find some interesting period buildings near **Svaneke Kirke**, a few minutes' walk south of Torv, the town square. The church, which has a rune stone, dates from 1350, although it was largely rebuilt during the 1880s.

If you're interested in crafts, there are a number of pottery and handicraft shops dotted around town, and at **Glastorvet** in the town centre there's a workshop where you can watch glass being melted into orange glowing lumps and then blown into clear, elegant glassware.

The easternmost town in Denmark, Svaneke is quite breezy and has a number of windmills. To the northwest of town you'll find an old **post mill** (a type of mill that turns in its entirety to face the wind) and a **Dutch mill**, as well as an unusual three-sided **water tower** designed by architect Jørn Utzon (of Sydney's Opera House fame). On the main road 3km south of Svaneke in the hamlet of **Årsdale**, there's a working windmill where grains are ground and sold.

Sleeping

Hullehavn Camping (☎ 56 49 63 63, www.hullehavn.dk in Danish, Sydskovvej 9; camping per person 55kr; ⏲ mid-May–mid-Sep) Has the more natural setting of Svaneke's two camping grounds, including its own sandy beach. Three-star rating and just 400m south of Danhostel Svaneke,

Danhostel Svaneke (☎ 56 49 62 42; www.danhostel-svaneke.dk in Danish; Reberbanevej 9; dm 115kr, s/d 400/450kr; ⏲ Apr-Oct; P ⊠ ▣) A squat, basic, low-roofed hostel 1km south of the centre of Svaneke.

Hotel Siemsens Gaard (☎ 56 49 61 49; www.siemsens.dk; Havnebryggen 9; s/d incl breakfast 495/790kr; P ⊠ ▣) If you like old-world character, ask for a room in the old wing. This 51-room hotel sitting right on the harbour has comfortable rooms (all with bath and refrigerator).

Eating & Drinking

Rogeriet i Svaneke (☎ 56 49 63 24; Fiskergade 12; counter items 25-50kr, buffet lunch/evening 82/92kr) You'll find a huge selection of excellent, smoked fare at the long counter including wonderful smørrebrød, great trout, salmon, herring and tasty fried fish cakes (20kr). Accompany it with remoulade and chips then wash it all down with the local ale. Choose to eat inside with a view of the massive, blackened doors of the smoking ovens or at the outdoor picnic tables overlooking the old cannons. It's by the water at the end of Fiskergade, north of the town centre.

Bryghuset (☎ 56 49 73 21, Torv 5; mains lunch 55kr, dinner 70-140kr; ⏲ lunch & dinner) Its own excellent

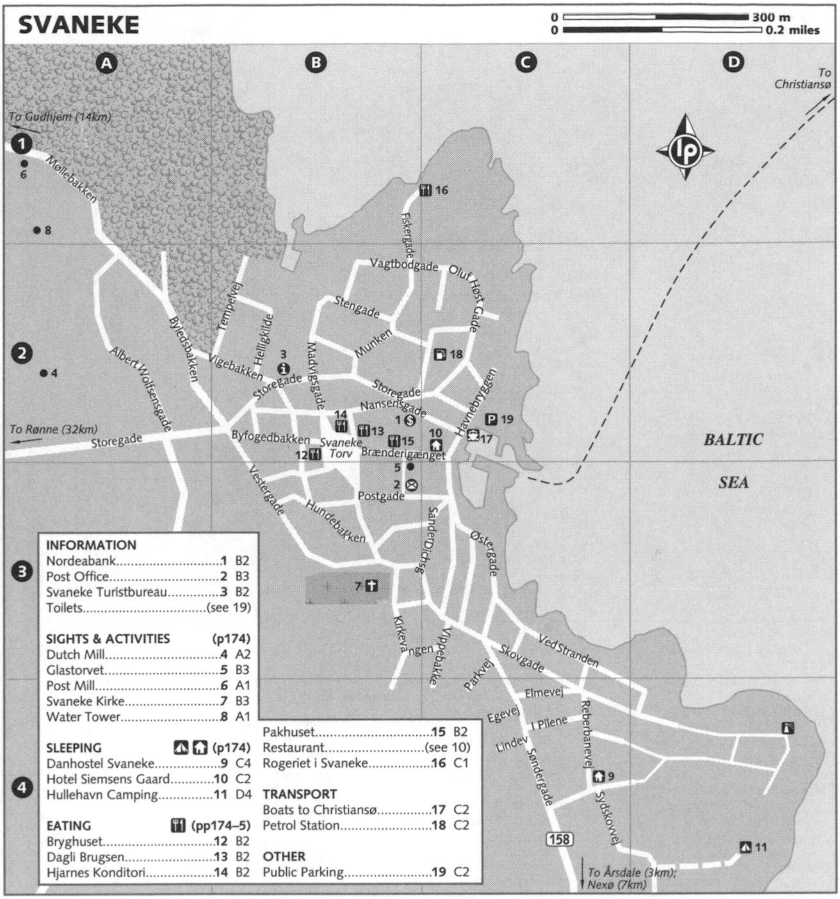
SVANEKE
0 300 m
0 0.2 miles
A
B
C
D
To Christiansø
To Gudhjem (14km)
Møllebakken
Tempelvej
Helligkilde
Byledsbakken
Albert Wolfsensgade
Vigebakken
Storegade
Madvigsgade
Vagtbodgade
Fiskergade
Stengade
Munken
Oluf Høst Gade
Nansensgade
Havnebryggen
To Rønne (32km)
Byfogedbakken
Svaneke Torv
Brænderigænget
Postgade
Vestergade
Hundebakken
SanderDichsg
Østergade
Kirkevangen
Vippebakke
Ved Stranden
Skovgade
Parkvej
Elmevej
Egevej
I Pilene
Lindev
Søndergade
Reberbanevej
Sydskovvej
158
To Årsdale (3km); Nexø (7km)
BALTIC SEA
INFORMATION
Nordeabank 1 B2
Post Office 2 B3
Svaneke Turistbureau 3 B2
Toilets (see 19)
SIGHTS & ACTIVITIES (p174)
Dutch Mill 4 A2
Glastorvet 5 B3
Post Mill 6 A1
Svaneke Kirke 7 B3
Water Tower 8 A1
SLEEPING (p174)
Danhostel Svaneke 9 C4
Hotel Siemsens Gaard 10 C2
Hullehavn Camping 11 D4
EATING (pp174–5)
Bryghuset 12 B2
Dagli Brugsen 13 B2
Hjarnes Konditori 14 B2
Pakhuset 15 B2
Restaurant (see 10)
Rogeriet i Svaneke 16 C1
TRANSPORT
Boats to Christiansø 17 C2
Petrol Station 18 C2
OTHER
Public Parking 19 C2

beers are brewed at this popular establishment. If you haven't already eaten, it also serves decent, hearty pub grub. A sampler of all three of its beers (a pilsner, an ale and a stout) costs 30kr.

Pakhuset (☎ 56 49 65 85; Brænderigænget 3; lunch buffet 59kr; lunch & dinner Tue-Sun) Very tasty home-made burgers (59kr) are served here and this restaurant has a wide range of reasonably priced beef dishes.

Hotel Siemsens Gaard (☎ 56 49 61 49; Havnebryggen 9; smørrebrød 36-68kr, mains lunch 72-98kr, dinner 100-160kr; lunch & dinner) With patio dining overlooking the harbour, this restaurant hotel makes an ideal lunch choice on a sunny day. It does good light lunches such as daintily presented smørrebrød, smoked and marinated salmon with crème fraiche and other more substantial fresh fish dishes.

Hjarnes Konditori (☎ 56 49 61 56; Torv 8) A handy place serving good pastries and coffee on Torvet, the town square where you'll also find the supermarket **Dagli Brugsen** (☎ 56 49 60 41; Mon-Fri).

GUDHJEM & MELSTED

pop 900

Gudhjem is an attractive seaside village crowned by a squat windmill standing over half-timbered houses and sloping streets that roll down to the pleasant harbourfront. In fact Gudhjem would make a good base for exploring the rest of Bornholm; it has cycle paths, walking trails, convenient bus

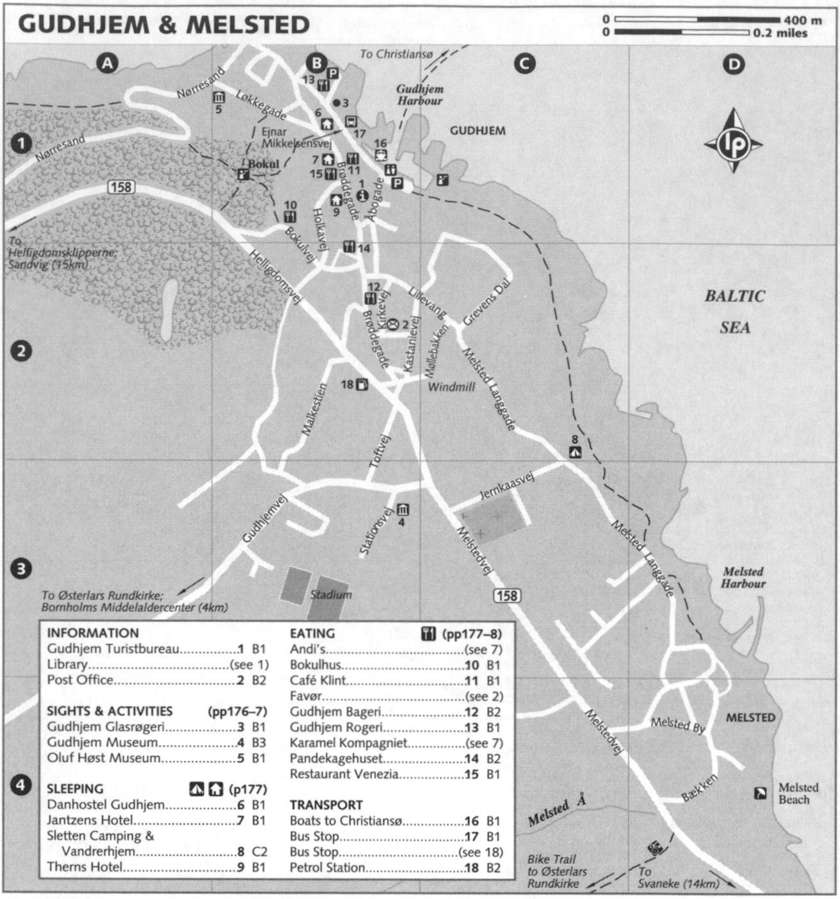
GUDHJEM & MELSTED
0 400 m
0 0.2 miles
To Christiansø
Gudhjem Harbour
GUDHJEM
BALTIC SEA
MELSTED
Melsted Harbour
Melsted Beach
Nørresand
Løkkegade
Ejnar Mikkelsensvej
Bokul
Brøddegade
Åbogade
Holkavej
Bokulvej
Helligdomsvej
Kirkevej
Kastanievej
Møllebakken
Lillevang
Grevens Dal
Melsted Langgade
Windmill
Malkestien
Toftvej
Jernkaasvej
Gudhjemvej
Stationsvej
Melstedvej
Melsted By
Bækken
Melsted Å
Stadium
158
To Helligdomsklipperne; Sandvig (15km)
To Østerlars Rundkirke; Bornholms Middelaldercenter (4km)
Bike Trail to Østerlars Rundkirke
To Svaneke (14km)
INFORMATION
Gudhjem Turistbureau 1 B1
Library (see 1)
Post Office 2 B2
SIGHTS & ACTIVITIES (pp176–7)
Gudhjem Glasrøgeri 3 B1
Gudhjem Museum 4 B3
Oluf Høst Museum 5 B1
SLEEPING (p177)
Danhostel Gudhjem 6 B1
Jantzens Hotel 7 B1
Sletten Camping & Vandrerhjem 8 C2
Therns Hotel 9 B1
EATING (pp177–8)
Andi's (see 7)
Bokulhus 10 B1
Café Klint 11 B1
Favør (see 2)
Gudhjem Bageri 12 B2
Gudhjem Rogeri 13 B1
Karamel Kompagniet (see 7)
Pandekagehuset 14 B2
Restaurant Venezia 15 B1
TRANSPORT
Boats to Christiansø 16 B1
Bus Stop 17 B1
Bus Stop (see 18)
Petrol Station 18 B2

connections, reasonably priced places to stay, a good range of restaurants and a boat service to Christiansø.

It is also an enjoyable place to just wander about and soak up the harbourside atmosphere. The harbour was one of the settings for the Oscar-winning film *Pelle the Conqueror* based on the novel by Bornholm writer Martin Andersen Nexø (p173).

Stroll the **footpath** running southeast from the harbour for a pleasant coastal view. Gudhjem's shoreline is rocky, though sunbathers will find a small sandy **beach** at Melsted, 1km east. A bike path leads inland 4km south from Gudhjem to the thick-walled, stoutly-buttressed **Østerlars Rundkirke** (p178), the most impressive of the island's round churches; bus No 3 goes by the church.

Information

Gudhjem Turistbureau (☎ 56 48 52 10; mail@ntbook.dk; Åbogade 7; ⏲ 10am-4pm daily Jul-Aug, 1-4pm Mon-Sat Sep & Mar-Jun) is at the library, just a block inland from the harbour. The **post office** (☎ 56 94 38 00) is inside the Favør grocery shop. There are toilets and showers at the harbour and a car park just northwest of it.

Sights & Activities

Gudhjem Glasrøgeri (☎ 56 48 54 68; Ejnar Mikkelsensvej 13A; ⏲ daily in summer) Watch top-quality Bornholm glass being hand-blown here at the dockside.

In the handsome former train station in the southern part of town, **Gudhjem Museum** (☎ 56 48 54 62, Stationsvej 1; adult/child 20/5kr; 🕑 10am-5pm Mon-Sat, 2-5pm Sun mid-May–mid-Sep) features local history displays, temporary art exhibits and outdoor sculptures.

Oluf Høst Museum (☎ 56 48 50 38; Løkkegade 35; adult/child 40/15kr; 🕑 1-5pm Tue-Sun Apr-Oct) contains the workshops and paintings of Oluf Høst (1884–1966), one of Bornholm's best-known artists. The museum occupies the home where Oluf lived from 1929 until his death.

A short five-minute climb up the heather-covered hill **Bokul** provides a fine view of the town's red-tiled rooftops and out to sea.

From the hill at the southeastern end of Gudhjem harbour you'll be rewarded with a **harbour view**. You can continue along this path that runs above the shoreline 2km south to Melsted, where there's a little **sandy beach**. It's a delightful nature trail, with swallows, nightingales and wildflowers.

Sleeping

Sletten Camping & Vandrerhjem (☎ 56 48 50 71; www.bornholm.org/sletten; Melsted Langgade 45; camping per person 48kr, d 295kr; 🕑 mid-May–mid-Sep; Ⓟ) It's the nearest camping ground to town and a 15-minute walk south of Gudhjem harbour. In addition to camping, this place also has a hostel-like building with comfortable double rooms and shared bathrooms.

Danhostel Gudhjem (☎ 56 48 50 35; www.danhostel-gudhjem.dk; Løkkegade 7; dm 118kr, s/d 325/375kr; 🕑 year-round; Ⓟ) Right by the harbour and has cosy, bright, six-bed dorms. The reception is at a small grocery shop on Løkkegade, about 75m northwest of the hostel. Mountain bikes can be hired for 70kr per day.

Therns Hotel (☎ 56 48 50 99; fax 56 48 56 35; Brøddegade 31; s/d incl breakfast with bathroom 500/800kr, with shared bathroom 350/550kr) Reasonably priced and very central hotel (under the same management as the hostel) has 30 pleasant rooms, most with TV, a small refrigerator and an extra sofa bed; some also have kitchenettes.

Jantzens Hotel (☎ 56 48 50 17; jantzenshotel@mail.dk; Brøddegade 33; s/d 525/925kr) Offers the most comfortable, stylish rooms in town and occupies an attractive old building. There's also a good fine-dining restaurant (below) in this centrally located hotel.

Eating

Gudhjem Rogeri (☎ 56 48 57 08; Gudhjem harbour; buffet lunch/dinner 82/92kr) Fine Bornholm smokehouse serves deli-style fish and salads. There's both indoor and outdoor seating, some of it very challenging (the upper floor is reached by rope ladder!). It has live folk, country and rock music most summer nights.

Restaurant Venezia (☎ 56 48 53 53; Brøddegade 33; pizza & pasta 65-110kr) Popular Italian restaurant underneath Jantzens Hotel has a pleasant atmosphere and serves very good food.

Bokulhus (☎ 56 48 52 97; Bokulvej 4; lunch specials 80kr, mains 180-220kr; 🕑 Tue-Sun) Gudhjem's top fine-dining choice, Bokulhus is an old-fashioned restaurant, highly regarded for its fish dishes.

Andi's (☎ 56 48 50 84; Brøddegade 33; menus 275/375kr) A close competitor to Bokulhus, Andi's has a more contemporary, adventurous menu. It's inside Jantzen's Hotel and serves complicated but accomplished dishes such as monkfish with a delicate bisque, asparagus and Bornholm-grown potatoes. There's a small but good wine list and some excellent desserts and cheeses.

BORNHOLM'S ROUND CHURCHES

Unique among Bornholm's sights are its four 12th-century *rundkirke* (round churches), constructed with 2m-thick whitewashed walls and black conical roofs.

The churches were built at a time when pirating Wends from eastern Germany were ravaging coastal areas throughout the Baltic Sea. They were designed not only as places of worship but also as refuges against enemy attacks – their upper storeys doubling as shooting galleries. They were also used as store houses to protect valuable possessions and trading goods from being carried off by the pirates. Each church was built about 2km inland, and all four are sited high enough on knolls to offer a lookout to the sea. These striking and utterly unique churches have a stern, ponderous appearance, more typical of a fortress than of a place of worship

All four churches are still used for Sunday services. You'll find them at Østerlars, Olsker, Nyker and Nylars.

Pandekagehuset (☎ 56 48 55 17; Brøddegade 15; light meals 20-65kr) Casual café specialises in omelettes and sweet and savoury pancakes with a good range of fillings.

Café Café Klint (☎ 56 48 54 59, Ejnar Mikkelsensvej 20; light meals 40-80kr) On a sunny day the patio is the spot for a leisurely cappuccino or beer, with a view of the harbour.

Karamel Kompagniet (☎ 56 44 22 55; Holkavej) Looking for all the world like the sweet factory in Chitty Chitty Bang Bang or a Willy Wonka franchise, you can see everything being made in shiny copper basins in this tiny sweet factory that turns out scrumptious caramel and chocolates.

Gudhjem Bageri (☎ 56 48 56 03, Brøddegade 16; bakery goods 6-20kr) You can enjoy your pastries and coffee on this bakery's rooftop patio.

There's a Favør grocery shop around the corner to the southeast on Kirkevej.

ØSTERLARS RUNDKIRKE

The largest and most impressive of the island's round churches is **Østerlars Rundkirke** (☎ 56 49 82 64; Vietsvej 25; adult/child 10kr/free; 9am-5pm Mon-Sat), which dates from 1150 (possibly even earlier) and is set amidst wheat fields and half-timbered farmhouses. Bulky and thick-walled with seven weighty buttresses and an upper-level shooting gallery, this odd, striking building is unmistakeably a fortress. The roof was originally constructed with a flat top to serve as a battle platform, complete with a brick parapet but, because of the excessive weight this exerted on the church walls, the roof was eventually replaced with its present conical one.

The interior is largely whitewashed, although a swath of medieval frescoes has been uncovered and restored. There's a rune stone dating back to 1070 at the church entrance and a sundial above it.

A cycle path to the church leads inland 4km south from Gudhjem; the church can also be reached on bus No 9.

BORNHOLMS MIDDELALDERCENTER

The 10.5-hectare **Bornholm's Medieval Centre** (☎ 56 49 83 19; Stangevej 1; adult/child 65kr/free; 75/30kr Jun-Aug; 9am-5pm May-Sep) re-creates a medieval fort and village and gives the Danes another chance to do what they love best: dressing up in period costume and hitting each other with rubber swords. They also operate a smithy, tend fields, grind wheat in a water mill and perform other chores of yore throughout the summer months. In July the activity schedule is beefed up to include falconry presentations, archery demonstrations and hands-on craft activities for children.

The medieval centre is 500m north of Østerlars Rundkirke and can be reached by bus No 9.

HELLIGDOMSKLIPPERNE

Perhaps because Denmark hasn't much in the way of hills or lofty rocks, those it does have are almost revered. Such is the case with Helligdomsklipperne (Sanctuary Cliffs), where moderately high coastal cliffs of sharp granite rock attract sightseers. About 5km north of Gudhjem on the eastern side of the main coastal road, the Helligdomsklipperne area also has **nature trails** and an art museum.

Bornholms Kunstmuseum (☎ 56 48 43 86; Helligdommen; adult/child 40kr/free; 10am-5pm Tue-Sun May-Oct, 1-5pm Tue, Thu & Sat Nov-Apr) On a great spot overlooking sea, fields and (weather permitting) the distant isle of Christiansø, this 100-year-old museum housed in a stylish modern building, exhibits paintings by artists from the Bornholm School, including Olaf Rude, Oluf Høst and Edvard Weie, who painted during the first half of the 20th century. The museum also has works by other Danish artists, most notably paintings of Bornholm, by Skagen artist Michael Ancher. There's a café on site. Buses stop in front of the museum (bus No 2 from Rønne or Sandvig, bus No 7 between Gudhjem and Sandvig).

SANDVIG & ALLINGE

pop 2700

Sandvig is a quiet little seaside hamlet with attractive older homes, many with rose bushes and tidy flower gardens. It's fronted by a sandy beach and borders a network of interesting walking trails (see p179).

Allinge, the larger and more developed half of the Allinge-Sandvig municipality, is 2km southeast of Sandvig. Although not as quaint as Sandvig, Allinge has the lion's share of commercial facilities, including banks, grocery shops and the area's tourist office, **Nordbornholms Turistbureau** (☎ 56 48 00 01; www.bornholmsbookingcenter.dk in Danish; Kirkegade 4; 10am-5pm Mon-Fri, Sat 10am-3pm May-Sep, 11am-5pm Mon-Fri, 11am-2pm Sat Oct-Apr).

Seven kilometres southeast of Sandvig, in the small village of **Olsker**, is the most slender of the island's four round churches. If you take the inland bus to Rønne, you can stop off en route to visit the church or catch a passing glimpse of it as you ride by.

Sleeping & Eating

Sandvig Familie Camping (☎ 56 48 04 47; Sandlinien 5; www.publiccamp.dk/sandvig; adult/child/tent 50/25/15kr) Occupies a great spot near the beach and is handy for tracks onto Hammeren.

Danhostel Sandvig (☎ 56 48 03 62; www.danhostel.dk/sandvig; Hammershusvej 94; dm 115kr, s/d 275/400kr; Jun-Oct) Midway between Hammershus Slot and Sandvig, this hostel has a pleasant, rural location just 10 minutes' walk from the ruins and 100m from a bus stop. Accommodation is in cosy four- or six-bed chalets. Breakfast is available.

Byskriviergarden (☎ 56 48 08 86; www.byskrivergasarden.dk; Løsebækegade 3; s/d 710/595kr, less in low season; P) Enchanting, white-walled, black-beamed converted farmhouse right on the water in Allinge is our choice of places to stay in the area. The rooms (try to get the sea-facing, and not the road-facing ones) are smartly, if sparsely decorated in contemporary style. There's a pleasant garden, a larger, cheerful breakfast room and kelp-filled rock pools nearby if you fancy braving the water.

Ella's Konditori (☎ 56 48 03 29, Strandgade 42; light meals 53-80kr) Offers good homemade food inside the picturesque cottage or out in the pretty garden. The menu includes fish and chips, grilled chicken and salads.

Café Værftet (☎ 56 48 04 34; Jernbanegade 3; meat mains around 85kr; dinner) An unmissable place for good company and delicious Christiansø herring dishes (from 35kr), this café is in an old boathouse whose entire front wall, complete with windows and coverings, can be raised at the touch of a button from behind the bar – an entertaining event, especially if you've had a *akvavit* (schnapps) too many.

HAMMERSHUS SLOT

The impressive 13th-century ruins of Hammershus Slot, dramatically perched on top of a sea cliff, are the largest in Scandinavia. Construction probably began around 1250 under the archbishop of Lund, who wanted a fortress to protect his diocese against the Crown, engaged at the time in a power struggle with the Church. In the centuries that followed, the castle was enlarged, with the upper levels of the square tower added on during the mid-16th century.

Eventually, improvements in naval artillery left the fortress walls vulnerable to attack and in 1645 the castle temporarily fell to Swedish troops after a brief bombardment. Hammershus served as both military garrison and prison – King Christian IV's daughter, Leonora Christine, was imprisoned here on treason charges from 1660 to 1661.

In 1743 the Danish military abandoned Hammershus and many of the stones were carried away to be used as building materials elsewhere. Still, there's much to see and you shouldn't miss a stroll through these extensive fortress ruins. The grounds are always open and admission is free.

Getting There & Away

There's an hourly bus (No 7) from Sandvig to Hammershus Slot, but the most enjoyable way to get there is via footpaths through the hills of Hammeren – a wonderful hour's hike. The well-trodden trail begins by the Sandvig Familie Camping ground and the route is signposted.

If you're coming from Rønne, bus No 1 makes the trip to Hammershus Slot about once an hour.

HAMMEREN

Hammeren, the hammerhead-shaped crag of granite at the northern tip of Bornholm, is crisscrossed by **walking trails** leading through hillsides thick with purple heather. Some of the trails are inland, while others run along the coast. The whole area is a delight for people who enjoy nature walks.

For adventure, follow the trails between Sandvig and Hammershus Slot. The shortest route travels along the inland side of Hammeren and passes **Hammer Sø**, Bornholm's largest lake, and **Opaløsen**, a deep pond in an old rock quarry. A longer, more windswept route goes along the rocky outer rim of Hammeren, passes a **lighthouse** at Bornholm's northernmost point and continues south along the coast to **Hammer Havn**.

From Hammershus Slot there are trails heading south through another heathered landscape in a nature area called **Slotslyngen**, and east through public woodlands to **Moseløkke granite quarry**. Moseløkke is also the site of a small **museum** (☎ 56 48 04 68; Moseløkkevej 4; adult/child 20kr/free; 10am-noon & 1-4pm Mon-Fri Apr-

Oct) where you can see demonstrations of traditional rock-cutting techniques.

For a detailed map of the trails and terrain, pick up the free *Hammeren og Hammershus, Slotslyng* forestry brochure at any one of the island's tourist offices.

CHRISTIANSØ

pop 100

Tiny Christiansø (about 500m long) is a charming 17th-century island fortress an hour's sail northeast of Bornholm and well worth a side trip. A seasonal fishing hamlet since the Middle Ages, Christiansø fell briefly into Swedish hands in 1658, after which Christian V turned it into an invincible naval fortress. Bastions and barracks were built; a church, school and prison followed.

Christiansø became the Danish Navy's forward position in the Baltic, serving to monitor Swedish trade routes and in less congenial days as a base for attacks on Sweden. By the 1850s, though, the island was no longer needed as a forward base against Sweden and the navy withdrew. Those who wanted to stay on as fishermen were allowed to live as free tenants in the old cottages. Their offspring, and a few latter-day fisherfolk and artists, currently comprise Christiansø's 100 residents. The entire island is an unspoiled reserve – there are no cats or dogs, no cars and no modern buildings – allowing the rich birdlife, including puffins, to prosper.

If the hectic pace of life on Christiansø is getting to you, try escaping to a smaller island, **Frederiksø**, by the footbridge.

Græsholm, the island to the northwest of Christiansø, is a wildlife refuge and an important breeding ground for guillemots, razorbills and other sea birds.

All of the Ertholmene Islands, including Christiansø and Frederiksø, serve as spring breeding grounds for up to 2000 eider ducks. The ducks nest near coastal paths and all visitors should take care not to scare mothers away from their nests because predator gulls will quickly swoop and attack the unattended eggs. Conservation laws forbid the removal of any plants from this unique ecosystem.

Sights & Activities

A leisurely walk of around an hour is all that's needed to explore both Christiansø and Frederiksø – an ideal day trip.

The main sights are the two stone circular defence towers. **Lille Tårn** (Little Tower) on Frederiksø dates from 1685 and is now the **local history museum** (☎ 56 46 20 71; adult/child 10/5kr; ⏰ 11.30am-4pm May-Sep). The ground floor features fishing supplies, hand tools and iron works; upstairs there are cannons, models and a display of local flora and fauna.

Christiansø's **Store Tårn** (Great Tower), built in 1684, is an impressive structure measuring a full 25m in diameter. The Great Tower's 100-year-old **lighthouse** offers a splendid 360-degree view of the island; for 4kr you can climb to the top.

The main activity on Christiansø is the **walk** along the fortified stone walls and cannon-lined batteries that mark the island's perimeter. There are skerries (rocky islets) with nesting sea birds and a secluded **swimming cove** on Christiansø's eastern side.

Sleeping & Eating

Duchess Battery (☎ 30 34 96 05; camping per person 45kr) Camping is allowed in summer in a small field called the Duchess Battery, at the northern end of Christiansø, limited space means it can be difficult to book a site.

Christiansø Gæstgiveriet (☎ 56 46 20 15; chr.hotel@post.tele.dk; d with breakfast 800kr; ⏰ Apr-late Oct) Built in 1730 as the naval commander's residence, this is the island's only inn. It has half a dozen cosy rooms all decorated in a homey early-20th-century style. All the rooms share bathrooms.

The inn has a moderately priced restaurant and there's a small food store and snack shop nearby.

Getting There & Away

Christiansøfarten (☎ 56 48 51 76; www.christiansoefarten.dk; adult/child return late Jun-late Aug 160/80kr, other times 150/75kr) operates passenger ferries to Christiansø from Gudhjem year-round and from Allinge in the summer.

A boat leaves Gudhjem at 10am daily (weekdays only in winter) and departs from Christiansø for the return trip at 2.15pm. Between mid-June and August there are also boats leaving Gudhjem at 9.45am (Monday to Friday) and 12.30pm daily.

A boat leaves Allinge at 12.45pm (Monday to Saturday, May to mid-September) and departs Christiansø at 4.30pm.

Dogs or other pets are forbidden on Christiansø.

Funen

CONTENTS

Take your time and don't let the main railway line or motorway from Copenhagen carry you straight through Funen, past its main city, Odense, and onwards west to Jutland. You'll miss so much by zipping through without stopping to explore more of Denmark's second largest island and the many other islands that cluster around it.

As well as Odense, places of special merit include the magnificent Renaissance Egeskov Slot, the historic maritime town of Faaborg and the unspoiled, unhurried island of Ærø. Most of bucolic Funen County is engagingly pretty, with picturesque rural scenery and thatched farmhouses.

Funen (Fyn) is both the name for the island and the county (Fyn Amt), which also includes about 90 neighbouring islands and there's immense pleasure to be had island hopping down south by ferry, yacht or charter boat. The largest three – Ærø, Langeland and Tåsinge – have appealing seaside towns and are fine destinations in themselves.

HIGHLIGHTS

- Experience the fairytale life of author Hans Christian Andersen, Odense's most famous son, at the excellent **HCA museum** (p185).
- Island hop by ferry to one of the small islands off Funen's **southern coast** (p201).
- Alternatively, simply sail around them on a **charter yacht** (p199).
- Escape to Ærø and cycle its undulating country lanes past picturesque farms, villages, woods and **ancient burial mound**s (p207).
- Spend a day exploring the grounds and interior of Egeskov Slot, a splendid moat-encircled **Renaissance castle** (p195).

Odense
Egeskov Slot
Svendborg
Skarø Drejø Hjortø
Ærø

FUNEN
0 20 km
0 12 miles
To Århus
JUTLAND
Æbelø
Fyns Hoved
Korshavn
Hindsholm
Store Bælt
ZEALAND
Fredericia
Bogense
Mårhøj
Strib
Otterup
Romsø
Odense Fjord
Viby
Måle
Båring
Middelfart
Søndersø
Munkebo
Kerteminde
Nørre Åby
Stige
Seden
Bullerup
Ladby
Korup
To Copenhagen
Lange-
skov
Ullerslev
Brandsø
Årup
Vissenbjerg
Odense
Bellinge
Nyborg
Korsør
Årslev
Knudshoved
Bågo
Glamsbjerg
Assens
FUNEN
Ørbæk
JUTLAND
Årø
Ringe
Hårby
Egeskov Slot
Kværndrup
Lille Bælt
Helnæs
Korinth
Lundeborg
Svanninge Bakker
Lohals
Faaborg
Bøjden
Bjørnø
Svendborg
Thurø
Nordborg
Lyø
Troense
Bregninge
Avernakø
Skarø
Valdemars Slot
Landet
Tranekær
ALS
Fynshav
Drejø
TÅSINGE
Sund
Skjoldnæs Fyr
Hjortø
Spodsbjerg
Mommark
Søby
Rudkøbing
Strynø
Siø
LANGELAND
Tårs
ÆRØ
Sønderborg
Ærøskøbing
Langelandsbælt
Nakskov
Marstal
Lindelse
Store Rise
Ristinge
Humble
Marstal Bugt
LOLLAND
GERMANY
Gelting
Bagenkop
E20
161
162
327
311
317
329
162
303
311
165
315
165
160
161
329
313
335
168
43
301
315
163
9
168
323
329
323
335
323
8
43
8
329
9
163
8
44
305
8
41
9
8
9
305

ODENSE

pop 185,000

The city makes much ado about being the birthplace of Hans Christian Andersen, but Andersen himself got out of Odense as fast as he could, after a fairly unhappy childhood. Now it's Denmark's third largest city; it is an affable place with lots of pedestrian streets and cycle paths, an interesting cathedral, a few lively nightspots and a rich concentration of good museums and galleries. It's also relatively light on the wallet, with two hostels and some good-value hotels.

Odense, which translates as 'Odin's shrine', was named after the powerful Nordic god of war, poetry and wisdom. The city's history dates back to pre-Viking times, with the first known reference to Odense appearing in a letter written by the German emperor Otto III in 988. By the middle of the 18th century Odense was the largest provincial town in Denmark, with 5000 inhabitants. But it was the only major Danish town without a harbour and thus failed to benefit directly from the maritime trade that prospered in coastal towns such as Faaborg.

In 1800, in the largest construction project of that era, a canal was dug to connect Odense to the Odense Fjord, 5km to the north. With the new sea link Odense became an industrial city with products ranging from refined sugar to textiles. Odense is the

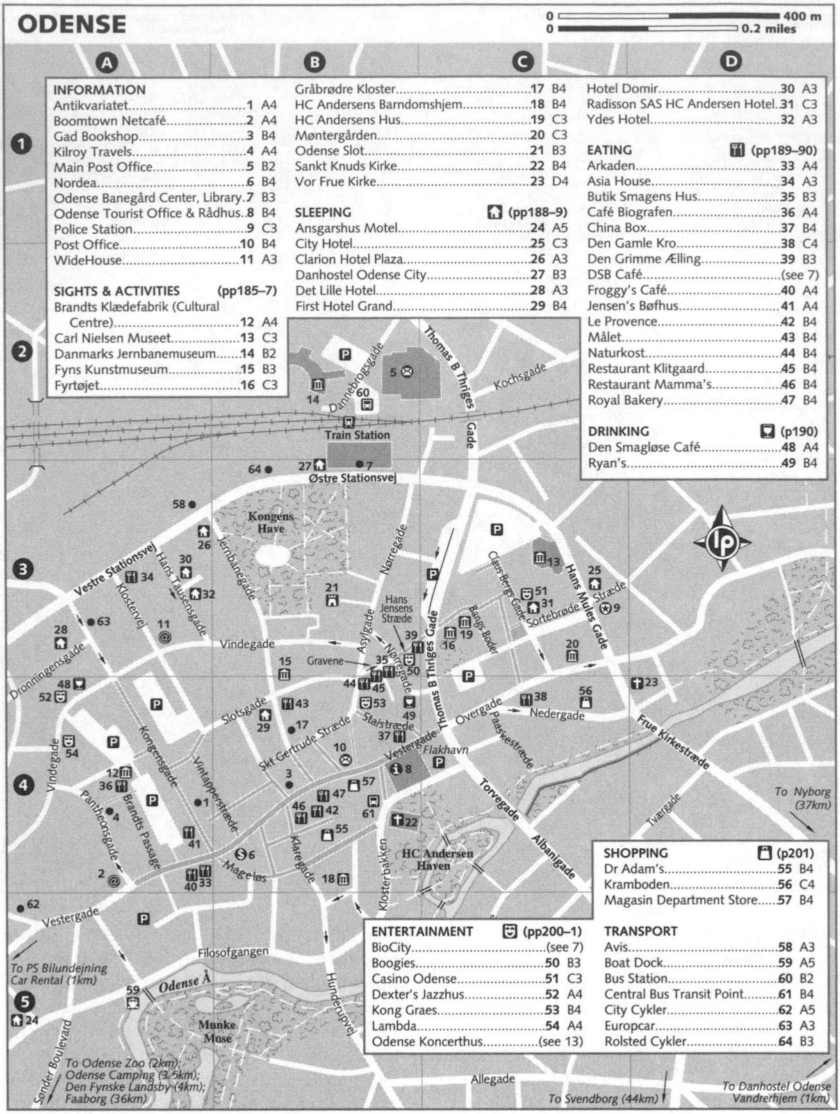
ODENSE
0 400 m
0 0.2 miles
A
B
C
D
1
2
3
4
5
INFORMATION
Antikvariatet....1 A4
Boomtown Netcafé....2 A4
Gad Bookshop....3 B4
Kilroy Travels....4 A4
Main Post Office....5 B2
Nordea....6 B4
Odense Banegård Center, Library..7 B3
Odense Tourist Office & Rådhus..8 B4
Police Station....9 C3
Post Office....10 B4
WideHouse....11 A3
SIGHTS & ACTIVITIES (pp185–7)
Brandts Klædefabrik (Cultural Centre)....12 A4
Carl Nielsen Museet....13 C3
Danmarks Jernbanemuseum....14 B2
Fyns Kunstmuseum....15 B3
Fyrtøjet....16 C3
Gråbrødre Kloster....17 B4
HC Andersens Barndomshjem....18 B4
HC Andersens Hus....19 C3
Møntergården....20 C3
Odense Slot....21 B3
Sankt Knuds Kirke....22 B4
Vor Frue Kirke....23 D4
SLEEPING (pp188–9)
Ansgarshus Motel....24 A5
City Hotel....25 C3
Clarion Hotel Plaza....26 A3
Danhostel Odense City....27 B3
Det Lille Hotel....28 A3
First Hotel Grand....29 B4
Hotel Domir....30 A3
Radisson SAS HC Andersen Hotel..31 C3
Ydes Hotel....32 A3
EATING (pp189–90)
Arkaden....33 A4
Asia House....34 A3
Butik Smagens Hus....35 B3
Café Biografen....36 A4
China Box....37 B4
Den Gamle Kro....38 C4
Den Grimme Ælling....39 B3
DSB Café....(see 7)
Froggy's Café....40 A4
Jensen's Bøfhus....41 A4
Le Provence....42 B4
Målet....43 B4
Naturkost....44 B4
Restaurant Klitgaard....45 B4
Restaurant Mamma's....46 B4
Royal Bakery....47 B4
DRINKING (p190)
Den Smagløse Café....48 A4
Ryan's....49 B4
SHOPPING (p201)
Dr Adam's....55 B4
Kramboden....56 C4
Magasin Department Store....57 B4
ENTERTAINMENT (pp200–1)
BioCity....(see 7)
Boogies....50 B3
Casino Odense....51 C3
Dexter's Jazzhus....52 A4
Kong Graes....53 B4
Lambda....54 A4
Odense Koncerthus....(see 13)
TRANSPORT
Avis....58 A3
Boat Dock....59 A5
Bus Station....60 B2
Central Bus Transit Point....61 B4
City Cykler....62 A5
Europcar....63 A3
Rolsted Cykler....64 B3
Train Station
Østre Stationsvej
Kongens Have
Vestre Stationsvej
Hans Tausensgade
Klostervej
Jernbanegade
Nørregade
Dannebrogsgade
Thomas B Thriges Gade
Kochsgade
Claus Bergs Gade
Hans Mules Gade
Sortebrødre Stræde
Vindegade
Dronningensgade
Slotsgade
Kongensgade
Vintapperstræde
Skt Gertrude Stræde
Stålstræde
Overgade
Nedergade
Paaskestræde
Frue Kirkestræde
Flakhavn
Torvegade
Albanigade
Tværgade
Vestergade
Pantheonsgade
Brandts Passage
Magelos
Klaregade
Klosterbakken
HC Andersen Haven
Filosofgangen
Odense Å
Munke Mose
Hunderupvej
Søndre Boulevard
Allegade
To Nyborg (37km)
To PS Bilundejning Car Rental (1km)
To Odense Zoo (2km); Odense Camping (3.5km); Den Fynske Landsby (4km); Faaborg (36km)
To Svendborg (44km)
To Danhostel Odense Vandrerhjem (1km)

capital of Funen county and a transportation hub for the region.

The city marked the 200th anniversary of Han Christian Andersen's birth in 2005.

ORIENTATION

The train station is in a large modern complex, the Odense Banegård Center, which contains restaurants, shops, the public library and travel-related facilities. The tourist office, at rådhus, is a short walk south from the train station. The cathedral, Sankt Knuds Kirke, is on Klosterbakken, a two-minute walk from the tourist office, and most other sights are also within walking distance of each other in the city centre.

INFORMATION

Bookshops

Antikvariatet (☎ 66 13 35 76; Kongensgade 13) A good place to pick up second-hand paperback novels at reasonable prices.

GAD Bookshop (☎ 66 13 17 42; Vestergade 37) Well stocked with English titles.

Internet Access

Boomtown Netcafé (Pantheonsgade 4; 10am-11pm) A plush gamers place with fast Internet connection.

Odense Central Library (Odense Banegård Center; 10am-7pm Mon-Thu, 10am-4pm Fri & Sat) Offers free use of the Internet and has a few foreign language newspapers.

WideHouse (Vindegade 43; per 30min/1hr 15/25kr 10am-midnight)

Left luggage

Left luggage Lockers at the train station cost 10kr for 24 hours.

Money

Nordea Bank (☎ 66 12 73 25; Vestergade 64)

Post

Main post office (Dannebrogsgade 2; 9am-6pm Mon-Fri, 9am-1pm Sat) North of the train station.

Post office (Gråbrødrestræde 1; 9am-6pm)

Tourist Information

Badstuen (☎ 66 13 48 66; Østre Stationsvej) A youth and community centre with café and information point.

Tourist office (☎ 66 12 75 20; www.visitodense.com; 9.30am-6pm Mon-Fri, 10am-5pm Sat & Sun mid-Jun–Aug; 9.30am-4.30pm Mon-Fri, 10am-3pm Sat & Sun Sep–mid-Jun) At rådhus, about 800m from the train station. Odense has a handy 'adventure pass' that allows free entry into museums and free bus transport. You can buy it at the train station or tourist office for 110/150kr for 24/48 hours. Staff at the tourist office can also arrange for foreign travellers to meet with a Danish family at home for tea and conversation. Because they try to match people of similar ages and interests, you should request the 'Meet the Danes' program at least a day in advance. There's no fee.

Travel Agencies

Kilroy Travels (☎ 66 17 77 80; Pantheonsgade 7) Specialises in youth and discount travel.

SIGHTS

Sankt Knuds Kirke

Odense's imposing 13th-century Gothic cathedral **Sankt Knuds Kirke** (☎ 66 12 03 92; Flakhaven; 9am-5pm Mon-Sat, noon-5pm Sun) reflects the city's medieval wealth and stature. The stark white interior has a handsome rococo pulpit and an ornate gilded altar dating from 1521 that's considered the finest work of master woodcrafter Claus Berg. An intricately detailed triptych, the altar stands 5m high and has nearly 300 carved figures, most depicting the life and death of Christ, although the bottom row also works in King Hans on the left and Queen Christine on the right. It was Christine, a friend of Berg's, who commissioned the work. Berg also created the large limestone sepulchral monument bearing the king's and queen's portraits in bas-relief.

The cathedral's most intriguing attraction lies in the cathedral's chilly crypt down an inconspicuous set of stairs descending from the right-hand side of the altar, where you'll find a glass case containing the 900-year-old skeleton of King Canute (Knud) II and another displaying the skeleton of his younger brother, Benedikt.

A few metres west of the coffin, stairs lead down to the remains of the original St Alban's church, to where the royals had fled and were killed by Jutland farmers during a revolt against taxes. Although less than saintly, in 1101 Knud was canonised Knud the Holy by the pope in a move to secure the Catholic church in Denmark.

HC Andersens Hus

The recently expanded and improved **HC Andersens Hus** (☎ 65 51 46 01; Bangs Boder 29; adult/child 50/20kr; 9am-7pm mid-Jun–Aug, 10am-4pm Tue-Sun Sep–mid-Jun) lies amid the picturesque little houses of the old poor quarter of Odense. It contains a thorough and lively telling of Andersen's amazing life, put into interesting historical context of the extraordinary era he lived through and leavened by some good audiovisual material, including a hugely entertaining audio clip of the great Shakespearean actor Sir Laurence Olivier wheeling out his finest chicken impressions in a rendering of Andersen's *It's Perfectly True,* a short tale of gossip and Chinese whispers in a henhouse.

There's a room with slide presentations on Andersen's life, a reconstruction of the author's Copenhagen study, displays of his fanciful silhouette-style paper cuttings and a voluminous selection of the author's books, which have been translated into more than 80 languages ranging from Azerbaijani to Zulu.

Fyrtøjet

Near the museum is the charming **Fyrtøjet – Et Kulturhus For Børn** (Tinderbox – A Cultural Centre for Children; ☎ 66 14 44 11; Hans Jensens Stræde 21; admission 60kr; 🕑 9am-7pm mid-Jun–Aug, 10am-4pm Tue-Sun Sep–mid-Jun), where youngsters can explore the magical world of Hans Christian Andersen through storytelling and music (in English as well as Danish during June to August) and by dressing up and playing Andersen characters. All the materials needed during a visit are included in the admission price.

HC Andersens Barndomshjem

In the centre of the city, **HC Andersens Barndomshjem** (Munkemøllestræde 3; adult/child 10/5kr; 🕑 10am-4pm mid-Jun–Aug, 11am-3pm Tue-Sun Sep–mid-Jun) has a couple of rooms of mildly diverting exhibits in the small house where Andersen spent much of his childhood.

Brandts Klædefabrik

The former textile mill on Brandts Passage has been converted into a huge, sprawling and impressive cultural centre and cinema complex, **Brandts Klædefabrik** (☎ 66 13 78 97; combined ticket 50kr; 🕑 10am-5pm Jul & Aug, 10am-5pm Tue-Sun Sep-Jun), with a photography museum, a modern art gallery and a museum of graphics and printing. The superb bright, capacious exhibition spaces often contain excellent temporary exhibitions from artists from all over the world. There's also an appealing roof terrace overlooking town.

Museet for Fotokunst (Museum of Photographic Art; ☎ 66 13 78 16; admission 25kr), dedicated to the art of photography, has both a permanent collection and changing exhibitions by national and international photographers.

Kunsthallen (☎ 66 13 78 97; admission 30kr), a modern art gallery, has four large halls with changing exhibitions focusing on new trends in the visual arts. Displays include paintings, sculpture and installations as well as exhibits on Scandinavian design. There's also a 'videotheque' with a library of art videos that can be viewed by visitors.

The **Danmarks Grafiske Museum/Dansk Pressemuseum** (Danish Graphic Museum/Danish Press Museum; ☎ 66 12 10 20; admission 25kr) traces the development of printing in Denmark over the last three centuries. One section covers the now old-fashioned lithography, engraving, bookbinding and paper-making; the other section concentrates on newspaper production. Retired workers demonstrate the techniques they used in their working days (such as setting cold metal type), made obsolete by computerised presses.

Fyns Kunstmuseum

In a stately, neoclassical building, the **Fyns Kunstmuseum** (☎ 65 51 46 01; Jernbanegade 13; adult/child 30/10kr; 🕑 10am-4pm Tue-Sun) has a serene atmosphere and contains a quality collection of Danish art from the 18th century to the present. Highlights include PS Krøyer's *Italieneske Markarbejdere,* 'Italian Field Workers', Gustava Emilie Grüner's cheerful *Portraegruppe Familien Leunbach* and HA Brendekild's harrowing, but powerful *Udslidt,* 'Finished', depicting a prostrate worker and distressed woman in a vast, despairingly flat field. There are small collections of fine sculptures and of contemporary art; changing exhibitions are also staged.

Carl Nielsen Museet

The **Carl Nielsen Museet** (☎ 65 51 46 01; Claus Bergs Gade 11; adult/child 25/5kr; 🕑 4-8pm Thu & Fri, noon-4pm Sun) in Odense's concert hall, details the career of the city's native son Carl Nielsen, Denmark's best known composer. Nielsen's music career began at the age of 14 when he became a trumpet player in Odense's military band. Four years later he moved to Copenhagen to undertake formal music studies and shortly afterwards, in 1888, his first orchestral work, *Suite for Strings,* was performed at the Tivoli concert hall to critical acclaim. It has become a regular piece in Danish concert repertories. Nielsen's music includes six symphonies, several operas and numerous hymn tunes and popular songs, some with patriotic themes.

The chronologically ordered exhibition details not only the life of Nielsen but also that of his wife, sculptor Anne Marie Brodersen. Displays include Brodersen's works and studio and Nielsen's study and piano. At various points you can don earphones and enjoy Nielsen's music.

Møntergården

Free city museum **Møntergården** (☎ 66 14 88 14; Overgade 48-50; 🕑 10am-4pm Tue-Sun) has various displays on Odense's history from the Viking Age and a couple of 16th- and 17th-century half-timbered houses. There are numerous rooms with period furnishings, medieval exhibits, church carvings and local archaeological finds.

Danmarks Jernbanemuseum

Railway buffs should not miss the collection of 19th-century locomotives at the **Danmarks Jernbanemuseum** (☎ 66 13 66 30; Dannebrogsgade 24; adult/child 40/16kr; 🕑 10am-4pm) just behind the train station. There are also mini-railways for children of all ages to ride on. It has a replica of a period station and about two dozen engines and saloon cars, as well as a royal carriage that once belonged to Christian IX. There are also displays of model trains and ferries.

Odense Slot

Kongens Have, the park directly opposite the train station, is the site of **Odense Slot**, a two-storey castle with red-tiled roofs and cobbled courtyard. Modest as castles go, it was erected in 1720 by Frederik IV to serve as a royal residence during his visits to Odense. The king died here in 1730, a victim of tuberculosis. Odense Slot was later converted into a governor's residence and now serves as administrative offices for the municipal and county governments. It's not open to visitors but you can stroll through the grounds.

Den Fynske Landsby

A delightful open-air museum, **Den Fynske Landsby** (☎ 65 51 46 01; adult/child 55/15kr; 🕑 10am-7pm mid-Jun–mid-Aug, 10am-5pm Tue-Sun Apr–mid-Jun & mid-Aug–Oct, 11am-3pm Nov-Mar) is furnished with period buildings authentically laid out like a small country village, complete with barnyard animals, a duck pond, apple trees and flower gardens.

The museum is in a green zone 4km south of the city centre via bus No 42. From May to September you can take a boat (adult/child 35/25kr) from Munke Mose down the river to Erik Bøghs Sti, from where it's a 15-minute woodland walk along the river to Den Fynske Landsby.

Odense Zoo

Denmark's second largest **zoo** (☎ 66 11 13 60; Sondre Blvd 306; adult/child 85/50kr; 🕑 9am-7pm Jul, 9am-6pm May, Jun & Aug, 9am to at least 4pm Sep-Apr; bus No 11, 12 or 31) borders the river, 2km south of the city centre. As zoos go the animals generally have large enclosures and the zoo supports various conservation and educational programs. It's home to tigers, lions, giraffes, zebras, chimpanzees and colourful African birds and there's a new 'oceanium' with penguins and manatees. There's plenty for children to enjoy in addition to the animals, including donkeys, to pet, a playground and lots of animal-related games.

Odense Åfart (p191) stops at the zoo during the peak season, or you could walk the entire way along the wooded riverside path that begins at Munke Mose.

WALKING TOUR

A leisurely paced walk is one of our favourite ways of exploring the city. The following route takes in many of the city's historic sights and museums. Although the walk itself takes only about an hour, if you stop at all the sights along the way it could easily take you the better part of a day to complete the tour.

From rådhus (the mainly 1950s town hall) head east on Vestergade, which becomes Overgade, and then turn right onto **Nedergade (1)**, a cobblestone street with leaning half-timbered houses and antique shops.

At the end of Nedergade, a left turn onto Frue Kirkestræde will bring you to **Vor Frue Kirke (2;** 🕑 10am-noon Mon-Fri), erected in the 13th century. It has a rather plain, whitewashed interior, though there's an ornate Baroque pulpit that dates from the mid-17th century.

From Vor Frue Kirke turn left back onto Overgade; you'll soon reach **Møntergården (3)**, the city museum, and then turn right into Claus Bergs Gade, where you'll pass the city's only casino. Immediately to the north is the **Odense Koncerthus (4),** the concert hall, and a museum dedicated to composer Carl Nielsen.

Just past the casino, turn left onto Ramsherred (which quickly changes into Hans Jensens Stræde) to reach the **HC Andersens Hus (5)**, the recently expanded and revamped museum dedicated to Hans Christian Andersen, and the children's cultural centre, **Fyrtøjet (6)**. The museum is in a pleasant neighbourhood of narrow cobbled streets and old tile-roofed houses.

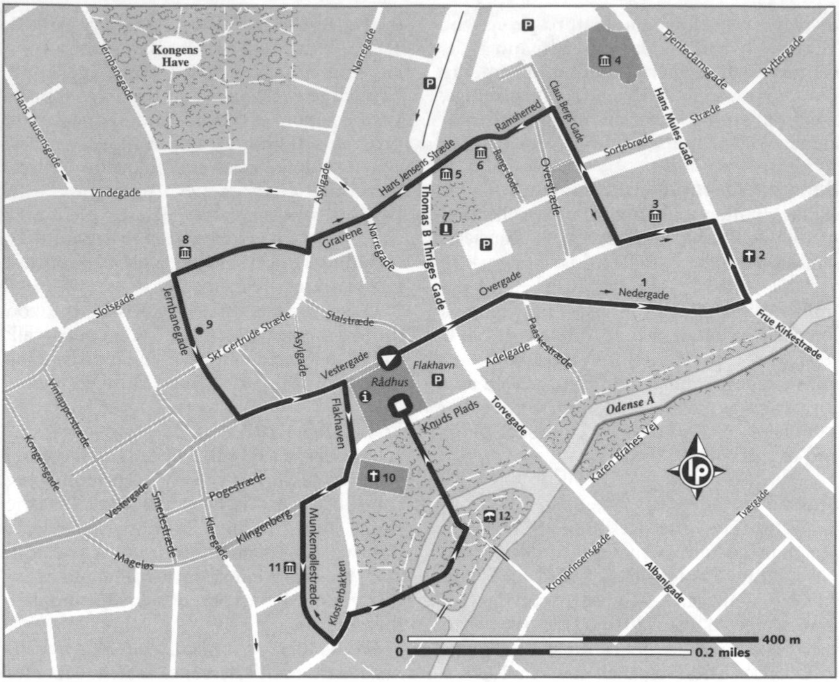
Kongens Have
Jernbanegade
Hans Tausensgade
Nørregade
Vindegade
Asylgade
Hans Jensens Stræde
Ramsherred
Claus Bergs Gade
Pjentedamsgade
Ryttergade
Hans Mules Gade
Stræde
Sortebrøde
Bangs Boder
Overstræde
Thomas B Thriges Gade
Gravene
Nørregade
Slotsgade
Jernbanegade
Skt Gertrude Stræde
Asylgade
Stalstræde
Overgade
Nedergade
Frue Kirkestræde
Vestergade
Flakhavn
Rådhus
Adelgade
Paaskestræde
Odense Å
Flakhaven
Knuds Plads
Torvegade
Karen Brahes Vej
Vintapperstræde
Kongensgade
Vestergade
Smedestræde
Pogestræde
Klingenberg
Klaregade
Munkemøllestræde
Klosterbakken
Mageløs
Kronprinsensgade
Albanigade
Tværgade
0
400 m
0
0.2 miles

There's a peaceful little **park and duck pond (7)** south of the museum.

Continue down Hans Jensens Stræde, cross Thomas B Thriges Gade and follow Gravene to Slotsgade; **Fyns Kunstmuseum (8)**, Odense's notable fine arts museum, is on the corner of Slotsgade and Jernbanegade. Turn left and proceed down Jernbanegade to Vestergade. Along the way you'll pass the site of **Gråbrødre Kloster (9)**, a medieval Franciscan monastery that has been converted into a home for the elderly.

When you reach Vestergade, turn east back to rådhus and then go south to **Sankt Knuds Kirke (10)**, Odense's intriguing cathedral. Opposite the cathedral, turn down Sankt Knuds Kirkestræde and then go south on Munkemøllestræde, where you'll pass **HC Andersens Barndomshjem (11)**, the writer's childhood home.

Loop back around on Klosterbakken and take the path into the **HC Andersen Haven (12)**, a riverside park with a prominent statue of the author. You can walk north through the park to get back to your starting point at rådhus.

SLEEPING

The tourist office books rooms in private homes at 250/350kr for singles/doubles, plus a 35kr booking fee.

Budget

Odense Camping (☎ 66 11 47 02; www.camping-odense.dk; Odensevej 102; adult/child/tent 64/32/20kr; bus No 21 or 22) Pleasant three-star camping ground is in a wooded area not far from Den Fynske Landsby, 3.5km south of the city centre.

Danhostel Odense City (☎ 63 11 04 25; www.cityhostel.dk; Østre Statiosvej 31; dm 118kr, s/d 360/450kr; year round;) You can't get more central than this bright, modern 140-bed place in a renovated 19th-century hotel with four- and six-bed dorms, a kitchen and laundry facilities alongside the train and bus stations. Each room has its own bathroom.

Danhostel Odense Vandrerhjem (☎ 66 13 04 25; Kragsbjergvej 121; dm 105kr, s/d 295/420kr; bus No 61 or 62) Attractive hostel in a half-timbered manor house surrounding a cobbled courtyard in an exclusive suburb 2km southeast of the city centre. The interior has been renovated and the rooms are modern. The 168 beds are mostly in four-bed rooms.

Det Lille Hotel (☎ 66 12 28 21; Dronningensgade 5; s/d incl breakfast 350/550kr, with shared bathroom 300/430kr) Located just a leisurely 10-minute walk west of the train station, this is a small friendly and inexpensive hotel. The 14 rooms are best descrived as standard. Det Lille is looking a little scruffy these days and smoking is allowed throughout the hotel, which can be irritating.

Mid-Range

Ansgarshus Motel (☎ 66 12 88 00; fax 66 12 88 65; Kirkegåds Allé; s/d 445/575kr, with shared bathroom s/d 350/495kr; P) A small, family-run place near the river and parkland with clean, welcoming rooms.

Hotel Domir (☎ 66 12 14 27; www.domir.dk; Tausensgade 19; s 420kr, d 495-585kr; 💻) One of the better mid-range options in town a short walk from the train station. Pleasant, good value rooms all with phone, desk, TV and bathroom, although some singles are a bit cramped.

Ydes Hotel (☎ 66 12 11 31; Hans Tausensgade 11; s 360kr, d 450-550kr) Sister hotel to the Domir, the Ydes has 26 smaller, but similarly appointed, spotlessly clean rooms with TV, desk and bathroom.

City Hotel (☎ 66 12 12 58; www.city-hotel-odense.dk; Hans Mulesgade 5; s/d 595/795kr; P) A comfortable modern hotel near the Hans Christian Andersen House Museum. Rooms have full amenities, and there's free parking, a good breakfast and friendly service.

Top End

First Hotel Grand (☎ 66 11 71 71; odense@firsthotels.dk; Jernbanegade 18; s/d from 753/1179kr; ⊠ 💻 P) An old-fashioned but welcoming place that's strong on service. The rooms are large and the décor a muted but not unappealing 1960s style. There's a sauna and solarium, in-room cable TV and minibar and WiFi access.

Clarion Hotel Plaza (☎ 66 11 77 45; www.choicehotels.dk; Østre Stationsvej 24; s/d 1125/1325kr; 💻 P ⊠) Overlooking the green spaces of Kongens, this hotel is good on friendly service and comfort. Its 68 rooms are decorated in a slightly pastoral Old English style and are fairly luxurious. There's WiFi access, a gym and a pleasant sunroom where a better-than-average breakfast is served.

Radisson SAS HC Andersen Hotel (☎ 66 14 78 00; www.radisson.com/odensedk; Claus Bergs Gade 7; s/d 1195/1395kr; ⊠ 💻 P) Rooms at this contemporary four-storey hotel are reasonably well equipped. There's a casino, a sauna and gymnasium.

EATING

Restaurants

There are moderately priced restaurants and cafés along both Vestergade and Kongensgade, which chalk up daily specials. One cluster can be found at the **Arkaden** complex, at the southern end of Kongensgade on Vestergade, which contains Greek, Italian, Brazilian and a few other ethnic restaurants offering lunchtime specials for around 50kr and full dinners for about 100kr.

Restaurant Klitgaard (☎ 66 13 14 55; Gravene 4; 2/3/4 courses 335/395/475kr; 🕑 dinner only) Small, newish, gourmet place, noted for its use of fresh, locally grown seasonal ingredients cooked by a locally grown chef is one of the best places we've eaten in Denmark. The pairings of ingredients are clever (slow-roasted and ever-so-tender-and-pink duck breast, for instance, with the merest sliver of foie gras for richness and roasted fennel to lighten it) and surprising (like the sensational rhubarb sorbet with pickled rhubarb and lavender oil).

Den Gamle Kro (☎ 66 12 14 33; Overgade 23; fish & meat mains 158-258kr; 🕑 lunch & dinner) One of Odense's most atmospheric restaurants spread throughout several rooms of a 17th-century house and with an old world feel, including the recipes, which are heavy, traditional Danish (good fish dishes such as fillet of sole stuffed with salmon and spinach) or French (eg Chateaubriand or pork with Lyonnaise potatoes). It's mostly meat-based fare, but tasty. There's also a huge wine list.

Den Grimme Ælling (☎ 65 91 70 30; Hans Jensens Straede 1; lunch buffet without drinks/with drinks 79-115kr, evening buffet with wine 245kr; 🕑 lunch & dinner) A charming little restaurant in a cobbled lane with a varied and high-quality buffet selection. Non-buffet lunch mains start at 75kr for herring and salad, while a hearty Danish hash – a typical fry-up with fried egg, meat and potatoes always with pickles – costs 65kr.

Restaurant Mamma's (☎ 66 14 55 40; Klaregade 4; lunch pizza or pasta mains 49kr, dinner mains: pizza 72-89kr, pasta 78-89kr; 🕑 lunch & dinner) A very decent pasta and pizza place offering a warm atmosphere, fresh ingredients and good lunch deals. It's tucked away behind the main shopping area.

Målet (☎ 66 17 82 41; Jernbanegade 17; schnitzel 79kr; 🕑 11am-10pm for food, 11pm for drinks) As long as it's one of 10 different varieties of schnitzel, this sports pub and restaurant will serve you anything.

Jensen's Bøfhus (☎ 66 14 59 59; Kongensgade 10; dinner mains around 100kr, lunch specials 50kr; 🕑 11am-11pm) Part of a smart, if uniform, nationwide chain, it offers grilled chicken and steaks at dinner, and cheap lunch specials.

Asia House (☎ 66 12 19 24; Østre Stationsvej 40; à la carte mains 100kr, buffet 139kr; 🕑 from 5pm) Head here for delicious, authentic Thai food. Best time is Friday or Saturday night, when there's a grand buffet spread.

Le Provence (☎ 66 12 12 96; Pogestræde 31; 3-course meal from 168kr; 🕑 5.30pm-midnight Mon-Sat). This pleasant French restaurant on a quiet back street in the city centre offers cosy candlelit dinners.

Cafés

Café Biografen (☎ 66 13 16 16; Brandts Klædefabrik; brunch 65kr 🕑 11am-midnight) Ducks waddle happily around the terrace tables at this cheerful place beside the cultural centre and cinema. The café does a good selection of baguettes for around 40kr and salads for about 60kr, as well as cakes, pastries, coffees, light meals and beer at reasonable prices.

Froggy's Café (☎ 65 90 74 47; Vestergade 68; light meals 45-70kr; 🕑 11am-2am) A good people-watching spot overlooking the main pedestrian street, Froggy's has reasonably priced burgers, pastas, omelettes and salads.

Quick Eats

You'll find fast-food outlets all around the city, especially along Kongensgade. At the train station you'll find a bakery with both eat-in and takeaway items, some fast-food places.

China Box (☎ 66 20 62 44; Vestergade; small/large takeaway box 25/38kr; 🕑 11am-9pm Mon-Sat) Close to the tourist office this takeaway does inexpensive noodles and other Chinese buffet food – all served in paper boxes.

Butik Smagens Hus (☎ 66 12 22 72; Nørregade 32; sandwiches 40-50kr; 🕑 10am-5.30pm Tue-Thu, 10am-6.30pm Fri , 10am-2pm Sat) A great little place to pick up gourmet deli supplies, good wine or sit and enjoy a delicious pressed apple juice, organic coffee or superb sandwich containing some of the delicious meats and cheeses on display at the counter.

Self-Catering

On Wednesday and Saturday mornings there's a produce market along Claus Bergs Gade, the pedestrian street that runs south from the Odense Koncerthus. Odense Banegård Center, which incorporates the train and bus stations, has low-priced options including a **DSB Café** (🕑 5am-10pm Mon-Fri, 8am-10pm Sat & Sun) and a small grocery store at the station that's open until midnight.

Restaurant Mamma's (☎ 66 13 13 03; 🕑 10am-5.30pm Mon-Fri, 10am-2pm Sat) Great deli is attached to the pizza place of the same name and sells a wide choice of upmarket treats for picnickers and self-caterers including good dried meats, cheeses and marinated vegetables.

Royal Bakery (Vestergadevej 28) For the best the best Danish pastries in town and tasty organic ice cream, this bakery is located just opposite Jernbanegade.

Naturkost (☎ 66 13 70 13; Gravene 8; 🕑 Mon-Sat) A well-stocked health-food store.

DRINKING

The **outdoor cafés** on Vintapperstræde are good spots for a quiet evening drink.

Ryan's (☎ 65 91 53 00; Fisketorvet 12) In the evening there's often live Irish folk music at this friendly Irish pub near rådhus – it has Guinness and Kilkenny on tap. It's a popular spot with local university students.

Den Smagløse Café (Vindegade 47; 🕑 1pm-2am Mon-Sat) A buzzing, atmospheric little place where a youngish, studenty crowd relaxes on beaten-up but comfortable old sofas.

ENTERTAINMENT

Nightclubs

Boogies (☎ 66 14 00 39; Nørregade 23; 🕑 11am-4.30am Tue-Sat) Boogies is a dance spot popular with students.

Kong Graes (☎ 66 11 18 16; Asylgade 7-9; average admission 50kr; 🕑 Thu-Sat) A dressier, less student orientated late-night dance club big on house and other repetitive beats.

Cinema

BioCity (☎ 70 13 12 11; Odense Banegård Center) If you're up for a movie this new cinema in the train station complex features the largest screen in Denmark.

Café Biografen (☎ 66 13 16 16; Brandts Passage 43) Located at Brandts Klædefabrik, this café screens first-run movies, and often has art-house flicks as well.

Gay & Lesbian

Lambda (☎ 66 17 76 92; Vindegade 100) Has a late-night café on Fridays and most Saturdays and a disco on the first and third Saturday of each month. It's in an unsigned, red-brick building, about 30m beyond the roundabout just past Jazzhus Dexter, and on the other side of the road.

Live Music

Dexter's Jazzhus (☎ 66 13 68 88; Vindegade 65; entry usually 40kr; ⏲ Thu-Sat) The place in town for jazz.

Casino Odense (☎ 66 14 78 10; Claus Bergs Gade 7; ⏲ 7pm-2am Mon-Fri, 7pm-4am Sat &Sun) At this casino in the Radisson SAS HC Andersen Hotel you can try your luck at blackjack, roulette and slot machines.

Odense Koncerthus (☎ 66 12 44 80; Claus Bergs Gade 9) Symphony orchestra and other classical music performances are conducted here, with .a program that commonly includes works by native son Carl Nielsen.

Brandts Klædefabrik (☎ 66 13 78 97; Brandts Passage) Open-air amphitheatre across from the arts complex hosts free summertime rock, jazz and blues concerts, particularly on Saturdays.

SHOPPING

A wide variety of clothing and speciality shops cluster in the city centre along Kongensgade and Vestergade.

Dr Adam's (☎ 66 14 55 59; Pogestræde 24-26) A smart men's and women's clothing boutique tucked behind the Magasin department store that sells posh designer labels, including a few Danish ones such as Munthe plus Simondsen.

Magasin (☎ 66 11 92 11; Vestergade 20) The city's largest and smartest department store, Magasin stocks just about everything from food delicacies to cosmetics and clothing.

Kramboden (☎ 66 11 45 22; Nedergade 24) Kramboden offers an interesting hotchpotch of items including porcelain, toys, glass and pewter, some of them antique.

GETTING THERE & AWAY

Odense is 34km west of Nyborg, 44km northwest of Svendborg, 37km northeast of Faaborg and 50km east of the bridge to Jutland.

Bus

Regional buses leave from Dannebrogsgade 6, at the rear of the train station. There are bus services from Odense to all major towns on Funen (see individual destinations for bus information).

Car & Motorcycle

Odense is to the north of the E20; you can exit the E20 and go into the city via Rte 9, 43 or 168. Odense is connected to Nyborg by Rte 160 and the E20, to Kerteminde by Rte 165, to Jutland by the E20, to Faaborg by Rte 43 and to Svendborg by Rte 9.

Car rental companies in town include:

Avis (☎ 66 14 39 99; Østre Stationsvej 37)
Europcar (☎ 66 14 15 44; Kongensgade 69)
PS Bilundejning (☎ 66 14 00 00; Middlefartvej 1)
A competitive local option (from 340kr per day) if you don't need to drop the car in another town or city.

Train

Odense is accessible by the main railway line between Copenhagen (207kr, 1½ hours), Århus (181kr, 1¾ hours), Aalborg (276kr, three hours) and Esbjerg (163kr, two hours). Trains between Odense and Copenhagen stop at Nyborg (42kr, 20 minutes). The ticket office is open from about 6am to 8.15pm most days, but closes at 5.15pm on Saturdays. Buses leave from the rear of the train station. The only other train route in Funen is the hourly run between Odense and Svendborg (59kr, one hour).

GETTING AROUND

Bicycle

Bicycles can be rented at **Rolsted Cykler** (☎ 66 17 77 36; Østre Stationsvej 33; ⏲ 10am-5.30pm Mon-Fri, 10am-2pm Sun) for 85kr per day, 500kr per week. Another hire place is **City Cykler** (☎ 66 13 97 83; www.citycykler.dk; Vesterbro 27; ⏲ 9am-5.30pm Mon-Fri, 10am-2pm Sat) west of the city centre. Bikes cost 99kr per day.

Boat

From May to August, **Odense Åfart** (☎ 65 95 79 96) runs a little covered boat down the Odense Å to Erik Bøghs Sti, a landing in the woods at

Fruens Bøge. The boat departs from Munke Mose, to the southwest of the city centre, at 10am, 11am, 1pm, 2pm, 3pm and 5pm (and also at noon and 4pm between June and mid-August). Take it as a 70-minute return excursion or break your journey at the zoo or the woods. The cost for adults is 35/55kr one-way/return, 24/35kr for children.

Bus

In Odense you board city buses at the front and pay the driver (12kr) when you get off. The driver may grumble if you don't have the correct change. The main transit point for city buses is in front of Sankt Knuds Kirke.

Car & Motorcycle

Outside rush hour, driving in Odense is not difficult, but many of the central sights are on pedestrian streets and it's best to park your car and explore on foot.

Near the city centre, there's metered parking along the streets, but spaces fill quickly. You can find substantial parking lots around Brandts Klædefabrik and the Carl Nielsen Museet Parking costs a minimum 1kr for about seven minutes, and around 8kr for one hour.

Taxi

Taxis are readily available at the train station, or you can order one by phoning **Odense Taxa** (☎ 66 15 44 15).

AROUND FUNEN ISLAND

The island of Funen is largely rural and green, with rolling woodlands, pastures, wheat fields and lots of old farmhouses. The terrain is gentler in the north, where it eventually levels out to marshland, and more hilly in the south. In May the landscape is ablaze with solid patches of yellow rapeseed flowers.

NYBORG

pop 1,500

Nyborg is the easternmost town on Funen and the western terminus of the Store Bælt bridge. While most people pass right through the town without pause, seeing little more than its industrial harbourfront, Nyborg can make an enjoyable stop for those with time to spare.

The most appealing part of town is around Torvet, the main square, where there is an attractive brick rådhus, the remains of a medieval castle and some classic half-timbered houses. All are just a few hundred metres apart and only a 10-minute walk west of the train station.

There are white-sand beaches on the east of town, about 1.5km from the centre.

Information

Nyborg Turistbureau (☎ 65 31 02 80; www.nyborgturist.dk; Torvet 9; 🕒 9.30am-5.30pm Mon-Fri, 9.30am-2.30pm Sat mid-Jun–Aug; 9am-4pm Mon-Fri, 9.30am-12.30pm Sat Sep–mid-Jun)

Sights

NYBORG SLOT

The main reason for stopping in town is **Nyborg Slot** (☎ 65 31 02 07; Slotsgade 11; adult/child 30/15kr; 🕒 10am-4pm Jun & Aug, 10am-5pm Jul, 10am-3pm Mar-May, Sep & Oct). It's one of half a dozen fortresses erected in strategic locations during the late 12th century to secure Denmark's coast but it has a far more important place in Danish history than the other castles.

In 1282 Erik V, under pressure from nobles who wanted to limit royal power, signed an important charter here that established Denmark's first constitution and an annual parliament known as the Danehof, which sat here until 1413. The castle was used as a royal residence for centuries.

The fortress once had an enclosing defence wall and four corner towers but only part of the original structure remains. Two of the towers fell victim to earlier modifications and in 1870 most of the ramparts were torn down to make room for the town's expansion.

Still, what does remain is fun to explore. The **Danehof room**, where the Danehof met, has walls painted with an intriguing 16th-century, three-dimensional cube design that seems strikingly contemporary. You'll find old royal paintings, suits of armour, antique guns and swords. You can climb a spiral staircase to the loft and walk along the running boards past the machicolations through which boiling tar was once poured onto attacking Swedes.

VOR FRUE KIRKE

Nyborg's central place of worship, **Vor Frue Kirke** (Gammel Torv 1; 🕒 9am-6pm Jun-Aug, 9am-

4pm Sep-May) dates from 1388 but has been altered many times over the years, most extensively in 1870. Its beautifully detailed Baroque pulpit was carved in 1653 by Anders Mortensen of Odense. From left to right the pulpit sections depict the birth of John the Baptist, Christ's baptism, the Transfiguration, the Resurrection and the Ascension. Entry is via the small southern door on Korsbrødregade.

Sleeping

Nyborg Strandcamping (☎ 65 31 02 56; www.strandcamping.dk; Hjejlevej 99; per person 60kr, per tent 20kr; 🕑 Apr-Sep) Impressively located three-star camping ground is on a white-sand beach about 2km east of the town centre, with a view of the Store Bælt bridge.

Hotel Villa Gulle (☎ 65 30 11 88; www.villa-gulle.dk, in Danish; Østervoldgade 44; s/d without bathroom 350/495kr, with bathroom 450/650kr; P ⊠) Cheapest hotel in town, with 26 straightforward rooms.

Hotel Hesselet (☎ 65 31 30 29; www.hesselet.dk; Christianslundsvej 119; s/d incl breakfast 1280/1780kr; 💻 ⊠ P) Built on a striking location 2km northeast of town looking out across the Great Belt road bridge. The Hesselet's interior exudes a grand old style from the leather sofas, billiards room and large fireplace to the plush carpets and the library lined with leather-bound tomes. The rooms are large and cosseting with big, firm beds. Most have ocean views. There are also an indoor swimming pool, tennis courts and two saunas. The hotel is accessible to people in wheelchairs.

Eating

There are several places to eat in the streets south of Torvet.

Restaurant Østervemb (☎ 65 30 10 70; Mellemgade 18; lunch mains 130kr, dinner mains 195kr; 🕑 lunch & dinner Tue-Sat) This atmospheric restaurant specialises in fresh seafood such as its fish plate with three kinds of fish, vegetables and potatoes. It cooks other non-fish home-style Danish and French dishes to a high standard too.

Gertz Conditori (☎ 65 31 00 96; Kongegade 16; light meals 25kr) Bakery doubles as a sandwich shop and café. On sunny days it's pleasant to sit outside at one of the pavement tables.

Fiskehallen (☎ 65 31 16 60; Korsgade 11; fish & chips 43kr; 🕑 10.30am-6.30pm Mon-Sat) Freshly caught and freshly cooked takeaway seafood is on offer at this fish shop.

Getting There & Away

Nyborg is on the E20, 34km east of Odense. Trains generally run about twice an hour between Nyborg and Odense (42kr, 20 minutes).

KERTEMINDE

pop 5500

Kerteminde is a seaside town which is well worth visiting simply for the chance to do some slow-paced, low-key ambling around its pastel-walled houses and its pleasing yacht-filled harbour. It's a good break for hectic sightseeing.

Inviting sandy beaches can be easily reached either side of town. Nordstranden extends from the northern end of the marina, Sydstranden begins on the southern side of the harbour. A statue of Amanda the fisher girl, a town symbol of sorts, stands on the southern side of Langebro, the bridge that crosses the Kerteminde Fjord and connects the northern and southern parts of Kerteminde.

Information

Danske Bank (☎ 63 32 07 00; Langegade 31)

Post office (Strandvejen 4) Immediately south of the bus station.

Kerteminde Turistbureau (☎ 65 32 11 21; www.kerteminde-turist.dk, in Danish; Strandgade 1B; 🕑 9am-5pm Mon-Sat mid-Jun & Aug; 9am-4pm Mon-Fri, 9.30am-12.30pm Sat Sep–mid-Jun)

Sights

Johannes Larsen Museet (☎ 65 32 31 27; Møllebakken 14; adult/child 40kr/free; 🕑 10am-5pm Jun-Aug, 10am-4pm Tue-Sun Sep-May) On the northern side of town, this museum is in the artist's former home and retains its original furniture and decor. Larsen (1867–1961), one of the Fynboerne painters, is known for his paintings of wildlife and provincial Danish scenes.

Also here is **Svanemøllen**, a windmill dating from 1853, and a modern 15-room exhibition centre with paintings by several dozen artists. This museum has parking spaces only for people with disabilities. The car park at the corner of Hindsholmvej and Marinavejen is handiest.

Activities

For a quiet outing, consider a visit to the island of **Romsø**, a mere 30-minute boat ride from Kerteminde. The only residents are the boatman's family, about 200 deer and numerous rabbits and birds. You can walk a 3km coastal trail around the 109- hectare island or just soak up the solitude. Bring a picnic lunch because there are no facilities.

The **Romsø-Båden boat service** (☎ 65 32 13 77; return adult/child 85/45kr) takes passengers to the island on Wednesday and Saturday, departing from Kerteminde at 9am and from Romsø at 3pm. Reservations are required.

Sleeping

Kerteminde Camping (☎ 65 32 19 71; www.dk-camp.dk; Hindsholmvej 80; camping per person 61kr; Apr-Sep) Three-star camping ground opposite the beach and just 1.5km north of the town centre.

Danhostel Kerteminde (☎ 65 32 39 29; www.dkhostel.dk; Skovvej 46; dm 118kr, d or tr 354kr; Jan–mid-Dec; ⊠ P) Nestled next to a delightful wooded area, this hostel sits just a five-minute walk from a sandy beach and 15 minutes south of the town centre. The 30 rooms each have a maximum of four beds, a shower and a toilet. With plenty of wholesome outdoor activities on the doorstep it's a good base for the outward bound and for families. Danhostel Kerteminde is accessible to people in wheelchairs.

Tornøes Hotel (☎ 65 32 16 05; www.tornoeshotel.dk; Strandgade 2; s/d 795/845kr; P ⊠) A great harbourside spot right in the centre of town makes this place worth considering, especially if you can bag a harbour-view room.

Eating

Restaurant Sejlklub (☎ 65 32 24 53; Marinavej 2; lunch mains 70-100kr, dinner mains 100-160kr; lunch & dinner) For affordable waterfront dining, Restaurant Sejlklub at the yacht marina on the northern side of town offers beef and seafood dishes, many of them Danish staples. There's indoor and patio seating. It's also a nice spot to have a cold beer on a sunny afternoon.

Rudolf Mathis (☎ 65 32 32 33; Dosseringen 13; mains lunch/dinner 175/250kr, lunch/dinner menus from 315/650kr; lunch & dinner) Waterside restaurant on the southern side of Kerteminde harbour specialises in fresh fish and is widely regarded as one of Funen's best restaurants. Shellfish are a strong point, including delights such as gratinated Norwegian lobster salad or scallops in a small pastry basket with spring onions. Specialities include a grilled five-fish platter with *beurre blanc* and seasonal veg or fried, deboned plaice stuffed with fish mousse.

Getting There & Around

Kerteminde is on Rte 165, 19km northwest of Nyborg and 21km northeast of Odense.

There are hourly bus services connecting Kerteminde with Odense (No 885 and 890) and Nyborg (No 890 and 891). Both of these routes take about 35 minutes and cost 35kr.

LADBYSKIBET

A Viking chieftain lay entombed for almost 1000 years in a 22m Viking ship that was laid here and covered with earth some time in the 10th century. **Ladbyskibet** (Ladby ship; ☎ 65 32 16 67; Vikingevej 123; adult/child 25kr/free; 10am-5pm Jun-Aug; 10am-4pm Tue-Sun Sep, Oct & Mar-May; 11am-3pm Wed-Sun Nov-Feb) was originally excavated in 1935 and remains the only Viking Age ship burial site uncovered in Denmark to date, surprisingly so perhaps, given that it was not uncommon for high-ranking Vikings to be buried in their wooden ships, along with supplies considered to be of use in the afterlife.

All the wooden planks from the Ladby ship decayed long ago, leaving the imprint of the hull moulded into the earth, along with iron nails, an anchor and the partial remains of the dogs and horses that were buried with their master. This may sound unpromising, and at first glance, the grassy hillock covering the site seems more like a bomb shelter from the outside, but as soon as the automatic entrance doors hiss open most people are captivated by this compelling relic.

The exhibition hall, which resembles a burial mound from the exterior, has been erected around the excavation. There's also a separate visitor centre near the car park with a 1:10-scale model of the ship and background information about the site.

Getting There & Away

In the little village of Ladby, 4km southwest of Kerteminde via Odensevej, turn north onto Vikingevej, a one-lane road through fields that ends after 1.2km at the Ladbyskibet car park. You enter through the little museum, from where it's a few minutes' walk along a field path to the mound.

Local bus No 482 (14kr, eight daily, Monday to Friday) makes the six-minute trip from Kerteminde to Ladby. Check the schedule with the bus driver, as the last return bus is typically around 4pm. Also, you'll have to walk the Vikingevej section.

HINDSHOLM

The Hindsholm peninsula, stretching north from Kerteminde, is a rural area of small villages boasting 16th-century churches and old half-timbered farmhouses. The most fetching village is **Viby**, which has a picturesque windmill and an early Gothic church with frescoes. Viby is at the southern end of the peninsula, only a 15-minute drive from Kerteminde.

Further to the north, in Mårhøj, is Funen's largest single-chamber **passage grave**, which dates from 200 BC; it consists of a 10m-long chamber that visitors can enter, but it's only about 1m high so bring a torch and be prepared to crawl. The mound is easy to spot, in a farmer's field about five minutes' walk from the road.

At the northernmost tip is **Fyns Hoved**, an island-like extension of the Hindsholm peninsula that's connected by a narrow causeway. You can walk to the edge of its 25m-high cliffs (high by Danish standards), from where there's a view of the northern Funen coast and, on a clear day, Jutland and Zealand as well.

Getting There & Away

Route 315 runs the length of the peninsula from south to north; villages and sightseeing spots along the way are signposted.

There are a couple of buses running from Kerteminde to Hindsholm. Bus No 481 connects Kerteminde with Viby, while Nos 484 and 483 run up the peninsula to Korshavn, ending about 1km shy of Fyns Hoved. Both routes are covered about half a dozen times a day on weekdays only and cost 18kr.

The best way to visit laid-back Hindsholm is by bicycle. There's a regional loop cycle route from Kerteminde to Fyns Hoved that makes a good day-long bike tour. You can get more information on cycling from the Kerteminde tourist office.

EGESKOV SLOT

There are plenty of sights and activities at **Egeskov Slot** (☎ 62 27 10 16; www.egeskov.com; combined ticket for all sights except the castle adult/child 85/45kr, plus castle interior 55/25kr; 🕑 10am-5pm May, Jun, Aug & Sep, 10am-7pm Jul) to keep anyone happily occupied for a day. It's a magnificent example of the lavish castles that sprang up during Denmark's 'Golden Age', complete with moat and drawbridge. Egeskov, literally 'oak forest', was built in 1554 in the middle of a pond on a foundation of thousands of upright oak trunks.

The grounds are perhaps the most impressive, although the castle interior does hold some attractions. It has antique furnishings, grand period paintings and an abundance of hunting trophies that include elephant tusks and the skins and heads of tigers, cheetahs and other rare creatures. Apparently former owner, Count Gregers Ahlefeldt-Laurvig-Bille, was one of the more active hunters of African big game of his day.

Designed in the 18th century, the expansive 15-hectare park that surrounds the castle includes century-old privet hedges, topiary, free-roaming peacocks and manicured English-style gardens.

The castle grounds usually stay open an hour longer than the castle. Admission to the grounds includes entry to a large antique **car museum**, which also features some vintage aircraft swooping from the rafters.

Getting There & Away

Egeskov Slot is 2km west of Kværndrup on Rte 8. From Odense take the Svendborg-bound train to Kværndrup Station (49kr) and continue on foot or by taxi. Alternatively, for 40kr take bus No 801 to Kværndrup Bibliotek, where you can switch to bus No 920, which stops at the castle on its regular run between Faaborg and Nyborg. If you're lucky, in the summer months (June to August) bus No 801 may run all the way to the castle.

FAABORG

pop 7300

Faaborg is a south-facing sun trap with a relaxing air. In the 17th century it was a bustling harbour town sustained by one of Denmark's largest commercial fleets. Today, Faaborg retains many vestiges of that earlier era in its picturesque, cobblestone streets and leaning, half-timbered houses. Three streets particularly notable for their attractive period buildings and hollyhock-trimmed doorways are Holkegade, Adelgade and Tårngade.

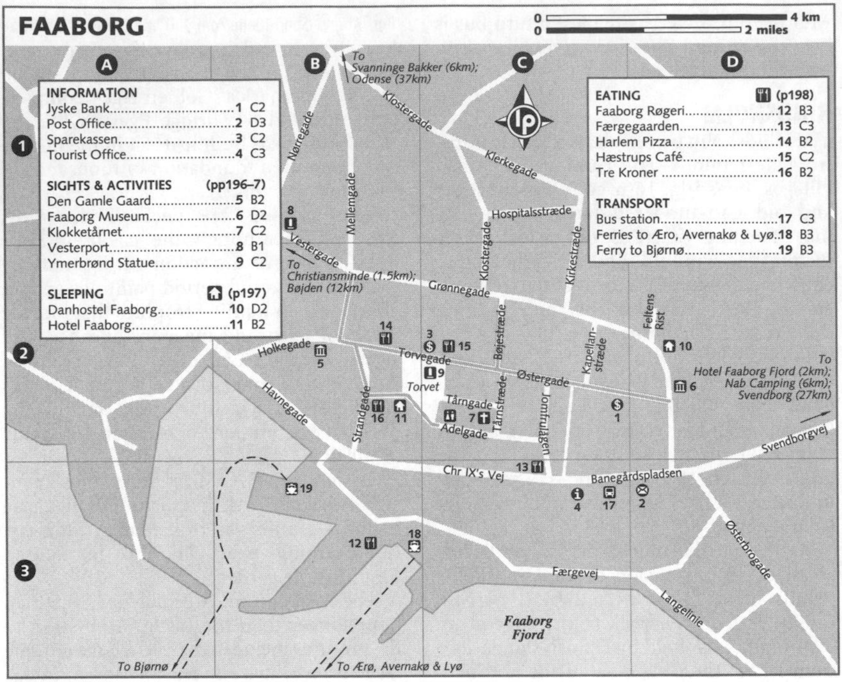
FAABORG
0 4 km
0 2 miles
A
B
C
D
1
2
3
INFORMATION
Jyske Bank 1 C2
Post Office 2 D3
Sparekassen 3 C2
Tourist Office 4 C3
SIGHTS & ACTIVITIES (pp196–7)
Den Gamle Gaard 5 B2
Faaborg Museum 6 D2
Klokketårnet 7 C2
Vesterport 8 B1
Ymerbrønd Statue 9 C2
SLEEPING (p197)
Danhostel Faaborg 10 D2
Hotel Faaborg 11 B2
EATING (p198)
Faaborg Røgeri 12 B3
Færgegaarden 13 C3
Harlem Pizza 14 B2
Hæstrups Café 15 C2
Tre Kroner 16 B2
TRANSPORT
Bus station 17 C3
Ferries to Ærø, Avernakø & Lyø 18 B3
Ferry to Bjørnø 19 B3
To Svanninge Bakker (6km); Odense (37km)
Klostergade
Klerkegade
Nørregade
Mellemgade
Hospitalsstræde
Klostergade
Kirkestræde
Vestergade
To Christiansminde (1.5km); Bøjden (12km)
Grønnegade
Feltens Rist
Kapellanstræde
Bøjestræde
Holkegade
Torvegade
Torvet
Østergade
Tårngade
Tårnstræde
Adelgade
Jomfrulågen
Havnegade
Strandgade
To Hotel Faaborg Fjord (2km); Nab Camping (6km); Svendborg (27km)
Svendborgvej
Chr IX's Vej
Banegårdspladsen
Østerbrogade
Færgevej
Langelinie
Faaborg Fjord
To Bjørnø
To Ærø, Avernakø & Lyø

Faaborg also has two rather interesting museums, one dedicated to town history and the other concentrating on regional art. It's well worth stopping at this small, charming town for a drink or lunch before moving on elsewhere on Funen or via the ferry to the southern islands.

Information

Jyske Bank (☎ 63 61 10 20; Østergade 36)

Post office (☎ 63 21 68 68; Banegårdspladsen 4; 🕑 10am-5pm Mon-Fri, 10am-noon Sat) It's just east of the bus station.

Sparekassen (☎ 63 61 18 00; Torvet 6) Bank.

Tourist office (☎ 62 61 07 07; www.visitfaaborg.dk; Banegårdspladsen 2A; 🕑 9am-5pm Mon-Sat Jun-Sep, 10am-5pm Mon-Fri, 10am-3pm Sat Oct-May) Also supplies bike hire, biking maps, fishing licences and telephone cards. Adjacent to the bus station and car park on the harbour front.

Sights

DEN GAMLE GAARD

This well-presented museum, just west of Torvet, **Den Gamle Gaard** (Holkegade 1; adult/child 30kr/free; 🕑 10.30am-4.30pm mid-May–Oct; 11am-3pm Sat & Sun Apr–mid-May), is in a timber-framed merchant's house that dates back to about 1725 and retains much of its original character. The 22 rooms are arranged to show how a wealthy merchant lived at the start of the 19th century; part of the house holds the family quarters and other sections contain workshops and storerooms. The museum is full of antiques, ranging from furniture, porcelain and toys to maritime objects and a hearse carriage. One room contains personal items that belonged to Riborg Voigt, a merchant's daughter with whom Hans Christian Andersen had a brief relationship and a lifelong infatuation. The mementos include one of Andersen's business cards and a lock of his hair.

FAABORG MUSEUM FOR FYNSK MALERKUNST

In an attractive neoclassical building, **Faaborg Museum** (Grønnegade 75; adult/child 35kr/free; 🕑 10am-4pm Apr-Oct) is a former winery which, though small, contains a fine collection of Funen art, including works by leading Funenite artists such as Peter Hansen, Jens Birkholm and Anna Syberg. Kai Nielsen's original granite sculpture of the *Ymerbrønd* is also here (see Torvet below).

TORVET

The main square, **Torvet**, is a pleasant spot to linger and have a drink outside at one of the cafés. It features the Svendborg sculptor Kai Nielsen's striking (some say disturbing) bronze fountain *Ymerbrønd*, a naked giant suckling at the udder of a cow – depicting a Norse fertility myth – which caused a minor uproar on its unveiling.

VESTERPORT

The brick town **Vesterport** (West Gate), which was erected in the 15th century to allow entry into the city, still spans Vestergade, 500m northwest of Torvet. One of only a handful of such gates remaining in Denmark, it owes its existence primarily to Faaborg's economic decline in the 19th century, a time when many town gates elsewhere were torn down to make room for wider roads and municipal expansion.

KLOKKETÅRNET

The **Klokketårnet** (cnr Tårngade & Tårnstræde; admission 10kr; 11am-4.15pm Mon-Fri mid-Jun–Aug), a belfry that was once part of a medieval church, now serves as the town's clock tower; in summer you can climb it.

Activities

Intruders and criminals beware: between mid-June and late August a costumed **night watchman** winding his way through the old town may sing comical nightwatchman songs at you in Danish. Visitors can follow in his footsteps. He begins his rounds at Klokketårnet at 9pm from Thursday to Sunday.

Syd Fyenske Veteranjernbane (☎ 63 63 36 96; adult/child 40/20kr; departs 10am, 1pm & 3pm Sun late Jun-early Aug), an antique train, makes three leisurely runs from the old Faaborg train station north to Korinth. The return trip lasts 80 minutes.

Svanninge Bakker, the countryside north of Faaborg, has some pretty rolling hills, dubbed the Funen Alps by local tourism authorities. Here you'll find cycling and walking trails and a golf course.

There's a good water-sports centre at the **Hotel Faaborg Fjord** (☎ 62 61 10 10; Svendborgvej 175; activities 60-100kr), 2km out of town, offering water-based fun such as kneeboarding and high-speed water-ski jumping. You can also cling on for dear life while being towed along behind a weaving speedboat – astride a giant inflatable banana.

Sleeping

There are a few camping grounds within a 10km radius of Faaborg but none within reasonable walking distance.

The tourist office books **rooms** in private homes for singles/doubles for 250/400kr for a 25kr fee.

Nab Camping (☎ 62 61 67 79; www.nabcamping.dk; Kildesgårdvej 8; camping adult/child 55/28kr; May-Aug) A basic two star spot right by the sea, about 6km southeast of town.

Danhostel Faaborg (☎ 62 61 12 03; www.danhostel.dk/faaborg; Grønnegade 71-72; dm 100kr, d 300kr; Apr-Sep) Close to the Faaborg Museum, this 69-bed hostel occupies two handsome historic buildings. One is a former public bathhouse and the other a half-timbered house.

Christiansminde (☎ 62 61 90 18; www.fynsiden.dk; Assensvej 66; s/d 395/450kr; ☒) This delightful guesthouse in a 19th-century home 1.5km west of Torvet has five cosy rooms with antique furnishings and lots of pleasant touches. A large breakfast is available for 65kr, a smaller one for 40kr. There's also a candlelit dining room where guests can, with advance notice, enjoy a home-made, three-course dinner for 125kr. In addition, Christiansminde has a nearby seaside house that can sleep up to eight people for 7500kr per week.

Hotel Faaborg (☎ 62 61 02 45; www.hotelfaaborg.dk; Torvet; s/d 575/650kr; P) In an old brick building overlooking Torvet, this small hotel has a dozen rooms, each with bath, TV and a refrigerator. If you need some sustenance, there's a bar and a restaurant on the ground floor which does tasty herring dishes for 80kr and smørrebrød for 38kr to 58kr.

Hotel Faaborg Fjord (☎ 62 61 10 10; www.hotelfaaborgfjord.dk, in Danish; Svendborgvej 175; s/d 795/1125kr) A member of the Quality Hotel chain, this large hotel on the eastern outskirts of town on a pleasant waterside spot has standard tourist amenities, including 131 modern chalet-style rooms, a restaurant, pool, sauna and water sports centre (see also activities p197).

Eating

Many cafés and restaurants cluster in or around Torvet.

Tre Kroner (☎ 62 61 01 50; Strandgade 1; sandwiches 37-50kr, omelettes 60-90kr) A pub-style café with a charming old-world character, Tre Kroner has moderately priced Danish food such as smørrebrød, herring or *æggekage* (69kr), a rich Funen omelette served with dark bread.

Færgegaarden (☎ 62 61 11 15; Chr IX's Vej 31; mains 2-/3-/4-course dinner 228/268/298kr) A good bet for fine dining, this pleasant restaurant has new energetic owners and dishes up good traditional Danish food at fair prices with the odd non-Danish treat such as tuna steaks thrown in.

Faaborg Røgeri (☎ 62 61 42 32; Vestkaj; fish dishes 19-66kr; daily) Serves cheap, tasty, home-smoked fish in a great spot by the harbour with a small outside dining area.

Hæstrups Café (☎ 63 61 00 20; Torvet 2; salads, burgers & sandwiches around 50kr; daily) A popular central spot for light meals and drinks on the square.

Harlem Pizza (☎ 62 61 41 62; Torvegade 10; pizza & pasta 30-40kr; 11am-11pm) Takeaway pizzeria has good pizza with a range of toppings, as well as reasonably priced pitta-bread sandwiches, lasagne and spaghetti.

Getting There & Away

Faaborg is 27km west of Svendborg and 37km south of Odense.

BOAT

Ferries run to and from Faaborg daily to the island of Ærø.

There are also ferries from Faaborg to the nearby offshore islands of Bjørnø, Lyø and Avernakø; see right.

BUS

Faaborg has no train service. Bus Nos 961 and 962 from Odense (56kr, 1¼ hours) run at least hourly to 11pm. Bus Nos 930 and 962 from Svendborg (42kr, 40 minutes) are also frequent throughout the day, running at least hourly. Faaborg's bus station is on Banegårdspladsen, at the old train station on the southern side of town.

CAR & MOTORCYCLE

Getting to Faaborg by car is straightforward: if you are coming from the north, simply follow Rte 43, which is called Odensevej as it enters the town. From Svendborg, Rte 44 leads directly west into Faaborg, entering the town as Svendborgvej.

Getting Around

Bicycles can be hired at the tourist office for 50kr per day.

BJØRNØ, LYØ & AVERNAKØ

If you are looking for a quiet getaway while you're in the Faaborg area, consider a day trip to one of the three small offshore islands, Bjørnø, Lyø and Avernakø. All three islands are rural, unspoilt and connected by a daily ferry service to Faaborg. If you're interested in staying overnight, staff at the Faaborg tourist office can arrange stays with local families.

The nearest and smallest island, Bjørnø, 3km south of Faaborg, is just 3km long and 1km wide. It has one small village with about 40 inhabitants. You can walk around the island but there are no real sights.

Lyø, about 10km southwest of Faaborg, is the most heavily populated of the islands – with all of 150 residents. Roughly 4km long and 2km wide, it has a small village perched in the middle of the island, with half-timbered houses, a school and a church with an unusual circular churchyard. It also has a few scattered sights, on the western side of the island, and enough narrow roads to make for an interesting day's cycling.

Avernakø, 6km south of Faaborg, is shaped a bit like a pair of spectacles, with two oval-shaped sides, both about 4km long, connected by a thin rim of land. There's a small village, Avernak, on the northwestern side of the island and scattered farmsteads throughout. In all, about 120 people live on Avernakø.

Getting There & Away

The M/S *Lillebjørn* (☎ 20 29 80 50), a little 20-passenger boat, shuttles between Faaborg and Bjørnø (return adult/child 40/20kr, bicycles 12kr, six daily Monday to Friday, four or five Saturday, three Sunday). The trip takes 20 minutes.

The M/F *Faaborg II* (☎ 62 61 23 07) can take 150 passengers and 12 cars and operates between Faaborg, Avernakø and Lyø (at least six daily; adult/child 85/40kr return, bicycle 20kr, motorcycle 60kr). From Faaborg it takes between 30 and 70 minutes to get to your destination, depending on which island the boat pulls into first.

Because the roads are narrow, visitors are not encouraged to bring cars to Avernakø or Lyø; there's no car ferry to Bjørnø.

SVENDBORG

pop 40,000

It's not a bad spot to spend a night before heading to the less developed and perhaps more alluring islands beyond – such as Tåsinge, Langeland and Ærø. Svendborg offers some historic buildings, several good hostels and hotels in its centre and a lively bar and restaurant scene along the quayside where yachties and landlubbers flock to in numbers.

During the 19th century Svendborg was a busy harbour town with nearly two dozen shipyards producing almost half of all of the wooden-hulled ships built in Denmark. AP Møller, one of the world's largest shipping companies, was founded in Svendborg in that period of peak activity. With its excellent port facilities, Svendborg also became the site of foundries, tanneries, tobacco-processing plants and mills.

Today Svendborg, the largest municipality in southern Funen, remains an industrial city with commercial port facilities. It also has a couple of shipyards that still build wooden ships and provide repair services to the scores of yachts that ply the waters off southern Funen.

Information

Danske Bank (☎ 63 21 43 30; Møllergade 2) A few minutes' walk from the train station.

Nordeabank (☎ 62 21 52 21; Centrumpladsen 8) Just south of the tourist office.

Post office (☎ 63 21 68 68; Klosterplads 11) South of the train station.

Tourist office (☎ 62 2 1 09 80; www.visitsydfyn.dk; Centrumpladsen 4; 🕒 9.30am-6pm Mon-Fri, 9.30am-3pm Sat mid-Jun–Aug; 9.30am-5pm Mon-Fri, 9.30am-12.30pm Sat Jan–mid-Jun & Sep-Dec) Has lots of information on South Funen as a whole.

Sights & Activities

At the southern end of Havnepladsen's cobbled quayside, opposite where the Ærø

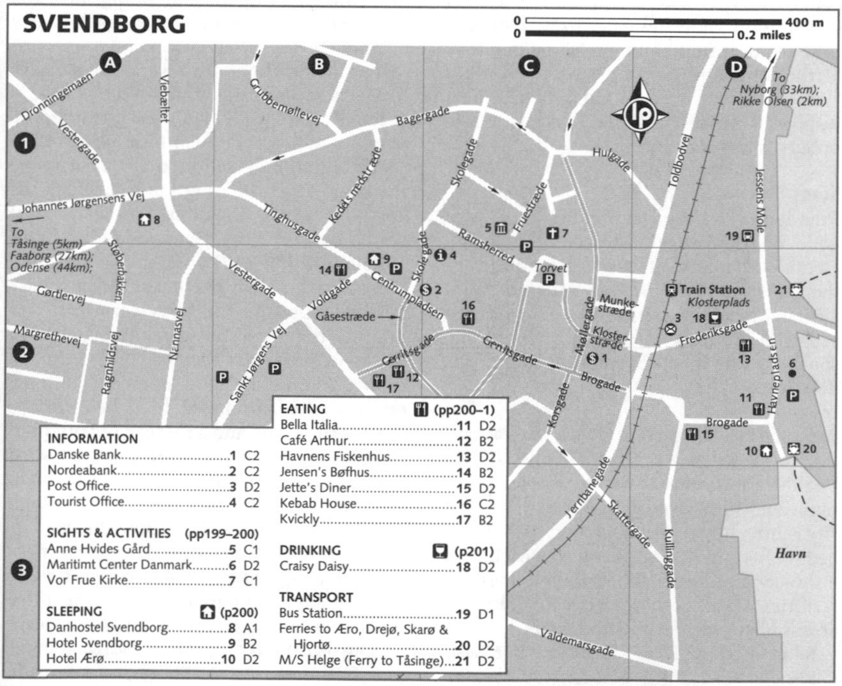
SVENDBORG
0 400 m
0 0.2 miles
A
B
C
D
1
2
3
To Nyborg (33km); Rikke Olsen (2km)
Dronningemaen
Vestergade
Viebæltet
Grubbemøllevej
Bagergade
Skolegade
Hulgade
Toldbodvej
Jessens Mole
Johannes Jørgensens Vej
To Tåsinge (5km) Faaborg (27km); Odense (44km);
Tinghusgade
Kedelsmedstræde
Fruestræde
Ramsherred
Torvet
Støberbakken
Voldgade
Centrumpladsen
Gåsestræde
Gørtlervej
Margrethevej
Ragnhildsvej
Nannasvej
Sankt Jørgens Vej
Gerritsgade
Møllergade
Munkestræde
Klosterstræde
Train Station
Klosterplads
Frederiksgade
Havnepladsen
Brogade
Korsgade
Jernbanegade
Skattergade
Kullinggade
Valdemarsgade
Havn
INFORMATION
Danske Bank 1 C2
Nordeabank 2 C2
Post Office 3 D2
Tourist Office 4 C2
SIGHTS & ACTIVITIES (pp199–200)
Anne Hvides Gård 5 C1
Maritimt Center Danmark 6 D2
Vor Frue Kirke 7 C1
SLEEPING (p200)
Danhostel Svendborg 8 A1
Hotel Svendborg 9 B2
Hotel Ærø 10 D2
EATING (pp200–1)
Bella Italia 11 D2
Café Arthur 12 B2
Havnens Fiskenhus 13 D2
Jensen's Bøfhus 14 B2
Jette's Diner 15 D2
Kebab House 16 C2
Kvickly 17 B2
DRINKING (p201)
Craisy Daisy 18 D2
TRANSPORT
Bus Station 19 D1
Ferries to Ærø, Drejø, Skarø & Hjortø 20 D2
M/S Helge (Ferry to Tåsinge) 21 D2

ferry docks, is **Sejlskibsbroen**, a jetty lined with splendidly preserved sailing ships and smaller vessels and with an adjoining marina that caters for the great number of yachts that sail local waters.

Take a sunset cruise, experience shipboard life on a historic wooden sailing ship, sail round Funen's southern isles, or take the kids aboard Captain Blood's ship to learn how to sing pirate songs, hunt for treasure and spit long distances – just like a real pirate – at **Maritimt Center Danmark** (☎ 62 80 02 14; post@maritimt-center.dk; Havnepladsen 2; cruises adult/child from 110/70kr; ⏰ Thu & Fri Jul & Aug only).

Near Torvet you'll find a couple of attractive period buildings. The handsome brick church, **Vor Frue Kirke** (Torvet 1; ⏰ 8am-4pm Jun-Aug, 8am-noon in low season), was originally built in the 13th century in Romanesque style, although subsequent alterations have given it a Gothic appearance. The church has a late-16th-century pulpit and altar.

Just west of Vor Frue Kirke, **Anne Hvides Gård** (☎ 62 21 02 61; Fruestræde 3; admission 25kr; ⏰ 10am-5pm Tue-Sun Apr-Aug) is the city's oldest secular building, a large and lovely bumble-bee-coloured timber-framed house that leans tipsily to one side and dates from 1560. It's now a local-history museum telling the story of the town and its people with the lively 'Old bones and treasure' exhibition. It also displays antiques, including locally made pottery, silverware and glass.

Sleeping

Svendborg and the surrounding area have good bed and breakfast accommodation. Details of many of them are found in the *Funen and the Islands* B&B brochure available from the tourist office. The nearest camping grounds are on Tåsinge, on the southern side of the Svendborg sound; for details see p202.

Danhostel Svendborg (☎ 62 21 66 99; www.danhostel-svendborg.dk; Vestergade 45; dm/r 118/375kr; Ⓟ 💻 ⊠) Highly rated hostel is in a pleasantly renovated 19th-century iron foundry in the city centre. It has 34 double rooms, 28 three-bed rooms and 22 four-bed rooms, each with a shower and toilet. The hostel has laundry facilities and also rents bicycles for 63kr. It is accessible to people in wheelchairs.

Rikke Olsen (☎ 20 16 55 56; Måroddevej 22, Thurø; r 450kr; ⏰ May-Oct; Ⓟ) A superbly located quiet B&B on the tiny island of Thurø (about 2km from town) and reached by a slender road bridge. All rooms have an en suite and a balcony with sea views looking across to Tåsinge. There's also a garden, and a beach and bathing jetty.

Hotel Ærø (☎ 62 21 07 60; www.hotel-aeroe.dk, in Danish; Brogade 1; s/d 650/775kr; Ⓟ) Right by the water, the Ærø has an annexe of large, modern chalet-style rooms with plush décor, big comfy beds, and a cosy bar and restaurant downstairs. In summer try to get a room as far from the bar as possible as noise can sometimes be a problem. There's a good restaurant serving top-notch traditional fare, including a great range of light lunches and smørrebrød (42kr to72kr).

Hotel Svendborg (☎ 62 21 17 00; www.hotel-svendborg.dk; Centrumpladsen 1; s/d with bathroom 695/795kr; Ⓟ ⊠) Modern five-storey hotel in the city centre has bright, cheerfully coloured rooms. It is accessible to people in wheelchairs.

Eating

The lion's share of restaurants in Svendborg are conveniently located along Brogade and Gerritsgade, which connect the ferry terminal with the city centre.

You'll find there are several inexpensive food places along the same stretch of road.

Jette's Diner (☎ 62 22 16 97; Kullinggade 1; mains 40-68kr; ⏰ noon-9.30pm) Popular local place, 200m south of the train station, that's a cut above the usual diner, offering sandwiches, salads and tasty burgers (including Ostrich burgers) served between tasty, generously filled buns.

Hotel Ærø (☎ 62 21 07 60; Brogade; daily special 75kr, lunch mains 42-78kr, dinner mains 95-182kr; ⏰ lunch & dinner) Opposite the ferry terminal, this popular restaurant has a refined air with a gracious, nautically themed, high-ceilinged dining room. The food is mostly unfussy classics such as minced fried beef on rye toast with pickles and a raw egg or with fried onion potatoes and gravy; fried plaice stuffed with prawns, asparagus and mushrooms in a lobster sauce, but it's prepared to a high standard using good, fresh ingredients.

Bella Italia (☎ 62 22 24 55; Brogade 2; mains 136-190kr; pizzas & pastas 60-99kr; ⏰ lunch & dinner) Really good pizza and pasta make this place justifiably the most popular Italian in town.

Jensen's Bøfhus (☎ 62 80 08 84; Tinghusgade 1; lunch specials 45kr, dinner mains 80-100kr; ⏰ lunch & dinner) In the complex opposite the Hotel Svendborg, this steak and chicken restaurant has a good salad bar and some cheap lunch deals.

Kebab House (☎ 62 22 99 00; Gerritsgade 28; burgers, kebabs & pitta bread sandwiches 20-30kr) Hole-in-the-wall place offers the standard quick snack.

Café Arthur (☎ 62 21 11 01; Gerritsgade 35; pastas & pizzas 50-65kr) Pleasant little café has good prices and is in a central location.

Havnens Fiskenhus (Frederiksgade; 7am-5.30pm Mon-Fri, 7am-1pm Sat) Almost opposite Crazy Daisy (see below), Havnens Fiskenhus sells a good range of fresh and smoked fish.

Kvickly (Vestergade 20; 9am-8pm Mon-Fri, 8am-5pm Sat) Central supermarket also has a decent bakery and a simple cafeteria.

Drinking & Entertainment

Hotel Ærø (☎ 62 21 07 60; Brogade) Cosy bar here has a roaring fire in winter and serves a good range of Danish beer all year.

Craisy Daisy (☎ 62 21 67 60; Frederiksgade 7; admission 50kr; Terrace bar Tue-Sat 7pm-at least 11am; Nightclub Fri & Sat 11pm-early hours) The place where Svendborg comes to party to music in the nightclub inside or outside on the more chilled-out terrace (June to August only).

Getting There & Away

For most travellers, Svendborg is the transit point between Odense and the southern Funen islands. It is 44km southeast of Odense on Rte 9, 33km southwest of Nyborg on Rte 163 and 27km east of Faaborg on Rte 44.

BOAT

Ferries to Ærøskøbing depart five times a day, the last at 10.30pm in summer. For more information see p210.

For information on the M/S *Helge*, which sails between Svendborg and Tåsinge, see p203.

BUS & TRAIN

There are frequent bus services between Svendborg and Faaborg (No 930; 38kr, 40 minutes), Rudkøbing (35kr, 25 minutes) and other Funen towns. Trains leave Odense for Svendborg about once an hour (58kr, one hour). The bus and train stations are a few streets north of the ferry terminal.

DREJØ, SKARØ & HJORTØ

Many of Svendborg's visitors are yachties who sail the protected waters along the southern Funen coast. Three popular local sailing spots are the small offshore islands of Drejø, Skarø and Hjortø, all 10km to 15km southwest of Svendborg.

Camping is allowed at designated sites on all three islands; Drejø has a restaurant and grocery shop, while Skarø has a small food shop and a snack bar.

Drejø (population 76) is the largest island, covering 412 hectares and extending about 5km in length. The island has some attractive old houses and a community church dating from 1535. It's largely given over to moors and meadows (home to the endangered fire-bellied toad) and has a large protected harbour with good mooring facilities.

Skarø (population 41) is shaped a bit like a rabbit's head, covers 189 hectares and reaches an altitude of just 9m at its highest point. Part of the island's salt meadows is set aside as a bird sanctuary, and it is home to about 50 species of breeding birds each summer. Skarø has mooring space for about 50 boats.

Car-free Hjortø (population 15) is the smallest of the three islands, measuring just 2km at its widest point and attracts lots of sea birds and shore birds. You can walk around the island in just a couple of hours. About 25 boats can moor in the Hjortø harbour.

Getting There & Away

If you don't have your own boat, it's possible to visit these islands on a day trip via small ferries that leave from Svendborg's harbour. The **Hjortø** ferry (☎ 62 54 15 18, 40 97 95 18) generally sails twice daily, while the ferry to **Drejø** and **Skarø** (☎ 62 21 02 62; adult/child return 70/45kr; bicycles 20kr) has three to five sailings daily (sailing time 30 to 75 minutes, depending on island and route). Detailed timetables are available at the Svendborg tourist office.

TÅSINGE

pop 2300

Tåsinge, the fourth largest island in Funen county, is connected by bridge to both Svendborg and Langeland. Most of the island is typically rural, a mix of woods and open fields.

The island's main road, Rte 9, cuts straight across Tåsinge, but it's well worth making a detour through the northeastern quarter of the island, where you'll find Tåsinge's main sights: the old sea captains' village of Troense and the 17th-century Valdemars Slot.

Sights

Troense is a well-to-do seaside village with lots of quaint thatched houses and a small yachting harbour. The main activity for visitors is just strolling around and admiring the old homes; two particularly interesting streets are Grønnegade and Badstuen.

Søfartssamlingerne i Troense (☎ 62 22 52 32; Strandgade 1; adult/child 25/10kr; 10am-5pm May-Sep) is a small maritime museum, housed in the old village schoolhouse (dating from about 1790), which sports a rooftop belfry. The museum displays paintings, photos, model ships, figureheads and items from China brought back by local merchant ships in the 19th century.

The lavish interior of **Valdemars Slot** (☎ 62 22 61 06; Slotsalléen 100; adult/child 60/30kr; combined ticket 110/60kr; 10am-5pm May-Sep) is crammed with paintings and eccentric objects. In the grounds are **Denmark's Toy Museum**, packed with candy-coloured vintage playthings and the **Danish Yachting Museum**. You can get to Valdemars Slot by bus but a better way is by the MS *Helge*, an old-style ferry that carries passengers from Svendborg to Troense and Valdemars Slot every few hours (70kr) from May to September.

The road leading from Troense passes right through the castle's two decorative gatehouses, which are open 24 hours. There is no admission charge to the castle grounds or to the sandy beach that's just outside the castle's southern gate.

About 1km southwest of the castle, look for a grand oak tree along the northern side of the road. **Ambrosius Egen** (Ambrosius' Oak), which is marked by a plaque, is named after Ambrosius Stub, a romantic poet who worked at Valdemars Slot about 1700 and who composed many of his verses while relaxing beneath the shade of this tree. The oak tree is thought to be at least 400 years old and has a girth of nearly 7m.

BREGNINGE

The small village of **Bregninge**, on Rte 9, is home to the medieval Bregninge Kirke. One of the church's three votive ships was built in 1727 as a replica of the battleship sailed by Niels Juel in the Battle of Køge Bay, but the main attraction is the panoramic view from the **church tower** (admission 5kr; 8am-10pm (theoretically) daily), which at 72m is the highest point on the island.

Tåsinge Skipperkjem og Folkemindesamling (☎ 62 22 71 44; Kirkebakken 1; admission 30kr; 10am-5pm Tue-Sun Jun-Aug), across the road from the church, is the thatch-roofed local-history museum that tells the story of Lieutenant Sixten Sparre and artist Elvira Madigan, Denmark's real-life Romeo and Juliet. They were tragic lovers who committed suicide together in 1889 rather than be separated. They are buried together on Tåsinge in the churchyard at Landet 3km south of Bregninge, where brides still throw their bouquets on their grave.

Sleeping

Vindebyøre Camping (☎ 62225425; www.vindebyoere.dk, Vindebyørvej 52; camping per person 60kr; Apr–mid-Sep) Three-star seaside facility is the closest camping ground to Svendborg. It has a coin laundry, a TV lounge and a guest kitchen. The local ferry, M/S *Helge*, docks out front and bicycles can be hired.

Det Lille Hotel (☎ 62 22 53 41; www.detlillehotel.dk; Badstuen 15; s/d with shared bath 420/550kr; P) Charming and friendly guesthouse has a few rooms in a picturesque half-timbered cottage with a roof of ancient mossy thatch and a tranquil garden.

Hotel Troense (☎ 62 22 54 12; www.hoteltroense.dk; Strandgade 5; s/d with breakfast 625/830kr; ☒ P) Perched above the harbour in the village centre, the hotel has 27 rooms in modern, white-painted blocks behind the main building, all with bath, TV and phone.

Slotspension Valdemars Slot (☎ 62 22 59 00; slot@valdemarsslot.dk; Slotsalléen 100; s 450-950kr, d 750-1200kr) If you've ever wanted to live like royalty, here's your chance. One wing of Valdemars Slot now has eight plush guestrooms with four-poster beds, courtyard views and full amenities. Rates include a fresh, hearty breakfast in the atmospheric Restaurant Valdemars Slot.

Eating

Troense village centre has a bakery and a minimarket.

Hotel Troense (☎ 62 22 54 12; Strand-gade 5; lunch mains 40-150kr, dinner mains 132-218kr) Classic Danish fare for lunch (mainly smørrebrød) and a wider-ranging, more adventurous selection of meat and fish for dinner. The hotel restaurant serves a tempting array, such as tournedos of red deer with red onion compote or lemon sole with

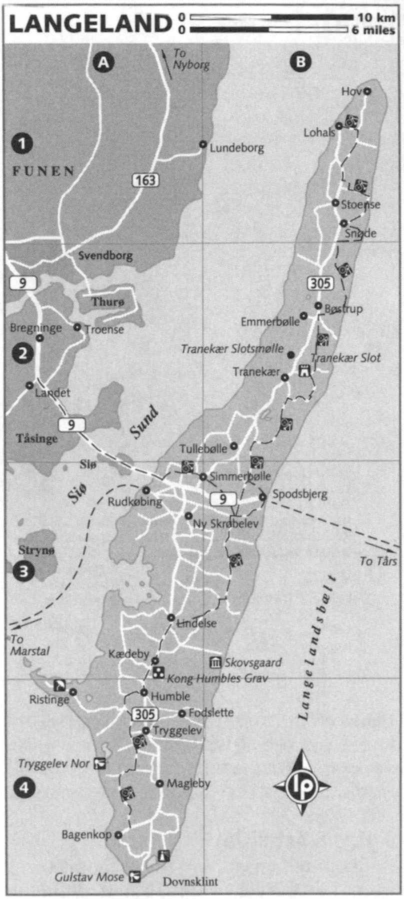
LANGELAND
0 10 km
0 6 miles
A
B
To Nyborg
Hov
Lohals
1
Lundeborg
FUNEN
163
Stoense
Snøde
Svendborg
9
Thurø
305
Bøstrup
Emmerbølle
Bregninge
Troense
2
Tranekær Slotsmølle
Tranekær Slot
Tranekær
Landet
Sund
9
Tåsinge
Tullebølle
Siø
Simmerbølle
Siø
Rudkøbing
9
Spodsbjerg
Ny Skrøbelev
Strynø
3
To Tårs
Langelandsbælt
Lindelse
To Marstal
Kædeby
Skovsgaard
Kong Humbles Grav
Ristinge
Humble
305
Fodslette
Tryggelev
Tryggelev Nor
4
Magleby
Bagenkop
Gulstav Mose
Dovnsklint

mushrooms and sun-dried tomatoes in a mustard *beurre blanc*. Plus there's some rather more humdrum vegie options.

Restaurant Valdemars Slot (☎ 62 22 59 00; Slotsalléen 100; light lunch dishes 40-72kr, lunch & dinner mains 98-195kr; 🕑 Wed-Sat) A lavish and atmospheric spot for hang-the-expense, romantic fine dining with a mostly French flavour (lobster bisque, foie gras terrine, beef and venison abound) and a high-quality wine list. There's also a less upmarket but still appealing day-time café-bistro.

Getting There & Away

Route 9 connects Tåsinge with Svendborg on Funen and Rudkøbing on Langeland; there are cycle paths running the entire way.

The Svendborg city bus service operates between the city and Tåsinge, but the most enjoyable public transport option is the vintage ferry M/S *Helge* (☎ 62 21 09 80), which operates mid-May to early September. The boat leaves Svendborg harbour at 9am, 11am, 1.30pm, 3.30pm and 5.30pm from June to mid-August. Ten minutes later it docks at Vindebyøre on the northern tip of Tåsinge and then crosses back across the sound to Christiansminde, a beach area to the east of Svendborg. The boat continues on to Troense and then to Valdemars Slot. Departures from Valdemars Slot are at 9.55am, 11.55am, 2.25pm, 4.25pm and 6.25pm. In May and late summer, the *Helge* operates the three middle sailings only. Fares range from 20kr to 40kr one way (children half price), depending on the distance. Bicycles are allowed on for an extra 20kr provided space is available.

LANGELAND

There's a satisfying sense of isolation on the long, narrow island of Langeland, connected by bridge to Funen via Tåsinge. It has some good beaches, enjoyable cycling and rewarding bird-watching.

It has an unhurried provincial character with small farming villages and countryside dotted with swishing windmills, both modern and vintage. There are ceramics shops and galleries selling local handicrafts scattered all around the island.

Langeland's only large town – Rudkøbing – has just a handful of historic sights, but the island's most frequented visitor attraction is the medieval castle at Tranekær.

RUDKØBING

pop 5000

Rudkøbing is Langeland's commercial centre and only sizable town. It's also the departure point for ferries to Ærø. North of the ferry harbour is a fishing harbour and a 260-berth marina that attracts German yachties during the summer and Danes year-round.

Information

Nordeabank (☎ 62 51 11 04; Østergade 39)
Post office (☎ 63 21 68 68; Brogade 9; 🕑 10am-5pm Mon-Fri, 10am-noon Sat)

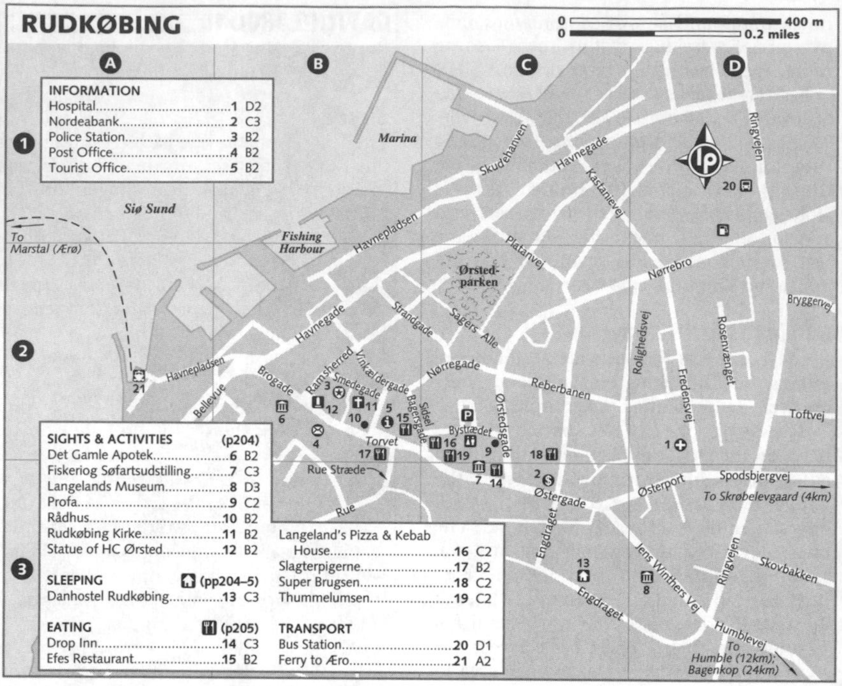
RUDKØBING
0 400 m
0 0.2 miles
INFORMATION
Hospital 1 D2
Nordeabank 2 C3
Police Station 3 B2
Post Office 4 B2
Tourist Office 5 B2
SIGHTS & ACTIVITIES (p204)
Det Gamle Apotek 6 B2
Fiskeriog Søfartsudstilling 7 C3
Langelands Museum 8 D3
Profa 9 C2
Rådhus 10 B2
Rudkøbing Kirke 11 B2
Statue of HC Ørsted 12 B2
SLEEPING (pp204–5)
Danhostel Rudkøbing 13 C3
EATING (p205)
Drop Inn 14 C3
Efes Restaurant 15 B2
Langeland's Pizza & Kebab House 16 C2
Slagterpigerne 17 B2
Super Brugsen 18 C2
Thummelumsen 19 C2
TRANSPORT
Bus Station 20 D1
Ferry to Ærø 21 A2
Marina
Siø Sund
To Marstal (Ærø)
Fishing Harbour
Ørsted-parken
Skudehavnen
Havnegade
Kastanievej
Ringvejen
Havnepladsen
Platanvej
Nørrebro
Bryggervej
Strandgade
Sagers Alle
Rolighedsvej
Rosenvænget
Fredensvej
Ramsherred
Vinkældergade
Smedegade
Brogade
Bellevue
Nørregade
Reberbanen
Toftvej
Bagergade
Sidsel
Bystrædet
Ørstedsgade
Torvet
Rue Stræde
Rue
Østergade
Engdraget
Østerport
Spodsbjergvej
To Skrøbelevgaard (4km)
Jens Winthers Vej
Skovbakken
Humblevej
To Humble (12km); Bagenkop (24km)

Tourist office (☎ 62 51 35 05; www.langeland.dk; Torvet 5, Rudkøbing; 9am-5pm Mon-Fri, 9am-3pm Sat mid-Jun–Aug; 9.30-4.30 Mon-Fri, 9.30-12.30 Sat Sep–mid-Jun) You can pick up information on the entire island here.

Sights & Activities

Rudkøbing can appear rather nondescript from the ferry harbour, but it definitely warrants a closer look. Just east of Havnegade, the main harbour road, is a series of one-lane carriage roads that date from medieval times and are lined with old houses. Three of the most interesting streets – Ramsherred, Smedegade and Vinkældergade – can be combined in a pleasant 15-minute stroll between Havnegade and Brogade.

The town also has a few sights along its main street, which begins inland of the harbour as Brogade and changes to Østergade after Torvet. On Brogade, just east of Ramsherred, is a **statue of HC Ørsted**, the Danish physicist who advanced the development of electromagnetic theory.

Across the street from the statue is **Det Gamle Apotek** (☎ 62 51 13 47; Brogade 15; adult/child 15kr/free; 11am-4pm Mon-Fri mid-Jun–Aug), where Ørsted was born. The old Rudkøbing Apotek now houses the small museum containing replicas of the interiors of two pharmacy shops, one from the 18th century and the other from the 19th century.

The Nautical museum, **Fiskeriog Søfartsudstilling** (☎ 62 51 13 47; Østergade 25; admission free; 10am-4pm Mon-Fri, 10am-1pm Sat), displays fishing gear, dinghies and model ships.

Langelands Museum (☎ 62 51 13 47; Jens Winthers Vej 12; adult/child 20kr/free; 10am-4pm Mon-Thu, 10am-1pm Fri), about 500m further east, is the region's history museum. Its displays are primarily archaeological finds from Langeland and Ærø, but it also has a collection of glass, silver and furniture from the 18th century.

On Torvet you'll find the 19th-century **rådhus** backed by the **Rudkøbing Kirke**, which dates from the early 12th century, although most of the current church building is from the post-Reformation era.

Sleeping

The tourist office can provide a list of private homes with **rooms** for rent. Some are in villages, others on farms; a few are in Rudkøbing, the rest spread around the island. Doubles cost 375kr to 400kr.

Danhostel Rudkøbing (☎ 62 51 18 30; www.danhostel.dk/rudkobing; Engdraget 11; camping per person 50kr, dm/r 100/325kr; ⏲ 15 Mar-31 Oct) Langeland's only hostel is just a 10-minute walk from Torvet in the town centre. Tents can be pitched in the field at the side of the hostel.

Skrøbelevgaard (☎ 62 51 45 31; www.skrobelevgaard.dk; Skrøbelev Hedevej 4; s 300-450kr, d 400-750kr) A fine option if you enjoy historic settings and the quiet ambience of the countryside. This stylish inn is 4km east of Rudkøbing in the village of Ny Skrøbelev. There are 10 cosy rooms for guests in this 17th-century manor house. The free city bus stops nearby on weekdays.

Eating

Thummelumsen (☎ 63 51 00 43; Østergade 15; lunch mains 50-70kr, dinner mains 135-145kr) The pick of the high street cafés/restaurants serving good, fresh, home-made light lunches, such as generously filled burgers, chilli, tortillas, meatballs with rye bread and more ambitious fare in the evenings such as carpaccio and gazpacho.

Efes Restaurant (☎ 62 51 22 23; Østergade 5; pasta, meat & fish mains 60-120kr; ⏲ lunch & dinner Mon-Sat, dinner Sun) A popular place to linger over a good, reasonably priced meal.

Drop Inn (☎ 62 51 42 20; Ostergade 29; sandwiches, salads & chicken dishes 25-50kr; ⏲ lunch) Cheery café has a nice variety of healthy light meals.

Langeland's Pizza & Kebab House (☎ 62 51 50 04; Østergade 11; pizza slices 20-25kr, other items 35-55kr; ⏲ daily til late) A good choice for inexpensive pizza, pitta-bread sandwiches and pastas.

Slagterpigerne (☎ 62 51 10 72; Torvet; sandwiches 20kr) Creative smørrebrød is prepared for takeaway at this butcher shop.

Super Brugsen (☎ 62 51 13 54; Ahlefeldtsgade 5) In the town centre, this grocery store has a good bakery and a café serving simple, cheap fare.

GETTING THERE & AWAY

Route 9, via the Langeland bridge, connects Langeland with Tåsinge and Svendborg.

Buses make the 20km run from Svendborg to Rudkøbing (35kr, 25 minutes) at least hourly.

There's a ferry service from Rudkøbing to Marstal on Ærø (see p210) and from Spodsbjerg to Tårs on Lolland (see p161).

GETTING AROUND

Route 305 runs from Lohals to Bagenkop, nearly the full length of the island.

Bicycle

There are asphalt cycle paths running from the Rudkøbing area north to Lohals, east to Spodsbjerg and south to Bagenkop. The tourist office in Rudkøbing sells a bicycle map of Langeland (15kr). In Rudkøbing you can hire bicycles at **Profa** (☎ 62 51 11 08; Ørstedsgade 5) and **Cykelsmeden** (Bystrædt 3; per day 60kr). Elsewhere on the island they can be hired at the camping grounds.

Bus

The buses are all marked No 910, so you'll need to check the destination sign on the bus to see in which direction it's headed. Buses travel from Rudkøbing north to Lohals and south to Bagenkop at least once an hour (about half as often at weekends), connecting all of Langeland's major villages en route. The maximum one-way fare from Rudkøbing to anywhere on Langeland is 40kr; the Lohals-Bagenkop fare is 70kr.

Within Rudkøbing there are special green buses that make a loop around the city outskirts, going as far east as the Spodsbjerg harbour, about a dozen times a day from Monday to Friday. There are no charges to use these buses. The whole loop takes about an hour; hop on for an interesting little tour.

All buses leave from the Rudkøbing bus station on Ringvejen.

NORTHERN LANGELAND

Northern Langeland has a run of small villages separated by farmland. You'll see the occasional sign advertising organic produce for sale and a few roadside windmills, but the main sights are at Tranekær, a quiet village surrounding a lovely medieval castle.

You could continue travelling north from Tranekær to Lohals, a fair-sized village near the northern tip of Langeland. It and the neighbouring seaside area of Hov have camping grounds and hotels, but Lohals lacks the charm of Tranekær and its beaches are not as good as those in the south.

Tranekær

Tranekær has a quaint character and quite a number of timber-framed houses, but its dominant sight is the salmon-coloured **Tranekær Slot,** which, reflected in its swan pond, looks like something torn from the pages of a fairytale.

The Tranekær Slot is a handsome 12th century medieval castle which has been in the hands of the one family since the late 1600s. The castle is not open to the public, but its grounds are home to the fascinating **TICKON** (Tranekær International Centre for Art & Nature; admission to grounds 25kr), a collection of striking art installations around the wooded grounds and lake. **Tranekær Slot Museum** and the **Souvenir Museum** are housed in the castle's old water mill and old theatre respectively. About 1km north of the castle is the **Castle Mill** (☎ 63 51 10 10; Lejbølleveje; adult/child 20kr/free; 🕑 10am-5pm Mon-Fri, 1-5pm Sat & Sun Jun–mid-Sep; 10am-4pm Mon-Fri, 1-4pm Sat & Sun mid-Sep–May), a 19th-century windmill, its remarkable wooden mechanics still intact.

Sleeping & Eating

Tranekær Gæstgivergaard (☎ 62 59 12 04; www.tranekaerkro.dk; Slotsgade 74; s/d with bathroom 500/650kr; P ⊠) Most of the rooms have peaceful garden views and there's one lovely, bright family apartment. This half-timbered village inn 200m south of the castle dates from 1802 and retains its period ambience.

Tranekær Gæstgivergaard's restaurant is strong on local game such as venison for around 180-290kr but always offers a vegetarian option too. Serves traditional Danish country dinners.

Café Herskabsstalden (☎ 62 59 14 26; Slotsgade 92; dishes 20-65kr) Large café fronting the castle offers rather grease-heavy fare such as chicken dishes, fish and chips, hot dogs and burgers.

SOUTHERN LANGELAND

Southern Langeland has the island's best beaches, several passage graves and a couple of bird sanctuaries.

Heading south from Rudkøbing you will pass a number of small villages. Three kilometres southeast of Lindelse is **Skovsgaard**, which is an estate managed by the conservation group Danmarks Naturfredningsforening; it contains an old manor house and a large organic farm complete with a windmill and thatched farm buildings. Visitors are welcome; there's an organic food café and the stable has been converted into a **carriage museum** (☎ 62 51 13 47; Kaagårdsvej 12; adult/child 35kr/free; 🕑 10am-5pm Mon-Fri, 1-5pm Sun mid-May–Oct) with 25 horse-drawn vehicles, ranging from a wedding carriage to farm wagons.

A few kilometres away, just south of Kædeby, is **Kong Humbles Grav**, the largest long dolmen on Langeland. Dating from approximately 3000 BC, the barrow is edged with 77 stones, extends 55m in length and has a single burial chamber. Its size has given rise to local folklore that a king was buried here, although historians give little credence to the tale. The dolmen is on private property in a field of grain and rapeseed, but visitors are free to walk to the site along a path that begins near the whitewashed church in Humble. To get to the dolmen walk northeast from the car park, which is just past the church, and bear left at the first intersection; follow that trail past the farmhouses. The walk takes about 20 minutes each way.

If the crops aren't too tall you'll also be able to see the site from Rte 305 about 150m south of Kædeby; the mounded dolmen is about 800m east of the road.

The village of **Humble**, the little commercial centre of southern Langeland, has a bank, a pizzeria and a petrol station. Humble is also the turn-off for Ristinge.

Ristinge, a little seaside village with thatched houses, is bordered by a long stretch of sandy beach backed by dunes and wild roses. Despite being the island's favourite bathing area, Ristinge is pleasantly low key, its main visitor facility being the camping ground.

At the southern end of the island is **Bagenkop**, an attractive little fishing village. Just beyond Bagenkop at the southernmost tip of the island is **Dovnsklint**, an area of 16m-high cliffs and pebble beaches that's popular with bird-watchers during the autumn southern migration. About 500m north of the cliffs is **Gulstav Mose**, a marshy bird sanctuary that provides a habitat for hawks, herons, ducks, reed buntings and small songbirds. East of the sanctuary are the adjacent woodlands **Gulstav Skov**. All three sites are connected by footpaths. Another area of interest to bird-watchers is **Tryggelev Nor**, a coastal nature reserve with a sighting tower, midway between Bagenkop and Ristinge.

Sleeping & Eating

Ristinge Camping & Feriecenter (☎ 62 57 13 29; www.ristinge.dk; Ristingevej 104, Humble; camping per person 62kr;

(mid-Apr–early Sep) Within walking distance of the beach in Ristinge, this three-star camping ground has a grocery shop and a snack bar.

Humble Hotel (☎ 62 57 11 34; www.humblekro.dk, in Danish; Ristingevej 2, 5932 Humble; s/d with bathroom 595/760kr; P) The nearest hotel to Ristinge, this small hotel is in Humble village centre. Breakfast is included in the room rate.

Larger villages, such as Humble and Bagenkop, have bakeries, grocery shops and at least a couple of places where you can stop for a meal.

ÆRØ

Undulating country roads wind past thatched houses, patchwork farms, ancient passage graves and old windmills on Ærø, an idyllic island well off the beaten track. Its almost-empty roads make it an ideal place to tour by bicycle, although it is fairly hilly.

Ærø is a favourite destination of yachties, and each of the island's three main towns of Ærøskøbing, Marstal and Søby has a modern marina. Sailing is so popular that, with a total of 800 berths, there are about four times as many yacht moorings as there are hotel rooms. Each of the three towns also has a commercial ferry harbour.

ÆRØSKØBING

pop 1050

Ærøskøbing was what the words 'higgledy' and 'piggledy' were invented to describe. A prosperous merchants' town in the late 1600s, Ærøskøbing has narrow, winding cobblestone streets tightly lined with 17th- and 18th-century houses, many of them gently subsiding, crooked, half-timbered affairs with old traditional hand-blown glass windows and decorative doorways beautified by plantings of hollyhocks. The tourist office has an illustrated leaflet, with a separate insert in English, describing the finest buildings, many of them very well preserved.

In addition to its engaging historic character, Ærøskøbing has a central location and good accommodation options, which makes it an ideal base for a stay on Ærø.

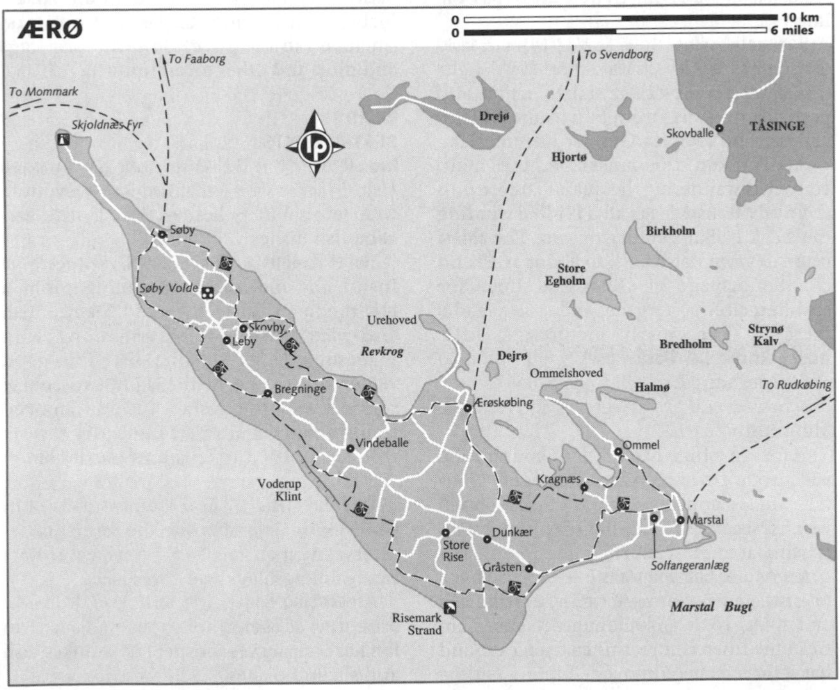
ÆRØ
0 10 km
0 6 miles
To Faaborg
To Mommark
To Svendborg
Skjoldnæs Fyr
Drejø
Hjortø
Skovballe
TÅSINGE
Søby
Søby Volde
Skovby
Leby
Birkholm
Store Egholm
Urehoved
Revkrog
Bregninge
Dejrø
Ommelshoved
Bredholm
Strynø Kalv
Halmø
To Rudkøbing
Ærøskøbing
Vindeballe
Ommel
Kragnæs
Voderup Klint
Marstal
Store Rise
Dunkær
Gråsten
Solfangeranlæg
Risemark Strand
Marstal Bugt

Information

Ærøskøbing tourist office (☎ 62 52 13 00; www.arre.dk, in Danish & German; Vestergade 1; 9am-5pm Mon-Fri, 10am-1pm Sat, 9.30am-12.30pm Sun Jun–Aug) The office is near the waterfront.

Danske Bank (☎ 63 52 25 40; Vestergade 56)

Post office (☎ 63 21 68 68; Statene 6; noon-4.30pm Mon-Fri, 10am-noon Sat)

Sights & Activities

In keeping with the town's character, sights are low key. A combined ticket for all three of the following museums for adults/children costs 50/15kr.

Flaske Peters Samling (☎ 62 52 29 51; Smedegade 22; adult/child 25/10kr; 10am-5pm Jun-Jul, 10am-4pm Aug–mid-Oct & Apr-early Jun) The former poorhouse is now a museum which displays local folk art but the most celebrated exhibits comprise the life's work of ship's cook Peter Jacobsen 'Bottle Peter', who crafted 1700 ships-in-a-bottle.

Ærø Museum (☎ 62 52 29 50; Brogade 3; adult/child 20/10kr; 10am-4pm Tue-Sun mid-Jun–late Aug, 10am-1pm April–mid-Jun & Sep) The antique furnishings, mid-19th-century paintings and other historical items displayed here are of passing interest.

Hammerichs Hus (☎ 62 52 27 54; Gyden 22; adult/child 20kr/free; 11am-3pm Tue-Sun Jun-Aug) A half-timbered house with antiques, china and period furnishings from Funen and Jutland collected by sculptor Gunnar Hammerich.

Apart from the museums, the main activity is wandering the quaint streets with their tidy houses – it's all a bit like winding the clock back a century or two. The **oldest house** in town dates back to about 1645 and is at Søndergade 36. Other fine streets for strolling are Vestergade and Smedegade; there's a particularly picturesque little house known as **Dukkehuset** (Doll's House) at Smedegade 37.

Sleeping

The tourist office has a list of countryside **B&Bs** around the island for around 250/375kr for singles/doubles. Staff can also book houses, cottages and flats by the week, starting at around 3400kr.

Ærøskøbing Campingplads (☎ 62 52 18 54; turistar@post1.tele.dk; Sygehusvej 40; camping per person 50kr; May-Sep) Near a shallow beach just 1km from the town centre, this camping ground has a three-star rating.

Danhostel Ærøskøbing (☎ 62 52 10 44; www.danhostel.dk; dm/r 105/270kr; Apr-Sep; ⊠ P) Just 1km out of town on the road to Marstal, this place is typically clean and modern but loudly slamming doors can irritate at night.

Hotel Ærohus (☎ 62 52 10 03; www.aeroehus.dk; Vestergade 38; s/d from 770/1090kr, with shared bath Dkr450/650; P) Occupies a large period building close to the harbour. It has comfortable, modernised rooms in the creaky, low-ceilinged, half-timbered main block and a smart, modern extension and garden annexe out back.

Vestergade 44 (☎ 62 52 22 98; pensionvestergade44@post.tele.dk; Vestergade 44; s/d with shared bathroom 450/680kr; P ⊠) An 18th-century house with very stylish, yet homely, interiors and a peaceful garden. The breakfast is tasty with freshly laid eggs and home-made jam. It's our pick of places in town. Book ahead.

Graasten Farm (☎ 62 52 24 25; graastenfarmb-b.com; Østermarksvej 20; s/d 350/450kr; P) For a homely country experience consider this working cattle farm run by a Danish-English couple, on the main road midway between Ærøskøbing and Marstal. It has three guest bedrooms and lots of common space, including a kitchenette. Feast at breakfast (included in the price) on fresh local eggs and milk and other local produce.

Eating

RESTAURANTS

Hos Grethe (☎ 62 52 21 43; Vertergade 39; mains around 115kr; lunch & dinner Tue-Sat, lunch Sun) A favourite with locals for its home-cooking style and good fish dishes.

Hotel Ærøhus (☎ 62 52 10 03; Vestergade 38) Inside the old-fashioned dining room a full menu of fairly standard Danish fish and meat dishes is served along with a reasonably good wine list. For good value choose one of the daily two-course specials. Sample dishes include smoked venison haunch with scrambled egg, steak with softly fried onions and pickle, and a vegetable tart.

Café Lille Claus (☎ 62 52 40 02; Havnepladsen; light meals 35-90kr) Café opposite the tourist office offers inexpensive (and unspectacular) sandwiches, salads and fish dishes.

Ærøskøbing Røgeri (☎ 62 52 40 07; Havnen 15; simple meals 20-66kr) Smokehouse adjacent to the harbour serves inexpensive smoked fish and shrimp dishes.

ENERGETIC ISLANDERS

Renewable energy isn't just an eco-friendly buzzword on Ærø, it's a centuries-old tradition as the scores of old windmills dotting the island illustrate. In the latter half of the last century, however, interest in renewable energy resurfaced here and across Denmark as the green movement emerged, anti-nuclear sentiment grew and the 1970s oil shocks made everyone worry about energy.

The industrious and ingenious islanders of Ærø have been blazing a modern renewable energy trail for decades now. They have made big strides forward in taking the island towards energy self-sufficiency by experimenting with ever larger and more efficient wind turbines to produce electricity. At the same time solar energy farms (such as the one just outside Marstal, now the world's largest solar power station), together with a series of experimental biomass burning projects, provide heat for Ærø's homes in winter.

The dream of self-sufficiency is not an idle or a distant one. It's estimated that seven modern wind turbines will provide enough electricity to light and power the island and Ærø is half way there: three massive new 100m-tall modern windmills already produce 50% of the island's electricity as they swish their elegantly feather-like blades high above Rise Mark Beach. Look out for them at the southern tip of the island on the main road linking Marstal and Søby or stand beneath them by heading south off the main road at Dunkær.

Ærøskøbing Bageri (☎ 62 52 10 31; Vestergade 62; sandwiches 25kr) Serves takeaway sandwiches and yummy pastries.

Netto (🕒 Mon-Fri) Get your self-catering supplies from this supermarket right by the harbour.

MARSTAL

pop 2500

Marstal, at the eastern end of the island, is a modern, nautical town with a busy shipyard and marina. There's a reasonably good beach, half sandy and half rocky, on the southern side of town a 15-minute walk – about 800m – from the centre.

Marstal is quieter today than in its 19th-century heyday when it was one of the region's busiest harbours, with more than 300 merchant ships pulling into port annually. The sea was such an integral part of people's lives that even the gravestones at the seamen's church on Kirkestræde are engraved with maritime epitaphs, the most frequently quoted being 'Here lies Christen Hansen at anchor with his wife; he will not weigh until summoned by God'.

Information

Danske Bank (☎ 63 52 60 00; Prinsensgade 8) Located one block inland from the tourist office.

Marstal tourist office (☎ 62 53 19 60; www.arre.dk, in Danish; Havnegade 5; 🕒 10am-6pm Mon-Fri, 10.30am-1.30pm Sat, 9.30am-12.30pm Sun) A few minutes' walk south of the harbour.

Post office (☎ 63 21 68 68; Havnegade 1; 🕒 10am-5pm Mon-Fri, 10am-noon Sat)

Sights

The **Marstal Søfartsmuseum** (☎ 62 53 23 31; Prinsensgade 1; adult/child 40/10kr; 🕒 9am-8pm Jul, 9am-5pm Jun & Aug, 10am-4pm Mar & Sep) has an absorbing collection of nautical artefacts including ships' models and full-size boats.

Sleeping

Marstal Camping (☎ 63 52 63 69; Egehovedvej 1; camping per person 59kr; 🕒 Apr-late Oct) Behind the marina, this camping ground is 1km south of the harbour.

Danhostel Marstal (☎ 63 52 63 58; danhostel@marstal.dk; Færgestræde 29; dm 100kr, s/d 210/250kr; 🕒 May-Sep) Adequate if rather basic 82-bed hostel is central, only 500m south of the ferry harbour and within walking distance of restaurants and the beach.

Hotel Marstal (☎ 62 53 13 52; www.hotelmarstal.dk, in Danish; Dronningestræde 1A; s/d 675/775kr, with shared bathroom 375/500kr) Near the harbour, this family-run place has inexpensive basic rooms in the old building and bright, modern, appealing en suite ones in the new annexe.

Eating

At the ferry harbour there's a small food shop and a grill restaurant serving inexpensive burgers, pizzas and other simple eats.

Hotel Marstal (☎ 62 53 13 52; Dronninge-stræde 1A; dinner mains 130-180kr) Substance rather than subtlety is the watchword here. The food is heavy and conventional with lots of steak and wiener schnitzel–style mains.

Super Brugsen (☎ 62 53 17 80; cnr Kirke-stræde & Skovgyden) Grocery shop, about 300m west of the ferry harbour.

STORE RISE

The village of Store Rise, in the middle of the island, has an attractive medieval **church**, though much of the current structure is from the 17th century. The churchyard is surrounded by a medieval circular wall and contains graves separated from each other by hedges. The church interior has an ornately carved Gothic altar. .

In a field behind the church is **Tingstedet**, a 54m-long Neolithic passage grave at least 5000 years old. The cup-like markings in the largest stone indicate that the grave may have belonged to a fertility cult. A footpath is marked from the church.

A couple of kilometres south of the village is **Risemark Strand**, the best of Ærø's few sandy beaches.

SØBY

pop 900

The shipyard at Søby (the island's biggest employer) dominates the town, which harbours a sizable fishing fleet and a popular marina. It's a pleasant enough place with some thatched houses, but the town doesn't pack the same charm as Ærøskøbing and most of its visitors are yachting folk.

Tourist office (☎ 62 58 13 00; www.arre.dk, in Danish; 🕑 9.30am-3.30pm Mon-Fri, 9.30am-2pm Sat Jun-Aug) is located at the harbour.

Sights & Activities

Five kilometres from Søby, at Ærø's northern most tip, is **Skjoldnæs Fyr**, a 19th-century, granite-block lighthouse with a narrow stairway; you can climb the lighthouse for a fine view of the sea. A few minutes' walk beyond the lighthouse is a pebble beach.

Along the main cross-island road, roughly 3km south of Søby, you'll see **Søby Volde**, the mounded-over earthen ramparts that were once part of a 12th-century fortress.

Sleeping & Eating

Søby Camping (☎ 62 58 14 70; sobycam@image.dk; Vitsø 10; camping per person 50kr; 🕑 all year) A small two-star facility about 1km west of town.

Søby Kro (☎ 62 58 10 06, 26 34 10 06; Østerbro 2; s/d with shared bathroom 225/395kr) Good fresh-fish dinners for 110kr are served at this small inn, in the centre of town three blocks south of the harbour .

There are a couple of fast-food kiosks near the harbour and a bakery 200m south of the harbour at Nørrebro 2.

GETTING THERE & AWAY

Det Ærøske Færgetrafikselskab (☎ 62 52 40 00; info@aeroe-ferry.dk) runs year-round car ferries to Søby from Faaborg, to Ærøskøbing from Svendborg and to Marstal from Rudkøbing. All run about five times a day, take about an hour and cost 81/43kr per adult/child, 22kr per bike and 179kr per car. If you have a car it's a good idea to make reservations, particularly at weekends and in July and August.

There's also a **ferry** (☎ 62 58 17 17; aero.als@get2net.dk) between Søby and Mommark that runs a few times daily from April to September, but much less frequently during the rest of the year. The trip takes one hour and costs 77kr for adults, 35kr for children, 20kr per bicycle and 350kr per car.

GETTING AROUND

Bicycle

CYCLE ROUTES

Cycling is a great way to enjoy Ærø, with three well-signposted cycle routes to follow. Cycle Route 91 begins at Marstal and continues along the southern side of the island up to Søby, while cycle Route 90 runs along the northern side of the island from Søby to Ærøskøbing and continues as Route 92 from Ærøskøbing to Marstal. The entire route would be about 60km. Ærø's tourist offices sell an inexpensive English-language cycling map of the island, listing sights along the routes.

RENTAL

You can **rent bikes** for 45kr per day at the **hostel** and **camping ground** in Ærøskøbing and at **Pilebækkens Cykel og Servicestation** (☎ 62 52 11 10; Pilebækken 11) opposite the car park on the outskirts of the town. In Marstal, **Nørremarks Cykelforretning** (☎ 62 53 14 77; Møllevejen 77) rents out bikes (45kr per day) from a stand at the harbour car park between 10am and 11am each morning. **Søby Cykelforretning** (☎ 62 58 18 42; Langebro 4) rents out bikes in Søby. The tourist office in Marstal sells a 20kr cycling map of a round-island route.

Bus

Fyns Amt (☎ 63 11 22 33) operates bus service No 990 from Marstal to Søby via Ærøskøbing. It runs hourly from 5.30am to 7.30pm on weekdays. Weekend buses are about half as frequent, with the first bus leaving Marstal at 8.30am. It takes about an hour to get from one end of the island to the other. Fares range from 12kr to 27kr, depending on the distance. A pass for unlimited one-day travel costs 50/25kr for adults/children.

Car

Cars can be rented at the harbourside **Q8 petrol station** (☎ 62 53 18 55) in Marstal.

Southern Jutland

CONTENTS

Southern Jutland offers visitors a host of fascinating insights into both past and present Denmark. Historically, attractions down here range from the lovingly restored old town of Ribe to Sønderborg, with its war-torn past. Visually, the west is covered in marshland and moors, while the east features deep fjords and rolling green fields. Economically, the area is industry-based – the harbour town Esbjerg is the centre for Denmark's North Sea oil activities as well as its largest fishing port.

Southern Jutland is the only part of Denmark connected to mainland Europe and the boundary has long been the subject of bitter conflict. Most notable was the 1864 Battle of Dybbøl, when German forces took control of the region with a devastating bombardment of Sønderborg. The current border dates from 1920, when Germany returned part of the Schleswig region to Denmark following a postwar referendum on self-determination.

Ribe is the standout spot of the south – its crooked, cobblestone streets, half-timbered buildings and imposing church charm some 1.5 million visitors each year. Also in the south are Crown Prince Frederik and Crown Princess Mary's majestic residence in Gråsten, and the castle of Prince Joachim and his family in Møgeltønder. Both have extravagant gardens.

Kolding, at the region's northeastern tip, has a magnificent castle and modern art museum that capture the imagination of curious travellers.

Unique to the south is the word *mojn*, which is used as 'hello', 'goodbye' and anything in between. Locals love the term and you can use it to put them at ease.

HIGHLIGHTS

- Step back in time in **Ribe** (p218), Denmark's oldest and best-preserved town
- Take a stroll around **Møgeltønder** (p229) and explore its lavish church
- Tour **Sønderborg** (p234) with its seaside castle and battlefield sites from 1864
- Take in the edgy and stylish ambience of **Kolding** (p230)
- Horse ride along one of the expansive beaches of **Rømø** (p225)

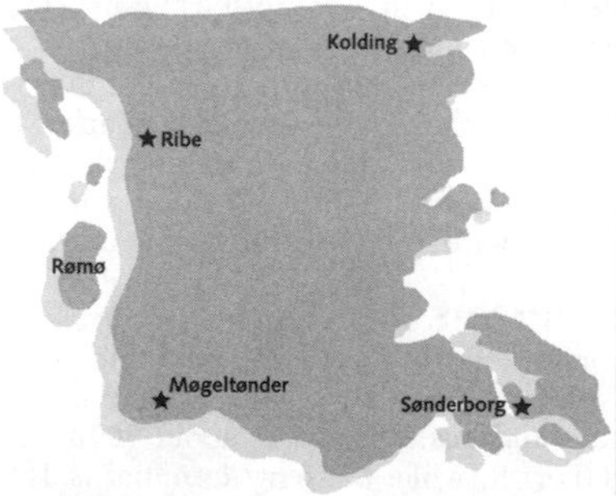
Kolding
Ribe
Rømø
Møgeltønder
Sønderborg

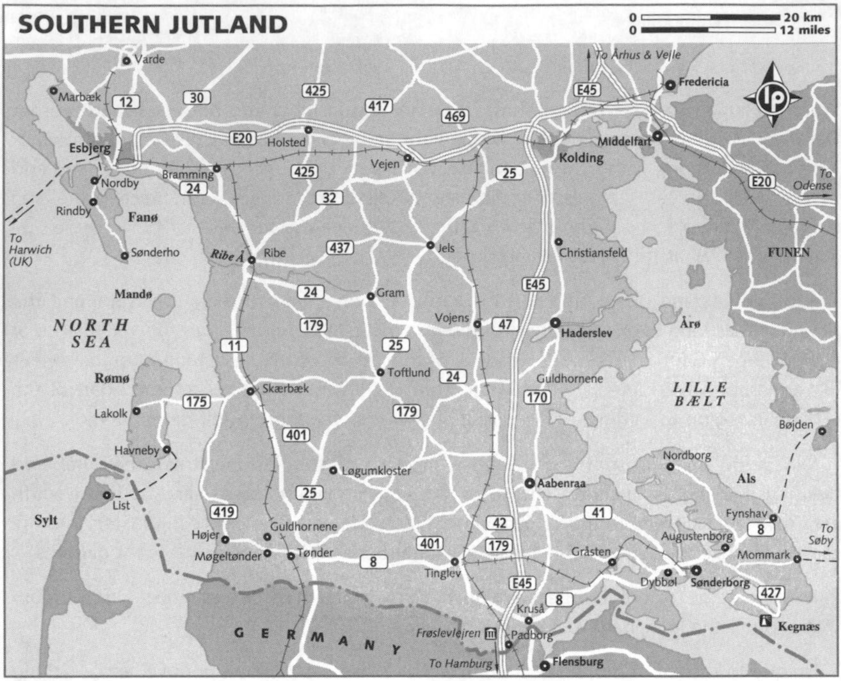
SOUTHERN JUTLAND
0 20 km
0 12 miles
Varde
Marbæk
Esbjerg
Nordby
Rindby
Fanø
To Harwich (UK)
Sønderho
Mandø
NORTH SEA
Rømø
Lakolk
Havneby
List
Sylt
Bramming
Holsted
Vejen
Ribe Å
Ribe
Jels
Gram
Vojens
Toftlund
Skærbæk
Løgumkloster
Guldhornene
Højer
Møgeltønder
Tønder
Tinglev
Kruså
Padborg
Frøslevlejren
To Hamburg
Flensburg
GERMANY
To Århus & Vejle
Fredericia
Middelfart
Kolding
To Odense
FUNEN
Christiansfeld
Haderslev
Årø
Guldhornene
LILLE BÆLT
Bøjden
Nordborg
Als
Fynshav
To Søby
Augustenborg
Mommark
Aabenraa
Gråsten
Dybbøl
Sønderborg
Kegnæs
E20
E45
12
30
425
417
469
24
32
437
179
25
11
175
401
419
8
47
170
42
41
427

ESBJERG

pop 83,000

Esbjerg is both Denmark's youngest city and largest port. It is also the hub of Denmark's North Sea oil activities. The visitor is greeted with an overwhelming odour of fish, and by the sight of heavy industrial plants. Historically, Esbjerg owes its existence to the German invasion of Schleswig and Holstein in 1864, which forced Danish farmers to find another harbour from which to export goods to Britain. Thus, in 1868, the city of Esbjerg was created and has since developed into a key industrial centre. With its grid layout, the town lacks the atmosphere afforded by the medieval quarters in Jutlands' tourist meccas. So travellers are inclined to transit Esbjerg, to or from the UK, rather than invest much time here.

Orientation

Torvet, the city square, can be found where Skolegade and Torvegade intersect. The train and bus stations are about 300m east of Torvet, while the ferry terminal is 1km to the south.

Information

Danske Bank (☎ 79 15 72 00; Torvet 18)
Esbjerg Turistbureau (☎ 75 15 55 99; www.visitesbjerg.com in Danish; Skolegade 33; 🕑 9am-5pm Mon-Fri, 9.30am-2.30pm Sat mid-Jun–Aug, 10am-5pm Mon-Fri, 10am-1pm Sat Sep–mid-Jun) On the corner of the main square, Torvet; tourist information and Internet access.
Krone Apoteket (☎ 75 12 92 11; Kongensgade 36) Pharmacy open 24 hours.
Nordea (☎ 79 12 60 00; Kongensgade 48) Bank.
Post office (☎ 79 12 12 12; Torvet 20)

Sights

ESBJERG KUNSTMUSEUM

There's an eye-opening modern art collection at **Esbjerg Kunstmuseum** (Esbjerg Art Museum; ☎ 75 13 02 11; Havnegade 20; adult/child 40kr/free; 🕑 10am-4pm) with notable works by Richard Mortensen, Robert Jacobsen and Per Kirkeby. It has a pretty comprehensive collection from the Cobra (Copenhagen–Brussels–Amsterdam) movement of the 20th century.

ESBJERG VANDTÅRN

Esbjerg attempted to manufacture a medieval appearance in 1897 when town architect

CH Clausen built **Esbjerg Vandtårn** (Esbjerg Water Tower; ☎ 75 12 78 11; Havnegade 22; adult/child 15/5kr; 🕑 10am-4pm daily Jun–mid-Sep, 10am-4pm Sat & Sun mid-Sep–May), an impressive and successful project. You can climb up the tower and look out over the sweeping harbour and the new-looking 'old' town.

FISKERI-OG SØFARTSMUSEET

For an up close and personal look at North Sea marine life head 4km northwest of the city centre to the 25-tank aquarium at **Fiskeri-og Søfartsmuseet** (Museum of Fishing & Shipping; ☎ 76 12 20 00; Tarphagevej; adult/child 75/35kr; 🕑 10am-6pm Jul & Aug, 10am-5pm Sep-Jun), where you'll see seals, sharks and other big fish getting along swimmingly. The seals are fed at 11am and 2.30pm daily. The aquarium can be reached by bus Nos 1 and 8.

MENNESKET VED HAVET

On the waterfront opposite the aquarium is Esbjerg's newest landmark, **Mennesket ved Havet** (Man Meets the Sea), comprising four stark-white, 9m-high, stylised human figures created by Danish sculptor Svend Wiig Hansen to commemorate the city's centennial. According to Wiig, the statues represent humans in their most innocent state – straight out of the womb – but as soon as they interact with society and get 'dirt' on their hands, however, it all goes horribly wrong. Strike a pose on their toes for a photo.

LIGHTSHIP

The old wooden **lightship** (☎ 21 62 11 04; adult/child 20/10kr; 🕑 10am-4pm Jun-Aug) moored at the fishing harbour is good fun to explore. See how sailors lived in the good old days.

Festivals & Events

Held throughout August every year, the **Esbjerg International Chamber Music Festival** (☎ 20 16 23 34; www.eicmf.dk in Danish) consists of chamber music concerts.

Sleeping

Staff at the tourist office can book **rooms** (per person B&B 180kr) in private homes, both in the city and in the surrounding countryside.

Danhostel Esbjerg (☎ 75 12 42 58; www.danhostel.dk/esbjerg; Gammel Vardevej 80; dm/d 118/400kr; P ⊠ 💻) Housed in a wonderful old folk high school it boasts compact, clean dorms and is 3km north of the city centre on bus No 4.

Ådalens Camping (☎ 75 15 88 22; www.adal.dk; Gudenåvej 20; per person 61kr; P) Well-decked-out camping ground 5km north of the city centre has crazy golf, modern facilities, a general store, TV room, barbecue, spa and good tent sites. Take bus No 1 or drive up Rte 447.

Hotel Britannia (☎ 75 13 01 11; www.britannia.dk; Torvet 24; s/d 800/900kr; P ⊠) Service is both professional and slick. 'Plush' hotel down by the harbour plans to double in size over the next couple of years. Rooms are light, modern and cosy.

Palads Cab Inn Esbjerg (☎ 75 18 16 00; www.cabinn.dk; Skolegade 14; s/d 510/630kr; P ⊠) The idea behind this new hotel group is copied from cabins of passenger ships. It's the best-value hotel in town. It occupies an attractive century-old building that has been thoroughly renovated. The 82 modern rooms all have bathroom, cable TV and phone.

Hotel Ansgar (☎ 75 12 82 44; www.hotelansgar.dk, Skolegade 36; s/d 640/880kr; P) Centrally located hotel has comfy rooms equipped with TV, telephone and bath. With the filling breakfast it's a good deal.

Eating

Dronning Louise (☎ 75 13 13 44; Torvet 19; lunch 90kr, dinner 140kr; 🕑 lunch & dinner) Great outdoor and indoor dining is available here. Try the Esbjerg delight *bakskuld*, a salted, smoked dab – a fish not unlike a flounder – fried in butter, followed by *kaffepunch*, coffee with Danish schnapps. If that's all too much there's also a great variety of meat and fish dishes. From Wednesday to Sunday there is live music.

Papa's Cantina (☎ 75 13 08 00; Torvet 17; steaks from 150kr, tacos 80kr; 🕑 dinner) Mexican tacos and Argentinean steaks are all the rage here and the restaurant is decked out in true Latino fashion – an enjoyable dining experience.

Restaurant hos Ingeborg (☎ 75 12 00 78; Kongensgade 22; mains 80kr; 🕑 lunch & dinner) A popular place for lunch serving traditional Danish fare in a cosy environment.

Sand's (☎ 75 12 02 07; Skolegade 60; lunch 100kr, dinner 140kr; 🕑 lunch & dinner) If you want to sample regional specialties that are predominately seafood-based in a tremendously lively setting, this place was made for you.

Baker Street (☎ 75 13 41 07; Kongensgade 25; sandwiches 25kr; 🕑 lunch) Big, mouthwatering

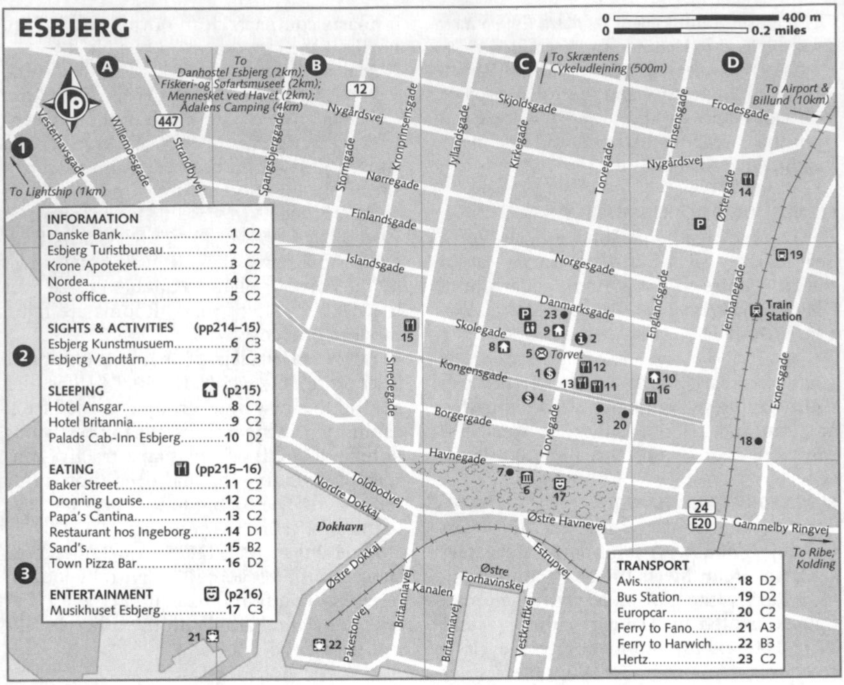
ESBJERG
0 400 m
0 0.2 miles
A
B
C
D
1
2
3
To Danhostel Esbjerg (2km); Fiskeri-og Søfartsmuseet (2km); Mennesket ved Havet (2km); Ådalens Camping (4km)
To Skræntens Cykeludlejning (500m)
To Airport & Billund (10km)
To Lightship (1km)
To Ribe; Kolding
12
447
24
E20
Vesterhavsgade
Willemoesgade
Strandbyvej
Spangsbjerggade
Stormgade
Kronprinsensgade
Nygårdsvej
Nørregade
Finlandsgade
Islandsgade
Jyllandsgade
Kirkegade
Skjoldsgade
Torvegade
Finsensgade
Frodesgade
Østergade
Norgesgade
Danmarksgade
Englandsgade
Jernbanegade
Skolegade
Kongensgade
Torvet
Borgergade
Smedegade
Havnegade
Exnersgade
Toldbodvej
Nordre Dokkaj
Dokhavn
Østre Havnevej
Gammelby Ringvej
Estrupvej
Østre Forhavinskej
Østre Dokkaj
Kanalen
Britanniavej
Pakestonvej
Vestkraftkej
Train Station
INFORMATION
Danske Bank 1 C2
Esbjerg Turistbureau 2 C2
Krone Apoteket 3 C2
Nordea 4 C2
Post office 5 C2
SIGHTS & ACTIVITIES (pp214–15)
Esbjerg Kunstmusuem 6 C3
Esbjerg Vandtårn 7 C3
SLEEPING (p215)
Hotel Ansgar 8 C2
Hotel Britannia 9 C2
Palads Cab-Inn Esbjerg 10 D2
EATING (pp215–16)
Baker Street 11 C2
Dronning Louise 12 C2
Papa's Cantina 13 C2
Restaurant hos Ingeborg 14 D1
Sand's 15 B2
Town Pizza Bar 16 D2
ENTERTAINMENT (p216)
Musikhuset Esbjerg 17 C3
TRANSPORT
Avis 18 D2
Bus Station 19 D2
Europcar 20 C2
Ferry to Fano 21 A3
Ferry to Harwich 22 B3
Hertz 23 C2

sandwiches on wonderfully crispy bread are a speciality at this bakery-café.

Town Pizza Bar (☎ 75 13 00 52; Kongensgade 9B; pizza slice 20kr; ⏰ lunch & dinner) Tiny pizzeria is a local favourite and serves giant slices of tasty pizza that are a meal in themselves.

Entertainment

Musikhuset Esbjerg (☎ 76 10 90 10; Havnegade 18) Famed Danish architect Jørn Utzon designed this performing arts centre, the city's main venue for classical music concerts.

Getting There & Away

Ryan Air provides inexpensive air services daily between London and Esbjerg (see p308).

For details of ferry services to the UK see the Transport chapter (p308). For information on boats leaving for Fanø, see p218.

Express bus No 980 leaves for Frederikshavn twice per day (280kr). Call ☎ 98 90 09 00 for more information.

Esbjerg is 77km northwest of Tønder, 59km southwest of Billund and 92km west of the Funen–Jutland bridge. If you're driving into Esbjerg, the E20 (the main expressway from the east) leads directly into the heart of the city and down to the ferry harbour. If you're coming from the south, Rte 24 merges with the E20 on the outskirts of the city. From the north, Rte 12 makes a beeline for the city, ending at the harbour.

All the major car rental agencies are in town including **Avis** (☎ 75 13 44 77; Exnersgade 19), **Europcar** (☎ 75 12 38 93; Jernbanegade 56-58) and **Hertz** (☎ 76 13 85 20; Storegade 246). They have booths at the airport although advance reservations are required.

Trains run hourly between Copenhagen and Esbjerg (287kr, 3¼ hrs) during the day. There's also a train service that runs north to Struer (233kr, three hours); south to Ribe (60kr, 35 minutes) and Tønder (84kr, 1½ hours); and east to Kolding (75kr, 55 minutes).

Getting Around

The airport is 10km east of the city centre. Public bus No 9 (17kr) runs about once an hour between the airport and the train station.

Bikes can be hired from **Skræntens Cykeludlejning** (☎ 75 45 75 05; cnr Skrænten & Kirkegade; per day 75kr). The tourist office has free English-language brochures detailing suggested cycling tours.

Most city buses can be boarded at the train station (1/10 rides 17/85kr).

There's free central parking with a two-hour limit west of Hotel Britannia (enter from Danmarksgade), and free parking with no time limit at the car park on Nørregade east of the library.

MARBÆK

Great for walking and even better for plant and wildlife enthusiasts is this area 12km north of Esbjerg. A little over 1200 hectares, it has many colour-coded walking tracks, such as the red track (5km, 1¼ hours) that starts at Hjerting and winds its way through the woodland. It's a rich area for wildlife – foxes, deer, rabbits, pheasants and hawks all call it home. There is also a wide variety of tree species in the woodland section that takes up about a third of the park. To get there drive north along Rte 475, turn left at Hjerting and continue on to Marbækgaard.

FANØ

pop 3400

A charmingly intimate island off the west coast, Fanø features heath land, windswept sand dunes and interesting wildlife. Accessible from Esbjerg, it makes for a great day trip. Beachgoers are blessed with wide, welcoming strips of quality sand on the exposed west coast, while historically minded visitors can explore the old sailor villages at each end of the island, Nordby and Sønderho. The howling westerly presents good windsurfing options on the waves south of Rindby Strand – you'll need to bring your own equipment.

Orientation

The villages of Sønderho and Nordby, lie at each end of the island. The best beaches are around Rindby Strand and Fanø Bad. Further north is the vast sand spit that marks the northernmost tip, Søren Jessens Sand. A nature reserve, Fanø Klitplantage is spread across the middle of the island.

Information

Danske Bank (☎ 76 66 07 20; Hovedgaden 74, Nordby)

Fanø Turistbureau (☎ 75 16 26 00; fax 75 16 29 03; Færgevej 1; 🕒 8.30am-6pm Mon-Fri, 9am-5pm Sat & Sun mid-Jun–mid-Aug, 8.30am-5pm Mon-Fri, 9am-1pm Sat 11am-1pm Sun rest of year) At the ferry harbour in Nordby.

Library (☎ 75 16 22 30; Niels Engersvej 5A) Internet access free.

Post office (☎ 75 16 20 18; Hovedgaden 15, Nordby)

Sights

Fanø's rich maritime history (see p218) is on display at **Fanø Skibsfarts-og Dragtsamling** (☎ 75 16 22 72; Hovedgaden 28; admission 15kr), 200m west of the tourist office in Nordby. Models of Fanø's proud fleet, local costumes and photos relating to Fanø's golden age make up this interesting museum.

Fanø Museum (☎ 75 16 61 37; Skolevej 2; admission 15kr), is housed in a 300-year-old building. As well as an impressive collection of period furniture there is an interesting array of sailors' mementoes. The museum is 300m east of Fanø Skibsfarts-og Dragtsamling

In Sønder, the 18th century **Sønderho Kirke** (☎ 75 16 40 32; Sønderho Strandvej 1) has the distinction of having the most votive ships of any church in Denmark – 15 in all. For art enthusiasts, **Fanø Kunstmuseum** (☎ 75 16 40 44; Nordland 5; admission 25kr) features paintings of Fanø. **Hannes Hus** (☎ 75 16 41 71; Øster Land 7; admission 12kr) is a 17th-century sea captain's home complete with décor from the period.

Activities

Fanø Golf Links (☎ 76 66 00 44; Golfvejen 5, Fanø Bad; 18 holes 300kr) is the only links course in Denmark and when the wind is up it gives Scotland's St Andrews a run for its high scores.

Wildlife watchers and nature lovers will feel at home in the centre of the island where 1162 hectares make up **Fanø Klitplantage**. Take to the walking tracks and you'll find birds, deer and rabbits in abundance.

Festivals & Events

The second week of July sees the town celebrate its maritime golden age Fannikerdage Festival - a folk festival with traditional costumes and shipping festivities.

Sleeping

There are nine camping grounds on Fanø, most of which have cabins for rent in addition to the usual tent and caravan sites.

For information on booking **summer holiday flats** (per wk 3000-5000kr), which typically sleep four to six people, contact the tourist office.

Tempo Camping (☎ 75 16 22 51; fax 75 16 12 51; Strandvejen 34, Nordby; 🕑 mid-May–mid-Sep; per person 55kr; P) Complete with a mini-market and plenty of tree cover, this is a good option 1km north of Nordby.

Feldberg Strand Camping (☎ 75 16 24 90; fax 75 16 33 33; Rindby Strand; 🕑 mid-Apr–mid-Oct; per person 61kr; P) A stone's throw from the beach, it gets very busy during the warmer months.

Fanø Krogaard (☎ 75 16 20 52; www.fanokrogaard.dk; Langelinie 11, Nordby; s/d 695/795kr; P) In operation since 1624, this charming option near the waterfront in Nordby has cosy rooms and an intimate atmosphere.

Sønderho Kro (☎ 75 16 40 09; sonderhokro@mail.dk; Kropladsen 11, Sønderho; s/d 760/960kr; P) Housed in a 1722 thatched-roof building, this rather delightful place has classy service, lovely old-fashioned rooms and great food is served downstairs

Eating

Bakeries and cafés abound in Nordby, Fanø Bad and Sønderho.

NORDBY

Fanø Krogaard (☎ 75 16 20 52; Langelinie 11, Nordby; mains 140kr; 🕑 dinner) Pleasant dining option offers a predominantly Danish-influenced menu that focuses upon fresh local produce, from Fanø marsh lamb to seafood.

Nordby Kro (☎ 75 16 35 89; Strandvejen 12; mains 160kr; 🕑 lunch & dinner) Locally adored for its seafood dishes, it also has a diverse menu that should satisfy most tastes.

Aage's Pizza (☎ 75 16 11 22; Valdemarsvej 14; pizzas 55kr; 🕑 lunch & dinner) A stock-standard pizzeria that has large, tasty pizzas.

SØNDERHO

Sønderho Kro (☎ 75 16 40 09; Kropladsen 11; mains 230k, 3-course meal 330kr; 🕑 dinner) Smoked fish and succulent local lamb are used in creative dishes that merge French and Danish influences.

Kromann's Fisherestaurant (☎ 75 16 44 45; Kropladsen, Sønderho; mains 140kr; 🕑 lunch & dinner) A great array of fresh seafood including the local speciality *bakskuld*, a dried, smoked and fried fish dish.

Getting There & Away

Scandlines (☎ 33 15 15 15; return adult/child 30/15kr, bike/motorcycle/car 30/85/320kr) shuttles a car ferry between Nordby and Esbjerg two or three times hourly from 5am to midnight.

Getting Around

There's a local bus service from the ferry dock that runs about once an hour in summer, connecting Nordby with Fanø Bad (15kr), Rindby Strand (15kr) and Sønderho (20kr). The schedule is heavily reduced in winter.

Bicycles can be hired in Nordby from **Fanø Cykler** (☎ 75 16 25 13; Hovedgaden 96; per day 60kr).

RIBE

pop 8000

Ribe is Denmark's oldest town and with its magnificent 12th-century cathedral, adored storks and cobblestone streets, encapsulates the country's golden past in exquisite style. Such is the overwhelming sense of living history that the entire 'old town' has been designated as a preservation zone, with more than 100 buildings registered by the

A CUNNING DEAL

Until 1741 the island of Fanø was Crown property but when Christian VI, in the midst of grand construction projects across Denmark, found the royal coffers running dry he decided to sell it. He put the island up for auction, much to the chagrin of the Fanø natives, who were convinced that wealthy Ribe merchants would purchase it and impose hefty taxes.

According to one oft-told tale, on the eve of the auction Fanø's attractive young women lured would-be bidders to a night of drink and merriment and, while they were distracted, wound the men's watches back an hour. When the auction took place the next day at 8am, only a contingent of Fanø islanders and a single lord from Tønder appeared. The Tønder lord was forcibly squeezed behind a door by a crowd of men and the Fanø islanders put in the sole bid.

This bit of local lore aside, history does record that the Fanø islanders were able to piece together enough money to buy their island from the Crown. Along with the land, the deed also bestowed the right to own and build ships and in the next 150 years, nearly 1000 sailing vessels were constructed on Fanø. During that time it had the largest fleet outside of Copenhagen.

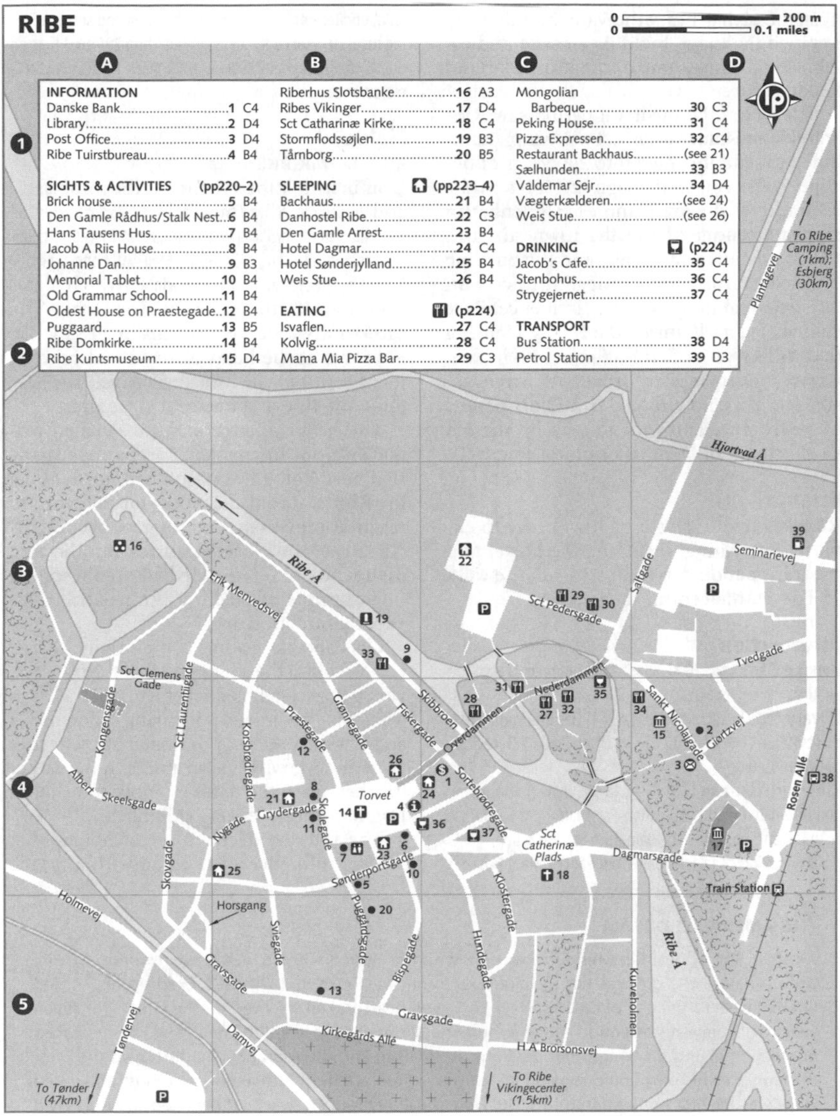
RIBE
0 200 m
0 0.1 miles
A
B
C
D
1
2
3
4
5
INFORMATION
Danske Bank.....1 C4
Library.....2 D4
Post Office.....3 D4
Ribe Tuirstbureau.....4 B4
SIGHTS & ACTIVITIES (pp220–2)
Brick house.....5 B4
Den Gamle Rådhus/Stalk Nest..6 B4
Hans Tausens Hus.....7 B4
Jacob A Riis House.....8 B4
Johanne Dan.....9 B3
Memorial Tablet.....10 B4
Old Grammar School.....11 B4
Oldest House on Praestegade..12 B4
Puggaard.....13 B5
Ribe Domkirke.....14 B4
Ribe Kuntsmuseum.....15 D4
Riberhus Slotsbanke.....16 A3
Ribes Vikinger.....17 D4
Sct Catharinæ Kirke.....18 C4
Stormflodssøjlen.....19 B3
Tårnborg.....20 B5
SLEEPING (pp223–4)
Backhaus.....21 B4
Danhostel Ribe.....22 C3
Den Gamle Arrest.....23 B4
Hotel Dagmar.....24 C4
Hotel Sønderjylland.....25 B4
Weis Stue.....26 B4
EATING (p224)
Isvaflen.....27 C4
Kolvig.....28 C4
Mama Mia Pizza Bar.....29 C3
Mongolian Barbeque.....30 C3
Peking House.....31 C4
Pizza Expressen.....32 C4
Restaurant Backhaus.....(see 21)
Sælhunden.....33 B3
Valdemar Sejr.....34 D4
Vægterkælderen.....(see 24)
Weis Stue.....(see 26)
DRINKING (p224)
Jacob's Cafe.....35 C4
Stenbohus.....36 C4
Strygejernet.....37 C4
TRANSPORT
Bus Station.....38 D4
Petrol Station.....39 D3
To Ribe Camping (1km); Esbjerg (30km)
Plantagevej
Hjortvad Å
Ribe Å
Erik Menvedsvej
Seminarievej
Saltgade
Sct Pedersgade
Tvedgade
Sct Clemens Gade
Sct Laurentiigade
Kongensgade
Korsbrødregade
Præstegade
Grønnegade
Fiskergade
Skibbroen
Overdammen
Nederdammen
Sankt Nicolajgade
Gl0rtzvej
Rosen Allé
Albert Skeelsgade
Torvet
Grydergade
Skolegade
Nygade
Sortebrødregade
Sct Catherinæ Plads
Dagmarsgade
Train Station
Skovgade
Sønderportsgade
Horsgang
Holmevej
Puggårdsgade
Sviegade
Bispegade
Klostergade
Hundegade
Kurveholmen
Gravsgade
Kirkegårds Allé
H A Brorsonsvej
Tøndervej
Damvej
To Tønder (47km)
To Ribe Vikingecenter (1.5km)

National Trust. In a word, Ribe is a must for any visitor to Denmark.

History

Founded around 700, Ribe evolved into a key post of the hailed Viking era. It began when the Apostle of the North, Ansgar, was given a parcel of land by the Danish king around 860 and permission to erect a church. It's not known when the church was built. The earliest record of the existence of a bishop in Ribe is 948 – and bishops have cathedrals. During the Viking era, Ribe, linked to the sea by its river, flourished as a centre of trade between the Frankish empire and the Scandinavian states to the north.

In the 12th century the Valdemar dynasty fortified the town, building a castle and establishing Ribe as one of the king's Jutland residences.

The end of the medieval period saw Ribe enter its most torrid time. Two factors combined to send the town into 250 years of decline. A fire ripped through in 1580 and the relocation of the royal family to Copenhagen saw royal money leave the town. In turn the population diminished, and the bustling trade port turned into a struggling town with little regional importance or influence. Ribe re-invented itself during the 1800's realising that its lack of modernisation could, in fact, attract tourists in their droves. A correct assumption, as nowadays 1.5 million people come from far and wide to soak up the old world charm of Denmark's oldest town.

Orientation

Ribe is a tightly clustered town, easy to explore. Everything, including the hostel and the train station, is within a 10-minute walk of Torvet, the central square.

Information

Danske Bank (☎ 76 88 68 20; Overdammen 4) Has an ATM.
Library (☎ 75 12 17 00; Giørtzvej 1) Has Internet access.
Post office (☎ 79 12 12 12; Sct Nicolajgade 12) Next to the art museum.
Ribe Turistbureau (☎ 75 42 15 00; www.ribetourist.dk; Torvet 3; 9am-6pm Mon-Fri, 10am-5pm Sat Jul & Aug, 9am-5pm Mon-Fri, 10am-1pm Sat Jun & Sep, 9.30am-4.30pm Mon-Fri, 10am-1pm Sat Oct-May) Has an abundance of information on the town and surrounding areas. It offers a Ribe Pass (adult/child 20/10kr) that grants the holder a 20% discount at many museums and restaurants.

Sights

RIBE DOMKIRKE

Dominating Ribe's skyline is the impressive and historic **Ribe Cathedral** (☎ 75 42 06 19; Torvet; adult/child 12/5kr; 10am-5.30pm Mon-Sat, noon-5.30pm Sun Jul & Aug, 10am-5pm Mon-Sat, noon-5pm Sun May, Jun & Sep, reduced hrs in winter) which dates back to 948, the oldest in Denmark. The cathedral was largely rebuilt in 1150 when Ribe was at the heart of royal and government money which in turn paved the way for some fine architectural structures.

The new cathedral was constructed primarily from tufa, a soft porous rock quarried near Cologne and shipped north along the Rhine. It took a century for the work to reach completion. The later additions included several Gothic features, but the core of the cathedral is decidedly Romanesque, a fine example of medieval Rhineland influences in architecture.

One notable feature is the original 'Cat's Head' door at the south portal of the transept, which boasts detailed relief work including a triangular pediment portraying Valdemar II and Queen Dagmar positioned at the feet of Jesus and Mary. At noon and 3pm the cathedral bell plays the notes to a folk song about Dagmar's death during childbirth.

The interior décor is a real hotchpotch of later influences. An organ with a façade

THE AMERICAN DREAM

Jacob A Riis, a local Ribe resident, was 21 when he lost his heart to the town's prettiest girl. Unfortunately, the girl was not as taken by young Jacob, so in 1870 he packed up his kit and headed west to the city of dreams, New York. Still heartbroken, he lived on the streets for seven years. This drew his attention to the inhumane slums that so many beaten New Yorkers called home. Combining his two potent passions, journalism and photography, he portrayed the poor through a series of graphic, moving slides that jolted a nation into action. His most acclaimed work was his first book printed in 1890, *How the Other Half Lives,* which depicted through vivid photographs and profound words the hopeless situation many immigrants faced in New York City during the late 19th century. Through such words, Riis, and close associate Theodore Roosevelt (later the USA's 26th president) helped clear the slums.

He was offered the post as Mayor of New York but turned it down to pursue matters closer to the heart. Having directly helped well over a million people off the streets, he returned to Ribe to woo and marry the love of his life – completing the fairytale in true Danish style. After his death in 1914 he was known as 'New York's most beneficial citizen'. You can walk past his former residence in Ribe on Skolegade (p223).

SEPULCHRAL MONUMENTS

In the Renaissance period, arranging for burial inside Ribe Domkirke became fashionable among those wealthy enough to buy the floor space. Most of these graves are marked by simple carved stones in the aisles, but there are also some more ostentatious memorials and chapels containing the remains of bishops and other distinguished citizens of the day. The highest-ranked bones within the confines of the cathedral are those of King Christopher I, who was buried in 1259 directly beneath the great dome in the middle of the sanctuary.

designed by renowned 17th-century sculptor Jens Olufsen and an ornate altar created in 1597 by Odense sculptor Jens Asmussen. You can find frescoes dating from the 16th century along the northern side of the cathedral, while in the apse are modern-day frescoes, stained-glass windows and seven mosaics created in the 1980s by artist Carl-Henning Pedersen.

For a towering view over the countryside, climb the 248 steps (52m) up the cathedral tower, which dates back to 1333. A survey of the surrounding marshland makes it easy to understand why the tower once doubled as a lookout station for floods.

SANKT CATHARINÆ KIRKE

Founded by Spanish Black Friars in 1228, **St Catharine's Church** (☎ 75 42 05 34; Sankt Catharinæ Plads; admission free; 10am-noon & 2-5pm May-Sep, 10am-noon & 2-4pm Oct-Apr) was originally built on reclaimed marshland, but this structure eventually collapsed. The present structure dates from the 15th century. Of the 13 churches built during the pre-Reformation period in Ribe, Sankt Catharinæ Kirke and Ribe Domkirke are the only survivors.

In 1536 the Reformation forced the friars to abandon Sankt Catharinæ Kirke and, in the years that followed, the compound served as an asylum for the mentally ill and a wartime field hospital, to name but a few incarnations. Currently, the abbey provides housing for the elderly.

In the 1920s Sankt Catharinæ Kirke was restored at tremendous cost (due to its still-faulty foundations) and was reconsecrated in 1934. The interior boasts a delicately carved pulpit dating from 1591 and an ornate altarpiece created in 1650.

DEN GAMLE RÅDHUS

First-timers may be bemused to see locals staring inquisitively at the **town hall** (☎ 76 88 11 22; Von Støckens Plads; adult/child 15/5kr; 1-3pm Mon-Fri May & Sep, 1-3pm daily Jun-Aug). Put simply, they're bird-watching, or more precisely have been caught up in the 'stork culture' this town cherishes and they are catching a glimpse of the nesting site (see the boxed text below). This is the oldest town hall (1496) in Denmark and is still used as a courthouse – as well as housing a small collection of historical artefacts, such as medieval weapons and the executioner's axe.

RIBE KUNSTMUSEUM

An undeniable benefit of being the oldest town in the land is the opportunity to amass a superb art collection, and **Ribe Kunstmuseum** (☎ 75 42 03 62; Sct Nicolajgade 10; adult/child 35kr/free; 11am-5pm Tue-Sun Jul/Aug, 11am-4pm Tue-Sun Feb-Jun & Sep-Dec) has been able to acquire some of Denmark's best works, including the works of the 19th-century Golden Age painters. The singing birds outside present a glorious backdrop to classics such as LA Schou's 1866 masterpiece *Chione Killed while Hunting the Offended Diana*. The collection also boasts pieces by Juel, Abildgaard, Eckersberg, Købke and Michael Ancher.

RIBES VIKINGER

An insightful and informative presentation is the **Vikings of Ribe** (☎ 77 88 11 22; Odin Plads 1; adult/child 50/20kr; 10am-6pm, Wed till 9pm Jul & Aug, 10am-4pm Sep-Jun) which takes you through Ribe's Viking and medieval history.

STORK WATCH

A look at the top of Den Gamle Rådhus in Ribe will reward you with the rare sight of a large, round nest built of sticks and spanning a couple of metres in diameter. Each year around 1 April a pair of storks return to this nest. Ribe residents enthusiastically follow the comings and goings of these great birds and even have a little ceremony on the first Thursday after the birds return. If you chance upon this ceremony while in Ribe, you're sure to be intrigued.

Two thoughtful rooms that bring the past to the present provide snapshots of the town in AD 800, and during medieval times in 1500. These portrayals are complemented by rare archaeological finds, which add real substance to the tales. This Viking experience finishes with a thought-provoking video of the legendary Viking era.

RIBE VIKINGECENTER

The **Ribe Vikingecenter** (☎ 75 41 16 11; Lustrupvej 4; adult/child 60/30kr; 🕑 10am-3.30pm Mon-Fri, falconer show 12.30pm May, Jun & Sep, 11am-5pm, falconer show 1pm & 4pm Jul & Aug) is more hands-on than the museum. It attempts to re-create a slice of life in Viking-era Ribe using various reconstructions, including a 34m Fyrkat-style longhouse. The staff, dressed in period clothing, bake bread over open fires, demonstrate Viking-era crafts, such as pottery and leatherwork, and offer falconry demonstrations. All of which you can actively partake in. The centre is 2km south of the town centre.

Riberhus Slotsbanke

One kilometre northwest of the town centre is **Riberhus Slotsbanke**, the moated site of a former 12th-century royal castle; it served as a fort until the 17th century and was then dismantled for its stones. In the southwestern corner of the grounds is a statue of Queen Dagmar.

Walking Tour

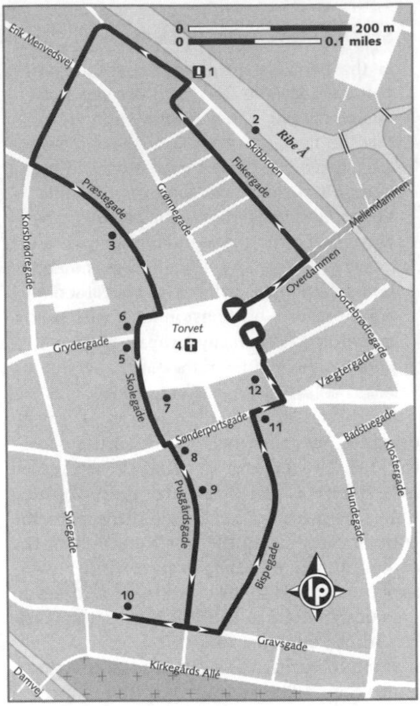
0 200 m
0 0.1 miles
Erik Menvedsvej
Ribe Å
Skibbroen
Fiskergade
Grønnegade
Præstegade
Korsbrødregade
Mellemdammen
Overdammen
Sortebrødregade
Torvet
Grydergade
Skolegade
Vægtergade
Sønderportsgade
Badstuegade
Klostergade
Puggårdsgade
Sviegade
Hundegade
Bispegade
Gravsgade
Kirkegårds Allé
Damvej
1
2
3
4
5
6
7
8
9
10
11
12

You can visit central Ribe's historic sights on a leisurely looped walk at a pace that takes a couple of hours. For more detail, drop by the tourist office and grab a copy of the walking guide (5kr).

The walk begins at Torvet and follows Overdammen east to Fiskergade, where you turn left. On Fiskergade you'll notice many alleys leading east to the riverfront. Take a look at the 'bumper' stones on the house corners; the alleys are so narrow that the original residents installed these stones to protect their houses from being scraped by the wheels of horse-drawn carriages.

At the intersection of Fiskergade and Skibbroen you'll come across **Stormflodssøjlen (1)**, a wooden flood column commemorating the numerous floods that have swept over Ribe. The ring at the top of the column indicates the water's depth during the record flood of 1634 (6m above normal!), which claimed hundreds of lives. Although these days a system of dykes affords low-lying Ribe somewhat more protection, residents are still subject to periodic flood evacuations.

At Stormflodssøjlen, look southeast along the waterfront and you'll spot **Johannes Dan (2)**, a replica of an 1867 sailing ship designed with a flat bottom that allowed it to navigate through the shallow waters of the Ribe Å; it's occasionally open in summer for boarding.

Continue northwest along Skibbroen, which skirts the medieval quay, now lined with small motorboats.

From Skibbroen, turn south onto Korsbrødregade and head southeast along Præstegade. About halfway down on the right, you'll pass this street's **oldest house (3)**, constructed in 1580, as noted on the plaque above the door; it was once the residence of the cathedral curate. Continue back to **Ribe Domkirke (4**; p220), skirting around the cathedral's western side and onto Skolegade.

On the corner of Skolegade and Grydergade is an **old grammar school (5)** that first opened in the early 16th century. Next door is the former residence of **Jacob A Riis (6**; p220) with a plaque on the wall. On the opposite side of Skolegade is one of Denmark's oldest bishops' residences, the two-storey **Hans Tausens Hus (7)**, which dates from the early 17th century. A statue of Hans Tausen, who helped spark the Danish Reformation, stands in the churchyard opposite.

From Skolegade continue south on Puggårdsgade, a cobbled street lined with older homes. The timber-framed **brick house (8)** on the corner of Sønderportsgade and Puggårdsgade has an interesting 2nd storey that overhangs the road. A couple of buildings down on the left is a 16th-century privately owned manor house, **Tårnborg (9)**. On the same side of the street, but a little further south, is a half-timbered house dating back to 1550.

When you reach Gravsgade go right for about 50m and on the northern side of the street you'll discover the brick **Puggaard (10)**, a canon's residence constructed in about 1500. From there turn around and walk east on Gravsgade, then turn north onto Bispegade.

On the corner of Bispegade and Sønderportsgade you'll find a **memorial tablet (11)** dedicated to Maren Spliid, burned at the stake on 9 November 1641, the last victim of Denmark's witch-hunt persecutions.

From that corner continue north past **Den Gamle Rådhus** (the old town hall, **12**; p221) and back to your starting point on Torvet.

Tours

To get a taste of Ribe's strong hold on the past, meet at the town square at 10pm for the **Night Watchman Tour** (1 May-15 Sep; free) for a merry and somewhat intriguing walk in the past. It's said that Ribe is an untouched historical museum, and this tour illustrates it wonderfully. Interesting facts, Danish singing and colourful stories of memorable Ribe people are just part of the act. Throw in narrow streets, thatched houses and a glorious summer's night and it's a great way to end an historical day. The night watchman is not without his own slice of history. The first written reference to him came in the form of a murder report, after two night watchmen were killed by a drunkard in the streets of Ribe. The offender soon met with the same fate.

The **Ghost Walk** (tourist office sells tickets) shows Ribe in a whole new light. Listen out for the tales of the last lady to be burnt to death in Ribe – she was accused of witchcraft by a paranoid community and faced a terrible fate.

Festivals & Events

Every May the town is colourfully invaded by the **Tulip Festival** (info@tulipanfest.dk), which climaxes in a Tulip parade where hundreds of people decorate themselves in tulips and take to the streets.

Only a new addition on the Ribe events calendar but certainly set for a long innings, the **Jazz Festival** (www.ribejazz.dk) is something to savour. Swing by in late July to join the jazz bonanza.

Sleeping

The tourist office distributes an annually updated brochure listing some 20 private homes in and around Ribe that rent **rooms and apartments** (town s/d 200/350kr, apt 400kr; outskirts s/d 150/250kr apt 300kr). An option is to book a **themed holiday** (www.ribetourist.dk; 2-person 3-nights from 2200kr) based around Vikings, art or history.

Danhostel Ribe (☎ 75 42 06 20; www.danhostel.dk/ribe; Sct Pedersgade 16; 🕑 Feb-Nov; dm 120kr, s/d 270/300kr; P 💻 ⊠) Ideal location, energetic staff and state-of-the-art rooms makes this a fine establishment suited to both backpackers and families. It has table tennis and Internet access, rents out bikes, and is a stone's throw from Ribe's historic centre.

Ribe Camping (☎ 75 41 07 77; www.ribecamping.dk; Farupvej 2; 🕑 Apr-Oct; per person 67kr; P ♿) Just 1.5km north of the town centre lies this well-equipped camp ground; a barbecue, swimming pool, mini-golf and shop are all at your disposal.

Hotel Dagmar (☎ 75 42 00 33; www.hoteldagmar.dk; Torvet 1; s/d 845/1045kr P ⊠) Central Hotel Dagmar is Denmark's oldest (1581) and exudes the old world charm you'd expect. Rooms have all the modern amenities and the cellar and restaurant don't disappoint. Settle in and enjoy an historic experience in this four-star hotel.

Den Gamle Arrest (☎ 75 42 37 00; www.dengamlearrest.dk; Torvet 11; s/d without bathroom 450/540kr, with bathroom 650/790kr; P ⊠) Experience waking up in a jail-turned-hotel. Old steel doors open up into charmingly renovated rooms that are sure to satisfy any 'lock-in' fantasy. That said, jail rooms make for cramped quarters, but the iron bars are complemented by typical Danish hospitality. It served as a jail right up until 1989.

Backhaus (☎ 75 42 11 01; www.backhaus-ribe.dk Grydergade 12; s/d 250/500kr; P ⊠) Small yet adequate rooms present good value in the heart of town. Accommodation is on the 2nd floor, above a restaurant.

Weis Stue (☎ 75 42 07 00; Torvet 2; s/d 395/595kr; P) Its position is outstanding and rooms cosy, though a touch cramped.

Hotel Sønderjylland (☎ 75 42 04 66; fax 75 42 21 92; Sønderportsgade 22; s/d 350/550kr P ⊠) Straightforward rooms are above a small pub 300m west of Torvet.

Eating

There's plenty of options for dining in Ribe – whether you select a quality restaurant or a café for a quick meal.

Restaurant Backhaus (☎ 75 42 11 01; Grydergade 12; mains 160kr; ⌚ lunch & dinner) Its trademark dish, *æggekage* (basically an omelette with a few Danish touches), draws Danes from far and wide. The stuffed plaice is also tempting .

Sælhunden (☎ 75 42 09 46; Skibbroen 13; mains 70-130kr, lunch/dinner 75/120kr; ⌚ lunch & dinner) Top choice for a leisurely meal is this atmospheric restaurant which has the best seafood in town and offers generous servings as well. Smoked ham and asparagus salad makes a delicious lunch, while the fried plaice with shrimp and mussels is the dinner favourite.

Vægterkælderen (☎ 75 42 00 33; Torvet 1; mains 145kr; ⌚ lunch & dinner) Sharing the same kitchen as the Dagmar's expensive dining room, the Night Watchman's Cellar turns out quality steaks, Danish spare ribs, veal and salmon at competitive prices.

Kolvig (☎ 75 41 04 88; Mellemdammen 13; mains lunch/dinner 80/145kr; ⌚ lunch & dinner) Gorgeously situated on the waterfront, this café serves international cuisine that is sure to indulge the senses. It's also great for a coffee and to soak up the tranquil surrounds with the water lapping nearby.

Weis Stue (☎ 75 42 07 00; Torvet; mains 140kr; ⌚ lunch & dinner) For old-fashioned dining head to this leaning, half-timbered tavern with wooden plank tables. It dates back to 1704, and serves excellent fish and a well-rounded selection of dishes.

Peking House (☎ 75 41 16 00; Nederdammen 21; lunch/dinner buffets 40/110kr; ⌚ lunch & dinner) An increasingly popular restaurant puts on a generous buffet which includes all the usual Chinese suspects.

Mongolian Barbeque (☎ 75 44 66 50; Sct Pedersgade 2; all you can eat 130kr; ⌚ lunch & dinner) Impressive buffet selection includes six different meats – great value if you're a little peckish.

Valdemar Sejr (☎ 75 42 42 03; Sct Nicolaj Gade 6B; mains 70kr; ⌚ lunch & dinner) With typical Danish cuisine and a splendid garden to dine in with occasional live music, this is certainly a winner on a summer's day.

Pizza Expressen (☎ 75 41 14 10; Nederdammen 28; pizza 20kr; ⌚ lunch & dinner) Deep-pan pizza is served long into the night.

Isvaflen (☎ 75 41 06 88; Nederdammen 18; cone 17kr; ⌚ 11am-10pm) You'll find tempting all-natural ice cream here.

Mama Mia Pizza Bar (☎ 75 41 17 67; Sct Pedersgade 4; slices 20kr; ⌚ lunch & dinner) Just up from the hostel, Mama Mia serves large slices of pizza – certainly a good option late at night.

Drinking

Stenbohus (☎ 75 42 01 22; Stenbogade 1; ⌚ till late) Long-standing venue is a great place to meet the locals and enjoy a wide selection of Danish and international beers. There's also live music once a week.

Strygejernet (☎ 75 41 13 51; Dagmarsgade 1) An institution in itself with its triangular shape. Enjoy a cold one and roll the dice in a game of backgammon.

Jacob's Café (☎ 75 42 42 30; Nederdammen 36) A wide selection of cocktails and neat seats on the cobblestone street, and a beer garden.

Getting There & Away

Ribe is 30km south of Esbjerg via Rte 24 and 47km north of Tønder via Rte 11.

Trains from Ribe run hourly during weekdays and less frequently at weekends to Esbjerg (60kr, 35 minutes) and to Tønder (58kr, 50 minutes).

Getting Around

There's parking with a two-hour limit on the southern side of Ribe Domkirke, a parking area with a three-hour limit at Ribes Vikinger and parking with no time limit at the end of Sct Pedersgade near the hostel.

Bicycles can be hired from Danhostel Ribe for 65kr per day.

RØMØ

pop 850

Summer sees the large island of Rømø fill with German tourists, which is hardly surprising given its wide, sandy beach that's ideal for horse riding, kite flying, windsurfing, seal watching and bird-watching. And the sunsets are magnificent. Inland are thatched houses, rolling grassland, and the odd historic building. Rømø is connected to the mainland by a 10km causeway (with cycle lane). During the colder months the island is a windswept sleeper.

Orientation

As you cross the causeway you continue straight to reach Lakolk, a large camping ground turned village on the central west coast. It's also where you'll find the most popular beach – Lakolk Strand. Heading left (south) immediately after reaching Rømø takes you to Kongsmark and onto the southern tip, Havnby. Havsand is the best beach, yet few make the pilgrimage over the dunes. If you head right (north) as you reach the island you will arrive at the historic centre, Toftum and Juvre. The far northern end of the island is a military zone and access is prohibited.

Information

Rømø Andelskasse (☎ 74 75 55 55; Havnebyvej 81) Has a 24 hour ATM.

Rømø Turistbureau (☎ 74 75 51 30; www.romo.dk; Havnebyvej 30, Tvismark; 🕒 9am-6pm Jul & Aug, 9am-5pm Feb-Jun & Sep-Dec, closed Jan) Is 1km south of the causeway and rents out cottages.

Sights

Kommandørgården (☎ 74 75 52 76; Juvrevej 60, Toftum; adult/child 15kr/free; 🕒 10am 6pm Tue-Sun May-Sep, 10am-3pm Tue-Sun Oct), 1.5km north of the causeway, is a sea captain's handsome house (c 1748) that is testimony to the prosperity that Rømø sea captains brought to the town through their work on German and Dutch whaling expeditions. It's fully restored inside and there are displays on local history.

Another remnant of the whaling era, a **whale jawbone fence**, can be seen 1km further north on the eastern side of the main road in the village of Juvre.

The island's 18th-century **Rømø Kirke**, is on the main road in Kirkeby, It's noted for its unique Greenlandic gravestones (which

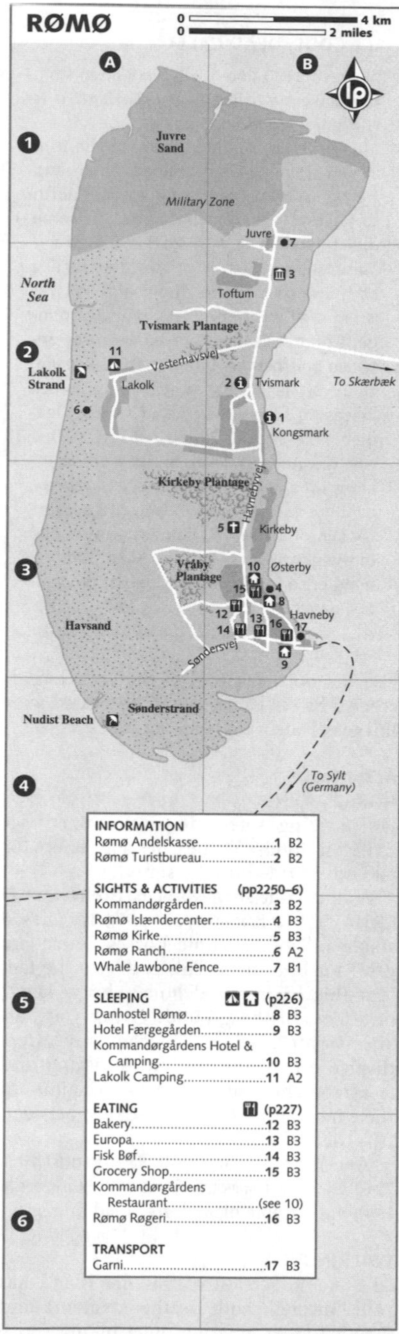
RØMØ
0 4 km
0 2 miles
A
B
1
2
3
4
5
6
Juvre Sand
Military Zone
Juvre
7
3
North Sea
Toftum
Tvismark Plantage
11
Vesterhavsvej
Lakolk Strand
Lakolk
2
Tvismark
To Skærbæk
6
1
Kongsmark
Kirkeby Plantage
Havnebyvej
5
Kirkeby
Vråby Plantage
10
Østerby
15
4
8
12
13
16
Havneby
14
17
Havsand
Søndersvej
9
Sønderstrand
Nudist Beach
To Sylt (Germany)
INFORMATION
Rømø Andelskasse.....1 B2
Rømø Turistbureau.....2 B2
SIGHTS & ACTIVITIES (pp2250–6)
Kommandørgården.....3 B2
Rømø Islændercenter.....4 B3
Rømø Kirke.....5 B3
Rømø Ranch.....6 A2
Whale Jawbone Fence.....7 B1
SLEEPING (p226)
Danhostel Rømø.....8 B3
Hotel Færgegården.....9 B3
Kommandørgårdens Hotel & Camping.....10 B3
Lakolk Camping.....11 A2
EATING (p227)
Bakery.....12 B3
Europa.....13 B3
Fisk Bøf.....14 B3
Grocery Shop.....15 B3
Kommandørgårdens Restaurant.....(see 10)
Rømø Røgeri.....16 B3
TRANSPORT
Garni.....17 B3

ICE COOL, DEAD CALM

Between 1650 and 1850, many men from Rømø went whaling near Greenland. It is still regarded as the golden age of this island. Skilled, confident and fearless fishermen from Rømø captained Dutch and German ships on dangerous voyages north to catch whales. Some returned rich, some didn't return at all. A trip to Rømø Kirke and Kommandørgården illustrates the sacrifice and rewards involved. The year 1777 was when it all went horribly wrong; a contingent of 450 seamen braved the seas between Spitsbergen and eastern Greenland. Of the 30 ships, 13 became perilously stuck in ice and 300 seamen died. Fifty local seamen were aboard, 20 did not return. One who did, Anders Mickelsen List, who was 12 at the time, and had witnessed this tragedy, continued to sail to Greenland and became captain of a ship. His name is also on one of the gravestones at Rømø Kirke. The ultimate price for an unforgiving yet prosperous passion.

line the northern wall of the churchyard) erected by sea captains and decorated with images of their boats and families.

Activities

HORSE RIDING

Horse riding is becoming a prominent activity on Rømø – its beaches are perfect for an endless ride into the sunset.

As the name suggests **Rømø Islændercenter** (☎ 74 75 51 22; Havnebyvej 201; per hr 85kr) has a stable full of Icelandic horses which are great for beginners. This is due to the fact that this Viking-bred horse always keeps one foot on the ground, giving you balance beyond belief. The company offers diverse excursions around the island and is a reputable outfit. The motto sums up the experience, 'Riding is a dance between two friends'.

Another reputable outfit, **Rømø Ranch** (☎ 74 75 60 52; www.romoranch.dk; Standen ved Lakolk; per hr 80kr), has a stable of well-groomed horses.

WALKING

The inland section of this flat island has trails through both heathered moors and wooded areas, offering quiet hiking spots. There are three forest zones, each with a couple of kilometres of trails: Tvismark Plantage, along Vesterhavsvej, the main east–west road; Kirkeby Plantage, to the west of Kirkeby; and Vråby Plantage, a less diverse area dominated by pines, about 1km further south.

OTHER ACTIVITIES

Windsurfing is a popular activity and the main area is south of Lakolk. Most enthusiasts arrive with their own equipment but if you come without, inquire at the tourist office (p225) about possibilities.

For those who think bathing suits are overrated there's a **nudist beach** at the southwestern tip of the island; follow Søndersvej to its western end and walk 2km over the sand dunes.

Festivals & Events

A **kite-flying festival** is held over three days in early September on Lakolk beach.

Sleeping

The vast majority of accommodation on Rømø is found in some 1300 **summer houses** (6-person cabin per wk 1500-3000kr, chalet per wk 3000-6000kr) scattered around the island. Prices vary, depending on the season and the degree of luxury. The tourist office can provide a catalogue and handle the bookings.

Kommandørgårdens Hotel & Camping (☎ 74 75 51 22; www.kommandoergaarden.dk; Havnebyvej, Østerby; camping 65kr, s/d 595/795kr, apt from 1700kr; P ⊠) From camping to comfortable rooms and apartments, this place has it all. It also has a mini-market, café, restaurant, swimming pool and tennis courts. Astonishingly big and impressively run.

Hotel Færgegården (☎ 74 75 54 32; Vestergade 1, Havneby; s/d 610/870kr; P) Rømø's most upmarket hotel is in a classically refurnished thatched house; some rooms have stunning views over the dunes.

Lakolk Camping (☎ 74 75 52 28; Lakolk; Apr–mid-Oct; per person 64kr; P) The sunsets are to die for and the tent sites are reasonably good. This caravan camping draw card is on the western side of town.

Danhostel Rømø (☎ 74 75 51 88; www.danhostel.dk/romo; Lyngvejen 7, Østerby; Mar-Oct; dm/d 118/280kr; P ⊠) A thatched-roof hostel that has inviting four-bed dorms and friendly, knowledgeable owners. There are 91 beds.

Eating

HAVNEBY

Rømø Røgeri (☎ 74 75 54 52; Havnevej 1; fish & chips 40kr, buffet 100kr; ⏲ lunch & dinner) Right next to the harbour, Rømø Røgeri fries up good fish and chips and the seafood buffet is great for fresh, tasty seafood and salad.

Fisk Bøf (☎ 74 75 55 65; Vestergade 6; mains 80kr; ⏲ dinner) Specialising in seafood. Great for families as an adjoining mini-golf course keeps the kids entertained for hours.

Europa (☎ 74 75 59 73; Vestergade 3; mains 70-110kr; ⏲ dinner) For Italian and Greek specialities this place is hard to beat; excessively popular during the warmer months.

ØSTERBY

There's a grocery shop and bakery in Østerby, within walking distance of the hostel. **Kommandørgårdens Restaurant** (☎ 74 75 51 22; Havnebyvej 201, Østerby; mains 130kr; ⏲ lunch & dinner) serves quality meat and fish dishes; try the mussels which are not only fresh but divine.

LAKOLK

There's a supermarket, bakery and various eateries at the Lakolk Butikcentre, which fronts Lakolk Camping; these include hot dog stands, a café, a pizzeria and a cafeteria.

Getting There & Away

Rømø is on Rte 175, about 14km west of Skærbæk.

Bus No 29 runs from Skærbæk to Havneby (16kr, 35 minutes) about once an hour on weekdays, and less often at weekends. From Skærbæk there are trains about once an hour to Ribe (46kr, 19 minutes), Tønder (52kr, 28 minutes) and Esbjerg (101kr, one hour).

Rømø-Sylt Linie (☎ 73 75 53 03) operates car ferries between Havncby and the German island of Sylt (46kr, one hour) several times daily.

Getting Around

From late May to early September bus No 29/591 (16kr) makes a 20-minute trip from Havneby up the east-coast road and over to Lakolk. There are about 10 runs on weekdays, and about half that at weekends.

The best choice, if you don't have your own transport, is to rent a bicycle, as Rømø is flat and small enough to explore. You can hire bikes from **Garni** (☎ 74 75 54 80; Nørre Frankel 15, Havneby; per day/wk 40/200kr) and at **Hotel Kommandørgåordens** (☎ 74 75 51 22; Østerby; per day/wk 50/250kr).

TØNDER

pop 8200

The record books say 1243 but talk to any local and the bloodlines run deeper into the past – so it's little wonder Tønder lays unofficial claim to the title of Denmark's oldest town. It's an inviting village that has had a rocky journey through the ages, from serious flooding to German invasions.

During the 16th century a series of dikes were erected to prevent the imminent threat of flooding. In doing so the town isolated itself from a sea-port connection and turned elsewhere for economic prosperity. Lace-making was introduced – an economic windfall that employed up to 12,000 workers during its peak in the 18th century.

Information

There are a couple of banks near Torvet, the central square.

Post office (☎ 73 22 40 00; Vestergade 83) A few minutes' walk north of the train station.

Tønder Turistbureau (☎ 74 72 12 20; www.visittonder.dk; Torvet 1; ⏲ 10am-5pm Mon-Fri, 10am-2pm Sat Jul & Aug, 9am-4pm Mon-Fri, 9am-noon Sat Sep-Jun) Has information on the town as well as Møgeltønder and Højo.

Sights

To glimpse into the past, head south from Torvet along Søndergade and turn right into Uldgade. The cobbled street has Tønder's best collection of unique gabled houses.

Tønder Museum (☎ 74 72 89 89; Kongevej 51; adult/child 40kr/free; ⏲ 10am-5pm daily Jun-Aug, 10am-5pm Tue-Sun Sep-May) has the replica of the golden horns (p228), and an impressive collection of delicate Tønder lace as well as the usual local history exhibits. In the adjacent wing is **Sønderjyllands Kunstmuseum**, featuring Danish surrealist and modern art, most notably by Kain Tapper whose sculptures are quite intriguing. The **water tower** on the other side is just as curious as it houses eight storeys of Hans J Wegner-designed chairs. A universal favourite is on the 5th floor, the classic 'Ox-Chair' from 1960. From the top are sweeping views of the town and countryside and it is well worth the climb. It's a 10-minute walk east of the train station.

The grand old **Kristkirken** (Torvet; admission free; ⏲ 10am-4pm Mon-Sat), on the northeastern side of Torvet dates back to 1592. Its decorative interior came courtesy of the town's rich cattle and lace merchants who invested heavily between the late 17th and 18th centuries. The church interior boasts impressive carvings and paintings, including a rare baptismal font from 1350, an ornate pulpit from 1586 and a series of memorial tablets from around 1600. The 47.5m-high tower, part of an earlier church that stood at the same site, doubled as a navigational marker in the days when Tønder was connected to the sea.

Det Gamle Apotek (☎ 74 72 51 11; Østergade 1; 9.30am-5.30pm), on Torvet, has an elaborate 1671 Baroque doorway flanked by two lions. If the lions entice you inside, prepare to be enchanted by an old-fashioned interior and an extensive gift shop collection.

Festivals & Events

Gaining in reputation and scale each year, the **Tønder Festival** (☎ 74 72 46 10; www.tf.dk) takes place in the last week of May and draws people from all corners of the country. Regarded by many as the best folk music festival in Europe, it's a great opportunity to let your hair down and dance with the locals.

Sleeping

The tourist office can provide a list of **rooms** (s/d 200/300kr) in private homes in the Tønder area.

Danhostel Tønder (☎ 74 72 35 00; www.tonder-net.dk.danhostel; Sønderport 4; Feb–mid-Dec; dm/d 118/355kr; P ⊠) Just a few minute's walk east of the town centre, this hostel has comfortable rooms, each with four beds and a bathroom.

Tønder Campingplads (☎ 74 72 18 49; Holmevej 2; Apr-late Sep; per person 57kr; P) East of the town centre and adjacent to the hostel, this three-star facility is part of Tønder Fritidscenter (sports centre), which includes tennis courts, a swimming pool and squash courts.

Hostrups Hotel (☎ 74 72 21 29; www.hostrupshotel.dk; Søndergade 30; s/d from 380/490kr; P ⊠) A well-priced hotel near the historic street of Ulgade, most rooms come with TV, bathroom and desk and some have a view of the lake.

Hotel Tønderhus (☎ 74 72 22 22; www.hoteltoenderhus.dk, Jomfrustien 1; s/d 795/950kr; P) Opposite the museum this four-star hotel has light, inviting rooms.

Eating

There are some good options around Torvet as well as the main pedestrian street that runs through town.

Café Victoria (☎ 74 72 00 89; Storgade 9; mains 75-100kr; lunch & dinner) Locally adored and with good reason: tasty meals, rich coffee and a typically cosy Danish environment. Also a good spot for a relaxing late night glass of vino.

Torvet Restaurant (☎ 74 72 43 73; Torvet; mains 80-110kr; lunch & dinner) Well suited to gourmet food lovers, this restaurant has a strong Danish menu that is sure to please.

Pizzeria Italiano (☎ 74 72 53 05; Østargaze 40; mains 55-70kr; lunch & dinner) The elder statesmen of the pizzerias around town and still the benchmark with generously topped pizzas and fulfilling pastas. It's a short walk east of Torvet.

Torve Bistroen (☎ 74 72 41 55; Torvet; fast food 35-50kr; lunch) Popular café serves fish and chips, vegetarian omelettes, sandwiches and burgers.

GOLDEN HORNS

Just north of Tønder is Guldhornene wherein lies a good yarn. The year was 1639 and a girl was strolling along to work when she tripped on something solid. On closer inspection she found she had stumbled across gold, literally. It came in the form of a horn, and this was presented to the king.

Almost 100 years later (in 1734) a farmer in a nearby paddock was ploughing his field to bring up a golden crop (pardon the pun), and a second horn was plucked out of this rich land and into the hands of Danish royalty. How they ended up in the pastoral lands of southern Jutland baffled historians, who were unable to examine the unique finds as the prince was using them as drinking vessels. The horns were later stolen and in 1802 were melted down by a goldsmith taking with them the truth about their origins. Still, it's a pleasant drive north of Tønder, and who knows, you may just stumble across gold yourself.

There's a market selling fruit, vegetables and cheese at Torvet on Tuesday and Friday mornings.

Getting There & Away

Tønder is on Rte 11, 4km north of the border with Germany and 77km south of Esbjerg.

The train station is on the western side of town, 1km from Torvet via Vestergade. Trains run hourly on weekdays and slightly less frequently at weekends from Ribe (52kr, 50 minutes) and Esbjerg (84kr, 1½ hours).

MØGELTØNDER

A royal castle, the most beautiful street in Jutland and a church rich in frescoes are just some of the joys to be found in this charming village 4km west of Tønder. Møgeltønderand should be high on any traveller's radar.

On the eastern edge of town is **Schackenborg**, a small castle that was presented by the Crown to Field Marshal Hans Schack in 1661 following his victory over the Swedes in the battle of Nyborg. Eleven generations of Schacks lived there until 1978 when it was returned to the royal family.

In 1995 Queen Margrethe's youngest son, Prince Joachim, married Princess Alexandra and the newlyweds made Schackenborg their primary residence, completing the fairytale town. You can see the grand old building from the street and while you can't join in for a lazy brunch, the moat-surrounded grounds on the opposite side of the street have been turned into a small public **park** that you're free to enjoy. During summer there are guided tours of the **Castle Gardens** (☎ 74 72 12 20; www.visittonder.dk; 11.30am & noon Wed, Thu & Sat May–mid-Jun, 11.30am & noon Wed-Sat mid-Jun–Aug).

Continue along Slotsgade and soak in the market-village feel of this street with its cutely packed, almost immaculate houses. Look behind the houses and you will notice that it opens into green fields – it's not a crammed market town at all, rather a purpose-built picturesque street.

At the western end of Slotsgade is **Møgeltønder Kirke** (Slotsgade 1; admission free; ⏲ 8am-5pm May-Sep, 9am-4pm Oct-Apr) which has one of the most lavish church interiors in Denmark. The Romanesque nave dates back to 1180 and the baptismal font is from 1200, however the church has had many additions as the Gothic choir vaults were built during the 13th century, the tower dates from about 1500 and the chapel on the northern side was added in 1763.

The interior is rich in frescoes, gallery paintings and ceiling drawings. Here, too, is the oldest functioning church organ in Denmark, dating from 1679. The elaborately detailed gilt altar dates back to the 16th century. Note the 'countess bower', a balcony with private seating for the Schack family, who owned the church from 1661 until 1970.

Sleeping & Eating

Schackenborg Slotskro (☎ 74 73 83 83; www.slotskro.dk; Slotsgade 42; s/d 845/1090kr Ⓟ) Within a stone's throw of the castle, this hotel has elegantly decorated rooms by none other than Princess Alexandra. The menu at the **restaurant** (light lunch 75kr, 3-course meal 345kr; ⏲ breakfast/lunch & dinner) is heavenly, with gourmet Danish and French cuisine. Grab a paper and a coffee at the hotel's al fresco café – it's a royal experience.

Getting There & Away

Møgeltønder is 4km west of Tønder on Rte 419. Bus No 66 connects Tønder with Møgeltønder (15kr, 10 minutes) about once every hour on weekdays, and less frequently at the weekend.

HØJER

Just 15km east of Møgeltønder is Højer, an attractive, well-groomed town that warrants a visit if you're in the area. The town sums up (and plays up to being) a typically traditional Danish village with a cracking old **windmill** as its centrepiece. Sitting just above sea level it's protected by a complex and historic network of 16th century sluice gates and dikes. Højer's most famous export is its sausages, which are nationally recognised as the land's best – duck down to the supermarket and throw a few Højer *pølser* on the barbecue.

Thatched roofs keep the rain off many of the red-brick houses and the town hall is claimed to be the only thatched town hall in the land. Commanding attention from far and wide is the **Dutch windmill** (☎ 74 78 29 11; Møllegade 13; admission 20kr; ⏲ 10am-4pm Mon-Fri Apr-Oct) that dates back to 1857 and is home to a well-laid-out history museum.

Bird-watchers will be delighted, as wading birds, sea birds and shore birds love the rich marshland habitat to Højer's west.

Getting There & Away

Højer is on Rte 419, about 7km west of Møgeltønder. Bus No 66 connects Højer with Møgeltønder (26kr) and Tønder (26kr) roughly on the hour.

KOLDING

pop 59,000

Kolding's mix of picturesque beauty and cutting-edge culture means the town is well on its way to fulfilling its enormous potential as a tourist hot spot. A striking hilltop castle, an engaging old town layout and a magnificent modern art museum have been the catalyst for this movement. The economy is based on industry and the town thrives on a philosophy of 'old meets new' which many neighbouring towns would do well to adopt.

Information

Danske Bank (☎ 76 34 35 00; Akseltorv 22) South of the tourist office

Kolding Turistbureau (☎ 76 33 21 00; www.visitkolding.dk in Danish; Akseltorv 8; ⌚ 9.30am-7pm Mon-Fri, 9.30am-2.30pm Sat Jul–mid-Aug, 9.30am-5.30pm Mon-Fri, 9.30am-2pm Sat mid-Aug–Jun) Knowledgeable staff and sells the Kulturkort Kolding Card (90kr) which offers substantial discounts to the town's attractions.

Post office (☎ 79 43 50 00) Next to the train station.

Sights

The tourist office marks the town centre and the curvy streets sprawl out from there. Akseltorv, the central square, is the site of **Borchs Gård**, a decorative Renaissance building which dates from 1595.

Helligkorsgade, a few minutes' walk south of Akseltorv at the end of Østergade, is a pleasant street for a stroll; here you'll find Kolding's **oldest house** at No 18, a lovely timber-framed affair built in 1589.

Just west of Akseltorv, on the other side of the rådhus, is **Sankt Nicolai Kirke** (Nicolai Plads; admission free), a medieval church that was largely rebuilt in the 19th century; it has a 16th-century altar and pulpit.

Koldinghus (☎ 76 33 81 00; Adelgade 1; adult/child 60/30kr; ⌚ 10am-5pm) is the town's extravagant showpiece. A fortress once occupied the land in 1248, but like so many other buildings in Denmark, it had a turbulent history. Parts of the masterpiece you see before you today can be traced to 1440. The year of its most recent mishap was 1808. At that time the castle was hosting Spanish soldiers during the Napoleonic Wars. Missing the Mediterranean summer they lit a fire to restore some inner heat. This heat soon turned into an inferno sending the castle up in a blaze of glory that left nothing but soot-covered walls. The tower then spectacularly caught fire and collapsed through the great wall and onto the castle chapel. At the time, the Danish state was at war and bankrupt and the common school of thought was that the castle would be left in ruins. If only they could see it now, shining like never before and supported by strikingly modern timber and steel structures. It houses exhibitions, collections of historic paintings and silverware, and the observation deck provides a great panoramic view of the area.

Trapholt Museum of Modern Art (☎ 76 30 05 30; Æblehaven 23; adult/child 60kr/free; ⌚ 10am-5pm) is housed in an edgy, architectural wonder that certainly gets the eye ready for a funky museum experience. Danes love interior design and inside you will see it at its very best. Look for Peter Blonde's powerful painting *Blow Hole*, from the tail end of the '60s movement. There's a couple of classics from the Skagen artists, Ann Ancher and PS Kroyer. Down in the furniture display section take a look at Verner Panton's 1969 red couch, highly impractical but highly desirable. All in all, it's one of the most impressive museums in Denmark. Take bus No 4 to get there.

Activities

Sail around the bay and take in Kolding from a different perspective on the **MS Tenna II** (☎ 76 33 21 00; Kolding Inner Harbour; adult/child 95/45kr; 11.30am & 1.30pm Tue 22 Jun-22 Aug). Departure and tickets are down at the harbour.

Festivals & Events

During summer there is a **classical music concert** in the castle about once a week, ask at the tourist office (left) about dates.

Sleeping

Kolding Byferie (☎ 75 54 18 00; www.kolding-byferie.dk; Kedelsmedgangen 2; apt from 675kr; Ⓟ) Designed in peculiar shapes and located on the waterfront, these are not your average apartments. They are a magnificent architectural addition to the town and a good talking point as well as a wonderful place to retire at the end of the day.

Kolding Youth Hostel (☎ 75 50 91 40; www.danhostel.dk/kolding; Ørnsborgvej 10; ⏲ Feb-Nov; dm/d 90/320kr; P ⊠) A compact hostel 1.5km north of the city centre, it is fitted with eight-bed dorms, kitchen, table tennis and a comfortable basement TV room.

Kolding City Camp Vonsild (☎ 75 52 13 88; Vonsildvej 19; per person 67kr; P) At 3km south of the town centre this is the closest camping ground. Facilities live up to its three-star rating.

Saxildhus (☎ 75 52 12 00; www.saxildhus.dk; Banegårdspladsen; s/d 745/895kr; P ⊠) Classic, period hotel opposite the train station has modern, individually decorated rooms in a prime central location.

Radisson SAS Koldingfjord Hotel (☎ 75 51 00 00; www.radissonsas.com; Fjordvej 154; s/d 1155/1455kr; P ⊠) Located just past Trapholt Museum this is a four-star hotel that is housed in a plush, classical building facing Kolding Bay.

Eating

The main cluster of eateries is near Akseltorv, the central square. Take Jernbanegade west from the station and it's just a 10-minute walk to Akseltorv.

Cafe Lucca (☎ 76 33 39 00; Låsbybanke 4; lunch 60kr, mains 150kr; ⏲ lunch & dinner) Swish café has tasty food, good drinks and a cosmopolitan ambience. A two minute walk northwest of the tourist office.

Den Blå Café (☎ 75 50 65 12; Lilletorv, Slotsgade 4; lunch 40-70kr; ⏲ lunch & dinner) Little café has fresh salads and fulfilling sandwiches and is just two minutes southeast of the tourist office.

Saxen (☎ 75 52 12 00; Banegårdspladsen; mains 160kr; ⏲ lunch/dinner) If you're after modern Danish cuisine Saxen has an imaginative menu and won't disappoint.

Café Piano (☎ 75 52 26 57; Akseltorv 3; lunch 40-70kr; ⏲ lunch) Opposite the tourist office, this café offers terrific outdoor seating and all the standard café fare.

China Garden (☎ 75 53 32 18; Østergade 19; mains 60-90kr; ⏲ lunch & dinner) Serves up all your Chinese favourites in generous proportions. Only 100m south of Akseltorv.

Getting There & Away

Kolding is 92km east of Esbjerg and 82km north of the German border. The E20 (which continues east to Funen) and the E45 connect Kolding with other major towns in Jutland. If you're travelling leisurely by road north to south, Rte 170 is a pleasant alternative to the E45.

There are regular train services from Kolding south to Padborg on the German border (93kr, 70 minutes) and north all the way to Frederikshavn (265kr, four hours). There's a second line to Esbjerg (75kr, 55 minutes). Trains run roughly hourly, except for services to Padborg (every two hours).

HADERSLEV

pop 30,000

While not a must-see on any Jutland adventure, Haderslev has a proud church that stands over the 13th-century old town and a relaxing time is assured. The heart of the town can be found around Torvet, a cobbled square bordered by half-timbered buildings enhanced with sculptures by Erik Heide.

Information

Danske Bank (☎ 73 22 46 46; Nørregade 23)

Haderslev Turistbureau (☎ 74 52 55 50; www.haderslev-turist.dk; Honnøkajen 1; ⏲ 9.30am-6pm Mon-Fri, 9.30am-2pm Sat mid-Jun–mid-Aug, 9.30am-4.30pm Mon-Fri, 9.30am-12.30am Sat rest of year) Down by the harbour.

Jyske Bank (☎ 73 53 12 00; Nørregade 22)

Post office (☎ 73 22 40 00; Gravene 8) North of the town centre.

Sights

Haderslev Domkirke (Apotekergade; admission free; ⏲ 10am-5pm May-Sep, 10am-3pm Oct-Apr) has exuded its presence over the town since the mid-13th century. The Gothic windows are an astonishing 16m high. Largeness continues inside with an organ comprised of 73 stops, 5000 pipes and a façade from 1652. The altar is much more recent, created during the 1941–51 restoration, yet the crucifix was made around 1300 and the alabaster figures of the 12 apostles in the 1400s.

Ehlers-samlingen (☎ 74 53 08 58; Slotsgade 20; admission 20kr; ⏲ 1-5pm Tue-Sun Sep-May, 1-5pm Tue-Sun Jun-Aug) is a classic case of a passion turning into an obsession. The Ehlers sought to trace the evolution of pottery through the ages and before they knew it they had collected Europe's largest display. If diverse pottery in large quantities hits a cord you will love this 1577 timber-framed museum.

Haderslev Museum (☎ 74 52 75 66; Dalgade 7; adult/child 15kr/free; ⏲ 10am-4pm Tue-Sun Jun-Aug, 1-4pm Tue-Sun Sep-May), 1km northeast of Torvet, features exhibits on southern Jutland's

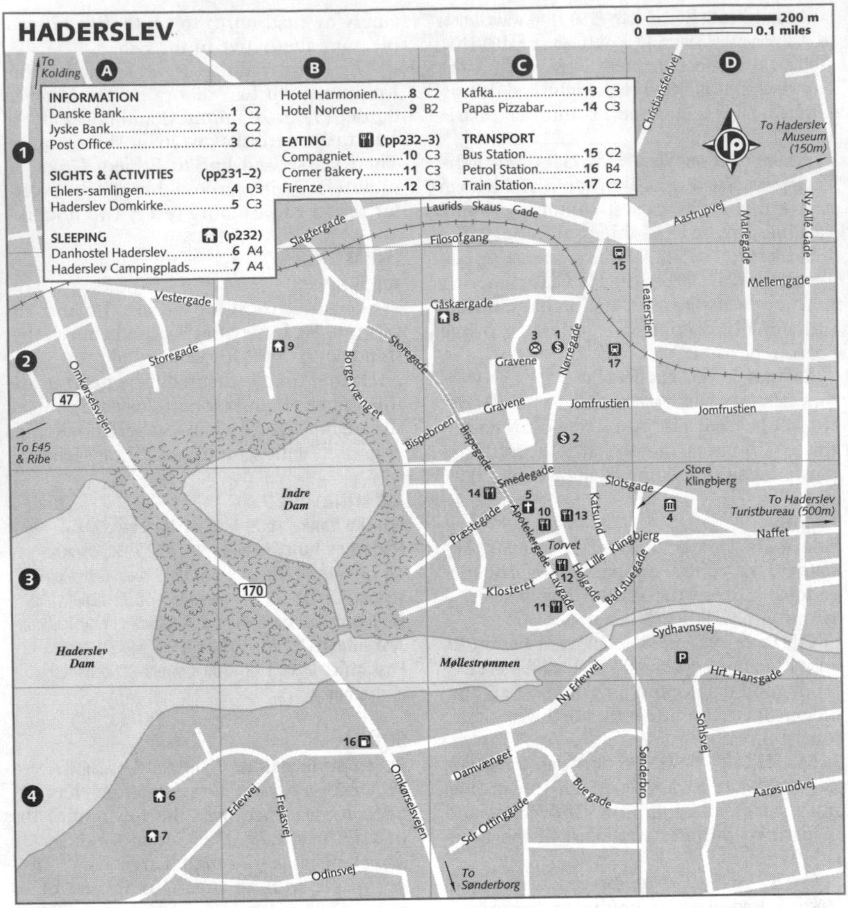

HADERSLEV
0 200 m
0 0.1 miles
INFORMATION
Danske Bank....1 C2
Jyske Bank....2 C2
Post Office....3 C2
SIGHTS & ACTIVITIES (pp231–2)
Ehlers-samlingen....4 D3
Haderslev Domkirke....5 C3
SLEEPING (p232)
Danhostel Haderslev....6 A4
Haderslev Campingplads....7 A4
Hotel Harmonien....8 C2
Hotel Norden....9 B2
EATING (pp232–3)
Compagniet....10 C3
Corner Bakery....11 C3
Firenze....12 C3
Kafka....13 C3
Papas Pizzabar....14 C3
TRANSPORT
Bus Station....15 C2
Petrol Station....16 B4
Train Station....17 C2
To Kolding
To Haderslev Museum (150m)
To E45 & Ribe
To Haderslev Turistbureau (500m)
To Sønderborg
Store Klingbjerg
Indre Dam
Haderslev Dam
Møllestrømmen
Torvet
Christiansfeldvej
Aastrupvej
Mariegade
Ny Allé Gade
Mellemgade
Laurids Skaus Gade
Slagtergade
Filosofgang
Vestergade
Gåskærgade
Storegade
Omkørselsvejen
Borgervænget
Nørregade
Teaterstien
Gravene
Jomfrustien
Bispebroen
Bispegade
Smedegade
Slotsgade
Præstegade
Apotekergade
Katsund
Lille Klingbjerg
Højgade
Badstuegade
Klosteret
Lavgade
Naffet
Sydhavnsvej
Hrt. Hansgade
Ny Erlevvej
Sohlsvej
Sønderbro
Damvænget
Buegade
Aarøsundvej
Sdr Ottinggade
Erlevvej
Frejasvej
Odinsvej
47
170

archaeological history as well as a small open-air museum with a windmill and a few other period buildings.

Sleeping

Hotel Harmonien (☎ 74 52 37 20; hotel.harmonien@mail.tele.dk; Gåskærgade 19; s/d 695/795kr; P ⊠) Proud of its royal connections (Queen Margrethe dropped by for a dinner party in 1988), this classically designed 1844 hotel boasts attractive rooms and great hospitality.

Hotel Norden (☎ 74 52 40 30; www.hotel-norden.dk; Storegade 55; s/d 900/1145kr; P ⊠) A touch pricey but the modern rooms, swift service and central location are the draw cards for this conference-oriented hotel. All rooms have a view of the lake.

Danhostel Haderslev & Haderslev Campingplads (☎ 74 52 13 47; www.danhostel.dk/haderslev; Erlevvej 34; ⏲ Feb-Nov; camping 59kr, dm/d 115/350kr; P ⊠) The camp sites are right on the water at this complex 1km west of the town centre. The hostel is user-friendly with small dorms, kitchen, TV room and plenty of space to move.

Eating

There are numerous places to grab a bite on or near the central square, Torvet.

Firenze (☎ 74 53 05 05; Torvet 13; pizza or pasta 75kr, meat or fish dishes 150kr; ⏲ lunch & dinner) Clearly the standout Italian place in town – great pizzas and hearty steaks await.

Papas Pizzabar (☎ 74 53 03 00; Bispegade 13; pizzas 55kr; ⏲ lunch & dinner) Slick café offers tasty, healthy pizzas and is popular with shoppers and workers.

Kafka (☎ 74 53 00 08; Nørregade 6; mains 65kr; ⏰ lunch & dinner) Stylish café serves good coffee and smørrebrød (Danish open sandwiches) and a variety of dishes including fish and pasta.

Compagniet (☎ 74 53 54 44; Torvet 7; mains lunch/dinner 50/160kr; ⏰ lunch & dinner) Upmarket café right on Torvet has good Caesar salads and sandwiches at lunch, steaks and fresh fish at dinner.

Corner Bakery (☎ 74 52 30 15; Lavgade 10; sandwiches 25kr; ⏰ lunch) A well-decked-out bakery that has some scrumptious bites as well as filling sandwiches.

Getting There & Away

Haderslev is 31km south of Kolding via Rte 170 or the E45, and 51km east of Ribe via Rtes 24 and 47. There's a large free car park at the southern side of Sydhavnsvej with no time limit.

Bus Nos 33 and 35 frequently run between Haderslev and Vojens (26kr, 25 minutes), the nearest train station. Trains to Vojens run about hourly from Fredericia (58kr, 45 minutes) and a bit less often from Sønderborg (78kr, one hour).

Bus No 34 runs hourly between Haderslev and Kolding (43kr, 45 minutes).

PADBORG

pop 4700

Padborg, near the German border, is the site of **Frøslevlejren** (Frøslev Camp), an internment camp opened near the end of WWII following negotiations with Germany to keep the Danish POWs in Denmark. Despite this agreement, 1600 Danish patriots were deported to the horrors of Concentration Camps in Germany. During its nine months in operation it held 12,000 prisoners.

Frøslevlejrens Museum (☎ 74 67 65 57; Lejrvejen 83; adult/child 30/5kr; ⏰ 10am-5pm daily Jul, 9am-4pm Tue-Fri, 10am-5pm Sat & Sun Feb-Jun & Aug-Nov, closed Dec & Jan) depicts the Danish Resistance movement and daily prison life at Frøslev. A shining light in the German POW camps Frøslev had ample food, no torture and no executions. The only horror was the threat of deportation across the border.

Frøslevlejren is on the northwestern outskirts of Padborg, 1km west of the E45 (take exit 76).

GRÅSTEN

pop 3300

For three weeks each year the town is abuzz as Queen Margrethe and Prince Henrik head down for some R&R away from the hectic capital.

The **Gråsten Turist Bureau** (☎ 74 65 09 55; www.turistbureauet.com; Kongevej 71; ⏰ 9am-4.30pm Mon-Fri, 9am-12.30pm Sat mid-Jun–Aug, 9am-4pm Mon-Fri Aug–mid-Jun) is at the train station 1km south of the castle.

Sights

Gråsten's major crowd puller is its majestic **Royal Castle** on the banks of Slotssøen lake. The castle itself has had a stormy upbringing. Originally built in the middle of the 15th century it was destroyed by fire in 1603 and rebuilt only to be ravaged by the same culprit in 1757. In 1842 the main building you see today was constructed and in 1935 the rights to the castle were handed to the royal family.

Romanticism is the theme of **Gråsten Castle Garden** (adult/child 20kr/free; ⏰ tour Wed Jun-Aug, garden 10am-dusk) and 40,000 flowers are here to greet you. Queen Ingrid designed the garden and drew on English influences in landscaping for inspiration. It's a wonderful place to wander and a perfect spot to bring a bottle of wine and have a picnic. Spend a leisurely afternoon soaking in the summer rays.

Gråsten Castle Church (⏰ 2-4pm Wed, Sat & Sun Jun-Aug) The only remaining building from the original Baroque castle following the 1757 fire. This 1699 church is an exact replica of the Jesuit Church in Antwerp.

Getting There & Away

Trains run to Gråsten from Kolding (102kr, 1¼ hours) and also continue on to Sønderborg (39kr, 15 minutes).

Gråsten is on Rte 8, 10km west of Sønderborg and 23km northeast of Padborg.

ALS

pop 60,000

The island of Als, separated from Jutland by the thin Als Sund, is relatively untouched by large-scale tourism and provides visitors with a snapshot of the laid-back Danish country lifestyle. Down south is where the best beaches lie while up the east coast you will encounter intimate, engaging little villages.

Sønderborg

pop 32,000

Sønderborg, nestled on both sides of the Als Sund, nurtures a modern, cosmopolitan ambience despite its medieval origins. In 1169 Valdemar I (the Great) erected a castle fortress along the waterfront and the town has since spread out from there with fishing as the economic mainstay.

The town has shaped Denmark to a degree, as the battleground for two wars against Germany in the middle of the 19th century. In 1864, during the Battle of Dybbøl, Danish forces gathered here while a bombardment of 80,000 German shells paved the way for the German occupation of Jutland for some 60 years. Reconstruction of the city since that fateful war has led to its modern feel and a bombardment of another kind – the annual descent of German and Danish holidaymakers.

Orientation

Sønderborg spreads along both sides of the Als Sund (Als Sound), which is joined by two bridges. The town centre and Sønderborg Slot are to the east, on the island of Als. The Dybbøl area and the train station are on the western side, which is part of mainland Jutland. There's a small, sandy beach right in town by the southern side of the castle.

Information

Jyske Bank (☎ 73 42 05 30; Perlegade 81A) On the pedestrian street Perlegade, immediately north of Rådhustorvet.

Post office (☎ 73 43 62 00; Perlegade 20)

Sønderborg Turistbureau (☎ 74 42 35 55; www.visitals.com; Rådhustorvet 7; 🕑 10am-6pm Mon-Fri, 8.30am-1pm Sat Jul & Aug, 10am-5pm Mon-Fri, 9.30am-1pm Sat Sep-Jun) On the main town square.

Sights

Sønderborg Slot (☎ 74 42 41 89; ghost tours Jun-Aug, inquire at tourist bureau) dates back to 1170, when it was a strategic stronghold in the defence against the Wends. Between 1532 and 1549 the castle was used to hold the deposed king, Christian II. Rather than be confined to the dungeon he was free to stroll the grounds and enjoy the royal chambers. The castle took on its quadrangular Renaissance appearance in 1718. During the German occupation it was used as a German barracks. In 1568 under the reign of Queen Dorothea, widow of King Christian III, Denmark's first Lutheran chapel was constructed. The chapel still stands today, and rates as one of Europe's oldest preserved royal chapels.

Nowadays the castle houses **Museet på Sønderborg Slot** (☎ 74 42 25 39; Slotsbakken; adult/child 30/15kr; 🕑 10am-5pm daily May-Sep, 1-4pm Tue-Sun Oct-Apr) which has exhibits on the wars of 1848 and 1864 as well as paintings from the Danish Golden Age and an insight into the political history of the country.

On the western edge of town is **Dybbøl Banke Battlefield Centre** (☎ 74 48 90 00; Dybbøl Banke 16; adult/child 45/18kr; 🕑 10am-5pm Easter & late-Apr–Sep) which gives you an informative insight into the bloody war of 1864. There are two multimedia rooms, and an impressive reconstruction of the battlefield – complete with cannons. Graphic sketches of medical procedures, namely amputations, demonstrate the ghastly realities of war in the 19th century. On April 18, 1864 the German army steamrolled the Danes and took control of Southern Jutland until the end of WWI. Danish men were forced to fight for Germany in WWI on both fronts.

Dybbøl Mølle (☎ 74 48 90 00; Dybbøl Banke 15; adult/child 25/5kr; 🕑 10am-5pm May-Aug, 10am-4pm Sep & Oct) is a windmill which has been bombed twice and now stands as a national symbol. The museum inside conveys the symbolism of the windmill - its great show of strength and that of the local people which gives further insight into the 1864 war.

SLEEPING

Hotel Sønderborg (☎ 74 42 34 33; www.hotelsoenderborg.dk; Kongevej 96; s/d 570r/820kr; Ⓟ) Occupies a classic 1904 building with all the charm of that era. All rooms have a bathroom, cable TV, telephone and mini-bar. It's a five minute walk southeast of the tourist office.

Comwell Sønderborg (☎ 74 42 19 00; www.comwell.com; Rosengade 2; s/d 795/895kr; Ⓟ ☒ 🖳) Modern four-star hotel lays on the luxury with spacious rooms, a gym, sauna and swimming pool (guests only).It's next to the castle.

Danhostel Sønderborg (☎ 74 42 31 12; www.danhostel.dk/sonderborg; Kærvej 70; 🕑 Feb-Nov; dm/d 118/325kr; Ⓟ ☒) Just 10 minutes north of the town centre, this modern hostel has heated, four-bed dorms with bathroom. There's also a sauna, a lounge with open fireplace, and sporting fields. Not surprisingly, it's a hit with school camps.

Sønderborg Camping (☎ 74 42 41 89; Ringgade 7; www.sonderborgcamping.dk in Danish; Apr-Sep; per person 61kr; P) In an idyllic position next to the yacht harbour, this is only 10 minutes' walk east of the town centre. There's a mini-market, laundry and TV lounge.

EATING

You'll find a selection of quality eateries down by the harbour and a few cheap eats around the tourist office.

Colosseum (☎ 74 42 23 06; Sønder Havnegade 24; smørrebrød 40-70kr, mains 135kr; lunch & dinner) Serves up traditional Danish fare and offers spectacular views of the harbour. Great for a feed or a drink as the yachts sail by. It's just up from the castle and does an enticing dish of salmon poached in white wine. The smørrebrød is pretty good for lunch.

Café au Lait (☎ 74 43 16 39; Sønder Havnegade 22; lunch 80kr; lunch & dinner) Antique café has great outdoor seating and dishes up both steak and seafood – the shellfish of the day comes highly recommended.

OX-EN Latino Steak House (☎ 74 42 27 07; Brogade 2; mains 160kr; dinner) Another harbour restaurant that gets packed with locals enjoying succulent Argentinean steaks with an imported Chilean wine. Great atmosphere and brilliant meat, South American style.

Maybe Not Bob (☎ 74 42 52 28; Rådhustorvet 5; sandwiches & snacks 25-40kr; lunch & dinner) With some outdoor seating on the square, Kilkenny beer on tap and reasonably priced sandwiches, Maybe Not Bob draws a young crowd.

GETTING THERE & AWAY

Sønderborg is 30km northeast of the German border crossing at Kruså, via Rte 8.

The airport is 6km north of town. The commuter airline Cimber Air offers daily direct flights to Copenhagen. For more information, see p305.

Sønderborg is connected by numerous trains each day to Kolding (119kr, 1½ hours) and the rest of Jutland. It's also possible to go from Sønderborg to Padborg (65kr), changing trains in Tinglev; with a good connection it takes about an hour.

GETTING AROUND

If you want to cycle between sights, bicycles can be hired from **Stavgaard Eft** (☎ 74 42 33 75; Lille Rådhusgade 41; per day 80kr), a block northeast of Rådhustorvet.

AROUND ALS

Tourism is fairly quiet and laid back on the island of Als. There are, however, plenty of great day outings.

Sights

AUGUSTENBORG SLOT

Eight kilometres northeast of Sønderborg along Rte 8, Augustenborg is one of Als' more easily accessible and interesting villages. Spend an afternoon wandering around the lush gardens of the grand **Augustenborg Slot** (☎ 74 47 17 20; admission free; church & museum 10am-6pm). You will be following in the footsteps of Hans Christian Andersen who used to visit the duke and his family and sought peace and tranquillity under the old linden tree. The castle is no longer used by the Duke of Augustenborg; rather it serves as a psychiatric hospital. There is a small exhibition in both the gatehouse and courtly palace chapel; if the chapel door is locked, borrow the key from the hospital caretaker.

DANFOSS MUSEUM & ADVENTURE PARK

Inside this **park** (☎ 74 88 59 77; Gammel Fabriksvej 7, Elsmark, Nordborg) you can not only learn about inventions that transformed Danfoss into Denmark's largest industrial company, you can enter the sensory room, which will take you from Antarctica to the Sahara in under 30 seconds, and allows you to compete in a Formula One race. Outside, the Experience Park (open spring, 2005) aims to convey the way nature and its forces have improved the quality of human life. From the Blue Cube to the Garden of Wisdom, it's set to be quite surreal.

KEGNÆS ISLAND

Kegnæs Island, has a lovely feeling of solitude with the narrow deserted roads and rolling fields making for a pleasant outing. In the south of Als, Kegnæs Island is great for cycling or driving around. The **lighthouse** just across the causeway can be climbed and provides a good panoramic view of mainland Germany.

Activities

FISHING

Keen anglers will always find a nice spot to throw a line and see what bites. Head to the western end of Kegnæs Island and there is plenty of trout and flounder. If you go 4.5km north of Fynshav to a spot called **Fladbæk** you can reel in some trout, cod and garfish for dinner. If you're after perch and eel, go 1km past Augustenborg to **Ketting Nor**. You can hire a boat and equipment from **WRS Charterboat** (☎ 74 47 36 35; Notmark 1; boats per day from 550kr) in Notmark, which is in the centre of the Als.

CYCLE TOURING

Why not hire a bike and see where it takes you? Quaint villages, cute whitewashed kirke and talkative locals await. A good route is to head out to **Regnæs** and then sweep up the coast to **Fynshav**. From there head inland to **Guderup** and wind your way down to Augustenborg via **Sebbelev**. It will take around five hours with stops.

GETTING THERE & AROUND

On weekdays bus No 13 leaves from the Sønderborg bus station about twice hourly for Augustenborg (26kr, 12 minutes).

Public buses elsewhere on the island are erratic but everything is easily accessible by bike or car.

The Sønderborg tourist office (p234) sells a map (30kr) with suggested cycling tours.

Central Jutland

CONTENTS

Home to Jutland's capital, Århus, central Jutland is an area rich in culture, wilderness and fun activities. The area stretches from the Limfjord in the north all the way to Fredericia in the south and across to the windswept west coast. The eastern side has rich, fertile soil and many farms, while the west is dominated by pasture and sugar beet fields.

Århus has been culturally enriched by the opening of ARoS, a new art museum that is an architectural wonder in itself. Add the café culture, great shopping, sensational restaurants and 40,000 students and you have a town that dances to its own unique beat.

Just west of the capital lies the Lake District (Søhøjlandet) and the landscape contrasts so vividly to the rest of Jutland it's little wonder that Danes love spending their holidays canoeing, hiking and biking out in the wilderness here.

The large peninsula north of Århus is home to Ebeltoft and Grenaa, both of which have individual charm and attract hordes of Swedish tourists during the warmer months. Inland there are amusement parks, manor houses and intimate villages to seduce the wandering traveller.

The northern area is also the location for Denmark's only national park, Rebild Bakker, and although you would be hard-pressed to get lost (it's only 77 sq km), it's a fantastic place to walk or bike around. A Viking fortress near Hobro also attracts history buffs.

Out on the west coast windsurfing is all the rage and Hvide Sande has some great spots while Ringkøbing adds some historical interest to this sandy stretch.

Legoland sees more tourists through its gates than any other tourist attraction outside Copenhagen, and Jelling's rune stones mark the origins of the Danish royal family.

HIGHLIGHTS

- Enjoy Århus' newest addition, **ARoS museum**, (p242) while soaking in the cosmopolitan ambience and wicked nightlife this university city offers
- Take a canoe trip through the **Lake District** (p255) and revel in the great outdoors
- Relive your childhood at the **Legoland amusement park** (p251), Denmark's most visited family destination
- Check out the rune stones at **Jelling** (p250), the spiritual home of the Danish royal family
- Get lost in Denmark's only national park, **Rebild Bakker** (p267)

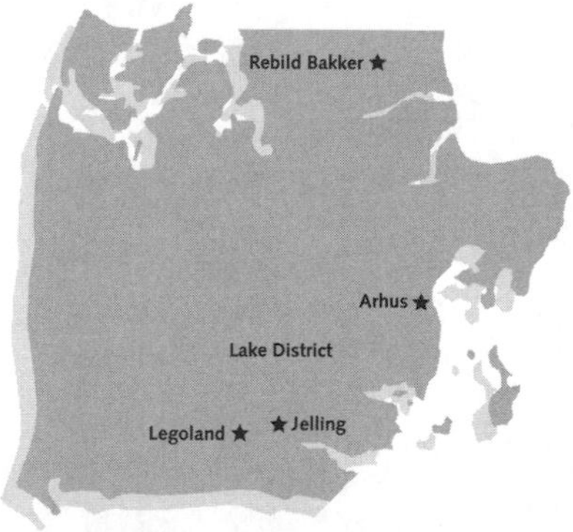
Rebild Bakker
Arhus
Lake District
Legoland
Jelling

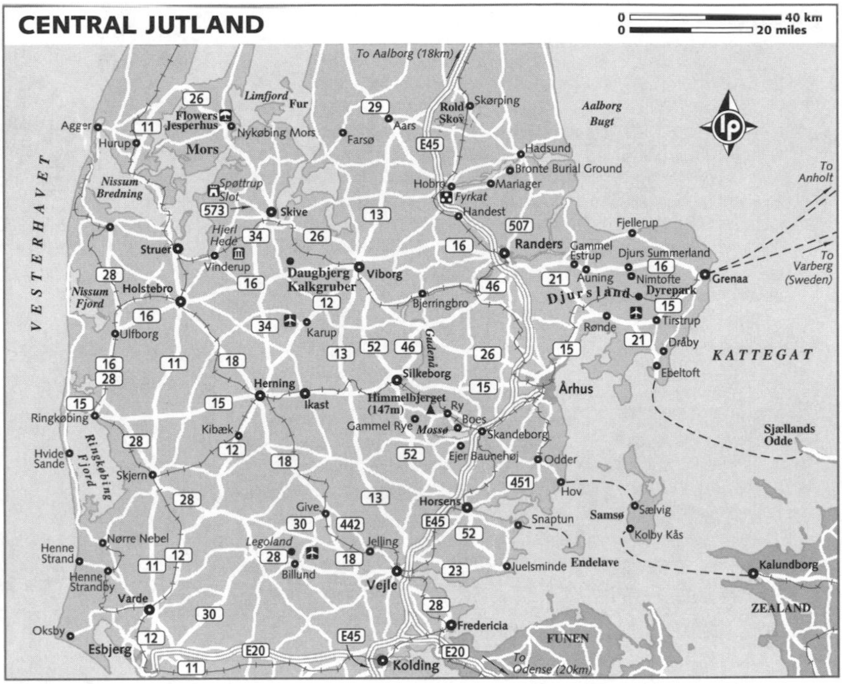
CENTRAL JUTLAND
0 40 km
0 20 miles
To Aalborg (18km)
Limfjord
Fur
Flowers
Jesperhus
Nykøbing Mors
Mors
Agger
Hurup
Farsø
Aars
Rold Skov
Skørping
Aalborg Bugt
Hadsund
Bronte Burial Ground
Mariager
Hobro
Fyrkat
Handest
To Anholt
VESTERHAVET
Nissum Bredning
Spøttrup Slot
Skive
Hjerl Hede
Struer
Vinderup
Daugbjerg Kalkgruber
Viborg
Bjerringbro
Randers
Gammel Estrup
Auning
Fjellerup
Djurs Summerland
Nimtofte
Dyrepark
Grenaa
To Varberg (Sweden)
Djursland
Tirstrup
Rønde
Dråby
Ebeltoft
KATTEGAT
Nissum Fjord
Holstebro
Ulfborg
Karup
Gudenå
Silkeborg
Herning
Ikast
Himmelbjerget (147m)
Ry
Boes
Gammel Rye
Mossø
Skanderborg
Århus
Ringkøbing
Ringkøbing Fjord
Kibæk
Hvide Sande
Skjern
Ejer Bavnehøj
Odder
Hov
Sjællands Odde
Give
Horsens
Snaptun
Samsø
Sælvig
Kolby Kås
Nørre Nebel
Legoland
Billund
Jelling
Henne Strand
Henne Stranby
Juelsminde
Endelave
Kalundborg
Varde
Vejle
ZEALAND
Fredericia
Oksby
Esbjerg
Kolding
FUNEN
To Odense (20km)
26
11
29
E45
573
13
34
26
507
16
16
46
21
28
12
16
34
52
46
26
15
16
28
11
18
21
15
15
15
12
18
52
451
28
13
30
442
E45
52
12
11
28
18
23
28
30
12
E20
E45
E20
11

ÅRHUS

pop 300,000

Great bars and cafés, massive museums, a lengthy church, sandy beaches and cheap flights have catapulted this cultural haven into the limelight. It's possibly the world's smallest big city. A vibrant student population brings alive its glorious parks, fills its cobblestone streets and complements its effervescent architecture. The cultural capital of Denmark has a brisk sea breeze that sweeps into the centre from its bustling port. Århus exudes a unique charm, little wonder that its popularity is indeed on the rise.

History

Due to its central seaside location, Århus has always been a busy trading town. Excavations from 1963 suggest the town was founded in around 900.

Medieval times were Århus' most turbulent as the town was wedged right in the middle of feuding neighbouring states. King Sweyn II of Denmark and King Magnus of Norway engaged in a major battle off Århus in 1043, and just a few years later in 1050 Århus was ravaged by the Norwegian warrior king Harald Hardrada. Prosperity was kept in check over the following centuries by raids from rival Vikings and attacks by fearsome Wend pirates.

Stability then ensued until the 1500s and it was during this time Århus flourished as a centre of trade, art and religion. Its natural asset, a large, protected harbour, drew attention from far and wide and in the process turned Århus into one of Jutland's most important transport hubs – a focus that remains to this day.

The university has a tale of its own as Århus established it against the wishes of the national government in 1928. However, by the time it was ready in 1933 the government had changed its tune and was in full support of the learned institution. Nowadays it is a cornerstone of the vibrant life of the city with students from the university, and those enrolled at Århus engineering college, dental school, business

ÅRHUS

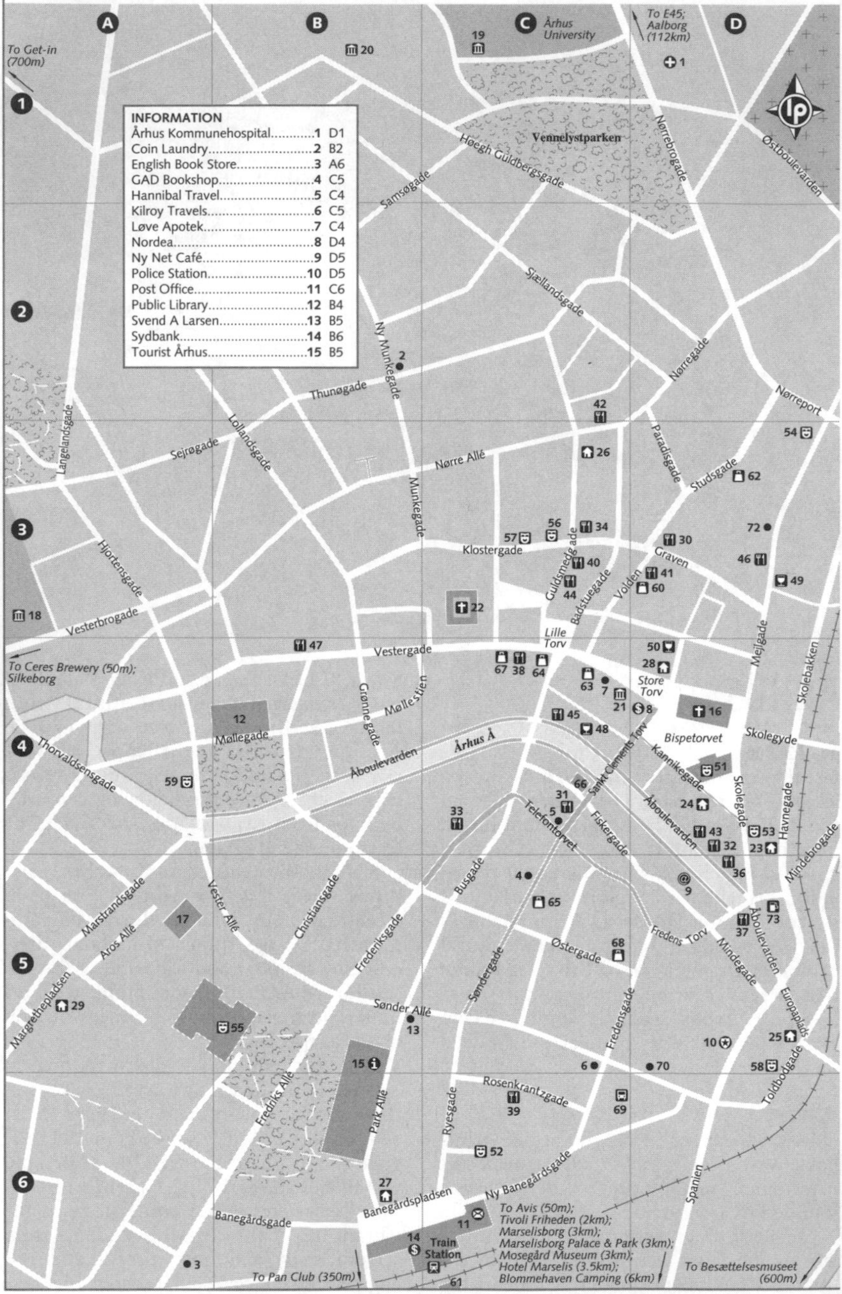
INFORMATION
Århus Kommunehospital....1 D1
Coin Laundry....2 B2
English Book Store....3 A6
GAD Bookshop....4 C5
Hannibal Travel....5 C4
Kilroy Travels....6 C5
Løve Apotek....7 C4
Nordea....8 D4
Ny Net Café....9 D5
Police Station....10 D5
Post Office....11 C6
Public Library....12 B4
Svend A Larsen....13 B5
Sydbank....14 B6
Tourist Århus....15 B5
To Get-in (700m)
Århus University
To E45; Aalborg (112km)
Vennelystparken
Høegh Guldbergsgade
Samsøgade
Nørrebrogade
Østboulevarden
Sjællandsgade
Nørregade
Nørreport
Ny Munkegade
Thunøgade
Lollandsgade
Sejrøgade
Langelandsgade
Nørre Allé
Paradisgade
Studsgade
Munkegade
Klostergade
Graven
Guldsmedgade
Badstuegade
Volden
Hjortensgade
Vesterbrogade
Vestergade
Lille Torv
Store Torv
To Ceres Brewery (50m); Silkeborg
Grønnegade
Møllestien
Møllegade
Århus Å
Åboulevarden
Thorvaldsensgade
Bispetorvet
Kannikegade
Sankt Clemens Torv
Skolegade
Skolegyde
Mejlgade
Skolebakken
Havnegade
Mindebrogade
Telefontorvet
Fiskergade
Busgade
Vester Allé
Christiansgade
Marstrandsgade
Aros Allé
Margrethepladsen
Fredensgade
Fredens Torv
Mindegade
Østergade
Søndergade
Sønder Allé
Fredensgade
Europaplads
Toldbodgade
Rosenkrantzgade
Ryesgade
Frederiks Allé
Park Allé
Spanien
Ny Banegårdsgade
Banegårdspladsen
Banegårdsgade
Train Station
To Avis (50m); Tivoli Friheden (2km); Marselisborg (3km); Marselisborg Palace & Park (3km); Mosegård Museum (3km); Hotel Marselis (3.5km); Blommehaven Camping (6km)
To Pan Club (350m)
To Besættelsesmuseet (600m)

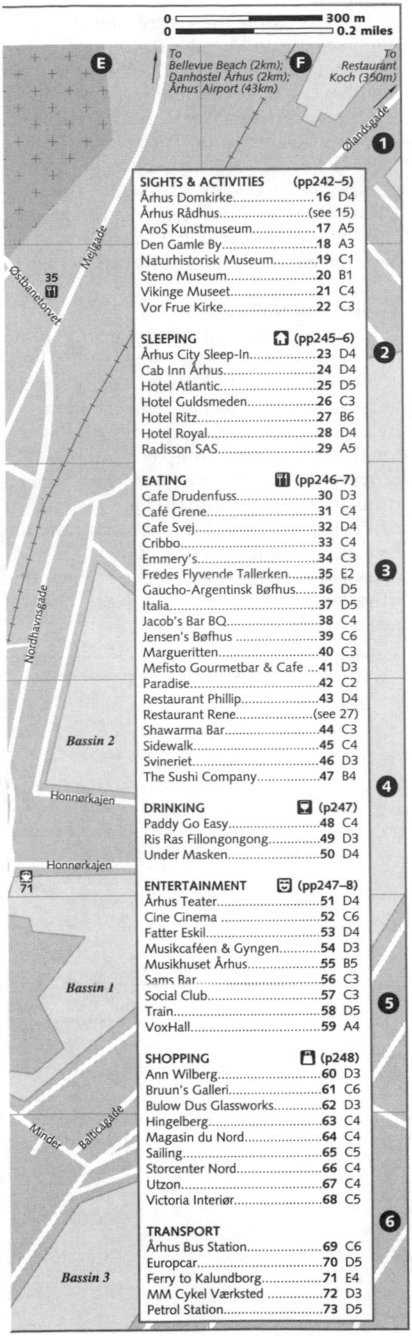
0 300 m
0 0.2 miles
To Bellevue Beach (2km); Danhostel Århus (2km); Århus Airport (43km)
To Restaurant Koch (350m)
Ølandsgade
Mejlgade
Østbanetorvet
Nordhavnsgade
Bassin 2
Honnørkajen
Honnørkajen
Bassin 1
Minder
Balticagade
Bassin 3
SIGHTS & ACTIVITIES (pp242–5)
Århus Domkirke....16 D4
Århus Rådhus....(see 15)
AroS Kunstmuseum....17 A5
Den Gamle By....18 A3
Naturhistorisk Museum....19 C1
Steno Museum....20 B1
Vikinge Museet....21 C4
Vor Frue Kirke....22 C3
SLEEPING (pp245–6)
Århus City Sleep-In....23 D4
Cab Inn Århus....24 D4
Hotel Atlantic....25 D5
Hotel Guldsmeden....26 C3
Hotel Ritz....27 B6
Hotel Royal....28 D4
Radisson SAS....29 A5
EATING (pp246–7)
Cafe Drudenfuss....30 D3
Café Grene....31 C4
Cafe Svej....32 D4
Cribbo....33 C4
Emmery's....34 C3
Fredes Flyvende Tallerken....35 E2
Gaucho-Argentinsk Bøfhus....36 D5
Italia....37 D5
Jacob's Bar BQ....38 C4
Jensen's Bøfhus....39 C6
Margueritten....40 C3
Mefisto Gourmetbar & Cafe....41 D3
Paradise....42 C2
Restaurant Phillip....43 D4
Restaurant Rene....(see 27)
Shawarma Bar....44 C3
Sidewalk....45 C4
Svineriet....46 D3
The Sushi Company....47 B4
DRINKING (p247)
Paddy Go Easy....48 C4
Ris Ras Fillongongong....49 D3
Under Masken....50 D4
ENTERTAINMENT (pp247–8)
Århus Teater....51 D4
Cine Cinema....52 C6
Fatter Eskil....53 D4
Musikcaféen & Gyngen....54 D3
Musikhuset Århus....55 B5
Sams Bar....56 C3
Social Club....57 C3
Train....58 D5
VoxHall....59 A4
SHOPPING (p248)
Ann Wilberg....60 D3
Bruun's Galleri....61 C6
Bulow Dus Glassworks....62 D3
Hingelberg....63 C4
Magasin du Nord....64 C4
Sailing....65 C5
Storcenter Nord....66 C4
Utzon....67 C4
Victoria Interiør....68 C5
TRANSPORT
Århus Bus Station....69 C6
Europcar....70 D5
Ferry to Kalundborg....71 E4
MM Cykel Værksted....72 D3
Petrol Station....73 D5

college, music academy and school of architecture, accounting for nearly 40,000 of the city's residents.

Orientation

Århus is fairly compact and easy to get around. The train station (Århus Hovedbanegård) marks the south side of the city centre. The pedestrian shopping streets of Søndergade and Sankt Clements Torv lead to Århus Domkirke in the heart of the old city. The small streets to the northwest of the cathedral are known as the Latin Quarter and are filled with cafés and shops.

Information

BOOKSHOPS

GAD bookshop (☎ 86 13 10 66; Søndergade 20)

Svend A Larsen (☎ 86 12 56 11; Sønder Allé 4) Has a comprehensive selection of English books.

English Book Store (☎ 86 19 54 55; Frederiks Allé 53) Specialises in both new and second-hand English-language books.

EMERGENCY & MEDICAL SERVICES

Århus Kommunehospital (☎ 87 31 50 50; Nørrebrogade 44) Has a 24-hour emergency ward.

Krisecenter for Voldsramtekvinder (☎ 86 15 35 22) Helps women in crisis and can provide a safe overnight haven if necessary.

Løve Apotek (☎ 86 12 00 22; Store Torv 5) A 24-hour pharmacy.

Police/ambulance (☎ 112)

INTERNET ACCESS

Ny Net Café (☎ 89 41 39 30; Åboulevarden 21; 11am-midnight) Lightning-fast access.

LAUNDRY

Coin laundry (cnr Thunøgade & Ny Munkegade) Just north of the city centre.

LIBRARY & MEDIA

Public library (☎ 86 12 48 44; Møllegade), where you can read internaional papers in the large modern facility off Vester Allé. International newspapers are on sale at the kiosk in the train station.

MONEY

Nordea (☎ 89 42 11 00; Sankt Clements Torv 6) Near Århus Domkirke.

Sydbank (☎ 86 12 40 88; Banegårdspladsen 1) At the front of the train station.

POST

Post office (☎ 89 35 80 00; Banegårdspladsen 1A) Beside the train station.

TOURIST INFORMATION

Tourist Århus (☎ 89 40 67 00; www.visitaarhus.com; Rådhuset, 8000 Århus C; 9.30am-6pm Mon-Fri, 9.30am-5pm Sat, 9.30am-1pm Sun mid-Jun–Aug, 9.30am-5pm Mon-Fri, 10am-1pm Sat May–mid-Jun, 9.30am-4.30pm Mon-Fri, 10am-1pm Sat Sep-Apr) Situated in the town hall.

TRAVEL AGENCIES

Kilroy Travels (☎ 86 20 11 44; Fredensgade 40) Specialises in youth and discount travel.

Hannibal Travel (☎ 86 76 00 99; Søndergae 10-12) A more upmarket option.

Sights

AROS KUNSTMUSEUM

ARoS (☎ 87 30 66 00; Aros Allé 2; adult/child 60kr/free; 10am-5pm Tue & Thu-Sun, 10am-10pm Wed), the new kid on the block, is not only large (nine floors), but impressive and profound in parts. If you like to be shocked, Bjørn Nørgaards' sacrificing of a horse can be seen in 112 jars, while the centre's most imposing piece is Ron Mueck's sculpture of a boy, crouching down and overlooking you from 5m above. The centre also has a wonderful selection of Golden Age works, as well as examples of Danish modernism from 1900 to 1960 and an abundance of obscure contemporary art to get the imagination ticking. Up on the roof there is great view looking back over Århus, yet a tad frustrating as the harbour views are not the feature here.

ÅRHUS DOMKIRKE

With a lofty nave spanning nearly 100m in length, **Århus Cathedral** (☎ 86 12 38 45; Bispetorv; admission free; 9.30am-4pm Mon-Sat May-Sep, 10am-3pm Mon-Sat Oct-Apr) is Denmark's longest. Its construction began in around 1200 and took 100 years to complete. In the 15th century the cathedral was transformed from its original Romanesque style to its current Gothic character. At that time the roof was raised over the nave, the landmark clock tower was erected, high Gothic windows were installed and the chancel extended.

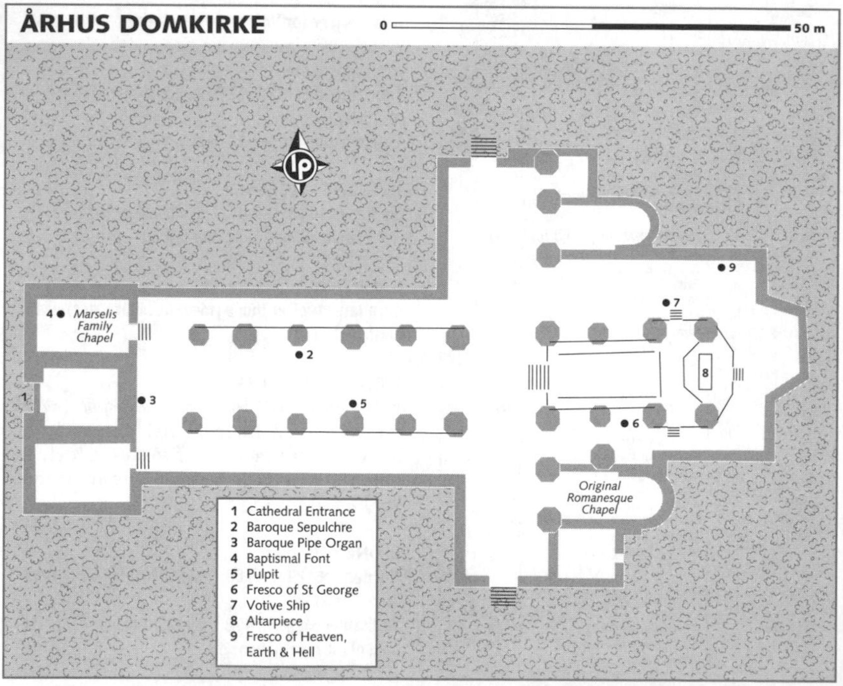
ÅRHUS DOMKIRKE
0
50 m
Marselis Family Chapel
Original Romanesque Chapel
1 Cathedral Entrance
2 Baroque Sepulchre
3 Baroque Pipe Organ
4 Baptismal Font
5 Pulpit
6 Fresco of St George
7 Votive Ship
8 Altarpiece
9 Fresco of Heaven, Earth & Hell

LIGHTS, CAMERA, TICKET

Student cards in Århus are a great asset so don't hesitate to flaunt them at every opportunity. From pubs to restaurants to museums, students with cards are given favourable prices. Interestingly, only two years ago students who rode their bikes without lights at night were fined 50% of the total fine because of their student status. That has now changed but discounts are widely available.

Like many other Danish churches, Århus Domkirke was once richly decorated with frescoes that were painted to convey biblical parables to illiterate peasants. After the Reformation in 1536 church authorities, who felt the frescoes embodied Catholicism, had them all whitewashed. Many of these frescoes, which range from tormented scenes of hell to fairytale-like paintings, have now been uncovered and painstakingly restored.

Just north of the altar is a powerful **painting of St George**, the patron saint of knights, slaying a dragon while a grateful princess looks on; the Arabic numerals in the corner date it to 1497.

A focal point of the cathedral is the ornate, five-panel gilt **altarpiece** (pentaptych) made in Lubeck by the renowned woodcarver Bernt Notke in the 15th century. In its centre panel, to the left of the Madonna and child, is a gaunt St Clement, to whom Århus Domkirke was dedicated. Rather ironically, Clement became the patron saint of sailors by having the inauspicious fate of drowning at sea with an anchor around his neck. The anchor, which has come to symbolise St Clement, can be found in many of the cathedral's decorations.

Other items worthy of special attention are the bronze **baptismal font** dating from 1481, the finely carved Renaissance **pulpit** created in 1588, the magnificent Baroque **pipe organ** made in 1730, the large **votive ship** from the 18th-century and the Baroque **sepulchre** in the Marselis family chapel.

DEN GAMLE BY

The **Old Town** (☎ 86 12 31 88; Viborgvej 2; adult/child 75/25kr; ⏲ 9am-6pm Jun-Aug; 10am-5pm Apr, May, Sep & Oct; 10am-4pm Jan; 11am-3pm Feb-Mar & Nov-Dec) is a proven heavyweight on the town's tourist circuit as some 75 restored buildings, located in the heart of the botanical gardens, come together to showcase all corners of Denmark. You can take a horse-drawn **carriage tour** (adult/child 35/25kr) around the gardens and then walk into each building to see what life was all about in these half-timbered 17th- and 18th-century buildings. Outside of opening hours you can stroll the cobbled streets for free and the light can often be ideal for photography.

The Old Town is 1.5km west of the city centre.

VIKINGE-MUSEET

In the mid-1960s this site was excavated and some impressive artefacts from 900 to 1400 were unearthed. It was established that Århus had been protected by a rampart since 900. Finds include a skeleton, 105,000 animal bones, 71 iron knives and other peculiar and important objects. The **museum** (☎ 89 42 11 00; Sankt Clements Torv 6; admission free; ⏲ 10am-4pm Mon-Fri, 10am-5.30pm Thu) takes up the basement of Nordea Bank, a stone's throw from the cathedral.

BESÆTTELSESMUSEET

For those interested in the German Occupation during WWII, this **museum** (☎ 86 18 42 77; Mathilde Fibigers Have 2; adult/child 20kr/free; ⏲ 11am-4pm Tue, Thu, Sat & Sun Jun-Aug, 11am-4pm Sat & Sun Sep-May) has well-presented displays of military equipment, Nazi and Danish propaganda and snippets into everyday life that are sure to keep you intrigued.

UNIVERSITY MUSEUMS

There are two museums in Universitetsparken, the grounds of Århus University. **Naturhistorisk Museum** (☎ 86 12 97 77; adult/child 40/15kr; ⏲ 10am-5pm Jul & Aug, 10am-4pm Sep-Jun) delves into the evolution of the Danish landscape since the Ice Age, and also has a comprehensive collection of stuffed birds from all corners of the globe.

Steno Museet (☎ 89 42 39 75; adult/child 40/15kr; ⏲ 10am-4pm Tue-Sun), a history of science museum, also features an outdoor garden comprising 350 herbs. Inside, you can take in the **planetarium show** (adult/child 40/20kr, incl museum 60/30kr) that looks into outer space at 11am, 1pm and 2pm.

Buses to Århus University include Nos 1, 2, 3 and 11.

VOR FRUE KIRKE

Set back from Vestergade, the **Vor Frue Kirke** (☎ 86 12 12 43; Frue Kirkeplads; admission free; ⏰ 10am-2pm Mon-Fri, 10am-noon Sat), is like a Russian *matryoshka* doll, opening to reveal multiple layers beneath the surface. It was here that the original Århus cathedral was erected shortly after 1060 when Sweyn II, bent on weakening the power of the archbishop who led the Danish church, divided Denmark into eight separate dioceses, one of which was Århus. The cathedral was constructed from rough stone and travertine, and stood until about 1240 when it was replaced by the current Vor Frue Kirke.

Built of red brick, the church has a largely whitewashed interior although the chancel features a few exposed frescoes depicting the coats of arms of wealthy families from the 14th century. There's also a detailed triptych altar carved by Claus Berg in 1530. However, the main treasure is in the church basement – the vaulted **crypt** of the original cathedral, which is the oldest surviving church interior in Denmark. Entered via the stairs beneath the chancel, the crypt was uncovered by chance in 1956 during a restoration by the national museum.

Vor Frue Kirke has yet another chapel, this one exhibiting early-16th-century frescoes, which can be entered through the garden courtyard; it's behind the first door on the left.

ÅRHUS RÅDHUS

Århus **city hall** (☎ 89 40 20 00; Rådhuspladsen; tour/lift 10/5kr; ⏰ tour 11am, lift to rooftop noon & 2pm) was designed by architect Arne Jacobsen, a pioneer of Danish modernism, and completed in 1942. This controversial building is ponderous, yet functional in design and is topped by a rectangular clock tower, the outer skeleton of which resembles forgotten scaffolding. The outer façade is dark Norwegian marble, while the inside has light, open spaces.

MARSELISBORG

A green belt begins 2km south of the city centre and runs nearly 10km south and is great for hiking, cycling and horse riding. It's divided into three sections, with the northern end known as Marselisborg, the midsection Moesgård and the southern end Fløjstrup – the names taken from the former estates that they were once part of.

Two standout features on the northern tip of the woodland are Tivoli Friheden (below) and **Jysk Væddeløbsbane** (a horse racing track).

Marselisborg Palace & Park (Kongevejen 100) is the summer home of the royal family and when they are not in residence the pubic is allowed to explore the grounds and the rose garden. When they are there, you can watch the changing of the guard at midday from a vantage point on the road. The palace can be reached by bus Nos 1, 18 and 19.

A further 1.5km southeast of the palace is **Dyrehaven** (Deer Park) which, as the name suggest, has an abundance of deer along with wild pigs. The park makes for a relaxing stroll on a sunny day.

MOESGÅRD

The Moesgård area is ideal for a half-day outing, taking in the museum and then an interesting walk around the area.

Moesgård Museum (☎ 89 42 11 00; Moesgård Allé 20; adult/child 45kr/free; ⏰ 10am-5pm daily Apr-Sep, 10am-4pm Tue-Sun Oct-Mar) is centred on Graubelle Man a 2000-year-old man discovered in a nearby bog in 1952. He is so well preserved you can see the wrinkles on his face as the bog literally tanned his hide, giving his skin a brown, leather-like appearance. The museum also has a room of rune stones, flint axes, tools and pottery.

An enjoyable **trail** dubbed the 'prehistoric track' leads from behind the museum through fields of wildflowers, grazing sheep and beech woods down to **Moesgård Strand**, Århus' best sandy beach. The trail, marked by red-dotted stones, passes reconstructed historic sights including burial sites and an Iron Age house. Before you head off, pick up a brochure at the museum. You can walk one way and catch a bus from the beach back to the city centre or follow the trail both ways as a 5km round trip.

Bus No 6 runs about twice an hour from the train station.

Activities

TIVOLI FRIHEDEN

It's over a hundred years old, yet fun times still abound at this amusement park. It's a great theme park with all the old favourites – Dodgem cars and merry-go-rounds – as well as the newer, faster additions such as the stomach-turning Sky Tower. It's a great way to break up the cultural bombardment if museums are wearing a little thin. Located at the northern edge of Marselisborg woods, it can be reached via Strandvejen (2km) or you can get there by bus No 4, 18 or 19.

HIKING & CYCLING

The best hiking and cycling can be found along the green belt south of the city. The tourist office sells a brochure, *Nature Around Århus South* (10kr) which outlines some great routes as well as giving an insight into local fauna and fauna.

For hardened cyclists, *Cyclist Turistkort* (80kr) details cycle routes over a mix of surfaced secondary roads, forest paths and abandoned railway tracks. If you're planning on notching up a few kilometres on the bike, this publication is a must.

SWIMMING

Sandy beaches lie on the outskirts of Århus. The most popular one to the north is Bellevue, about 4km from the city centre (take bus No 6 or 16), while the favourite of the south is Moesgård Strand, 8km from the centre on bus No 19.

WINDSURFING

Windsurfers will find suitable spots in Århus Bay to the north of the city centre near Risskov and to the south at Marselisborg. For more on windsurfing, including information on classes, call **Surfline** (☎ 86 17 67 65).

OTHER SPORTS

Tourist Århus has a **Tourist Sport Program** (☎ 89 40 67 00); staff can help to arrange various sporting activities including sailing, tennis, golf, ice-skating and windsurfing.

Tours

If all the cultural sites have worked up a thirst then a **brewery tour** (Vesterbrogade; adult/child 25kr/free; 2pm Tue & Wed mid-Jun–Jul, 2pm Wed year-round) is just the medicine. It takes you through the wonders of beer production and finishes with a tasting session. Tickets are sold at the tourist office and sell like hot cakes so pick one up on arrival.

A **city tour** (☎ 89 40 67 00; adult/child 45kr/free; 10am daily from tourist office) provides a good overview of Århus' main sites and a detailed tour of Århus Domkirke conducted by knowledgeable multilingual guides (2½ hours). It's a cute way to begin your Århus experience as the price includes free public transport for the rest of the day.

Festivals

Every August sees the **Århus Festival** (www.aarhusfestuge.dk) transform the town into a celebration of life. An annual marathon takes place, along with a number of cultural performances, many of which are free.

Jazz lovers will be in heaven during **Århus Jazz Festival** (www.jazzfest.dk in Danish) in mid-July when 170 concerts take place over eight days. A number of big-name acts have made this a ritual since 1989.

Sleeping

BUDGET

Århus City Sleep-In (☎ 86 19 20 55; sleep-in@citysleep-in-dk, Havnegade 20, 8000 Århus C; dm/d 105/325kr;) Central, clean and has friendly staff. Add to that, this fine hostel has small dorms sleeping four, a pool table, TV room, guest kitchen, courtyard, 24-hour reception and laundry facilities and you have a top-quality hostel in the heart of Århus.

Get-in (☎ 86 10 86 14; www.get-in.dk; Jens Baggesensvej 43; s/d 250/350kr; P) Just north of the city centre near Århus University, this guesthouse is a rich man's hostel (or a poor man's hotel, depending on your point of view). The rooms are colourful, basic and there is a communal TV room and guest kitchen.

Danhostel Århus (☎ 86 16 72 98; www.danhostel.dk/aarhus; Marienlundsvej 10, 8240 Risskov; dm/d 111/472kr; 5 Jan-15 Dec; P) Situated in woods north of the city centre, this spacious, clean hostel was an 1850s dancehall in a previous lifetime. Take bus Nos 1, 6 or 9 and then it's a 300m walk east along Marienlundsvej.

Blommehaven Camping (☎ 86 27 02 07; info@blommehaven.dk, Ørneredevej 35, 8270 Århus; per person 61kr; Apr–mid-Sep; P) Camping ground 5km south of the centre fronts the beach in the Marselisborg woods. It's also home to a minimarket, making this spacious camp ground a solid option. Take bus No 19 from the train station.

MID-RANGE

Hotel Guldsmeden (☎ 86 13 45 50; www.hotelguldsmeden.dk in Danish; Guldsmedgade 40, 8000 Århus C; s/d without bathroom 495/745kr, with bathroom 795/945kr; P ☒) Twenty French colonial-style rooms delight with four-poster beds, good art and an intimate feel that is nonexistent in the bigger city hotels. The owner is an architect who has creatively added modern Scandinavian aspects to an older building. Pleasant touches include a hearty organic breakfast.

Cab Inn Århus (☎ 70 21 62 00; www.cabinn.dk; Kannikegade 14, 8000 Århus C; s/d 435/630kr; P ☒) A fantastic position overlooking Åboulevarden and competitive prices have seen this hotel bursting with English tourists taking advantage of cheap flights. Rooms come with all the amenities and service is swift and obliging.

Hotel Ritz (☎ 86 13 44 44; www.hotelritz.dk; Banegårdsplads 12, 8100 Århus C; s/d 895/1085kr; P ☒) Occupying a grand old building opposite the train station, the Ritz creaks with old world charm. Although some rooms can be cramped it's a comfortable option on the southern side of town.

CENTRAL JUTLAND

TOP-END

Hotel Royal (☎ 86 12 00 11; www.hotelroyal.dk; Store Torv 4, 8100 Århus C; s/d 1145/1295kr; P ☒) On the same square as Århus Domkirke is Århus' premiere hotel. The casino downstairs entertains high rollers and the rooms upstairs come complete with marble bathrooms. It's a charming 1838 hotel that has a real old money feel about it. You almost feel like lighting up a fat Havana just to fit in.

Hotel Atlantic (☎ 86 13 11 11; www.choicehotels.dk; Europaplads 12, 8000 Århus C; s/d 1075/1165kr; P ☒) An imposing hotel that has 102 inviting rooms equipped with all the creature comforts associated with a top-end hotel.

Hotel Marselis (☎ 86 14 44 11; www.marselis.dk; Strandvejen 25, 8000 Århus C; s/d 1195/1395kr; P ☒) Popular holiday and conference resort. The rooms are well furnished and have ocean-view balconies. You can literally walk out into the waves. The hotel is about 4km south of the city centre on the beach.

Radisson SAS (☎ 86 12 86 65; www.radisson.dk; Margrethepladsen 1; s/d 995/1295kr; P ☒) A four-star hotel that has some wonderfully plush rooms along with all the predictable Radisson luxury.

Eating

RESTAURANTS

Restaurant Rene (☎ 86 12 12 11; Banegårdspladsen 12; 3-course meal 300kr; lunch & dinner) Upmarket, classically furnished and offers exquisite food ranging from light lunches to gourmet, extravagant dinners. Certainly a place foodies will love.

Restaurant Koch (☎ 86 18 64 00; Pakkerivej; mains 250kr; lunch & dinner) Internationally recognised twin chefs, Jesper and Michael Koch, have set up this fine dining experience down at the harbour. There's a flamboyant use of fresh seafood and a menu that is sure to send diners into seventh heaven.

Restaurant Phillip (☎ 87 32 14 44; Åboulevarden 28; 3-course meal 250kr; lunch & dinner) Candle-lit tables, old school furnishings and a genuine 19th-century feel complement the great steaks and fresh seafood on offer. It's owned by former Danish Soccer International star Marc Rieper.

Gaucho-Argentinsk Bøfhus (☎ 86 13 70 65; Åboulevarden 20; 3-course meal 155kr; lunch & dinner) Lavestone South American steaks are on offer as well as plenty of imaginative dishes to keep most taste buds entertained.

Svineriet (☎ 86 12 30 00; Mejlgade 35; 3 courses 280kr; lunch & dinner) Quality dining in fine surrounds with food influences from Italy. The ambience is self-described as 'a dash of sophistication and humour from east Jutland'.

Italia (☎ 86 19 80 22; Åboulevarden 9; pizza & pasta from 60kr, mains 100kr; lunch & dinner) Italian restaurant boasts a wood-fired pizza oven for an authentic flavour.

Jensen's Bøfhus (☎ 86 12 44 88; Rosenkrantzgade 23; mains lunch/dinner 45/100kr; lunch & dinner) Great family option as the service is slick and the options plentiful.

Margueritten (☎ 86 19 60 33; Guldsmedgade 20; mains 130kr; lunch & dinner) Danish, French and Italian cuisine is on offer and there is both indoor and outdoor seating.

Jacob's Bar BQ (☎ 86 12 20 42; Vestergade 3; mains 100kr; lunch & dinner) In an historic merchant's house, this bustling place is known for its grilled steaks, and also has fish, lamb and kebab dishes.

CAFÉS

Sidewalk (☎ 86 18 18 66; Åboulevarden 56; brunch 75kr; breakfast, lunch & dinner) Brilliantly positioned café sits on the edge of the scenic canal. It's always full of atmosphere and is renowned for its brunch.

Café Svej (☎ 86 12 30 13; Åboulevarden 25; light meals 55kr; lunch & dinner) A ridiculously long bar, plus lovely outdoor seating and freshly prepared meals from the open kitchen make this place hard to beat.

Café Drudenfuss (☎ 86 12 82 72; cnr Graven & Studsgade; mains 30kr; breakfast & lunch) One of the more popular meeting places, this café has inexpensive sandwiches, empanadas and drinks.

Mefisto Gourmetbar & Cafe (☎ 86 13 18 13; Volden 28; mains 140kr; breakfast & lunch) Great wine, a diverse menu and a soothing atmosphere results in a trendy café that gets a lot of attention at weekends.

Café Grene (Søndergade 11; light snacks 35kr; lunch) For the traveller at heart, here is a café lined with memorabilia collected from all over the globe by the Grene sisters, Ane and Clara.

Emmery's (☎ 86 13 04 00; Guildsmedgade 24; snacks 30kr, mains 100kr; breakfast & lunch) A trendy café that focuses on organic produce and has plenty of healthy options.

The Sushi Company (☎ 86 13 73 83; Vestergade 48; sushi 35kr; lunch) A sharp, stylish little café that also has sushi to go – immaculately prepared and very tasty.

Fredes Flyvende Tallerken (☎ 86 16 92 57; Østbanetorvet 2; sandwiches 40kr; lunch & dinner) A focus upon homemade ingredients and fresh produce result in an engrossing sandwich experience that is a hit with Århus locals.

QUICK EATS

Shawarma Bar (☎ 86 19 49 25; Guildsmedgade 8; light meals from 30kr; breakfast, lunch & dinner) Popular hole-in-the-wall Middle Eastern sandwich shop commonly has a queue out the door – but it's worth the wait for falafel or the shawarma pitta-bread sandwiches.

Cribbo (Frediksgade 32; 2 scoops 18kr; 10am-9pm) Italian ice cream at its very best. The indulgent should try the tiramisu, and *brombær* (blackberry) mix.

Paradise (Nørregade 40; 2 scoops 16kr; 11am-6pm) One of the more comprehensive ranges of quality ice cream with every flavour under the sun.

The train station houses a supermarket, a few cafés in the adjoining shopping mall and some fast-food outlets.

Drinking

Ris Ras Filliongongong (☎ 86 18 50 06; Mejlgade 24; bottled beer 35kr) Leather couches, a comprehensive beer selection and an intimate atmosphere make this establishment a perfect place to chill out.

Under Masken (☎ 86 18 22 66; Bispegade 3; bottled beer 35kr) Ships hanging from the ceiling and a hippy, arty vibe in cosy surrounds makes this a pub with a difference.

Paddy Go Easy (☎ 86 13 83 33; Åboulevarden 60; pints 45kr) Not surprisingly, this authentic Irish pub has live Irish music at weekends and is also a spot to watch football games on a wide-screen TV.

Entertainment

Århus' large student contingent guarantees the bars fill up Wednesday onwards and the vibe is always happening. Pick up either *Musik Kalenderen* or *What's On in Århus* from the tourist office for bands and specific celebrations.

NIGHTCLUBS

Much of the vibrant music scene is centred on backstreet cafés that offer a variety of choices.

Train (☎ 86 13 47 22; Toldbodgade 6; cover charge 70kr) One of the hottest spots in town, Train features good rock, pop and jazz bands from Denmark and the UK, and also has a disco.

VoxHall (☎ 87 30 97 97; Vester Allé 15) A popular music venue which features a wide range of quality music, from rock and metal to world music and jazz.

Sams Bar (☎ 86 13 21 31; Klostergade 28) Part bar, part disco, old classics and current hits combine to set the tone for large times in this basement of fun.

Social Club (☎ 86 19 42 50; Klostergade 34; admission free with student card) Attracts students in droves, perhaps due to the ever-popular free beer (for students) before midnight. Afterwards, it turns into a packed, sweaty and sometimes a little raunchy dance affair with plenty of trance and hard tunes.

Fatter Eskil (☎ 86 19 44 11; Skolegade 25) Jazz or blues music most nights at his café.

Musikcaféen and **Gyngen** (☎ 86 76 03 44; Mejlgade 53) These are part of Kulturgyngen, a youth and culture centre that occupies a renovated factory on the northern side of the city centre. Both places offer an interesting alternative scene with a wide range of music including rock, techno and world music.

Pan Club (☎ 86 13 43 80; Jægergårdsgade 42) is a café and weekend disco just a short walk southwest of the train station. It's the city's main gay and lesbian hang-out.

OPERA

Musikhuset Århus (☎ 89 40 40 40; Thomas Jensens Allé) comprises two concert halls, the main one seating 1600 with events including dance performances, opera and musicals. Drop past the ticket office at the front to pick up a monthly guide. From international pop stars to classical symphonies, the offerings cut a broad swathe through the taste barometer.

THEATRE

Århus Teater (☎ 89 33 26 22; Bispetorv; season Sep-mid-Jun) is a splendid century-old building richly embellished with gargoyles and other extravagant décor, including a scene from a Ludvig Holberg play. It's also Jutland's largest theatre with five stages, a permanent theatre troupe, and an affiliated drama school.

CINEMA

Nine-screens **Cine City** (☎ 86 13 70 90; Sankt Knuds Torv 15) show all the latest Hollywood hits.

CASINO

Royal Scandinavia Casino (☎ 86 19 21 22; Store Torv 4; 2pm-4am daily, entrance 50kr after 7pm) All the traditional games and a rather cosy environment in which to invest your money in lady luck. Proper dress is required and men can hire jackets at the front door.

Shopping

Århus has the best shopping outside of Copenhagen. Søndergade, a busy pedestrian street, and the Latin Quarter are the two main shopping areas. There are two main department stores, **Magasin du Nord** (☎ 86 12 33 00; Immervad 2) and **Sailing** (☎ 86 12 18 00; Søndergade 27), which should cover most people's shopping needs from Danish silverware to tax-free gift items.

There are two busy shopping malls in town, Bruun's Galleri, which is connected to the train station and has 90 specialist shops, and Storcenter Nord, down near the canal, which houses some 45 specialist shops.

If you like top-quality glassware **Bulow Dus Glassworks** (☎ 86 12 72 86; Studsgade 14) has an exciting range of products. If you are on a romantic weekend and want to seal the deal with an expensive rock, drop by **Hingelberg** (☎ 86 13 13 00; Store Torv 3), which has been creating masterpieces since 1897.

Scandinavian interior design is always the envy of the rest of Europe and to catch a glimpse of the latest fashion **Victoria Interiør** (☎ 86 12 79 39; Østergade 33) stocks all the big names.

Renowned Danish designer **Ann Wilberg** (☎ 86 19 90 22; Volden 10-12) has a shop in the Latin Quarter and her designs are gaining prominence on catwalks around the globe. To wrap yourself in a good fur or leather coat for when the weather turns chilly drop by **Utzon** (☎ 86 13 60 88; Vestergade 5) which is refreshingly imaginative with its coveted coat selection.

Getting There & Away

AIR

Århus airport, in Tirstrup 44km northeast of the city (70kr, 45 minutes by airport bus), is primarily a domestic airport. Scandinavian Airlines (SAS) has numerous daily flights to and from Copenhagen, and Ryan Air has twice-daily bargain basement flights from London.

BOAT

Mols-Linien (☎ 70 10 14 18; adult/child/car 140/70/200kr) runs car ferries between Århus and Kalundborg six times per day on weekdays and three times per day at weekends (2¾ hours). It also runs thrice-daily trips up to Odden (65 minutes) with a similar price structure.

BUS

All long-distance buses stop at Århus bus station, 500m northeast of the train station. The bus station has lockers, a small grocery shop and an inexpensive café.

Express buses **Abildskous Rutebiler** (☎ 70 21 08 88) run four times daily between Copenhagen's Valby station and Århus (220kr, 2¾ hours).

CAR & MOTORCYCLE

The main highways to Århus are the E45 from the north and south, and Rte 15 from the west. The E45 curves around the western edge of the city as a ring road. There are several turn-offs from the ring road into the city, including Åhavevej from the south and Randersvej from the north.

TRAIN

Trains to Copenhagen (287kr, 3½ hours), via Odense, leave Århus roughly hourly from early morning to midnight. There's an hourly train service north to Frederikshavn

(189kr, 2½ hours) and south to Fredericia (110kr, one hour). There are also regular trains to Grenaa (76kr, 1½ hours), and hourly trains to Silkeborg (via Ry) in the Lake District (60kr, 50 minutes).

Getting Around

BICYCLE

MM Cykel Værksted (☎ 86 19 29 27; Mejlgade 41; per day/wk 3-speed 85/300kr, mountain bike 100/450kr) has a good range of bikes and is knowledgeable about surrounding bike routes.

BUS

Århus has an extensive public bus system and most buses depart twice hourly. Unlike the rest of Denmark, you get on the back of the bus and buy your ticket from the machine (17kr, two hours). Most city buses stop in front of the train station or around the corner from it on Park Allé. Dial ☎ 89 46 56 00 for information on bus routes and departure times.

Tourist Århus, hotels and camping grounds sell the **Århus pass** (adult/child 2 days 121/61kr, 7 days 171/83kr) allowing unlimited transport on municipal buses as well as admission to most city sights, including Den Gamle By, ARoS Museum, Kunstmuseum, Moesgård Museum, the two university museums, Det Danske Brandværnsmuseum, Kvindemuseet and Tivoli Friheden.

CAR & MOTORCYCLE

A car is quite convenient for getting to sights such as Moesgård on the city outskirts, although the city centre is really best explored on foot.

Århus has numerous *billetautomats* (parking meters) along its streets. Parking costs around 10kr per hour from 8am to 6pm Monday to Thursday, 8am to 8pm on Friday and 8am to 2pm on Saturday. Outside those hours parking is usually free of charge.

Car parks around town include large ones in front of and beneath the conference centre, Scandinavia Center Århus.

Cars can be rented in town from **Avis** (☎ 86 16 10 99; Spanien 63) or **Europcar** (☎ 89 33 11 11; Sønder Allé 35).

TAXI

Taxis are readily available at the train station or you can order one (☎ 89 48 48 48, 86 16 47 00).

EAST CENTRAL JUTLAND

This section of the Jutland region has two significant albiet dissimilar tourist destinations. Children who have played with Lego blocks will undoubtedly want to make a beeline for Legoland, Jutland's most visited attraction, while kid free adults may be more interested in Jelling, one of Denmark's most important historic sites and declared a World Heritage site in 1994.

FREDERICIA

pop 36,700

Fredericia's significance lies in its history and in the character of its old city. Industry is the dominant feature, but a concerted effort by the council to commemorate its war-torn history brings life into an otherwise dull city (for tourists, at least).

Fredericia's birth date was 1650, when Frederik III established a military stronghold on mainland Jutland with the construction of a fortress. The fortress played significant roles in the subsequent wars between Denmark and its neighbours. In the winter of 1657–58, Swedish troops, on their way to Copenhagen, overran the fortress and killed the entire garrison before marching on across the frozen waters of the Lille Bælt. The most celebrated battle took place two centuries later when, in 1849, the successful Danish defence of Fredericia from German assault halted the northward advance of the Schleswig-Holstein troops. The fortified ramparts are still standing today and spearhead the town's attractions.

Orientation

The train and bus stations are together to the west of the town centre. To get to the tourist office, walk north from the stations, turn right onto Vesterbrogade and follow it to the ramparts, then enter the old town gate at Danmark's Port through the rampart wall to Danmarksgade. The walk takes approximately 10 minutes.

Information

There are several banks on Gothersgade, just a few minutes' walk southeast of the tourist office.

Fredericia Turistbureau (☎ 75 92 13 77; www.visitfredericia.dk; Danmarksgade 2A; 🕑 9am-6pm Mon-Fri,

9am-2pm Sat mid-Jun–Aug, 10am-5pm Mon-Fri, 10am-1pm Sat Aug–mid-Jun) is in the centre of town and well signposted.

Post office (☎ 80 20 70 30) is on the northern side of the train station.

Sights & Activities

Fredericia's old earthen **ramparts** are the town's major draw card. They remain largely intact forming a mounded park-like green belt around the oldest section of the city. The ramparts extend 2km, walking along the top of them provides an insight into the significant role they played in the defence of the Danish border. Along the way are cannons, war memorials and lush green trees. For an overview, head to the western end of Danmarksgade and climb the water tower.

Fredericia Museum (☎ 72 10 69 80; Jernbanegade 10; adult/child 20kr/free; 🕒 11am-4pm mid-Jun–Aug, noon-4pm Oct–mid-Jun) has local military and civilian history in an attractive collection of historic buildings, just a few minutes' walk south of the train station.

Sleeping

Danhostel Fredericia (☎ 75 92 12 87; www.danhostel.dk/fredericia; Vestre Ringvej 98; dm/d 118/420kr; 🕒 mid-Jan–mid-Dec; P ⊠) Modern, cushy and with a great view of the area, is this five-star hostel 1km northwest of the train station.

Kronprinds Frederik (☎ 75 91 00 00; www.kronprindsfrederik.dk; Vestra Ringvej 96; s/d 995/1175kr; P ⊠) Just next to the hostel is this plush Best Western affiliate with ultramodern rooms that come with a gorgeous view. It's usually crowded with businesspeople.

Eating

In the town centre along Danmarksgade (which runs east from the tourist office) you'll find a variety of places to eat to suit all budgets.

Ti Ten Ned (☎ 75 93 33 55; Norgesgade 3; 2 courses 280kr; 🕒 lunch & dinner) Gourmet food-lovers will be at home here as top-notch meat and meticulously prepared dishes dazzle in this atmospheric restaurant in town.

Simon's Café & Restaurant (☎ 75 91 49 66; Torvegade 2; mains 140kr; 🕒 lunch & dinner) Traditional Danish fare is served here throughout the day and into the night with a focus on seasonal, fresh ingredients.

Café Den 7.Himmel (☎ 75 91 04 05; Gothersgade 7; lunch 60kr, dinner 130kr; 🕒 lunch & dinner) An oh so outrageously popular café in the heart of town with unbeatable outdoor seating and a varied menu.

Getting There & Away

Fredericia has good train connections, being on the north–south line between Padborg (110kr, 1¼ hours) and Frederikshavn and also on the Copenhagen (253kr, 2¼ hours) to Århus (110kr, one hour) route.

Fredericia is north of the E20, 80km from Nyborg and 92km from Esbjerg.

JELLING

postcode 7300

Revered as the birthplace of the monarchy and all that is truly Danish, it is little surprise this village is bustling with character and intrigue. People come to pay homage at Jelling Kirke, inspect the two nearby rune stones and climb the burial mounds. The town once served as the royal seat of King Gorm during the Vikings' most dominant era. Gorm the Old was the first in a millennium-long chain of Danish monarchs that continues unbroken to this day. The site of Gorm's ancient castle remains a mystery but other vestiges of his reign can still be found at Jelling Kirke.

Information

In the museum is **Jelling Turistbureau** (☎ 75 87 23 50; www.visitjelling.dk; Gormsgade 23; 🕒 10am-5pm daily mid-Jun–Aug, 1-4pm Tue-Sun Aug–mid-Jun).

Sights

Jelling Kirke (cnr Gormsgade & Vejlevej; admission free; 🕒 church 8am-5pm Mon-Fri, 8am-2pm Sat; grounds year-round), erected in about 1100, is one of Denmark's most significant historical sites. Inside this small whitewashed church you'll find some vividly restored 12th-century **frescoes** that are among the oldest in Denmark. The main attractions, however, are the two well-preserved **rune stones** just outside the church door.

The smaller stone was erected in the early 10th century by Gorm the Old in honour of his wife. The larger one, raised by Gorm's son, Harald Bluetooth, is adorned with the oldest representation of Christ found in Scandinavia and reads:

> Harald king bade this be ordained for
> Gorm his father and Thyra his mother,

the Harald who won for himself all Denmark and Norway and made the Danes Christians.

Harald Bluetooth did, in fact, succeed in routing the Swedes from Denmark and began the peaceful conversion of the Danish people from the pagan religion celebrated by his father to Christianity. The larger stone, commonly dubbed 'Denmark's baptismal certificate', not only represents the advent of Christianity but also bids a royal farewell to the ancient gods of prehistoric Denmark. One side of the stone, which depicts a snake coiled around a mythological creature, is thought to symbolise this change of faith.

Two huge **burial mounds** flank Jelling Kirke. The barrow to the north was long believed to contain the bones of Gorm and his queen Thyra, but when it was excavated in 1820 no human remains were found. In 1861 Frederik VII oversaw the excavation of the southern mound but, again, only a few objects were found with no mortal remains among them.

In the 1970s a team of archaeologists dug beneath Jelling Kirke itself and hit pay dirt. They found the remains of three earlier wooden churches; the oldest is thought to have been erected by Harald Bluetooth. A burial chamber was also unearthed at this time and human bones and gold jewellery were discovered. The jewellery was consistent with pieces that had been found earlier in the northern burial mound.

Archaeologists now believe that the skeletal remains found beneath the church are those of Gorm, who had originally been buried in the northern mound but was later re-interred by his son. Presumably Harald Bluetooth, out of respect, moved his parents' remains from pagan soil to a Christian place of honour within the church. The bones of Queen Thyra have yet to be found.

The Jelling burial mounds, church and rune stones are a designated Unesco World Heritage site.

Jelling Kirke is in the centre of town, just a two-minute walk due north from the train station along Stationsvej.

Kongernes Jelling (☎ 75 87 23 50; Gormsgade 23; adult/child 40/15kr; ⏰ 10am-4pm Tue-Sun Sept-mid-Jun; 1pm-4pm Tue-Fri Dec), opposite the church, provides further insight into the town's magnificent monuments and its importance in Danish royal history.

Sleeping & Eating

Jelling Kro (☎ 75 87 10 06; jellingkro@mail.dk; Gormsgade 16; 2 courses 170kr; s/d 395/495kr; ⏰ breakfast, lunch & dinner; P) In a 1780 yellow, half-timbered building bristling with character is Jelling's most appealing hotel. The rooms are simple, inviting and comfy. Downstairs the restaurant serves up tasty fish and meat dishes that are imaginative in creation and flavour.

Jelling Camping (☎ 75 87 16 53; www.jellingcamping.dk; Mølvangvej 55; per person 58kr; ⏰ Apr-Sep; P) Just 1km west of Jelling Kirke, this camping ground has great facilities including a minimarket, coin laundry and TV room.

Harald Blåtand (☎ 75 87 10 03; Gormsgade 11; mains 80kr; ⏰ lunch & dinner) Close to the church it has a wide array of dishes on offer and is also good for a coffee.

Getting There & Away

Jelling is 10km northwest of Vejle on Rte 442. From Vejle trains run at least hourly on weekdays, slightly less frequently at weekends (28kr, 15 minutes).

LEGOLAND

Wildly exciting rides, mind-blowing Lego models and the magic associated with great theme parks has transformed Legoland into Denmark's most visited tourist attraction outside of Copenhagen. It's a great day outing and sits in the middle of Jutland, 1km north of the town of Billund.

You should set aside one day to 'do' Legoland but truly dedicated Lego buffs might need more time in this remarkable park.

Information

There is no government tourist office, however at the front gate of Legoland, the park has ample information on surrounding activities and accommodation.

Legoland has its own bank, post office, tourist office, hotel and restaurants, and even its own airport.

Sights & Activities

The paramount attraction of the **park** (☎ 75 33 13 33; www.legoland.dk; Aastvej; adult/child 180/160kr, under 3 free; ⏰ 10am-8pm daily Apr–mid-Jul & mid-Aug–early Sep, 10am-9pm daily mid-Jul–mid-Aug, 10am-6pm Mon-Fri, 10am-8pm Sat & Sun early Sep-end Oct; closed rest of year) is **Miniland** – the 45 million plastic Lego blocks snapped together to create miniature cities. Take a trip around the Lilliputian world and see the Statue of Liberty, Bangkok's Grand Palace, Amsterdam or perhaps a quick trip around Denmark taking in Møgeltønder, Copenhagen's port, Billund airport and Ribe. The reconstructions are on a scale of 1:20 and the attention to detail is incredible.

The park employs up to 40 'builders' to maintain and piece together these showpieces. The tallest piece, a model of the American Indian chief, Sitting Bull, reaches 14m in height and contains 1.4 million Lego blocks.

Adventure Land is where the heart really starts pumping. X-treme Racers throw you around in all directions as they crank up to a speed of 60km/h. Then for the individualistic adrenalin junkie, why not design your own horror ride on the **Power Builder**, where *you* set the parameters for a wild old time.

For the chilled park goer there are rides aplenty to keep the blood pressure down, from merry-go-rounds to the **Lego Canoe** ride to a tranquil train ride. Once the entrance fee is paid, all rides are free. The only exception is the **Lego Driving School** (30kr) that lets kids obtain their driving licences and puts them out onto the 'open road' (that is, the open Lego road).

Other sections in the park include the **Knights' Kingdom**, where a grand old castle awaits; **Duplo Land** that consists of rides for the little ones; **Imagination Zone**, where kid's can realise their secret Lego desires, and **Pirate Land** which hosts ships and sword play.

Activities and rides shut down two hours before Legoland closes, so it's a good idea to indulge in the rides in the morning and spend the latter hours soaking up Miniland over an ice cream or two. Once the rides have stopped the gates swing open and curious Lego enthusiasts who just want to enjoy the sights are free to stroll in without reaching for the hip pocket.

Sleeping

If you are coming during high season, advance bookings are highly recommended.

Danhostel Billund (☎ 75 33 27 77; www.legoland-village.dk; Ellehammer Allé 2; dm/f 200/860kr; Ⓟ ☒) You'll find themed Lego rooms at this modern five-star facility run in conjunction with the park. Family rooms sleep four.

Billund FDM Camping (☎ 75 33 15 21; www.billundcamping.dk; Ellehammer Allé 2; per person 65kr, 5-person chalet 480kr; Ⓟ) One of the largest camping grounds, with 550 sites, a food store, sitting rooms and playground. Three-star facility is 400m east of the Legoland gate.

Hotel Legoland (☎ 75 33 12 44; www.hotellegoland.dk; Aastvej 10; s/d 1120/1425kr, incl park entrance 1265/1715kr; Ⓟ ☒) As Legoland's official hotel, all rooms are themed around the product and you can roll out of bed and onto a roller coaster. The hotel offers very reasonable packages and has knowledgeable staff.

Hotel Propellen (☎ 75 33 81 33; www.propellen.dk; Nordmarksvej 3; s/d 985/1105kr; Ⓟ ☒ 🖳) Large, comfy rooms situated a stone's throw from the action of Legoland. This hotel has the best value and quality accommodation.

Hotel Svanen (☎ 75 33 28 33; www.hotelsvanen.dk; Nordmarksvej 8; s/d 950/1050kr; Ⓟ ☒) Attractive, affordable rooms 700m from the action, along with a generous buffet breakfast to set you up for an action-packed day.

Eating

Legoland has about a dozen food stands serving amusement park fare. The names given to these simple eateries – Hotdogs, Burger House, Coffee & Pastry, Pizza Slice, Pancakes and Soft Ice – simply reveal the menus. You can snack for around 50kr.

Hotel Legoland Restaurant (☎ 75 33 12 44; Aastvej 10; buffet lunch/dinner 170/210kr; 🕑 breakfast, lunch & dinner) For the kids there are Lego chips that can be put together and then into the mouth. For the adults the buffet has a wide selection that is sure to appeal to most taste buds.

Café & Bistro (☎ 75 33 27 77; Ellehammer Allé 2; buffet adults/kids 130/60kr; 🕑 breakfast, lunch & dinner) Economical way to fill up with smoked salmon, roast meat and a good salad.

Getting There & Away

Billund is on Rte 28, 59km northeast of Esbjerg and 28km west of Vejle.

AIR

Billund's airport sits right outside Legoland's gate, serving not only Legoland but most of southern Jutland. Because of its central location, it has grown into Denmark's second busiest airport.

PLASTIC FANTASTIC

Ever thought that you're only one good idea away from a million big ones? Well, Ole Kirk Christiansen probably didn't, but that's all it took. A carpenter by trade, when business was slow during a Depression-era slump in 1934 he turned his hammer to making wooden toys. What followed was a heart-warming story showing that 'from little things big things grow'. The same year he came up with the business name Lego (a contraction of *leg godt*, meaning 'play well' in Danish), and play well they did. By the late 1940s Lego became the first Danish company to acquire a plastics-injection moulding machine, and began making interlocking plastic blocks called 'binding bricks' – the forerunner of today's Lego blocks.

However, every rags to riches story has its tragedy and this one is no exception. In 1960 the wooden-toy warehouse went up in flames. Lego decided to focus upon its plastic toys instead, an idea that proved to be the cornerstone of the company's success. Lego blocks soon became the most popular children's toy in Europe.

It's estimated that in the past 50 years some 300 million children worldwide have at one time or another played with Lego toys. Lego goes hand in hand with growing up: one foot in front of the other, one block on top of the other; incredibly simple yet a constant that is as perennial as the grass.

As Lego building blocks are passed from generation to generation the company is following that same formula. Currently headed by Ole Kirk's grandson, Lego is now one of the world's most recognisable companies.

Maersk Air (☎ 70 10 74 74) and **SAS** (☎ 32 32 68 00) operates a heavy schedule with numerous daily flights to Billund from Copenhagen (900kr return); daily international services to Billund from many European cities such as Amsterdam, Frankfurt and London.

BUS

There's no train service, but if you're travelling by train, the most common route is to get off at Vejle and catch a bus from there. Bus No 907 (49kr, 40 minutes) runs hourly from Vejle to Legoland.

You could also hop onto one of the airport buses, timed to meet scheduled flights between Billund and Århus (150kr, 1½ hours) or Fredericia (78kr, one hour).

CAR

Four international car rental agencies have booths at Billund: **Avis** (☎ 75 33 29 99), **Budget** (☎ 75 35 39 00), **Europcar** (☎ 75 33 15 33) and **Hertz** (☎ 75 33 82 50).

THE LAKE DISTRICT

Jutland's most prized area is the Lake District, Sohojlandet, as it dazzles with hills, forests and lakes not found anywhere else in Denmark. The area is one to please the statisticians, as it has Denmark's longest river, the Gudenåo, Jutland's biggest lake, Mossø, and Denmark's highest point, Ejer Baunehøj. All of which may not make you quiver with astonishment, but are facts nonetheless.

SILKEBORG

pop 54,000

Silkeborg is the black sheep of Jutland, surrounded by hills, sitting on an expansive lake and spaciously laid out. It's tremendously popular with Danes as they return each summer to canoe, hike and revel in the great outdoors. The town's spacious layout can be attributed to its relatively late arrival in 1846. It was founded by Michael Drewson who built a paper mill on the eastern side of the river. The mill and other industries have since formed the backbone of the local economy. If you're strolling through the town at night walk past the lake which is lit up by a northern Europe's largest colour fountain.

Information

Coin laundry (☎ 86 80 57 51; Hostrupsgade 21)
Jyske Bank (☎ 89 22 22 22; Vestergade 16)
Library (☎ 86 82 02 33; Hostrupsgade 41) Has a central location and ample computers with Internet access.
Nordea (☎ 86 82 53 33; Vestergade 13)
Pharmacy (☎ 86 82 15 00; Vestergade 9)
Post office (☎ 76 26 86 00; Drewsensvej 1) Next to the train station.

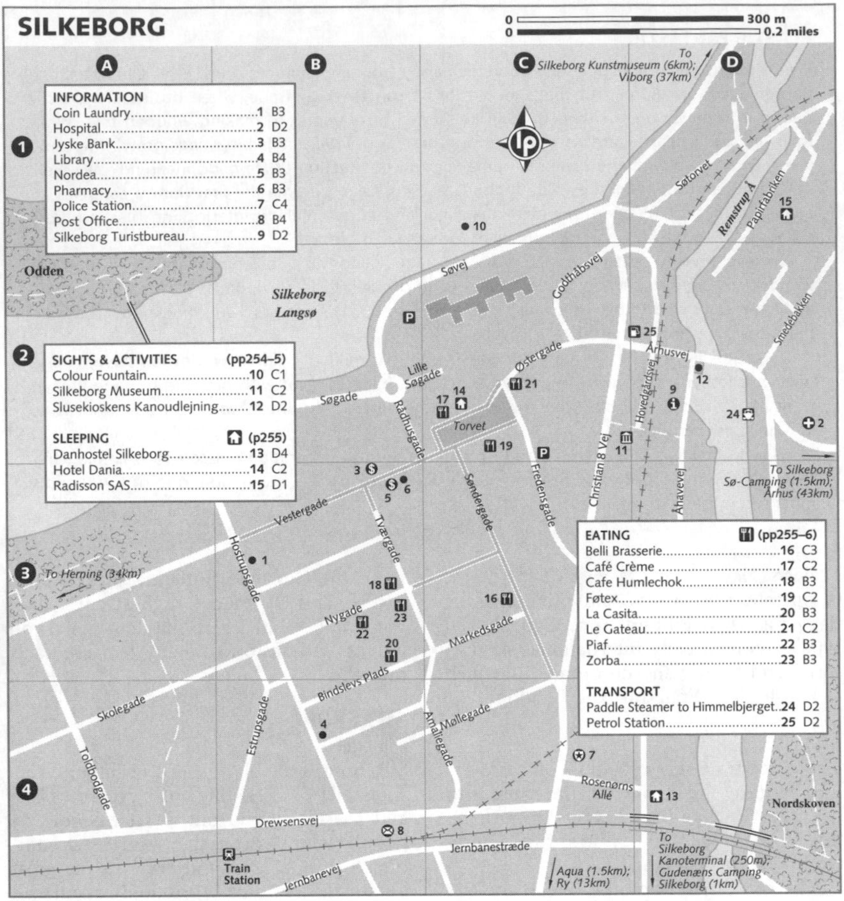
SILKEBORG
0 300 m
0 0.2 miles
A
B
C
D
1
2
3
4
To Silkeborg Kunstmuseum (6km); Viborg (37km)
INFORMATION
Coin Laundry 1 B3
Hospital 2 D2
Jyske Bank 3 B3
Library 4 B4
Nordea 5 B3
Pharmacy 6 B3
Police Station 7 C4
Post Office 8 B4
Silkeborg Turistbureau 9 D2
SIGHTS & ACTIVITIES (pp254–5)
Colour Fountain 10 C1
Silkeborg Museum 11 C2
Slusekioskens Kanoudlejning 12 D2
SLEEPING (p255)
Danhostel Silkeborg 13 D4
Hotel Dania 14 C2
Radisson SAS 15 D1
EATING (pp255–6)
Belli Brasserie 16 C3
Café Crème 17 C2
Cafe Humlechok 18 B3
Føtex 19 C2
La Casita 20 B3
Le Gateau 21 C2
Piaf 22 B3
Zorba 23 B3
TRANSPORT
Paddle Steamer to Himmelbjerget 24 D2
Petrol Station 25 D2
Odden
Silkeborg Langsø
Søvej
Søtorvet
Remstrup Å
Papirfabrikken
Smedebakken
Godthåbsvej
Østergade
Århusvej
Hovedgårdsvej
Lille Søgade
Søgade
Rådhusgade
Torvet
Christian 8 Vej
Åhavevej
Fredensgade
Søndergade
Vestergade
Hostrupsgade
Tværgade
Nygade
Markedsgade
Bindslevs Plads
Skolegade
Estrupsgade
Møllegade
Arnalilegade
Toldbodgade
Rosenørns Allé
Drewsensvej
Jernbanestræde
Jernbanevej
Train Station
Nordskoven
To Herning (34km)
To Silkeborg Sø-Camping (1.5km); Århus (43km)
Aqua (1.5km); Ry (13km)
To Silkeborg Kanoterminal (250m); Gudenæns Camping Silkeborg (1km)

Silkeborg Turistbureau (☎ 86 82 19 11; www.silkeborg.com; Aahavevej 2A; 9am-5pm Mon-Fri, 10am-2pm Sat & Sun mid-Jun–Aug, 9am-4pm Mon-Fri, 10am-1pm Sat Oct–mid-Jun) Faces the river and is next to the museum.

Sights

Silkeborg Museum (☎ 86 82 14 99; Hovedgårdensvej 7; adult/child 30/10kr; 10am-5pm daily May-Oct, noon-4pm Wed, Sat & Sun in winter) is housed in the oldest building in Silkeborg which dates back to 1767. Speaking of old, inside you can check out **Tollund Man**, the oldest Danish man. Good at solving murder mysteries? Try this one. It hasn't been solved for 2400 years. The Tollund Man, aged 40, strolled around the outskirts of Silkeborg in 400 BC during the Iron Age, and his remains were found in 1950. The autopsy suggested he had been hanged, yet he was placed as though lying asleep with only a leather hat over his face. At the museum you can literally confront this man, as his skin has been so well preserved that you can see the wrinkles on his forehead. The autopsy also revealed he was a vegetarian, living off a mixture of grain and wheat. Surviving 2400 years in his original shape puts modern pop stars to shame, and his immortality is set to continue within the confines of this museum as he is the central star to an otherwise predictable collection.

If you like modern art, or, more specifically modern art by world-renowned Dane Asger Jorn, you are going to love **Silkeborg**

Kunstmusem (☎ 86 82 53 88; Gudenåvej 7; adult/child 30kr/free; 10am-5pm Tue-Sun Apr-Oct, noon-4pm Tue-Fri, 10am-5pm Sat & Sun Nov-Mar). His work provides the backbone to the museum's paintings and sculptures, though the collection also features works by 150 international artists. Look out for Asger Jorn's *The Moon Dog* from 1953, and John Halbek's *A Gentlemen & the Sea* from 1884.

Aqua (☎ 89 21 21 89; Vejsøvej 55; adult/child 65/35kr; 10am-6pm daily Jun-Aug, 10am-4pm Mon-Fri, 10am-5pm Sat & Sun Sep-May) is one for the kids on a rainy day. Enthusiastic staff entertain and educate the masses on feeding, ecology and the sustainability of freshwater fauna. It's certainly not a must-do, but if the heavens open, it will keep everyone entertained for a few hours.

Activities

Danes come to Silkeborg to be active on their summer break each year and you're sure to see thousands out and about during the hotter months.

CANOEING

There are a number of companies that hire out canoes, the most central being **Slusekioskens Kanoudlejning** (☎ 86 80 08 93; Haven; per hr/day 60/250kr). You can take to the waters and have quite an outing up the river. **Silkeborg Kanoterminal** (☎ 86 80 30 03; Åhave Alle 7; per hr/day 60/250kr) also has plenty of robust canoes for rent.

The tourist office organises popular, all-inclusive canoe tours that take you through some magnificent country. Tours range from three to six days. The **Family Tour** (6 days, 2 people 2550kr) takes you from Tørring to Silkeborg, staying in camping grounds; while the shorter **Ry to Silkeborg Tour** (3 days, per canoe 1150kr) covers 18km through rich forests. For the luxury-orientated canoeist, hotel accommodation can be arranged at atmospheric old hotels.

Alternatively you can plan your own tour and consult the various canoe hirers for the finer details – they are a wealth of information.

HIKING

To get to **Nordskoven**, a beech forest with hiking and cycling trails, simply walk over the old railway bridge at the eastern end of Jernbanestræde.

Festivals

The town comes alive with jazz concerts in every corner during **River Boat Jazz Festival** (☎ 86 80 16 17) in mid-June. You can buy a ticket and take a cruise down the river, or stroll the streets and take advantage of the free jazz. It's immensely popular with Århus people. Some 40,000 people venture here each year, attracted by the slogan 'New Orleans comes to Silkeborg'.

Sleeping

The tourist office has a list of private homes that let rooms ranging from 150kr to 400kr.

Danhostel Silkeborg (☎ 86 82 36 42; www.danhostel.dk/silkeborg; dm/d 118/290kr; Mar-Nov; P ☒) Gorgeously situated on the banks of the river and extremely popular. Four-bed dorms and a well-decked-out kitchen make this a great hostel.

Silkeborg Sø-Camping (☎ 86 82 28 24; www.seacamp.dk; Århusvej 51; per person 67kr; Apr–mid-Sep; P) Only 1.5km east of the centre, these grounds boast a private beach on the lake, canoes, barbecue and a real family feel.

Gudenæns Camping Silkeborg (☎ 86 82 22 01; www.gudenaaenscamping.dk; Vejlsøvej 7; per person 64kr; P) Right next to the river, this site has a pool, bouncy cushion and plenty of tree cover for pleasant camping.

Hotel Dania (☎ 86 82 01 11; www.hoteldania.dk; Torvet 5; s/d 1090/1265kr; P ☒) On the main square, this hotel has a traditional feel and the rooms overlooking the lake or square are cosy, clean and colour-coordinated. Downstairs the bar is charmingly old and the service is elegantly professional.

Radisson SAS (☎ 88 82 22 22; www.radisson.com; Papirfabrikken 12; s/d 795/895kr; P ☒) Right on the river, with rooms with all the luxuries, this modern hotel is representative of both the commercial and tourist-oriented nature of the town.

Eating

Café Humlechok (☎ 86 81 91 03; Nygade 16; mains 80kr; lunch & dinner) Focaccia, sandwiches, salads and burgers are of the highest quality here, and at weekends it often has live music and a young, fashionable crowd.

Zorba (☎ 86 81 21 55; Nygade & Tvaergade; lunch 70kr; dinner 160kr; lunch & dinner) A cosy candlelit affair specialising in Greek food – grilled lamb and moussaka take centre stage.

Café Crème (☎ 86 80 38 11; Torvet 3; lunch 80kr; ⏲ breakfast/lunch) On the main square and a great place for a late breakfast or relaxing coffee.

Le Gateau (☎ 86 82 03 37; Torvet 14; pastries 15kr; ⏲ breakfast/lunch) Fantastic selection of pastries and sandwiches. Also brews a strong, good coffee.

Belli Brasserie (☎ 86 82 40 97; Søndergade 20; sandwiches 40kr, tapas 80kr; ⏲ lunch & dinner) An inviting restaurant that has a Spanish-oriented menu with mouthwatering tapas on offer.

La Casita (☎ 86 81 38 12; Bindslevs Plads 6; 3-course meal 220kr; ⏲ dinner) Fulfilling, tasty Mexican food is served here and the atmosphere is jovial and entertaining.

Piaf (☎ 86 81 12 55; Nygade 31; 3-course meal 290kr; ⏲ dinner) Upmarket French restaurant has a changing menu such as fish soup, beef medallions and sumptuous gateaux.

For self-caterers, there's a **Føtex** (☎ 86 82 50 88; Torvet 4) supermarket on Torvet.

Entertainment

Nygade is where all the after-dark clubs and pubs are located, so just take a stroll down and you're sure to find a lively spot.

Getting There & Away

Silkeborg is 37km south of Viborg on Rte 52 and 43km west of Århus on Rte 15.

Hourly trains connect Silkeborg with Århus (60kr, 50 minutes) via Ry.

A paddle steamer sails from Silkeborg to Himmelbjerget daily during the summer. See opposite for details of departure times and costs.

Getting Around

You can park along the streets in the town centre and at Torvecentret on Fredensgade, as well as car parks on the western side of the rådhus.

Bicycles can be hired at the camping grounds and hostel; they cost around 60kr per day.

RY

pop 4800

Ry lies in the heart of the Lake District and has a pretty port along with many activities around town to keep you entertained. Hiking, canoeing, swimming and climbing are all on offer as well as cycling the area and discovering the quaint villages.

Information

Danske Bank (☎ 87 88 00 44; Klostervej 2)

Post office (☎ 76 26 86 00; Klostervej 1)

Ry Turistbureau (☎ 86 89 34 22; www.visitry.com; Klostervej 3; ⏲ 7am-4pm Mon-Fri, 9am-2pm Sat Jun-Aug, 7am-4pm Mon-Fri, 10am-noon Sat Sep-May) In the train station.

Activities

CLIMBING

Denmark's tallest tree has been turned into a climbing pole that sits just outside Ry at an impressive height of 45m. The Ry tourist office manages the tree and for 100kr you can climb to the top to get a bird's eye view of the area.

HIKING

The tourist office sells an English-language brochure called *On Foot in Ry and Environs* (10kr) that maps out and briefly describes 10 hikes in the Ry area. One of the nicest hikes from Ry is the two-hour, 7km walk to Himmelbjerget. The starting point is the dirt road that begins off Rodelundvej about 400m south of the Ry bridge. The path, which is signposted, leads to the Himmelbjerget boat dock before climbing the hill to the tower. A pleasant idea is to hike out there and catch a boat back to Ry or onto Silkeborg.

CYCLING TOUR

A solid ride takes you around Denmark's largest lake and up to Denmark's tallest point and through some quirky villages. Set out west bound on Rte 445 to **Gammel Rye**, where you can have a breather at the **Windmill & Wooden Shoe Museum** (☎ 86 89 81 94; Møllestien 5; adult/child 20kr/free; ⏲ 10am-5pm May-Sep). It has an 1872 Dutch windmill to complement the surprisingly interesting insight into 19th-century shoemaking. From there head south along Rte 461 for the town of **Klostermølle** which is surrounded by a lovely little forest and fronts onto the lake. Follow the lake through the township of **Dørup** and then take a right at Hemvej, which will take you to **Yding**. Take a left there and follow the signs to climb up to **Ejer Baunehøj**, Denmark's highest natural point at 170.89m. There are sweeping views from the top, but you can also climb a grand, four-pillared tower (10kr honesty box) for an even better view. During 1848–64, fires were lit to warn of unrest in the region and men fit for battle had a formal duty to assemble here. From there you sweep back down to the lake through the towns of **Ejer, Lille Tåning** and **Tåning** and onto the lake. Follow the edge of the lake to the tiny hamlet of **Boes** that boasts an array of picturesque thatched houses and bounteous flower gardens. For the final leg it's a mellow climb back up to Ry. This ride is about 40km in length and takes the best part of a day to enjoy.

CANOEING

If you want to explore the surrounding lakes and rivers, **Ry Kanofart** (☎ 86 89 11 67; Kyhnsvej 20; per hr/day 60/300kr) has canoes for hire.

Sleeping

Staff at the tourist office can book rooms from 200kr in private homes around Ry. They also book cottages in the Ry area, most of which can sleep four people and cost from 2400kr a week.

Birkhede Camping & Motel (☎ 86 89 13 55; info@birkhede.dk; Lyngvej 14; per person 59kr, motel from 280kr; P) A great park just north of Ry, the grounds are green and facilities include a water slide, heated pool and kitchen. There are also inviting hikes around the area.

Ry Park Hotel (☎ 86 89 19 11; ryparkhotel@mail.dk; Kyhnsvej 2; s/d 590/790kr; P) Exudes an elegant feel with some bathrooms finished in marble. Rooms are decked out with all the expected amenities.

Eating

Cafe Alberto (☎ 86 89 30 99; Randersvej 1; snacks 45kr; lunch) Pleasantly situated opposite the train station, this café is perfect for a light lunch or a coffee in the sun.

Pizzeria Italia (☎ 86 89 31 33; Skanderborgvej 3; pizza & pasta 55kr; lunch & dinner) Large serves are good value here; the pasta is done with Italian pizzazz and comes up a treat.

Bagergaarden (☎ 86 89 10 48; Klostervej 12; pastries 15kr, sandwiches 25kr; breakfast & lunch) Opposite the train station this bakery has good sandwiches and pastries.

Peking Grill (☎ 86 89 24 84; Klostervej 26; mains 55kr; lunch & dinner) Good-value Chinese dishes star at this simple place just west of the train station.

Getting There & Around

If you have your own transport, Ry is on Rte 445, 24km southeast of Silkeborg and 35km west of Århus.

Hourly trains connect Ry with Silkeborg (26kr, 20 minutes) and Århus (40kr, 30 minutes).

Ry Cykel (☎ 86 89 14 91; Parallelvej 9B; per day/wk 60/300kr) is a couple of kilometres west of town.

HIMMELBJERGET

This is possibly the only place on Jutland that has a real forest feel, so much so that you could be part of an American summer camp. Scaling heights of 147m, the Danes have appropriately named the site Himmelbjerget (Sky Mountain). Once you have completed the five-minute pilgrimage from the car park you can climb the 25m tower (10kr) for a fine 360 degree view of the lakes and countryside. On a clear day it's a lovely vista.

There are marked hiking trails in the woodland area, including one that leads 1km down to the lake.

The parking area (10kr) for Himmelbjerget is next to a hotel, restaurant and souvenir kiosks, and the area is open from Easter to the end of October.

Sleeping & Eating

Hotel Himmelbjerget (☎ 86 89 80 45; www.hotel-himmelbjerget.dk; Ny Himmelbjergvej 20; s/d 495/595kr; P) Rustic lodge has 18 rooms with shared bathrooms. The pleasant rooms are basic but do boast great views of the surrounding woods. The restaurant serves up Danish and French cuisine that reaches its pinnacle with fried *sander*, a local fish that does wonders for the taste buds.

Getting There & Away

Bus No 311 runs from Ry train station to Himmelbjerget four to seven times per day; check the schedule with the Ry tourist office as it varies with the day of the week. Himmelbjerget is a 10-minute drive west of Ry on Rte 445.

It can also be reached by a pleasant 7km hike from Ry or by a scenic boat ride from either Ry or Silkeborg.

BOAT

The paddle steamer **Hjejlen** (☎ 86 82 07 66; return adult/child 92/46kr), sails from Silkeborg to Himmelbjerget twice daily at 10am and 1.45pm. An ordinary boat also plies this route up to six times per day, so be sure to request the *Hjejlen* when you book.

A PADDLE STEAMER CRUISE

The **Hjejlen** (☎ 86 82 07 66; return adult/child 92/46kr), the world's oldest operating paddle steamer, has been faithfully plying the waters of the Lake District since it was first launched in 1861. King Frederik VII was among the passengers on that inaugural cruise.

Built by the Burmeister & Wain shipyard in Copenhagen, the boat is so old that, when the engine needed rebuilding a few years ago, an engineer had to be called out of retirement to do the work. These days the boat makes a couple of daily runs shuttling tourists from Silkeborg to Himmelbjerget during the summer season. The 15km route takes in a wealth of river and lake scenery along the way and is one of the most popular outings in the Lake District.

Ry Turistbåde (☎ 86 82 88 21; return adult/child 70/35kr) operates boats from Ry to Himmelbjerget daily in summer, leaving Ry at 10am, noon and 2pm, and leaving Himmelbjerget one hour later.

DJURSLAND & MOLS

Djursland and Mols are the names of the northern and southern halves of the large peninsula northeast of Århus. The area's standout tourist towns are Ebeltoft and Grenaa, both of which attract hordes of beach-going Swedish tourists each summer. Inland activities range from soaking up the atmosphere in an historic manor house, to riding wild rides at a fun park or checking out big grizzly bears. It's an entertaining area that has a little bit of something for everyone.

If you happen to be travelling between Ebeltoft and Grenaa take the rural route that leads through Dråby – the countryside is interspersed with rich woodland and charming villages.

EBELTOFT

pop 5300

Ebeltoft has all the right ingredients for a great summer getaway. Historic cobblestone streets, white sandy beaches and a classic warship attract large numbers of ice-cream eating holidaymakers each year.

Ebeltoft's golden age was during medieval times when it was a central trader with Zealand, Germany and Sweden. Bitter relations with Sweden in 1659 resulted in the Swedish navy torching its fleet and sacking Ebeltoft. Economic stagnation lingered for nearly 200 years until the Swedes came flooding back as tourists. The economic downturn has, however, had one undeniably positive effect: the old town has remained virtually untouched for 200 years, and its half-timbered houses and winding streets give the town a solid, historic ambience.

Orientation

The tourist office, *Fregatten Jylland* and harbour are along Strandvejen. From the harbour walk east on Jernbanegade to reach Adelgade, the main shopping street. Torvet, the town square, is at the southern end of Adelgade. All of these places are within a five-minute walk of each other.

Information

Ebeltoft/Mols Turistbureau (☎ 86 34 14 00; www.visitdjursland.com; Strandvejen 2; 🕐 9am-5pm Mon-Fri, 9am-2pm Sat mid-Jun–mid-Aug, 9am-4pm Mon-Fri, 9am-1pm Sat rest of year) Next to *Fregatten Jylland*.

Nordea (☎ 86 34 17 11; Jernbanegade 7).

Post office (☎ 87 12 89 00; Ndr. Strandvej 1) On the waterfront north of the tourist office.

Sights

Fregatten Jylland (☎ 86 34 10 99; Strandvejen 4; adult/child 50/20kr; 🕐 10am-7pm mid-Jun–Aug, 10am-5pm Sep–mid-Jun) is the biggest wooden ship in the world and played an instrumental role in Denmark's navy during the 19th century. Step inside and see the life of a crew member, and experience the sense of pride this great old vessel seems to exude.

Glasmuseum (☎ 86 34 17 99; Strandvejen 8; adult/child 40/5kr; 🕐 10am-5pm year-round, until 7pm in Jul) is the Danish headquarters for glass sculptors. It's very modern in design and pretty much everything you can do with glass is demonstrated here, from the production of stylish vases to eccentric and colourful pieces.

Ebeltoft Museum (☎ 86 34 55 99; Torvet; adult/child 25/5kr; 🕐 11am-4pm daily Jun-Aug, 11am-3pm Tue-Sun in spring & autumn) houses an interesting exhibition of local history and also lays claim to being Denmark's smallest town hall. Civil marriage ceremonies have become immensely popular and if you are here on a Saturday morning you will be hard-pressed to miss one. The hall was built in 1789 when the town had only 600 inhabitants and has survived many attempts at demolition. Now the half-timbered building is something of a town treasure.

Activities

Ebeltoft sits on a calm, protected bay fringed with white-sand beaches; you'll find a nice stretch right along Strandvejen, the coastal road that leads north from the town centre. Another bathing area begins on the southern side of Ebeltoft.

Sleeping

Hotel Hvide Hus (☎ 86 34 14 66; www.hhh-hotel.dk; Strandgårdshøj 1; s/d 825/125kr; P ⊠) Just north of the town centre, this hotel has spacious, light rooms and slick service. All rooms come with the expected necessities.

Ebeltoft Parkhotel (☎ 86 34 32 22; www.ebeltoftparkhotel.dk; Adelgade 44; s/d 600/720kr; P ⊠) A five-minute walk east of Torvet, this hotel has cosy, modern, clean rooms that have typical Danish design. Along with a heated indoor pool.

Danhostel Ebeltoft (☎ 86 34 20 53; www.danhostel.dk/ebeltoft; Søndergade 43; dm/d 118/290kr; Feb-Nov; P ⊠) Friendly owners and comfy rooms. There is also a kitchen, TV room and parking.

Vibæk Camping (☎ 86 34 12 14; www.vibaekcamping.dk; Strandvej 23; per person 67kr; P) Good sites on a lovely beach, perfect position and a child-friendly layout, just north of town

Eating

You'll find several places to eat along Adelgade between Jernbanegade and Torvet.

Restaurant Vigen (☎ 86 34 14 33; Adelgade 5; mains 160-190kr; dinner) An upmarket dinner option that merges French and Danish influences and is renowned for its fish dishes.

Italia (☎ 86 34 44 30; Nedergade 14; mains 70-90kr; lunch & dinner) A tidy little restaurant opposite the water, Italia serves great pizza and pasta but mediocre red wine.

Fellini (☎ 86 34 61 62; Nytorv 1; mains 60-110kr; lunch & dinner) Another Italian café just off Adelgade with tables sprawling out into the sunshine. Great for a late afternoon refreshment.

Restaurant Panorama (☎ 86 34 14 66; Strandgårdshøj 1; buffet 160kr; dinner) During summer it has a themed buffet each night, featuring everything from Danish to Italian. Good-quality food in a pleasant setting.

Gryden (☎ 86 34 13 00; Adelgade 32; fast food 25-60kr; lunch & dinner) All the usual fried food as well as delicious ice cream, pleasant outdoor seating and free Internet access.

Getting There & Away

Ebeltoft is on Rte 21, 54km east of Århus and 35km southwest of Grenaa.

Bus No 123 runs between Århus and Ebeltoft (64kr; 1½ hours). There's also the No 351 regular bus service between Ebeltoft and Grenaa (42kr, 40 minutes).

Mols-Linien (☎ 70 10 14 18; adult/child/car 205/60/455kr) operates a large hydrofoil car ferry between Ebeltoft and Odden in northwestern Zealand 12 to 16 times daily.

Getting Around

Bicycles can be hired from **LP Cykler** (☎ 86 34 47 77; Nørreallé 5; per day 75).

GRENAA

pop 14,400

A purpose-built harbour complete with roaming sharks, an historic old town and 7km of sandy beaches are the defining elements of this town that offers a little bit of everything. Its old town is some 3km east, and is the economic and shopping hub of the district, while the waterfront is for holiday-makers and Sweden-bound ships.

Kattegatcentret is an impressive shark centre that dominates the harbour. The old town radiates out from Torvet, which is the central square and meeting point of three pedestrian streets.

Information

Djurslands Bank (☎ 86 32 16 22; Strandgade 2) Opposite the fishing harbour.

Grenaa Tourist Bureau (☎ 87 58 12 00; www.visitdjursland.com; Torvet 1; 9am-5pm Mon-Fri, 9.30am-1pm Sat mid-Jun–mid-Aug, 9am-4.30pm Mon-Fri, 10am-1pm Sat mid-Aug–mid-Jun) Opposite the cathedral in the main square.

Post office (☎ 87 12 89 00; Stationsplads 2) West of the train station.

Sights & Activities

Grenaa's 7km of beach runs south out of town and is where it's at on hot days. To get there just follow the coast from the port south and you can't miss it. If you want to be surrounded by holiday makers the northern end of the beach is always a hive of activity but as you run south it becomes a little more private but still packed.

If you fancy being 6cm from a shark and in total control then you'll love **Kattegatcentret** (☎ 86 32 72 00; Færgevej 4; www.kattegatcentret.dk; adult/child 100/55kr; 10am-6pm daily mid-Jun–Aug, 10am-4pm Sep-May). Sharks are at the top of the food chain in Danish seas and this is a brilliant chance to see just why. There is also a seal pool, and a touch pool for those with a fetish for touching stingrays and other sea life. If you want to go diving it can be organised through the centre, for everyone from beginners to experts.

Character oozes out of the **Djurslands Museum & Dansk Fiskerimuseum** (☎ 86 32 48 00; Søndergade 1; adult/child 30kr/free; 10am-4pm Mon-Fri, 1-4pm Sat & Sun Jun-Aug; 1-4pm Tue-Fri & Sun rest of year). It's in an old merchant's house, and exhibits inside tell the tale of local peasant hero Søren Kanne. The museum houses artefacts discovered in the region and includes plenty of model boats to keep the budding builder entertained. It's just down from Torvet and well worth a visit.

The Gothic-style **Grenaa Kirke** (Torvet; free admission; 2-5pm) has undergone extensive renovations in recent times. Some parts of it date back to 1300. During its makeover in 2001 it inherited one of Northern Europe's best organs along with a glockenspiel that has 21 bronze bells.

CENTRAL JUTLAND

Sleeping

The tourist office maintains a list of private homes that rent rooms from 150kr per person in the Grenaa area. It also has information on beachside holiday cottages that are rented by the week.

Danhostel Grenaa (☎ 86 32 66 22; www.danhostel.dk/grenaa; Ydesvej 4; dm/d 118/290kr; Jan–mid-Dec; P) Located in a sports centre, this clean, comfy and well-run hostel is just 1.5km southeast of the centre.

Grenaa Strand Camping (☎ 86 32 17 18; Fuglsangvej 58; per person 65kr; Apr-Sep; P) Very close to the beach, this well-equipped ground has a minimarket and restaurant.

Hotel Grenaa Strand (☎ 86 32 68 14; www.grenaastrand.dk; Havneplads 1; s/d 495/695kr; P) Rooms in this atmospheric little 1912 hotel opposite the harbour have a private bathroom and TV.

Hoed Kro (☎ 86 33 70 12; Hoedvej 53; d 450kr; P) For a real Danish experience head here. Downstairs they fry up a mean eel and upstairs the accommodation is basic but inviting with individual charm.

Eating

Den Gyldne Krus (☎ 86 32 47 22; Lillegade 18; mains 60-90kr; lunch & dinner) Cosy indoor seating and sunny outdoor pavement tables with good, hearty meals make this pub-restaurant a solid option. Steaks, pizza and pasta make up the menu.

Huset (☎ 86 32 00 32; Østergade 24; mains 110-140kr; lunch & dinner) An old-school steakhouse where meat is an institution – great for an injection of protein.

Skakkes Holm (☎ 86 30 09 89; Lystabådehavnen; mains 130kr; lunch & dinner) Eat top-class fish, and be surrounded by a harbour full of yachts. Locals love this place and it's justified as the seafood is fresh, tasty and immaculately prepared.

Fiskerestauranten (☎ 86 30 03 07; Kystvej 14; mains 150kr; dinner) A pleasant option for a relaxing upmarket dinner, this popular fish restaurant is by the harbour.

Otto's Bageri (☎ 86 32 12 06; Lillegade 10; light meals 20-40kr; breakfast & dinner) Bakery-café combo has good sandwiches, pizza and salads.

Getting There & Away

Grenaa is 63km northeast of Århus on Rte 15 and 57km east of Randers along Rte 16.

Both bus (No 121 or 122) and train services run throughout the day between Århus and Grenaa (76kr, 1½ hours).

For information on boats between Grenaa and Varberg, Sweden, see p311.

Getting Around

Both buses and trains leave from the DSB station at Stationsplads 4.

Bicycles can be hired from **Viggo Jensen** (☎ 86 32 06 83; Strandgade 14; per day 60kr) near the harbour.

AROUND GRENAA

Gammel Estrup

On the outskirts of Aunning, 33km west of Grenaa, is the magnificent manor house **Gammel Estrup** (☎ 86 48 30 01; www.gl-estrup.dk; Randersvej 2; manor & museum adult/child 70kr/free; 10am-5pm daily Apr-Oct, 10am-4pm Tue-Sun Nov-Mar). Two museums, exquisite gardens and an aura of the Danish upper class await you. For nearly 400 years the Skeel/Scheel family owned the manor, selling it in 1926 when 11 different Scheels decided to sell it on inheritance. Recent renovations and extra exhibitions have had an immense effect upon the presentation.

The moat-encircled manor house, known as **Jyllands Herregårdsmuseum**, has been preserved and presented in much the same way as it was in the 17th century, with spacious rooms, antique furniture, elaborate tapestries, historic portraits, glorious views and creaking floorboards that tell a thousand stories. The old beds will arouse your curiosity as will the chapel on the ground floor.

For farm lovers, the **Dansk Landbrugsmuseum** has a mammoth collection of old farm equipment including a few classic, early 20th-century Massey Ferguson tractors. The museum also attempts to recreate the workings on the farm, like the forced transition in the 19th century from producing grain to butter and bacon. It's an interesting window into the past although the displays can be a touch phoney.

In its jubilee year (2005), the manor house plans to showcase 25 different exhibitions throughout the year and many into the following year. At the time of writing, a silver exhibition is to be the centrepiece to a packed schedule of events.

To get Gammel Estrup, take bus No 119 from Århus. The bus goes right to the door. If you are driving take Rte 16 between Greena and Randers and it's just west of Aunning.

Djurs Sommerland

Terrifyingly fast roller coasters and a plethora of water slides await you at **Djurs Sommerland** (☎ 86 39 84 00; Randersvej 17; adult/child 150/150kr; 🕑 10am-6pm May-Aug). Once the entry fee is paid you are free to play until your hearts content, and the park has arguably the best outdoor rides in Jutland.

The park lies 20km west of Grenaa in Nimtofte.

Dyrepark

Scandinavisk Dyrepark (☎ 86 39 13 33; www.skandinaviskdyrepark.dk; Nødagervej 67B; adult/child 95/55kr; 🕑 10am-5pm May-Oct) If you were to be a caged bear, this is where you would want to be, with endless space and plenty of playmates to fill in the days. This is a great set-up and if you haven't seen these incredibly big, hairy, cuddly, scary bears you are doing yourself an injustice.

Along with the big friendly giants there are snakes, wolves, elk, foxes and roe deer wandering about. Pack a picnic basket and make a day of it. You certainly won't forget it in a hurry.

The park is 2km north of Tirstrup on the road to Kolind. Follow the A15 to Tirstrup and then it is just north and well signposted. Bus No 120 runs between Arhus and Greena and it stops at the entrance to the wildlife park. Buses run once an hour.

THE INTERIOR

Prepare to be educated at the Viking ring fortress stronghold of Fyrkat near Hobro, enchanted by Viborg's glowing appeal on the banks of two idyllic lakes, and charmed by the lovely hamlet of Mariager. The landscape of Jutland's interior ranges from hilly woodland up the middle to rolling fields in the east. Industry, including vehicle manufacturing, is prominent throughout the area.

RANDERS

pop 62,000

Randers' tourist appeal lies partly in its impressive old town and partly in its most flaunted attraction, a triple-domed zoo, which mesmerises families and wildlife enthusiasts alike. Industrial pursuits are still the heartbeat of the city (Denmark's sixth largest) and range from vehicle manufacturing to woodcarving and silversmithing. If you're heading north it's well worth investing a day here.

History

Randers was founded in 1302 and its central location has made it an important trading town ever since. It's situated on the spot where the river Gudenå and Randers Fjord merge. The German occupation of Randers saw local folk pay exorbitant taxes and a deterioration in their quality of life. A patriot by the name of Neil Ebbesen made it his task, in 1340, to liberate Jutland. His action was both swift and effective, slicing off Count Gert's head and with it German rule

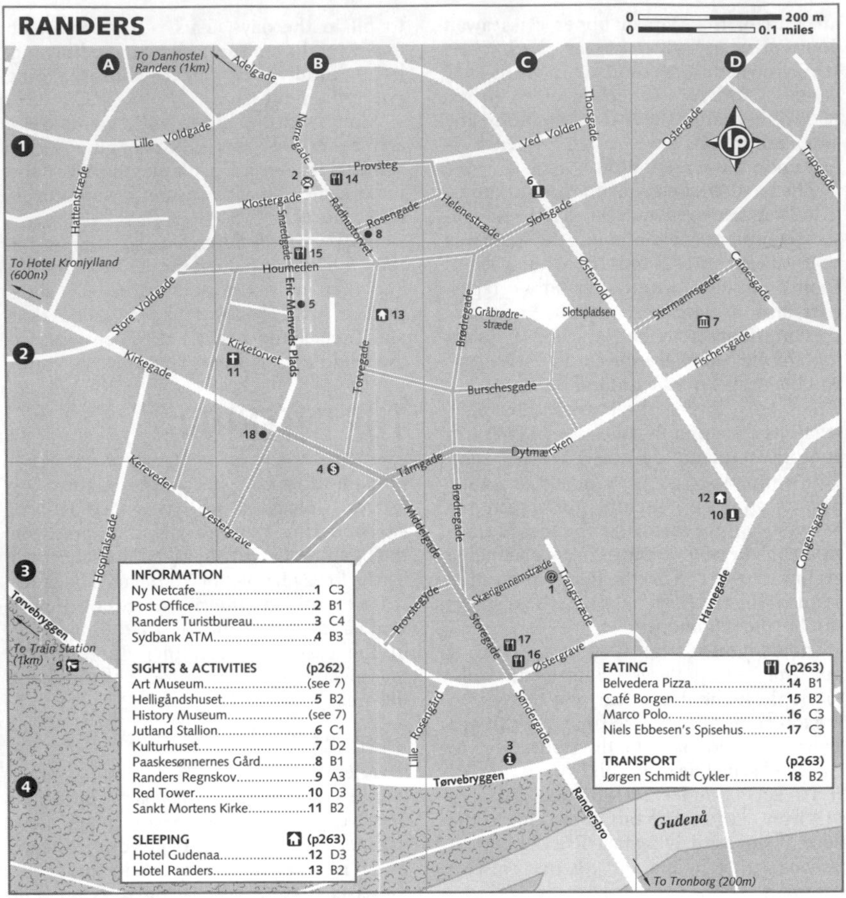
RANDERS
0 200 m
0 0.1 miles
To Danhostel Randers (1km)
To Hotel Kronjylland (600m)
To Train Station (1km)
To Tronborg (200m)
Adelgade
Lille Voldgade
Hattenstræde
Nørregade
Provsteg
Klostergade
Snaregade
Rådhustorvet
Rosengade
Houmeden
Eric Menveds Plads
Store Voldgade
Kirketorvet
Kirkegade
Torvegade
Helenestræde
Slotsgade
Ved Volden
Thorsgade
Østergade
Trapsgade
Østervold
Gråbrødre-stræde
Brødregade
Slotspladsen
Burschesgade
Stermannsgade
Carøesgade
Fischersgade
Dytmærsken
Tårngade
Middelgade
Kereveder
Vestergrave
Hospitalsgade
Tørvebryggen
Provstegyde
Skærigennemstræde
Trangstræde
Storegade
Østergrave
Søndergade
Lille Rosengård
Randersbro
Havnegade
Congensgade
Gudenå
INFORMATION
Ny Netcafe 1 C3
Post Office 2 B1
Randers Turistbureau 3 C4
Sydbank ATM 4 B3
SIGHTS & ACTIVITIES (p262)
Art Museum (see 7)
Helligåndshuset 5 B2
History Museum (see 7)
Jutland Stallion 6 C1
Kulturhuset 7 D2
Paaskesønnernes Gård 8 B1
Randers Regnskov 9 A3
Red Tower 10 D3
Sankt Mortens Kirke 11 B2
SLEEPING (p263)
Hotel Gudenaa 12 D3
Hotel Randers 13 B2
EATING (p263)
Belvedera Pizza 14 B1
Café Borgen 15 B2
Marco Polo 16 C3
Niels Ebbesen's Spisehus 17 C3
TRANSPORT (p263)
Jørgen Schmidt Cykler 18 B2

in one stroke. Unsurprisingly, he is regarded as a hero in this region and throughout town you will notice many things named in his honour. In 1940 the Germans returned and occupied the town until the closing days of WWII.

Orientation

The train station is west of the city centre. It's a 15-minute walk to the tourist office (go east on Jernbanegade and Tørvebryggen) or a 10-minute walk via Vestergade to Rådhustorvet, the central square.

Information

Ny Netcafé (☎ 86 40 77 22; Trangstraede 7; half hr 15kr) Has quick computers.

Post office (☎ 87 12 89 00; Nørregade 1) At the northern end of the city centre.

Randers Turistbureau (☎ 86 42 44 77; www.visitranders.com; Tørvebryggen 12; ⏲ 10am-4pm Mon-Fri, 10am-1pm Sat mid-Aug–mid-Jun, 10am-5.30pm Mon-Fri, 10am-1pm Sat mid-Jun–mid-Aug) Has great information and hints on exploring the town and surrounding area.

Sydbank ATM (Kirkegade)

Sights & Activities

The city's most visited attraction is **Randers Regnskov** (☎ 87 10 99 99; www.randers-regnskov.dk; Tørvebryggen 11; adult/child 90/50kr; ⏲ 10am-6pm daily mid-Jun–mid-Aug, 10am-4pm Mon-Fri, 10am-5pm Sat & Sun rest of the year), a dome-enclosed tropical zoo. Trails within the sultry domes pass through enclosures housing crocodiles, monkeys, pythons, iguanas, orchids, hibiscus and other rainforest flora and fauna. The South American dome is a standout as waterfalls and an abundance of wildlife engulf you. It is astounding how well done this eco-sphere is, considering it's on the wrong side of the equator.

By far the most interesting part of Randers is its central area, where there is a cluster of period brick and half-timbered buildings. Three buildings that date from the late 15th century are **Paaskesønnernes Gård** (Rådhustorvet), a lavish three-storey brick building; **Helligåndshuset** (Eric Menveds Plads) which was once part of a medieval monastery; and the imposing red medieval **Sankt Mortens Kirke** (Kirketorvet). Interestingly, the area around the church used to be a cemetery which was abolished in 1812 and has since been replaced with a festive marketplace. In 1882 a statue of Neils Ebbesen was constructed at Rådustorvert 1. All are within a few minutes' walk of each other and give you a good feel for times gone by.

At night take a stroll down Østervold, which will take you past a rather large, imposing bronze **Jutland stallion** and onto the ever-intriguing **Red Tower**. This fantastic display of creative art was made in 2002 and incorporates a fountain, house and lights. According to its artist, Ingvar Cronhammar, the work means 'anything and everything'.

The local-history and art museums are at **Kulturhuset.** The **art museum** (☎ 86 42 29 22; Stemannsgade 2; adult/child 40kr/free; 🕑 11am-5pm Tue-Sun) features Danish paintings from around 1800 to the present and is rich in Danish naturalism, realism and symbolism. The **history museum** (☎ 86 42 86 55; Stemannsgade 2; admission free; 🕑 11am-5pm Tue-Sun) has a prehistory section and collections of church art, period interiors, weapons and glass.

Sleeping

The tourist office can provide a list of private homes with double rooms for rent for 300kr in the Randers area.

Danhostel Randers (☎ 86 42 50 44; www.danhostel.dk/randers; Gethersvej 1; 🕑 15 Feb-1 Dec; dm/d 90/255kr; ⊠) Modern and large, this hostel is on the edge of a sweeping park. It has 136 beds in 30 rooms and is family-friendly. Be advised that advanced bookings are essential outside of the summer months.

Hotel Randers (☎ 86 42 34 22; www.hotel-randers.dk; Torvegade 11; s/d Sun-Thu 695/995kr, Fri & Sat 595/770kr; Ⓟ ⊠) Randers' oldest hotel is full of charm and is filled with old-fashioned service with unique rooms that house all the modern conveniences. Its position in the heart of the old town will enrich your Randers experience.

Hotel Gudenaa (☎ 86 40 44 11; www.hotel-gudenaa.dk in Danish; Østervold 42; s/d 560/675kr; Ⓟ ⊠) Great position and rooms with ever-changing (and sometimes bizarre) artwork. Each room has a TV, bathroom and phone.

Hotel Kronjylland (☎ 86 41 43 33; www.hotelkronjylland.dk in Danish; Vestergade 53; s/d Sun-Thu 735/945kr, Fri & Sat 595/755kr; Ⓟ) Spacious, modern and comfortable hotel has everything you could expect. Rooms come complete with large TV, phone, bathroom and a crisp, fresh feel from recent renovations.

Eating

Niels Ebbesen's Spisehus (☎ 86 43 32 26; Storegade 13; mains 100-220kr; 🕑 lunch & dinner) Upmarket restaurant occupies a charming period building offering good steak and fish dishes.

Marco Polo (☎ 86 40 30 35; Storegade 15; 🕑 dinner; mains 140kr) Its trademark steak dish, the tender Tournedos al Marco Polo, is produced with care and delivered elegantly in this cosy, candle-lit restaurant.

Hotel Randers (☎ 86 42 34 22; Torvegade 11; mains 200kr; 🕑 breakfast, lunch & dinner) One of Randers' finer restaurants, the Danish-style lamb comes highly recommended.

Café Borgen (☎ 86 43 47 00; Houmeden 10; mains 35-50kr; 🕑 breakfast & lunch) A favourite with the locals as tables sprawl out onto the pavement. Home to rich coffee and lazy lunches on a sunny day.

Tronborg (☎ 86 40 89 11; Grenaavej 2; mains 150kr; 🕑 lunch & dinner) An all-you-can-eat buffet that is sure to satisfy the empty stomach with a great array of meats, salads and vegetables.

Belvedera Pizza (☎ 86 40 79 75; Rådhustorvet 6; pizza slice 20kr, kebabs 35kr; 🕑 lunch & dinner) Great value to the slice and perfect for a quick bite.

Getting There & Around

All trains between Århus (44kr, 35 minutes) and Aalborg (84kr, 50 minutes) stop in Randers.

Randers is 76km south of Aalborg and 36km north of Århus on the E45 and 57km west of Grenaa and 41km east of Viborg on Rte 16.

> **GOLDEN PIPES**
>
> The fact that Randers produces its own beer is not a great surprise. What is surprising, indeed inspiring, is that Randers' Thor beer is distributed straight from beer house to local restaurants and bars through a network of underground pipes. This astonishing situation resulted from a decision to re-lay the inner city roads, and, at the same time, lay pipes to provide the freshest beer in the world to dedicated Thor drinkers. The system works like a charm, with Thor's client establishments being automatically topped up when the drinkers do the proper thing. By the way, Thor is an immensely popular drop.

Jørgen Schmidt Cykler (☎ 86 41 29 03; Vestergade 35; per day 50kr) hires bicycles.

HOBRO

pop 10,800

Hobro's biggest asset is **Fyrkat**, a recently discovered 10th-century Viking ring fortress. The town itself has little historical and visual enchantment due to a history of fires. Nowadays, it primarily acts as a service town to the surrounding farms.

The train station lies on the western edge of the town. To reach the centre walk 1km east along Jernbanegade using the church tower as your central reference.

Information

Hobro Turistbureau (☎ 96 57 66 13; www.visithobro.dk; Adelgade 30; 🕓 9am-5pm Mon-Fri, 9am-2pm Sat Jun-Aug, 9am-4pm Mon-Fri, 9am-noon Sat Sep-May) In the public library; has plenty of information on Fyrkat and the town.
Jyske Bank (☎ 98 52 41 11; Adelgade 10) Has a 24 hour ATM
Post office (☎ 80 20 70 30; Adelgade 8)

Sights

Over the centuries, fires have robbed Hobro of its finer buildings. The oldest building is the **Vicar Spur's Vicarage** (cnr Adelgade & Skibsgade) erected in 1772.

An 1821 merchant's house is home to the **Hobro Museum** (☎ 98 51 05 55; www.sydhimmerlandsmuseum.dk; Vestergade 23; adult/child 25/5kr; 🕓 11am-5pm May-Sep), which has some excavated items of interest from Fyrkat and a detailed history of Hobro.

Follow Brogade south out of town and turn left at Mariagervej which brings you to **Hobro's churchyard**. It's immaculately kept with hedges and flowers adding to its allure, and there are wonderful views of the surrounding district. The town's **war memorial**, with a monument paying respect to Danish soldiers who fought bravely against the Germans can also be seen here.

FYRKAT

Although it's somewhat smaller than the better known Trelleborg in southern Zealand, the 1000-year-old **Fyrkat fortress** (☎ 98 51 19 27; Frykatvej 45; adult/child 55/20kr incl entry to Vikingegården Fyrkat; 🕓 10am-5pm Jun-Aug, 10am-4pm Sep-May) south of Hobro so closely resembles Trelleborg that both are presumed to have been built by the Viking king mastermind, Harald Bluetooth, around 980.

When archaeologists discovered the fortress in 1950 they realised its importance and excavated the area over the following decade. Fyrkat was found to be a military stronghold used to monitor 'traffic' movement throughout Jutland. Evidence indicates that 800 Vikings and their families lived within the fort. The site is thought to have been abandoned when it was destroyed by fire just after its completion; many objects uncovered were singed, confirming that fire was the probable culprit.

Today as you walk out onto the grass-covered circular ramparts you can almost envisage the bloodthirsty Viking warriors roaming the fortress. Absorb the fort's impressive symmetrical design and marvel at the four cuts in its earthen walls, formerly imposing gates that faced the four points of the compass. Within the rampart walls the fortress was divided into four quadrants, each with a central courtyard surrounded by four symmetrical buildings which housed the inhabitants of Fyrkat. Stone foundation blocks show the outline of these elongated buildings. Sheep grazing in the fields add a timeless backdrop to it all.

Although no structures still stand in the ramparts, just outside is a replica Viking house built of oak timbers utilising a stave-style construction technique.

At the entrance to Fyrkat there are some period farm buildings, including a 200-year-old working water mill and a half-timbered house with an old-fashioned restaurant.

Fyrkat is 3km southwest of Hobro's town centre via Fyrkatvej and about a 90kr taxi ride from the train station. If the weather is good, stop at the Viking farmstead and then walk the last kilometre to the fortress site. There is no bus service.

VIKINGEGÅORDEN FYRKAT

Complementing Fyrkat fortress is a Viking-style farmstead 1km north along Fyrkatvej. Archaeologists believe such farms existed around the fortress walls, supplying encamped Vikings with fresh produce.

The complex took over a decade to erect using only materials and hand tools authentic to the period. The 33m longhouse is particularly impressive. It has a frame made of oak hewn by hand using an adze, a roof constructed of reeds fastened by willow shoots, a ridge of local peat and walls made from a mixture of cow dung, blue clay and straw.

Costumed interpreters provide demonstrations of silverwork, archery and other Viking activities. Many of these folk are volunteers who come to Fyrkat every year for a week or so to live as the Vikings did: sleeping in the longhouse, eating grains and smoked fish that they prepare for themselves, and mastering Viking-era crafts. They'll be happy to answer any questions you might have and most of them also speak English. The Viking-style farm is normally bustling with school trips and enthusiastic volunteers.

The farmstead area has the same opening hours as the Fyrkat fortress site. Admission is also included in the cost of entry to the fortress.

Events

Fyrkat annually hosts a **play** put on by a local amateur theatre troupe, Fyrkatspillet, over a two-week period in late May/early June. Although performed in Danish, the general theme is easy to follow – expect to see beautiful damsels, sword-wielding Viking warriors, conflicts and resolutions, and lots of light-hearted laughter. A new play is performed each year but a constant theme involving Viking kings is assured. For tickets (80kr) contact Hobro Turistbureau and book in advance as it's an outrageously popular event on the local calendar.

Sleeping

The tourist office can provide a list of rooms for 300kr per double in private homes.

Danhostel Hobro (☎ 98 52 18 47; www.danhostel.dk/hobro; Amerikavej 24; dm/d 115/330kr; ⏲ 15 Jan-15 Dec; Ⓟ ⊠) A large modern hostel that attracts school groups in their droves. It's clean, spacious and there's a kitchen, TV room, six-bed dorms and its run by engaging and welcoming hosts.

Hobro Camping Gattenborg (☎ 98 52 32 88; Skivevej 35; per person 70kr; ⏲ Apr-Sep; Ⓟ) Three-star camping ground has a swimming pool and is just 1km south of the train station.

Hotel Amerika (☎ 98 45 42 00; www.hotelamerika.dk in Danish; Amerikavej 48; s/d 650/800kr; Ⓟ ⊠) Nestled in a forest this hotel has a luxurious feel with classically furnished rooms equipped with all the necessities. The restaurant (mains 160kr) focuses on fresh ingredients and has a great array of international and local dishes. It's 2.5km east of town.

Eating

Fyrkat Møllegaard (☎ 98 52 10 65; Frykatvej 45; mains lunch/dinner 90/200kr; ⏲ lunch & dinner) Atmospheric red restaurant in a period building at Fyrkat offers Danish country meals including omelettes, minced beef with pumpkin and dinner steaks.

Musikcafé en Hobro (☎ 25 51 52 07; Havnen; lunch 70kr; ⏲ lunch) Café at the harbour offers good, reasonably priced Danish food and occasional live jazz.

Bæch's Conditori (☎ 98 52 48 00; Adelgade 38; sandwiches 25kr; ⏲ breakfast & lunch) On the pedestrian street running through the town centre, this bakery with café tables sells hearty sandwiches.

Getting There & Away

Route 180 runs straight through Hobro, connecting it with Randers, 27km to the southeast and to Aalborg, 49km to the north. The speedier E45 runs along the outskirts of Hobro connecting with the same cities.

Hobro is on the main Frederikshavn–Århus railway line. There are trains about twice hourly to Randers (32kr, 15 min) and Aalborg (62kr, 36 minutes).

MARIAGER

pop 2500

Perched on the Mariager Fjord, this picturesque village is great for a romantic escape or family fun. Cobblestone streets, roses galore, a vintage steam train and a paddle steamer all add to the historical charm of the town. There's also a Salt Museum that has a relaxing salt pool and an interactive display.

Information

Mariager Turistbureau (☎ 98 54 13 77; www.visitmariager.dk; Torvet 1 B; 9am-5pm Mon-Fri, 9am-2pm Sat mid-Jun–Aug, 9am-4pm Mon-Fri, 9am-noon Sat rest of year) Has friendly staff who are enthusiastic about the area.

Sights & Activities

HC Andersen once said that 'humour was the real salt of my fairytales'. Well, there is any amount of real salt at Mariager's biggest tourist attraction on the harbour, **Denmarks Saltcenter** (☎ 98 54 18 16; www.saltcenter.com in Danish; Havnen; adult/senior/child 75/65/55kr; 10am-6pm daily 19 Jun-18 Aug, 10am-4pm Mon-Fri, 10am-5pm Sat & Sun 3 Jan-18 Jun & 19 Aug-23 Sep). Home to a salt laboratory, garden, interactive display and underground mine, two aspects stand out. Firstly, the **Dead Sea** pool, where you can float (it's 30% salt) and relax at a toasty 38 degrees Celsius, and secondly, a collection of salt cellars that is about to be inducted into the Guinness Book of World Records. The adjoining café (light meals 60kr) has some tasty snacks.

You'll find the best collection of old buildings around Torvet, the central square, a five-minute walk south of the harbour. The **Mariager Museum** (☎ 98 54 12 87; Kirkegade 4; adult/child 15kr/free; 1-5pm 15 May-15 Sep), just a minute's walk south of Torvet, occupies an 18th-century merchant's house and contains the usual collection of historical artefacts plus a mini-reconstruction of Abbey Church.

The 21m-long *Svanen* **paddle steamer** (☎ 98 54 14 70; adult one way/return 45/75kr, children half-price) plies the Mariager Fjord in summer and takes you past some glorious country, making a return journey between Mariager and Hobro. The departure times may vary, but are usually Tuesday, Thursday and Sunday in August, but Sunday only from late June to July.

In summer, the smoke-belching *Veteranjernbane* **steam train** (☎ 98 54 18 64; www.jernbaner.dk/mhvj in Danish/; return adult/child 70/35kr) is taken out of its winter mothballs to carry passengers on a 45-minute joyride to the village of Handest, where it stops for 30 minutes before making the return journey. Departures are 11am, noon, 2pm and 3pm daily in summer.

The Mariager Turistbureau sells a ticket that enables you to cruise down the fjord on the paddle steamer, take a steam train to Handest and then a connecting bus to Hobro (120kr, three hours, July and August only). This is very popular, so book in advance and soak up the triangle of transport on a summer's day.

Sleeping

Hotel Postgaarden (☎ 98 54 10 12; fax 98 54 24 64; Torvet 6; s/d incl breakfast 550/750kr; P) The elder statesman of Mariager, this restored 300-year-old hotel is renowned for its elegance, old world charm and warm ambience. All rooms have a bathroom, TV and phone. It is next to the town square.

Motel Langangen (☎ 98 54 11 22; Oxendalen 1; s/d 350/550kr; P ☒) On the eastern edge of the harbour this motel has clean rooms with TV, bathroom, telephone and sweeping harbour views.

Mariager Camping (☎ 98 54 13 42; www.mariagercamping.dk; Ny Havnevej 5A; per person 70kr; Apr-Sep; P) You can camp right beside the water. This fjordside, three-star camping ground has some stunning views and it's just a few hundred metres west of the boat dock and the steam train station.

Eating

Hotel Postgaarden (☎ 98 54 10 12; Torvet 6; lunch 110kr, dinner 170kr; breakfast, lunch & dinner) A fun place to soak up the village atmosphere, this restaurant has traditional Danish fare and tables right on the cobbled square – a 'must-do' for any Mariager visit.

Motel Langangen (☎ 98 54 11 22; Oxendalen 1; lunch 90kr, dinner 140kr; lunch & dinner). A favourite among locals, the simple, yet enticing range of meat and fish dishes satisfy hungry punters.

Opposite the harbour there's a grill serving hot dogs and burgers. There's also a grocery shop in this area.

On Torvet you'll find a bakery, an ice-cream shop and a pizzeria.

Getting There & Around

Mariager is 15km east of Hobro on Rte 555. Other than the vintage tourist steam train, there's no train service to Mariager. Buses run every couple of hours from Hobro

BRONZE BURIAL MOUND

Hohøj is the largest burial mound from the Bronze Age (310–410) in Scandinavia. It is 110m above sea level and back in 1870 one could see 75 churches and castles from the vantage point. Today the view is partially blocked by trees. It functioned as a beacon during the Middle Ages, with the beacon lit to warn the surrounding inhabitants of trouble. Legend has it that one day a local man was taking a siesta near Hohøj and was awoken by a voice shouting, 'The water is hot and the knife has been sharpened. I will stab the pig who lies on the mound.' Needless to say, the local man quickly ran back to town to tell the tale. It added to the town's suspicion that there resided at Hohøj a mountain troll who ate people and boiled them in a pot. Hohøj is about 2km southeast of Mariager. Follow Havndalvej and turn right at Hohøj Skovvej.

(23kr, No 234, Monday to Friday) and hourly from Randers (34kr, No 235, daily); both routes take about 30 minutes.

At the time of writing the turistbureau was purchasing a number of bikes to hire out.

REBILD BAKKER

As most Danes will proudly exclaim, they are a small country that has achieved a lot, and their only national park illustrates this covering a mere 77 sq km. The story of Rebild Bakker dates back to 1912 when a group of Danish Americans presented 200 hectares of (previously privately owned) forest to the Danish government on the proviso that it would remain in a natural state, be open to all visitors and be accessible to Danish Americans for the celebration of US holidays.

This act of good will inspired the Danish forest service to acquire adjacent woodland and collectively the area is known as **Rold Skov**. The area is lovely and has mild undulating walks that take you through country covered with heather, juniper, crowberry, blueberry, cranberry, mountain tobacco and club moss, while its woods contain European aspen, beech and oak trees.

The **turistbureau** (☎ 99 82 84 40; Kulturstationen; www.roldskovturist.dk; ⏲ 9am-5pm Mon-Fri, 9am-2pm Sat Jun-Aug, 9am-4pm Mon-Fri, 9am-noon Sat rest of year) is at Skorping, 3km east of Rebild Bakker.

Sights & Activities

The **Lincoln Log Cabin** (Cimbrervej 3; adult/child 20kr/free), just west of the car park at the start of the trails, contains bits of Americana as seen through Danish eyes, plus displays on Danish emigration to the USA. Modelled on the log cabin that US president Abraham Lincoln grew up in, the cabin is itself a replica, the original having been destroyed by arsonists in 1993.

At the car park is **Spillemandsmuseet** (Fiddlers' Museum; ☎ 98 39 16 04; Cimbrervej 2; adult/child 20/5kr), a simple regional museum featuring a varied collection of exhibits including guns and traps, 19th-century kitchen textiles and fiddles.

There are numerous walking **trails** crisscrossing the park. One pleasant 4km route begins in a sheep meadow west of the car park. It goes past Tophuset, a small century-old thatched house that was built by the first caretakers; the Lincoln log cabin; a large glacial boulder called Cimbrerstenen, sculpted in the form of a Cimbrian bull's head by Anders Bundgaard; the hollow where the 4th July celebrations are held; and Sønderland, the park's highest hill at 102m. It's a particularly lovely area in summer and autumn when the heather adds a purple tinge to the hillsides.

Festival & Events

Rebild Festival (www.visitaalborg.dk) is an annual 4th July celebration (held since 1912, excluding world wars) that is the biggest outside the USA. Singing, dancing, country music and guest speakers (recently George Bush Snr and Bill Clinton) are in abundance and festivities normally span a week ending in the merry city of Aalborg. The festival is the Dane's way of thanking a land which has welcomed more than 300,000 immigrants and aims in this way to retain this special bond between the two countries.

Sleeping

Rold Storkro (☎ 98 37 51 00; www.roldstorkro.dk; Vaelderskoven 13; s/d 725/925kr; P ⊠ 🅿 ⛶). The only hotel in Rold Scov, Storkro is overflowing with luxury including an indoor swimming pool, sauna, solarium, pool table, atrium garden, open fire place in the lounge and a sun baked terrace.

Danhostel Rebild (☎ 98 39 13 40; www.danhostel.dk/rebild; Rebildvej 23; dm/d 115/375kr; ⏲ Feb-Nov;

CENTRAL JUTLAND

(P ⊠) Thatched, 94-bed hostel has a handy location right next to the park entrance.

Safari Camping (☎ 98 39 11 10; safari@dk-camp.dk; Rebildvej 17A; per person 70kr; P) Three-star facility is just a few minutes' walk from the entrance to Rebild Bakker.

Eating

Panorama (☎ 98 37 51 00; Vaelderskoven 13; mains 190kr; ⏲ breakfast, lunch & dinner) Situated in Rold Storkro hotel the menu at this restaurant is an exciting combination of Danish and French cuisine and the service is first class. Fresh and smoked venison is a speciality.

Bette Grill (☎ 98 39 12 00; Cimbrervej 1; snacks 25-50kr; ⏲ breakfast & lunch) Fries up all the predictable fast foods such as burgers, hot dogs, fried chicken and fish and chips to satisfy hungry parkgoers.

Rebild Hus (☎ 98 39 12 00; Cimbrervej 1; mains 100kr; ⏲ lunch & dinner) Adjacent to the grill, this is the park's sit-down restaurant, featuring moderately priced meat dishes.

Getting There & Away

Route 180 runs through the Rold Skov forest, connecting Rebild Bakker with Hobro, 23km to the south.

From Aalborg, Århus-bound trains stop in Skørping (51kr, 20 minutes), 3km west to Rebild Bakker. Bus No 104 runs between Aalborg and Rebild Bakker (41kr, 45 minutes) via Skørping hourly on weekdays, less often at weekends. Trains run from Hobro to Skørping (30kr, 15 minutes).

VIBORG

pop 12,700

Rich in religious history and bordering two idyllic lakes, Viborg is a superbly romantic getaway. During its holiest period (just prior to the Reformation), 25 churches lined the streets. Nowadays, however, only two can be found in the town centre.

The town's origins can be traced back to the 8th century but it was in 1060 that it became one of Denmark's eight bishoprics and a century later, in 1150, granted municipal charter. Refreshingly hilly for a Danish town it provides a welcome relief from the flat, almost monotonous coastal areas. The local women's handball team, Viborg HK, has collected plenty of silverware over the years and watching a game is a must if you visit during the season (September to April).

Orientation

The old part of town consists of the streets around Viborg Domkirke. Sankt Mogens Gade, is between the cathedral and the tourist office, and has some handsome homes, including Hauchs Gård at No 7 and the Willesens House at No 9, both dating from around 1520.

The train station is about 1km southwest of the tourist office.

Information

Jutland National Archive (☎ 86 62 17 88; www.sa.dk; Sct Hans Gade 5; ⏲ 9am-4pm Mon-Sat) If you have Danish roots this impeccable archive centre has records as far back as 1100.

Viborg Turistbureau (☎ 86 61 16 66; www.visitviborg.dk; Nytorv 9; ⏲ 9am-4pm Mon-Fri, 9.30am-12.30am Sat Sep-May, 9am-5pm Mon-Fri, 9am-2pm Sat Jun-Aug) Is clued up on the area.

Sights

This striking twin-towered **Viborg Domkirke** (☎ 87 25 52 50; Sankt Mogens Gade 4; admission free; ⏲ 10am-5pm Mon-Sat, noon-5pm Sun Jun-Aug, 11am-3pm Mon-Sat, noon-5pm Sep-May) is equally impressive inside and out, with exquisite frescoes by Joakim Skovgaard evocatively portraying the story of the protestant bible. In 1876 the cathedral was almost entirely rebuilt, becoming the largest granite church in Scandinavia, an enduring claim to fame. The crypt is all that survives from its birth date, 1100.

Of the paintings inside, two are especially notable: God creating women (on the right as you enter) and the 12 apostles and four evangelists with St Paul replacing Judas (the centrepiece on the roof). They're well worth absorbing as the detail is astounding.

The impressive exterior features the massive walls and semicircular arches common to Norman-style buildings.

The work of Joakim Skovgaard is the cornerstone of **Skovgaard Museet** (☎ 86 62 39 75; Domkirkestræde 4; adult/child 10kr/free; ⏲ 10am-12.30pm & 1.30-5pm May-Sep, 1.30-5pm Oct-Apr) though his family have also contributed pieces. It has some exciting changing exhibitions and warrants a visit for Skovgaard's work alone.

Viborg Stiftsmuseum (☎ 87 25 26 20; Hjultorvet 9; adult/child 20kr/free; ⏲ 11am-5pm Jun-Aug, 11am-4pm Sep-May) is the local history museum and provides more insight into Viking times and the town's religious phases.

Activities

The women's handball team, **Viborg HK** (☎ 86 62 91 06; Tingvej 8; tickets 80kr, season runs Sep-Apr), is renowned far and wide for its success. It is the Manchester United of the league, supplying many players to the national side. Go along and watch a game at the sports centre as it's highly addictive viewing. The centre is 800m northeast of the church.

Jump on board **Margrethe I** (☎ 87 25 30 75; Viborg Turistbureau; adult/child 35/25kr; 2pm May-mid-Jun; 12.45pm, 2pm & 3.15pm mid-Jun–Jul, 2pm & 3.15pm Aug) during summer and soak up the sun and Viborg from out on the lake.

Sleeping

Staff at the tourist office can book rooms in private homes for around 200/275kr for singles/doubles, plus a 25kr booking fee.

Golf Hotel Viborg (☎ 86 61 02 22; www.golf-hotel-viborg.dk; Randersvej 2; s/d 995/1095kr; P ⊠) Right on the lake, this modern hotel features an indoor pool, sauna, bar, canoes, rowing boats and a whole lot more. Substantially sized rooms come with all the required necessities and a few luxuries for good measure. Cable TV, modern bathrooms, comfy beds, great views, a solarium, Jacuzzi, billiard room, and a bar overlooking the lake.

Danhostel Viborg (☎ 86 67 17 81; www.danhostel.dk/viborg; Vinkelvej 36; Mar-Nov; dm/d 118/290kr; P ⊠) Comprising four buildings, this hostel has modern, four-bed dorms and is 3km from the town centre, up the road from the camping ground.

Viborg Sø Camping (☎ 86 67 13 11; www.camping-viborg.dk; Vinkelvej 36; Apr-Sep; per person 65kr; P) Great position close to the waterfront on the eastern side of lake Søndersø and set in picturesque surrounds.

Eating

Latinerly (☎ 86 62 08 81; Sct Mathias Gade 78; lunch & dinner; mains 80kr) Attracts a young crowd and grills up some fantastic fish and steaks. The atmosphere is best described in Danish as *hygge* – cosy. Later on it transforms into a trendy bar.

Brygger Bauers Grotter (☎ 86 11 44 88; Sct Mathias Gade 61; mains 130kr; lunch & dinner) A unique dining experience in 'cave rooms' that date back over 100 years. The caves are the work of a Hungarian master brewer who believed that they would provide an ideal maturing environment for home-brewed Bavarian beer. Why not have a cold one in honour of its founder?

Café Morville (☎ 86 60 22 11; Hjultorvet; mains 100kr; lunch & dinner) Funky café is ideal for a coffee and light lunch or a cold beer to soothe the nerves.

Kafé Arthur (☎ 86 62 21 26; Vestergade 4; lunch 60kr, dinner mains 160kr; lunch & dinner) Romantic restaurant serves dishes from a broad Danish-international menu.

Drinking

Music Café Chaplin (☎ 86 62 66 94; Vesterbrogade 3; bottled beer 30kr) Cruisy café has plenty of live music throughout the week and attracts an alternative crowd at weekends.

Getting There & Away

Viborg is 66km northwest of Århus on Rte 26 and 41km west of Randers on Rte 16. Trains from Århus (102kr, 70 minutes) run hourly on weekdays, less frequently at weekends.

AROUND VIBORG

Daugbjerg Kalkgruber

Just 22km west of Viborg on Rte 16 this is Denmark's oldest **limestone quarry** (☎ 97 54 83 33; Dybdalsvej, 7850, Lånum; adult/child 40/10kr; 10am-4pm mid-Apr–Oct, 10am-6pm Jul & Aug), and is great fun to explore. Two hundred years ago the infamous outlaw Jens Langkniv hid out in the caves and today you can see some ghostly reminders of his seedy haunts, as well as exploring the caves 60m recess. Limestone has been mined in the area for over 900 years. For the kids there's a daily treasure hunt and there are maps to find hidden prizes. While the kids are seeking out the darkest corners the adults can savour some prime cheese that has been curing in the humid quarry, and is available to buy along with quality plonk. It's a great outing and walking around these caves is an eerie yet utterly enjoyable experience.

Hjerl Hede

Seven kilometres east of the small village of Vinderup is **Hjerl Hede** (☎ 97 44 80 60; Hjerl Hedevej 14; adult/child 40/20kr; 9am-5pm Apr-Oct;), an open-air museum that traces the development of a typical Danish village from 1500 to 1900. Scenically set against a lake and moors, it has a collection of about 50 period buildings, many of them timber-framed with thatched roofs, which were brought here from around

Jutland. They include a forge, a dairy, a bakery and village school.

From mid-June to late-August about 100 traditionally costumed men, women and children act as villagers doing such tasks as baking bread, dipping candles and tilling the fields. There's also a small settlement where 'Stone Age people' in costume make flint instruments and pottery and practise spear fishing from dugout canoes.

Because of the re-enactments the summer high season – mid-June to late August – is by far the most interesting time to go. The nearest train station is at Vinderup. There's no bus service from Vinderup; a taxi costs around 100kr. Trains run hourly between Viborg and Vinderup (58kr, 55 minutes).

Spøttrup Slot

Castle lovers with a sense of occasion are sure to enjoy this place. Nestled in the middle of nowhere, and with plenty of character, **Spøttrup Slot** (☎ 97 56 16 06; Slotsvej 1; adult/child 40/15kr; ⏰ 10am-6pm May-Aug, 10am-5pm Sep, 10am-4pm Oct) gives an intriguing insight into Danish life in the 1500s. It has the distinction of a double moat because when it was erected, Denmark was besieged by bitter in-fighting, and its creator, Jørgen Friis (the region's last Catholic bishop), ensured his safety by meticulous defensive planning.

What it lacks in scale and splendour it makes up for in genuine character. It has survived centuries without any significant alteration and stands as arguably the best-preserved medieval castle in Denmark. The national government has managed Spøttrup Slot for 50 years and you are able to walk freely around the castle and soak up the atmosphere in the expansive rooms laid out with minimal furnishings and décor.

The nearest train station is in Skive; from there you can take bus No 43 or 44 (26kr) which leave hourly on weekdays, less frequently at weekends. Trains run hourly between Skive and Viborg (37kr, 23 minutes).

Flowers Jesperhus

On the island of Mors **Flowers Jesperhus** (☎ 96 70 14 00; www.jesperhus.dk; Legindvej 30, Nykøbing Mors; adult/child 135/95kr; ⏰ 10am-5pm May–mid-Oct) has blossoming flowers in abundance along with child-friendly monkeys, parrots and the odd mellow joy ride. You will also find three acres of immaculately kept gardens along with the largest butterfly habitat in Scandinavia where some 1000 butterflies fly freely. And to really capture the imagination the Jungle Garden has crocodiles (at a safe distance) and other tropical wonders. It's great fun and if you're driving in the area certainly one to consider. You take Rte 26 across the Sallingsund Bridge and onto the island of Mors. It is just over the bridge on the right and very well signposted. Driving from Viborg it is a pleasant 35 minute drive.

CENTRAL WEST COAST

The windswept, sweeping coastline of the central west is dotted with an array of summer towns that cater to German tourists. The coast's most flaunted area is Holmsland Klit, the thin neck of sand and dunes stretching nearly 35km from north to south and separating the North Sea from the Ringkøbing Fjord. Windsurfers flock to Hvide Sande as its reputation for the best wind conditions in Denmark spreads.

HVIDE SANDE

pop 3200

Hvide Sande owes its existence to the wind. Wind caused the sand migration that forced the construction of a lock here in 1931 to assure a North Sea passage for the port of Ringkøbing. And wind continues to be the big draw card for the large number of tourists who come here for sailboarding.

Hvide Sande has a busy deep-sea fishing harbour, with trawlers, fish-processing factories and an early-morning fish auction. There's also a little fishing museum adjacent to the tourist office.

Information

Holmsland Klit Turistbureau (☎ 97 31 18 66; post@hkt.dk; Nørregade 2; ⏰ 10am-5pm Mon-Fri, 9am-1pm Sat) On the northern side of the channel.

Activities

WINDSURFING

A consistent, howling westerly coupled with both an invitingly safe lake in Ringkøbing Fjord and the wild North Sea around Hvide Sande make this area ideal for windsurfers of all levels.

Surfcenter Hvide Sande Nord (☎ 97 31 25 99; www.westwind.dk in Danish; Gytjevej 15; ½ day board rental

200kr), a Westwind operation on the northern side of Hvide Sande, offers a three-hour introductory course (4000kr) as well as the latest fad, kite surfing (750kr). Children nine years and over are welcome (but need to weigh at least 30kg to uphaul the sail).

A well-informed website about windsurfing in the area can be found through www.ringkobingfjord.dk.

HORSE RIDING

Hvide Sand is perfect for glorious rides at sunrise and as the sun sets over the water. Contact **Reiterof Vinterlejegaard** (☎ 97 31 51 63; www.vinterlejegaard.dk in Danish; Vesterledvej 9; 1hr ride 120kr) for details.

Events

A big weekend on this stretch of coast is the annual **beach marathon** (www.beachmarathon.com) at the end of June. It attracts international names as well as local punters who take part in one of the many events.

In the second weekend in June each year a **cycle race** is held around the Ringkøbing Fjord. All can join in or simply watch the fun.

Sleeping

The tourist office rents out a number of state-of-the-art houseboats as well as summer cottages and rooms in private homes.

Danhostel Hvide Sande (☎ 97 31 21 05; danhostel@hvidesande.dk; Numitvej 5; dm/d 118/425kr; P) Modern, 88-bed hostel has a central location at a sports centre on the northern side of the harbour. It has comfortable rooms, many with shower and toilet. The centre has a large indoor swimming pool, handball and badminton courts.

Beltana Camping (☎ 97 31 12 18; beltana@dk-camp.dk, Karen Brandsvej 70; Apr–mid-Oct; per person 65kr; P) If you're here for the windsurfing this is the camping ground for you. It's right on the water on the southern side of town and has a two-star rating. There are other camping grounds both to the north and south.

Hvide Sande Sømandshjem (☎ 97 31 10 33; www.hssh.dk in in Danish; Bredgade 5; s/d 425/595kr; P) The only hotel in town offering simple rooms with a TV and bathroom. It's on the southern side of the harbour.

Eating

There are bakeries on the southern side of town on the corner of Metheasvej and Stormgade and on the northern side of town at Nørregade 50.

Restaurant Slusen (☎ 97 31 27 27; Bredgade 3; mains 300kr; dinner) The steak at this upmarket restaurant justifies its price, it's both succulent and big. The chef is great with his flamboyant use of fish in the Danish/French menu.

Edgar Madsen (☎ 97 31 14 33; Metheasvej 11; snacks 15-30kr; lunch) Sells smoked fish by the piece, deli salads and a few other takeaway items. It's near the waterfront street Auktionsvej on the southern side of town.

Bella Italia (☎ 97 31 30 00; Parallelvej 3; pizza 60kr, mains 90kr; lunch & dinner) On the northern side of the harbour has a good steak-and-chips lunch deal, plus pizza and meat dishes.

Getting There & Away

Hvide Sande is on Rte 181. Bus No 58 runs to Hvide Sande from Ringkøbing train station (24kr, 20 minutes) and Nørre Nebel train station (32kr, 35 minutes) about hourly on weekdays, half as frequently at weekends.

There is also a ferry that runs to Ringkøbing from April to October four times daily (adult/child 60/30kr, one hour).

RINGKØBING

pop 9100

Ringkøbing nurtures the strongest hold on the past of any town on the west coast and in doing so presents itself as an enjoyable base. It was once a prominent North Sea port, until shifting sands caused the mouth of the fjord to slowly migrate south and threatened to cut off the town's lifeline to the sea. In 1931 the town acquired a constant North Sea passage when a lock was built at Hvide Sande. Today the port is not a big player in exports, and the town is surrounded by industry, namely windmills, and feeds off these natural energy sources as well as the regional administration offices.

Information

Post office (☎ 96 26 74 00; Nørredige 1) West of the train station.

Ringkøbing Turistbureau (☎ 97 32 00 31; www.ringkobingfjord.dk; Vestergade 2; 9am-5pm Mon-Fri, 10am-2pm Sat mid-Jun–Aug, 9.30am-5pm Mon-Fri, 10am-1pm Sat Aug–mid-Jun) At Torvet, the main square.

Sights

There are a few **period buildings** in the centre of town around Torvet, the oldest of which is Hotel Ringkøbing, whose timber-framed wing dates from 1601. The church northwest of the hotel dates from medieval times and has a sundial from 1728 on its western buttress. The **Lindetroer trees** in the square are a healthy 175 years old.

Ringkøbing Museum (☎ 97 32 16 15; Østerport; adult/child 20kr/free; ⌚ 11am-5pm Jul & Aug, shorter hrs rest of year), east of Torvet, features displays on the Greenland expedition (1906–08) of Mylius Erichsen and intriguing local items such as a chastity belt from 1600.

Sleeping

Hotel Ringkøbing (☎ 97 32 00 11; www.hotelringkobing.dk; Torvet 18; s/d 695/796kr; Ⓟ ⊠) Dates back to 1601 and has just been renovated resulting in modern, spacious rooms in a charismatic old building.

Danhostel Ringkøbing (☎ 97 32 24 55; www.rofi.dk; Kirkevej 28; dm/d 118/320kr; Ⓟ ⊠) Up there with the best of them – a great socialising/relaxing area, modern layout, activities in abundance (it's in a sports centre) and very reasonably priced. It's 1.5km north of the train station via Holstebrovej.

Ringkøbing Camping (☎ 97 32 08 38; info@ringk-camp.dk, Vellingvej 56; per person 58kr; ⌚ Apr-Oct; Ⓟ) Holds an outstanding position east of the town on the fjord with safe swimming and ideal windsurfing areas aplenty. There's also a minimarket, TV room and activity room.

Eating

Hotel Ringkøbing (☎ 97 32 00 11; Torvet 18; lunch mains 80kr, 3-course dinner 228kr; ⌚ lunch & dinner) You can really get a taste of the town's history and charm at this fine dining experience overlooking Torvet. Try the Watchmans Steak, a nice cut covered in whisky sauce along with fresh veggies and fried potatoes.

Café Victoria (☎ 97 32 42 01; Torvet 12; light meals 55kr; ⌚ lunch & dinner) Dine in the courtyard of this pleasant café on sunny days with a menu offering sandwiches, omelettes and salads.

Italia (☎ 97 32 01 23; Algade 11; mains 60-90kr; ⌚ lunch & dinner) Pizzeria has pizza, pasta and Italian meat dishes at moderate prices.

Peking House (☎ 97 32 63 50; Ved Fjorden 2A; all you can eat 145kr; ⌚ lunch & dinner) What more could you want? All the Chinese classics.

Getting There & Around

Ringkøbing is on Rte 15, 46km west of Herning and 9km east of the North Sea.

By rail it's between Esbjerg (84kr, 1½ hours) and Struer (53kr, one hour).

A ferry runs to Hvide Sande from April to October four times daily (adult/child 60/30kr, one hour). Bus No 58 runs to Hvide Sande from Ringkøbing train station (24kr, 20 minutes) about hourly on weekdays, less frequently at weekends.

Taxis (☎ 26 73 73 26) are at the station or can be called.

Northern Jutland

CONTENTS

Split from the rest of Jutland by the Limfjord, northern Jutland possesses rich light, rolling landscape and contrasting images. Aalborg is the 'capital' of the north, a city that boasts a wealth of cultural activities, as well as Denmark's most recognisable party street, Jomfru Ane Gade. Along with these appealing facets is the industrial district that provides a contrasting yet complimentary backdrop to the cosmopolitan ambience.

The area's most coveted tourist destination, Skagen, lies at Denmark's northern tip. Naturally it receives more daylight hours than its counterparts further south yet it is the light which makes this town unique. So unique, in fact, that Skagen became a haven for artists in the second half of the 19th century who flocked there to 'paint the light'. It was this movement that thrust Skagen into the limelight with soon-to-be household names such as PS Krøyer and Michael and Anna Ancher preserving the area in Danish masterpieces. They say blue tones transcend belief when the light is right.

Around the same time, a little further down the east coast, writers discovered the hamlet of Sæby. Summer after summer, literary minds like those of Herman Bang and Gustav Weid found inspiration in the lonely landscapes and bustling cobblestone streets to create classic Scandinavian novels.

Another defining aspect of the north is the howling westerly wind that has shaped this region; its effects can be seen on the locals' weather-beaten faces, in the permanently leaning trees, in the number of windmills and even in the sporting pursuits. Klitmøller, on the northwestern coast, has been labelled one of Europe's premier windsurfing locations and the town attracts enthusiasts from far and wide.

All in all, northern Jutland will enthral you with its magnificent light, intimidate you with its barrenly beautiful landscape and intrigue you with its bluntly infectious characters. All awaits on the northern side of the Limfjord.

HIGHLIGHTS

- Let your hair down while checking out the nightlife on **Jomfru Ane Gade in Aalborg** (p275)
- Experience the rich art and great seafood in **Skagen** (p285)
- Ride **Icelandic horses** (p289) into the sunset on the windy, western beaches
- Enjoy the windsurfing action at **Klitmøller** (p291)
- Bike around the traditional island of **Læsø** (p282)

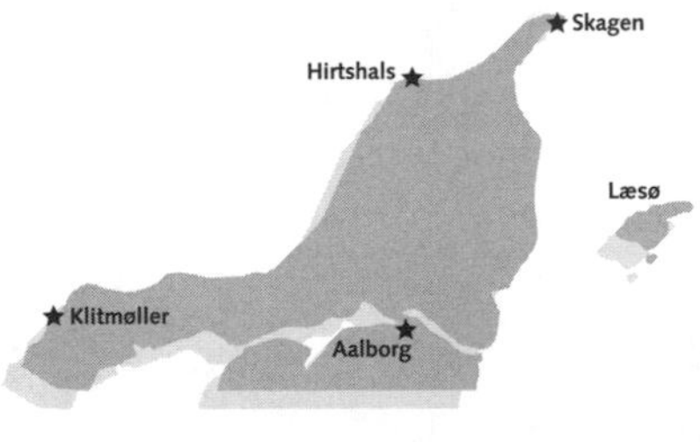
Skagen
Hirtshals
Læsø
Klitmøller
Aalborg

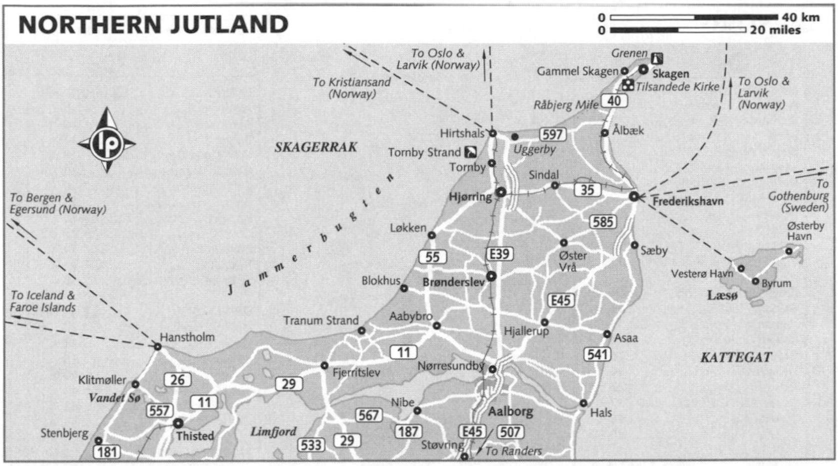
NORTHERN JUTLAND
0 40 km
0 20 miles
To Oslo & Larvik (Norway)
To Kristiansand (Norway)
Grenen
Gammel Skagen
Skagen
Tilsandede Kirke
To Oslo & Larvik (Norway)
Råbjerg Mile
40
SKAGERRAK
Hirtshals
597
Ålbæk
Tornby Strand
Uggerby
Tornby
Sindal
To Bergen & Egersund (Norway)
Hjørring
35
Frederikshavn
To Gothenburg (Sweden)
Jammerbugten
Løkken
585
Østerby Havn
55
E39
Øster Vrå
Sæby
Blokhus
Brønderslev
Vesterø Havn
Byrum
Læsø
To Iceland & Faroe Islands
E45
Tranum Strand
Aabybro
Hjallerup
Hanstholm
Asaa
11
541
KATTEGAT
Fjerritslev
Nørresundby
Klitmøller
26
29
Vandet Sø
11
557
Nibe
567
Aalborg
Hals
Thisted
Limfjord
187
E45
507
Stenbjerg
533
29
Støvring
To Randers
181

AALBORG

pop 169,000

Aalborg is famous within Denmark for its vivacious street, Jomfru Ane Gade (Virgin Ane Street) which draws young party goers from around the country for one-night hit-and-run extravaganzas. Naturally, *akvavit* (world-famous Danish schnapps) is consumed in vast quantities.

Aside from grand fiestas, Aalborg's 'old town' has a refreshingly spacious layout that lets the buildings (and you) breathe, and allows individual structures to bathe in their own rightful glory. Traditionally its been ignored by foreign travellers yet there's an abundance of sights and activities, ranging from Viking burial grounds to stunning museums to outrageously fun 'fun parks'. The city sits at the narrowest point of the Limfjord, the long body of water that slices Jutland in two.

History

A thousand years ago the Vikings founded Aalborg and used it as a base for their glorious, if sometimes brutal, expeditions. Through the ages it has been a busy trade town which is still evident in industrial pursuits such as shipbuilding and cement and steel manufacturing.

Orientation

Aalborg spreads along both sides of the Limfjord, with its two halves linked by both bridge and tunnel. The heart of the city and most traveller amenities are on the southern side. These include the tourist office which is about 1km north of the train and bus stations along Boulevarden.

Information

BOOKSHOPS

Vigeo Madsens Boghandel (☎ 98 13 21 44; Bispengade 10) An international bookshop selling a wide selection of maps and guides.

INTERNET ACCESS

Boomtown NetCafe (☎ 98 19 07 09; Nytrov 13A; per hr 30kr; 🕑 11am-midnight)
Public library (☎ 99 31 44 10; Nytov; free)

MONEY

Nordea (☎ 99 33 20 00; Algade 41)
Jyske Bank (☎ 98 12 31 22; Nytorv 1)

LAUNDRY

Coin laundry (☎ cnr Christiansgade & Rantzausgade; 🕑 9am-8pm) On the southern edge of town.

MEDICAL SERVICES

Budolfi Apotek (☎ 98 12 06 77; cnr Vesterbro & Algade; 🕑 24 hr) A well-stocked pharmacy.

POST

Post office (☎ 99 35 44 00; Algade 42) West of Budolfi Domkirke.

TOURIST INFORMATION

Aalborg Turistbureau (☎ 99 30 60 90; www.visitaalborg.dk in Danish; Østerågade 8; 🕑 9am-4.30 Mon-Fri,

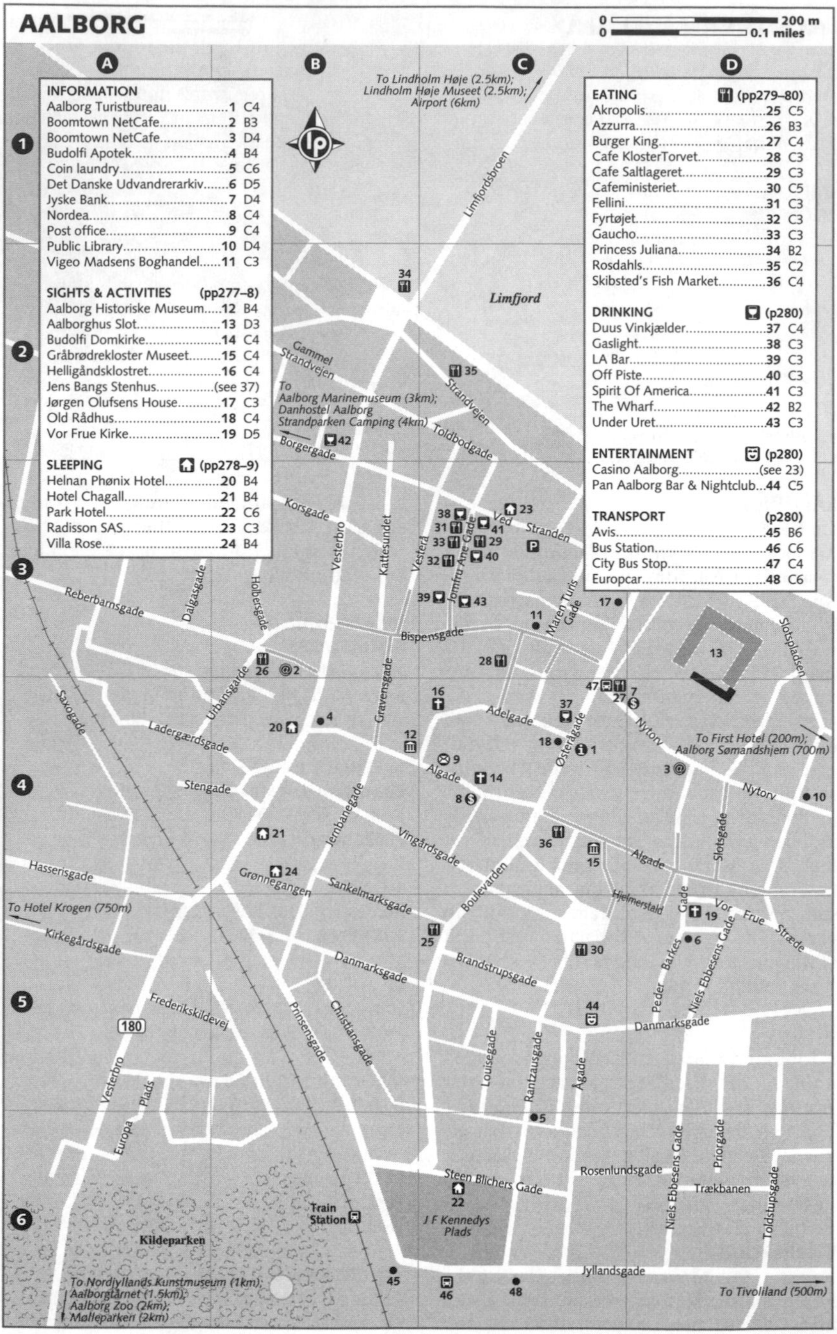

AALBORG
0 200 m
0 0.1 miles
A
B
C
D
1
2
3
4
5
6
INFORMATION
Aalborg Turistbureau....1 C4
Boomtown NetCafe....2 B3
Boomtown NetCafe....3 D4
Budolfi Apotek....4 B4
Coin laundry....5 C6
Det Danske Udvandrerarkiv....6 D5
Jyske Bank....7 D4
Nordea....8 C4
Post office....9 C4
Public Library....10 D4
Vigeo Madsens Boghandel....11 C3
SIGHTS & ACTIVITIES (pp277–8)
Aalborg Historiske Museum....12 B4
Aalborghus Slot....13 D3
Budolfi Domkirke....14 C4
Gråbrødrekloster Museet....15 C4
Helligåndsklostret....16 C4
Jens Bangs Stenhus....(see 37)
Jørgen Olufsens House....17 C3
Old Rådhus....18 C4
Vor Frue Kirke....19 D5
SLEEPING (pp278–9)
Helnan Phønix Hotel....20 B4
Hotel Chagall....21 B4
Park Hotel....22 C6
Radisson SAS....23 C3
Villa Rose....24 B4
EATING (pp279–80)
Akropolis....25 C5
Azzurra....26 B3
Burger King....27 C4
Cafe KlosterTorvet....28 C3
Cafe Saltlageret....29 C3
Cafeministeriet....30 C5
Fellini....31 C3
Fyrtøjet....32 C3
Gaucho....33 C3
Princess Juliana....34 B2
Rosdahls....35 C2
Skibsted's Fish Market....36 C4
DRINKING (p280)
Duus Vinkjælder....37 C4
Gaslight....38 C3
LA Bar....39 C3
Off Piste....40 C3
Spirit Of America....41 C3
The Wharf....42 B2
Under Uret....43 C3
ENTERTAINMENT (p280)
Casino Aalborg....(see 23)
Pan Aalborg Bar & Nightclub....44 C5
TRANSPORT (p280)
Avis....45 B6
Bus Station....46 C6
City Bus Stop....47 C4
Europcar....48 C6
To Lindholm Høje (2.5km); Lindholm Høje Museet (2.5km); Airport (6km)
Limfjordsbroen
Limfjord
Gammel Strandvejen
To Aalborg Marinemuseum (3km); Danhostel Aalborg Strandparken Camping (4km)
Strandvejen
Toldbodgade
Borgergade
Korsgade
Ved Stranden
Vesterbro
Kattesundet
Vesterå
Jomfru Ane Gade
Maren Turis Gade
Slotspladsen
Reberbansgade
Dalgasgade
Holbergsgade
Bispensgade
Urbansgade
Saxogade
Ladegærdsgade
Gravensgade
Adelgade
Østerågade
Nytorv
To First Hotel (200m); Aalborg Sømandshjem (700m)
Algade
Stengade
Jernbanegade
Vingårdsgade
Slotsgade
Hasserisgade
Grønnegangen
Sankelmarksgade
Boulevarden
Hjelmerstald
Gade
Vor Frue Stræde
To Hotel Krogen (750m)
Kirkegårdsgade
Danmarksgade
Brandstrupsgade
Peder Barkes
Niels Ebbesens Gade
Frederikskildevej
Prinsensgade
Christiansgade
180
Louisegade
Rantzausgade
Ågade
Vesterbro
Europa Plads
Niels Ebbesens Gade
Priorgade
Rosenlundsgade
Steen Blichers Gade
Trækbanen
Toldstupsgade
Train Station
J F Kennedys Plads
Kildeparken
Jyllandsgade
To Nordjyllands Kunstmuseum (1km); Aalborgtårnet (1.5km); Aalborg Zoo (2km); Mølleparken (2km)
To Tivoliland (500m)

NORTHERN JUTLAND

10am-1pm Sat Sep–mid-Jun, 9am-5.30pm Mon-Fri, 10am-1pm Sat mid-Jun–Aug) Professional, clued-up service.

Det Danske Udvandrerarkiv (☎ 99 31 42 20; www.emiarch.dk; Arkivstræde 1; ⏰ 9am-4pm Mon-Thu, 9am-2pm Fri & Sat) Keeps records of Danish emigration history and help foreigners of Danish descent trace their roots.

Sights

BUDOLFI DOMKIRKE

This 12th-century **cathedral** (Algade 40; admission free; ⏰ 9am-4pm Mon-Fri, 9am-2pm Sat May-Sep, 9am-3pm Mon-Fri, 9am-noon Sat Oct-Apr) marks the centre of the old town and its elegant carillon can be heard throughout town every hour, on the hour. Its whitewashed interior creates an almost Mediterranean ambience.

As you enter the cathedral from Algade, look up at the foyer ceiling to see colourful frescoes. The interior boasts some beautifully carved items, including a gilded Baroque altar and a richly detailed pulpit. Interestingly, despite their different appearances, both were created by Danish sculptor Lauridtz Jensen; apparently the altar, carved in 1689, was too flashy for the parish so in 1692 Jensen used an older Renaissance style for the pulpit.

AALBORG HISTORISKE MUSEUM

A block west of Budolfi Domkirke is the **Aalborg Historiske Museum** (☎ 96 31 04 10; Algade 48; adult/child 20/10kr; ⏰ 10am-5pm Tue-Sun). Expect to see excavated artefacts, the requisite Renaissance furnishings and fine collections of silver and ancient Danish coins. It also displays some interesting oddities, such as a mid-18th-century hearse embellished with motifs of a skull and crossbones.

GRÅBRØDREKLOSTER MUSEET

Underground **museum** (☎ 96 31 04 10; Algade 19; 20kr per 250kg in the lift; ⏰ 10am-5pm) examines the life of a Franciscan friary in Aalborg. Excavations in 1994–95 provide the basis for these archaeological assumptions of life in Aalborg from the 11th century through to the 14th century. Well worth a look.

OTHER CENTRAL SIGHTS

An alley between the Aalborg Historiske Museum and post office leads to the rambling **Helligåndsklostret** (Monastery of the Holy Ghost), which dates from 1431. It's the oldest social institution in Denmark and home to some fascinating frescoes. The interior can only be visited on a **guided tour** (☎ 99 30 60 90; ⏰ 1.30pm Mon, Wed & Fri; adult/child 40/20kr) arranged through the tourist office.

East of Budolfi Domkirke on Østerå gade there are three rather noteworthy historic buildings: the Baroque-style **old rådhus** (c 1762), **Jens Bangs Stenhus** (c 1624), and **Jørgen Olufsens House** (c 1616) at Østerågade 25. The latter two are lovely Renaissance buildings, one was built by a wealthy merchant, Jens Bang, and the other by a wealthy mayor, Jørgen Olufsen.

In addition, the neighbourhoods of half-timbered houses around **Vor Frue Kirke** on Peder Barkes Gade are worth seeing, particularly the cobbled street Hjelmerstald. **Aalborghus Slot**, near the waterfront, is more an administrative office than a castle but there's a small dungeon you can visit (admission free).

Ask at the tourist office for the English-language *Good Old Aalborg* booklet, which maps out two suggested walking tours and provides details of buildings and sights along the way.

LINDHOLM HØJE

Aalborg's paramount attraction is this majestic hill-top graveyard that dates back to the Iron Age and Viking era. **Lindholm Høje** (admission free; ⏰ dawn-dusk) consists of 682 graves, most of which are Viking graves marked by stones placed in an oval ship shape, with two principal stones at stem and stern. At the end of the Viking era the whole area was buried under drifting sand and thus preserved until modern times. The Vikings were buried in the graves fully clothed along with their respective dogs. Nowadays, it's a great place to explore; there's almost something spiritual about it. It's the largest Viking burial ground in Scandinavia and has plaques in both Danish and English explaining the intricacies of the site.

Lindholm Høje Museet (☎ 96 31 04 28; Vendilavej 11; adult/child 30/15kr; ⏰ 10am-5pm daily Apr-Oct, 10am-4pm Tue-Sun Nov-Mar) This museum adjoins the site and displays archaeological finds made during its excavation. Using panorama reconstructions, illustrations, maps and text it builds a strong image of Viking life. The museum café serves up reasonably priced, filling sandwiches and tossed salads.

Lindholm Høje is 15 minutes from Aalborg via bus No 2; cross the fence 50m beyond the bus stop and you'll be in the burial field. If you have your own transport, head north from the city centre over Limfjordsbroen to Nørresundby, and following Lindholmsvej head north to Hvorupvej. After Hvorupvej intersects with Vikingevej take the first left, which will bring you up the driveway to the museum.

NORDJYLLANDS KUNSTMUSEUM

A striking marble building designed by Finnish architect Alvar Aalto houses this regional **museum of contemporary and modern art** (☎ 98 13 80 88; Kong Christian Allé 50; adult/child 35kr/free; 🕑 10am-5pm Tue-Sun). It has a fine collection of Danish art dating from the late 19th century to the present day, including works by JF Willumsen, Asger Jorn, Richard Mortensen and Edvard Weie. The display incorporates naturalism, abstract and experimental art and offers a diverse experience for the art enthusiast.

To get there take the tunnel beneath the train station, which emerges into Kildeparken, a green space with statues and water fountains. Go directly through the park, cross Vesterbro and continue through a wooded area to the museum, a 10-minute walk in all.

AALBORGTÅRNET

The hill behind Nordjyllands Kunstmuseum is topped with **Aalborgtårnet** (☎ 98 77 05 11; Søndre Skovvej; adult/child 20/10kr 🕑 11am-5pm Apr-Sep, weather-permitting 10am-7pm Jul), a rather grotesque-looking tower offering a panoramic view of the city's smokestacks and steeples .Good on a clear day only.

Aalborgtårnet sits at the edge of an expansive wooded area, **Mølleparken**, which has walking trails, views and also the Aalborg Zoo.

AALBORG ZOO

Bubbling with wildlife, it's no surprise this **zoo** (☎ 96 31 29 29; Mølleparkvej 63; adult/child 70/35kr; 🕑 9am-6pm May-Aug, 10am-4pm Apr, Sep & Oct, 10am-2pm Nov-Mar) is one of Denmark's most popular. Some 1600 animals call it home, including tigers, zebras, giraffes, orang-utans, crocodiles and polar bears. It is a leader in the breeding of near-extinct animals and the successful reproduction of the Siberian Tiger illustrates its success. It's also accessible to people in wheelchairs so go along and check out the sea lion show at 11am each day. The zoo is southwest of the city and can be reached by taking bus No 1 from the centre.

AALBORG MARINEMUSEUM

Waterfront museum (☎ 98 11 78 03; Vestre Fjordvej 81; adult/child 60/30kr; 🕑 10am-6pm May-Aug, 10am-4pm Sep-Apr), 3km west of the city centre, features a 54m submarine, a torpedo boat, model ships and other maritime exhibits. It displays over 200 years of maritime history and is a perfect place to have a picnic. Take bus No 13 to get there.

Activities

TIVOLILAND

Roller coasters, gravity towers, bumper cars and fairy floss sum up this **amusement park** (☎ 98 11 12 55; Karolinelundsvej; adult/child 50/25kr; 🕑 vary, usually 10am-10pm Apr-Sep). Kids adore it and adults get a few kicks along the way, a great way to break up the historical and cultural bombardment for the youngsters. To get there take bus No 11 from the centre.

Festivals

Each year in late May, 100,000 people descend upon this city to partake in the **Aalborg Carnival** (☎ 98 13 72 11; www.karnevaliaalborg.dk). Festivities include a street parade, fireworks display and the inaugural 'Battle of Carnival Bands' which see the city at its effervescent best.

Sleeping

There are some 2600 beds in Aalborg and quite often they are not full, so asking for a discount or pursing a few leads can be beneficial to the hip pocket. Tourist office staff can book rooms (s/d 200/300kr plus booking fee 25kr) in private homes.

BUDGET

The following facilities are in the marina area about 4km west of the centre of Aalborg. Take bus No 13.

Danhostel Aalborg (☎ 98 11 60 44; www.danhostel.dk/aalborg; Skydebanevej 50; dm/d 120/330kr; 🅿 ⊠) Its only detraction is its distance from town. This hostel has 35 rooms, each with four beds and a bath.

Strandparken Camping (☎ 98 12 76 29; www.strandparken.dk in Danish; Skydebanevej 20; 🕑 17 Apr-19 Sep; per person 65kr; 🅿) A three-star camping ground on the eastern side of the marina that has a playground, kitchen and plenty of room to move. It's 300m from Fjordparken.

MID-RANGE

Villa Rose (☎ 98 12 13 38; www.villarosa.dk/english; Grønnegangen 4; from 500kr; P) The Hunter Room and the Skipper Room are just a couple of themed rooms on offer in these private villas. Situated smack bang in the centre, these villas possess real character.

Hotel Krogen (☎ 98 12 17 05; www.krogen.dk; Skibstedsvej 4; s/d without bathroom450/600kr, with bathroom 650/800kr; P) Old world charm in a well-to-do neighbourhood of Aalborg. Rooms are elegant, light and airy, and the dining and lounge rooms have wonderful high ceilings and classic furniture.

Aalborg Sømandshjem (☎ 98 12 19 00; www.hotel-aalborg.com; Østerbro 27; s/d 550/740kr; P ⊠) Geared towards families, this hotel has modern rooms, clean layout and is only 1km east of the centre. It has 54 rooms, each with phone, bathroom and large TV. There's also a pool table and table tennis in the basement for the kids. A hearty buffet breakfast is included.

Park Hotel (☎ 98 12 31 33; www.park-hotel-aalborg.dk; JF Kennedys Plads 41; s/d 785/915kr; P) Traditional and perhaps a touch tardy, this hotel is conveniently positioned opposite the train station and has a fitness room. A tip: ask for a courtyard (*til gaarden*) room if you're a light sleeper.

TOP END

Hotel Chagall (☎ 98 12 69 33; www.hotel-chagall.dk.com; Vesterbro 36; s/d 850/1050kr; P ⊠) The Chagall is central, comfortable and has 72 rooms with TV, phone and mini-bar. There's also a sauna, solarium and spa for indulgent types, and an exercise room for fitness fanatics.

First Hotel (☎ 80 88 04 11; www.firsthotels.com; Rendsburggade 5; s/d 1040/1290kr; P ⊠) Refreshing views overlooking the harbour and the rooms come with all the amenities you would expect. Each floor even has its own shoe-polishing machine; it is a haven for Danish businessmen. A mere 400m east of the city centre.

Radisson SAS (☎ 98 16 43 33; www.radissonsas.com; Ved Stranden 14; s/d 795/895kr; P ⊠) Best known as the site of the local casino, the rooms are both spacious and modern with some overlooking the harbour. Its position is outstanding.

Helnan Phønix Hotel (☎ 98 12 00 11; www.helnan.dk; Vesterbro 77; s/d 940/1140kr; P ⊠). Good old-fashioned service and the rooms have great character. Maybe a touch pricey for what you get. However, if you like wood finishes, you'll love the bar.

Eating

The best place to head at meal-time is Jomfru Ane Gade, a boisterous pedestrian street lined with cafés and restaurants, some with alfresco dining. With so much competition you can always find tempting deals, simply stroll the street and see what tickles your taste buds. A few favourites are listed here.

RESTAURANTS

Gaucho (☎ 98 13 70 30; Jomfru Ane Gade 21; mains 80-130kr; lunch & dinner) Fancy a succulent world-renowned Argentinean steak? Look no further.

Fellini (☎ 98 11 34 55; Jomfru Ane Gade 23; buffet 49kr, mains 50-90kr; lunch) Italian restaurant best known for its good-value buffet lunch of pizza, pasta and salad.

Fyrtøjet (☎ 98 13 73 77; Jomfru Ane Gade 17; mains 50-100kr; lunch & dinner) If it looks like it might be going to rain, consider this place, which has a glass-roofed courtyard, competitive prices and good food.

Princess Juliana (☎ 98 11 55 66; Vestre Havnepromenade; mains 230kr, set menu 350kr; lunch & dinner) Dine on this classic old ship and enjoy gourmet Danish and French cuisine. Simply divine.

Rosdahls (☎ 98 12 05 80; Strandvejen; mains 200kr, 6-course menu 495kr; lunch & dinner) A classy affair overlooking the harbour where quality fish and juicy steaks are on offer.

CAFÉS & QUICK EATS

Café KlosterTorvet (☎ 98 16 86 11; CW Obels Plads 4; mains day 40-60kr, night 80-120kr; breakfast, lunch & dinner) A funky café that is perfect for some fried eggs or a sandwich and a game of backgammon.

Caféministeriet (☎ 98 19 40 50; Mølleplads; mains 50-80kr; lunch & dinner) If you're after authentic Danish cuisine, head to this stylish, cosmopolitan café. It also does tasty sandwiches and fat, juicy burgers.

Café Saltlageret (☎ 98 12 59 77; Jomfru Ane Gade 16; 2 courses 100kr; breakfast, lunch & dinner) Great value, they offer efficient, hearty meals that are presented in style.

Azzurra (☎ 98 16 41 22; Jens Bangs Gade 15; mains 70-110kr; ⏲ lunch & dinner) All your favourite pizzas and pastas served in an Italian environment.

Skibsted's Fish Market (☎ 98 12 35 92, Algade 23; dishes 15-20kr; ⏲ lunch) Here you can get fresh takeaway salmon burgers and fish and chips.

Akropolis (☎ 98 11 44 08; Sankelmarksgade 1A; mains 70-110kr; ⏲ lunch & dinner) Authentic Greek food and drinks at moderate prices.

Drinking

When it comes to nightlife, tourist brochures describe Aalborg as 'the Paris of the north'. Danish folk describe the night scene as the only place in Denmark where you're likely to see a good, old-fashioned bar fight. The truth lies somewhere in between but whatever your experience, you're assured plenty of *akvavit* a locally produced spirit that means 'water of life'. There are enough bars up here to send a drunk delirious and it's a town the party purist will embrace immediately. Here are a few places to get warmed up.

LA Bar (☎ 98 11 37 37; Jomfru Ane Gade 7) Great place to start the night as cheap drinks are in abundance.

The Wharf (☎ 98 11 70 10; Borgergade 16) A popular pub with an impressive beer selection.

Off Piste (☎ 98 13 07 666; Jomfru Ane Gade 14) Chilled atmosphere and well-priced drinks.

Duus Vinkjælder (☎ 98 12 50 56; Østerågade 9; ⏲ midnight-close Mon-Sat) A superb way to cap off the evening is with a glass of wine at this smoulderingly romantic 300-year-old candlelit wine cellar in Jens Bangs Stenhus.

Entertainment

If you're interested in drinking and dancing (and perhaps a spot of gambling), there are a few places to pick from.

Under Uret (☎ 98 10 33 10; Jomfru Ane Gade 10) Massive club that gets going around midnight.

Gaslight (☎ 98 10 17 50; Jomfru Ane Gade 23) Always cranking out fat beats and if you want to cut up a dance floor this is your calling.

Spirit of America (☎ 98 12 47 55; Jomfru Ane Gade 16) Bar during the day, outrageously fun disco by night.

Casino Aalborg (☎ 98 10 15 50; Ved Stranden 14; ⏲ 8pm-4am) Roulette, blackjack and poker are part of the entertainment offered.

Pan Aalborg Bar & Niteclub (☎ 98 12 22 45; Danmarksgade 27A; ⏲ Thu-Sat) Aalborg's main gay venue, with a bar and dance club.

Getting There & Away

Aalborg airport is 6km northwest of the city centre. International flight normally go via Copenhagen and connect with one of Scandinavian Airlines many daily flights.

An airport bus (31kr) coincides with flight times and runs between the airport and the bus station on Jyllandsgade. A taxi between the airport and the city centre costs about 120kr.

Express buses (☎ 70 10 00 10; 290kr) run to Copenhagen two to four times daily (five hours).

Trains run about hourly to Frederikshavn (83kr, one hour) and a little more frequently to Århus (145kr, one hour).

Aalborg is 112km north of Århus and 65km southwest of Frederikshavn. The E45 bypasses the city centre, tunnelling under the Limfjord, while Rte 180 (which links up with the E45 both north and south of the city) leads into the centre.

To get to Lindholm Høje, or points north of the centre of Aalborg, take Rte 180 (Vesterbro), parallel to the E45, which crosses Limfjordsbroen.

Hertz, Avis and Europcar have booths at the airport. **Avis** (☎ 98 13 30 99; JF Kennedys Plads 3A) has an office at the train station and **Europcar** (☎ 98 13 23 55; Jyllandsgade 4) is also in town.

Getting Around

Almost all city buses leave from Østerågade and Nytorv, near Burger King. The standard bus fare is 15kr, or you can buy a 24-hour tourist bus pass (80kr). Grab a detailed bus map from the tourist office or call the **bus information line** (☎ 98 11 11 11).

Apart from a few one-way streets that may have you driving in circles a bit, Aalborg is easy to travel around by car. There's free parking along many side streets, and metered parking in the city centre. If you're unable to find a parking space, there are several large commercial car parks, including one at Ved Stranden 11.

You can order a **taxi** (☎ 98 10 10 10, 98 12 12 12), or just pick one from the rank at the train station (these coincide with flight times).

FREDERIKSHAVN

pop 25,700

Frederikshavn shuffles more than three million people through its port each year making it Jutland's busiest international ferry terminal. The majority of visitors are overtaxed Scandinavians raiding Denmark's supplies of relatively cheap booze and meat. The town itself lacks the historical glamour of its coastal neighbours but can successfully entertain you for a few hours with its feature attraction, Bangsbo.

Orientation

An overhead walkway leads from the ferry terminals to the tourist office, which sits at the edge of the central commercial district. The train station and the adjacent bus terminal are a 10-minute walk north of the ferry terminals.

Information

Danske Bank (☎ 96 20 61 60; Danmarksgade 70)
Frederikshavn Sømandshjem (☎ 98 42 09 77; Tordenskjoldsgade 15B; Internet access half-hour 20kr)
Frederikshavn Turistbureau (☎ 98 42 32 66; www.frederikshavn-tourist.dk; Skandiatorv 1; 9am-4pm Mon-Fri 11am-2pm, Sat Sep–mid-Jun, 8.30am-5pm daily mid-Jun–Aug) has the lowdown on town.
Post office (☎ 98 42 32 66; Skippergade) Beside the train station.

Sights

If you're waiting for a train it's an ideal time to climb the nearby whitewashed **Krudttårnet** (Gunpowder Tower; ☎ 98 42 31 11, Kragholmen 1; adult/child 15/5kr; 10.30am-5pm Jun–mid-Sep), a remnant of the 17th-century citadel that once protected the port. Until 1974 this squat round tower stood 270m to the east of its present position but an expansion of the shipyards necessitated its move further inland. Within the tower's 2m-thick walls are a few displays of antique swords, helmets and guns, and a steep stairway leading to a top galley mounted with cannons. Local naval hero Tordenskiold kept his gunpowder dry in this tower during Denmark's epic battles with Sweden.

BANGSBO

Bangsbo is on the southern edge of town and comprises a manor house, parkland and some wonderful gardens. The **museum** (☎ 98 41 09 37; Margrethesvej 1; adult/child 30/5kr; 10.30am-5pm daily, closed Mon in winter) looks at

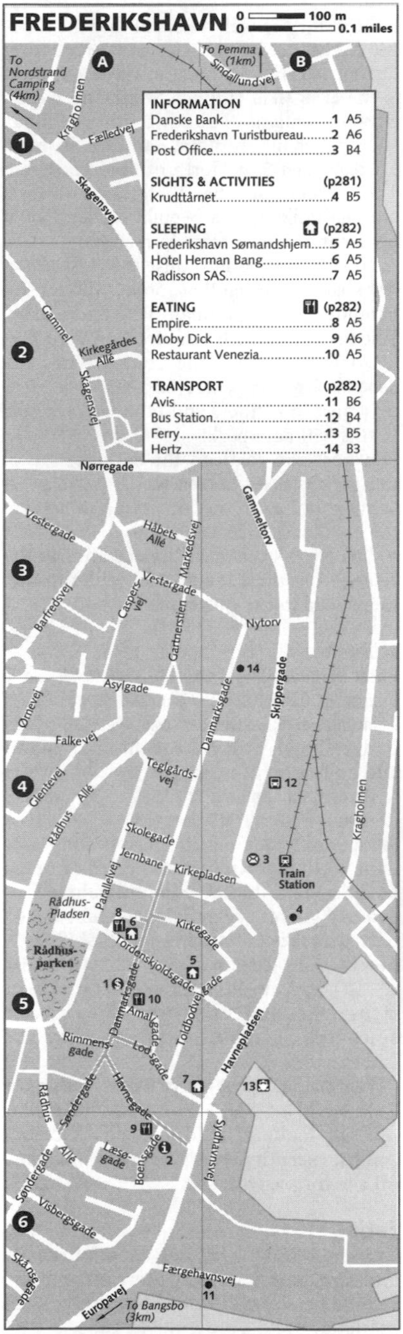
FREDERIKSHAVN
0 100 m
0 0.1 miles
INFORMATION
Danske Bank....1 A5
Frederikshavn Turistbureau....2 A6
Post Office....3 B4
SIGHTS & ACTIVITIES (p281)
Krudttårnet....4 B5
SLEEPING (p282)
Frederikshavn Sømandshjem....5 A5
Hotel Herman Bang....6 A5
Radisson SAS....7 A5
EATING (p282)
Empire....8 A5
Moby Dick....9 A6
Restaurant Venezia....10 A5
TRANSPORT (p282)
Avis....11 B6
Bus Station....12 B4
Ferry....13 B5
Hertz....14 B3
To Nordstrand Camping (4km)
To Pemma (1km)
Sindallundvej
Kragholmen
Fællesvej
Skagensvej
Gammel
Kirkegårdes Allé
Nørregade
Vestergade
Håbets Allé
Markedsvej
Gammeltorv
Barfredsvej
Caspers Vej
Gartnerstien
Nytorv
Skippergade
Asylgade
Danmarksgade
Ørnevej
Falkevej
Teglgårdsvej
Glentevej
Rådhus Allé
Skolegade
Jernbane
Kirkepladsen
Train Station
Parallelvej
Rådhus-Pladsen
Kirkegade
Rådhusparken
Tordenskjoldsgade
Toldbodvej
Amalgade
Havnepladsen
Rimmensgade
Lodsgade
Søndergade
Havnegade
Sydhavnsvej
Læsøgade
Boensgade
Visbergsgade
Skansevej
Færgehavnsvej
Europavej
To Bangsbo (3km)

local history as well as examining the Danish Resistance to the German occupation during WWII. The most intriguing exhibit is the **Ellingåskib** (Ellingå Ship), the reconstructed remains of a 12th-century, Viking-style merchant ship that was dug up from a stream bed 5km north of Frederikshavn. The museum also has Victorian furniture, antique dolls, and a peculiar collection of ornaments woven from human hair.

Next to the manor house is **Bangsbo Botaniske Have**, a garden that soothes the senses. Famous authors Herman Bang and Gustav Wied spent many hours strolling here.

To the south of the complex lies the **Bangsbo Dyrepark** where 50 or so roe deer play host to runners and other active souls in this 250-acre park.

Across the road on the eastern side of the park is **Pikkerbakken** which has a great vantage point to look out to Læsø and up the east coast to Skagen.

Bus No 3 stops near the entrance to the estate; from there it's a 500m-walk through the woods to the museum.

Sleeping

Hotel Herman Bang (☎ 98 42 21 66; www.hermanbang.dk in Danish, Tordenskjoldsgade 3; s/d without bathroom295/395; s/d with bathroom 395/495kr; Ⓟ) A budget hotel with run-of-the-mill rooms and a pleasant atmosphere.

Nordstrand Camping (☎ 98 42 93 50; nordstrand-camping.dk in Danish, Apholmenvej 40; Apr-Oct; per person 69kr; Ⓟ) Set in an appealing area 4km north of town it offers decent camping facilities. Take the north-bound train to Skagen and get off at Strandby, the first stop.

Frederikshavn Sømandshjem (☎ 98 42 09 77; www.fshotel.dk; Tordenskjoldsgade; 15B; s/d 575/695kr; Ⓟ) A fresh, modern hotel with spacious rooms that come with all the expected amenities. There's also a fitness centre and Internet café.

Radisson SAS (☎ 98 42 42 00; www.radissonsas.com; Havnepladsen 1; s/d 975/1165kr; Ⓟ) An impressive-looking building with luxurious rooms, exceptional service and a nightclub on site for party goers.

Eating

You can pick up a hot dog at both the train and ferry terminals. For more imaginative cuisine head into town to Lodsgade, Danmarksgade and Tordenskjoldsgade.

Pemma (☎ 98 43 82 98; Norde Strandvej 48; mains 200kr; lunch & dinner) Renowned for its fresh fish and panoramic views of the harbour, Pemma is a hit with locals – always a good sign.

Moby Dick (☎ 98 43 01 01; Havnegade 5; mains 160kr; lunch & dinner) A cellar restaurant that has a strong international menu, Moby Dick is great for fish or a hearty steak. On a fine day the courtyard is a nice place to dine.

Restaurant Venezia (☎ 98 42 37 50; Danmarksgade 73; pizza & pasta 50-90kr; lunch & dinner) Head here for excellent Italian food in a pleasant atmosphere.

Empire (☎ 98 42 60 02: Tordenskjoldsgade 3; burgers 55kr, mains 110kr; lunch & dinner) Specialises in designer burgers (such as pineapple, basil, chilli etc) and also has steaks and ribs.

Getting There & Away

For information on ferries from Frederikshavn to Sweden see p311, and to Norway see p310.

Frederikshavn is the northern terminus of the **Danske Statsbaner** (DSB; ☎ 70 13 14 15; www.dsb.dk) railway line. Trains depart about hourly south to Aalborg (83kr, one hour), Århus (189kr, 2½ hours) and Copenhagen (340kr, five hours).

Bus and rail routes in northern Jutland extend as far afield as Skagen, Råbjerg Mile, Hirtshals, Hjørring and Løkken. **Nordjyllands Trafikselskab (NT)** (☎ 98 90 09 00) has trains and buses to Skagen (45kr, one hour). You can by a *klipperkort* (clip card) for 120kr worth of travel (which several people can use), or there is also a 24-hour travel card (adult/child 80/40kr).

Express bus No 980 travels to Esbjerg twice per day.

Frederikshavn is 65km northeast of Aalborg on the E45 and 41km south of Skagen on Rte 40.

As Frederikshavn is a port of entry, there are several car-rental offices, including **Avis** (☎ 98 43 19 77; Paradiskajen 1) and **Hertz** (☎ 98 42 86 77; Danmarksgade 15).

LÆSØ

pop 2400

Læsø's appeal lies in its ability to stay firmly entrenched in the past. Just 28km off the coast (southeast) of Frederikshavn, it seems 100 years in arrears. It's an island of small farms, sandy beaches, heathlands, dunes, much-loved traditions and, of course, a contagiously charming community – it's 'capital' is Kattegat.

Fittingly, legend has it that Queen Margrethe 1 was saved from a shipwreck off Læsø in the 14th century and rewarded her rescuers with a stunning dress, giving them the right to adapt it as an island costume. Although such regional customs had largely disappeared elsewhere in Denmark by the 19th century, Læsø women wore their traditional island dress daily until just after WWII. Today they still wear the costume on special occasions.

Another island tradition continues in the making of Læsø salt. At one time an island export, salt is now sold in small souvenir bags for tourists.

Læsø is free of large resort hotels and attracts visitors looking for a low-key summer holiday. The island has a few small towns (including Vesterø Havn, Byrum and Østerby Havn), two medieval churches, a seaweed-roofed farm museum and a straw-roofed fishing museum.

Sights

MUSEUMSGÅRDEN

Now the official museum, **Museumsgården** (☎ 98 49 80 45; Museumsvej 3; open pm May-Sept or by appointment; adult/child 20kr/free) is a classic quadrangle farmstead from the 1600's that was predominately built out of shipwrecks with a seaweed roof.

THE SHALLOWS

The **Shallows** is a conservation area aiming to preserve the local seaside habitat and shrubs.

LÆSØ SALTSYDERI

It's not quite a salt mine but now a museum – **Læsø Saltsyderi** (☎ 98 49 13 55; Hornfiskrønvej 1, Byrum; adult/child 40/20kr 🕑 pm May-Sept or by appointment). Salt was manufactured here for over 500 years and this museum lets you taste, buy and learn about the importance of salt to the people of Læsø. In the middle ages salt was produced here for the Bishop of Viborg in Central Jutland.

VESTERØ HAVN

A Gothic altarpiece from 1475 has pride of place at **Vesterø Havn** (☎ 98 49 96 66; Vesterø Sdr. Kirke, Præstevejen 37) a medieval church. Fresco paintings tell the story of the Three Wise Men

Information

Læsø Turistbureau (☎ 98 49 92 42; Vesterø Havnegade 17; 🕑 9am-4pm Mon-Fri, 10am-3pm Sat 10am-noon Sun Jun-Aug) is 200m east of the ferry terminal in Vesterø Havn.

Tours

A good way to experience this unique island is by doing a day trip from Frederikshavn. Book at the **Frederikshavn ferry office** (☎ 98 49 92 42; Havnepladsen 1) for the tours described below. Both tours run daily from June to August, less frequently during the rest of the year.

The **bus tour** (☎ 98 49 92 42; 180kr) takes you around the island in four hours and shows you all the main sights including the saltworks, museum and the Shallows.

Another fine way of touring the island is the **bike tour** (☎ 98 49 92 42; 220kr), and you enjoy a gorgeous lunch at Bakken Restaurant, Byrum.

Sleeping & Eating

Læsø Turistbureau can organise holiday cottages and flats for hire around the island. Vesterø Havn and Kattegat are the best villages with the most variety and quality.

Danhostel Læsø (☎ 98 49 91 95; www.laesoe-vandrerhjem.dk; Lærkevej 6, Vesterø Havn; dm/d 120/400kr; Ⓟ ⊠) Situated 500m southeast of the ferry harbour, this hostel has 90 beds.

Hotel Havnbakken (☎ 98 49 90 09; Havnbakken 12; s/d 550/795kr; 🕑 breakfast, lunch & dinner; Ⓟ) Centrally located in a cosy white building, this hotel has light, comfy rooms at a reasonable rate. There's also a restaurant downstairs that serves up fresh fish and other Danish fare.

Læsø Camping (☎ 98 49 94 95; laesoe@dk-camp.dk; Agersigen 18, Vesterø Havn; per person 65kr; 🕑 May-Sep; Ⓟ) Three-star camping ground on the northwest side of the island also hires out cabins that are in pretty good shape.

Getting There & Away

Færgeselskabet Læsø (☎ 98 49 90 22; www.laesoe-line.dk; return trip adult/child 120/60kr) sails two to six times per day between Læsø and Frederikshavn year-round (1½ hours).

Getting Around

A public bus runs about hourly on weekdays and less frequently at weekends between the villages of Vesterø Havn, Byrum and Østerby Havn.

Bicycles can be rented from **Jarvis Cykelservice** (☎ 98 49 94 44; Vesterø Havnegade 29; per day 80kr) in Vesterø Havn.

SÆBY

pop 8500

While Skagen is the inspiration behind world-renowned Scandinavian artists, Sæby is the spiritual home of Danish literature. In summer, its gorgeous port, whitewashed church and historic old town are packed with sunburnt Danish holiday-makers. It's a great place to unwind with wide, safe, child-friendly beaches and good restaurants.

Sæby was the inspiration behind Hernan Bang's *Sommerglæder* (Summer pleasure), Gustav Wied's novel *Fædrene æde* (The Fathers Eat Grapes) and Henrik Ibsen's renowned work *Fruen fra havet* (The Lady from the Sea).

Orientation & Information

The bus station is 300m southwest of the town centre. The **Sæby Turistbureau** (☎ 98 46 12 44; www.visittoppen.com; Krystalgade 3; ⏲ 9am-4pm Mon-Fri, 10am-1pm Sat Sep-May, 9am-5pm Mon-Sat, 10am-1pm Sun mid-Jun–Aug) is smack bang in the middle of town – just walk down the main shopping street Vestergade and you can't miss it. Continue down on Søndergade and turn right into Algade to reach the church and port, about five minutes on foot from the centre.

There's an ATM at the **Danske Bank** (☎ 98 89 89 00; Vestergade 35) on the main shopping street.

Sights & Activities

Next to the port is **Sæby Klosterkirke** (☎ 98 46 39 37; Strandgade 5), the remains of an impressive four-winged Carmelite monastery from 1470. Its visually imposing exterior is coupled with an interior that boasts beautiful frescoes from the Middle Ages and a 16th-century altarpiece. For those disappointed with the physical size of the Little Mermaid in Copenhagen, Sæby's symbol of protection **The Lady from the Sea** has presence *and* stature. It's based on Henrik Ibsen's play of the same name, which he wrote after a summer spent walking along the beach and up into the woods around Sæby. On the way into town stop at Algade 7, the former **home of Adda Ravnkilde**, who wrote three very powerful novels regarding female artists in a male-dominated domain and then tragically took her life at the age of 21.

Just north of the turistbureau is the **Sæby Museum** (☎ 98 46 10 77; Algade 1-3; ⏲ 10am-5pm Tue-Sun Jun-Aug, 10am-5pm Tue-Fri Sep-May; adult/child 30/15kr), occupying a charming 17th-century timber-frame house. Expect to see an amber collection, a 1920s classroom and a classically refurnished Victorian sitting room.

Herregårdsmusset Sæbygård (☎ 98 46 10 77; Sæbgårdvej 51; ⏲ 10am-5pm Tue-Sun Jun-Aug; adult/child 30/15kr), 3km west of town, is a classic Danish Renaissance manor house. The furniture (from around 1700–1900) still presides in the house which is being restored.

Sleeping

Aahøj (☎ 98 46 11 27; www.aahoj-saebyhotel.dk; Hans Aabelsvej 1; s/d 475/625kr; P) Flushed with elegance, this 1896 villa offers classically furnished rooms, a pleasant sun-room/lounge and a rich, green garden. It is 200 metres west of the tourist office.

Sæby Fritidscenter-Danhostel (☎ 98 46 36 50; www.saebyfritidscenter.dk; Sæbygaardvej 32; dm/d 85/300kr; P ⊠), located a mere kilometre east of town at the sports centre, it's clean, large and friendly. Dorms sleep six.

Sæby-Strand Camping (☎ 98 46 20 90; Frederikshavnsvej 96A; per person 67kr; P) North of town, this camping ground has beach frontage and plenty of activities in playgrounds and crazy golf. There is also a mini-market and café on site.

Eating

Café Smeden (☎ 98 46 29 90; Haven 2; mains 60-120kr; ⏲ lunch & dinner) Offers a wide range of fresh seafood. Try the shrimp, garlic and parsley risotto, which is both filling and tasty.

Jensens Fiskerestaurant (☎ 98 46 11 56; mains 120-150kr; Haven; ⏲ lunch & dinner) In the heart of the harbour area there's some great seafood on offer. The yachts make a nice backdrop for a plate of smoked herring.

Frøken Madsen's Spisehus (☎ 98 40 80 36; Pindborggade 1; mains 150-230kr; ⏲ dinner) Up in town in an intimate old building near the stream, this restaurant offers a wide variety of gourmet food from an impressive international menu.

Getting There & Away

Sæby is 12km south of Frederikshavn on Rte 180. The E45 bypasses it but if you drive from Aalborg you can pull off at Syvsten and take the 180 into town.

There is no train line here but the hourly No 73 buses between Aalborg and Frederikshavn stop at Sæby.

SKAGEN

pop 11,000

In the late 19th century, artists flocked to Skagen (Skane), infatuated with the radiant light's impact on the rugged, yet beautiful landscape. Now tourists flock here every summer to soak up the light which inspired many famous paintings and poems. Skagen has been a fishing port for centuries and its Nordic sailors add immense character to the town. The intimate, older neighbourhoods are filled with distinctive yellow-wash houses, petite white picket fences and red-tiled roofs. Skagen, with its rich art, fresh seafood and classic characters, is an utterly delicious slice of Denmark.

Orientation

Sankt Laurentii Vej, the main street, runs almost the entire length of this long, thin town and is never more than five minutes' walk from the waterfront. The train station is 100 metres north of the town centre.

Information

Internet access is at **Jakobscafé Café & Bar** (☎ 98 44 16 90; Havnevej 4A; free).

There are several banks in town, including an **Egnsbank Nord** (☎ 98 48 86 66; Sankt Laurentii Vej 39) and a **Danske Bank** (☎ 96 79 10 50; Havnevej 1).

> **FISHY BUSINESS**
>
> They say the early bird catches the worm but if you want to catch the heartbeat of this fishing community head down to the fish auctions at the port when the boats return with their catch (6am to 7am). The theatre of it all is infectious, as the auctioneers and buyers go toe to toe in rapid Danish. The Nordic fishermen have harsh, weather-beaten faces and while proud, are surprisingly approachable. They have some fantastic yarns up their sleeves and it's well worth sparking up a conversation once the sales are over. All in all, the auction is a cornerstone of Skagen society and definitely worth the early-morning rise.

The **post office** (☎ 98 44 23 44; Christian X Vej 8) is 100m west of the station.

The **Skagen Turistbureau** (☎ 98 44 13 77, www.skagen-tourist.dk; Sankt Laurentii Vej 22; 9am-5pm Mon-Fri, 10am-2pm Sat Jun-Aug, 9am-4pm Mon-Fri, 10am-1pm Sat Sep-May) is at the train station and is bustling with activities to keep you entertained for days. It has information on a popular kids program that runs each week during summer.

Sights & Activities

SKAGENS MUSEUM

Fabulous **museum** (☎ 96 44 64 44; Brøndumsvej 4; adult/child 50kr/free; 10am-6pm Jun-Aug, 10am-5pm May & Sep, reduced low-season hrs) showcases the outstanding art that was produced here between 1830 and 1930. PS Krøyer, Anna and Michael Ancher, Christian Krohg and Oscar Bjørck were the artists that placed Skagen firmly in the international art scene with their naturalistic representation of the landscape. PS Krøyer's work is quite incredible – he came here to 'paint the light' and certainly succeeded on that level, but in the process evoked an atmospheric sense of place. Take a close look at *Johannisfeuer*, Krøyer's early-20th-century work that shows a bonfire on the Skagen beach. Among the notable Skagen residents depicted on the left side of the painting are Anna Ancher, in a blue cape, and Holger Drachmann, in a brown cloak with a white beard and cane. The museum is about 300 metres east of the train station and well signposted.

ARTISTS' HOUSES

If you want to dig a little deeper into the world of infamous Skagen artists, the former houses of the Anchers and Holger Drachmann have been restored as museums. The **Anchers' house** (☎ 98 44 30 09; Markvej 2; adult/child 40/10kr; 10am-5pm May-Sep, 10am-6pm mid-Jun–mid-Aug, 11am-3pm Oct-Apr), 300m north-east of the station, was preserved after the death of their only child Helga in 1964 and appears much in the same way as it would have during the artists' lives, with antique furniture and vivid paintings.

Holger Drachmann's house (☎ 98 44 51 88; Hans Baghs Vej 21; adult/child 25/5kr; 11am-3pm daily Jun–mid-Sep, reduced hrs low-season), is west of the town centre near Sankt Laurentii Vej, and was his home for the last six years of his life. There's a photographic exhibition in the annex, and the house has many of the oil paintings that were there when he died.

SKAGEN BY OG EGNSMUSEUM

Evocatively presented, the open-air **Skagen By og Egnsmuseum** (☎ 98 44 47 60; PK Nielsen Vej 8; adult/child 30/5kr; 10am-4pm daily May-Sep; 11am-4pm Mon-Fri Mar, Apr & Oct), 200m southwest of the harbour, depicts Skagen's maritime history. Interesting displays on Skagen's lifeboat rescue service, include dramatic photos of ships in distress, as well as the preserved homes of fisherfolk with their original furnishings, and a picturesque Dutch windmill.

GRENEN

Northern Jutland on the whole is a rough and barren in parts landscape, but if you dig deep enough there is a reassuring calm in it all. It is epitomised in Grenen in stunning fashion as the Kattegat and Skagerrak seas clash at the country's most northerly point. The wind is ferocious yet refreshing, while the strikingly blue skies contrast with the barren, sandy landscape. The 30-minute walk up the long, thin, sweeping stretch of sand passes Holger Drachmann's (1846–1908) grave. Yachts and blue water make an irresistible postcard image. Skagen's light comes into its own here, as the earth, water and sky combine to enrich the senses.

The **Sandormen** (☎ 98 44 36 84; Apr-Oct; adult/child return 15/10kr) can take you out to the point if it's raining or if time is not on your side.

In summer, buses run between Skagen station and Grenen (15kr) hourly until 5pm.

TILSANDEDE KIRKE

Prepare to be bemused yet amused by the tale of Tilsandede Kirke (Buried Church). Erected during the mid-14th century and once the biggest church in the region, it fell victim to a sand drift in the 16th century. So much so that by the end of the 18th century, church goers had to dig their way into God's sacred building. In 1795 the relentless sand drift broke the will of the congregation and the church was closed by royal decree. The main part of the church was torn down in 1810 but the lofty **tower** (adult/child 8/4kr; 11am-5pm Jun-Aug) still stands. It was used as a navigational tool for sailors back in the early days.

The picturesque church tower and the surrounding area comprise part of **Skagen Klitplantage**, a nature reserve. It's 5km south of Skagen and well signposted from Rte 40. The nicest way to get there is by bike; take Gammel Landevej from Skagen. You could also take the train (15kr) to Højen, a rural stop near the church; in Skagen, let the conductor know you want to get off in Højen (on the return you'll need to push the button on the platform in Højen that signals the train to stop).

GAMMEL SKAGEN

Renowned for its gorgeous sunsets and well-heeled summer residents, Gammel Skagen is a fine place to head late in the afternoon. It was a fishing hamlet before sandstorms ravaged this windswept area and forced many of its inhabitants to move to Skagen on the more protected east coast. It's a pleasant bike ride 4km west of Skagen: just head towards Frederikshavn and turn right at Højensvej, which will take you to the waterfront. Bus No 79 runs infrequently between Skagen and Gammel Skagen (15kr).

Festivals

Since 1971 the **Skagen Festival** (☎ 98 44 40 94) has transformed this artistic fishing village into a music lover's paradise, with acts ranging from modern day rock to folk music. It's held on the last weekend of June, but be warned – the town is always booked out at this time so book ahead if you're keen to join the celebrations.

Sleeping

Tourist office staff can book rooms (s/d 200/350kr, plus booking fee 50kr) in private houses.

Danhostel Skagen Ny (☎ 98 44 22 00; www.danhostel.dk/skagen; Rolighedsvej 2; mid-Feb–Nov; dm/d 118/300kr; P ⊠) Always a hive of family activity, the rooms here are both clean and light. Book ahead as it's very popular on weekends. It's 1km towards Frederikshavn from the train station and has 112 beds.

Grenen Camping (☎ 98 44 25 46; grencamp@post6.tele.dk; Fyrvej 16; May-Sep; per person 70kr; P) Ideal seaside location and plenty of tree cover make this the pick of the camping grounds. It's on the outskirts of town towards Grenen.

Brødums Hotel (☎ 98 44 15 55; Anchersvej 3; www.broendums-hotel.dk in Danish; s/d 575/875, with bathroom 795/1095kr; P) When artists first discovered

Skagen this is where they stayed, painting awe-inspiring images in the 'Blue Room' that still exists today. The hotel has retained the atmosphere of yesteryear and is rich in history, culture and warm hospitality. Rooms are how they were 70 years ago with no TV or bath but plenty of charm. Danish royalty as well as world-famous artists have stayed here.

Marienlund Badepension (☎ 98 44 13 20; badepension@marielund.dk, Fabriciusvej 8; s/d 400/750kr; P) Light, white rooms, comfy beds and incredibly hospitable hosts make this a solid option on the western side of town. It's a five-minute walk from the centre along Sankt Laurentii Vej.

Finns Hotel Pension (☎ 98 45 01 55; info@finnshotelpension.dk, Østre Strandvej 63; s/d 400/675kr, with bath 700/875kr; P ☒) A very striking black and white house that is gay-friendly and a stone's throw from the ocean. There are six delightful rooms furnished with antiques available at Finns.

Clausens Hotel (☎ 98 45 01 66; www.clausenshotel.dk in Danish; Sankt Laurentii Vej 35; s/d without bathroom 525/645kr, with bathroom 550/795kr; P) In a grand old building, Clausens has airy rooms and holds a handy position opposite the train station, though in the height of summer the passing traffic can be a touch noisy.

Color Hotel (☎ 98 44 22 33; www.colorhotels.dk in Danish; Gammel Landevej 39; s/d 895/1150kr; P ☒) One of Skagen's top-of-the-range hotels, this has all the usual amenities and a great pool.

Eating

Stroll down to the harbour for fantastically fresh seafood in the open-air waterfront cafés. All have cheap fish and chips and pricier specialities. Havnevej, the main road connecting the harbour and the town centre, has the best cluster of inexpensive eateries.

Pakhuset (☎ 98 44 17 46; Rødspættevej 6; mains café 90-120kr, restaurant 150-230kr; lunch & dinner) Arguably the best seafood in town, upstairs is where the discerning seafood lover is at home as oysters, lobster, mussels and fine fish are meticulously prepared. Downstairs is your stock-standard café option that has some good, appetising bites.

Skagen Fiskerestaurant (☎ 98 44 35 44; Fiskehuskaj 13; mains 50-80kr, platter 250kr; lunch & dinner) Tremendously popular with tourists and the calamari is certainly a dish to savour.

Brødums Hotel (☎ 98 44 15 55; Anchersvej 3; lunch smørredrød 50kr, dinner mains 140kr; lunch & dinner) Sit in the sheltered courtyard or fine dine inside the majestic 1874 hotel building. Plenty of fresh seafood is used throughout the Danish menu. Delight your tastebuds with the fish soup, a timeless classic.

Jakobscafé Café & Bar (☎ 98 44 16 90; Havnevej 4A; mains 80-120kr; lunch & dinner) Relaxed café-pub with hearty meals that should satisfy most hungers – the steak is a winner. During summer the place is full of young Danes having a few warm-up drinks.

Trattoria Toscana (☎ 98 45 12 13; Havnevej 14; mains 70-120kr; lunch & dinner) Locals adore this

A MARINER'S NIGHTMARE

The waters off northern Jutland have always been extremely treacherous for mariners and have claimed hundreds of ships and thousands of lives over the centuries. Not only are the waters tempestuous and the currents strong, but the land is flat and devoid of landmarks, offering few navigational reference points.

Historically, when ships washed up on shore, local residents would go straight to work pillaging the contents and dismantling the ships for their timber. Some unscrupulous souls are even said to have hung lanterns in such a manner as to imitate waterways and lure captains into venturing too close to the shoreline.

The situation got so out of hand that in 1521 a decree was passed to control salvaging. Gallows were erected along the coast to remind would-be pillagers of the new penalty for the looting of shipwrecks.

At the same time, simple wooden seesaw-style 'lighthouses' called *vippefyret* were erected along the coastline. Each had a basket that could be pulled down and filled with coal, and a counterweight that raised the basket high where it burned throughout the night. These forerunners of present-day lighthouses helped to guide ships safely around the point.

Although none of the original coal lights still exist, there's a reconstructed one at Skagen above the beach at the northeastern end of Østre Strandvej.

Italian restaurant and its pizzas are topped with fresh, juicy ingredients. Always full on weekends.

Clausens Hotel (☎ 98 45 01 66; Sankt Laurentii Vej 35; mains 120kr; ⌚ lunch & dinner) Old-fashioned hotel-restaurant, opposite the train station, has some tasty seafood on offer and is great for a late afternoon beer.

Stendys Is-Café (☎ 98 44 38 78; Sankt Laurentii Vej 37; ice cream 20kr; ⌚ 10am-10pm) Has a wide variety of Italian ice cream and is just opposite the train station.

Getting There & Away

Skagen is 41km north of Frederikshavn on Rte 40 and 49km northeast of Hirtshals via Rtes 597 and 40.

Nordjyllands Trafikselskab (NT) has trains or buses to Frederikshavn about once an hour (45kr, one hour). NT's seasonal Skagerakkeren bus (No 99) operates about six times per day from Skagen to Hirtshals (37kr, 1½ hours) between mid-June and mid-August. The same bus also continues on to Hjørring and Løkken.

Getting Around

Skagen Cykeludlejning (☎ 98 44 10 70; Banegårdspladsen; 24hr hire 75kr) is adjacent to the train station and has a wide range of bikes.

Taxis (☎ 98 43 34 34) are available at the station and charge about 60kr from Skagen town centre to Grenen.

RÅBJERG MILE

Denmark's largest expanse of drifting sand dunes, Råbjerg Mile, is an amazing natural phenomenon. These undulating, 40m-high hills are great fun to explore and almost big enough to lose yourself in. The dunes were formed on the west coast during the great sand drift of the 16th century and have purposefully been left in a migratory state (moving towards the forest at a rate of 15m per year). The dunes leave a low, moist layer of sand behind, stretching westwards to Skagerrak.

Råbjerg Mile is 16km southwest of Skagen, off Rte 40 on the road to Kandestederne. Between mid-June and mid-August the Skagerakkeren bus (No 99) runs six times daily from Skagen station to Råbjerg Mile (23kr, 25 minutes) and on to Hirtshals. The dunes themselves are a 750m walk from the Råbjerg Mile bus stop.

HIRTSHALS

pop 6900

Adored by discount-hungry Norwegians and largely inhabited by hardened Hirtshals seamen, this town is a good base for sightseeing. If sharks and sea life get you going you won't be disappointed either – Hirtshals boasts an impressive aquarium.

West of the town the coast is comprised of harsh cliffs and a lighthouse which are good fun to explore on a bike or horse. But if beaches are more to your liking, head south to Tornby Strand (opposite) where endless amounts of sand await.

Information

Danske Bank (☎ 96 56 10 00; Jørgens Fiblers Gade 23) One block south (inland) of the train station.

Hirtshals Turistbureau (☎ 98 94 22 20; Nørregade 40; www.visithirtshals.dk; ⌚ 9am-4pm Mon-Fri, 9am-7pm Sat mid-Jun–Aug, 9.30am-3.30pm Mon-Thu, 9am-4pm Fri, 9am-3pm Sat Sep–mid-Jun) At the end of the far pedestrian walk, about five minutes' walk from the train station.

Post office (☎ 98 94 17 33) Part of the train station.

Sights

Nordsømuseet (☎ 98 94 44 44; Willemoesvej 2; adult/child 90/45kr; ⌚ 10am-10pm mid-Jun–mid-Aug, 9am-5pm mid-Aug–mid-Jun) is an aquarium that is home to the largest tank in Europe. The focus is on North Sea marine life, as sharks and schools of fish share the gigantic tank. The central viewing platform is an amphitheatre that looks into the circular tank through an 8m-high window. Every day at 1pm a diver enters the tank to feed the marine life, a seemingly improbable sight that creates a real sense of danger. The seal pool outside comes alive during feeding time at 11am and 3pm daily.

Sleeping

Hotel Hirtshals (☎ 98 94 20 77; fax 98 94 21 07; Havngade 2; s/d 695/795kr; Ⓟ ⊠) Modern rooms with pleasant views over the town's fishing fleet. Comfy beds coupled with a bathroom, TV and phone make it Hirtshals' best.

Danhostel Hirtshals (☎ 98 94 12 48; danhostel.hirtshals@adr.dk; Kystvejen 53; ⌚ Mar-Apr; dm/d 120/340kr; Ⓟ ⊠) Indicative of this hostel chain, Danhostel Hirtshals is of high quality with friendly staff and a family atmosphere. It's just 1km south of the train station.

Hirtshals Camping (☎ 98 94 25 35; fax 98 94 33 43; hirstshals@dk-camp.dk; Kystvejen 6; ⌚ Apr-mid–Sep; per

ICELANDIC HORSES

Cantering along the windswept west coast beaches on an Icelandic horse is an unforgettable experience. The horse – or pony to be exact – has provided the only means of transport in Iceland for about a thousand years. The pony is short, stocky, smart and tough, but also docile and friendly. And if you get lost, it will, on request, simply take you home.

A great ride takes you through Uggerby Klitplantage and onto the beach on these magnificent beasts. It's a top outing for riders of all skill levels and is well suited for a family outing or a romantic escape. A well-respected outfit is **Vestkystens Ridecenter** (☎ 98 97 54 80; www.vestkystens-ridecenter.dk; Digetvej 28, Uggerby; 2-hr ride 225kr) which is 7km east of Hirtshals on Rte 597.

Northern Jutland is a great place for horse riding with 175km of horse trails meandering around the region. Many establishments offer half-hour rides or you can simply hire a horse and go out west.

person 64kr; P) There are 170 camp sites on this flat, exposed piece of land 150m south of the hostel.

Eating

You'll find the following eateries close together in the town centre.

Lilleheden & Café 2 (☎ 98 94 45 38; Hjørringgade 2; downstairs 30-70kr, gourmet 110kr; lunch & dinner) Great for a light lunch or a gourmet dining experience, this place has two levels and two menus that should cover most needs. Sit outside during summer and soak up the sun, harbour and excellent food.

Restaurant Rosa (☎ 98 94 19 44; Nørregade 4; pizza 40kr, dinner mains 65kr; lunch & dinner) Specialises in pizza but also has Mexican dishes.

Jasmine (☎ 98 94 35 55; Hjørringgade 4; fish & chips 40kr, Chinese dishes 50kr; lunch & dinner) A good-value place that has both Danish fast food and Chinese fare.

Getting There & Around

Hirtshals is 49km southwest of Skagen via Rtes 40 and 597 and 41km northwest of Frederikshavn via the E39 and Rte 35.

Mosquito Cykelcenter (☎ 98 94 21 96; Nørredage 34; per day 100kr) is a reputable outfit.

Color Line (www.colorline.com) operates ferries year-round to the Norwegian ports of Oslo, Kristiansand and Larvik (see p310).

The summer Skagerakkeren bus runs between Hirtshals station and Skagen six times daily (37kr, 1½ hours).

Hirtshals' train station is 500m south of the ferry terminal, but trains connecting with ferry services continue down to the harbour. A private railway, operated by Hjørring Privatbaner, connects Hirtshals with Hjørring hourly between 6am to 10pm (22.50kr, 20 minutes). At Hjørring you can connect with a DSB train to Aalborg (67.50kr, 40 minutes) or Frederikshavn (45kr, 30 minutes).

AROUND HIRTSHALS

If all you're after is a long stretch of untouched white sand **Tornby Strand** delivers it in buckets. It's 5km south of Hirtshals and attracts both locals and tourists attempting to beat the heat of summer. During colder times it's a beach desert. As the sand is compact enough to drive on, many park next to the breakers. You can drive 4km south to where the river slices the sand in two but use caution as it's easy to misjudge the tides or hit a soft spot. Hiking is also possible in the high mounded dunes and into the coastal woodlands that back the southern side of the beach.

Tornby Strand can be reached from Hirtshals via Rte 55 and Tornby Strandvej. In summer the bus (15kr) from Hirtshals to Hjørring stops at Tornby Strand six times daily.

HJØRRING

pop 24,800

Hjørring is a regional centre with a difference – 150 statues and bronze sculptures placed randomly throughout the town. If you find yourself in the region with a couple of spare hours drop in and grab a bite to eat in the market area of its old town.

Hjørring's old town is around its main square, Springvandspladsen, and runs north up to Sankt Olai Plads, which is bordered by the three medieval churches. Springvandspladsen is a five-minute walk north of the train station along Jernbanegade; stroll 200 metres further north on the pedestrian walk Strømgade to reach Sankt Olai Plads.

Information

Danske Bank (☎ 96 23 63 60; Springvandspladsen 2)

Hjørring Turistbureau (☎ 98 92 02 32; www.visithjoerring.dk; Markedsgade 9; 9am-4pm Mon-Fri, 9am-noon Sat mid-Jun–mid-Aug, 9am-5pm Mon-Fri, 9am-2pm Sat mid-Aug–mid-Jun) Is 750m east of the train station and has knowledgeable staff.

Post office (☎ 80 20 70 30) On the western side of the train station.

Sights

Hjørring is unique in that it managed to retain three medieval churches despite the thinning out that occurred throughout Denmark following the Reformation. All three churches are within 200m of each other, on the northern side of Sankt Olai Plads.

The oldest, **Sankt Olai Kirke**, dates from the 11th century and has a Romanesque chancel, a late Gothic porch and a 16th-century altarpiece. **Sankt Catharinæ Kirke**, the current parish church, retains traces of its medieval beginnings in the transept and has a 13th-century Gothic crucifix, although the church has been altered over the centuries and was largely rebuilt in the 1920s. Check out the 1651 altarpiece depicting the Last Supper. The Romanesque **Sankt Hans Kirke** has a nave built from medieval brick, a fresco painted in 1350 and an altarpiece and pulpit dating from the early 17th century.

On your walk through town look out for the imposing bronze sculptured bull and the imaginative fountains.

Sleeping & Eating

Hotel Phønix (☎ 98 92 54 55; hotel@phoenix-hjoerring.dk; Jernbanegade 6; s/d 550/750kr; restaurant mains 185kr; breakfast, lunch & dinner; P) In a lovely old 1887 building this hotel has both inviting rooms and an upmarket restaurant downstairs featuring quality steak and fish dishes. It's 300m north of the train station.

Danhostel Hjørring (☎ 98 92 67 00; www.danhostel.dk/hjoerring; Thomas Morildsvej 11; Mar-Oct; dm/d 118/350kr; P ☒) Well equipped with spacious dorms and a TV room, this hostel is 2.5km north of the train station.

Pizza King (☎ 98 92 23 00; Jernbanegade 24; pizza 30kr; lunch & dinner) An ideal place for a quick bite. There is plenty of value to the slice, as well as kebabs and hot dogs.

Getting There & Away

Hjørring is 35km west of Frederikshavn on Rte 35 and 17km south of Hirtshals on Rte 55 or the E39.

Hjørring is served by Nordjyllands Trafikselskab (NT; ☎ 98 90 09 00), which operates bus services to Skagen, Løkken, Frederikshavn and Hirtshals. The bus station is 150m northeast of the train station, near the intersection of Jernbanegade and Asylgade.

Hjørring is on the Århus–Frederikshavn DSB railway line and is also the terminus of a private railway line to Hirtshals (p289). Destinations include Hirtshals (22.50kr, 20 minutes), Frederikshavn (45kr, 30 minutes), Aalborg (67.50kr, 40 minutes) and Århus (172kr, 2¼ hours).

LØKKEN

pop 1300

Løkken is dubbed the 'Danish Ibiza' during summer, and rightly so as wild teenagers transform this sleepy town into a sea of loud parties. In fact, the local economy is somewhat dependent upon the teenagers and they are welcomed with open arms. The town's draw card is its wide, sandy beach, and the requisite shops, ice-cream stands and cafés welcome the summer bombardment. Colder months see the town go into hibernation.

Information

Løkken Turistbureau (☎ 98 99 10 09; www.loekken.dk; Harad Fischers Vej 8; 9am-5pm Mon-Sat Jun-Aug, 9am-4pm Mon-Fri, 10am-1pm Sat Sep-May) is 200m east of the main square Torvet. It has a wealth of knowledge on the area and can book hotels and apartments, change money and even send your postcards. Outstanding.

Sleeping

There is a string of camping grounds along Søndergade, the street that runs south from Torvet.

Josefines Camping (☎ 98 99 13 26; josefines-camping@post.tele.dk; Søndergade 57; Apr-Sep per person 67kr; P) Only 300 metres to the beach and close to the town centre. Good facilities at the site and it gets plenty of attention in summer.

Hotel Klitbakken (☎ 98 99 11 66; klitbakken@loekken.dk, Nørregade 3; s/d 550/700kr; P ☒) Close to Torvet and a solid option with en suite rooms that also have a balcony.

NORTHERN JUTLAND

Eating

There are several places to eat on Torvet and along Nørregade and Strandgade, which radiate out from Torvet.

Asia House Restaurant (☎ 98 99 25 10; Norgesvej 10; mains 40-70kr; lunch & dinner) Does a mean fried rice and all your Asian favourites.

Løkken Badehotel (☎ 98 99 27 12; Torvet; mains lunch/dinner 90/150kr; lunch & dinner) On the main square, serving traditional Danish fish and beef dishes.

Getting There & Away

Løkken is on Rte 55, 18km southwest of Hjørring. Buses run every couple of hours between Løkken and Hjørring (30kr, 40 minutes) and between Løkken and Aalborg (60kr, 1¼ hours).

HANSTHOLM

pop 3200

Its impressive commercial harbour was completed in 1967 and since then the town has developed into one of Denmark's largest fishing ports and prominent industrial centres. The only reason you would be here is to jump on a ferry to Norway or Iceland.

Information

Hanstholm Turistbureau (☎ 97 96 12 19; www.hanstholmturist.dk; Bytorvet 9; 10am-5pm Mon-Thu, 10am-3pm Fri, 10am-12.30pm Sat mid-Jun–Aug, 10am-4pm Mon-Thu, 10am-3pm Fri Sep–mid-Jun) is right in the centre of town.

Sights

Hanstholm was a key player in the German occupation and a **museum** (☎ 97 96 17 36; Molevej 29; adult/child 50/20kr; 10am-5pm Jun-Aug, 10am-4pm Apr-May & Sep-Oct) is based around a German bunker. In the bunker is one of four 38cm guns used to fire across the channel. It had a range of 55km and with the other three guns made up the German battery known as 'Hanstholm II'. Hitler used this as part of his 'Atlantic Wall' system, which was a system of fortifications that spread from Kirkenes in Norway to the Pyrenees. Along with the bunker you can visit The Documentation Centre that outlines this in more detail and also provides an insight into the way of life for the people under Hitler's rule. The museum is 300m west of the centre and well signposted. After negotiating the bunker you might want to climb the **lighthouse**, which claimed to beam the world's most powerful beacon when it was first erected in 1843. It now contains local-history exhibits.

Sleeping & Eating

Hotel Hanstholm (☎ 97 96 10 44; www.hotelhanstholm.dk; Christian Hansens Vej 2; s/d 650/795kr; P) Hanstholm's best hotel with renovated rooms and staff that are both well-informed and welcoming. The hotel is situated in forest inland from the harbour near the shopping hub, Hanstholm Centret.

Havnehotellet Sømandshjem (☎ 97 96 11 45; www.hshh.dk; Kai Lindbergsgade 71; 395/550kr; P) Simplicity is the best word to describe this seamens hotel on the harbour; the basic rooms would satisfy the budget-orientated traveller.

Steak House/Centergrillen (☎ 97 96 18 05; Bytorvet 19; mains 90kr; dinner) Presents good value if you're after a hearty steak. It's just up from the tourist office.

Getting There & Away

Hanstholm is at the terminus of Rtes 181, 26 and 29.

Thisted, 21km to the south via Rte 26, has the nearest train station. Bus No 40 runs to Thisted train station from Hanstholm harbour roughly every hour on weekdays, less often at weekends (23kr, 45 minutes).

There are car ferries from Hanstholm to the Norwegian cities of Bergen and Egersund, as well as to Iceland and the Faroe Islands (p310).

KLITMØLLER

pop 900

Klitmøller's windy ways and curving waves have transformed the small fishing village into one of Europe's premier windsurfing destinations. In 1998 it hosted the first official world championship of the sport. However, don't despair if you are not world championship material, Vandet lake is only a few kilometres inland and an ideal spot to learn the fundamentals. If such tumultuous weather does not appeal, Klitmøller should be bypassed en route to the calmer bathing spots available north and south of the town.

Windsurfing

In addition to the challenging waves of the North Sea, Vandet Sø, to the east of Klitmøller, is a popular windsurfing lake, with conditions suitable for all levels.

Surfzone Klitmøller (☎ 97 97 56 56; Ørhagevej 151; equipment per day 300kr, 4hr lesson incl gear 500kr) is just up from the beach and has enthusiastic surfers who can show you the sails of this exciting sport.

Sleeping & Eating

Strandgaarden Klitmøller (☎ 97 97 54 42; www.strandgaarden-klitmoeller.dk; dm/d 200/300kr; P ⊠) A youth hostel, B&B and holiday house rolled into one, its freshly presented rooms are perfect for families.

Nystrup Camping (☎ 97 97 52 49; fax 97 97 57 52; Trøjborgvej 22; Mar-Oct; per person 69kr; P) Three-star camping ground has plenty of trees as well as mini-golf, horse riding and a sauna. It also has a mini-market and café.

Klitmøller Røgeri (☎ 97 97 55 66; Ørhagevej 152; mains 40-70kr; lunch & dinner) Offers a sensational selection of fresh seafood right next to the beach – grab some smoked fish and a cold beer and watch the water acrobatics in full swing.

Neils Juel (☎ 97 97 51 88; Ørhagevej 150; 3-course menu 245kr; dinner) Klitmøller's best restaurant offers steak as well as strikingly fresh seafood.

Getting There & Away

Klitmøller is 10km southwest of Hanstholm on Rte 181, and 15km northwest of Thisted on Rte 557. From Klitmøller, bus No 22 (22kr, hourly Monday to Friday) goes to Thisted, which has the nearest rail connections.

Directory

CONTENTS

ACCOMMODATION

Denmark has a wide range of lodgings, from camping grounds to opulent.

Truly cheap hotels are virtually unknown, but if you're on a tight budget you'll save money staying in camping grounds, hostels or private homes. Self-catering flats and cottages are also available if you're with a group and are planning to stay in one place for a while.

Staff at local tourist offices can provide you with lists of local accommodation and may be able to arrange bookings, although there could be a nominal fee.

During July and August it's advisable to book ahead. Even camping grounds can fill up.

Camping

Camping is restricted to established camping grounds or private land with the owner's permission. Camping in a car or caravan at the beach, in a car park or along the street can result in a fine.

There are more than 500 camping grounds around the country. In resort areas camping grounds are commonly found right in the thick of it all, while in cities and large towns they tend to be more on the outskirts.

PRACTICALITIES

- Newspapers and magazines: *Jyllandsposten* and *Politiken* are the leading Danish-language newspapers (of some 50 nationwide). English listings available in *Copenhagen Post*. Other English-language publications include the *International Herald Tribune, Guardian, Wall Street Journal, Financial Times, Economist* and *Time*.
- Radio: Radio Danmark International at 1062MHz (five-minute news briefs in English at 10.30am, 5.05pm and 10pm Mon-Fri). Other stations play a mix of Danish-language news and cultural programming, and music. BBC radio is available via shortwave.
- TV: Danish TV broadcasts local and international programs, with English-language programs usually presented in English with Danish subtitles. International cable channels such as CNN and BBC World are available in many hotels.
- Video system: PAL
- Electric current: 220V (volts), 50Hz (cycles) AC, Europlug (two round plugs).
- Weights and measures: metric system (see conversion chart on inside front cover). Fruit is often sold by the piece (*stykke* or 'stk').
- Numbering: a comma indicates a decimal point; points indicate thousands. So 12,345.67 in English would be written 12.345,67 in Denmark.

Camping is most popular for people with their own vehicles, as transit into the town centre can cancel out any savings.

Particularly in seaside resort areas, some camping grounds are open only in the summer months, while others operate from spring to autumn. About 100 stay open year-round and some offer off-season rates.

A camping pass is required for stays at all camping grounds. A Camping Card International will do, or you can buy a Danish carnet at the first camping ground you visit or from tourist offices. The cost for an annual pass is 80kr; it covers all accompanied children aged under 18.

The per-night charge to pitch a tent or park a caravan typically ranges from 45kr to 65kr for each adult and about half that for each child. In summer, some places also tack on a surcharge of 15kr to 30kr per tent/caravan.

Many Danish camping grounds also rent simple cabins (and/or on-site caravans) sleeping four to six people, often with cooking facilities, though rarely with bed linens and blankets – bring your own sleeping bag. Toilet and shower facilities are shared with other campers.

Backpackers and cyclists, note: even if a campground is signposted as fully booked for motorists, sometimes there are sites for light-travelling campers.

Pick up either *Camping Danmark* (95kr), published by **Campingrådet** (Danish Camping Board; ☎ 29 27 88 44; www.campingraadet.dk) or *DK Camping*, listing details of the 325-member camping grounds of **DK-Camp** (www.dk-camp.dk).

Homestays

Homestays can be a great way to see the countryside and meet local people. Rates vary widely but average about 300/400kr for singles/doubles between Copenhagen and the countryside. In most cases, breakfast is available for around 40kr more per person.

Staff at many tourist offices can help with bookings, or **Dansk Bed & Breakfast** (☎ 39 61 04 05; www.bbdk.dk; Sankt Peders Stræde 41, 1453 Copenhagen K) publishes a booklet *Bed & Breakfast in Denmark* (mail-order outside of Scandinavia 95kr, at tourist offices 20kr to 30kr, or at bookstores).

Farm Stays

Landsforeningen for Landboturisme (☎ 45 86 35 50; www.bondegaardsferie.dk; Lerbakken 7, 8410 Rønde) books stays on more than 130 farms throughout Denmark. There's an interesting variety of farmhouses, ranging from modern homes to traditional straw-roofed, timber-framed places. The cost, including breakfast, averages 200kr per person per day (half-price for children under 12 years old). The options also include self-contained flats and small rural houses that can accommodate up to six people and cost around 2500kr to 4500kr per week. Upon request, the organisation will mail you a booklet containing a colour photo and brief description of each place as well as booking details.

Although it's best to plan in advance, if you're cycling or driving around Denmark you may well come across farmhouses displaying *værelse* (room) signs.

IT'S IN THE STARS...

Camping grounds in Denmark are rated by the Danish Camping Board using a star system. Some examples are as follows.

- One star: running water, toilets, at least one shower and at least one electricity outlet for shavers.
- Two stars: at least one shower for every 25 sites, kitchen with hot water tap and hotplates, playground for children, location within 2km of a grocery shop.
- Three stars: hot water in the washbasins, communal lounge, large play area for children, nursing rooms, sinks or washing machines for laundry, location within 1km of a grocery shop. Four- and five-star ratings indicate further upgraded facilities.

Hostels, too, are categorised by a star system (one to five). A one-star hostel will be pretty basic, two stars will get you luggage storage and a small shop, while four- and five-star facilities have TV lounges and a minimum of 75% of rooms with shower and toilet.

SEASONS

For purposes of this book, 'high season' generally refers to July and August, while 'low season' is April through June and September and October.

Manor Houses

Danske Slotte & Herregaarde (☎ 86 60 38 44; danskeslotteogherregaarde@mail.dk; Frederiksberggade 2.1, 1459 Copenhagen) books rooms in two dozen manor houses and small castles around Denmark. Singles range from 450kr to 1425kr, doubles range from 640kr to 2050kr, including breakfast. Brochures are available by mail at larger tourist offices in Denmark.

Hostels

Some 100 hostels make up the **Danhostel association** (☎ 33 31 36 12; www.danhostel.dk; Vesterbrogade 39, Copenhagen), it is affiliated with the Hostelling International (HI).

Danish hostels appeal to guests in all age categories and are oriented as much towards families and groups as to budget travellers. Typical costs are 80kr to 120kr per person in dorm beds. For private rooms, expect to pay 125kr to 480kr per single, 210kr to 480kr per double, or between 35kr and 50kr per each additional person in larger rooms.

Facilities vary, but most newer hostels have two-bed rooms, four-bed rooms and dormitory rooms. During busier periods, some are loathe to rent private rooms to individuals or couples who won't pay for all beds in the room.

Typically you can expect single bunk-style beds with comfortable foam mattresses. Blankets and pillows are provided, but you'll have to bring or hire (around between 35kr and 60kr per stay) your own sheets. All Danish hostels provide an all-you-can-eat breakfast costing 46kr maximum, and many also provide dinner (75kr maximum). Most hostels also have guest kitchens with pots and pans.

Travellers without an international hostel card can buy one for 160kr (annual fee). Hostelling cards may be purchased via Danhostel or at individual hostels. You may also pay 35kr per night above the overnight charges for a one-night 'guest card'. Six guest cards can be redeemed for an annual hostelling card.

Advance reservations are advised, particularly in summer. In a few places, reception closes as early as 6pm. In most hostels the reception office is closed, and the phone not answered, between noon and 4pm.

Between May and September, hostels can get crowded with children on school excursions. Most Danish hostels close for at least part of the off-season.

Hotels

Hotels can be found in the centre of all major Danish cities and towns. This book considers hotel rooms under 1000kr (double with bathroom) in the budget category, 1000kr to1700kr per night mid-range and over 1700kr top end, though these are 'rack rates' and specials are often available.

Although the cheapest places are fairly Spartan, Danish hotels are rarely seedy or unsafe. Interestingly, standard top-end hotels generally cost only about a third more than budget hotels, particularly if you use weekend rates or other hotel schemes.

A *kro,* a name that implies a country inn but is more commonly the Danish version of a motel, is typically found along major motorways near the outskirts of town. A *kro* tends to be cheaper and simpler than a hotel. Generally they're not a practical option unless you have your own transport.

Both hotels and *kro*s usually include an all-you-can-eat breakfast, which can vary from a simple meal of bread, cheese and coffee to a generous full-table buffet.

HOTEL SCHEMES

The **Danske Kroer & Hoteller** (☎ 75 64 87 00; www.krohotel.dk) group offers 'cheques' valid at some 86 accommodations. The cheques can be purchased at Danish tourist offices and travel agencies, and cost from 689kr for one night in a double room to 1399kr for two nights in a room for two adults and two children; all rooms include private facilities and breakfast. Note that there are blackout periods, while at other times there's a surcharge of up to 350kr.

The **Best Western Hotels** (www.bestwestern.dk) group has a weekend and holiday discount that doesn't require vouchers or advance payment. A room sleeping up to two adults and two children costs from 795kr per night including breakfast. The rate is effective weekends year-round and on weekdays

THE MARGUERITE ROUTE

A special network of scenic routes recommended for people touring by car and motorcycle has been designated and signposted throughout Denmark. Known as the Marguerite Route, it is not a single route that can be taken from end to end but rather a series of routes comprising 3500km of roads in all. Some roads have been chosen for their rural appeal, others have been selected because they pass tourist attractions.

Most of the Marguerite Route is along secondary highways and minor country roads and, consequently, it usually makes an enjoyable alternative to a mundane zip along the main motorways.

The route is marked by a road sign consisting of a white daisy set against a brown backdrop. Virtually all Danish highway maps show the route, either with heavy green dots or solid green outlines. While it's fun to include sections of the Marguerite Route in any self-drive itinerary, at times you'll find alternative country roads parallel to the route to be just as scenic.

The Marguerite Route is not intended for cars pulling trailers, as some of the roads are narrow and cross small bridges. For more details on the route and sights along the way, pick up the small self-touring book the *Marguerite Route*, which is published in English, Danish and German by the Danish Tourist Board. The book can be purchased in larger tourist offices and at Statoil petrol stations.

during school holiday periods, including from mid-June to early August. It's best to book as far in advance as possible as the offer covers a limited number of rooms.

Rental Accommodation

Many seaside resort areas are filled with cottages and flats. These are generally booked by the week and require reservations. Rates vary greatly, depending on the type of accommodation and the season, but generally they're cheaper than hotels.

DanCenter (☎ 70 13 16 16; www.dancenter.dk) handles hoiliday cottage bookings nationwide Many tourist offices can also help make reservations.

ACTIVITIES

OK, so 'Ski Denmark' is never going to be a tourist board slogan, but Denmark is a fine destination for lovers of water and flatland activities. For more information on the type of activities on offer, see pp54-9.

BUSINESS HOURS

Office hours are generally 9am to 4pm Monday to Friday. Most banks are open 9.30am to 4pm Monday to Friday (to 6pm on Thursday), though bank hours can be longer at airports and major train stations.

Shops are typically open from 9.30am to 5.30pm on weekdays (7pm on Friday) and to 2pm on Saturday. Shops tend to stay open until around 5pm on the first and last Saturday of each month. In general, the trend in larger cities is towards longer opening hours.

Restaurants and cafés tend to open 11am to 11pm or midnight, and bars and nightclubs until 1am Monday to Wednesday and until 3am or 5am Thursday to Saturday.

Post offices are open from 9am or 10am to 5pm or 5.30pm Monday to Friday, and until noon or 1pm on Saturday.

CHILDREN

Denmark is a family-oriented place. Even stuffy history museums often have hands-on sections for the kids, camping grounds commonly have playgrounds, cities have duck ponds and gardens that invite picnics, and you'll find amusement parks nationwide. Staff at tourist offices can help with suggestions and occasionally provide information on babysitting services.

Lonely Planet's *Travel with Children* is loaded with tips and information, and don't forget to ask advice of locals and other travellers with (happy) children.

Practicalities

Highchairs and cots (cribs) are standard in many restaurants and hotels, and many public toilets have nappy (diaper)-changing facilities. Car rental firms hire out children's safety seats at a nominal cost, but it's essential that you book them in advance. Danish supermarkets offer a relatively wide choice of baby food, infant formulas, and disposable nappies etc. Breastfeeding in public is rare (especially in the colder months), but would not cause offence.

CLIMATE CHARTS

Given that Denmark sits at quite a northerly latitude, it's surprisingly warm. See also When to Go (p9).

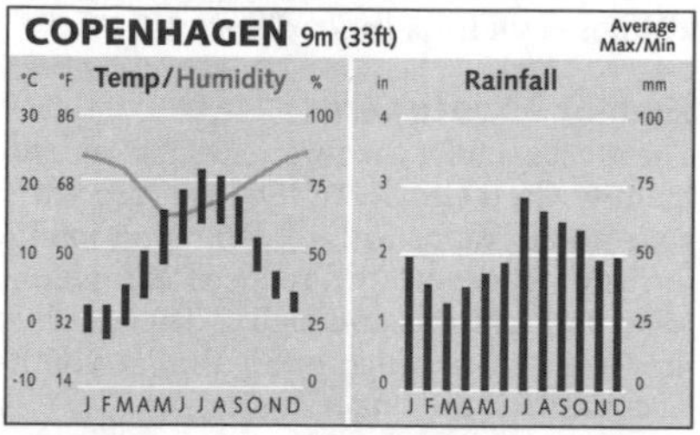
COPENHAGEN 9m (33ft)
Average Max/Min
°C °F Temp/Humidity %
Rainfall
in mm
J F M A M J J A S O N D
J F M A M J J A S O N D

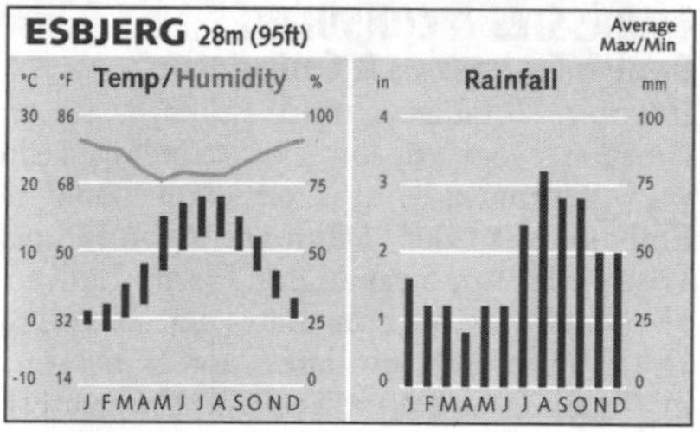
ESBJERG 28m (95ft)
Average Max/Min
°C °F Temp/Humidity %
Rainfall
in mm
J F M A M J J A S O N D
J F M A M J J A S O N D

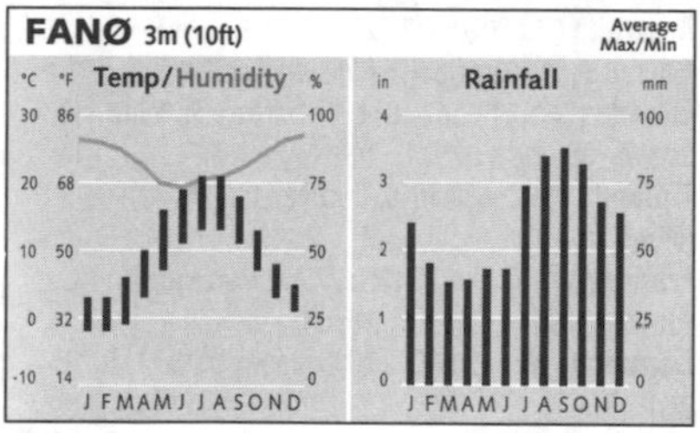
FANØ 3m (10ft)
Average Max/Min
°C °F Temp/Humidity %
Rainfall
in mm
J F M A M J J A S O N D
J F M A M J J A S O N D

COURSES

Scandinavia's unique folkehøjskole, literally 'folk high school' (the 'high' denotes an institute of higher learning), provides a liberal education within a communal living environment. Folk high schools got their start in Denmark, inspired by philosopher Nikolai Grundtvig's concept of 'enlightenment for life'. The curriculum includes such things as drama, peace studies and organic farming.

People aged 17½ and older can enrol; there are no entrance exams and no formal qualifications such as degrees. Tuition, including room and board, averages €110 per week (about 820kr). For more information, on the nearly 100 schools, contact **Højskolernes Sekretariat** (☎ 33 13 98 22; www.folkehojskoler.dk; Nytorv 7, 1450 Copenhagen K).

While most folk high schools teach in Danish, the **International People's College** (☎ 49 21 33 61; www.ipc.dk; Montebello Allé 1, 3000 Helsingør) has students and teachers from around the world, and most instruction is given in English. Foreigners are welcome to enrol in short-term courses that typically last for two to eight weeks and in summer these include an intensive Danish language and culture program.

Language

Want to learn Danish? Contact the nearest Danish embassy or consulate, or a local university language department, to inquire about language courses that might be offered in your home country.

In Denmark, there are a number of schools set up to teach Danish to foreigners, but most focus on teaching immigrants or other long-term residents. Expect to pay around 80kr per hour for language instruction.

Following are four of the schools that offer Danish language courses to foreigners:

AOF (☎ 39 16 82 00; Lersø Park Allé 44, 2100 Copenhagen Ø)

HOF (☎ 33 11 88 33; Købmagergade 26, 1150 Copenhagen K)

KISS (☎ 35 36 25 25; www.kiss.dk; Nørrebrogade 32, 2200 Copenhagen N)

Studieskolen (☎ 33 14 43 22; www.studieskolen.dk; Antonigade 6, 1106 Copenhagen K)

CUSTOMS

One litre of spirits and 200 cigarettes can be brought into Denmark duty-free if you're coming from outside the EU. Those coming from an EU country are allowed to bring in 300 cigarettes and 1.5L of spirits.

DANGERS & ANNOYANCES

Denmark is by and large a very safe country and travelling presents no unusual dangers. Travellers should nevertheless be careful with their belongings, particularly in busy places such as Copenhagen's Central Station.

In cities, you'll need to quickly become accustomed to the busy cycle lanes that run beside roads between the vehicle lanes and the pedestrian pavement, as these cycle lanes (and fast-moving cyclists) are easy to veer into accidentally.

Throughout Denmark, dial ☎112 for police, fire or medical emergency.

Theft

Be careful even in hotels; don't leave valuables lying around in your room. Hostellers should bring a padlock to secure their belongings in the hostel lockers.

Never leave your valuables unattended in parked cars. If you must leave your luggage in a vehicle, be sure that your car has a covered area that keeps bags out of sight and carry the most important items with you. Remove all luggage overnight, even if the car is left in a garage.

If you are unfortunate enough to have something stolen, immediately report it to the nearest police station. If your credit cards or travellers cheques have been taken, notify your bank or the relevant company immediately.

DISABLED TRAVELLERS

If you have a physical disability, get in touch with your national support organisation (preferably the 'travel officer' if there is one). They often have libraries devoted to travel and can put you in touch with travel agents who specialise in tours for disabled travellers.

Most Danish tourist literature, such as the Danish Tourist Board's hotel guide, the camping association listings and the hostel booklet, indicates which establishments have wheelchair-accessible rooms and facilities. Disabled travellers may wish to consult www.visitdenmark.com/and click 'Accessible Denmark' under 'Inspiration'.

Once in Denmark, disabled travellers who have specific questions can contact **Dansk Handicap Forbund** (☎ 39 29 35 55; Kollektivhuset, Hans Knudsens Plads 1A, 2100 Copenhagen Ø).

DISCOUNT CARDS

Copenhagen Card

Visitors to Copenhagen, especially those planning to cover a lot of territory in a short time, will want to invest in the **Copenhagen Card** (24/72hr adult 199/399kr, child 129/229kr). This tourist pass allows unlimited travel on buses and trains in Copenhagen and throughout North Zealand, as well as free admission to about 60 of the region's museums and attractions. It's available at Central Station, tourist offices and some hotels. See p101 for details.

Hostel Cards

A Hostelling International card will get you discounts at some museums and sightseeing spots. See p294 for details and visit www.danhostel.dk for a list of discounts.

Student & Youth Cards

The most useful is the International Student Identity Card (ISIC), an ID-style card with your photograph, with discounts on many forms of transport and reduced admission to some museums and sights. There's also the GO25 card, which offers similar youth discounts for the under 25s.

EMBASSIES & CONSULATES

Danish Embassies & Consulates

If you're unable to find an embassy or consulate near you on the list below, visit www.denmark.dk and click on 'Danish Embassies' under 'Denmark Around the World'. In some cases, there is more than one embassy or consulate per country. Note: there are consulates, not embassies, in Australia and New Zealand; the nearest embassy is in Singapore.

Australia (☎ 02-9247 2224; Level 4, Gold Fields House, 1 Alfred St, Circular Quay, Sydney NSW 2000)
Canada (☎ 613-562 1811; 47 Clarence St, Suite 450, Ottawa, Ontario K1N 9K1)
Finland (☎ 9-684 1050; Centralgatan 1A, 00100 Helsingfors)
France (☎ 01 44 31 21 21; 77 Ave Marceau, 75116 Paris)
Germany (☎ 030-5050 2000; Rauchstrasse 1, 10787 Berlin)
Iceland (☎ 57 50 300; Hverfisgata 29, 101 Reykjavik)
Ireland (☎ 1-475 6404; 121-122 St Stephen's Green, Dublin 2)
Netherlands (☎ 70-302 5959; Koninginnegracht 30 (Postbus 85654), 2508 CJ Den Haag)
New Zealand (☎ 4-471 0520; Level 7, Forsyth Barr House, 45 Johnson St, Wellington 6063)
Norway (☎ 22 54 08 00; Olav Kyrres Gate 7, 0244 Oslo)
Singapore (☎ 6355 5010; 101 Thompson Rd, United Sq, Singapore 307591)
Sweden (☎ 08-406 7500; Jakobs Torg 1, 11186 Stockholm)
UK (☎ 020-7333 0200; 55 Sloane St, London SW1X 9SR)
USA (☎ 202-234 4300; 3200 Whitehaven St NW, Washington, DC 20008)

Embassies & Consulates in Denmark

The following embassies and consulates are in and around Copenhagen:

Australia (Map p103; ☎ 70 26 36 76; Dampfaergevej 26, Copenhagen)
Canada (Map pp70-1; ☎ 33 48 32 00; Kristen Bernikows Gade 1, Copenhagen)
Finland (☎ 33 13 42 14; Sankt Annæ Plads 24, Copenhagen)
France (Map pp70-1; ☎ 33 67 10 00; Kongens Nytorv 4, Copenhagen)
Germany (Map pp62-3; ☎ 35 45 99 00; Stockholmsgade 57, Copenhagen)
Iceland (☎ 33 18 10 50; Dantes Plads 3, Copenhagen)
Ireland (Map p103; ☎ 35 42 32 33; Østbanegade 21, Copenhagen)
Netherlands (Map pp62-3; ☎ 33 70 72 00; Toldbodgade 33, Copenhagen)
Norway (☎ 33 14 01 24; Amaliegade 39, Copenhagen)
Poland (☎ 39 62 72 45; Richelieus Allé 12, Hellerup)
Russia (☎ 35 42 55 85; Kristianiagade 5, Copenhagen)
Sweden (☎ 33 36 03 70; Sankt Annæ Plads 15A, Copenhagen)
UK (Map p103; ☎ 35 44 52 00; Kastelsvej 40, Copenhagen)
USA (Map pp62-3 ☎ 35 55 31 44; Dag Hammarskjölds Allé 24, Copenhagen)

FESTIVALS & EVENTS

January

New Year Concerts Classical music is performed in major cities in early January by the Zealand, Århus, Odense, Aalborg and West Jutland symphony orchestras.

February & March

Night Film Festival (☎ 33 12 00 05; www.natfilm.dk) Held in Copenhagen in early March over 10-days shows more than 100 international films in their original languages.

April

Queen Margrethe's Birthday Celebrated on 16 April at Amalienborg in Copenhagen, with the royal guards in full ceremonial dress and the queen waving from the palace balcony at noon.

Tivoli (☎ 33 15 10 01; www.tivoligardens.com) and **Legoland** (☎ 75 33 13 33; www.legoland.dk) Tivoli in Copenhagen and Legoland in Billund, Denmark's major amusement parks, open for the season in April.

May

Carnival in Aalborg (☎ 98 13 72 11; www.karnevali aalborg.dk) The 'Battle of Carnival Bands' and the parade are features of this four-day celebration that ends with a grand fireworks display. Up to 100,000 visitors share in the excitement.

June

Riverboat Jazz Festival (☎ 86 80 16 17; www.river boat.dk) Held in Silkeborg in mid-June. Some 50 bands enliven the city with numerous performances, some taking place on land, others on river boats.

Midsummer Eve (23 June) Known as Sankt Hans eve, the night sky is alight with bonfires on beaches all around Denmark.

Skagen Festival (☎ 98 44 40 04; www.skagenfestival .dk) Held over four days at the end of June. This festival in Skagen features folk and world music performed by Danish and international artists.

Round Zealand Boat Race (☎ 49 21 15 67) Held over three days in late June. This substantial yacht race circles the island of Zealand, starting and ending in Helsingør.

Roskilde Festival (☎ 46 36 66 13; www.roskilde -festival.dk) Northern Europe's largest music festival rocks Roskilde for four consecutive days each summer on the last weekend in June. Advance sales start in December, and the festival usually sells out!

Frederikssund Viking Festival (☎ 47 31 06 85; www.vikingespil.dk) Held in Frederikssund over a two-week period in late June and early July. Costumed 'Vikings' present an open-air drama, followed by a banquet with Viking food and entertainment.

July

Copenhagen Jazz Festival (☎ 33 93 20 13; www .jazzfestival.dk) This is the biggest entertainment event of the year in the capital, with 10 days of music beginning on the first Friday in July. The festival features a range of Danish and international jazz, blues and fusion music, with 500 indoor and outdoor concerts.

Viking Moot (☎ 89 42 11 00) Held for two days in late July at the Moesgård Museum in Århus, it features a Viking-style market with crafts, food and equestrian events.

August

Hamlet Summer Plays (☎ 49 28 20 44; www.hamlet sommer.dk) Held the first two weeks in August. Theatre performances of Shakespeare's Hamlet take place at Kronborg Slot in Helsingør.

Copenhagen Pride Parade (www.copenhagen-pride .dk) Held on the first or second Saturday in August. This festive gay pride parade marches with Carnival-like extravagance through the centre of Copenhagen.

Tønder Festival (☎ 74 72 46 10; www.tf.dk) Held in Tønder for four days in late August, this is one of northern Europe's largest folk festivals, featuring numerous indoor and outdoor performances and lots of hilarity.

Århus Festival Week The 10-day Århus Festuge (☎ 89 40 91 91; www.aarhusfestuge.dk) bills itself as Denmark's largest annual multicultural festival. It begins the last Friday of August and features scores of music performances, theatre, ballet, modern dance, opera, films and sports events at indoor and outdoor venues.

Golden Days in Copenhagen (☎ 35 42 14 32; www.goldendays.dk) Held over two weeks in late August and early September. The city celebrates with art exhibits, poetry readings, theatre, ballet and concerts that focus on Denmark's 'Golden Age' (1800-50).

December

Christmas Fairs Held all around Denmark throughout December, with food booths, arts and crafts stalls, and sometimes parades. Particularly atmospheric is the Christmas fair held for two days in early December at Den Gamle By in Århus.

FOOD & DRINK

While Denmark does not have the depth of international cuisines present in other countries, there's a fair representation of world cuisines in addition to Denmark's own specialties.

We have determined our eating categories using the price of a main course as a rough estimate. For places where smørrebrød or set menus predominate, we have gone with the cost of a full meal.

Eating listings are generally broken down in the following price ranges: Budget with mains under 100kr, Mid-Range from 101-190kr; Top End from 190kr. Prices may be a little less in the outer regions.

GAY & LESBIAN TRAVELLERS

Given Denmark's high degree of tolerance for alternative lifestyles of all sorts, it's hardly surprising that Denmark is a popular destination for gay and lesbian travellers. Copenhagen in particular has an active gay community and lots of nightlife options, but you'll find gay and lesbian venues in other cities as well.

Landsforeningen for Bøsser og Lesbiske (LBL, Danish National Association for Gays & Lesbians; ☎ 33 13 19 48; www.lbl.dk; Teglgårdsstræde 13, Copenhagen; office 🕑 11am-3pm Mon-Fri) has a **library** (🕑 5-7pm Mon-Fri), support groups, religious services and **counselling** (🕑 6-8pm Thu). LBL also has a branch in **Århus** (% 86 13 19 48) and publishes the magazine *PAN bladet*, which covers gay-related issues, upcoming events and entertainment in Danish, most months.

Two useful websites for travellers, with visitor information and listings in English, are www.gayguide.dk and www.copenhagen-gay-life.dk.

The main gay and lesbian festival of the year is the **Copenhagen Pride Parade** (fka Mermaid Pride Parade; www.copenhagen-pride.dk), a big Mardi Gras–like bash that takes place in Copenhagen on a Saturday in August. There's also the **Copenhagen Gay & Lesbian Film Festival** (www.cglff.dk), held each October.

HOLIDAYS

Many Danes take their main work holiday during the first three weeks of July, but there are numerous other holidays as well.

Public Holidays

Banks and most businesses are closed on public holidays, and transport schedules are commonly reduced.

New Year's Day (Nytårsdag) – 1 January
Maundy Thursday (Skærtorsdag) – Thursday before Easter
Good Friday (Langfredag) – Friday before Easter
Easter Day (Påskedag) – Sunday in March or April
Easter Monday (2.påskedag) – day after Easter
Common Prayer Day (Stor Bededag) – fourth Friday after Easter
Ascension Day (Kristi Himmelfartsdag) – sixth Thursday after Easter
Whitsunday (Pinsedag) – seventh Sunday after Easter
Whitmonday (2.pinsedag) – eighth Monday after Easter
Constitution Day (Grundlovsdag) – 5 June
Christmas Eve – 24 December (from noon)
Christmas Day (Juledag) – 25 December
Boxing Day (2.juledag) – 26 December

School Holidays

In addition to the public holidays noted above, schools generally have off as follows:

Winter holidays – a week in February or March
Easter holidays – a week around Easter time
Summer holidays – around 20 June to around 10 August
Autumn holidays – a week in mid-October
Christmas and New Year – two weeks

INSURANCE

A travel insurance policy to cover theft, loss and medical problems is a good idea, but policies vary widely in terms, conditions and requirements on you, the policy holder. Be sure to read the fine print. For example, some policies specifically exclude 'dangerous activities', which can include motorcycling, and a locally acquired motorcycle licence may not be valid under some policies.

Check that the policy covers ambulances or an emergency flight home.

INTERNET ACCESS

A growing number of hotels in Denmark are adding modem hook-ups in guest rooms, so if you intend to use your own computer, inquire when making reservations. Many hostels also have facilities for guests to check their email accounts. Where a lodging has an Internet terminal for guest use (from free use to quickly check email, to an elaborate business centre), we've noted it with the icon 🖳 in the listing.

Public libraries have computers with Internet access, though access policies vary and you may need to book in advance.

As most families in Denmark have their own computers, Internet cafés are not terribly abundant and they usually tend to be short-lived.

LEGAL MATTERS

Authorities are very strict about drink-driving, and even a couple of drinks can put you over the legal limit of 0.05% blood-alcohol. Drivers detected under the influence of alcohol are liable to receive stiff penalties and a possible prison sentence.

Always treat drugs with a great deal of caution. There is a fair bit of marijuana and hashish available in the region, sometimes quite openly, but note that in Denmark all forms of cannabis are officially illegal.

If you are arrested for any punishable offence in Denmark, you can be held for up to 24 hours before appearing in court. You have the right to know the charges against you and the right to a lawyer, and you are not obliged to answer police questions before speaking to the lawyer. If you don't know of a lawyer, the police will provide a list.

You can get free legal advice on your rights from **EU Legal Aid** (% 33 14 41 40) or **Emergency Legal Aid** (% 35 37 68 13), both in Copenhagen.

LEGAL AGES FOR...

- Drinking: 18
- Driving: 18
- Voting: 18
- Consensual sex: 15
- Marriage: 18

MAPS

Excellent maps of Denmark's larger cities can be picked up free from tourist offices, and include the cities of Copenhagen, Odense, Århus and Aalborg, Staff at the tourist offices in smaller cities and towns can generally provide simpler maps that are suitable for local sightseeing.

For road maps, try the quality foldout, four-colour *Map of Denmark – ferry guide & attractions* can be obtained free from Denmark's overseas tourist offices. Car rental agencies usually also have good, free maps.

Those maps will suit most travellers' needs, but for exploring back roads, nooks and crannies you may also want to pick up the detailed road map of Denmark published by Kort-og Matrikelstyrelsen in a handy atlas format and labelled *Færdselskort 1:200,000 Danmark*. It's readily found in Danish bookshops.

MONEY

Although Denmark is an EU member nation, Denmark's citizens rejected adopting the euro in a referendum in 2000. Denmark's own currency, the krone, is most often written with the symbol DKK in international money markets, Dkr in northern Europe and kr within Denmark. Throughout this guide we've used kr.

One krone is divided into 100 øre. There are 25 øre, 50 øre, one krone, two kroner, five kroner, 10 kroner and 20 kroner coins. Notes come in denominations of 50, 100, 200, 500 and 1000 kroner.

The krone is pegged to the euro, so its value relative to other currencies fluctuates with that of its neighbours to the south. See Inside Front Cover for exchange rates and p10 for information on costs.

ATMs

Most banks in Denmark have automated teller machines (ATMs) that give cash advances on Visa and MasterCard credit cards as well as Cirrus and Plus bank cards. Although ATMs are accessible outside normal banking hours, not all are open 24 hours; particularly outside of Copenhagen, many Danish ATMs shut down for some part of the night, often from around 1am to 6am.

Typically you'll get a good rate when withdrawing money directly from a Danish ATM, but keep in mind that your home bank may charge you a fee for international transactions or for using another bank's ATM – check before you leave.

Cash

Exchange booths at Copenhagen Airport are open to meet all scheduled incoming flights. If you're on an international ferry to Denmark, you can not only exchange US dollars and local currencies to Danish kroner on board but, if you buy a meal or use one of the shops, regardless of the currency you pay in, many will give you change in Danish kroner upon request.

The US dollar is generally the handiest foreign currency to bring. Danish banks will convert a wide range of currencies including the euro, UK pound, Canadian dollar, Swiss franc, Australian dollar, Japanese yen and kroner from Norway and Sweden. Banks seldom accept foreign coins.

A few banks, especially in Copenhagen, have 24-hour machines that change major foreign currencies into Danish kroner.

Credit Cards

Credit cards such as Visa and MasterCard (also known as Access or Euro-card) are widely accepted in Denmark, although don't expect to use anything other than a Danish domestic card at supermarkets. American Express and Diners Club are also accepted, but not as often.

If a card is lost or stolen, inform the issuing company as soon as possible. Here are Copenhagen numbers:

AmEx (☎ 70 20 70 97)
Diners Club (☎ 36 73 73 73)
MasterCard, Access, Eurocard (☎ 80 01 60 98)
Visa (☎ 80 01 85 88)

Tipping

Restaurant bills and taxi fares include service charges in the quoted prices. Further tipping is unnecessary, although rounding up the bill is not uncommon when service has been especially good.

Travellers Cheques

The main benefit of travellers cheques is that they can provide protection from theft. Large companies such as American Express and Thomas Cook generally offer efficient replacement policies.

Keeping a record of the cheque numbers and those you have used is vital when it comes to replacing lost cheques. You should keep this information separate from the cheques themselves along with the emergency phone number in case cheques need to be replaced.

POST

You can receive mail c/o poste restante at any post office in Denmark, but it's usually held for only two weeks.

Standard letters up to 50g sent within Denmark cost 4.50kr. To Europe, such letters cost 6kr and to the rest of the world it's 7kr. International mail sent from Copenhagen generally leaves Denmark within 24 hours.

For more information, inquire at post offices or visit www.postdanmark.dk.

SHOPPING

Few people come to Denmark for the shopping because prices tend to be rather high. However, there are some distinctively Danish products.

Danish amber, which washes up ashore on Jutland's west coast beaches, makes lovely jewellery and prices are relatively reasonable. Other popular purchases are silverwork, ceramics and hand-blown glass, all in the sleek style that typifies Danish design. Georg Jensen silverworks, Royal Copenhagen Porcelain and Holmegaard Glass & Crystal are among the biggest names in their fields. You'll find their products along Strøget, Copenhagen's famed shopping street.

As well as speciality shops, larger cities have substantial department stores, such as Magasin du Nord and Salling, that stock virtually everything from souvenir picture books to Scandinavian-designed furniture and fluffy goose-down quilts.

Bargaining is not a common practice in Denmark.

TELEPHONE

Denmark has an efficient phone system, and payphones abound in busy public places such as train stations and shopping areas.

You have a choice of using either card phones or coin phones, although card phones are coming to predominate. Coin phones take all Danish coins in denominations of

1kr to 20kr but won't return change from larger coins.

Denmark's *Yellow Pages* are also on the Internet at www.degulesider.dk. You can use the website to search for business, government and residential details – although it is in Danish. Note that the letters æ, ø and å are placed at the end of the Danish alphabet, and so come after z in the hard copy of telephone directories.

Mobile Phones

Denmark uses the worldwide GSM network, so you shouldn't have any problem getting your phone to work here. As befits a techno-savvy Scandinavian country, many locals carry a mobile phone – but they also know how to use them politely, and judiciously. Please follow their custom.

Service providers include the following:

Orange (☎ 80 40 40 40)
Sonofon (☎ 80 29 29 29)
TDC-mobil (☎ 80 80 80 20)
Telia (☎ 80 10 10 80)

Phone Codes

All telephone numbers in Denmark have eight digits; there are no area codes. This means that all eight digits must be dialled, even when making calls within the same city.

All domestic calls are charged the same rate whether you're calling across town or across the country. Rates are 0.25kr per minute between 8am and 7.30pm between land line phones (public or private). Rates are half between 7.30pm and 8am.

For local directory assistance dial ☎ 118 (5kr per minute). For overseas inquiries, including for rates and reverse charge (collect) calls, dial ☎ 113.

The country code for Denmark is ☎ 45. To call Denmark from another country, dial the international access code for the country you're in followed by ☎ 45 and the local eight digit number.

The international access code in Denmark is ☎ 00. To make direct international calls from Denmark, dial ☎ 00 followed by the country code for the country you're calling, the area code, then the local number.

You can also dial direct to an operator in your home country with the following services: to the UK, dial BTI at ☎ 80 01 04 44 or, for credit cards only ☎ 80 01 02 90. To the USA, dial ☎ 80 01 00 10 for AT&T or ☎ 80 01 08 77 for Sprint. To Canada, dial ☎ 80 01 00 11 to be connected to reach multiple services. To Australia, Telstra at ☎ 80 01 00 61; to New Zealand, NZ Telecom at ☎ 80 01 00 64.

Phonecards

If you're going to be making many calls, consider using a debit phonecard *(telekort)*, sold in denominations of 30kr, 50kr and 100kr. These cards can be used for making both local and international calls and are sold at post offices and many kiosks, especially at train stations.

Card phones work out slightly cheaper than coin phones because you pay for the exact amount of time you speak; an LCD screen shows how much time is left on the card. It's possible to replace an expiring card with a new card without breaking the call. Card phones have information in English detailing their use as well as the location of the nearest place that sells phonecards.

TIME

Time in Denmark is normally one hour ahead of GMT/UTC, the same as in neighbouring European countries. When it's noon in Denmark, it's 11am in London, 6am in New York and Toronto, 3am in Los Angeles, 9pm in Sydney and 11pm in Auckland.

Clocks are moved forward one hour for daylight-saving time from the last Sunday in March to the last Sunday in October. Denmark uses the 24-hour clock system and all timetables and business hours are posted accordingly. *Klokken*, which means o'clock, is abbreviated kl (kl 19.30 is 7.30pm).

Dates are written with the day followed by the month, thus 3/6 means 3 June and 6/3 means 6 March.

TOILETS

Public toilets are generally free and easy to find at such places as train stations, town squares and ferry harbours.

TOURIST INFORMATION

Denmark is extremely well served with tourist offices at major transit points – see local listings. Important websites for visitors to Denmark include www.denmark.dk and www.visitdenmark.com. Regional tourist offices include the following

Bornholm (☎ 70 23 20 77; www.bornholminfo.dk; Nordre Kystvej 3, Rønne)
Copenhagen & Northern Zealand (☎ 70 22 24 42; www.visitcopenhagen.dk; 4A Vesterbrogade, Copenhagen)
Funen (☎ 66 11 11 11; www.fyn.dk; Blangstedgårdsvej 4, Odense)
Eastern Jutland (☎ 87 33 33 33; www.visiteastjutland.com; Åhavej 5, Viby)
Northern & Central Jutland (www.visitnord.dk)
Southern Jutland (☎ 75 83 59 99; www.sej.dk; Vestre Engvei 21, Vejle)

VISAS

Citizens of the USA, Canada, Australia and New Zealand need a valid passport to enter Denmark, but they don't need a visa for tourist stays of less than three months. In addition, no entry visa is needed by citizens of EU and Scandinavian countries.

Citizens of many African, South American, Asian and former Soviet bloc countries do require a visa. The Danish Immigration Service publishes a list of countries whose citizens require a visa at its website at www.udlst.dk/english/Via/who_needs_visa.htm.

If you're in the country and have questions on visa extensions or visas in general, contact the Danish Immigration Service: **Udlændingestyrelsen** (☎ 35 36 66 00; www.udlst.dk; Ryesgade 53, Copenhagen; 🕑 8.30am-noon Mon-Fri, 3.30-5.30pm Thu).

WOMEN TRAVELLERS

Women travellers are less likely to encounter problems in Denmark than in most other countries. However, use common-sense when it comes to potentially dangerous situations such as hitching and walking alone in cities at night.

Center for Information om Kvinde-og Kønsforskning (KVINFO, Danish Centre for Information on Women & Gender; ☎ 33 13 50 88; www.kvinfo.dk; Christians Brygge 3, Copenhagen) is a good place to get involved in feminist issues. It houses the Kvindehuset – a help centre and meeting place for women.

In Århus, contact the **Kvindemuseet i Danmark** (Womens Museum in Denmark; ☎ 86 13 61 44; www.womensmuseum.dk; Domkirkeplads 5; adult/student or senior/child 30/25kr/free; 🕑 10am-5pm Mon-Fri (until 8pm Wed), 11am-5pm Sat & Sun Jun-Aug, 10am-4pm Tue-Fri, 11am-4pm Sat & Sun Sep-May), which has exhibits both historic and topical. There's also a café (admission free).

Dial ☎ 112 for rape crisis assistance or in other emergencies.

There are several good websites for women travellers, including those at www.passionfruit.com and www.journeywoman.com, and the women travellers' page on the Lonely Planet website's **Thorn Tree** (www.thorntree.lonelyplanet.com).

WORK

In terms of qualifying to work in Denmark, foreigners are divided into three categories: Scandinavian citizens, citizens of EU countries, and other foreigners. Essentially, Scandinavian citizens have the easiest go of it, as they can generally reside and work in Denmark without restrictions. It's best to visit the very informative website www.workindenmark.dk for more information about legalities.

Work Visas

Citizens of EU countries are allowed to stay in Denmark for up to three months while searching for a job and it's generally straightforward to get a residency permit if work is found. The main stipulation is that the job provides enough income to adequately cover living expenses.

Citizens of other countries are required to get a work permit before entering Denmark. This means first securing a job offer then applying for a work and residency permit from a Danish embassy or consulate while still in your home country; permits are usually limited to people with specialised skills in high demand.

Transport

CONTENTS

Getting to Denmark is simple. The capital Copenhagen has copious worldwide air links, and some low-cost carriers fly into other airports around the nation. Train, road and bridge links exist to Germany and Sweden, and there are numerous ferry connections to several countries.

What's more, once you get to Denmark the transport stays hassle-free. Most journeys by rail, car or bus are so short that you can reach regional destinations before your next meal.

GETTING THERE & AWAY

ENTERING THE COUNTRY

If you're arriving by air, there are no forms to fill out in advance as long as you're from a country that does not require a visa. If you're from a country that does require a visa, immigration officials may give you marginally more scrutiny. See p304 for more information on visas.

There are no border crossings at the land border with Germany and Denmark or on the bridge from Sweden.

If you're arriving by ferry, passports are not checked unless you're arriving from Poland (until 2007 as of this writing).

Passport

If you're from a non-visa holding country, then your passport must be valid for at least three months after you intend to leave Denmark. There are no countries for which a stamp in one's passport would bar a visitor from entering Denmark.

AIR

Airports & Airlines

The vast majority of overseas flights into Denmark land at **Copenhagen International Airport** (code CPH; ☎ 32 31 32 31; www.scph.dk). One of Europe's most important hubs, this up-to-date airport is conveniently located in Kastrup, about 9km southeast of central Copenhagen, just a 12-minute train ride south of the city centre. It has good eating, retail and information facilities, plus left luggage and banking options. Note that this is a 'silent' airport and there are no boarding calls, although there are numerous monitor screens.

A growing number of international flights, mostly those coming from other Scandinavian countries or the UK, land at smaller regional airports in **Århus** (code AAR;

WARNING

The information in this chapter is particularly vulnerable to change. Prices for international travel are volatile, routes are introduced and cancelled, schedules change, special deals come and go, and rules and visa requirements are amended.

Airlines and governments seem to take a perverse pleasure in making price structures and regulations as complicated as possible. You should check directly with the airline or a travel agent to make sure you understand how a fare (and ticket you may buy) works. The travel industry is highly competitive and there are many lurks and perks.

Get opinions, quotes and advice from as many airlines and travel agents as possible before you part with your hard-earned cash. The details given in this chapter should be regarded as pointers and are not a substitute for your own careful, up-to-date research.

☎ 87 75 70 00; www.aar.dk), **Aalborg** (code AAL; ☎ 98 17 11 44; www.aal.dk), **Esbjerg** (code EBJ; ☎ 76 12 14 00; www.esbjerg-lufthavn.dk) and **Billund** (code BLL; ☎ 76 50 50 50; www.billund-airport.dk).

Denmark's (and Norway's and Sweden's) flag carrier, Scandinavian Airlines (SAS), has the most services to Denmark. SAS has an admirable safety record, with only one fatal crash since 1970 despite being one of the busiest airlines in Europe.

AIRLINE OFFICES

Here is contact information for the major airlines serving Danish airports. More than 60 airlines serve Copenhagen; the airport websites have up-to-date information on all the carriers. All airline offices are in Copenhagen proper (clustered near the Central Train Station) unless otherwise indicated:

Aer Lingus (code EI; ☎ 33 12 60 55; www.flyaerlingus.com; Jernbanegade 4)
Air China (code CA; ☎ 33 14 92 22; Rådhuspladsen 16)
Alitalia (code AZ; ☎ 70 27 02 90; www.alitalia.it; Vesterbrogade 6D)
British Airways (code BA; ☎ 80 20 80 22; www.britishairways.com; Rådhuspladsen 16)
Finnair (code AY; ☎ 33 36 45 45; www.finnair.com; Nyropsgade 47)
Iberia (code IB; ☎ 33 12 22 22; www.iberia.com; Jernbanegade 4)
Icelandair (code FI; ☎ 33 70 22 00; www.icelandair.com; Frederiksberggade 23)
KLM-Royal Dutch Airlines (code KL; ☎ 70 10 07 47; www.klm.com; Copenhagen Airport)
Lufthansa Airlines (code LH; ☎ 70 10 20 00; www.lufthansa.com; Hammerichsgade 1)
Maersk Air (code DM; ☎ 33 14 60 00; www.maersk-air.com; Rådhuspladsen 16)
Ryanair (code FR; ☎ Ireland 353-1-249-7000; www.ryanair.com; no local office)
Scandinavian Airlines (SAS; code SK; ☎ 70 10 20 00; www.sas.dk; Hammerichsgade 1)
Swiss (code LX; ☎ 70 10 50 64; www.swiss.com; Copenhagen Airport)

Tickets

Air fares can gouge anyone's budget but you can reduce the cost by finding discounts. For long-term travel there are plenty of discount tickets valid for 12 months, allowing multiple stopovers with open dates. Short-term travellers can snag cheaper fares by travelling midweek, staying away at least one Saturday night or taking advantage of quickie promotional offers.

When you're looking for bargain air fares, the Internet offers a wealth of options from online booking agencies, travel agents and the airlines themselves. No-frills carriers operating in Europe sell direct to travellers and regularly undercut the major airlines.

The travel industry has been battered in recent years, but leading travel agents such as STA Travel (which has offices worldwide) and Council Travel in the USA appear to have weathered the storm. And they do offer good prices to many destinations.

COURIER FLIGHTS

Courier flights are a great bargain if you're lucky enough to find one. Many air-freight companies expedite delivery of urgent items by sending them with you as your baggage allowance. You are permitted to bring along only one carry-on bag, but you get a steeply discounted ticket in return.

Booking a courier ticket takes quite a lot of effort. They are not readily available and arrangements have to be made a month or more in advance. You won't find courier flights to all destinations either – just on the major air routes.

It doesn't happen often, but courier flights are occasionally advertised in the newspapers, or you can contact air-freight companies listed in the phone book. Another possibility is to join the International Association of Air Travel Couriers (IAATC). The membership fee (US$45 or UK£32) gets members access to online lists of courier companies and updated schedules, daily updates of last-minute specials and *Shoestring Traveler*, the bimonthly magazine . Contact **IAATC** (US ☎ 308-632-3273; UK ☎ 0800-0746 481; www.courier.org). Joining this organisation, however, doesn't guarantee that you'll get a courier flight.

DEPARTURE TAX

Departure taxes, which equal approximately US$20, are included with all the other fees that you pay when you purchase your ticket. There are no separate departure taxes to pay when leaving Denmark.

FREQUENT FLYERS

Most airlines offer frequent-flyer deals that can earn you a free air ticket or other goodies. To qualify, you have to accumulate sufficient mileage with the same airline or airline alliance. Many airlines have 'blackout periods', or times when you cannot fly for free on your frequent-flyer points (Christmas and Chinese New Year, for example), and even if you accumulate enough mileage, airlines tend to allocate only a certain number of seats for free tickets. Also, frequent-flyer programs tend to lock you into one group of airlines, and that group may not always have the cheapest fares or most convenient flight schedule.

STUDENT & YOUTH FARES

Full-time students and people aged under 26 can get better deals than other travellers. This doesn't always mean cheaper fares but can include more flexibility to change flights and/or routes. Generally travellers must present a document proving date of birth or a valid International Student Identity Card (ISIC) when buying a ticket or boarding a plane.

Airlines usually allow infants under two years of age to fly for free or 10% of the adult fare. For children between the ages of two and 12, the fare on international flights is usually 50% of the regular fare or 67% of a discounted fare.

Travellers with Special Needs

Most international airlines can cater to people with special needs – travellers with disabilities, people with young children and even children travelling alone.

Travellers with special dietary preferences (vegetarian, kosher etc) can request meals on advance notice. If you are travelling in a wheelchair, most international airports can provide an escort from the check-in desk to plane where needed, and ramps, lifts, toilets and phones are generally available.

Reputable international airlines usually provide nappies (diapers), tissues and other items needed to keep babies bouncy.

Africa

Both **Rennies Travel** (www.renniestravel.com) and **STA Travel** (www.statravel.co.za) have offices located throughout Southern Africa. Check their websites for branch locations.

Asia

It's a good idea to shop around as there are often some good deals on offer. From Bangkok, return fares to Copenhagen are around US$1500. Return fares from Singapore start at US$850, from Hong Kong expect to pay around US$1250 and US$1100 from Tokyo for a return fare.

A number of travel agents including **STA Travel** (☎ 02-236 0262; www.statravel.co.th) are located in Bangkok.

In Singapore, the best bet is still **STA Travel** (☎ 65-737 7188; www.statravel.com.sg).

In Hong Kong good agencies include **Hong Kong Student Travel** (☎ 2730 0888; www.hkst.com.hk, in Chinese) and **STA Travel** (☎ 2736 16180; www.statravel.com.hk).

Recommended agencies in Japan include **No 1 Travel** (☎ 3205 6073; www.no1-travel.com) and **STA Travel** (☎ 5391 3205; www.statravel.co.jp).

Australia

Flights from Australia to Copenhagen generally touch down at one of the Southeast Asian capitals such as Kuala Lumpur, Bangkok or Singapore, and occasionally another European city. Expect to pay in the vicinity of A$1700 for a return fare in low season, but shop around as there are often good deals on offer.

Quite a few travel offices specialise in discount air tickets. Some travel agents, particularly smaller operators, advertise a range of cheap air fares in the travel sections of the major weekend newspapers, such as the *Age* in Melbourne and the *Sydney Morning Herald*.

You can also contact **STA Travel** (☎ 1300 360 960; www.statravel.com.au). **Flight Centre** (☎ 131 600; www.flightcentre.com.au) has offices throughout Australia. For online bookings, try www.travel.com.au.

Canada

Fares vary from C$400 in winter to C$700 in summer.

Canadian discount air ticket sellers are also known as consolidators. The *Globe & Mail, Toronto Star, Montreal Gazette* and the *Vancouver Sun* carry travel agents' ads and are good places to look for cheap air fares.

Travel CUTS (☎ 866-246 9762; www.travelcuts.com) is Canada's national student travel agency and has offices in all major cities.

Continental Europe

Copenhagen is well connected to almost all other European cities with airports. SAS and the major airlines of each country all serve each other. You should be able to find return fares from the major hub airports such as Frankfurt, Paris and Madrid for €75 to €175.

Generally, there is not much variation in air-fare prices for departures from the main European cities. All the major airlines are usually offering some sort of deal, and travel agents generally have a number of deals on offer, so shop around.

Across Europe dozens of travel agencies have ties with **STA Travel** (www.statravel.com), where cheap tickets can be purchased and STA-issued tickets can be altered (usually for a US$25 fee).

France has a network of student travel agencies which can supply discount tickets to travellers of all ages. **OTU Voyages** (☎ 01 44 41 38; www.otu.fr, in French) has 27 offices around the country. General travel agencies in Paris which offer some of the best services and deals include **Nouvelles Frontières** (☎ 0825 000 747; www.nouvelles-frontieres.fr) and **Voyageurs du Monde** (☎ 01 42 86 16 00; www.vdm.com in French).

In the Netherlands, one recommended agency is **Airfair** (☎ 020 620 5121; www.airfair.nl, in Dutch).

Belgium, Switzerland and Greece are also good places for buying discount air tickets. In Belgium, **Airstop** (☎ 070-233 188; www.airstop.be) offers great cut-rate deals for both students and non-students.

New Zealand

Reaching Copenhagen from Auckland means you have a choice of transiting though Los Angeles or via a Southeast Asian city, and usually one other European city. Low season return fares start from around US$2199.

Both **Flight Centre** (☎ 0800 243 544; www.flightcentre.co.nz) and **STA Travel** (☎ 0800 874 773; www.statravel.co.nz) have branches nationwide. For online bookings try www.travel.co.nz.

UK & Ireland

British Airways, BMI and SAS fly to Denmark from the UK. Budget airlines easyJet and Ryanair do too, and have made big inroads into business of the mainstream carriers. Watch for special fares that can be as low as UK£1 for a single, although €40 to €60 is more likely in peak periods.

Known as bucket shops in the UK, discount air travel is big business and advertisements for many travel agents appear in the travel pages of the weekend broadsheets, such as the *Independent* on Saturday and the *Sunday Times*. Also look out for the free magazines such as TNT.

Popular travel agencies include **STA Travel** (☎ 0870-1600 599; www.statravel.co.uk), with offices throughout the UK. It sells tickets to all travellers but caters especially to young people and students. Other recommended British agencies include **Trailfinders** (☎ 020-7938 3939; www.trailfinders.co.uk) and **Bridge the World** (☎ 0870-443 23 99; www.bridgetheworld.co.uk).

USA

Fares from the USA to Copenhagen vary by season, from a low of US$300/500 from the east/west coast in winter to a high of US$700/900 in summer.

Discount travel agents in the USA are known as consolidators (although you probably won't see a sign on the door saying 'Consolidator'). The *New York Times*, the *Los Angeles Times*, the *Chicago Tribune* and the *San Francisco Chronicle* all produce Sunday travel sections in which you will find consolidators' ads.

Council Travel (☎ 800-226 8624; 205 E 42 St, New York, NY 10017; www.counciltravel.com), America's largest student travel groups, has around 100 locations in the USA. **STA Travel** (☎ 800-777 0112; www.statravel.com) has offices in Boston, Chicago, Los Angeles, Miami, New York, Philadelphia, San Francisco and other major cities.

LAND

The only land crossing is with Germany, although the bridge over the Øresund from Sweden functions similarily. Traffic flows freely among EU countries so border posts are largely a thing of the past. Customs officials still make spot checks, however, of vehicles that draw their attention.

Bicycle

You can carry your bicycle into Denmark aboard boat, plane or train. Ferries into

Denmark are all well equipped for passengers with bicycles, usually for a nominal fee.

Bicycles can also travel by air, taken apart and put in a bike bag or box, but it's much easier simply to wheel your bike to the check-in desk, where it should be treated as a piece of baggage. You may have to remove the pedals and turn the handlebars sideways so that it takes up less space in the aircraft's hold; check with the airline well in advance, preferably before you pay for your ticket.

On regular trains, bike space varies and at busy times you may have to wait for a train with room for your bike.

Bus

Copenhagen is well connected to the rest of Europe daily (or near daily) in the summer peak season and between two and five times a week the rest of the year.

The most extensive European bus network is maintained by **Eurolines** (☎ 33 88 70 00; www.eurolines.com) a consortium of coach operators.

There's a 10% discount for passengers aged 12 to 26. Children aged four to 11 pay 50% of the adult fare and those three and under pay 20%. Return fares for all age groups are about 15% less than two one-way fares. Advance reservations are advised.

To	One-way fare	Duration	Frequency
Stockholm	370kr*	8hr	most days
Oslo	305kr*	7hr	daily
Amsterdam	517/555kr*	10¾hr	daily
Frankfurt	683/720kr*	14¾hr	twice weekly (more in summer)
Paris	660/699kr*	18hr	daily
London	724/756kr*	20½hr	most days

*low/high season

Gullivers Reisen (☎ 030-31 10 21 10, outside Germany 00800-45 5548 37; www.gullivers.de) links Berlin to Århus (single/return €53/93, 8¼ hours, three times weekly) with stops in Abenra, Kolding, Vejle and Horsens en route.

Car & Motorcycle

The E45 motorway is the main route to Germany, although there are several smaller crossings as well.

Two ambitious, relatively new bridge-tunnels link Copenhagen with Germany and Sweden: the 18km Storebælts-forbindelsen (the Store Bælt Bridge) connects Zealand with the Jutland peninsula and Germany, and the 16km Øresundsforbindelsen (Øresund Fixed Link) joins Copenhagen with Malmö, Sweden, via the E20 motorway. These bridges each charge tolls for cars of 230kr. There are no other toll roads in Denmark.

Car ferries are still the most efficient way to arrive from Norway and the UK. See p310 for more information.

Train

The Danish state railway, **Danske Statsbaner** (DSB; ☎ 70 13 14 16 international, ☎ 70 13 14 15 domestic; www.dsb.dk) can provide schedule and fare information.

All Eurail, Inter-Rail and Scanrail tickets are valid on the DSB. That said, it's hard to get your money's worth on a rail pass if you're travelling solely in tiny Denmark, although a pass may make sense if you're visiting other countries as well. There's a dizzying variety of passes, depending on where you reside full time and where you're travelling. For comparison purposes, standard 2nd-class train fares from Copenhagen are 557kr to Oslo or 1000kr to Frankfurt.

See p313 for more about trains within the country.

TRAIN PASSES

There are several train pass options for people living outside Scandinavia. You'll need to show your passport. Categories for age groups vary, but are generally up to 12 years, 12 to 25, 25 to 59, 60 and over.

Scanrail (www.scanrail.com) passes cover travel in Denmark, Norway, Sweden and Finland and must be purchased before arrival in Scandinavia.

The Scanrail pass also includes free or discounted travel on international

WARNING!

If you buy a rail pass, read the small print. If you fail to validate the pass properly, you risk a fine and possible forfeiture of the pass.

TRANSPORT

boats travelling between Denmark and its neighbours.

Inter-Rail (www.interrailnet.com) passes are good for people who can show they've lived in Europe for at least six months.

For purposes of the Inter-Rail pass, Europe is split into eight zones covering countries from Scandinavia and the British Isles to Eastern Europe and North Africa. Prices are based on the number of zones you plan to travel in; Denmark is in the same zone as Germany, Switzerland and Austria.

Outside Europe the Eurailpass is heavily marketed. Good for 17 countries, it's more than overkill if you're just visiting Denmark. A 15-day pass costs US$414 for youths in 2nd class. Adults pay US$498, but only for 1st-class travel with at least one other adult (who pays the same price). You can buy these at travel agents or via **Europe Rail** (www.europerail.com).

Hitching

Hitching is never entirely safe anywhere in the world and we don't recommend it. Travellers who decide to hitch should understand that they are taking a small but potentially serious risk.

At any rate, hitching is not a common practice in Denmark and generally not a very rewarding one. It's also illegal on motorways.

The car fares on the Harwich–Esbjerg ferry (right) include passengers, so you can hitch to the Continent for nothing at no cost to the driver.

Looking for a ride out of the country? Try the notice boards at universities, public libraries and youth hostels. **Bugride** (www.europe.bugride.com) is a good meeting place for European drivers and those who are driven.

SEA

Ferries can be a pleasant way to travel as the boats are generally of a high standard. Long-distance boats usually have lounges, nightclubs, duty-free shopping, cafeterias and formal restaurants. Many of the boats between Denmark and other Scandinavian countries have floating casinos and small grocery shops on board. If you take an overnight ferry, you can save on hotels.

Fares in this section are for one-way travel unless noted. Discounts are often available, including for return tickets, passengers in a car on board, rail passes or student card holders and seniors. Child fares are usually half of the adult fares. Car fares given in this section are for a standard car (generally up to 6m in length and 2m in height); inquire about packages that include passengers with car transport.

Fares on the same ships vary wildly, by the season and the day of the week. Highest prices tend to occur on summer weekends and the lowest on winter weekdays.

Particularly if you are bringing along a vehicle, you should always make reservations well in advance – this is doubly true in summer and on weekends.

The following reservation information is for the larger ferry companies operating international routes to and from Denmark.

Faroe Islands & Iceland

Smiryl Lines (www.smyril-line.fo) serves the busy ports of Tórshavn and Seyðisfjörður on a circuitous, week-long route from the Danish port of Hanstholm. Check out the website for the latest schedules and fares.

Germany

Scandlines (www.scandlines.de) operates ferries between Puttgarden and Rødbyhavn (adult peak/off-peak €6/4, cars from €48, 45 minutes), Rostock and Gedser (passengers peak/off-peak €8/5, cars from €63, two hours), and Sassnitz and Rønne (passengers peak/off-peak €18/12, cars from €70, 3¾ hours).

Rømø-Sylt Linie (www.sylt-faehre.de) operates several ferries between Sylt and Rømø (passengers peak/off-peak €6.50/4.75, cars from €37, 45 minutes). Note, though, that this line's website is only in Danish and German.

Norway

Color Line (www.colorline.com) connects Kristiansand and Oslo with Hirtshals (4½ and 6½ hours respectively) and Larvik with Frederikshavn (6¼ hours). Sailings take place daily for most of the year. Fares on all of Color Line's routes between Norway and Denmark range from a high of €58 (weekends during summer) to a low of €24 (mid-week October to April). Costs per car and up to five passengers are between €89 and €225.

DFDS Seaways (www.dfdsseaways.com) connects Oslo with Copenhagen daily via Helsingborg, Sweden (passengers peak/off-peak Nkr995/685–875, cars from Nkr340 passengers extra, 14¼ hours).

Stena Lines (Norway ☎ 02010; www.stenalines.com) sails between Oslo and Frederikshavn (passengers peak/off-peak Nkr385–525/315–345, cars peak/off-peak Nkr775–1525 435–575 passengers extra, 12 hours) daily in peak season and daily except Monday in off-season.

Poland

Polferries (www.polferries.com) offers 10½-hour trips between Świnoujście and Copenhagen about five times per week (passengers peak/off-peak 425/395kr, cars from 595/550kr). There are daytime and overnight ferries to choose f rom depending on the day of the week. Polferries also offers weekly service from Świnoujście to Rønne (passengers 225kr, cars 550kr).

Sweden

Bornholmstrafikken (www.Bornholmstrafikken.dk) runs between Ystad and Rønne, on Bornholm, Denmark (passengers €20, cars peak/off-peak €122/91, fast ferry 1¼ hours, regular ferry 2½ hours).

HH Lines (www.hhferries.se, in Swedish & Danish) makes the quick journey from Helsingborg to Helsingør dozens of times daily, mostly on the hour and half-hour. Adult fares are Skr20 each way.

Stena Lines (Sweden ☎ 31-704 00 00; www.stenalines.com) sails between Gothenburg and Frederikshavn (3¼ hours) and between Varberg and Grenaa (four hours). Fares for both of these services are passengers Skr140–210, cars Skr745–1195. Fares vary greatly according to time of year and day of the week (winter weekdays are lowest, summer weekends are highest). There's also a high-speed ferry (passengers Skr170–250, cars Skr845–1395, two hours) between Gothenburg and Frederikshavn.

UK

DFDS Seaways (☎ 08705 333 111, www.dfdsseaways.com) offers passenger and car ferries three times per week between Harwich and Esbjerg (adults peak/off-peak £49/29, cars peak/off-peak £57/47). The journey takes about 18 hours.

GETTING AROUND

AIR

Denmark's small size and efficient rail network means that domestic air traffic is quite limited, usually to business travellers and people connecting from international flights through Copenhagen. Still, domestic carriers offer frequent services between Copenhagen and a few of the more distant corners.

Cimber Air (☎ 70 10 12 18; www.cimber.dk) flies from Copenhagen to Aalborg (from 1050kr), Karup (Central Jutland, 1025kr), Rønne (Bornholm, 1050kr) and Sønderborg (1075kr). Again, there are frequent discounts available.

Scandinavian Airlines (☎ 70 10 30 00; www.scandinavian.net) flies from Copenhagen to Århus (1030kr one-way), Aalborg (1140kr) and Billund (1090kr). Ask about discounts such as youth fares and weekend getaway fares.

If you're holding an international ticket on the same carrier, you may receive a discount even if you travel one way to Copenhagen, connect by land with the other city and then fly back through Copenhagen (or vice-versa).

BICYCLE

It's easy to travel with a bike anywhere in Denmark, even when you're not riding it, as bicycles can readily be taken on ferries and trains for a modest fee. Be aware on DSB trains, reservations should be made at least three hours prior to departure because bikes generally travel in a separate section of the train.

Cyclists are well catered for in Denmark and there are excellent cycling routes throughout the main islands. See p56 for more information on cycling routes

If you prefer to leave your bike at home, it's easy to hire bikes throughout Denmark. Prices average around 50/275kr per day/week for something basic. Note that helmets are not included with most hired bicycles.

Always lock up your bike, especially if you're travelling with an expensive model, as bike theft is common, particularly in larger cities such as Copenhagen and Århus.

BOAT

There's an extensive network of ferries linking Denmark's many populated islands. See local listings for details.

BUS

Long-distance buses run a distant second to trains. Still, some cross-country bus routes work out to about 25% cheaper than trains.

Daily express buses include connections between Copenhagen and Århus (220kr, 2¾ hours) and Copenhagen and Aalborg (290kr, five hours). There's also twice-daily express-bus service between the Jutland port cities of Frederikshavn and Esbjerg (280kr, five hours). See local listings for details.

CAR & MOTORCYCLE

Denmark is a pleasant country for touring by car. Roads are good and almost invariably well signposted. Except during rush hour, traffic is quite light, even in major cities.

Access to and from Danish motorways is straightforward: roads leading out of town centres are named after the main city that they lead to (eg the road heading out of Odense to Faaborg is called Faaborgvej). Petrol stations, with toilets, nappy-changing facilities and minimarkets, are at 50km intervals on motorways.

Denmark's extensive ferry network carries motor vehicles at quite reasonable rates. Fares for cars average three times the passenger rate. It's always wise for drivers to make ferry reservations in advance, even if it's only a couple of hours ahead of time. On weekends and holidays ferries on prime crossings can be completely booked. See destination chapters for more information on car ferries.

Unleaded and super petrol as well as diesel fuel are available. You'll generally find the most competitive prices at petrol stations along motorways.

The **Danish Road Directorate** (☎ 70 10 10 40) offers a helpful 24-hour telephone service that can provide nationwide information on traffic conditions, road works, detours and ferry cancellations; available in English.

Driving Licence

Many foreign driving licences are accepted in Denmark including those issued in the USA,

ROAD DISTANCES (KM)

Note: Distances between Jutland & Zealand are via Funen

	Aalborg	Copenhagen	Esbjerg	Frederikshavn	Grenaa	Helsingør	Kalundborg	Kolding	Næstved	Nyborg	Odense	Ringkøbing	Rødby	Skagen	Thisted	Tønder	Viborg	Århus
Aalborg	---																	
Copenhagen	402	---																
Esbjerg	216	298	---															
Frederikshavn	65	465	278	---														
Grenaa	136	367	216	193	---													
Helsingør	443	47	339	506	408	---												
Kalundborg	345	103	241	408	310	139	---											
Kolding	199	230	72	261	164	271	173	---										
Næstved	342	85	238	405	307	125	71	152	---									
Nyborg	274	228	170	337	239	169	71	102	68	---								
Odense	243	165	139	306	208	206	108	71	105	37	---							
Ringkøbing	174	336	81	236	188	377	279	115	276	208	177	---						
Rødby	410	181	306	473	375	221	176	238	105	136	173	344	---					
Skagen	105	505	319	41	233	546	448	302	445	377	346	277	513	---				
Thisted	90	399	185	138	186	440	342	196	339	271	240	123	407	172	---			
Tønder	284	315	77	347	249	356	258	86	255	187	156	148	323	387	252	---		
Viborg	80	323	136	142	100	354	266	119	263	195	164	94	331	183	87	205	---	
Århus	112	304	153	171	63	345	ferry	101	244	176	145	127	312	212	153	186	66	---

CAMPER VAN

Although your camper van can be your home away from home – eating, sleeping and entertainment centre – note that free camping, such as in motorway rest areas, is illegal in Denmark.

Canada, the UK and other EU countries so bring your home driving licence.

Hire

Rental cars are expensive in Denmark – you could easily pay as much to hire a car for just one day in Denmark as it would cost to hire one for a week across the border in Germany; some visitors do just that…and then drive across the border.

If Germany's not on the cards, a little research can mean big savings. You may get the best deal on a car rental by booking with an international rental agency before you arrive in Denmark. Be sure to ask about promotional rates, pre-pay schemes, etc. In Denmark, walk-up rates start at about 650kr per day, somewhat less for longer rentals.

Rental companies' weekend rates, when available, offer real savings. About 1000kr allows you to keep the car from Friday afternoon to Monday morning, including VAT and insurance. Be sure to request a plan that includes unlimited kilometres; some plans tack on an extra fee after 250km.

Avis, Budget, Europcar and Hertz are among the largest operators in Denmark, with offices in major cities, airports and other ports of entry.

Road Rules

- Drive on the right-hand side of the road.
- Cars and motorcycles must have dipped headlights on at all times.
- Drivers are required to carry a warning triangle in case of breakdown.
- Seat belt use is mandatory; fine for violation: 500kr per person.
- Children aged three and under must be secured in an infant seat or approved child restraint appropriate to the child's age, size and weight. Child seats are required for children aged from four to six.
- Motorcycle riders must wear helmets.
- Speed limits: 50km/h in towns and built-up areas, 80km/h on major roads, 110km/h on motorways. Maximum speed for vehicles with trailers: 70km/h.
- Speeding fines can be up to 8000kr; severe speeding can result in immediate confiscation of your driver's licence.
- Using a hand-held mobile phone while driving is illegal, carries a 500kr fine.
- It's illegal to drive with a blood-alcohol concentration of 0.05% or greater; driving under the influence will render drivers liable to stiff penalties and a possible prison sentence.
- Motorways have emergency telephones every 2km intervals, indicated by arrows on marker posts.
- From other telephones, dial ☎ 112 for emergencies.

HITCHING

Hitching is never entirely safe anywhere in the world and we don't recommend it. Travellers who decide to hitch should understand that they are taking a small but potentially serious risk.

At any rate, hitching is not a common practice in Denmark and generally not a very rewarding one. It's also illegal on motorways.

LOCAL TRANSPORT

Taxi

Taxis are generally readily available for hire throughout Denmark in city centres, near major shopping centres and at train stations. If you see a taxi with a lit *fri* sign, you can wave it down, but you can always phone for a taxi as well.

Fares average around 23kr at flag fall and 10kr per kilometre (13kr at night and at weekends). Tipping is not needed because a service charge is included in the fare.

TRAIN

Denmark has a reliable train system with reasonable fares and frequent services. The map on p100 shows the rail network. Most long-distance trains on major routes operate at least hourly throughout the day. **DSB** (☎ 70 13 14 15; www.dsb.dk) runs virtually all trains in Denmark. DSB trains include the following:

InterCity (IC) – ultramodern comforts, cushioned seats, reading lights, headphone jacks, play areas for children.

DSB1 (first class) is 50% more than standard fares.

TIP!

Nearly all Danish train stations have lockers (20kr for 24 hours).

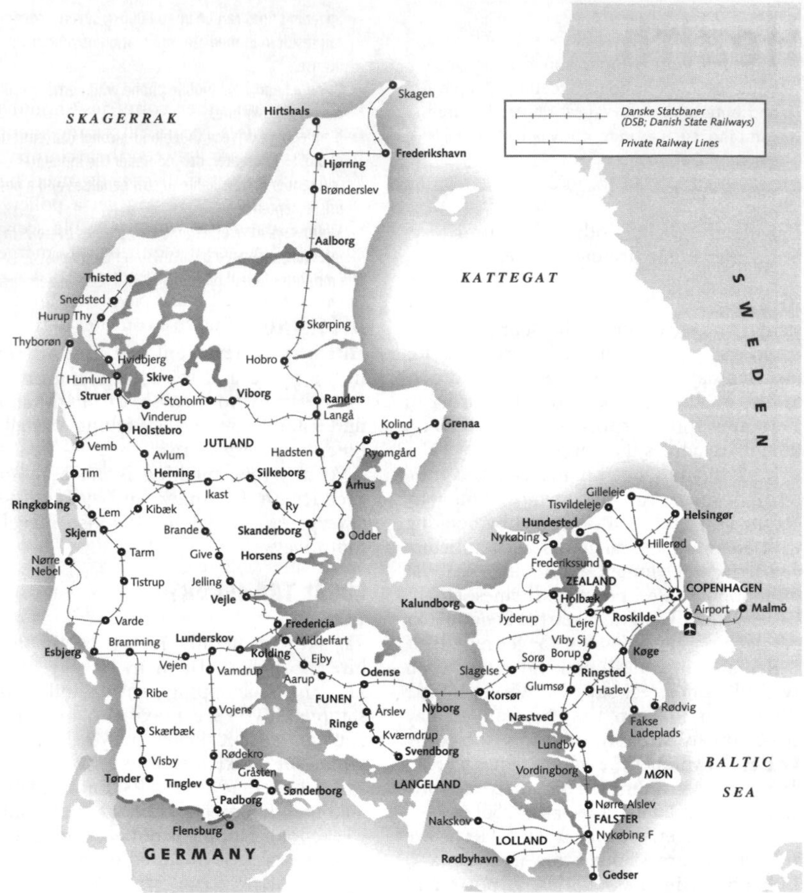
Danske Statsbaner (DSB; Danish State Railways)
Private Railway Lines
SKAGERRAK
KATTEGAT
SWEDEN
BALTIC SEA
GERMANY
JUTLAND
FUNEN
ZEALAND
LANGELAND
LOLLAND
FALSTER
MØN
Skagen
Hirtshals
Frederikshavn
Hjørring
Brønderslev
Aalborg
Thisted
Snedsted
Hurup Thy
Thyborøn
Skørping
Hobro
Hvidbjerg
Humlum
Skive
Struer
Stoholm
Viborg
Randers
Langå
Vinderup
Holstebro
Kolind
Grenaa
Vemb
Avlum
Hadsten
Ryomgård
Tim
Herning
Ikast
Silkeborg
Århus
Ringkøbing
Lem
Kibæk
Ry
Skjern
Brande
Skanderborg
Odder
Tarm
Give
Horsens
Nørre Nebel
Tistrup
Jelling
Vejle
Varde
Fredericia
Middelfart
Esbjerg
Bramming
Lunderskov
Kolding
Vejen
Ejby
Vamdrup
Aarup
Odense
Ribe
Vojens
Årslev
Nyborg
Ringe
Skærbæk
Kværndrup
Svendborg
Visby
Rødekro
Tønder
Tinglev
Gråsten
Sønderborg
Padborg
Flensburg
Gilleleje
Tisvildeleje
Helsingør
Hundested
Nykøbing S
Hillerød
Frederikssund
COPENHAGEN
Holbæk
Kalundborg
Airport
Malmö
Jyderup
Lejre
Roskilde
Viby Sj
Borup
Sorø
Køge
Slagelse
Ringsted
Korsør
Glumsø
Haslev
Næstved
Rødvig
Fakse Ladeplads
Lundby
Vordingborg
Nørre Alslev
Nakskov
Nykøbing F
Rødbyhavn
Gedser

Reservations not required, but recommended if you want a guaranteed seat.

InterCityLyn – on certain well-travelled routes. Same facilities as InterCity, but with fewer stops.

InterRegional (IR) – older, slower, simpler. Reservations not accepted.

Costs

Standard fares are about 2kr per kilometre, with the highest fare possible between any two points in Denmark topping out at just 331kr. Reservation fee for seats is 20kr. Discounts include the following:

Seniors (65 and over) 20% discount on Friday and Saturday and a 50% discount on other days.

Children (aged 12 to 15) half the adult fare at all times.

Children (under 12) free if they are with an adult.

Group discounts for eight or more adults travelling together.

Youth (aged 16 to 25) can buy a DSB WildCard (youth card) for 175kr; it allows half-price train fares Monday to Thursday and Saturday.

Health

CONTENTS

Travel health depends on your predeparture preparations, your daily health care while travelling and how you handle any medical problem that does develop. Denmark is a relatively healthy place and travellers shouldn't need to take any unusual health precautions.

BEFORE YOU GO

Prevention is the key to staying healthy while abroad. A little planning before departure, particularly for pre-existing illnesses will save trouble later. See your dentist before a long trip. Carry a spare pair of contact lenses or glasses, and take your optical prescription with you. Bring medications in their original, clearly labelled, containers. A signed and dated letter from your physician describing your medical conditions and medications, including generic names, is also a good idea. If carrying syringes or needles, be sure to have a physician's letter documenting their medical necessity.

INSURANCE

If you're an EU citizen, an E111 form, available from health centres or, in the UK, post offices, covers you for most medical care. E111 will not cover you for non-emergencies or for emergency repatriation home. Citizens from other countries should find out if there is a reciprocal arrangement for free medical care between their country and the country visited. If you do need health insurance, make sure you get a policy that covers you for the worst possible scenario, such as an accident requiring an emergency flight home. Find out in advance if your insurance plan will make payments directly to providers or reimburse you later for overseas health expenditures.

RECOMMENDED VACCINATIONS

The World Health Organisation (WHO) recommends that all travellers should be covered for diphtheria, tetanus, measles, mumps, rubella and polio, as well as Hepatitis B, regardless of their destination. Since most vaccines don't produce immunity until at least two weeks after they're given, visit a physician at least six weeks before departure. There are no specific vaccinations requirements for entry to Denmark, other than against yellow fever if you're coming from an affected area.

INTERNET RESOURCES

The WHO's publication *International Travel and Health* is revised annually and is available online at www.who.int/ith/.

> **GOVERNMENT WEBSITES**
>
> It's usually a good idea to consult your government's travel health website before departure, if one is available:
>
> **Australia** www.dfat.gov.au/travel/
> **Canada** www.travelhealth.gc.ca
> **United Kingdom** www.doh.gov.uk/traveladvice/
> **United States** www.cdc.gov/travel/

FURTHER READING

Health Advice for Travellers (currently called the 'T6' leaflet) is an annually updated leaflet by the UK Department of Health and is available free in post offices. It contains some general information, legally required and recommended vaccines for different countries, reciprocal health agreements and an E111 application form. Lonely Planet's *Travel with Children* includes advice on travel health for younger children. Other recommended references include *Traveller's Health* by Dr Richard Dawood (Oxford University Press) and *The Traveller's Good Health Guide* by Ted Lankester (Sheldon Press).

IN TRANSIT

DEEP VEIN THROMBOSIS (DVT)

Blood clots may form in the legs during plane flights, chiefly because of prolonged immobility. The longer the flight, the greater the risk. The chief symptom of DVT is swelling or pain of the foot, ankle or calf, usually but not always on just one side. When a blood clot travels to the lungs, it may cause chest pain and breathing difficulties. Travellers with any of these symptoms should immediately seek medical attention.

To prevent the development of DVT on long flights you should walk about the cabin, contract the leg muscles while sitting, drink plenty of fluids, and avoid alcohol and tobacco.

IN DENMARK

AVAILABILITY & COST OF HEALTH CARE

Good health care is readily available and for minor self-limiting illnesses pharmacists can give valuable advice and sell over the counter medication. They can also advise when more specialised help is required and point you in the right direction. The standard of dental care is usually good, however, it is sensible to have a dental check-up before a long trip.

INFECTIOUS DISEASES

Tickborne encephalitis is spread by tick bites. It is a serious infection of the brain and vaccination is advised for those in risk areas who are unable to avoid tick bites (such as campers, forestry workers and ramblers). Two doses of vaccine will give a year's protection, three doses up to three years'.

ENVIRONMENTAL HAZARDS

Heat Exhaustion & Hypothermia

Denmark has a fairly mild climate year round and visitors are not at excessive risk from either of these conditions. It is surprisingly easy however, to become over-exposed to the sun in a temperate climate, even on a cloudy day, and to become dangerously cold in mild, damp weather if out cycling or hiking.

Heat exhaustion occurs following excessive fluid loss with inadequate replacement of fluids and salt. Symptoms include headache, dizziness and tiredness. Dehydration is already happening by the time you feel thirsty – aim to drink sufficient water to produce pale, diluted urine. To treat heat exhaustion drink replacement fluids with water and/or fruit juice, and cool the body with cold water and fans. Treat salt loss with salty fluids such as soup or Bovril, or add a little more table salt to foods than usual.

Acute hypothermia follows a sudden drop of temperature over a short time. Chronic hypothermia is caused by a gradual loss of temperature over hours. Hypothermia starts with shivering, loss of judgment and clumsiness. Unless rewarming occurs, the sufferer deteriorates into apathy, confusion and coma. Prevent further heat loss by seeking shelter, warm dry clothing, hot sweet drinks and shared bodily warmth.

Insect Bites & Stings

Mosquitoes are found in most parts of Europe, they may not carry malaria but can cause irritation and infected bites. Use a DEET-based insect repellent. Bee and wasps stings only cause real problems to those with a severe allergy (anaphylaxis.) If you have a severe allergy to bee or wasp stings carry an 'epipen' or similar adrenaline injection.

TRAVELLING WITH CHILDREN

All travellers with children should know how to treat minor ailments and when to seek medical treatment. Make sure the children are up to date with routine vaccinations, and discuss possible travel vaccines well before departure as some vaccines are not suitable for children under a year.

In hot moist climates any wound or break in the skin is likely to let in infection. The area should be cleaned and kept dry.

Remember to avoid contaminated food and water. If your child has vomiting or diarrhoea, lost fluid and salts must be replaced. It may be helpful to take rehydration powders for reconstituting with boiled water.

Children should be encouraged to avoid and mistrust any dogs or other mammals because of the risk of diseases. Any bite, scratch or lick from a warm blooded, furry animal should immediately be thoroughly cleaned.

WOMEN'S HEALTH

Emotional stress, exhaustion and travelling through different time zones can all contribute to an upset in the menstrual pattern. If using oral contraceptives, remember some antibiotics, diarrhoea and vomiting can stop the pill from working and lead to the risk of pregnancy – remember to take condoms with you just in case. Time zones, gastrointestinal upsets and antibiotics do not affect injectable contraception.

Travelling during pregnancy is usually possible but always consult your doctor before planning your trip. The most risky times for travel are during the first 12 weeks of pregnancy and after 30 weeks.

SEXUAL HEALTH

Emergency contraception is most effective if taken within 24 hours after unprotected sex. The **International Planned Parent Federation** (www.ippf.org) can advise about the availability of contraception in different countries.

When buying condoms, look for a European CE mark, which means it has been rigorously tested, and then keep them in a cool dry place or they may crack and perish.

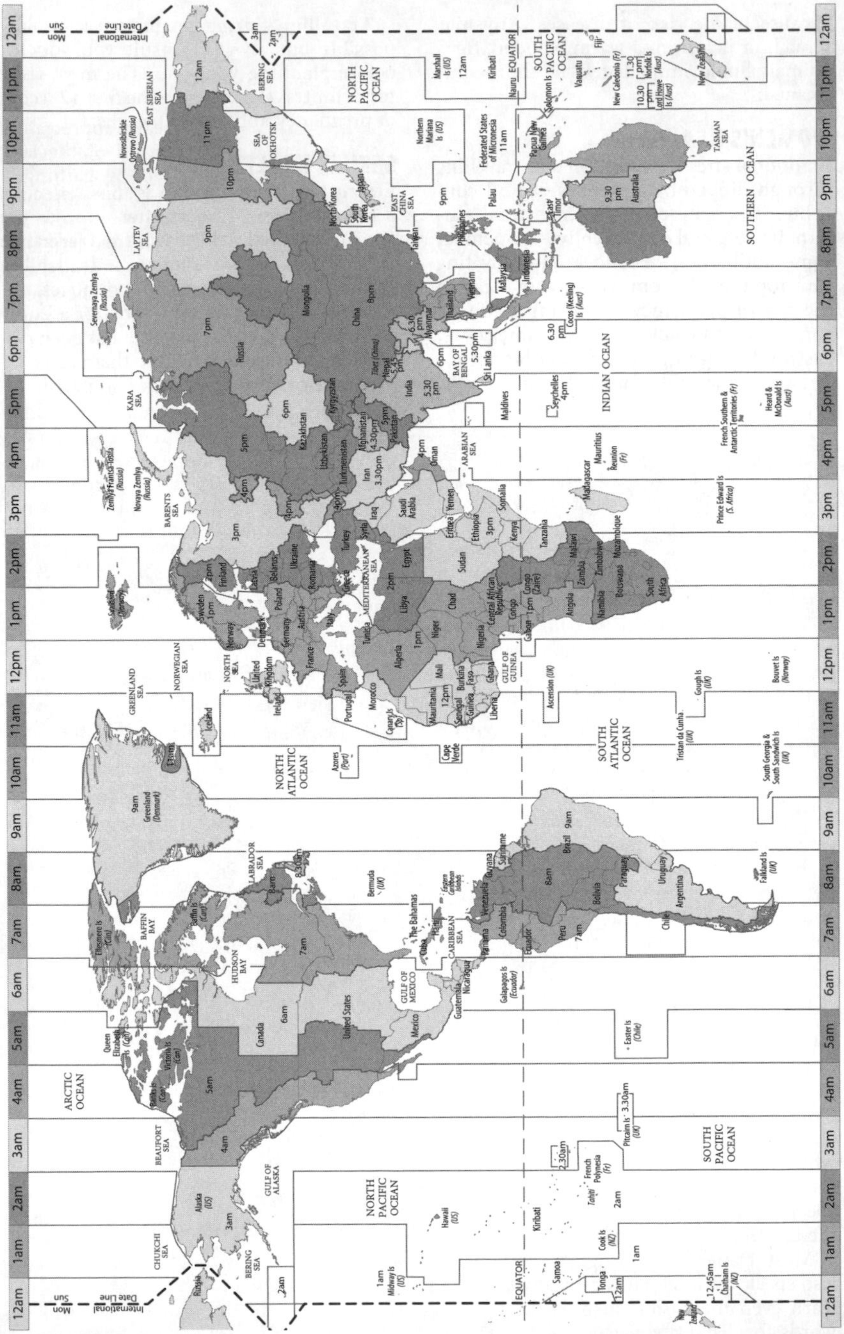
12am
1am
2am
3am
4am
5am
6am
7am
8am
9am
10am
11am
12pm
1pm
2pm
3pm
4pm
5pm
6pm
7pm
8pm
9pm
10pm
11pm
12am
International Date Line
Mon
Sun
EQUATOR
ARCTIC OCEAN
BEAUFORT SEA
CHUKCHI SEA
BERING SEA
GULF OF ALASKA
NORTH PACIFIC OCEAN
SOUTH PACIFIC OCEAN
HUDSON BAY
BAFFIN BAY
LABRADOR SEA
GULF OF MEXICO
CARIBBEAN SEA
NORTH ATLANTIC OCEAN
SOUTH ATLANTIC OCEAN
GREENLAND SEA
NORWEGIAN SEA
NORTH SEA
BARENTS SEA
KARA SEA
LAPTEV SEA
EAST SIBERIAN SEA
SEA OF OKHOTSK
EAST CHINA SEA
MEDITERRANEAN SEA
ARABIAN SEA
BAY OF BENGAL
INDIAN OCEAN
GULF OF GUINEA
SOUTHERN OCEAN
TASMAN SEA
Alaska (US)
Canada
United States
Mexico
Greenland (Denmark)
Iceland
Brazil
Argentina
Chile
Peru
Bolivia
Paraguay
Uruguay
Colombia
Venezuela
Ecuador
Guyana
Suriname
Cuba
The Bahamas
Haiti
Panama
Nicaragua
Guatemala
Bermuda (UK)
Azores (Port)
Canary Is (Sp)
Cape Verde
Ireland
United Kingdom
Portugal
Spain
France
Germany
Norway
Sweden
Finland
Denmark
Poland
Austria
Italy
Latvia
Belarus
Ukraine
Romania
Greece
Turkey
Syria
Iraq
Iran
Saudi Arabia
Yemen
Oman
Egypt
Libya
Tunisia
Algeria
Morocco
Mauritania
Mali
Niger
Chad
Sudan
Ethiopia
Eritrea
Somalia
Kenya
Tanzania
Nigeria
Ghana
Liberia
Senegal
Guinea
Burkina Faso
Gabon
Congo
Central African Republic
Angola
Zambia
Malawi
Mozambique
Zimbabwe
Botswana
Namibia
South Africa
Madagascar
Mauritius
Russia
Kazakhstan
Uzbekistan
Turkmenistan
Kyrgyzstan
Afghanistan
Pakistan
India
Nepal
Sri Lanka
Maldives
Mongolia
China
Tibet (China)
Myanmar
Thailand
Vietnam
Malaysia
Indonesia
Philippines
Taiwan
North Korea
South Korea
Japan
Australia
New Zealand
Papua New Guinea
East Timor
Palau
Federated States of Micronesia
Northern Mariana Is (US)
Marshall Is (US)
Kiribati
Nauru
Solomon Is
Vanuatu
Fiji
New Caledonia (Fr)
Hawaii (US)
Midway Is (US)
Samoa
Tonga
Cook Is (NZ)
French Polynesia (Fr)
Tahiti
Pitcairn Is (UK)
Easter Is (Chile)
Galapagos Is (Ecuador)
Falkland Is (UK)
South Georgia & South Sandwich Is (UK)
Tristan da Cunha (UK)
Gough Is (UK)
Bouvet Is (Norway)
Ascension (UK)
Prince Edward Is (S. Africa)
French Southern & Antarctic Territories (Fr)
Heard & McDonald Is (Aust)
Seychelles
Cocos (Keeling) Is (Aust)
Novaya Zemlya (Russia)
Severnaya Zemlya (Russia)
Novosibirskie Ostrova (Russia)
Zemlya Frantsa-Iosifa (Russia)
Ellesmere Is (Can)
Baffin Is (Can)
Victoria Is (Can)
Queen Elizabeth Is (Can)
Banks Is (Can)
Chatham Is (NZ)
Norfolk Is (Aust)
Lord Howe Is (Aust)
Reunion (Fr)

Language

CONTENTS

Together with Swedish, Norwegian, Icelandic and Faroese, Danish belongs to the northern branch of the Germanic language group. Consequently, written Danish bears a strong resemblance to all these languages. Spoken Danish, however, has evolved in a different direction, developing sounds and quirks of pronunciation that aren't found elsewhere.

Grammatically, Danish has the same general rules and syntax as the other Germanic languages of Scandinavia. There are two genders: common (or 'non-neuter'), and neuter. Articles ('a/an' and 'the' in English) are suffixed to the noun: *-en* for common singular nouns and *-et* for neuter singular nouns.

Danish has both a polite and an informal mode of address (where English uses the universal 'you'); the polite form uses the personal pronouns *De* and *Dem*, the informal, *du* and *dig*. The translations in this chapter are mostly in the informal, except where it's appropriate to use the polite form. In general, use the polite form when speaking to senior citizens and officials, and the informal in all other instances.

Most Danes speak English, and many also speak German. However, any effort to learn even the basics, such as the Danish words for 'Thank you', 'Goodbye', 'Hello' and 'I'm sorry', will be greatly appreciated. With an increased command of the language, you'll be rewarded by gaining a greater insight into the people and their country.

Note that Danish has all of the letters of the English alphabet plus three others: **æ, ø** and **å**. These come at the end of the alphabet and we have used this order thoughout the book.

PRONUNCIATION

You may find Danish pronunciation difficult. Consonants can be drawled, swallowed and even omitted completely, creating, in conjunction with vowels, the peculiarity of the glottal stop or stød. Its sound is rather as a Cockney would say the 'tt' in 'bottle'. Stress usually falls on the first syllable. As a general rule, the best advice is to listen and learn. Good luck!

Vowels

Danish	Pronunciation Guide	
a	**a**	as in 'act'
	aa	as the 'a' in 'father'
e/æ	**e**	a short, flat 'e' as in 'met'
eg	**ai**	as in 'aisle'
i	**i**	as in 'hit'
	ee	as the 'ee' in 'bee'
o	**o**	a short 'o' as in 'pot'
ov	**ow**	as the 'ow' in 'growl', but shorter
u	**oo**	as in 'book'
	a	before 'n', as the 'a' in 'walk
y	**ew**	a long, sharp 'u' – purse your lips and say 'ee'
ø	**er**	as the 'er' in 'fern', but shorter
øj	**oy**	as in 'toy'
å	**or**	as the 'a' in 'walk'

Consonants

Consonants are pronounced as in English with the exception of the following:

Danish	Pronunciation Guide	
d	**d**	as in 'dog'
	th	as in 'these'
g	**g**	before vowels, a hard 'g' as in 'get'

j	**y**	as in 'yet'
r	**r**	a rolling 'r' in the throat, abruptly cut short
ch	**sh**	as in 'ship'

ACCOMMODATION

I'm looking for a ...
Jeg leder efter ...
yai *li*·thaa *ef*·daa ...

campground
en campingplads — in *kam*·ping·plas
guesthouse
et pensionat — it pang·sho·*naat*
hotel
et hotel — it ho·*tel*
youth hostel
et vandrehjem — it *van*·dra·yem

Where is a cheap hotel?
Hvor er der et billigt hotel?
vor er daa it *bee*·leed ho·*tel*
What is the address?
Hvad er adressen?
va er a·*draa*·sen
Could you write it down, please?
Kunne De/du skrive adressen ned? (pol/inf)
koo·ne dee/doo *sgree*·ve a·*draa*·sen nith
Do you have any rooms available?
Har I ledige værelser?
haa ee *li*·thee·e *verl*·saa

I'd like (a) ...
Jeg vil gerne have ...
yai vi *ger*·ne ha ...

bed
en seng — in seng
single room
et enkeltværelse — it *eng*·geld·verl·se
double-bed
en dobbeltseng — in *do*·beld·seng
room
et værelse — it *verl*·se
double room
et dobbeltværelse — it *do*·beld·verl·se
room with a bathroom
et værelse med bad — it *verl*·se me bath
to share a dorm
plads i en sovesal — plas ee in *sow*·saal

How much is it ...?
Hvor meget koster det ...?
vor *ma*·eth *kos*·daa di ...

per night
per nat — per naad
per person
per person — per per·*son*

MAKING A RESERVATION
(for written and phone inquiries)

To ...
Til ... — ti ...
From ...
Fra ... — fraa ...
date
dato — *da*·to
credit card
kreditkort — kre·*deed*·kord
number
nummer — *noom*·ma
expiry date
udløbsdato — *ooth*·lerbs·da·to

I'd like to book ... (type of room)
Jeg vil gerne reservere ...
yai vi *ger*·ne re·ser·*ve*·re ...
Please confirm availability and price.
Vær så venlig at bekræfte ledighed og pris.
ver sor *ven*·lee at be·*krerf*·de *li*·thee·hith o prees

May I see the room?
Må jeg se værelset?
mor yai si *verl*·seth
Where is the toilet?
Hvor er toilettet?
vor er toy·*le*·deth
I'm/we're leaving now/tomorrow.
Jeg/Vi rejser nu/i morgen.
yai/vee *rai*·sa noo/i morn

CONVERSATION & ESSENTIALS

Hello.
Goddag/Hej. — go·*daa*/hai
Goodbye.
Farvel. — faa·*vel*
Yes.
Ja. — ya
No.
Nej. — nai
Thank you.
Tak. — taag
You're welcome.
Selv tak. — sel taag
Excuse me.
Undskyld. — *orn*·sgewl
Sorry.
Beklager. — bi·*kla*·aa
What's your name?
Hvad hedder De/du? — va *hi*·thaa dee/doo (pol/inf)
My name is ...
Mit navn er ... — mit naa·oon er ...

LANGUAGE

Where are you from?
Hvor kommer De/ du fra? — vor *kom*·aa dee/ doo fraa (pol/inf)
I'm from ...
Jeg er fra ... — yai er fraa ...
I like ...
Jeg kan lide ... — yai kan lee ...
I don't like ...
Jeg kan ikke lide ... — yai kan ig lee ...
Just a minute.
Et øjeblik. — it *oy*·e·blig

DIRECTIONS

Where is ...?
Hvor er ...? — vor er ...
Go straight aead.
Gå lige ud. — gor *lee*·e ooth
Turn left.
Drej til venstre. — drai ti *vens*·draa
Turn right.
Drej til højre. — drai ti *hoy*·yaa
at the next corner
ved næste hjørne — vi *nes*·de *yer*·ne
at the traffic lights
ved trafiklyset — vi traa·*feeg*·lew·seth

SIGNS

Indgang	Entrance
Udgang	Exit
Information	Information
Åben	Open
Lukket	Closed
Forbudt	Prohibited
Politi	Police
Toilet	Toilet/WC
Herrer	Men
Damer	Women

behind	*bag*	baa
in front of	*foran*	*for*·an
far (from)	*langt (fra)*	laangd (fraa)
near (to)	*nær (ved)*	ner (vi)
opposite	*modsat*	*moth*·sat

beach	*strand*	sdraan
bridge	*bro*	bro
castle	*slot*	slod
cathedral	*katedral*	ka·de·*draal*
church	*kirke*	*keer*·ge
island	*ø*	er
lake	*sø*	ser
main square	*hovedtorv*	*ho*·veth·torw
market	*marked*	*maa*·geth
old city (town)	*den gamle bydel*	den *gaam*·le *bew*·dil
palace	*palads*	pa·*las*
quay	*kaj*	kai
riverbank	*flodbred*	*floth*·breth
ruins	*ruiner*	roo·*ee*·naa
sea	*hav*	*haa*·oo
square	*torv*	torw

EMERGENCIES

It's an emergency!
Det er en nødsituation! — di er in *nerth*·si·too·a·shon
Help!
Hjælp! — yelb
There's been an accident!
Der er sket en ulykke! — daa er skit in *oo*·ler·ge
I'm lost.
Jeg er faret vild. — yai er *faa*·aeth vil
Go away!
Forsvind! — for·*svin*

Call ...!
Ring efter...!
ring *ef*·daa ...
a doctor
en læge — in *le*·e
the police
politiet — po·li·*tee*·eth

HEALTH

I'm ill.
Jeg er syg. — yai er sew
It hurts here.
Det gør ondt her. — di ger ond hir

I'm ...
Jeg har ...
yai haa ...

asthmatic	*astma*	*asd*·ma
diabetic	*diabetes*	dee·a·*bi*·tes
epileptic	*epilepsi*	e·pee·leb·*see*

I'm allergic to ...
Jeg er allergisk over for ...
yai er a·*ler*·geesg *ow*·aa for ...

antibiotics	*antibiotika*	an·tee·bee·*o*·tee·ka
aspirin	*aspirin*	as·bee·*reen*
penicillin	*penicillin*	pin·ee·see·*leen*
bees	*bier*	*bee*·aa
nuts	*nødder*	*nerth*·aa
peanuts	*peanuts*	*pee*·nuts

antiseptic	*antiseptisk*	an·tee·*seb*·tisg
condoms	*kondomer*	kon·*do*·maa
contraceptive	*prævention*	pre·ven·*shon*
diarrhoea	*diarré*	dee·a·*re*
medicine	*medicin*	mi·dee·*seen*
nausea	*kvalme*	*kval*·me
sunblock cream	*solcreme*	*sol*·krem
tampons	*tamponer*	taam·*pong*·aa

LANGUAGE DIFFICULTIES

Do you speak English?
Taler De engelsk?
ta·laa dee *eng*·elsg

Does anyone here speak English?
Er der nogen der taler engelsk?
er daa *no*·en daa *ta*·laa *eng*·elsg

How do you say ... in Danish?
Hvordan siger man ... på dansk?
vor·*dan see*·aa man ... por dansg

What does ... mean?
Hvad betyder ...?
va bi·*tew*·thaa

I understand.
Jeg forstår.
yai for·*sdor*

I don't understand.
Jeg forstår ikke.
yai for·*sdor* ig

Could you speak more slowly, please?
Kunne De/du tale langsommere? (pol/inf)
koo·ne dee/doo *ta*·le *laang*·som·aa

Can you show me (on the map)?
Kunne De/du vise mig det (på kortet)? (pol/inf)
koo·ne dee/doo *vee*·se mai di (por *kor*·deth)

NUMBERS

0	*nul*	norl
1	*en*	in
2	*to*	tor
3	*tre*	tre
4	*fire*	feer
5	*fem*	fem
6	*seks*	segs
7	*syv*	*see*·ew
8	*otte*	*o*·de
9	*ni*	nee
10	*ti*	tee
11	*elve*	*el*·ve
12	*tolv*	tol
13	*tretten*	*tra*·den
14	*fjorten*	*fyor*·den
15	*femten*	*fem*·den
16	*seksten*	*sais*·den
17	*sytten*	*ser*·den
18	*atten*	*a*·den
19	*nitten*	*ni*·den
20	*tyve*	*tew*·we
21	*enogtyve*	*in*·o·tew·we
30	*tredive*	*trath*·ve
40	*fyrre*	*fer*·e
50	*halvtreds*	haal·*tres*
60	*tres*	tres
70	*halvfjerds*	haal·*fyers*
80	*firs*	feers
90	*halvfems*	haal·*fems*
100	*hundrede*	*hoo*·naath
1000	*tusind*	*too*·sen

PAPERWORK

name	*navn*	*naa*·oon
nationality	*nationalitet*	na·sho·na·lee·*tit*
date of birth	*fødselsdato*	*fer*·sels·da·to
place of birth	*fødested*	*fer*·the·sdeth
sex/gender	*køn*	kern
passport	*pas*	pas
visa	*visum*	*vee*·sorm

QUESTION WORDS

Who?	*Hvem?*	vem
What?	*Hvad*	va
What is it?	*Hvad er det?*	va er di
When?	*Hvornår*	vor·*nor*
Where?	*Hvor*	vor
Which?	*Hvilket*	*vil*·geth
Why?	*Hvorfor?*	*vor*·for
How?	*Hvordan?*	vor·*dan*

SHOPPING & SERVICES

I'd like to buy ...
Jeg vil gerne have ... yai vi *ger*·ne ha ...

How much is it?
Hvor meget koster det? vo *maa*·eth *kos*·daa di

I don't like it.
Det kan jeg ikke lide. di kan yai ig li

May I look at it?
Må jeg se det? mor yai si di

I'm just looking.
Jeg kikker bare. yai *kee*·gaa baa

It's cheap.
Det er billigt. di er *bee*·leet

It's too expensive.
Det er for dyrt. di er for dewrt

I'll take it.
Jeg tager det. yai taa di

Do you accept ...?
Tager I ...? plur
taa ee ...

credit cards
kreditkort kre·*deed*·kort

travellers cheques
rejsechecks *rai*·se·shegs

LANGUAGE

more	*mere*	*mi*·a
less	*mindre*	*min*·dra
small	*lille*	*lee*·le
big	*stor*	stor

I'm looking for ...
Jeg leder efter ...
yai *li*·thaa *ef*·daa ...

a bank	
en bank	in bank
the church	
kirken	*keer*·gen
the city centre	
centrum	*sen*·trom
the ... embassy	
den ... ambassade	den ... am·ba·*saa*·the
the hospital	
hospitalet	hors·bi·*ta*·leth
the market	
et marked	it *maa*·geth
the museum	
museet	moo·*se*·eth
the police	
politiet	po·lee·*tee*·eth
the post office	
postkontoret	*post*·kon·tor·eth
a public toilet	
et offentligt toilet	it *o*·fend·leed toy·*let*
the tourist office	
turistinformationen	too·*reest*·in·for·ma·sho·nen

TIME & DATES

What time is it?

Hvad er klokken?	va er *klo*·gen

It's ... o'clock.

Klokken er ...	*klo*·gen er ...

in the morning

om morgenen	om *mor*·nen

in the afternoon

om eftermiddagen	om *ef*·daa·mi·da·en

in the evening

om aftenen	om *aafd*·nen

When?	*Hvornår?*	vo·*nor*
today	*i dag*	ee da
tomorrow	*i morgen*	ee morn
yesterday	*i går*	ee gor

Monday	*mandag*	*man*·da
Tuesday	*tirsdag*	*teers*·da
Wednesday	*onsdag*	*ons*·da
Thursday	*torsdag*	*tors*·da
Friday	*fredag*	*fre*·da
Saturday	*lørdag*	*ler*·da
Sunday	*søndag*	*sern*·da

January	*januar*	*yan*·oo·aa
February	*februar*	*feb*·oo·aa
March	*marts*	maards
April	*april*	a·*preel*
May	*maj*	mai
June	*juni*	*yoo*·nee
July	*juli*	*yoo*·lee
August	*august*	aa·oo·*gorsd*
September	*september*	sib·*tem*·baa
October	*oktober*	og·*to*·baa
November	*november*	no·*vem*·baa
December	*december*	di·*sem*·baa

TRANSPORT
Public Transport

What time does the ... leave/arrive?
Hvornår går/ankommer ...
vor·*nor* gor/*an*·kom·aa ...

boat	*båden*	*bor*·then
bus	*bussen*	*boo*·sen
plane	*flyet*	*flew*·eth
train	*toget*	*tor*·weth
tram	*metroen*	*me*·tro·en

I'd like a ... ticket.
Jeg vil gerne have en ... billet.
yai vi *ger*·ne ha in ... bi·*let*

one-way	*enkelt*	*eng*·geld
return	*retur*	re·*toor*
1st class	*første klasse*	*fers*·de *kla*·se
2nd class	*anden klasse*	*an*·en *kla*·se

I want to go to ...
Jeg vil gerne til ...
yai vi *ger*·ne ti ...

The train has been delayed/cancelled.
Toget er forsinket/aflyst.
tor·weth er for·*sing*·geth/*aa*·oo·lewsd

the first	*første*	*fers*·de
the last	*sidste*	*sees*·de
platform	*perron*	paa·*rong*
ticket office	*billetkontor*	bi·*let*·kon·tor
timetable	*køreplan*	*ker*·plan
train station	*togstation*	*torw*·sda·shon

Private Transport

Where can I rent a ...?
Hvor kan jeg leje en ...?
vor kan yai *lai*·e in ...

car	*bil*	beel
4WD	*firehjulstrækker*	*fee*·ya·yools·trer·gaa
motorbike	*motorcykel*	*mo*·tor·sew·gel
bicycle	*cykel*	*sew*·gel

LANGUAGE

ROAD SIGNS

Vigepligt	Give Way
Parkering Forbudt	No Parking
Omkørsel	Detour
Indgang	Entry
Indkørsel Forbudt	No Entry
Ensrettet	One Way
Udgang	Exit
Motorvej	Freeway
Selvbetjening	Self Service
Vejarbejde	Roadworks

Is this the road to ...?
Fører denne vej til ...?
fer·aa *den*·ne vai ti ...

Where's the next service station?
Hvor er næste benzinstation?
vor er *nes*·de ben·*seen*·sda·*shon*

Please fill it up.
Fyld den op, tak.
fewl den up taag

I'd like ... litres.
Jeg vil gerne have ... liter.
yai vi *ger*·ne ha ... *lee*·ta

diesel
diesel
dee·sel

unleaded petrol
blyfri benzin
blew·free ben·*seen*

(How long) Can I park here?
(Hvor længe) må jeg parkere her?
(vor *leng*·e) mor yai par·*ki*·aa hir

Where do I pay?
Hvor betaler jeg?
vor be·*ta*·laa yai

I need a mechanic.
Jeg har brug for en mekaniker.
yai har broo for in mi·*ka*·ni·gaa

The car/motorbike has broken down at ...
Bilen/motorcyklen er brudt sammen ved ...
bee·len/*mo*·tor·sew·glen er broot *saa*·men vi ...

The car/motorbike won't start.
Bilen/motorcyklen vil ikke starte.
bee·len/*mo*·tor·sew·glen vi ig *sdaar*·de

I have a flat tyre.
Jeg er punkteret.
yai er porng·*ti*·aath

I've run out of petrol.
Jeg er løbet tør for benzin.
yai er *ler*·beth ter for ben·*seen*

I've had an accident.
Jeg har været ude for en ulykke.
yai har *ver*·eth *oo*·the for in *oo*·ler·ge

TRAVEL WITH CHILDREN

Is there (a/an) ...?
Er der ...?
er daa ...

I need a ...
Jeg har brug for ...
yai haa broo for ...

baby change room	
et sted at skifte babyen	it sdeth at *sgeef*·de *bay*·bee·en
car baby seat	
et baby bilsæde	it *bay*·bee *beel*·se·the
child-minding service	
børnepasning	*ber*·ne·pas·ning
children's menu	
en børnemenu	in *ber*·ne·me·new
disposable nappies/diapers	
engangsbleer	*in*·gaarngs·bli·aa
formula (infant milk)	
noget erstatning	*nor*·eth er·*stat*·ning
(English-speaking) babysitter	
en (engelsktalende) babysitter	in *eng*·elsg·ta·le·naa *bay*·bee·see·taa
highchair	
en høj stol	in hoy storl
potty	
en potte	in *por*·de
stroller	
en klapvogn	in *klaab*·vown

Do you mind if I breastfeed here?
Må jeg amme her? mor yai *aa*·me hir

Are children allowed?
Er børn tilladt? er bern *ti*·lat

Glossary

Note that the Danish letters æ, ø and å fall at the end of the alphabet.

akvavit – schnapps
amt – county
apotek – pharmacy, chemist

bageri – bakery
bakke – hill
banegård – train station
bibliotek – library
billetautomat – automated parking-ticket dispenser
bro – bridge
bugt – bay
by – town
børnemenu – children's menu

campingplads – camping ground
cykel – bicycle

dag – day
dagens ret – special meal of the day
Danmark – Denmark
Dansk – Danish
domkirke – cathedral
DSB – abbreviation and common name for Danske Statsbaner (Danish State Railway), Denmark's national railway

EU – European Union

folkehøjskole – folk high school
Fyn – Funen, both a county and an island
færge – ferry
færegehavn – ferry harbour

gade – street
gammel – old
gård – yard, farm

have – garden
havn – harbour
HI – Hostelling International, the main international hostel organisation (formerly IYHF)
hygge – cosy

IC – intercity train
IR – inter-regional train

jernbane – railway
Jylland – Jutland

keramik – ceramic, pottery
kirke – church
kirkegård – churchyard, cemetery
klint – cliff
klippekort – a type of multiple-use transport ticket
kloster – monastery
koldt bord – buffet-style meal, mostly cold food
konditori – bakery with café tables
kro – inn
København – Copenhagen
køreplan – timetable

lur – Bronze Age horn

morgenmad – breakfast
museet – museum
møntvask – coin laundry

nord – north

plantage – plantation, tree farm, woods
prefect – chief administrative officer of the county government
pølsemandens – wheeled food carts

rådhus – town hall, city hall
rundkirke – fortified round church, found on Bornholm
røgeri – fish smokehouse

samling – collection, usually of art
Sjælland – the island of Zealand
skov – forest, woods
slagter – butcher
slot – castle
smørrebrød – open sandwich
strand – beach, shoreline
stykke – piece (fruit)
sund – sound
svømmehal – swimming pool
syd – south
sø – lake

telekort – phonecard
tog – train
torv, torvet – square, marketplace
tårn – tower

uge – week

vandrerhjem – youth and family hostel
vej – street, road
vest – west
værelse – room (to rent)

wienerbrød – Danish pastry, literally 'Vienna bread'

ø – island, usually attached as a suffix to the proper name
øl – beer
øst – east

å – river

Behind the Scenes

THIS BOOK

This 4th edition of *Denmark* was prepared in Lonely Planet's Mebourne office. It was researched by Andrew Bender (coordinating author), Michael Grosberg, Sally O'Brien, Rick Starey and Andrew Stone. Glenda Bednure and Ned Friary wrote the 1st edition and updated the 2nd and 3rd editions. Dr Caroline Evans reviewed and contributed to the Health chapter.

THANKS from the authors

Andrew Bender Thank you first of all to my co-authors for working so hard and so agreeably, to Lillian Hess, the Davidsen family, and the friendly folks at the DSB and Danish utilities for their information. Thanks also to Judith Bamber for the opportunity, Margedd Heliosz and Chris Love for their patience, and whoever invented smørrebrød for the inspiration.

Michael Grosberg Thanks go out to Gerd Thomsen for her insight, recommendations, and enthusiasm for all of Zealand. To Brett Skolnick for his info and contacts around Copenhagen, Agnes Manford on Møn, Ester Langholt in Roskilde, Jan Edslev in Helsingør, Matias Jensen in Hornbaek, Olga Madsen for a fun day at the beach in Hornbæk, and especially to the incredibly well-organised and informative staff at tourist offices throughout the region.

Sally O'Brien *Tilsund tak* to my colleague and good friend Carolyn Bain, who provided more laughs in Copenhagen than seems decent for work. Thanks also to Judith Bamber, Margedd Heliosz and everyone at Lonely Planet who toiled on this book. Many thanks to Sita Linddahl for all her help with accommodation scouting, weather enquiries and email access, and Susanne Juul and Karen Tjur for my fabulous living quarters in Nørrebro and Christianshavn.

Rick Starey A big thanks to Judith Bamber for sending me to Denmark. Glass-smashing cheers to Richard Plunkett. You're a gun and I appreciate all your support; Erik Øhren, a sensational bloke with a heart the size of Australia. Cheers to the people who make up the magic that is Laugagisgade 12. Simone and Soren, brilliant in the Amazon and Højer. Alexandra, effervescent effort. Anne, Simon, Sune, Helene, Jacob: all sensational. Thanks to the Jutland Turistbureaux for their knowledge and help, Susanne at Ribe and Anne at Århus. Boydo and Dicko, you boys set me up for this one so beer's on me. Byron Jones, a hero. Miss Charles, three votes. Madre, super effort. Dad, bloody fantastic. T, outstanding, brilliant, tireless! Love it. Coba, cool calm and collective.

Andrew Stone The research on this trip was made so much easier thanks to the Danish, Bornholm and Odense tourist offices. Special thanks to Charlotte Harder at the Danish Tourist Board and Pernille Kofod Larsen at Destination Bornholm for their assistance, suggestions, tips and recommendations. My main thank you must go to Lissen and Michael, generous friends who have put me up in Copenhagen and Funen so many times, and served me

THE LONELY PLANET STORY

The story begins with a classic travel adventure: Tony and Maureen Wheeler's 1972 journey across Europe and Asia to Australia. There was no useful information about the overland trail then, so Tony and Maureen published the first Lonely Planet guidebook to meet a growing need.

From a kitchen table, Lonely Planet has grown to become the largest independent travel publisher in the world, with offices in Melbourne (Australia), Oakland (USA) and London (UK). Today Lonely Planet guidebooks cover the globe. There is an ever-growing list of books and information in a variety of media. Some things haven't changed. The main aim is still to make it possible for adventurous travellers to get out there – to explore and better understand the world.

At Lonely Planet we believe travellers can make a positive contribution to the countries they visit – if they respect their host communities and spend their money wisely. Every year 5% of company profit is donated to charities around the world.

wonderful meals, great wine and delicious *krengle*. *Tusind tak* to you both for all the fun times.

CREDITS

This edition was commissioned and developed in Lonely Planet's London office by Judith Bamber. Cartography for this guide was developed by Mark Griffiths. The project manager was Chris Love. Editing was coordinated by Margedd Heliosz, with assistance from Miriam Cannell, Nick Tapp and Linda Suttie. Cartography was coordinated by Jovan Djkunanovic, with assistance from Tony Dupcinov. Vicki Beale laid out the colour pages and Wibowo Rusli laid out the book. The cover was designed by Wendy Wright and Yukiyoshi Kamimura did the cover artwork. Quentin Frayne and Karin Vidstrup Monk coordinated the language content. Thanks also to Kate McDonald, Sally Darmody and Stephanie Pearson.

THANKS from Lonely Planet

Many thanks to the travellers who used the last edition and wrote to us with helpful hints, useful advice and interesting anecdotes:

A Ben Arthur **B** Arris Blom, Helene Boeck, Michael and Sammie Buben **C** Patricia Capone, Signe Gry Clemmensen, Rob Cussons **D** Annemieke De Man, Paul Docherty, Michael T Donnellan, Mat Donnelly **E** Robert Edmunds, Keith Ellis **F** Lila French **G** Serge Gielkens, Sam Golledge, Ron Grant, Gary Gregerson **H** David Hallam, Arthur Hay, David and Mairin Herman, Emma Horton **J** Lykke Jensen, Sandra Josephson **K** Tomas Kocka, Zdenka Kockova **L** Dot Lodge, Richard and Liz Lower **M** Jan Malmstrom, Anne Marimuthu, Julie Martin Hansen, Margaret Mehl, Jean-Philippe Meloche, Judith Miller, Zoe Miller-Lee, Grant Mitchell, Alberto Moreira, Del Morgan, Thomas Murray **N** Evan Nass **O** Torsten Onderwater, Frank Opray **P** Sandra Pagano, Tracy Powis **R** Colin Ready, Jose Ruivo **S** Valine Saberton, Nanna Schacht, Solveig Schoenecker, Larry Schwarz, Jonathan Smith, David Szylit **T** Terence Tam, Marianne Teglengaard, Ruud van Trijp **W** Mike Winterer, Allen Wright.

ACKNOWLEDGMENTS

Many thanks to the following for the use of their content:

Globe on back cover © Mountain High Maps 1993 Digital Wisdom, Inc.

SEND US YOUR FEEDBACK

We love to hear from travellers – your comments keep us on our toes and help make our books better. Our well-travelled team reads every word on what you loved or loathed about this book. Although we cannot reply individually to postal submissions, we always guarantee that your feedback goes straight to the appropriate authors, in time for the next edition. Each person who sends us information is thanked in the next edition – and the most useful submissions are rewarded with a free book.

To send us your updates – and find out about Lonely Planet events, newsletters and travel news – visit our award-winning website: **www.lonelyplanet.com/feedback**

Note: We may edit, reproduce and incorporate your comments in Lonely Planet products such as guidebooks, websites and digital products, so let us know if you don't want your comments reproduced or your name acknowledged. For a copy of our privacy policy visit www.lonelyplanet.com/privacy

Index

DANISH ALPHABET

Note that the Danish letters æ, ø and Å fall in this order at the end of the alphabet

000 Map pages
000 Location of colour photographs

000 Map pages
000 Location of colour photographs

G

H

INDEX

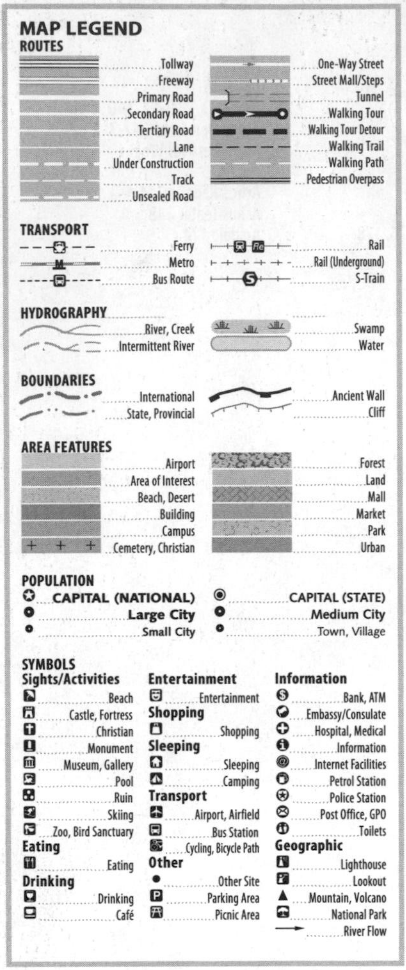
MAP LEGEND
ROUTES
Tollway
Freeway
Primary Road
Secondary Road
Tertiary Road
Lane
Under Construction
Track
Unsealed Road
One-Way Street
Street Mall/Steps
Tunnel
Walking Tour
Walking Tour Detour
Walking Trail
Walking Path
Pedestrian Overpass
TRANSPORT
Ferry
Metro
Bus Route
Rail
Rail (Underground)
S-Train
HYDROGRAPHY
River, Creek
Intermittent River
Swamp
Water
BOUNDARIES
International
State, Provincial
Ancient Wall
Cliff
AREA FEATURES
Airport
Area of Interest
Beach, Desert
Building
Campus
Cemetery, Christian
Forest
Land
Mall
Market
Park
Urban
POPULATION
CAPITAL (NATIONAL)
CAPITAL (STATE)
Large City
Medium City
Small City
Town, Village
SYMBOLS
Sights/Activities
Beach
Castle, Fortress
Christian
Monument
Museum, Gallery
Pool
Ruin
Skiing
Zoo, Bird Sanctuary
Eating
Eating
Drinking
Drinking
Café
Entertainment
Entertainment
Shopping
Shopping
Sleeping
Sleeping
Camping
Transport
Airport, Airfield
Bus Station
Cycling, Bicycle Path
Other
Other Site
Parking Area
Picnic Area
Information
Bank, ATM
Embassy/Consulate
Hospital, Medical
Information
Internet Facilities
Petrol Station
Police Station
Post Office, GPO
Toilets
Geographic
Lighthouse
Lookout
Mountain, Volcano
National Park
River Flow

LONELY PLANET OFFICES

Australia

Head Office
Locked Bag 1, Footscray, Victoria 3011
☎ 03 8379 8000, fax 03 8379 8111
talk2us@lonelyplanet.com.au

USA

150 Linden St, Oakland, CA 94607
☎ 510 893 8555, toll free 800 275 8555
fax 510 893 8572, info@lonelyplanet.com

UK

72–82 Rosebery Ave,
Clerkenwell, London EC1R 4RW
☎ 020 7841 9000, fax 020 7841 9001
go@lonelyplanet.co.uk

Published by Lonely Planet Publications Pty Ltd
ABN 36 005 607 983

Cover photographs by Lonely Planet Images: Tilsandede Kirke (Buried Church) in sunset, Jon Davidson (front); Visitors to Copenhagen enjoy a tour of Nyhavn, Anders Blomqvist (back). Many of the images in this guide are available for licensing from Lonely Planet Images: www .lonelyplanetimages.com

Printed by SNP SPrint (S) Pte Ltd, Singapore